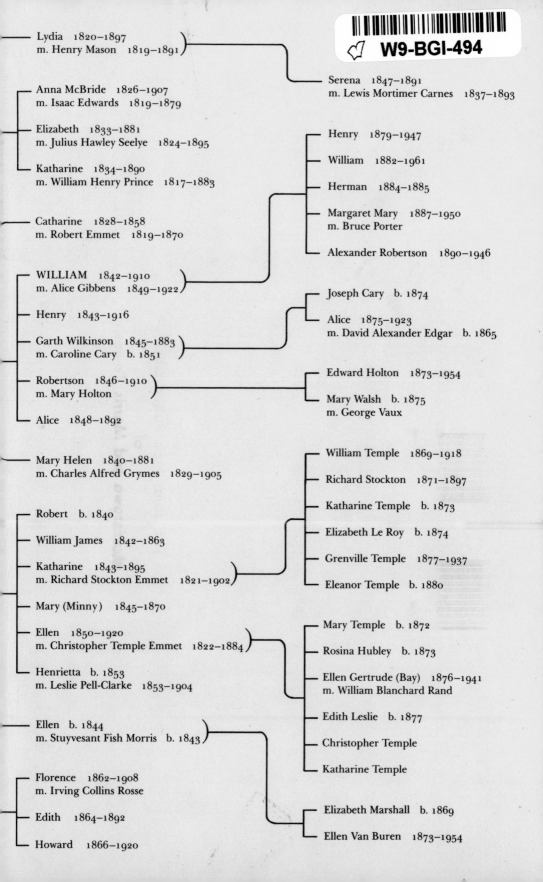

Lydia   1820–1897
m. Henry Mason   1819–1891

Serena   1847–1891
m. Lewis Mortimer Carnes   1837–1893

Anna McBride   1826–1907
m. Isaac Edwards   1819–1879

Elizabeth   1833–1881
m. Julius Hawley Seelye   1824–1895

Katharine   1834–1890
m. William Henry Prince   1817–1883

Henry   1879–1947

William   1882–1961

Herman   1884–1885

Margaret Mary   1887–1950
m. Bruce Porter

Alexander Robertson   1890–1946

Catharine   1828–1858
m. Robert Emmet   1819–1870

WILLIAM   1842–1910
m. Alice Gibbens   1849–1922

Henry   1843–1916

Garth Wilkinson   1845–1883
m. Caroline Cary   b. 1851

Joseph Cary   b. 1874

Alice   1875–1923
m. David Alexander Edgar   b. 1865

Robertson   1846–1910
m. Mary Holton

Edward Holton   1873–1954

Mary Walsh   b. 1875
m. George Vaux

Alice   1848–1892

Mary Helen   1840–1881
m. Charles Alfred Grymes   1829–1905

William Temple   1869–1918

Richard Stockton   1871–1897

Katharine Temple   b. 1873

Elizabeth Le Roy   b. 1874

Grenville Temple   1877–1937

Eleanor Temple   b. 1880

Robert   b. 1840

William James   1842–1863

Katharine   1843–1895
m. Richard Stockton Emmet   1821–1902

Mary (Minny)   1845–1870

Ellen   1850–1920
m. Christopher Temple Emmet   1822–1884

Henrietta   b. 1853
m. Leslie Pell-Clarke   1853–1904

Mary Temple   b. 1872

Rosina Hubley   b. 1873

Ellen Gertrude (Bay)   1876–1941
m. William Blanchard Rand

Edith Leslie   b. 1877

Christopher Temple

Katharine Temple

Ellen   b. 1844
m. Stuyvesant Fish Morris   b. 1843

Florence   1862–1908
m. Irving Collins Rosse

Edith   1864–1892

Howard   1866–1920

Elizabeth Marshall   b. 1869

Ellen Van Buren   1873–1954

The Correspondence of
WILLIAM JAMES

This edition of the Correspondence of William James is sponsored by
the American Council of Learned Societies.

The Correspondence *of* William James

VOLUME 1

WILLIAM AND HENRY

1861–1884

Edited by

Ignas K. Skrupskelis *and* Elizabeth M. Berkeley

with the assistance of

Bernice Grohskopf *and* Wilma Bradbeer

University Press of Virginia
Charlottesville and London

THE UNIVERSITY PRESS OF VIRGINIA
Copyright © 1992 by the Rector and Visitors
of the University of Virginia

First published 1992

COMMITTEE ON
SCHOLARLY EDITIONS

AN APPROVED EDITION

MODERN LANGUAGE
ASSOCIATION OF AMERICA

Frontispiece: Henry James and William James
ca. 1900. (Photograph by permission of the
Houghton Library, Harvard University)

Library of Congress Cataloging-in-Publication Data

James, William, 1842–1910.
[Correspondence]
The correspondence of William James / edited by Ignas K.
Skrupskelis and Elizabeth M. Berkeley with the assistance of Bernice
Grohskopf and Wilma Bradbeer.
p. cm.
Includes bibliographical references (p.) and index.
Contents: v. 1. William and Henry, 1861–1884.
ISBN 0-8139-1338-1 (cloth)
1. James, William, 1842–1910—Correspondence. 2. Philosophers—
United States—Biography. 3. Psychologists—United States—
Correspondence. 4. James, Henry, 1843–1916—Correspondence.
I. Skrupskelis, Ignas K., 1938–. II. Berkeley, Elizabeth M.
III. James, Henry, 1843–1916. IV. Title.
B945.J24A4 1992
191—dc20

[B]

91-35923

CIP

Printed in the United States of America

To Fredson Bowers
(1905–1991)

Contents

1869

1870

1872

1873

1874

1875

1876

1877

1878

1884

Illustrations following page 202

Foreword

This is the first volume of the Critical Edition of the Correspondence of William James. The subsequent two volumes will continue the epistolary relationship between the brothers, William and Henry James. The present projection of this project is to publish the remaining correspondence of William James with members of his immediate and extended family as well as with his friends and professional colleagues. Having completed nineteen volumes of *The Works of William James* in a Critical Edition, the editors and the editorial staff are pleased and privileged to commence the publication of an edition devoted to the correspondence of one of America's finest philosophers and writers, a person who stood four-square at the center of Euro-American thought for some fifty years.

The Editor of this edition is Ignas K. Skrupskelis of the University of South Carolina. Professor Skrupskelis is responsible for obtaining the letters and checking their legitimacy, place of origin and chronology, for the annotations, and for the preparation of the index. His discussion of the letters is detailed in his Bibliographical Note, below. The Associate Editor is Elizabeth M. Berkeley, who supervises transcription of the letters, is responsible for the textual apparatus, and sees the volumes through the press. The standards of transcription are detailed in the Note on the Editorial Method. She has been ably assisted in the preparation of this volume by Bernice Grohskopf, Wilma Bradbeer, Ann Goedde, Mary Mikalson and Judith Nelson.

This edition is sponsored by the American Council of Learned Societies, to whom we are grateful in the persons of Stanley N. Katz, Douglas Greenberg, and Hugh O'Neill.

Financial and advisory support for the edition has been provided by the National Endowment for the Humanities, specifically, Lynne V. Cheney, Chairperson, Kathy Fuller, Program Specialist, David Nichols, former Program Officer, and Douglas Arnold, Program Officer. The support of the Endowment for the earlier edition of *The*

Works of William James and for the present edition is a powerful testament to the importance of the American literary and philosophical tradition.

The editors are grateful to the University of Virginia for editorial office space in the Alderman Library, whose Reference Room staff has provided valuable assistance in locating source material pertinent to the project. We have received enthusiastic and caring support from Nancy C. Essig, Director of the University Press of Virginia, publisher of this edition. We express gratitude to the University of South Carolina, especially to George Terry, Vice-President for Libraries and Collections, who assisted the Editor with office space in the Cooper Library.

Invaluable help was provided by the Houghton Library of Harvard University and by Rodney Dennis, Curator of Manuscripts, for permission to use that William James material subject to permission of the Houghton Library. The Reading Room staff of the Houghton Library has been very helpful, especially Jennie Rathbun. We also were assisted by the Director of the Library of the Boston Athenaeum, Rodney Armstrong, and by Henry Katz, Librarian of the Print Room. We are grateful to Joan Klein, Historical Collection Librarian at the Claude Moore Health Sciences Library of the University of Virginia. Foreign language passages and medical terms were checked by George Crafts, Angelika Schmiegelow Powell, Luciana Wlassics, Jon Mikalson, Forrest Voight, and William A. Geary. Glenn and Gilberte Van Treese provided a French transcription of the letter of 3 May 1867. Anthony D. Townsend and Cristina Sharretts of the University of Virginia provided valuable technical advice and assistance. Professor Robert H. Hirst of the University of California at Berkeley, who reviewed the volume for the seal of the Committee on Scholarly Editions, made useful suggestions.

Important assistance was received from the James family: Alexander R. James, Henry James, Michael James, and Henry James Vaux. In this regard, we are deeply thankful to Roberta Sheehan-Taylor, who shared her extensive collection of James memorabilia and her intimate knowledge of the extended James family. Sylvia Watson provided important information about the Watsons of James's time. Frederick H. Burkhardt, the General Editor of the *Works*, was a motivating and consulting person in the decision to go forward with the *Correspondence* project.

John Lachs of Vanderbilt University graciously and professionally served as Interim General Editor in 1989–90, for which we are deeply grateful. The General Editor gives thanks for assistance from Kathryn Presley, Patricia A. Garner, and also to the Advisory Committee for this edition.

We are especially indebted to Gerald E. Myers, Professor Emeritus of Queens College and the Graduate Center, City University of New York, and member of the Advisory Committee, for his introduction to this volume.

Alexander R. James, William James's grandson and literary executor, gave the editors permission to publish materials on which he holds copyright.

Grateful acknowledgment is offered to the Rector and the Board of Visitors of the University of Virginia, who hold the copyright to the volumes in this edition.

John J. McDermott

The editors announce with sadness and a profound sense of loss the death on 11 April 1991 of Fredson Bowers, Linden Kent Professor of English, Emeritus, University of Virginia, who was the textual editor for *The Works of William James* and a consulting editor to the present edition. Fredson Bowers was world-renowned as a scholar and a superb master of textual editing, with an extraordinary knowledge of the William James materials. His contribution to the project has been incalculable, and the entire staff will miss his vitality and his enthusiasm.

Introduction
GERALD E. MYERS

William James collected fame by being a collection in himself. Variously called America's leading philosopher, our greatest psychologist, and our finest writer on religion, James is also one of our most fascinating intellectual personalities. The Jamesian charisma, to which his writings owe much of their durability, is never more evident than in his letters. He thus enjoys the further distinction of ranking among America's favorite correspondents, and in adventuring through his voluminous correspondence we better appreciate James's prominent place in our intellectual history.

What is not always understood, even by philosophers and psychologists, whose interests are often specialized, is James's significance to cultural historians and students of literature. Their ongoing attention to James's life and writings ensures his standing in our cultural history; with Ralph Waldo Emerson, he represents the establishment of nineteenth-century philosophical thought in America. Because of the astonishing range of interests that James commanded, and because of the elusiveness with which that command defies definition, he becomes increasingly an American culture hero, a mythical figure for succeeding generations to mythologize further in their successive tilts at demystification.[1]

---

[1] See the recent interesting work by George Cotkin, *William James: Public Philosopher* (Baltimore: Johns Hopkins Univ. Press, 1990). See also the recent and interesting work by Cornel West, *The American Evasion of Philosophy: A Genealogy of Pragmatism* (Madison: Univ. of Wisconsin Press, 1989).

For a comprehensive study of the development of philosophy at Harvard and of James's place in it, see Bruce Kuklick's influential *The Rise of American Philosophy* (New Haven and London: Yale Univ. Press, 1977).

An influential revival of pragmatism in contemporary philosophy is Richard Rorty's *Consequences of Pragmatism* (Minneapolis: Univ. of Minnesota Press, 1982). For literature about James, see Ignas K. Skrupskelis, *William James: A Reference Guide* (Bos-

James's star did not shine alone. He was one of a constellation of other stars, near stars, and nonstars; and his commentators ever sweep that firmament telescopically for his relationships to all of them. The other major star was his brother Henry James, Jr., often extolled as America's greatest writer of fiction. Other luminaries in James's orbit, briefly sampled, included John Dewey, Charles Sanders Peirce, Oliver Wendell Holmes, Jr., W. E. B. DuBois, Booker T. Washington, Gertrude Stein, John D. Rockefeller, Henri Bergson, John La Farge, Henry Adams, and Theodore Roosevelt. Important but less refulgent were G. S. Hall, E. B. Titchener, Frederic W. H. Myers, and Edmund Gurney. Barely flickering for public gaze were Wincenty Lutoslawski, B. P. Blood, and Thomas Davidson; yet these and others even less stellar, some of them admired by James despite their being cranks or quacks, somehow illuminate the Jamesian constellation—and, accordingly, scholars pursue the most peripheral light-casting clues.

The dominant cluster in James's constellation was the most intimate one, his family, and so pointed were their connections, inwardly and externally, that biographical tracking is as irresistible as it is opportune. To reach certain destinations in William, we start from his father, Henry James, Sr., and in process we connect with such paternal friends as Emerson and Thoreau. Or, for locating William in other ways, we begin with brother Henry, coming upon fraternal acquaintances like Flaubert, Turgenev, Tennyson, and Zola. The family relationships are intrinsically engaging while simultaneously introducing us to a whole galaxy of fin-de-siècle artists, intellectuals, and professionals, so the biographical attention continuously received by the James family is readily explained. The seductiveness of the family for biographers has made its own contributions toward sustaining the reputation of William James as author and person.[2]

ton: G. K. Hall, 1977). See also John J. McDermott's Introduction to his edited volume *The Writings of William James* (New York: Random House, 1967), pp. xiv–xliv.

For contemporary psychologists on James, see Michael G. Johnson and Tracy B. Henley, eds., *Reflections on the Principles of Psychology: William James after a Century* (Hillsdale, N.J.: Erlbaum, 1990).

[2] Important biographical and bibliographical sources are Ralph Barton Perry, *The Thought and Character of William James*, 2 vols. (Boston: Little, Brown, 1935); Gay Wilson Allen, *William James: A Biography* (New York: Viking, 1967); Frederic Harold Young, *The Philosophy of Henry James, Sr.* (New York: Bookman Associates, 1951); Leon Edel, *The Life of Henry James*, 5 vols. (Philadelphia: Lippincott, 1953–72); F. O. Matthiessen, *The James Family* (New York: Knopf, 1947); F. W. Dupee, ed., *Henry James: Autobiography* (Princeton: Princeton Univ. Press, 1956); Howard M. Feinstein, *Becom-

The sleuthing impulses of scholars investigating the James family enjoy a field day with the James Collection at Harvard's Houghton Library and lesser though not insignificant romps with what can be found elsewhere. Thousands of letters, notes and scraps, diaries, annotated books and articles, unpublished lectures, photos, and memorabilia await the magnifying glass. This archival vastness seems always to yield a new bit of information, a fresh insight, a basis for some reinterpretation; what is so richly preserved from the family preserves abundant interest in it. The letters between William and Henry that constitute this book, though but a fragment of the family letters, are essential for recounting how the brothers began their careers and related to each other in their development. These letters are more fully appreciated if surrounding factual background, beginning with family data, is before us.

The brothers failed uniqueness in one respect, to Henry's consternation especially, and that was in their names. Their father was Henry James, Sr. (1811–1882), the son of William James (1771–1832), who emigrated in his youth from Ireland to New York City and then to Albany. There he began a series of successful business ventures, including real estate and shares in the Erie Canal, that grew into an estate of some three million dollars, one of New York's wealthiest. It was his third wife, Catharine Barber, of an affluent upstate New York Scotch-Irish family, who mothered Henry James, Sr.

The family scene during this period looks somewhat chaotic: the wealthy patriarchal William with a succession of three wives, at odds with both a son (another William) from his first marriage and his son Henry James, Sr., who later explained his youthful rebelliousness as a reaction against his father's strict Calvinism.[3] Add to this Henry's terrible accident at age thirteen; he was injured in a fire during some game-playing that left him with an amputated right leg. His making it through Union College did not placate father William, who willed him (and half brother William) only a small annuity. The will was successfully challenged, however, and Henry received an equal share

---

ing William James (Ithaca and London: Cornell Univ. Press, 1984); Jean Strouse, *Alice James: A Biography* (Boston: Houghton Mifflin, 1980); Jane Maher, *Biography of Broken Fortunes: Wilkie and Bob, Brothers of William, Henry, and Alice James* (Hamden, Conn.: Archon, 1986); Mark R. Schwehn, James William Anderson, Robert J. Richards, and Eugene Taylor, in Mark R. Schwehn, ed., *A William James Renaissance: Four Essays by Young Scholars, Harvard Library Bulletin,* 30, no. 4 (Oct. 1982); and Gerald E. Myers, *William James: His Life and Thought* (New Haven and London: Yale Univ. Press, 1986).

[3] See William James, ed., *The Literary Remains of the Late Henry James* (Boston: James R. Osgood & Co., 1885), pp. 145–91.

amounting to an annual income of ten thousand dollars. As the letters of this volume show, it became his turn, albeit for very different reasons, to have his will renegotiated by his sons.

The appearance of Jamesian disarray—to be remembered as we discuss below the brothers William and Henry, Jr.—figured prominently in the latter's recollections: "Our father's family was to offer such a chronicle of early deaths, arrested careers, broken promises, orphaned children."[4] F. O. Matthiessen made this dismal summary of the chronicle referred to: "Of the eleven of [Grandfather] William James's sons and daughters who reached maturity, seven were dead by forty. Variously genial, charming, dissipated, or unstable," these Jameses resembled, Matthiessen observed, the forbears described in *The Wings of the Dove* as an "extravagant unregulated cluster, with free-living ancestors, handsome dead cousins, lurid uncles, beautiful vanished aunts, persons all busts and curls."[5]

Henry James, Sr., was a vibrant personality, and many acknowledged his distinct influence, but especially his own family, notably the sons William and Henry. His presence was substantial, combining the effects of an expansive and genial oval face, sensitive direct eyes, balding pate on top and ample beard below, a leg's absence accentuated by a cane in hand, and a conversational language bound to catch attention. He had, besides family, a single compelling interest: religion. His filial rebellion turned on itself over time, taking him to Princeton Theological Seminary for three years, then, in his iconoclastic mode, to finding his own theological convictions after reading the eighteenth-century mystic Emanuel Swedenborg.

In 1840 Henry Sr. married Mary Robertson Walsh, an Irishwoman from a well-established New York City family, whose photos and descriptions suggest similarities with Henry's mother. Stolid, patient, and dutiful, she had the not inconsiderable resources needed for managing husband and children. Henry by himself was a full-time assignment by being a constant companion. Never employed, because of his independent income and preference for reading, writing, and talking religion and metaphysics, yet of a restless spirit that loved traveling with its promise of new friends and places, he required Mary Walsh's care. Eventually, the same, allowing for certain differences, could be said of his son, William James, and his wife.

The first child born to Henry and Mary, while living in New York City's Astor House, was William (1842–1910), and Henry Jr. (1843–

[4] Henry James, *A Small Boy and Others* (New York: Scribners, 1913), p. 14.
[5] Matthiessen, p. 5.

1916) was the second. The brothers got their first taste of their father's restlessness during a family voyage in 1843 to Europe. Returning to New York City and then purchasing a brownstone at West Fourteenth Street, Henry Sr. fathered three family additions—Garth Wilkinson (1845–1883), Robertson (1846–1910), and Alice (1848–1892). Although William and Henry Jr. became the famous ones, all except mother Mary Walsh have received extensive biographical attention. Apart from William and Henry Jr., Henry Sr. received the earliest attention; daughter Alice's celebrated literary diary was published in 1964, followed by a book-length study of her in 1980, and six years later a book on Garth and Robertson appeared.[6]

During 1852–55, while residing in New York City, William and Henry were either at private schools or with tutors at home. *Culture* descended upon them early in life. They studied French, learned the names of writers and artists, and took dancing lessons at a Fourteenth Street school. Emerson and Thackeray were among distinguished houseguests, and at the dinner table the children learned geography, literature, and the art of (often bantering) conversation. Actively encouraged by their father, they made conversation the occasion for exploration, criticism, and debate. They studied penmanship and drawing for which William displayed an impressive talent. When not regularly visiting Albany and upstate relatives, the family absorbed Manhattan's offerings. They attended the opera, even more the theater, where both traditional and contemporary dramas could be seen, including *A Midsummer's Night Dream, Uncle Tom's Cabin,* and adaptations of Dickens's novels. Museums and art exhibits also figured importantly in the Jamesian cultural agenda. Less exalted forms of urban amusement were available, such as circuses, carnivals, and roaming the streets around Washington Square.[7]

A decade had passed since the previous trip to Europe, so Henry Sr. decided that, if his children's education was to surpass that of New York City streets, he must take the family to England and France in 1855 for a three-year sojourn. Besides a French governess, the traveling troupe included Catharine Walsh, the sister of Mrs. James and known as Aunt Kate, who became a family figure after her divorce and is treated like one in family correspondence. The children were again entrusted to private schools in England and France, tutors, and

[6] Besides the references already cited, see Leon Edel, ed., *The Diary of Alice James* (New York: Dodd, Mead, 1964).

[7] For these details, see Allen, pp. 27 ff.

governesses. These—in combination with scenes from ships, trains, and carriages, excursions to museums for "discoveries" of Delacroix and other artists, and prolonged encounters with European manners and customs—exposed William and Henry Jr., sufficiently mature to absorb it, to a cosmopolitanism that conspicuously shaped the brothers' lives in ways unavailable to less affluent and adventuresome Americans.

In spring of 1858 Henry Sr. decided to depart Boulogne, where the family had resided for a time and where William had shown his teachers a scientific bent with his interests in Bunsen burners, marine animals, and early photography, for Newport, Rhode Island. Newport beckoned because, in addition to hosting a summer colony that included Henry Wadsworth Longfellow, the painter William Morris Hunt, and various Harvard professors, it was home to other friends and relatives, such as Edmund Tweedy and wife. The Tweedys are repeatedly mentioned in family letters because they also made European trips that sometimes coincided with the Jameses' in later years and because they had generously assumed the responsibility of rearing Henry Sr.'s four orphaned nieces. Two of these—Kitty (Katharine) and Minny (Mary) Temple, daughters of Henry's sister—were William's and Henry Jr.'s favorite cousins. William did a very competent painting of Kitty; and Minny, as has been so often remarked by James scholars, inspired the character of Milly Theale in *The Wings of the Dove*. Among the Newport friends (and frequently mentioned in this volume's letters) were Thomas Sergeant Perry and John La Farge, who became one of America's leading painters. An engaging portrait of La Farge by William now belongs to one of William's descendants.

During 1858–59 William and Henry were enrolled in a somewhat odd private school in Newport, a tolerable year for William but boring for Henry. Then, abruptly, the father uprooted the family at summer's end in 1859 for a European return, again explaining the move as needed if the children were to be adequately educated. Settling in Geneva, William was stimulated by an anatomy course at the academy, and, unlike Henry, had a decent social and academic year.[8] But father Henry intervened again, moving them to Bonn for the summer so that they could learn German. Plans for a continuing education in Germany, however, were eventually aborted, and after an interim stay in Paris they returned to Newport in October 1860.

[8] Ibid., pp. 56–57.

The James's 1860–61 year in Newport is considered an important one by biographers, especially for then eighteen-year-old William. It was the year when, with John La Farge, he (and Henry Jr. also trying his hand) practiced painting at William Morris Hunt's studio. To do this, he had to overcome paternal objections to pursuing an artistic career, and at the year's end he decided to leave Newport and Hunt's tutelage to enroll at Harvard's Lawrence Scientific School. This decision has caused biographers to speculate about the possible motives and effects of that decision. Some view it as the result of Henry Sr.'s unsympathetic insistence on science instead of art as a career for his son, resulting for William in enormous emotional costs, depression, and unresolved emotional conflicts.[9]

The record shows that William and his father differed temporarily over the suitability of an artistic career, but, as I have urged elsewhere, the record shows neither that hostility soured their relationship nor that William's health problems were produced by a forced decision to abandon painting. Henry Jr. apparently never did understand his brother's resolve to study with Hunt in the first place, and his only explanation for William's giving up that resolve was a lack of real interest. That is probably true, given that William was unsure of his talent and, as he told his own son William years later, he had listened to Hunt's reservations about the fortunes of a painter's life in America. The "most serious" doubt that Ralph Barton Perry uncovered on William's part about his opting for science instead of art occurs in a letter from William to brother Henry of 24 August 1872 (this vol., p. 165).[10] But other than envying Henry's museum visits in Switzerland and Italy and paying tribute to the world of art, he wrote merely: "I feel more and more as if I ought to try to learn to sketch in water-colours, but am too lazy to begin. Perhaps I will at Mrs. Tappans." A more lackadaisical "seriousness" is hardly imaginable, nor, we may add, a more lackadaisical display of motivation.

We have brought the James family into the decade of the 1860s, when the letters of this volume begin, and, since these letters refer copiously to William's and Henry Jr.'s health problems that are often traced to family tensions allegedly created, some of them anyway, by Henry Sr., one is bound to wonder about the extent of his responsibility for his offspring's problems. William and Henry Jr. exhibited

---

[9] See, for example, Feinstein and Schwehn, ed.
[10] See Allen, pp. 68–70; Perry, 1:200; Schwehn, p. 428; and Myers, pp. 19, 493–94.

physical and mental frailties, afflictions of eyes, back, stomach, skin, and more, descriptions of which abound in this volume's letters. These problems (seemingly) kept them from serving during the Civil War. The younger brothers, Wilky (Garth Wilkinson) and Bob (Robertson), did fight. Wilky, with the famous 54th Massachusetts Black Regiment under Colonel Shaw, was badly wounded while attacking Fort Wagner in 1863 and was sent home to Newport. One of William's more poignant drawings is of Wilky at this time. At the war's conclusion, Wilky and Bob failed in a Florida plantation business venture, losing funds borrowed from their father, with the resultant drafting of his will as described in the correspondence between William and Henry after his death in December 1882. Wilky became a rather pathetic figure, a naive man defeated in his efforts to succeed in the commercial world and, in his nonintellectualism, looking alienated from the James family. Bob impressed his brother Henry and others as bright and having artistic talent, but alcohol repeatedly marred his life, to the point where William had to care for him personally. William's warnings about alcoholism in his writings were partly based on events close to home.[11]

The daughter, Alice, also exhibited mental and physical problems as a teenager. Prone to depressions and hysterical attacks, unable to form normal friendships, she seemed locked in the family. During the mid sixties, after the Jameses had moved from Newport to Boston and later to Cambridge, she was taken to New York City for medical treatment; but this was mostly ineffective, she being doomed to increasing invalidism. She eventually enjoyed a lasting relationship with a woman almost her own age, Katharine Loring, who became her caretaker-companion. Photos of them together in the late 1880s in England, when Alice joined Henry Jr., to whom she felt closest among her siblings, show bedridden Alice with Katharine hovering beside her. Whether this was a lesbian relationship has been a matter of unresolved speculation, almost matching for interest the question whether her brother Henry was always passively and perhaps occasionally actively homosexual.[12]

Henry Jr. did not escape the health traps that fate set for the Jameses, but he survived them less noisily than did William and with fewer threats to launching his career. What he called an "obscure hurt" resulting from an accident in Newport in 1861 has provoked

[11] For more on this, see Maher.
[12] See Strouse, pp. 248–53.

much conjecturing about what it was beyond being a back injury of some sort. It seems plausible, reading Henry's own allusions to the injury, to infer that it kept him from soldiering in the Civil War, but the plausibility dims before Leon Edel's account of the matter.[13] Why the younger brothers Wilky and Bob fought and William and Henry did not is never definitively explained. We might guess, on the slim data available, that the younger brothers wanted to serve and that Henry Sr. did not oppose them, that William and Henry, perhaps because of very limited physical strength (neither was large) and chronic health difficulties, did not want to serve and that Henry Sr. did not oppose them but might have done so had they offered to join up. To say this naturally incites more speculation; but absent more evidence, such conjecture is ultimately futile.[14]

Henry Jr.'s "problems," besides headaches, constipation, and other symptoms that are frequently complained about in this volume's letters, were shyness, hypochondria, feelings of inadequacy, concern about effeminacy, and "down" moods susceptible of various characterizations. After reflecting on how withdrawn and secretive his life had been, how much he reserved for a private consciousness wherein reality and imagination intermingled as only he (if anyone) could decipher, we surmise that those darker moods could be very dark indeed. Writing from Cambridge to William (22 Nov. 1867, p. 25), he admitted, in referring to his not being well, simply: "It is plain that I shall have a very long row to hoe before I am fit for anything—for either work or play." When looking back at himself in those mid 1860s, he recalled "the joy of youth" but also—more severely expressed than in the 1867 letter—he remembered the "suffering tortures from my damnable state of health. It was a time of suffering so keen that that fact might . . . give its dark colour to the whole period."[15]

If creativity demands psychical and physical distress, then William James could attribute his later successes to sharing family woes during the 1860s. After three years at Harvard's Lawrence Scientific School where biology had become his primary interest, William en-

[13] See Edel, *Life,* 1:167–83.

[14] My interpretation is based not only on the fact that Henry Sr. apparently did not want his two oldest sons to enlist but also that there is nothing in the record to indicate that they regretted not serving or not serving because of parental interference. One assumes that had such intervention occurred, it would have been mentioned at some point. See also notes 40 and 41 and accompanying text.

[15] Quoted by Edel, *Life,* 1:239.

tered Harvard Medical School in 1864. He interrupted his study
there to spend a year (1865–66) in Brazil with a team led by Louis
Agassiz, the famous Harvard naturalist, on a specimen-collecting expedition. The three Brazilian letters in this volume, besides conveying
travel impressions of the Amazon, reveal William's misgivings about
Agassiz, a noted opponent of Darwinian theory; whether these figured in his later differences with Agassiz on the merits of evolution-
ism is uncertain but interesting to contemplate, also keeping in mind
William's more redemptive remarks about Agassiz in other letters
from Brazil to his parents. Those letters deserve mention, too, for
showing William's realization that he was temperamentally not an
Agassiz-like scientist but was suited instead for "a speculative rather
than an active life," and, as he wrote Henry (3 May 1865, p. 8), "When
I get home I'm going to study philosophy all my days." [16]

After returning from the Brazilian expedition in February 1866,
William spent the summer as an undergraduate intern at Massachusetts General Hospital. In the fall he resumed his studies at Harvard
Medical School. But the following spring he again interrupted his
medical studies for eighteen months of recuperation and study in
Germany. Besides the thermal baths in Dresden that might relieve
chronic psychical-physical distress, there were the German universi-
ties that, he thought, would better prepare him in physiology and
psychology. The letters of 1867–68 in this volume show the brothers'
concerns for each other's health and ideas, lives, and careers—without, however, quite revealing how apparently "critical" this year was
for William. The same may be said, after his resuming at Harvard
and receiving his M.D. in 1869, of the year 1869–70. These are the
two periods most often examined in analyzing the psyche of William
James.

Whatever its proper name, depression or anxiety, despair or neu-
rasthenia, William tried to shake its grasp via the Germany visit, illus-
trating again his habit of seeking relief through travel. In a revealing
letter of 1868 to his friend Thomas Ward, he recalled that during the
previous year he had been "on the continual verge of suicide"; he
suggested how certain attitudes might combat despair, remarking
"What a preacher I'm getting to be!" [17] A preacher he was indeed, and

---

[16] Henry James III, ed., *The Letters of Williams James* (*LWJ*), 2 vols. (1920; reprint,
New York: Kraus, 1969), 1:62; also pp. 53–70.

[17] Ibid., pp. 127–33.

while symptomatic of his problems, such preaching seemed helpful in coping with them.

Another episode, perhaps even more critical, occurred in 1869–70. A notebook drawing of himself probably done about this time shows him seated on a chair, hands on knees, bending forward toward the floor, his face obscured, with the words "Here I and Sorrow Sit" appearing above him.[18] During this period, while he was still living with parents and sister in Cambridge and Henry Jr. was taking his European turn, William kept a diary that attributes his "crisis" to a philosophical loss of belief in free will but also credits his surviving the crisis to reading the French philosopher Charles Renouvier and adopting his definition of free will as "the sustaining of a thought *because I choose to* when I might have other thoughts." "My first act of free will," the diary continues, "shall be to believe in free will."[19] In Renouvier, William found his earliest support for a hallmark of his mature philosophy: that each of us has the right to choose our fundamental moral, religious, and metaphysical beliefs; it is a matter of choice, not of coercion by objective factors.

Although this volume's letters do not express the same melancholic depths disclosed in the diary or in letters to friends, such as Thomas Ward, they (together with other clues) alerted brother Henry to his ongoing troubles. William was deliberately restrained in what he wrote to Henry ("Harry") because, as he said in a candid acknowledgment of the difficulties to his father, "it will be just as well for you not to say anything to any of the others about what I shall tell you of my condition hitherto, as it will only give them useless pain, and poor Harry especially (who evidently from his letters runs much into that utterly useless emotion, sympathy, with me) had better remain ignorant."[20] Restraint was also required, he perhaps implied, because having compared in a letter to Thomas Ward his own symptoms with Henry's as being a "family peculiarity," to be utterly frank about them might have exacerbated Henry's possible anxiety that a curselike condition was inescapable. To Oliver Wendell Holmes, Jr. (17 Sept. 1867), William wrote, admitting his depression, "Since I have been here [Bad-Teplitz] I have admired Harry's pluck more and more."

[18] This is reproduced in an interesting article by James William Anderson, in Schwehn, ed., p. 375.

[19] Quoted in Myers, p. 46.

[20] *LWJ*, 1:95.

William was apparently resolved not to burden that pluck further by confessing all to Henry,[21] although he did not conceal his admiration for such pluck from Henry himself, as a letter in this volume (2 Oct. 1869, p. 100), written when William was low, touchingly shows.

Focusing on the Jamesian gloomier side before refocusing for a more balanced picture tempts us to ask why?—to speculate in particular about Henry Sr.'s influence. Whatever the causes, his five children were nervous, edgy, sensitive, if not physically or psychologically ill; by comparison, their parents appear more composed. Henry Sr. was indeed restless, conversationally hyperbolic, and often judgmental, but basically congenial and kindly. He supplied a comfortable home for his family, for William and Henry Jr. into their thirties, and for Alice even longer. He provided all of them, including Wilky and Bob, with financial support well into their adult lives, and he was their devoted father and correspondent. To find paternal faults in him, one has to dig the psychoanalytic soil rather deeply. He and his wife apparently agreed in mind and heart, and she, while occasionally vexed by her children's problems and complaints, was the stout, patient, dependable mother. Because there is some suggestion that she found Henry Jr.'s a gentler (less openly hypochondriachal) presence than William's, it is pertinent to note that, as William (when twenty-six) wrote from Teplitz to Henry (12 Feb. 1868, p. 31), she nevertheless had invited him "to come home & be nursed instead of remaining a lone outcast among the unfeeling foreigners."

Although Henry Sr. and Mary Walsh James were "good" parents, each of their five children, as adolescents and adults, felt a remarkable sense of inadequacy. Maybe genetic inheritance explains it, or that combined with other factors, such as the "rootlessness" (lack of neighborhood, etc. by the children during early family travels) and the puzzlement they felt when asked what their father did for a living. This probably did contribute to the sons' ability-anxieties, because Henry Sr., musing away his days on an independent income and an equally independent conviction that the here-and-now is an unworthy match for the hereafter, was in no position to inspire confidence in his career advice. The sons, unable to drift leisurely like their father (although, in William's case, some imitative efforts are decipherable), forced into vocation-seeking but without the benefit of paternal models and experiences as guides, might naturally wonder if they could compete in commercial and professional worlds. William's con-

---

[21] See Allen, pp. 134–35, for letters to Ward and Holmes.

cern about making a living is striking, so often was it voiced. In an 1867 letter to his friend Thomas Ward, for example, he lamented his failure over the prior six years to prepare himself for a career.[22] That failure, he thought was due partly to poor health but also to inferior training and education. Feeling ill-equipped and without special talents or the health and stamina to compensate for a late start in life, fearful of a weak psyche possibly born from deficient genes, any of us might verge on panic when confronted by our own ambitions.

Not that William's ambitions were exclusively his own, because though unspecified, they were shared and inspired by parental expectations. William and Henry had always seemed destined in Henry Sr.'s vision for achievements closed to Wilky and Bob.[23] Like their father, William and Henry chose an intellectual life. The sons had been reared on their father's linguistic inventiveness, and they came to believe, as did Socrates in Plato's *Phaedo,* that "to express oneself badly is not only faulty as far as the language goes, but does some harm to the soul." The careers of William and Henry were modeled on the paternal demonstration that the "feeling" mind is measured not by computations, gadgets, or deals but by the verbal style that it invents for itself. What language can do for nuancing ideas was not lost on these sons of a father who could complain to a newspaper editor about "the stagnant slipslop which your weekly ladle deals out" or about a traditional concept of God: "Against this lurid power—half-pedagogue, half-policeman, but wholly imbecile in both aspects—I . . . raise my gleeful fist, I lift my scornful foot."[24]

William and Henry, while distancing themselves from their father's aesthetic tastes, picked up his inclination, more like an obligation, to design one's reportage as an aesthetic reaction. In William's psychology and Henry's fiction the "evanescent" in experience is all-important; overlooked by the casual glance, the evanescent has to be displayed in a pictorial language that frames it. "Impressions" were their professional materials in which the reported and the reporting mixed indistinguishably, as the letters of this volume often demonstrate. William, coming to France from Germany, registered how "the tarnal smartness in the way the R. R. depôt counters for example are dressed up, the narrowish waists and white caps of the female servants, the everlasting 'monsieur' and 'madame,' and especially the ra-

---

[22] *LWJ,* 1:119.
[23] For more on this, see Maher and Myers, p. 30.
[24] Quoted by Matthiessen, p. 14; see also pp. 101–12.

pidity and snappishness of enunciation suggesting such an inward impatience made me feel uncomfortable" (26 Aug. 1868, p. 55). Making note, he said, of his "impressions" before they faded, Henry once wrote (26 Apr. 1869, p. 68) from Oxford that "the Warwickshire scenery is incredibly rich & pastoral," "one teeming garden" yet "too monotonously sweet & smooth—too comfortable, too ovine, too bovine, too English, in a word. But in its way its the last word of human toil." Not to catch (create?) such impressions for the James brothers was aesthetically culpable, morally vulgar.

For much of this time, as their correspondence shows, William and Henry enjoyed teeming gardens of impressions that tended to outdo the gloomy periods; far from being immobilized or withdrawn, they eagerly met new persons and scenes while nudging their careers ahead. We know that Henry's travels and readings, after he abandoned law school, during the 1860s and 1870s directly fed his reviews, travel articles, and tales for such as the *Nation, North American Review,* and *Atlantic Monthly,* as well as his first novel, *Roderick Hudson,* in 1875. He went straight for his goal, to be a self-supporting writer, and before 1880 had published impressively, including *The American, The Europeans,* and *Daisy Miller.*

But, compared to Henry, was William only marking time until his appointment at Harvard in 1872 as a physiology instructor? Never intending to practice medicine with his M.D. and still subject to "recuperating" spells, notably during 1869–72 and 1873–74, while searching for an intellectual and teaching focus, he was hiking a blinder path than Henry's. He knew what to read for teaching basic physiology, anatomy, and related psychology, but he was not preparing himself for laboratory expertise in those fields. His thought always drifted toward their philosophical fringes, and insofar as these became the site of his major achievements, the 1860s and 1870s and certainly the early 1880s—the years represented by this volume's correspondence—were professionally fruitful. The aesthetic interest shared with Henry is especially relevant; and what is a sizable piece of unfinished scholarship is a comprehensive interpretation of the aesthetic in William's philosophy and psychology; my own effort in that direction is merely a beginning.[25] The claim, for instance, that philosophical preferences are aesthetically motivated recurs in James's work, including the final chapter of *The Principles of Psychology,* appearing years earlier in an 1878 essay that scolded Thomas Henry

[25] Myers, pp. 239–40, 415–22.

Huxley and W. K. Clifford for not recognizing, in their praise of *disinterested* information, that "the love of consistency in thought . . . and the ideal fealty to Truth . . . are all so many particular forms of æsthetic interest."[26] Even physical science, James claimed, ultimately rests on decisions that are partly aesthetic and therefore partly subjective.

William's world of "impressions," whether gathered in reading Browning and Goethe, by savoring Paris, Rome, or London, or by sizing up friends and strangers, was vitally continuous with the "real" world that his philosophy and psychology sought to interpret. His third publication (referred to in a 26 Sept. 1867 letter to Henry, p. 18) was a review (to which Henry gave a helping hand) of a novel by Hermann Grimm, whom he had met by carrying a letter of introduction from Emerson. So it is not strange that "literary" modes of thought permeate James's formulations, whether in his philosophy of the self or in his psychology of experience (see, for example, "The Stream of Thought" chapter in *Principles of Psychology*). Using tropes and verbal devices of imaginative writers, creating verbal pictures worthy of a painter, he developed a genuinely "impressionistic" philosophy that appeals to similar temperaments but not to those wanting real precision or logical rigor. His thought both began and ended in impressions. *The Principles of Psychology* closes with an emphasis on psychology's explanatory limits, noting that the more we seek a scientific, less impressionistic understanding of ourselves, "the more clearly one perceives 'the slowly gathering twilight close in utter night.'"[27] Like the world of books and travels and "the tension of perception" that it generates (Henry's phrase, 26 Apr. 1869, p. 68), the world of philosophy and psychology is a kaleidoscope of impressions out of which a temporary, fragile conceptual collage is the best explanatory "system" that can be hoped for.

Religion was William's main concern all his life, and through the ups and downs of his twenties and thirties he pondered its validity, especially in his father's version of it. The relevance of these ponderings to his mature religious philosophy is another reason for not summarizing this early period, fragmented with recuperative flights to Europe, as only marking time. Religion was a further aspect of the aesthetic and impressionistic; it was an impressionistic way of giving

---

[26] "Remarks on Spencer's Definition of Mind as Correspondence" (1878), in William James, *Essays in Philosophy* (Cambridge: Harvard Univ. Press, 1978), p. 21.

[27] *The Principles of Psychology* (Cambridge: Harvard Univ. Press, 1981), p. 1280.

meaning to impressions recorded in letters, diaries, memories. I work "impressionistic" hard here, because the religion espoused by William in *The Varieties of Religious Experience* (1902) is, at best, mistily suggested. To appreciate this, one need only try to explain it to literal-minded students; they blink when told about the celebrated "directness" of William's language because what they find is an oblique, impressionistic exposition more commonly associated with brother Henry. Of course, William's idea was that religion is beyond the grasp of the literal-minded, and countless others, including Henry, have enthusiastically agreed.

The merger of the aesthetic, the impressionistic, and the religious in James's work ensured the authority of subjectivity. The aesthetic is partly *there*, but also partly here and mine; beauty is not entirely in the beholder's eye, yet it is not wholly outside it either. So with truth, the right, and the good—these, James declared in his mature writings, are determined by both objective and subjective factors. It was the latter feature, however, that his famous pragmatism emphasized; not to be overlooked is how his pragmatism was developed mainly as a subjective defense of religion.

William was mulling "the problem of evil" in his letters to Henry during the 1860s and 1870s, and the capability of religion, including Henry Sr.'s, of solving the problem. In a provocative letter (5 Apr. 1868, p. 41) he wrote: "The real brothers of the Greeks are the glorious Venetians—in both does the means of expression the artist is able to dispose of seem to cover all he wants to say—the Artist is adequate to his universe." But, he continued, Homer and the Greeks had no adequate concept of evil, and their stoic acceptance of fate (a point reiterated in *The Varieties of Religious Experience*) neither acknowledged evil nor met the modern demand for some "reason" for it. The artist depicts but does not explain, I take him to mean, and I suppose that he chose not art but philosophy because, besides doubting his talent, he was temperamentally driven to explain. The aesthetic is essential but not self-sufficient, a point also asserted, for instance, in an 1898 essay that introduced pragmatism.[28]

Can religion fulfill our explanatory needs? Answering this involved the son's assessing Henry Sr.'s theology and his book *The Secret of Swedenborg* (1869). Swedenborg, who claimed communion with spirits and angels and direct access to divine doctrines, was a challenge to any

[28]"Philosophical Conceptions and Practical Results," in William James, *Pragmatism* (Cambridge: Harvard Univ. Press, 1975).

would-be interpreter, so it is not surprising that one reviewer observed that Henry Sr. wrote about Swedenborg's secret while also keeping it. William tended to agree, indicating his discomfiture with his father's amateurishness in philosophical theology (2 Oct. 1869, p. 102). When he performed his "filial duty" in 1884 of publishing his father's writings, *The Literary Remains of the Late Henry James*, William relieved as best he could in his introduction the dogmatic amateurishness.

He called his father, despite his intellectual shallows, "a religious genius," as he had in a letter to Henry (1 Nov. 1869, p. 120). The concept of religious genius is central in *The Varieties of Religious Experience* in that it allows for genuine religious insight gained through the intuitive, prophetic grasp of unusual experiences. William might deplore Henry Sr.'s lack of intellectual sophistication, his neglect of evil, and confidence in salvation, but he understood the *experiential* and temperamental sources of his father's beliefs. In 1844 Henry Sr. had an eerie, semihallucinatory "fear and trembling" experience that left him shaken. This experience, making him receptive to Swedenborg, he later called a "vastation," and it has often been noted that William underwent a similar vastation that he described, but without admitting it as his own, in *The Varieties of Religious Experience*.[29]

William was outraged by dogmatism of any kind, charging it with ignorance and intolerance. The only tolerable viewpoints were those confessing *uncertainty*, and this he could detect in his father's vastation experience as in his own. He could also discern it in his father's theology, and whether he ever saw himself reflected in the seesaws of the paternal thinking, Henry and sister Alice evidently did. Alice wrote in her diary (18 Nov. 1889): "[William] is just like a blob of mercury, you can't put a mental finger upon him. H. and I were laughing over him and recalling Father and William's resemblance in these ways to him . . . in Wm., an entire inability or indifference 'to stick to a thing for the sake of sticking,' as some said of him once, whilst Father, the delicious infant! couldn't submit even to the thraldom of his own whim."[30] What William appreciated was his father's *need* of religious hope; he appreciated less the temptation to be consoled through doctrine. William wanted, but never enjoyed, genuine mystical experi-

[29] For more on Henry Sr.'s and William's religious views, see Perry, 1:20–38, 144–66, and 2:705–16. See also Matthiessen, pp. 136–89. And see *Diary of Alice James*, ed. Edel, pp. 149–50, for descriptions of "vastation" type experiences; and Edel's *Life*, 4:89–90, on the relation of Henry Sr.'s experiences to Henry Jr.'s.

[30] Edel, ed., *Diary of Alice James*, p. 57.

ence, nor did he find certainty of belief. The source of his subsequent vague and uncertain theology was the gut-level "fear and trembling" experience like his father's; this produced a *need* of which he said that "if I had not clung to scripture-texts like 'The eternal God is my refuge, etc . . .' I think I should have grown really insane."[31]

Abnormal psychology as well as religion was an area of interest for which William's experiences during his twenties and thirties were preparations. Impressed by the panoramic sweep of psychology in *The Principles of Psychology,* one easily forgets how much of that huge two-volume work is given to mental pathology. A number of early reviews in the *Nation* and the *Atlantic Monthly* focused on issues in abnormal psychology. A later article, "The Consciousness of Lost Limbs" (1887), summarizing amputees' reports of the phenomenon signified by the title, indicated William's interest in a type of experience that was familiar to his father. When his subsequent inquiries in psychical research are added, which in James's case were closely associated with psychology and philosophy, the growth of his intellectual output from the germ of those earlier experiences is distinctly visible.

The year 1878 looms large in William James's biography. By then he had published some forty-five short notices and review articles that pointed toward what he would begin in 1878, with such essays as "Remarks on Spencer's Definition of Mind as Correspondence," "Quelques considérations sur la méthode subjective," and "Brute and Human Intellect," as his own theoretical statements. He had been appointed assistant professor in physiology at Harvard, teaching what today would be considered a peculiar mix of physiology, psychology, and philosophy. His subsequent Harvard appointments indicate as much: professor of philosophy in 1885, of psychology in 1889. In 1878 he also contracted with Henry Holt to write *The Principles of Psychology,* beginning a fascinating episode both in James's career and in publishing history that culminated twelve years later. After the recuperative year 1873–74 he had remained on the job, declining a psychology appointment at Johns Hopkins University after lecturing there on "The Senses and the Brain." As always, the arguable independence of the mental was his antimaterialistic theme.

The momentous event of 1878 was his marriage to Alice Howe Gibbens. She was twenty-nine, a teacher at a Boston girls' school, helping to support her widowed mother and two younger sisters. She was "discovered"—an intriguing fact in itself—by Henry Sr., at a

[31] See Myers, p. 455.

function in Boston, as the wife for William. The marriage followed a rather awkward, drawn-out courtship. Pleasant, attractive, and strong like William's mother, Alice was an attentive, supportive spouse.[32] They had five children—Henry, William, Herman (died in infancy), Margaret Mary (Peggy), and Alexander Robertson—the first three born between 1879 and 1884, Margaret in 1887, and Alexander three years later.

These events are not recounted for us by William in this volume's correspondence, because William's letters to Henry from August 1876 to October 1882 are lost, with the exception of a single letter of 2 August 1880. Henry, who could not have known of course that William's new wife would one day, in 1916, personally and with some daring involved, return the ashes of his cremated body from England to the Cambridge Cemetery, was somewhat taken aback by "the abruptness of your union" (15 July 1878, p. 304). And though he regretted learning more about the marriage from his mother than from William, he was congratulatory in expressing confidence in the match. He also remarked in anticipating the wedding, "I had long wished to see you married; I believe almost as much in matrimony for most other people as I believe in it little for myself—which is saying a good deal" (29 May 1878, p. 303). Apart from some dismay at the identity-confusion occasioned by two Alices, sister and sister-in-law, and later by the names given to William's children, Henry (who never liked being Junior) was pleased, as was the family (save for sister Alice, if Jean Strouse's diagnosis is correct) by the great change in William's life.[33]

Henry, as his letters demonstrate, was actively writing and almost as actively establishing himself in the literary and social circles of England and Europe. It was a dazzling scene, meeting Herbert Spencer, William's intellectual preoccupation, at George Eliot's, chatting with Anthony Trollope, lunching at Lord Houghton's Cosmopolitan Club, conversing with Thomas Henry Huxley, dining with Gladstone and Tennyson; yet he felt another year or two were required for becoming a London "insider" (1 May 1878, pp. 300–301). After living and writing in Paris in 1875–76, and moving to London in 1876, he continued to develop the "international theme," to contrast nationalistic upper-middle-class manners, and to gather fame through such stories as *Daisy Miller* in 1878. Then, during 1879–80, he published *The Euro-*

[32] See Allen, pp. 214–31.
[33] See Strouse, pp. 178–230, 296–317.

peans, Washington Square, and *Confidence.* He managed, while traveling the next year in Switzerland and Italy, to finish *Portrait of a Lady.* The energy and flow of his talent were quite as dazzling as the life they served.

One is struck, in reading the extant full correspondence of William and Henry James by how energetic and active both men were. In this respect their prodigious publication records speak for themselves, but what went on additionally is no less noteworthy. When not writing, Henry was busy—endlessly traveling, walking London, on horseback in Rome's countryside, negotiating publications, visiting museums, attending theatre, dining and conversing with the rich and famous in Paris or wherever, registering impressions for his writings, as well as performing a bachelor's time-consuming personal and domestic chores.

By focusing too narrowly on their downside moments, we mistakenly fancy them, like their sister Alice, as reclusive semiinvalids. In William's instance, besides the travels there were social intercourse, hiking mountains here and abroad, taking public stands on political and social issues, contributing to special projects, carrying the daily burdens of a full Harvard teaching schedule, entertaining students, colleagues, and visiting scholars, and fathering a substantial family. The *practical* side of this pragmatic philosopher shows clearly in the letters and diaries that refer to such nonintellectual matters.

Another practical distraction of both brothers that at times siphoned their productive energies was their family obligations. Henry took over the family concern for sister Alice by escorting her (and Aunt Kate) in 1872 for six months on her first European trip. Henry wrote to William with obvious relief: "The great satisfaction of it all, of course, has been the sight of Alice's immense improvement. . . . You will probably see a great change in her when she gets home—if the second half of our journey is as propitious as the first—as it can hardly fail to be" (24 July 1872, p. 161). Seeing American friends such as Elizabeth (Lizzie) Boott, who later married the Cincinnati painter Frank Duveneck, assisted Henry's efforts on behalf of his sister. While beneficial, the trip did not, of course, solve deep-seated problems of health and depression. Her condition worsened, culminating in a breakdown in 1879. That, on Jean Strouse's analysis, was triggered by distress over William's marriage.[34] Experiencing further difficulties after her parents' deaths, she left in 1884 with Katharine

---

[34] Ibid.

Loring for England to be near Henry, where she died of breast cancer in 1892 at forty-four. It was no small thing, the compassionate attention that Henry gave his sister during those last eight years of her life. It was a prescient impulse that prompted Alice and her mother long before to call him "angel."

William was not the first of the family to marry; Bob married in 1872, Wilky the next year, both residing in Wisconsin and taking women from that state as brides. These events and their enduring effects troubled the Jameses. They disliked Wilky's wife Carrie (Caroline) Cary because of her gaudy clothes and jewels and lack of conversational, intellectual abilities. Wilky and Bob had moved to Wisconsin, taking clerk-type jobs with railroads such as the Chicago, Milwaukee and St. Paul Railway, after their postwar financial disaster in trying to run a cotton plantation in Florida. Another business venture, undertaken by Wilky with his usual but misplaced optimism, ended in bankruptcy in 1877. William visited him in Milwaukee, and Henry Sr. continued to send him funds, also inviting him home when his chronic health problems worsened. In 1883, assisted in travel by Henry Jr., Wilky went to Cambridge for a recuperative stay and then returned to family and Milwaukee, where he died at thirty-eight of kidney disease.

It is ironic that Wilky was the first of the Jameses to die and in such circumstances. Although bankrupt himself, he had married into an affluent family as had Bob, so the Jamesian connections with people of means continued, and to the benefit of Wilky's and Bob's wives and children. (Wilky's son, Joseph Cary James, for instance, became a prominent, wealthy member of Milwaukee society.) Wilky had always seemed, in Jean Maher's words, "the healthiest and happiest of all the James children."[35] Good-natured and well-intentioned, plumpish in body and temperament, the least artistic and cerebral of the five children, he is hard to place in the James family; but, as their correspondence shows, "poor" Wilky was constantly their concern.

Bob's wife, Mary Holton James, was liked by the Jameses, but not her wealthy father, who was most amusingly described by Henry Sr.: "He is an animated town clock, and if he could only get a position where every one would be content to listen to him 24 times a day, his happiness would be complete. He did nothing but orate and gesticulate with arms borrowed from a windmill all the time he was here."[36]

[35] Maher, p. 163.
[36] Letter of 7 August 1881, from Henry Sr. to William, quoted by Maher, p. 116.

(This again brings to mind the similarities of William's style and his judgmental bluntness to Henry Sr.'s.) Bob had always been a "problem," prone to drinking and violent outbursts. From his photos he appears the most athletic, masculine, and ruggedly handsome of the James children. Although physically active, William by contrast was small, wiry, and increasingly "professorial" in appearance. Confirming the family's belief that he was talented, Bob published a poem in 1885 in *Atlantic Monthly,* and in his final years he painted in Concord, Massachusetts, having moved there from Wisconsin. I have seen his paintings (most were in storage) in the Concord Free Public Library, and they compare favorably with much that I have looked at in New England galleries and auction houses.[37]

Whatever the proper diagnosis of Bob's mental problems, he exhibited the Jamesian restlessness. In Wisconsin he took, quit, and retook railroad jobs, filled a curator's position for a short time at the embryonic art museum in Milwaukee, after that tried farming. Then it was back east and seeking to be an artist. His wife Mary endured his philandering, alcoholism, temporary absences, general erratic behavior, and repeated offers of divorce. This was partly owing to her own financial independence. That allowed her some psychic distance as well. They had two children who did well subsequently. The son, Edward Holton James, a highly interesting and still remembered personality, married into the prominent Cushing family of Boston, one of his daughters marrying the sculptor Alexander Calder.

William's concern for Bob began as early as 1868 when, hearing that he was secretly engaged to a cousin, William wrote him about the dangers of such a marriage.[38] Between the early 1870s and 1885, when Bob settled in Concord, William and Henry Sr. monitored Bob's life through letters, William's traveling to him in Wisconsin or making temporary sanctuaries of their own homes when, in desperate moods, he needed such. Alice disliked her brother, wanting nothing to do with him. He was also a trial for William's wife, who feared his sudden drunken arrivals and outbursts that, were it not for William, might have ended even more disastrously. William deposited him in 1898 at Dansville Asylum in upper New York State; although he seemed quieter upon returning to Concord in 1901, the problems, including drinking, never disappeared entirely, and William's over-

[37] An intriguing portrait of Bob as a youth by John La Farge is reproduced in Maher.

[38] Ibid., p. 110.

sight continued until both gradually weakened into death in 1910—
Bob in July, William in August.

The letters in this volume reflect William's and Henry's interest in
their siblings, but at one point that interest becomes concentrated:
in December 1882 when Henry Sr. died, following his wife's death in
January of the same year. All five children attended the mother's funeral, their first (and last) time together since before the Civil War.[39]

Henry Sr.'s death—and will—produced the most focused series of
letters in this volume, beginning with William's of 20 December 1882,
telling that he learned through the newspapers of his father's death.
The brothers, anticipating their father's demise, had agreed that
Henry would sail to Massachusetts, leaving William free to continue
his year's leave from Harvard and with the use of Henry's London
lodgings. William's letter also betrays some guilt about his decision to
remain abroad. Henry's letter of 26 December tells of missing the funeral on the morning of the twenty-first (he arrived that evening), two
days after the day of their father's death. Bob had come from Wisconsin for the funeral and returned the next day, leaving Henry (with
Alice and Aunt Kate) essentially alone to fill the executor's role as-
signed him by their father.

The estate approximated $95,000, representing three business
properties in Syracuse and the rest in railway bonds and shares. (I
was told a few years ago by a James descendant that income is still
received from the Syracuse properties.) Alice was bequeathed the parental Mt. Vernon Street house in Boston and the income from stocks
and bonds. The sticky issue was Wilky's exclusion from the will because Henry Sr. had recently sent him $5,000 in addition to the mon-
eys given him in prior years. Another, but less sticky issue, was Henry
Sr.'s deducting $7,000 from Bob's inheritance, an amount given him
in 1874 to buy a farm. Besides the letters exchanged between William
and Henry on these matters, there were many more involving other
family members.

Wilky was upset, writing a (most untypical) bitter letter to Bob the
day after Christmas 1882, saying: "It was a base cowardly act of father's, . . . a death stab at the only two of his children who dared fight
through the war for the defense of the family and the only two who
attempted while very young to earn their own living and have earned
it steadily ever since."[40] Jane Maher seems correct, if we waive indirect

[39] Ibid., p. 140.
[40] Maher reproduces the letter in full, pp. 149–50.

allusions, in stating that this is "the only reference ever made by any of the Jameses to this sensitive issue."[41] And she persuasively infers that Wilky's letter resulted from shock, expecting his inheritance share to alleviate extreme financial pressures, rather than from long-standing resentment. In any event, as this volume's correspondence manifests, Henry and William were at odds for a time over the Wilky issue.

The episode has certain queer-looking aspects—Henry Sr.'s exclusion of Wilky; Henry Jr.'s being designated executor instead of William; William's holding out against the others, including his wife, in defending Henry Sr.'s will; Henry Sr.'s being even interested in drafting a will; Henry Jr.'s intense pleadings for William not to come home but to remain in London; and William's being by himself away from his family for a year's travels. It is interesting that Leon Edel does not magnify this episode as one might expect, given his well-known conviction that a serious Jacob-Esau sibling rivalry undercut the surface affections between William and Henry. He does say that when Henry instead of William was chosen by the father to administer the estate, "Jacob had indeed supplanted Esau—and Esau at this moment was in a far-away land."[42] But he treats the episode briefly, and in another place where he might emphasize the Jacob-Esau theme, he remarks lightly on William's and Henry's disagreement over the will, referring to Henry's "quarrel with William James (if one can use so violent a word for their verbal sparring)."[43] The seemingly queer aspects of the episode are explicable, I believe, in ways that justify Edel's light treatment of it.

Wilky suspected that Aunt Kate (Catharine Walsh) had manipulated Henry Sr., who scoffed at rituals and devices like wills, into both making a will and specifying its contents.[44] He may have guessed correctly in this, but if not, and Henry Sr. acted on his own, not malice but concern for fairness, it is fair to conclude, motivated his actions. Henry's appointment as estate executor, if Wilky's suspicions were true, could be attributed to Aunt Kate who, possibly with sister Alice's agreement, perhaps assumed that Henry, a bachelor with no family interests to defend and more docile than William, would act as instructed. Or Henry Sr. could have reasoned similarly, but, as it even-

[41] Ibid., p. 150.

[42] Edel, *Life,* 3:62; see also pp. 63–65.

[43] Edel, ed., *Henry James Letters,* 4 vols. (Cambridge: Belknap Press of Harvard Univ. Press, 1974–84), 2:328.

[44] See Maher, pp. 150–52.

tuated, only to have Henry Jr. (docilely) upset expectations. Whether Henry's generosity, extended to sister Alice and even to Wilky's wife Carrie, was foreseen is unknown. With relief, one gathers, Henry transferred the estate's administrative duties to William that summer upon returning to England. As for William's and Henry's disagreement about the will's merits, it must be said on William's behalf that, besides protecting his own family's interests, he had good reason to believe that money for Bob and Wilky was wasted and that, unlike himself, Bob and Wilky had affluent wives. His initial impulse, as evidenced in his letter of 9 January 1883 (p. 344), was to change the will, as was finally done, and restore Wilky's share. His change of heart seems due to the considerations just mentioned, but, as the successive letters indicate, he soon withdrew his alternative proposals, accepting a simple redivision of the estate with Wilky included. One gets the impression that the will was hardly the main thing on William's mind, that it was an irritating distraction. But the one most irritated and saddened by the "affair of the will" was Wilky who, within a few months of it, received his final "liberation."

Henry's letter (1 Jan. 1883, p. 342), which is often cited, describes his reading a "farewell" letter from William to Henry Sr. by the latter's graveside. The letter had arrived too late: the father never saw it. It is perhaps the most famous of William's letters, arresting one's attention by its direct, almost matter-of-fact acceptance of his father's imminent death, joined with an eloquent tribute to Henry Sr.'s influence.[45] One senses the strength of the delicate bond between the brothers—and the family through the father—in Henry's wanting to stand "beside his grave a long time & read him your letter of farewell—which I am sure he heard somewhere out of the depths of the still, bright winter air." One senses it even more when made aware of Henry's appreciation of William's choice of a line from Dante to be inscribed on sister Alice's urn after her death in 1892—"ed essa da martiro e da essilio venne a questa pace" (from martyrdom and exile she came to this peace). Calling the inscription William's "divine gift to us, and to *her*," it took him, Henry said, "at the throat with its penetrating *rightness*."[46]

But in that same letter of 1 January 1883, Henry also wrote: "Your letter makes me nervous in regard to your dispositions of coming home. *Don't for the world think of this, I beseech you*—it would be a very idle step." And he went on in this vein, more so in successive letters,

<hr />

[45] *LWJ*, 1:218–20.
[46] Edel, ed., *Diary of Alice James*, p. 21.

provoking William to sharp-toned replies. We can magnify Henry's resistance to William's interrupting his leave and returning home if we assume, as some do, unconscious anxieties in Henry about William. But we are warranted, I believe, in taking Henry at his word, sincere and sensible in reasoning as he did in his 1883 letters of 11 January and 23 January (that crossed with William's of the same day), 6 February and 11 February. From William's regular correspondence at the same time with his wife Alice, we know that she agreed with Henry. If William returned, he would dislike their awkward living situation at home (described in this volume's correspondence), and would probably regret having interrupted his leave's research as well as risking health and temperament under such circumstances.

William's temptation to return from England was apparently motivated not by the terms of his father's will but by remorse for being absent at his father's death and the ensuing events. He also missed his wife and children and felt some guilt there as well; and he was bored with life in England. Like Henry's, William's reasons, too, can be taken at face value. Finally, as we learn, he fell in with Henry's and Alice's advice, leaving us wondering, however, why he was apart from his family in the first place.

A fairly standard opinion has it that William's marriage to Alice Howe Gibbens in 1878 had an ongoing positive effect on his health and disposition, and, taken cautiously, that is probably true. But it should not be exaggerated, for, as might be anticipated, such problems as had haunted William tend to be stubborn visitors. Trying to progress with his psychology book for Holt while teaching and parenting his first child Harry (Henry III) in 1879 was difficult. The following year he left wife and year-old Harry for the summer to attend lectures in Berlin that would contribute to his book. But, as Henry's 1880 letters to him indicate, William's eye problems (among others) had recurred, and travel for "escape" as well as intellectual stimulation may be suspected. After William sojourned briefly with him in London at that time, Henry worried in a letter to their mother that William "takes himself, and his nerves, and his physical condition too hard and too consciously."[47]

When Henry Sr. died, William was thus away from wife and children a second time, and his second son, William, was just an infant. His habit of departing somewhere after a child's birth, according to James descendants, was legendary. It was another of William's

[47] Allen, p. 233.

"flights," since any perching-place was soon uncomfortable, including his own home. His marriage worked, wonderfully in many respects, and the mutual devotion of husband and wife seems evident. But it was not always easy, as I discovered in surveying the intimate correspondence between him and wife Alice. He appreciated the anxieties that his temperament inflicted on anyone at close quarters over time; with loving responses, Alice accepted his apologies while often reproving herself for being a contributory cause.[48] Alice's and Henry's worries about William's returning home under trying circumstances were based on considerable past experience.

What stung William in Henry's admonitions was the expressed fear of how William's returning would look to friends and colleagues in Cambridge and at Harvard, and the candor of William's reply, especially in his letter of 6 February 1883 (p. 362), is noteworthy. Knowing that such persons, including President Charles Eliot of Harvard, had long been (sympathetically) aware of his "problems," William reacted sensitively to the thought that they might judge his return a "confession of failure" or an "appearance of vacillation." Henry struck a nerve with these expressions, as he likely anticipated but risked, for anxieties about failures and vacillations dogged William, and openly. He had yet to prove himself; only recently had he begun to teach philosophy; his contracted book on psychology would wait another seven years before completion, and the quest for his own intellectual voice had far to go. To notice the defensiveness, however, is not to ignore his affectionate regard for Henry. True, he was needlessly harsh on Henry's beloved England, also needling in blaming the darkness of Henry's London lodgings for his "acute brain-fag"; yet, despite homesickness and all, he was on top of the situation in responding (23 Jan. 1883, pp. 353–54) to Henry's arduous efforts: "It makes my heart bleed that the relation of brother should entail such sacrifices. & I know now just how one's half-crazy relations feel when they get letters of good counsel."

How did these eminent brothers "really" relate to each other? This question is asked as often as the question about their relationship to Henry Sr., and some of the continuing interest in it may be credited to Leon Edel's monumental five-volume *Life of Henry James*. This remarkable and unmatched study of the life and career of Henry Jr. develops the idea mentioned earlier, that an unconscious rivalry between the brothers seriously conflicted with their conscious feelings

[48] See Myers, pp. 36–40.

of fraternal affection. Because William seems to take some unwarranted hits from Edel in his analysis, I offered a rebuttal in my study of William's life and career. Since the present volume's contents focus on the brothers' relationship, Edel's novel interpretation, which has been so influential, must be acknowledged. Debating it, however, is too complex to attempt here, so I settle for a few observations additional to the arguments advanced in my *William James: His Life and Thought*.[49]

No one questions the genuine fraternal affection displayed by this volume's correspondence, at most only whether it was ambivalent. That the brothers' "problems" sometimes recurred when together is presented in support of the ambivalence hypothesis. But this was surely coincidental to some extent, and the other instances of headaches, eye problems, and the like were probably due to their chronic edginess and inability to sustain daily intimacy with anyone. Both were essentially private persons who relished a full social life but one that terminated at their private precincts.

William's responses to Henry's writings are often mentioned on behalf of the claim that he (unconsciously) resented the younger brother's early successes and accompanying parental laudations. But we should remember that *criticism* had been learned at Henry Sr.'s dinner table as an intellectual, even moral duty; for William not to react critically would be reprehensible, whether applauding Henry's 1867 story "Poor Richard," admiring "Madame de Mauves" in 1875, anticipating *Roderick Hudson*'s ending (which he liked) the next year, or warming to *Daisy Miller* soon thereafter; or, on the other hand, responding negatively to such as "The Romance of Certain Old Clothes" for being "*thin*" and giving "a certain impression of the author clinging to his gentlemanlyness tho' all else be lost, and dying happy provided it be *sans déroger*" (4 Mar. 1868, p. 36)—the kind of evaluation, charging overrefinement, indirectness, and a "want of blood" that recurred in William's letters to Henry.

William's negative appraisals were echoed elsewhere, and, while perhaps not equaling Max Beerbohm's or H. G. Wells's, they have scored well with some of Henry's critical admirers (occasionally including Henry himself).[50] William certainly appreciated Henry's lit-

[49] Ibid., pp. 22–29.

[50] See Richard A. Hocks, *Henry James and Pragmatic Thought* (Chapel Hill: Univ. of North Carolina Press, 1974). Hocks, referring to a 1907 letter by William to Henry about the latter's *American Scene,* calls it "simply one of the most beautifully exact descriptions of the late 'Jamesian' method to be found" (pp. 21–22).

erary genius; in 1868 he requested, without embarrassment, Henry's help for some of his own writing projects, and, keeping abreast of Henry's prolific output, tried in his critical observations to be responsive. I think there can be no doubting William's worry that the odds were against a person's making a living via writing fiction, that he feared for Henry's future, and that he submitted what he believed was likely to be the most helpful advice protecting that future. Whether there is some figure in the carpet of his criticisms, some ruling concept behind his preferences among Henry's writings, I cannot say. Perhaps, in line with some thinking, it may be discovered that William's approvals correspond to the fictional use of the "pragmatic method," although I doubt it.[51] Certainly, let it be said, no correlation exists between William's approvals and just any use by Henry of the "stream of consciousness" device!

Henry relied less on criticisms of William's writings than on "impressions" of people and places to ensure a richer content in their correspondence—in 1869, for example, when it might have been reduced merely to reporting "my moving intestinal drama." Temperamentally less blunt than William, he was, although interested and encouraging, less engaged by William's publications, which accumulated slowly compared to his own, than William was by his; an understandable fact since fiction, unlike physiological psychology, turns everyone into impromptu critics. Henry became more openly resistant to William's fraternal lecturing while also waxing more enthusiastic about William's latest philosophical works, *Pragmatism* (1907) and *The Meaning of Truth* (1909). He, too, could play with the Jamesian badinage,

---

See also Virginia Fowler, *Henry James's American Girl* (Madison: Univ. of Wisconsin Press, 1984). About William's response to *The Golden Bowl* (1904) she writes: "William's acuteness as a critic asserts itself here, especially in his description of Henry's 'method of narration by interminable elaboration of suggestive reference,' though for some readers this method elicits as much praise as it does censure from the practical and direct William" (p. 97).

And see Matthiessen for the brothers' literary relationship.

[51] But Richard Hocks's book, cited above, seems to promise such, making Henry's fiction instantiate William's pragmatism. Hocks's discussion of the reasons for Henry's liking William's *Pragmatism* and *The Meaning of Truth* is persuasive at a general level, but the more specifically the link is made with Henry's fiction, the less persuasive it becomes.

See Nicola Bradbury's " 'Nothing That Is Not There and the Nothing That Is': The Celebration of Absence in *The Wings of the Dove*" for relating the "deconstructive text," at a certain place in *The Wings of the Dove*, with William's pragmatic method, in Ian F. Bell, ed., *Henry James: Fiction as History* (London and Totowa, N.J.: Vision and Barnes & Noble, 1984), pp. 89–90.

drop the offhand remark that is not totally offhand as when he signed off to William: "By this time I suppose you have begun to lecture or teach or preach, or whatever it is. Amen!" (8 Jan. 1873, p. 188). Their occasional differences were due to genuine divergences of taste and opinion, I think, rather than to unconscious rivalry; their temperaments and professions were sufficiently disparate to foreclose competitiveness.

The brothers shared art and literature as interests from the beginning, and once these became Henry's professional domain, William's familiarity with it and Henry's development in it naturally stimulated the critical conversations that he sometimes initiated. William was reading George Sand in the 1860s and later comparing impressions of George Eliot with Henry who, notwithstanding his debts to this author, called Eliot's *Daniel Deronda* an "amiable failure."[52] Because of their shared reverence for the aesthetic and its moral implications, William's entries into what Graham Greene called Henry's "private universe" were inevitable.[53] One such entry, William surmised, was unintended, but the unflattering reception given it by Henry was taken by William good-naturedly; he wrote, after reading the second installment of *The American:* "The morbid little clergyman is worthy of Ivan Sergeitch. I was not a little amused to find some of my own attributes in him—I think you found my 'moral reaction' excessive when I was abroad" (5 July 1876, p. 268).

William was impulsively "judgmental," quick to revise the judgment, showing a Hegelian-like inclination to reach a balanced conclusion through synthesizing opposing sentiments that seem deliberately looked for. Examples are found throughout his correspondence, and they may startle readers who encounter his caustic side for the first time. I think it significant, therefore, that in surveying some eighteen hundred letters between William and wife Alice I found, in that most confidential exchange, no signs of snideness or hostility toward Henry, not even in the 1882–83 period when if at any time such might be expected.

Being near Henry for a sustained time following Henry Sr.'s death was a new experience for wife Alice, and she wrote to William about some tension between Henry and herself caused apparently by their trying to excel each other's politeness and sensitivity for the other's

---

[52] For a recent discussion of George Eliot's influence on Henry James, see Roger Sale, *Literary Inheritance* (Amherst: Univ. of Massachusetts Press, 1984), pp. 155–201.

[53] "The Private Universe," in Leon Edel, ed., *Henry James: A Collection of Critical Essays* (Englewood Cliffs, N.J.: Prentice-Hall, 1963), pp. 111–23.

benefit. She wrote (1 Jan. 1883), "How wide these differences of nature are, and how I thank God for yours—your nature darling—which shelters mine so warmly!" A few days later she wrote "of Harry who is to me like a strange perfume, very pleasant but leaving a curious lassitude behind. And he is so good!" (11 Jan. 1883). William responded: "Yes, Harry is a queer boy, so good, & yet so limited, as if he had taken an oath not to let himself out to more than half of his humanhood, in order to keep the other half from suffering, & had capped it with a determination not to give anyone else credit for the half he resolves not to use himself. Really it is not oath or resolve, but helplessness" (31 Feb. [? 31 Jan.] 1883). William did worry about what he saw as Henry's helplessness, an inertness before life's practicalities that might require someone's caring for him as Katharine Loring did for sister Alice. William fretted about money and financial obligations, including, I believe (because of what his correspondence with wife Alice contains), those that Henry might come to represent. But in this, certainly, we see no symptoms of fraternal rivalry or resentment bubbling underneath.

The fraternal correspondence in this volume is to be read of course for more than what it tells us about the brothers' personal relationships. Henry's 29 March 1870 letter (p. 153) about cousin Minny Temple's death is an important example; it and Henry's *Notes of a Son and Brother* are drawn upon for scholarly findings of Minny in various Jamesian female guises but especially in Milly Theale in *The Wings of the Dove*.[54] Another instance is Henry's of 30 October 1869 (pp. 116–17), a letter much quoted and, as Leon Edel says, is sure to be quoted "again and again"[55]—reporting his first impression of Italy and of Rome where "I went reeling & moaning thro' the streets, in a fever of enjoyment."

In addition to the letters that tell about fellow writers such as Turgenev and Flaubert, letters having received much scholarly attention, others will attract notice for their glimpses of Oliver Wendell Holmes,

[54] For more on this, see Edel, *Life*, 1:313–33; Fowler, pp. 10–11, 86–88; and Tony Tanner, *Henry James* (Amherst: Univ. of Massachusetts Press, 1985), pp. 111–16.

[55] Leon Edel, "The Italian Journeys of Henry James," in James W. Tuttleton and Agostino Lombardo, eds., *The Sweetest Impression of Life: The James Family and Italy* (New York: New York Univ. Press, 1990), p. 14.

See also in the same volume, for material relevant to this Introduction, James W. Tuttleton's " 'Dipped in the Sacred Stream': The James Family in Italy," pp. 22–48; Gerald E. Myers's "The Influence of William James's Pragmatism in Italy," pp. 162–82; and Claudio Gorlier's "Listening to the Master: William James and the 'Making of the New' in Italian Culture," pp. 182–97.

Jr., Charles Sanders Peirce, Henry Adams, and John Singer Sargent. (Sargent, I was told, referred clients occasionally to William's son, another William, who was a portrait painter.)[56]

For William's followers, letters of special interest include his of 12 February 1868, from Teplitz (p. 32) that refers to an attractive woman "here for her rheumatism, an actress, a very handsome & agreeable jewess, who speaks german beautifully." He drew a likeness of her that is a fine example of his artistic skill; it is reproduced in my *William James*. Something may still be learned about William's views on marriage and women by reexamining his grounds for disliking his father's articles on these subjects (19 Jan. 1870, p. 141) which Henry, on the other hand, liked (8 Mar. 1870, p. 152).

We hear about visits to Concord to see the Emerson family, Louisa May Alcott, or an evening at the Longfellows, and about the publicity given to the Henry Ward Beecher adultery scandal. William to Henry (25 June 1874, p. 238): "I think Parisian lewdness is purity itself compared with this Puritanic pruriency." Puritanism had perhaps something to do with his citing, as the latest example of American "humor," the exclamation of a child lost at a fair, "Where's my mother? I told the darned thing she'd lose me" (12 Dec. 1875, p. 248). The 1883 letters provide anecdotal information on William's meetings with Thomas Davidson, an important philosophical ally of James's, in Florence; with Felix Adler, founder of the Ethical Culture movement, in William's favorite mountain sanctuary, Keene Valley in the Adirondacks.

This volume's correspondence takes us through 1884; by then Henry was internationally famous, his first collected edition of novels and tales in fourteen volumes having just been published in London. As he wrote to William (26 May 1884, p. 382), he was starting two "big & important" novels, identifying one of them thereafter as *The Bostonians*. It and the other, *The Princess Casamassima*, appeared two years later. His essay "The Art of Fiction" appeared in 1884. This was not only a marvelous explication of his own fiction but, as has been said, "it marks a turning point in the history of the theory of the novel."[57] The distinguished writer's distinguished social life continued, one day lunching with Arthur Balfour (whom William admired) and the next with Louis Pasteur. His friends included the psychologist-philosopher Alexander Bain, who could, he thought, be persuaded

---

[56] I was told this by Dr. Roberta Sheehan-Taylor, of Boston, who has researched the history of the Boston art scene, including the presence of James family members.

[57] Tanner, p. 72.

to obtain a copy of F. H. Bradley's *Ethical Studies* for William. In sister Alice and Katharine Loring, who were now in England near him, Henry James had the closest he would ever approximate to a family of his own.

William wrote (18 Oct. 1884, p. 385) that he was finishing his father's book, *The Literary Remains of the Late Henry James,* for publication the next month. His Harvard teaching duties were tolerable, but progress toward *The Principles of Psychology* was slow because of eye problems again. Nevertheless, during the previous six years he had several chapters of the book essentially in place. His thinking had crystallized on such topics as the differences between human and animal consciousness, automatism and free will, the perception of space, association of ideas, the feeling of effort, and numerous specialized topics, such as the sensibility of articular surfaces, monocular and binocular vision, and the physiology of the semicircular canals. Besides his father's book, William published two very important articles in 1884: "On Some Omissions of Introspective Psychology" and "What Is an Emotion?" Both would give his *Principles* a distinct Jamesian imprint. Two others appeared the same year: "Absolutism and Empiricism" and "The Dilemma of Determinism." Both would give his mature philosophy a distinct Jamesian stamp.

In 1884 William was instrumental in founding the American Society for Psychical Research, two years after Edmund Gurney, Frederic W. H. Myers, and Henry Sidgwick—names that occur in this volume's letters—had created the British society. William ever pleaded for tolerance in evaluating psychical research, but Henry was not so easily persuaded. "I went the other night to a *soirée* of Gurney & Myers's Psychical Society; & found it very dull & even repulsive, owing to the fearful verdigreased human & social types congregated there" (25 Jan. 1884, p. 373). A few months later he wrote that he did not see Gurney often. "I am afraid he is besotting himself with his ghost-hunting" (26 May 1884, p. 381). William wanted to believe in it, as did his wife, Alice, but the lack of good evidence kept him cautious on the subject. Sometimes he thought it was wasted effort, yet who could predict what it might yield? And it was valuable insofar as it stimulated, through various associations, his thinking and research in abnormal psychology.

In 1884, William's and Alice's third child was born, an event that prompted Henry's energetic concern about what to name him (see 20 Feb., 26 Mar., 21 Apr. 1884), "Herman" (after a Harvard professor) being finally acceptable to all. Eighteen months later Herman died of pneumonia. The family's sadness and Alice's devotion to the dying child were eloquently conveyed in William's correspondence.[58] He had lost both parents in 1882, brother Wilky the next year, and Herman two years later. As William's letters reveal, resisting morbidity under those circumstances took some doing. Daughter Margaret Mary (Peggy) was born in 1887, Alexander Robertson in 1890, the year that *The Principles of Psychology* at last appeared. The William James family was complete and the writing project of twelve years was finished—all that was needed was in place for forwarding the subsequent life and career of a philosopher who taught that the subject of his philosophy, the cosmos, is ongoing and never complete.

[58] Allen, pp. 279–80.

Bibliographical Note

Immediately after the death of William James in 1910, members of his family began the tedious work of collecting letters and preparing them for publication. The responsibility was shared by his widow, Alice Gibbens James, and his son Henry James. The family sought to retain control of James's reputation by presenting to the public its own version of his life and character. In his unpublished memoir of his mother, preserved at the Houghton Library, Henry notes that the attic of the house on Irving Street was crammed with papers and that in the evenings Alice would take down some bundles, sort through them, and destroy what she thought should not be preserved. No records were kept, although in the case of some of James's letters to her she made extracts before destroying the originals. Henry's job was to contact his father's correspondents and ask them either to lend the originals or to provide transcripts.

The first to benefit from these efforts was the brother Henry James who included some William James letters in his autobiographical volumes, especially in *Notes of a Son and Brother* (1914). Henry James treated the letters with considerable freedom, but his versions are helpful because he sometimes provides complete names of persons obscurely alluded to in the letters. The son Henry James's labors, interrupted by the war, resulted in the publication of the two volumes of *The Letters of William James* (1920). The letters were heavily edited. Henry deleted mentions of what seemed to him unimportant details, softened or omitted harsher judgments made about living persons, normalized spelling and punctuation, and fleshed out numerous abbreviations. Some years later, Ralph Barton Perry made extensive use of the letters in *The Thought and Character of William James* (1935), but Perry had to make the letters fit his narrative and rarely included complete texts.

Somewhat fewer than 1,000 letters were published in this way, about 10 percent of the surviving total. The texts provided by the two

Henry Jameses and by Perry are not reliable. There are significant omissions, and James's often slangy and informal epistolary style is normalized. James often used misspellings, abbreviations, slang expressions, and sloppy punctuation for humorous effect or to emphasize to recipients that the letters were written in great haste, in moments snatched from very busy days. Normalization often weakens the intended effect of the letters. In the present edition, letters generally are reproduced as written, without corrections. For a detailed account of the methodology of transcription the Note on the Editorial Method should be consulted.

Family members were by no means the only ones publishing James's letters. Other recipients of the letters have included many of them in essays and books. Of the scholars who have published James letters two deserve special mention: Robert C. Le Clair, who published *The Letters of William James and Theodore Flournoy* (Madison: Univ. of Wisconsin Press, 1966), and the late Frederick J. Down Scott, who carried out an extensive search for unknown letters. Scott's work resulted in the publication of some 500 letters in *William James: Selected Unpublished Correspondence: 1885–1910* (Columbus: Ohio State Univ. Press, 1986). Scott also published a number of letters on several occasions in *San Jose Studies* and *The New Scholasticism*. Although he added much to our knowledge of James's correspondence, Scott did not remedy any of the defects in earlier publications because his work included only letters not previously published.

Through the efforts of the family, the bulk of James's correspondence was saved and is now housed in the Houghton Library of Harvard University. When Henry James began collecting his father's letters, some of the recipients permitted him to keep the originals. Others, who wished to retain the originals, allowed him to have transcripts made. Unfortunately, some letters were returned to their owners without any detailed record kept of their contents. Over the years, the letters and other manuscripts were deposited at Harvard. The initial collection has grown through purchases and gifts from the estates of recipients. In addition to the Houghton Library, 114 institutional libraries in the United States, Canada, and Europe are known to have James letters. There are also numerous letters in the hands of private collectors, family members, and descendants of recipients.

As this volume goes to press, about 9,200 letters have been recorded. They will be published in the present edition in twelve volumes. It is virtually certain that as the edition progresses, additional letters will be found. Should they be located too late for inclusion in their proper place in the chronology, such letters will appear in an appendix to the last volume. The first three volumes of the edition are devoted to the correspondence between William James and his brother Henry James. At this writing, 737 letters are known; these will be published in their entirety. There are about 2,400 items of correspondence with other members of the family: parents, brothers, sister, cousins, aunts, children, and relations by marriage. The remaining 6,000 letters consist of business correspondence and correspondence with friends and professional acquaintances. Because publishing all of the letters is not feasible and because not all of them are worth publishing, about 3,000 letters will be calendared. Thus, every known letter will be either published in its entirety or listed with information about its provenance and a summary of its contents. Some of the letters between the two brothers mentioned in the correspondence as either received or sent have not been located, probably because they were lost or destroyed. Generally no note is made of their disappearance. This fact can be assumed from their absence in their proper place in the chronology.

The notes for the present volume are written from the point of view of William James. In the case of Henry James, a great deal of information is already available in the four volumes of Leon Edel's *Henry James Letters* (Cambridge: Belknap Press of Harvard Univ. Press, 1974–84) and in Robert L. Gale, *A Henry James Encyclopedia* (New York: Greenwood, 1989). The latter work is especially useful because it presents the full range of Henry James's comments about the persons mentioned in the letters.

For purposes of annotation, each volume of letters is treated independently of the others. When a person is mentioned in only one letter in a volume, full biographical information is given in a note attached directly to the letter. When a person is mentioned in more than one letter, the information is given in the Biographical Register. If a name is misspelled in a letter or if only initials are given, the full name is provided in the notes. In matters of spelling and transliteration of names, the *National Union Catalog* was followed. The notes also provide information about what is presently known concerning surviving correspondence with William James and thus serve the additional function of referring to volumes in which the letters are to appear.

James himself and his brothers and sister are referred to by initials. Complete names are used for other members of the family. Where the citation of a book includes a call number, in all cases the call number is that of the copy from James's library preserved at the Houghton Library.

The letters once published will provide a record of over fifty years of American cultural history from the perspective of an observer who had a vast range of interests and who was in the midst of most of the great events and movements of his time. University reform, the professionalization of philosophy, women's education, the development of modern psychology, psychical research, magazine and book publishing, unorthodox medical practices, the status of blacks in the United States, the pragmatism controversy, American imperialism, and other topics in literature, art, religion, and science are commented upon by James and his correspondents, American as well as European. Many of his correspondents were themselves eminent and those who did not attain to eminence are often interesting, for James, as has often been pointed out, had a talent for attracting interesting cranks.

I.K.S.

A Note on the Editorial Method

This Edition of the Correspondence of William James is intended for the general reader as well as the scholar. It follows that readability is given priority so long as it does not interfere with scholarly procedures. The letters are reproduced according to a system that may be described as modified diplomatic transcript, or clear text, which represents a faithful reproduction of the final text of the original except for the lineation and the positioning of inserted or marginal additions. All alterations in letters both *from* and *to* James are recorded in the Textual Apparatus. The letters are printed in chronological order; recipients and senders are identified.

The copy-text and provenance for each letter are given in an unnumbered note following the letter. In the case of dictated letters, the name of the amanuensis within parentheses follows the copy-text designation. The names of repositories are abbreviated according to the designations found in the *National Union Catalog*. Every effort has been made to find and print the original letters. Some letters, however, are known only from copies or entries in catalogs of manuscript dealers or published sources. In such cases, all known information about the letter and its source is supplied. A list of the abbreviations used in editing the letters is found on p. lxi.

Addresses and postal markings on envelopes (when preserved) and on postcards are printed immediately below the provenance line. Enclosures mentioned in letters are to be taken as no longer extant unless commented upon in the notes.

The principal objective of the editors is to provide complete and accurate texts of the letters. The capitalization, punctuation, and spelling of the original letters have been preserved. (Readers will note that James usually doubled the *c* in the various forms of the word *necessary*.) Although the utmost in readability would suggest the correction of inadvertent errors like *the the* and *restlessless* for *restlessness* and the expansion of ampersands and of abbreviations like *wh.* to *which* and *A.K.* to *Aunt Kate,* the text will faithfully transcribe these on the theory that they have some interest as representing James's haste or else his assumption of informality as against formality.

James's various idiosyncrasies in orthography are followed, whether or not consistent, such as his *tho* or *tho'.* His use of "reform" spellings such as *enuff* for *enough* is honored, as is his preference for minuscules in certain names and adjectives, such as *english, hegelian, greek,* and the like. James sometimes wrote contractions and possessives without apostrophes and abbreviations without periods; occasionally, he used dashes instead of periods at the ends of sentences.

Silent editorial intervention is limited to the resolution of certain forms of ambiguity. As with many writers, James's placement of punctuation in relation to quotation marks varied. His normal practice was to follow the standard American system of placing periods and commas inside quotation marks and colons and semicolons outside. But at times he violated his usual practice either by placing punctuation inside or outside the quotation marks according to context as in the British system or by placing punctuation immediately below the quotation marks. To attempt to copy James's careless variation in his customary procedures would be distracting, and often impossible, since, as with many writers, James might thoughtlessly place such punctuation directly under the quotation mark. Often it is impossible to adjudicate whether the relative position of the punctuation is a shade in one direction or the other. To reproduce such anomalies would be pedantic. In order to avoid what would eventually become misleadingly firm transcription into print of what are untranscribable ambiguities, the editors have followed James's usual and conventional practice.

Another form of ambiguity involves the spacing of certain compounds and of some abbreviations. No question of intent can arise for some words—as when James occasionally spaced words like *together* as *to gether*—since he was by no means careful to link syllables, especially initial ones. All such anomalies are regularized since it is clear that authorial intent is not involved. Nevertheless, problems of intention do arise owing to this habit of James's when a legitimate question can be posed whether a division or a compounding was intended in certain words like *anyone* or *any one* and *everyone* or *every one.* Frequently his intention may be inferred from the incidence of a narrow space, when he intended the syllables to be linked, or of the normally wide space such as he was accustomed to use between two different words. Difficulties come when there is ambiguity in the spacing for words where he had a preference but might at random unthinkingly violate his custom either of separation or of linkage, such as may occur even with his usual *anyone* and *everyone*. Such textual ambiguities the editors have ordinarily resolved in favor of retaining James's usual practice whenever the spacing is in legitimate doubt whether as intended linkage or separation.

Similarly, whether James was or was not observing the contemporary though fading convention of separating such abbreviations as *didn't* to *did n't* or *wouldn't* to *would n't* is often in doubt. Without question his usual practice was not to separate, but on rare occasions convention would guide him. When the spacing is without ambiguity it is reproduced; when there is doubt, James's usual practice is followed.

James's hand is generally clear and offers few difficulties to the transcriber. He was likely, however, to form certain initial letters without much if any distinction between majuscule and minuscule, especially the letters *c* and *s*, and even *a*, *g*, *m*, and *n*. Where there is no question of intent, initial letters are transcribed as capital or lower case according to context and syntactical position, and no attempt is made to transcribe an obviously intended lower-case initial letter as a capital because of its formation. Problems do arise in distinguishing minuscule from majuscule, however, when the words in question are conceptual nouns, words of region, titles, names, and certain adjectives (mentioned above) for which James might use either a capital or a lower case. Occasional ambiguities also occur in punctuation as when a hastily formed comma is so shortened as to resemble a period. Once again, editorial interpretation of James's intention, based on context and his custom, must guide the transcription.

James's typewritten letters posed a special problem. He was not a skilled typist and in his struggle to master the typewriter, made numerous mechanical errors that include run-on words, inadvertent strikeovers, odd spacing, and misplaced punctuation. No justification can be found for transcribing these mechanical errors, and they have been corrected without record. The letters, typed by James on a typewriter containing capital-letter keys only, have been printed conventionally; the capitalization of words in these letters, therefore, is the responsibility of the editors.

The procedure used in transcribing William James's holographs is followed in transcribing letters *to* James. Henry James's hand, while more challenging to the reader than William's, offers few serious problems. Henry's idiosyncratic way of forming letters caused some early transcribing difficulties: for example, the tail of his *y*, in a word such as *eyes,* might curve up and under the word, making it appear as if the word were underlined. When written hastily, Henry's lower-case initial *s* resembles a lower-case *d;* at times, his lower-case *o* and *a* are indistinguishable from his lower-case *v* and *u,* respectively. In order to pack as much text as possible into a letter, Henry frequently wrote to the edge of the right margin, crowding the last two or three letters of the final word on the line into so many squiggles. In these as in all other instances of ambiguity, the writer is given the benefit of the doubt. Henry, more than William, followed the convention of placing an apostrophe before the final *s* in words like *your's.* His use of ampersands, superscripts, and abbreviations, such as *Ld.* for *Lord, do.* for *ditto,* and *gt.* for *great,* was more frequent than William's, as was his use of the archaic long *s,* typically when the consonant is doubled. The long *s* has been normalized to the modern *s* in the present edition.

Most of the letters in the *Correspondence* are recipients' copies. In those rare instances when a draft also exists, the recipient's copy is printed and the variants are recorded in the Textual Apparatus. When there are letters bearing the same date, the letter *from* James precedes the letter *to* James. A letter misdated by the sender is printed in the correct chronological sequence, with the correct date supplied within inferior brackets after the sender's date.

Each letter is prefaced by an editorial heading, giving the name of the recipient or sender. The formal elements of the letters have been standardized. The address and date, occasionally written by James at the foot of a letter, are placed at the head and positioned flush right. Missing dates are supplied within inferior brackets by the editors. The salutation is positioned flush left; the closing and signature are positioned flush right. A letterhead imprinted on stationery is represented in print by small capitals. (This is the only occasion for small capitals in the dateline.) In the case of hotel stationery, only pertinent information such as the name of the hotel and the city and state are reproduced. To conserve space, addresses and dates are printed on the same line, as are closings and signatures. Vertical lines indicate line breaks between these elements in the original, except when these elements have been squeezed-in or written around the margins of a letter and no clearly defined line break is evident. The vertical line is not used between a printed letterhead and a handwritten date. Underlines, graphic embellishments and flourishes, whether in the dateline or signature, are not reproduced. Quotation marks that appear at the beginning of successive lines of a quoted passage are not reproduced. Unindented paragraphs are printed with the conventional em indentation.

The parentheses and standard brackets in the letters are James's. Inferior brackets [ ] enclose editorial interpolation; '[*sic*]' is not used. Descriptions of the state of the manuscript, such as '[*end of letter missing*]', are italic within inferior brackets; the description '[*blank space for name*]' indicates space left for a name that was either deliberately or inadvertently omitted. Missing opening or closing quotation marks and parentheses are supplied within inferior brackets, as are words and letters in words where authorial intent is not in question. Angle brackets ⟨ ⟩ indicate material that is irrecoverable because the manuscript is torn or otherwise damaged; text supplied within angle brackets is obviously the responsibility of the editors.

Internal and terminal dashes, set closed-up, are one em; exceptionally long dashes or lines, used occasionally by James to indicate transition, are three-ems. In the body of the letter, words with single underlines are printed in italic; those with double underlines for emphasis are printed in small capitals (or large and small capitals, as the case may be). Dots or hyphens to indicate ellipses are always the writer's with the exception of the letter of 23 January 1883 from Henry to William, which was reprinted from Ralph Barton Perry's *Thought and Character of William James*.

When a letter in the hand of an amanuensis also contains text in James's hand, the autograph portion is signaled by '[*WJ's hand*]'. Text added by the sender either in the margins after a letter was completed or on the back of the envelope is printed in the position of a postscript; a note appended to a letter by someone other than the sender is reproduced in the notes. Annotations made by James on letters he received, as well as those made by recipients of James's letters, are printed in the notes. Markings made by archivists or others who have worked with the letters through the years are not noted. The presence or absence of page numberings is not recorded, nor are directions such as 'P.T.O.' or 'over.'

Whether in personal correspondence or in manuscripts intended for publication, William James was perennially conscious of his style and so had no compunction in deleting, interlining, and even writing over words to accommodate his choice. The development of any Jamesian sentence, therefore, has an interest all its own apart from its end product. In all cases of alterations, the final reading has been transcribed as representing the latest intention, the altered earlier

readings then being recorded in the Textual Apparatus. James seldom wasted space, especially in the letters to his brother Henry, and
frequently completed a letter by writing around the margins. Since
these endings cannot be considered as alterations or additions, they
are not recorded in the Textual Apparatus. The position of text is
recorded, however, when the addition was written on the back of an
envelope or inserted as an afterthought in the margin of a completed
letter. An error created in the text as a result of an alteration, as might
occur when James misplaces a caret intended to indicate the position
of an interlineation or duplicates punctuation when interlining or neglects to reduce a capital after inserting a new word to begin a sentence, is corrected and the correction noted in the listing of the alteration. The basic system for recording the apparatus is detailed in
Fredson Bowers, "Transcription of Manuscripts: The Record of Variants," *Studies in Bibliography* 29 (1976): 212–64. This system, with
some emendations since 1976, is that used in the various volumes of
The Works of William James for recording his alterations in manuscript.
Its use of condensed description instead of arbitrary signs is grateful
for the general reader as well as the scholar. The chief characteristics
of this system are spelled out in the headnote to the Textual Apparatus.

A special section of the apparatus treats hyphenated word-
compounds. The first list shows those in the present text, with the
form adopted, that were broken between lines in the copy-text and
thus partake of the nature of emendations. The second lists the correct copy-text form of those broken between lines by the printer of
the present edition. Consultation of the second list will enable any
user to quote from the present text with correct hyphenation of the
original letter.

F. B.

E. M. B.

Abbreviations

AGJ	Alice Gibbens James (wife)
AJ	Alice James (sister)
AJB	Jean Strouse, *Alice James: A Biography* (Boston: Houghton, Mifflin, 1980)
AL	Autograph Letter (in the hand of the sender)
ALS	Autograph Letter Signed (signed by sender)
AP	Autograph Postcard
APS	Autograph Postcard Signed
BBF	Jane Maher, *Biography of Broken Fortunes* (Hamden, Conn.: Archon Books, 1986)
C	Copy (handwritten)
ECR	William James, *Essays, Comments, and Reviews* (Cambridge: Harvard Univ. Press, 1987)
GWJ	Garth Wilkinson James (brother)
HJ	Henry James (brother)
HJL	*Henry James Letters,* ed. Leon Edel, 4 vols. (Cambridge: Belknap Press of Harvard Univ. Press, 1974–84)
MH	Harvard University
ML	Manuscript Letter (in the hand of an amanuensis)
MLS	Manuscript Letter Signed (signed by sender)
NSB	Henry James, *Notes of a Son and Brother* (New York: Charles Scribner's Sons, 1914)
RJ	Robertson James (brother)
TC	Typed Copy
TCWJ	Ralph Barton Perry, *The Thought and Character of William James,* 2 vols. (Boston: Little, Brown, 1935)
TL	Typed Letter
TLS	Typed Letter Signed (signed by sender)
WJ	William James

The Correspondence of William James

William and Henry
1861–1884

To Henry James

Drear & Chill Abode | Cambridge Saturday Eve. [September 7, 1861][1]

Dear Harry

Sweet was your letter & grateful to my eyes. I had gone in a mechanical way to the P.O. not hoping for anything (though "on espère alors qu'on désespère toujours") & finding nothing was turning heavily away when a youth modestly tapped me & holding out an envelope inscribed with your well known characters, said "Mr. James!—this was in our box!." T'was the young Pasco,[2] the joy of his mother, but the graphic account I read in the letter he gave me of the sorrow of *my* mother almost made me shed tears on the floor of the P.O. Not that on reflection I should grieve, for reflexion shows me a future time when she shall regard my vacation visits as "on the whole" rather troublesome than otherwise; or at least when she shall feel herself as blessed in the trouble I spare her when absent, as in the glow of pride and happiness she feels on seeing me, when present. But she need never fear that *I* can ever think of *her* when absent with such equanimity. I ought not to "joke on such a serious subject" as Bobby would say, tho', for I have had several pangs since being here at the thought of all I had left behind at Newport, especially gushes of feeling about the *place*. I have not for one minute had the feeling of being at home here. Something about the room precludes the possibility of it. I don't suppose I can describe it to you. As I write now even, writing itself being a cosy cheerful looking amusement, and an argand gas burner with a neat green shade over it merrily singing beside me, I still feel unsettled. I write on a round table in the middle of the room with a red and black cloth upon it. In front of me I see another such-covered table of oblong shape against the wall capped by a cheap looking glass & flanked by 2 windows, curtainless and bleak, whose shades of linen flout the air as the sportive wind impels them. On my left hand are two other such windows with a horsehair covered sofa between them, at my back a 5th window and a vast wooden mantel piece with nothing to relieve its nakedness, but a large cast looking much plumbagoed Franklin. On my right *The Bookcase*, imposing and respectable with its empty drawers and with my little array of printed wisdom covering nearly *one* of the shelves.   I hear the people breathing as they go past in the street, and the roll & jar of the cars is terrific.   I have accordingly engaged the other room from Mrs Pasco,[3] with a little sleeping room up stairs. It looks infinitely more cheerful than this & if I do not find the grate sufficient I can easily have a Franklin put up.   She says that the grate will make an oven of it though.   The room is on the South side of the house & with the sleeping room costs only 120$ per annum.   This just balances the increased expense of Mrs. Upham's table,[4] where I am to start on Monday.   I have not made many acquaintances yet.   Ropes I met the other eveg. at Quincy's room[5] & was very much pleased with him.   Don't fail to send on Will Temples letters[6] to him & Mason,[7] which I left in one of the libraries' mantelpiecejars, to use the Portuguese idiom.   Storro Higginson[8] has been very kind to me, making inquiries about tables &c.   He is a very nice fellow.   We went this morning to the house of the Curator of the Gray collection of engravings[9] who is solemnly to unfold its glories to us to morrow.   He is a most serious stately German gentleman, fully sensible to the deep vital importance of the collection of engravings & to the weightiness of a visit to them.   Had I though[t] it was to have been such a tremendous formal affair, I hardly think I should have ventured to call.   He spoke of Mr Hunt[10] & said he expected to have seen him this summer, as Mr Hunt had promised to put him in the way of getting some photographs.   You may as well tell Mr. Hunt if you see him.   Jenks[11] seems a nice kind of fellow.   Tom Ward pays me a visit almost every evening.   Poor Tom seems a cold too.[12]   His deafness keeps him from making acquaintances.

Sunday 9 A.M.   Splendid morning.   The same Tom has just left me having walked home from breakfast with me.   Bkfst. at 8 on Sundays.   I have not made many acquaintances at the Sc. School. Young Atkinson, nephew of Miss Staiggs[13] friend seems a nice boy. Prof. Eliot is a fine fellow, I suspect, a man who if he resolves to do a thing will do it.   I find analysis[14] very interesting *so far*   The library has a reading room where th[e]y take the magazines, Rev. des 2 Mondes[15] &c.   I shall have plenty of time to myself here I suspect.   I am perfectly independent of everyone.   Went into the Boston Atheneum Gallery yesterday afternoon.   There was not much there worth seeing.   Some curious big things of Allston, & the casts.[16] Please tell Father to send me some more money immediately.   Necessary expenses have reduced me to borrowing $2 to pay up my score to night at the boarding house, & don't forget to send the letters of introduction.   Heaps of love to all, to poor desolate Niobe of a Mother, to Father, to the noiseless Alice, and last and least (but *multum in parvo*) to Bobby.   Aunt Kate must be home now.   Plenty of love for her.   Ask everybody to write often.   I don't feel much like writing now but will write soon again.

I remain with unalterable sentiments of devotion ever my dear Harry, your

Big Brother | Bill

Sunday eveg.   I went to Church in the Chapel of the College this morning, & to Mt. Auburn[17] this afternoon.   Delicious day   I have nothing more to say now.   Pray write soon Harry.   I am going to write to Wilky & then study

Address

Box 575

Cambridge

Mass

ALS: MH bMS Am 1092.9 (2547)

[1] After a year of studying painting in Newport, R.I., in fall 1861 WJ entered the Lawrence Scientific School of Harvard University, leaving the family behind in Newport.

[2] Apparently, the son of WJ's landlady.

[3] Mrs. John Pasco, whose house was on the corner of Linden and Harvard streets.

[4] Mrs. Upham's was located near the corner of Oxford and Kirkland streets.   The Cambridge directory lists her as Miss Catharine Upham.

[5] Henry Parker Quincy (1838–1899), physician, graduated from Harvard in 1862, the Harvard Medical School in 1867, later a Harvard professor.

[6] William James Temple (1842–1863), for a year a student at Harvard, at the time of the letter, a captain in the United States infantry, killed in battle at Chancellorsville, 1 May 1863, one of six Temple children, cousins of the Jameses.

[7] Herbert Cowpland Mason (1840–1884), a captain in the Union army, wounded at Gettysburg, 3 July 1863.   Identified in *NSB*, 126.

[8] Samuel Storrow Higginson (b. 1842) attended the Sanborn school in Concord with GWJ and RJ, was a student at Harvard, chaplain in a black regiment, later a businessman.

[9] A collection of engravings acquired by Francis Calley Gray (1790–1856), given to Harvard in 1857, at the time housed in Gore Hall, now part of the Fogg Art Museum. Access to the collection, especially by undergraduates, was severely restricted out of fear that careless viewers would cause damage.   The curator was Louis Thies.

[10] William Morris Hunt (1824–1879), American painter, opened a studio in Newport in 1856 and moved to Boston in 1862.   WJ studied painting with Hunt in 1858–59 and 1860–61.

[11] Henry Fitch Jenks (1842–1920) attended Harvard in 1859–63, later a Unitarian minister.

[12] From *King Lear*, act 3, sc. 4, line 57.

[13] Miss Staigg is either a sister or a daughter of Richard Morrell Staigg, an artist residing in Newport, or an error for Mrs. Staigg.   On 19 May 1873 HJ wrote WJ that Richard Staigg's wife gave him news of C. Atkinson.

[14] WJ was studying chemistry.

[15] *Revue des Deux Mondes.*

[16] The Boston Athenæum had an extensive collection of casts of classical sculptures.

[17] It is not clear whether he means the street of that name or Mount Auburn Cemetery on the outskirts of Cambridge.

To Henry James

Cambridge Sunday Eveg. [October 27, 1861]

Dear Baretha

I write a short note to let you know that all is well & to remind you to come and see me this week.   You had better leave Newport[1] on Friday mng.   You get into Boston at ½ past 12.   I will be at the depôt to meet you.   Thus you will have Saturday and Sunday with me (longer if you like but I suspect you'll get sick of it) and Monday & Tuesday with Wilky.[2]   You shall be an inmate of my parlor & bedroom, one of the family in fact with the run of the bookcase and of Miss Upham's board, a repetition of the old fat of the land scenes.   I think you will enjoy it that is if you don't mind sleeping thus— 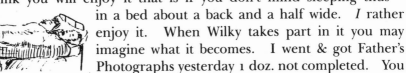 in a bed about a back and a half wide.   *I* rather enjoy it.   When Wilky takes part in it you may imagine what it becomes.   I went & got Father's Photographs yesterday 1 doz. not completed.   You can get them when you come.   I will send them to morrow either by post or Kinsley[3] whichever I can.   I left one big one at Fishers.[4]   The woman at Black's[5] gave me to understand that they intended to drive a business in them, at least she said something which I did not comprehend about *printing* a good many of them and then said with a rather sheepish smile that she thought the gentleman was a "public character" which I rather contradicted, but thought it prudent to order the negative of the Silenus[6] one to be destroyed as the P.C. seemed rather ashamed of it.   I think the others are very good, all of them.   I was in hopes I would be able to tell you something about Miss Watson[7] but the rain prevented me from getting there.   I promised Mrs Atkinson[8] that I would find out when I wrote whether Miss Anthony[9] could take her in for a couple of days, next Saturday and Sunday I think.   She is going to Newport and wants to avoid a Hotel. Will you be so good as to inquire and let me know before Saturday? Five weeks to Thanksgiving, then the Voluptuous Winter Vacation from Jany. 15th to March 1st!! I suppose the Temples are fully started in their new home. Tell Father there was nothing in the P.O. or at the Revere H.[10] I have heard nothing of his sermon[11] from anyone. Ask mother to write and the little babe too. Aunt Kate has one more chance to redeem her reputation, through you—M.S.[12]— she knows. Love to all big & small, & write about your coming

Your true bretha Wm. Jas.

ALS: MH bMS AM 1092.9 (2548)

[1] HJ left for Cambridge on Thursday, 31 October.

[2] At the time GWJ was a student at the Sanborn School in Concord, Mass. For a description of the school see *BBF*, 17–22.

[3] Kinsley's Express service, which operated between Newport and Boston.

[4] Fisher Brothers, "Photographists," on Washington St., Boston.

[5] James Wallace Black (1825–1896), American photographer, maintained a studio on Washington St., Boston. Black's copied pictures and finished pictures in "oil, india ink, and water colors." No published book of photographs from Black's studio was found.

[6] In Greek mythology, one of the satyrs, often depicted as a fat, drunken, old man, but sometimes as dignified and inspired.

[7] In an 1863 letter to his parents (bMS Am 1092.9 [2509]), WJ describes a visit to the Watsons in Milton, Mass., and mentions a Miss Watson who especially wants to be remembered to HJ. Most likely, Miss Watson is one of the daughters of Robert Sedgwick Watson (1809–1888) of Milton. Of his six daughters, several could be the Miss Watson in question: Sylvia Hathaway Watson (1834–1917), later wife of William Ralph Emerson, Mary Forbes Watson (1836–1891), Jane Sedgwick Watson (1838–1912), later wife of Edward Cranch Perkins, and Anna Russell Watson (1843–1909), later wife of William Jones Ladd.

[8] There are several possible Mrs. Atkinsons. Charles Follen Atkinson's mother was Sarah C. Parkman Atkinson (d. 1892), and perhaps she is the one WJ means.

[9] Newport directories list a Mary Anthony who operated a boarding house at 42 Church St.

[10] Revere Hotel, Bowdoin Square, Boston.

[11] WJ could be referring to Henry James's well-known oration "The Social Significance of Our Institutions: Oration Delivered by the Request of the Citizens of Newport, R. I., July 4, 1861."

[12] Nothing was found explaining this.

To Henry James

Encampment of Savans | Rio de Janeiro[1] | May 3rd 1865 | 9 P.M. My dearest Harry.

Another chance to write home presents itself; the Colorado[2] has been detained here by an accident to her machinery till now nearly 2 weeks have elapsed, so I can send by her. Although we have been

here so long, we have only just begun to get systematically at work.   I
confess that the unchartered freedom did me tire.   I had to stay a
week at the hotel, which was very dear and bad.   Many of the party
are there yet.   My life for 8 or 9 days has left a pretty unique impression of unlimited perspiration; unlimited itching of the skin caused
by fleas & mosquitoes, and worst of all, on both cheeks and one side
of neck, by virulent ring-worms which appeared on board ship &
which "still wave" with undiminished fire; great repletion & consequent discomfort produced by the excellent french cooking of the
various restaurants wh. I have felt it my duty to try, about town before
settling down to any one; considerable swipy-ness of evenings there
being absolutely no place to sit at the hotel and nothing to do but "go
around," & partake of cooling beverages.   (Do not think, I beg, however, that I have ever been intoxicated)   Now I think all that "facti-
tious life" is over for good.   We have a laboratory established over
Mr. Davis's store,[3] and we have 3 bedrooms just off it, in wh. 6 of us
sleep.   Tom Ward is my chum.   I wish I had a drawing or photograph of our premises to send you.   They are truly picturesque.
The laboratory surrounds a great well wh. is covered by a sky light to
illuminate the two lower stories. 4 very wide arched windows without
sashes open into our work shop
fm. the well & give us light.
The walls are all of stone about 3 feet thick covered with rough.   All
our furniture in our rooms are our trunks beds, & some nails.   In
the shop, some barrels, boxes & planks.   Tom has a cot.   I have slept
in my hammock for the last 2 nights & find it very agreeable indeed.

Our water is contained in great red
earthen jars & we drink out of earthen
beakers such as you see upon the
stage, holding a quart each. Prof. has
given me the marine critters of the bay
(except fishes) while I am here, wh. is
delightful, but it will cut me off of most of the excursions wh. the
other men will make while we are here.   You can imagine nothing
wh. will equal the profusion of the lower forms of life here at low
water.   I shall keep on now working as steadily as I can, in every way
& trying to be of as much use as I can to the Professor.   Altho' several
bushels of different things have already been collected, *nothing* has
been done wh. cd. not have been done just as well by writing fm. Boston.   To morrow, however 3 excursions are going off.   Professor is a
very interesting man.   I don't yet understand him very well.   His
charlatanerie is almost as great as his solid worth; and it seems of an

unconscious childish kind than you can't condemn him for as you wd most people.   He wishes to be too omniscient.   But his personal fascination is very remarkable.   I dont know whether after all, our expedition will accomplish as much as it promised to.   Prof. himself is a first rate captain to be sure & can organize splendidly.   But of his 11 assistants,[4] 3 are absolute idiots; Tom Ward, Dexter[5] & myself know nothing; of the 5 who know something, one is superannuated & one in such a feeble condition that the least exertion renders him unwell.   Remain 3 whole men.   I don't want to find fault with anyone but merely to show that the real strength of the party is by no means proportioned to its size; so that it will not be able to do as much work as many wd. expect fm. merely hearing the number of people of wh. it was composed.   It is as well however not to speak of this abroad.   It may turn out very well;   all I fear is that people are rather inclined to be too sanguine about it.   Tuesday May 10th.[6]   My dearest family.   The steamer[7] sails to morrow, so I am forced to finish now the very stupid letter wh. I began a week ago.   I am sorry to be obliged to write to day, for my physical being is in the process of undergoing that convulsion wh. we must all go through before being acclimatized, better sooner than later.   I suppose I shall be about again to morrow.   I have been so hard at work as to have had not a moment's time to write or read, not even a moment to study portuguese.   On Sunday 4 of us ascended a mountain called the Corcovado, near here.   The finest view I ever saw—the mountain having a narrow summit, from wh. three sides went sheer down.   The sea and mountains and clouds, & forests, together, made a scene wh. can be neither imagined nor described, so I think I shall not attempt to say anything about it.   The affluence of nature here is wonderful.   The ease with wh. vegetation invades every thing, with wh. moss grows on every wall a few years old for instance, and weds what is artificial to what is natural, makes everything very beautiful & very different from the colorless state of things at home.   The color of the vegetation is peculiarly vivid.   I have not been into the virgin forest yet. Prof. told me yesterday he was going to send four of us overland to Para,[8] one, a geologist the others must settle among themselves who shall go.   I think it probable now that Tom Ward & I will make two. The 4th is undecided.   If you take the map of Brazil you will see the province of minas Geraes, a little north of Rio; we go through that to the R. San Francisco.   After going down that River some distance two, probably Tom & no 4 cross over to the river Tocantins & go down it to Para, while the other two, probably St. Johns & myself, go further down the river & then go up over land into the Province of Ceara in wh. Prof wants some geological work to be done. Prof. has told us nothing about it. All I know is, it will be a tough journey of about 5 mos. mostly on mule-back. How we can transport collections, I know not, as the country is most uninhabited & very little travelled. The Emperor[9] wanted to send Agassiz over that route for the moral effect on the Brazilians, but it is much too long a journey for him to take. Something is said of the Emperor furnishing transportation & an escort. I hope he will. I wish I cd. tell you something definite about it at this date, for if I start, you will probably not hear from me, with the exception of my farewell letter, wh. will go by Europe, for many months. I think that I shall probably return home after the end of this journey, if I make it without going to the Amazons. I shall have seen enough on the journey. Since seeing more of Agassiz, my desire to be with him, so as to learn from him has much diminished. He is doubtless a man of some wonderful mental faculties, but such a politician & so self-seeking & illiberal to others that it sadly diminishes one's respect for him. Don't say anything about this outside, for heaven's sake, as my judgment is a very hasty one. Dexter is a very good fellow, and I get on very well with Tom Ward, who though inclined to question the use of what he is doing, is very active & tough, and a most pleasant companion. I never saw such physical energy. He already knows all the country round about. We have discovered a delicious little restaurant kept by a french family, *a la bourgeoise* where the cooking is perfect & every thing marvellously cheap. Good eating is the forte of the people of Rio, but things are very dear almost every where. I guess I will stop. I wonder what you are all doing now. It is at Rio 5 P.M. I suppose you are just sitting down to dinner or waiting for the bell, as it must be about 3 o'clock in Boston. Oceans of love to every one of you F., & M., & A.K, & Harry, & Wilky, & Bob, and the sweet clean faced Alice. You've no idea how I pine for war news. When I get home I'm going to study philosophy all my days. I hope this letter has not a sombre tone. If it has it is owing to my digestive derangement. I have only written to day from sheer neccessity. I never looked forward to any thing with more pleasure than to the making of this overland journey. Good bye! beloved family. I hope Harry is getting strong. Give my love to T.S.P., the Lafarges & every one of my friends. Once more, adieu. I sent The things I bought for the Tappan's by Mr. Harris, of the U.S. ship Onward.[10] He said he was going to Cambridgeport & wd. send the box to father. Perhaps it wont get to you till after this letter does.

Adieu   Your loving   W.J.

ALS: MH bMS AM 1092.9 (2549)

[1] WJ was on a naturalistic expedition in Brazil; see the Introduction, p. xxvi.

[2] The *Colorado*, a paddle-wheel steamer belonging to the Pacific Mail Steamship Co., left New York with the expedition on 1 April 1865, reaching Rio de Janeiro on 23 April. On her first voyage, the *Colorado* was equipped with guns in case of attack by pirates. WJ was an unpaid volunteer. For a detailed account of WJ's travels in Brazil see Carleton Sprague Smith, "William James in Brazil," in *Four Papers Presented in the Institute of Brazilian Studies* (Nashville: Vanderbilt Univ. Press, 1951).

[3] Elizabeth Cary Agassiz, *A Journey in Brazil* (Boston: Ticknor and Fields, 1868), 59, describes this as a "large empty room over a warehouse in the Rua Direita, the principal business street of the city."

[4] Agassiz, *Journey*, vii, lists the following assistants: Jacques Burkhardt, an artist, associated with Agassiz for many years; John Gould Anthony (1804–1877), conchologist; Charles Frederick Hartt (1840–1878), geologist; Orestes St. John, geologist; Joel Asaph Allen (1838–1921), ornithologist; George Sceva, preparator. There were also several unpaid volunteers, including WJ, Newton Dexter, Edward Copeland, a student at the Lawrence Scientific School, Thomas Wren Ward, Walter Hunnewell (1844–1921), and Stephen V. R. Thayer, son of Nathaniel Thayer, the expedition's sponsor. Other members were Thomas G. Cary, Agassiz's brother-in-law, and Benjamin Eddy Cotting (1812–1897), a physician, and his wife. Anthony and Allen went home early because of poor health, while the Cottings after several months continued on to Europe.

[5] Simon Newton Dexter (1848–1899), graduated from Harvard in 1870, a journalist.

[6] 10 May was a Wednesday.

[7] The *Colorado* continued on to California.

[8] The long journey was not made.

[9] Dom Pedro II de Alcântara (1825–1891), emperor of Brazil from 1831.

[10] The steamship *Onward* left Rio de Janeiro on 5 May and was in New York on 14 June. In his letter to AJ, 27 April 1865 (bMS Am 1092.9 [1093]), WJ identifies Harris as the storekeeper on the *Onward* and lists the contents of the packages.

To Henry James

Original Seat of Garden of Eden July 15th [1865]

Darling Harry

This place is not 20 miles fm. Rio, wh. damnable spot I left this mrng at six and now (11 P.M) am sitting on a stone resting fm. my walk and thinking of thee and the loved ones in Bosting.[1] No words, but only savage inarticulate cries can express the gorgeous loveliness of the walk I have been taking. Houp la la! The bewildering profusion & confusion of the vegetation, the inexhaustible variety of its forms & tints (& yet they tell us we are in the winter when much of its bril-

liancy is lost) are *literally* such as you have never dreamt of.   The brilliancy of the sky & the clouds, the effect of the atmosphere wh. gives
their proportional distance to the diverse planes of the landscape
make you admire the old Gal nature.   I almost thought my enjoyment of nature had entirely departed, but here she strikes such massive & stunning blows as to overwhelm the coarsest apprehension.   I
am sitting on a rock by the side of a winding mule-path.   The mule-
path is made over an "erratic drift"[2] wh. much delighteth Agassiz, but
makes it truly erratic to the traveller.   On my left up the hill there
rises the wonderful, inextricable, impenetrable forest, on my right
the hill plunges down into a carpet of vegetation wh. reaches to the
hills beyond, wh. rise further back into mountains.   Down in the valley I see 3 or four of the thatched mud hovels of negroes, embosomed
in their vivid patches of banana trees.

The hills on both sides & the path descend rapidly to the shores of
a large lagoon separated by a forest clad strip of land from the azure

sea, whose surf I can hear continuously roaring at
this distance.   Would I could get so far, but the
road is too long.   A part of the path hither lay
through an orange thicket where the great hard
sweet juicy fruit strewed the ground more than
ever did apples the good old Concord turnpike.
Out in the sea are a few rocky islands on wh. a few
palm trees cut against the sky & give the whole a
tropical look.   How often my dear old Harry wd. I
have given every thing to have you by my side to
enjoy the magnificent landscape of this region.   As

for the rest I dont enjoy so much.—But I will write more before the
next steamer—Au revoir at present

AL: MH bMS Am 1092.9 (2550)

[1] A slip for 'Boston'.

[2] In a letter quoted in Agassiz, *Journey*, 86, Agassiz begins a description of his first
view of a Brazilian "drift hill with innumerable erratic boulders" by noting that it was
"one of the happiest days" of his life.

To Henry James

Rio de Janeiro | July 23rd '65

My dear old Harry
The French Steamer wh. arrived 5 days ago brought me letters fm.
you and father written while the Perkinses[1] were in the house.   You
cannot tell how much I enjoyed them.   But by them you say you had

just rec.^d my first, written exactly 3 months ago.   It is very discouraging to have to wait such a time for an answer.   I feel as if I cd. write page after page this morning, for I pine for human intercourse, but my eyes imperatively say no!   Blast them!   At last the various postponements are over & we start for Para² day after to morrow without fail, wh. will bring us 1500 miles or more nearer home.   I have no idea what kind of a time we shall have there.   I anticipate however a better one on the whole than we have had here, cheaper & simpler living, and even richer, if more monotonous scenery.   I enclose a slip³ I wrote to you the other day.   Since then I have seen some more scenery & been on two large plantations in the interior.   Very interesting.   I pine for some conversation of an intellectual character, & I cant read.   Would I might hear your articles on Goethe & Arnold.⁴ Would I might hear Fathers on F. & Sc. or his letter to the E.P. on Johnson's drunkenness,⁵ would I might hear Chauncey Write⁶ philosophize for one evening, or see Lafarge, or Perry or Holmes, or Washburn.   After working at the Cooper's trade all day the only thing I can do in the evening is to go to a place called the Alcazar, a sort of French Café Chantant or "Bouffes" wh. becomes finally even more dismal than silence & darkness.   But I *must* stop.   Thanks for your letters 50 times.   Love to all Great & small.

Your affect. bro.   W.J.

ALS: MH bMS Am 1092.9 (2551)

¹ Not identified.   Helen Wyckoff, a cousin related through WJ's maternal grandmother, was married to a Perkins.   But there is almost no information about this side of the family and several different Perkinses are mentioned in other letters.

² According to Agassiz, *Journey*, 126, the party sailed on the steamer *Cruzeiro do Sul* on 25 July.

³ Apparently the letter of 15 July.

⁴ HJ, review of Matthew Arnold, *Essays in Criticism*, in *North American Review* 101 (July 1865): 206–13; review of Goethe's *Wilhelm Meister's Apprenticeship and Travels*, in *North American Review* 101 (July 1865): 281–85.

⁵ Henry James, "Faith and Science," *North American Review* 101 (October 1865): 335–78.   President Andrew Johnson (1808–1875) was sometimes accused of excessive drinking.   Apparently Henry James wrote a letter to the *New York Evening Post* about this, but the letter has not been located.

⁶ Chauncey Wright.

To Henry James

Gd. Hotel May 3 67 | Paris

Chéri de frère

J'ai écrit à soeur¹ il y a 3 jours mais j'ai manqué le courrier, en sorte qu'il me reste le temps de t'écrire également qq.ˢ mots.   J'ai cru sortir

de Paris aujourd'hui, mais je crois maintenant que n'en serai pas
quitte avant après demain.   Je me trouve tellement fatigué aujour-
d'hui de toutes mes courses que je me donnerai demain pour me reposer.   je n'ai pas fait grand chose, il est vrai, mais les distances sont
si énormes que la matinée s'en va on ne sait comment, puis il faut
se reposer et le soir on va au theatre.   J'ai été au Palais royal & au
Gymnase.   Au Palais royal 5 "low-comedians," *tous* de la force de Warren[2] *pour le moins*.   C'etait à étouffer de rire.   Au Gymnase j'ai
vu "les idées de Mme. Aubray" de Dumas fils.[3]   *Jamais*, au grand jamais, je n'ai éprouvé un si rich intellectual treat!   Je tressaillais, je
grillais, je débordais d'aise du commencement jusqu'à la fin. Chaque
detail, chaque syllabe, chaque regard dans le jeu des acteurs et ac-
trices était *fini*, parachevé, et d'une grace! d'une beauté!   Je ne croy-
ais pas que les hommes pussent être si naturels, si bien élevés que ces
comédiens l'étaient.   La comedie elle même est très forte, faite de
main de maître.   Je voudrais que tu la lusses pour te mettre plus en
rapport avec moi—mais vraiment ça ne vaut guère la peine de l'acheter, et le *vif* du charme pour moi, c'était tout dans le jeu des acteurs.
C'est une comédie morale, Mme. Aubray veut "reconstituer l'amour
en France"—mais ils ont tant d'esprit, ces Parisiens, qu'ils finissent
par n'en point avoir: Il n'est pas un jeune homme vivant comme nous
vivons à Boston qui ne sente ou plutot l'inanité, l'ineptitude essen-
tielle qui est dans les phrases les plus archi vertueuses de ce drame.
& pourtant M. Dumas & Cie regarderaient ce jeune homme en general comme une personne excessivement grossière & bête.   Ah! mon
cher frere combien j'aurais donné pour que tu fusses la à côté de moi
pour nous rejouir ensemble.—

Je suis allé ce matin consulter le Dr. Duchenne (de Boulogne)[4] qui
est l'autorité en France pour tout ce qui concerne les muscles.   Il dit
avoir vu beaucp. de cas comme les nôtres.   Il conseille comme Brown
Séquard[5] la contre irritation, non par la glace qu'il dit être dangereux
mais par la faradisation cutaneé.   Je viens d'acheter un appareil pour
180 fr.   Je t'en ecrirai des nouvelles.   J'ai fait trotter la glace tous les
jours jusqu' aujourd'hui.   Il est certain que cela soulage enormément
pendant plusieurs heures, mais il me paraît certain que l'effet n'est
pas permanent et qu'il y a même une reaction qui se trahit par une
faiblesse plus grande.   Duchenne advises un *corset* pour venir en aide
à ses muscles dans la station et la marche.   C'est ce que je te écrivais
de New York.   Faites faire un par Taylor pour vous, & envoye moi
l'addresse que Taylor aura ici, s'il te plaît.[6]   Adieu.   Chéri je n'ai que
juste le temps de courir avec ceci à la poste en bas, puis je vais diner

Je me porte a peu prés comme à New York, *certainement* pas plus mal, nonobstante tout le fatigue que j'ai eu.

Oceans of love to Father Mother Aunt Kate & Alice, to whom I will write fm. Dresden.

W.J.

ALS: MH bMS Am 1092.9 (2552)

[1] On 16 April 1867 WJ sailed from New York to Brest, France, on the *Great Eastern*, a paddle-wheel steamer known for extraordinarily heavy rolling, placed in passenger service for the Paris World Exhibition. WJ wrote to his sister on 27 April, while still at sea. Jules Verne was a passenger on the *Great Eastern* to the United States and described the voyage in *A Floating City*. Verne was WJ's fellow passenger on the return trip.

[2] William Warren (1812–1888), actor, spent most of his career in and around Boston.

[3] Alexandre Dumas *fils*, *Les idées de Madame Aubray*, a comedy in four acts first performed on 16 March 1867 at the Gymnase-Dramatique theater in Paris.

[4] Guillaume-Benjamin Duchenne de Boulogne (1806–1875), French physician, initiator of the application of electricity to muscles in therapeutic and diagnostic medicine.

[5] Charles Édouard Brown-Séquard (1817–1894), professor of physiology and pathology at Harvard, later succeeded Claude Bernard to the chair of experimental physiology at the Collège de France.

[6] Taylor, perhaps a manufacturer of corsets, has not been identified.

From Henry James

Cambridge—May 10th [1867]

Dear Willie—We have not heard from you yet, altho' we daily expect a letter; but I nevertheless venture to presume upon your being alive and well—well enough at least to care get a line from home. I am more anxious than I can say to hear how you endured your journey & in what condition you found yourself at the end of it.—I hope your letter when it comes will be very explicit on this point. We had the satisfaction of learning thro' the Cable of the safe arrival of the G.E.[1]—which was a great blessing; but the message didn't mention whether you had been sick or not.—But your back, *that* is what I want to hear about. However, there is no use in treating you to all this insipid conjecture—What you will care about is facts concerning ourselves. Nothing has happened since your departure, but the return of Alice[2] and Kate. The former is very well and of course rejoices in being home. She is a great blessing to all of us. The latter has gone into town to be treated by Doctor Monroe[3] and to live in his house meanwhile. She has been there but a few days, but is already much

encouraged.   I questioned Aunt Kate and Alice as to your doings in
N.Y. & came to the conclusion that you must have had a fierce ordeal.—It is dismally unsatisfactory and difficult to write to you in this
way—in ignorance of your condition, feelings &c; but I imagine for
the best; and fancy you resting from your wanderings in some decent
German household.—The Spring arrives with little steps; the grass is
green but the air is almost as cold as March.   Nothing has befallen
us.   We continue to hear from the boys, who were much surprised (&
gratified) at your departure. Wilkie has a prospect of being nomi-
nated to a political convention in the state & means to accept.   Aunt
K. got a most characteristic letter from him yesterday, in wh. he says
that in the last four months he has done "more *solid reading* than usually falls to the lot of man in twice that time."—We heard from Elly
Van Buren that she is *engaged* to one Dr. Morris of New Rochelle, a
young physician, who has "cared for" her for 4 years & "never been
attentive to any girl in the interval."   I should think Elly's own conscience would sting her.—Father seems quite well since you left &
writes a little daily. He has finished his Swedenborg for the N.A.R. &
is at work on his book.[4]   Mother is the perfection of health as of every
thing else.—I have felt quite strong since you sailed—and have read
several useful books.   I have been trying the *Ice* assiduously, but I
think rather overdid the application (in length & frequency) & am
now content to apply it less often & for a shorter time—every other
day, for 8 or 10 minutes.—I feel as if my letter were very much like
that one of Mr. Dexter's.[5]—We receive nothing but wars[6] and rumors
of war from Europe.   I hope you will not be incommoded.—I repeat
that I hope more than I can say to hear of your being well, cheerful,
comfortable, settled and satisfied.   Time will show.   *En attendant*, I
think of you often and miss you much.—On the arrival of your letter
I shall immediately write again.   You will probably be disappointed,
as it is, that this doesn't acknowledge the receipt of it.   Adieu.

À toi   H.

ALS: MH bMS Am 1094 (1924)

[1] *Great Eastern.*

[2] AJ had been in New York for treatment; for details see *AJB*, 98–99, 106–10.

[3] It was common for doctors to have rooms available for patients undergoing more
extensive treatment.   Aunt Kate was being treated by a Dr. Munroe.

[4] Henry James, "Swedenborg's Ontology," *North American Review* 105 (July 1867):
89–123; *The Secret of Swedenborg* (Boston: Fields, Osgood and Co., 1869).

[5] There is a well-known pamphlet by Timothy Dexter (1747–1806) first published
without any punctuation.   When readers objected, Dexter published a second edition
with several pages of nothing but punctuation marks while telling readers to "pepper

& salt" as they please.   Except for this remote possibility, nothing was found explaining the allusion.

[6] HJ was writing after the Austro-Prussian War (1866) and before the Franco-Prussian War (1870–71).

From Henry James

Cambridge, May 21 [1867]

Dear Will—I drop you a line by the *China*, wh. leaves Boston tomorrow.   We recd. your two letters at once, some 5 or 6 days ago & with immense satisfaction.   The private one to me was successfully concealed; & you may imagine that it was the most interesting.   I groaned in spirit as I thought of your fatigue & your weariness, but I was glad enough to think it was no worse than when here.   Of course I could not have expected it to be less.—Heaven protect you!   I hope by this time you have got some permanent repose, & we await your Dresden letter with great anxiety.   No news.   It seems but yesterday that you left—Father, Mother, & Alice are very well & (apparently) happy.   We hear often from the boys,[1] who are beginning to suffer from the heat & hard work.   We expect one of them home before long, & then the other, on his return.   They were equally surprised & delighted by your departure.   We have sent them your letter.   I must not forget to say how delighted we were to hear of your not having been sick!   Bravo!   I remember Pratt well.   Also *Grogan*.[2] What has become of the latter?—Your acct. of Paris was strange & moving.   I wish indeed I could have been at the theatre with you.   I had read M*me* *Aubray* when your letter came & was keenly sensible both of its merits & defects.   It's hard to say which prevail.   Wendell Holmes is gone salmon-fishing in Maine.   The Spring is well started as to verdure; but the air is cold & the skies gray.   I have been feeling essentially better since you left; but have given up the ice[3] as pernicious.   I was of course much interested in your acct. of the advice you had recd. & wait to hear what are the results.   I shall proba[b]ly go to N.Y. next week & get a *corset* from Taylor.   A. Kate is still staying at Dr. Munro's.   Jeff Davis[4] is released on bail—chiefly that of H. Greely.   I have seen no one and done nothing—except receive a day or two ago, new overtures from the *Nation*.   But I shall not be led into any imprudent promises.   It were a platitude to say that we miss you. Nevertheless we do.   But I try to think that you are feeling very cheerful; instead of, as is probable, very dismal.   I can only entreat you to watch yourself & do nothing imprudent (as walking, sightseeing &c)   I am curious to know what you have heard from T.S.P.—to whom I shall soon write.   But of course I am more eager still to hear your own personal news; prospects sensations, impressions of Dresden and so forth.   I sympathise with you both in your privations & discomforts, and in your hopes of profit & pleasure whatever they may be.—Have patience & courage and you will manage to keep comfortable.—Farewell.   I envy you chiefly the Dresden pictures— if you are able to look at any.   I have been reading Taine's Italy[5]— which made me hungry for works of art.   Father seems especially well just now.   Alice is extraordinary sweet.   Adieu.   I shall write often.

Tout à toi—H.J.jr

ALS: MH bMS Am 1094 (1925)

[1] After the Civil War, GWJ purchased substantial amounts of land in Florida, hoping to resell it to settlers from the North and raise cotton.   The enterprise failed with great losses.   GWJ visited Cambridge in late July to mid-August.   RJ, who assisted his brother in running the plantation, returned in mid-October.   He did not go back to Florida.

[2] The only Grogan at Harvard during this period was Alexander Edward Grogan, a student in the Lawrence Scientific School in 1866–69.

[3] See letter of 10 May 1867.

[4] Jefferson Davis (1808–1889), president of the Confederacy, was released on 13 May 1867.   Horace Greeley was one of ten signers of the bond.

[5] Hippolyte-Adolphe Taine, *Voyage en Italie* (1866).

To Henry James

Dresden June 27. 1867

My dear Harry

I have rec.d since my last a long letter from you written in reply to my first fm. Dresden, for wh. accept my hearty thanks.   The most important event wh. has occurred besides that has been the arrival of T. S. Perry fm. his "Italiänische Reise"[1]   He got here a week ago yesterday, and has a moment ago wrung my hand in mute farewell on his way to Switzerland; he will not be back before October probably as he has to be with his mother till she returns home. It is hard in the stiff language of pen and ink to gratify your curiosity as to how he seems, but if we were discoursing as of yore in your room, I could very easily give you an idea.   Owing to a gratuitous pre-expectation on my part, arising either from his letters, or from myself having grown rather precipitately old in the last year, I was considerably disappointed in finding him so little matured, ballasted and improved. He of course *is* so considerably but is still very puerile in many things, and has the old gift of his of wasting time in trifling and trifling reading, in perfection. (All this to you in confidence of course) he said he had not read a single substantial book since he had been abroad. All last winter in Paris he read nothing but the froth of Parisian-ism. He seems delighted beyond measure with Italy wh. he says is *the* part of Europe to see if you can't see everything—and has evidently been as thoroughly *doing*, helped by ware,² the fine Arts there, as he could. He evidently knows and cares a good deal about pictures now. He was extremely pleasant and affectionate and is alive to the neccessity of working hard soon. I hope next winter he'll begin. He sends you much love and will soon write to you again.

I have been for the last few days looking up a room and have seen lots of picturesque courts and stairs and so forth. The quarter of the town in wh. I now am is bran new, and the houses are just like the new ones in Paris, perfectly uninteresting. I at last engaged one this morning, tho' it was very difficult to decide, just by the Alt Markt, a most convenient situation, for 7 Thalers a month. I shall get breakfasts there for 3 groschen a day, or 3 Thlrs. a month, and dinners at a hotel for 15 gr. a day or 15 Thlrs. a month Suppers average 7 or 8 Thlrs. a month. This, the extreme, a little more than 30 dollars currency a month. The Germans are certainly a most *gemüthlich* people. The way all the old women told me how "*freundlich*" their rooms were, "so *freundlich* möblirt," and so forth, melted my heart. Whenever you tell an inferior here to do anything (e.g. a cabman) he or she replys "Schön!" or rather "*Schēhn!*" with an accent, not quick like a frenchman's "*bien*," but so protracted, soothing, and reassuring to you, that you feel as if he were adopting you into his family.—I am getting on, in a dorsal point of view, *bully*, and am feeling quite hopeful of recovery. I hope next week to write you some details thereupon. You say I have said nothing about the people in the house— There is nothing to say about them. Dr. Semler³ is an open hearted, excellent man as ever was, and wrapped up in his children. Mrs. S. a sickly, miserly, petty spirited non entity. The children perfectly uninteresting, though the younger Anna, or Aennchen is very handsome and fat, aged 5. The following short colloquy which I overheard after breakfast a few days since may amuse you as a piece of local color. Ännchen drops a book wh. she is carrying across the room & exclaims:

—"Herr Jē—sus!"

Mother   "Ach! das sagen *Kinder* nicht, Anna!"

Ännchen. (reflectively to herself, sotto voce) "Nicht für Kinder!"

[*end of letter missing*]

AL incomplete: MH bMS AM 1092.9 (2553)

[1] Johann Wolfgang von Goethe, *Italienische Reise*.

[2] William Robert Ware (1832 – 1915), American architect.

[3] From remarks made by WJ in a letter to his parents, 27 May 1867 (bMS Am 1092.9 [2519]), it is clear that this is Christian Semler (b. 1828) who published several works on Shakespeare and Homer.   He was WJ's first landlord in Dresden.   Dresden directories show a J. Jacob Christian Semler residing at 6 Christianstrasse.

To Henry James

                                       12^{III} Mittel Strasse, Berlin | Sept 26. 1867

Beloved Arry

I hope you will not be severely disappointed on opening this fat envelope to find it is not *all letter*.   I will first explain to you the nature of the enclosed document and then proceed to personal matters.— The other day as I was sitting alone with my deeply breached letter of credit, beweeping my outcast state, and wondering what I could possibly do for a living, it flashed across me that I might write a "Notice" of H. Grimms novel wh. I had just been reading.[1]   To conceive with me is to execute, as you well know.   And after sweating fearfully for three days, erasing, tearing my hair, copying, recopying &c, &c, I have just succeeding in finishing the enclosed.   I want you to read it, and if after correcting the style & thoughts, with the aid of Mother, Alice & Father, and re-writing it if possible, you judge it to be capable of interesting in any degree any one in the world but H. Grimm himself, to send it to the Nation or the round table.[2]   I feel that a living is hardly worth being gained at this price.   Style is not my forte, and to strike the mean between pomposity & vulgar familiarity is indeed difficult.   Still, an the rich guerdon accrue, an but 10 beauteous dollars lie down on their green and glossy backs within the family treasury in consequence of my exertions, I shall feel glad that I have made them. I have not seen Grimm yet as he is in Switzerland.   In his writings he is possessed of real imagination and eloquence, chiefly in an ethical line, and the novel is really *distingué*, somewhat as Cherbuliez's are, only with rather a deficiency on the physical & animal side.   He is, to my taste, too idealistic, & father would scout him for his arrant moralism.   Goethe seems to have mainly suckled him, and the manner of

this book is precisely that of Wm M.^r or Elect. Aff.³ There is something not exactly *robust* about him, but per contra, great delicacy, and
an extreme belief in the existence and worth of truth, and desire to
attain it justly & impartially. In short a rather painstaking liberality
and want of careless animal spirits—wh. by the bye seem to be rather
characteristics of the rising generation. But enough of him. The
notice was mere taskwork. I cd. not get up a spark of interest in it,
and I shd. not think it wd. be *d'actualité* for the Nation. Still I cd.
think of nothing else to do, and was bound to do something. I was
overjoyed yesterday morning to get a mighty & excellent letter from
you (Sept 6) with 2 Nations and a Tribune,⁴ and an amusing letter
from Elly Van Buren. By the same mail a fat letter from Charles
Atkinson & one from T.S.P. I have in fact been flooded with letters
of late. I can't get over that 4 sheeter wh. the gentle Babe sent me,
and wh. I have not yet answered! You can't tell how glad I am to
hear you are feeling so well. I only hope it will go on. I am a new
man since I have been here, both from the ruddy hues of health wh.
mantle on my back, and from the influence of this live city on my
spirits. Dresden was a place in which it always seemed afternoon,
and as I used to sit in my cool and darksome room, and see through
the ancient window the long dusty sunbeams slanting past the roof
angles opposite down into the deep well of a street, and hear the distant droning of the market and think of no reason why it shd. not
thus continue *in secula seculoram*, I used to have the same sort of feeling as that which now comes over me when I remember days passed
in Grandma's old house in Albany.⁵ Here on the other hand, it is just
like home. Berlin I suppose is the most American looking city in
Europe. In the quarter which I inhabit, the streets are all at right
angles, very broad, with dusty trees growing in them, houses all new
and flat roofed, covered with stucco, and of every imaginable irregularity in height, bleak, ugly, unsettled looking, *werdend.* Germany is,
I find, as a whole, (I hardly think more experience will change my
opinion) very nearly related to our country. And the German nature
and ours so akin in fundamental qualities, that to come here is not
much of an experience. There is a general colorlessness and bleak-
ness about the outside look of life, and in artistic matters a wide
spread manifestation of the very same creative spirit that designs our
kerosene lamp models, for instance, at home. Nothing in short that
is worth making a pilgrimage to see. To travel in Italy, in Egypt, or
in the Tropics, may make creation widen to one's view, but to one of
our race all that is *peculiar* in Germany is mental, and *that* Germany

can be brought to us. (thro.' de Vries & others)[6]   If I were you I would consequently not fret much at any delay in coming here, and even not feel very badly if I never came, but I would now begin and get accustomed to reading German.   It will hardly take any larger number of hours to acquire a given proficiency at home, than here, living as you would live, and you will find it worth while.   It seems to me the only gain here wh. is unattainable by staying home, might be the acquaintance of certain individuals—but that is precarious, and you are just as likely to meet those you are in need of in one country as in another.

(After dinner.)   I have just been out to dine.   I am gradually getting acquainted with all the different restaurants in the neighborhood, of wh. there are an endless number, and will presently choose one for good, certainly not the one where I went to day, where I paid 25 groschen for a soup, chicken & potatoes, and was almost prevented from breathing by the damned condescension of the waiters.   I fairly sigh for a home table.   I used to find a rather pleasant excitement in dining "'round" but that is long since played out.   Could I but find some of the honest florid and ornate ministers that wait on you at the Parker house[7] here, I wd. stick to their establishment no matter what the fare.   These indifferent reptiles here, dressed in cast off wedding suits, insolent and disobliging and always trying to cheat you in the change are the plague of my life.   After dinner I took quite a long walk under the Linden, and round by the Palace & Museum.[8]   There are great numbers of statues, (a great many of them "equestrian") here & you have no idea how they light up the place.   What you say about the change of the seasons wakens an echo in my soul.   To day is really a harbinger of winter, and felt like an october day at home, with an N.W. wind.   Cold and crisp with a white light, and the red leaves falling and blowing everywhere.   I expect T. S. Perry in a week.   We shall have a very good large parlor & bedroom, *together*, in this house, and steer off in fine style right into the bowels of the winter.   I expect it to be a stiff one, as every one speaks of it here with a certain solemnity.   We are in the same latitude as london and I believe the sun sets at ½ past 3 P.M. in December, and most of the landladies whose apartments I visited on my arrival assured me that there *never* was any sunshine in winter here.   However as they all happened to be living on what would have been the shady side of the street if there were any, I conceived that this was a slight slander devised by their cupidity, and intended to prevent my giving a prefer-

ence to rooms over the way. Our rooms are on what ought to be the sunny side.

I wish you wd. articulately display to me in your future letters the names of all the books you have been reading. "A great many books, none but good ones" is provokingly vague. On looking back at what *I* have read since I left home it shows exceeding small, owing in great part I suppose to it being in German. I have just got settled down again—after a nearly two months debauch on french fiction, during which time Mrs Sand, the fresh, the bright, the free, the somewhat shrill, but doughty Balzac, who has risen considerably in my esteem or rather in my affection, and Théophile Gautier the good, the golden mouthed, in turn captivated my attention, not to speak of the peerless Erckmann Chatrian who renews one's belief in the succulent harmonies of creation, and a host of others. I lately read Diderot: Oeuvres Choisies, 2 vols. wh. are entertaining to the utmost from their animal spirits and the comic modes of thinking, speaking and behaving of the time. Think of meeting continually such delicious sentences as this—he is speaking of the educability of beasts—"Et peut on savoir jusqu'ou l'usage des mains porterait les singes s'ils avaient le loisir comme la faculté d'inventer, et si la frayeur continuelle que leur inspirent les hommes ne les retenait dans l'abrutissement."!!![9] But I must pull up, as I have to write to father still. On the other page you will find a rather entertaining extract from Grimm wh. I have copied for you. It relates to young Americans at Berlin. I enclose a photograph of M. Babinet,[10] wh. I weakly bought because it looked so intensely french.

Adieu, lots of love from your aff. Wilhelm.

—All with the intention of getting a european culture, but each with a more or less peculiar method of his own in choosing what best suited him. One, who, without knowing latin or Greek, studied Basque & Sanscrit, and at the same time worked at the model of an original sort of ship; another who drove music, and at the same time attended the mathematical & theological lectures at the University; a 3rd. who gave no utterance of the nature of the direction of his studies but bought masses of engravings of every kind; but *all* distinguished by this, that altho' they entered upon their subjects for the most part without the preliminary studies wh. seem to *us* neccessary, they notwithstanding advanced rapidly, and always had marked out to themselves distinctly their direction & their end.[11]

I have just been enjoying a 3 days visit from Henry Tuck on his way to Vienna.   A rich treat, altho' I suppose you will sneer at the idea

I enclose the letter I got from T.S.P not because it is particularly good, but it is characteristic & will help you to "realize" our existence here.   I wrote him I had the room fm. the 1st instead of the 9th. Your article on Historical novels was very good.   I look as yet in vain for the Atlantic with the $200 story.[12]   You must send them.

ALS: MH bMS Am 1092.9 (2554)

[1] Herman Grimm, *Unüberwindliche Mächte*, 3 vols. (Berlin: Wilhelm Hertz, 1867), review in *Nation* 5 (28 November 1867): 432–33 (*ECR*).

[2] A weekly review of politics, literature, and art published in New York in 1863–69.

[3] Johann Wolfgang von Goethe, *Wilhelm Meisters Lehrjahre*, *Wilhelm Meisters Wanderjahre*, and *Die Wahlverwandtschaften*.

[4] *New York Daily Tribune*.

[5] HJ describes the house as "a big much-shadowed savoury house" (*A Small Boy and Others* [New York: Charles Scribner's Sons, 1913], 4).

[6] Not identified.

[7] A hotel in Boston, at 60 School St.

[8] Mittel Strasse was a short street parallel to Unter den Linden.   WJ would have walked through the university area to the Royal Museum.   The Brandenburg Gate was nearby, in the opposite direction.

[9] Denis Diderot, "Instinct," in *Œuvres choisies de Diderot*, 2 vols. (Paris: Firmin Didot Frères, Fils, et Cie., 1862), 1:267.

[10] There are several noted individuals of that name.

[11] Herman Grimm, *Unüberwindliche Mächte*, 2d ed., 2 vols. (Berlin: Wilhelm Hertz, 1870), 1:124.   A copy of the first edition (1867) was not available.

[12] HJ, unsigned reviews of Anne E. Manning, *The Household of Sir Thomas More* and *Jacques Bonneval*, in *Nation* 5 (15 August 1867): 126–27; "Poor Richard: A Story in Three Parts," *Atlantic Monthly* 19 (June 1867): 694–706; (July 1867): 32–42; (August 1867): 166–78.

To Henry James

Mittel Strasse 12[III] | Oct 17. 67

My dear Harry

I did not write last week as usual because I had nothing particular to say, and all the evening before the mail I wrote to C. F. Atkinson. I have entered on a new phase of my transatlantic existence, viz. that of living in company with T. S. Perry, and you've no idea how it lightens the burden of life to have some one to talk to an hour or two a day.   He has been here nearly a fortnight now, and has entered energetically upon the study of German.   He is in "rude health" and has lost to a great extent that peculiar sensitiveness that used to make

him at certain times difficult to talk freely with, and is good natured
all day long.   He has not, I confess, made as much intellectual progress as he might have done since he left home and has not outgrown
his old laziness.   This damned Parisian feuilleton & chronique literature I think has harmed him.   It is to the mind what drinking &
smoking are to the body, and renders it incapable of doing justice to
more substantial pabulum.   He is now probably under the influence
of the dying out waves of his summer's vacation, and when they pass
off may show more vigor.   I am very glad to be with him.———I
enclose you a photograph wh. Grimm gave me the other night and
which is interesting artistically even if of no historical worth.   One
Prof. Becker of Darmstadt found a picture representing a laurel-
crowned-corpse lying by the side of a candelabrum and dated 1637,
in the house of a resident of that city, with a modern label "Den trad-
itionen nach, *Shakspeare*."   The picture had been bought at the auction of the collection of antiquities and curiosities of the "Kesslstadt"
family, after the death of the last member thereof, some years previously.   The Professor judged from the definiteness of the face in the
picture that it must have been copied either from nature or a cast and
his zeal being aroused he ransacked all the garrets & junk shops in
Darmstadt for 2 years, after which time there turned up in one of the
latter the mask in question, wh. turned out to have come also from
the same auction, and wh. bore on its back in figures of the period,
scratched in the soft plaster ✝ Ao. Dm̃. 1616.   This is the date of
Shakespeare's death.   No other clue exists, nor has any information
been obtained, either positive or negative about the relations of any
member of the Kesselstadt family 250 years ago with England.[1]
There is evidently no attempt at deception on any one's part, the only
question is as to the worth of the "traditions."   Internal evidence is
favorable.   The mask has been critically compared, by *J. Hain
Friswell*[2] with the other portraits of the poet & found to agree in all
essential particulars with the Stratford bust.   The only difference
being in the fulness of the chaps of the latter.   It does not seem unnatural to suppose that the sculptor of the bust, even if using the
mask for a model, should have wished to substitute the healthy forms
of the "fat peasant of Stratford" for those of the mask, wasted by
illness and pinched by death.   If you take a piece of transparent paper, and letting the mask shimmer through it, trace around it the
outline of the head with the long side locks, the collar & shoulders,
the resemblance becomes very striking, and the fullness of the cheeks
and jaws seems much greater.—At any rate it is a superb head, and

could have belonged to no common man.   It looks more like a
gentleman & a man of action than a man of Shakespeare's disposition, but the dead are so apt to put on an eagle like expression that
that cannot go for much.—I am going to write to Alice & will here
pause.   I got a bully 5 sheet letter from you recently.   I don't know
whether I acknowledged it in my last or not—(I now remember that
I *did*)   T.S.P. received your long letter a few days ago and thoroughly
appreciated it.   He will enclose a note to you in this.

Ever yr. loving   Wm. James

ALS: MH bMS Am 1092.9 (2555)

¹The so-called Kesselstadt death mask was discovered by Ludwig Becker, a librarian at Darmstadt, in 1849.   For an account giving many of the details supplied by WJ
see John S. Hart, "The Shakespeare Death-Mask," *Scribner's Monthly* 8 (July 1874):
304–17.   Hart mentions an article by Grimm published in 1867.

²James Hain Friswell (1825–1878), British essayist, *Life Portraits of William Shakespeare* (1864).

From Henry James

Cambridge, Nov. 22ᵈ [1867]

Dear Willy—I haven't written to you for some time, because the others seemed to be doing so.   We at last got some little news about your
health.   Praised be the Lord that you are comfortable & in the way
of improvement!—I recd. about a fortnight ago—your letter with the
review of Grimm's novel—after a delay of nearly a month on the
road, occasioned by I know not what.   I am very sorry for the delay
as it must have kept you in suspense, and even yet I am unable to give
you a satisfactory reply.   I liked your article very much & was delighted to find you attempting something of the kind.   It struck me
as neither dull nor flat, but very readable.   I copied it forthwith &
sent it to the *Nation*.   I recd. no answer—which I take to be an affirmative.   I expected it to appear in yesterday's paper; but I see it is
absent, crowded out I suppose by other matter.   I confess to a dismal
apprehension that something *may* have happened to it on the road to
N.Y. & have just written to Godkin to tell me whether he actually recd.
it.   But I have little doubt he has done so & that it is waiting, & will
appear next week.—Were it not for the steamer I would keep your
letter till I get his answer.—I hope you will try your hand again.   I
assure you it is quite worth your while.   I see you scoffing from the
top of your arid philosophical dust-heap & commission T.S.P. to tell
you (in his own inimitable way) that you are a d——d fool.   I very

much enjoy your Berlin letters. Don't try to make out that America & Germany are identical & that it is as good to be here as there. It can't be done. Only let me go to Berlin & I will say as much. Life here in Cambridge—or in this house, at least, is about as lively as the inner sepulchre. You have already heard[1] of Wilkie's illness—chills & fever. It finally became so bad that he had to come home. He arrived some 10 days ago & is now much better; but he must have had a fearfully hard time of it. He eats, sleeps & receives his friends; but still looks very poorly & will not be able to return for some time. Bob went a few days ago out to his old railroad place at Burlington.[2] He was very impatient to get something to do, but nothing else turned up, altho' he moved heaven & earth, *more suo.* I have no news for you. A. Kate is in N.Y., attending "Em" Walsh's wedding.[3] The rest of us are as usual—whatever that may be called. I myself, I am sorry to say, am not so well as I was some time since. That is I am no worse; but my health has ceased to improve so steadily, as it did during the summer. It is plain that I shall have a very long row to hoe before I am fit for anything—for either work or play. I mention this, not to discourage you—for you have no right to be discouraged when I am not myself—but because it occurs to me that I may have given you an exaggerated notion of the extent of my improvement during the past 6 mos. An important element in my recovery, I believe, is to strike a happy medium between reading &c, & "social relaxation." The latter is not to be obtained in Cambridge—or only a ghastly simulacrum of it. There are no "distractions" here. How in Boston, when the evening arrives, & I am tired of reading & know it would be better to do something else, can I go to the theatre! I have tried it *ad nauseam.* Likewise *"calling."* Upon whom?—Sedgwick's, Nortons, Dixwells, Feltons.[4] I can't possibly call at such places oftener than 2 or 3 times in 6 months; & they are the best in Cambridge. Going into town on the winter nights puts a chill on larger enterprizes. I say this not in a querulous spirit, for in spite of these things I wouldn't for the present leave Cambridge, but in order that you may not let distance falsify your reminiscences of this excellent place. To night par example, I am going into town to see the French actors, who are there for a week, give Mme. Aubray.[5] Dickens has arrived for his readings.[6] It is impossible to get tickets. At 7 o'clock, A.M. on the 1ˢᵗ day of the sale there were 2 or 3 hundred people at the office, & at 9, when *I* stroled up, nearly a thousand. So I don't expect to hear him. Tell Sargy I got his little note, enclosed by you, & am anxiously awaiting his letter. I *hope* (for his sake<)> he will be able to extend his absence. If not &

he comes in March, I shall be 1ˢᵗ to welcome him.   I haven't a creature to talk to. Farewell.   I wanted to say more about yourself, personally, but I cant.   I will write next week.

—Je t'embrasse—H.J.jr

ALS: MH bMS Am 1094 (1926)

[1] Letter to WJ from his mother, 21 November 1867, see *BBF*, 99.

[2] Burlington, Iowa.   For details see *BBF*, 77–78, 99.

[3] Emilie Belden Walsh married Thomas Cochran, Jr., on 28 November 1867.   She was the daughter of Alexander Robertson Walsh, WJ's mother's brother.

[4] Cornelius Conway Felton (1807–1862), American classical scholar, president of Harvard at the time of his death.   His second wife was Mary Louisa Cary, sister-in-law of Louis Agassiz.   Felton had three daughters, of the same age group as WJ and HJ, and two younger sons.

[5] H. L. Bateman's Parisian Comedy Company, from New York, performed a number of plays at Chickering's Hall, Boston, including *Madame Aubray* on 22 November.

[6] Charles Dickens arrived in Boston on 19 November 1867 and gave his first reading on 2 December.   Speculators were selling tickets to the first reading for $50.

To Henry James

[Berlin December 1867]

[*beginning of letter missing*] I have a strong personal affection—but our ways are so far apart that I doubt if we ever really get intimate.   If I were you, (unless you get *perfectly* well) I shd give up all tho't of com-ing to germany   The atmosphere is uninteresting and uninstructive, and to know individuals is so difficult as to make me (who still can easier fall in with strangers than you) despair of doing it.   Even if you never read it fluently, I am not sure that you will lose so much. You are able now to read the untranslateable poems &c, and the rest, unless you need to keep abreast of some particular Science and read the Zeitschriften thereupon, is either translated or to be dispensed with.   I find now with all the practice I've had in reading that it goes about twice (if not more) as slowly as english, and I get over very little breadth of ground in my studies.—I have just been much refreshed by read͟g Swinburne's article on Arnold in the Fortnightly for Oct.[1] wh. T.S.P. sent for.   He seems much more real and innocent than I had supposed.   Of course the article is without judgment or any con-structive power and is intemperate like a boys.   But what freshness of perception and richness and ease of expression—such happy expressions as "compromise with the nature of things," "air" in Ar-nold's descriptions and not in those of the Tennysonian school, are worth pages of painful discrimination.   Poets can write good prose.

Stirling's article[2] is also big.   I presume you have read both.   I read
M. de Camors[3] the other day, wh. you speak in a letter to T.S.P. of
having read.   I must say that with every acknowledgment of its excellence in secondary qualities, good taste, concision, wit, and limpid
style, it was exceedingly repulsive to me, both from the exclusiveness
of the story, in wh. after all the hero's character is left a mere blank,
and from the perfect heartlessness of the author.   Personally he gives
me an impression of cold & fashionable corruption greater than any
one I know.   I shd. not have felt this perhaps so much in M. de C. if I
had not read the idiotic "Jeune homme Pauvre" this summer.   I find
as I grow older that I need something of beauty and refreshment in
novels more and more, and this of course is the general taste of those
who read them for relaxation and not for study.   Though of course
the "*étude*" style of novel cannot be judged from that point of view
and condemned, yet I think that the highest style of novel is the one
that satisfies that craving for refreshment.   Adieu, I hope that that
fat letter is the only one of mine that has been lost.   Lots of love to all
from

Yrs   W.J.

   I wrote at length to Charley Atkinson the 1st week in Oct. I think.

ALS incomplete: MH bMS AM 1092.9 (2556)

[1] Algernon Charles Swinburne, "Mr. Arnold's New Poems," *Fortnightly Review*, n.s.
2 (1 October 1867): 414–45.

[2] James Hutchison Stirling (1820–1909), Scottish philosopher, "De Quincey and
Coleridge upon Kant," *Fortnightly Review*, n.s. 2 (1 October 1867): 377–97.

[3] Octave Feuillet (1821–1890), French dramatist and novelist, *Monsieur de Camors*
(1867) and *Le roman d'un jeune homme pauvre* (1858).

To Henry James

Berlin Dec. 26. 67

My dear Harry

   Another fat pseudo letter.   T.S.P. bought the book of Feydeau[1] the
other night and after sitting up to read it, it occurred to me that my
irrepressible & venal pen might "compliquer" an article out of it wh.
shd. be more readable than the other two.   So with a mighty sweat
and labor I forged the accompanying, wh. I beg you will take care of
& smooth if possible the style.   I strove to imitate the Saturday Rev.,[2]
I fear unsuccessfully, but the writing is good practice.   I am now
more than ever convinced that I was not born for it.   Don't read the
book, it is as vile and weak as they make 'em.   For the last year, I

know not why I have found myself growing to despise the french in many ways.   Paris seems now to be in a state of moral & intellectual debasement, of wh. it really seems hard to imagine any peaceful issue. Every cord is tightly screwed up, to a hair of the snapping point; every thing *screams* falsetto, the point seems coming when pleasure must be bloody to be felt at all.   TS.P. takes the *figaro*[3] daily.   It is the most hideous little sheet I ever saw.   One part *bons-mots*, personal *can-cans*, and bawdy anecdotes, spun out with that infernal grinning flip-pancy & galvanized gaiety ye wot of, the rest devoted to executions, murders & crimes generally in different countries, and theatrical gos-sip.   I seriously think our Police Gazette[4] is a higher paper.   It is the organ of naturally coarse & low minds, but this Fig. is that of minds lost & putrefying.   Bah!

By the way it may please you to know that your health was drunk here the other night at a tea party by Herr u. Frau Geheimrath some-body, Frl. & Dr. Bornemann, a Miss Adams & Mrs Hopkins aus Amerika[5] & myself.   Miss Borneman told me she had been read§ some Atlantic monthlies.   I asked to see them, when lo! among them were "Friend Bingham"[6] and no ii of the great $200 story.[7]   She had read both & was vexed at not getting the whole of the latter.   Imagine the enthusiasm when I announced the author's name.   Er lebe hoch!

Christmas has passed quietly.   Every house in town whether of old or young has had its tree.   The maid-servant said to me last week as she was heating up the stove "Das schöne weihnachtsfest ist bald da," and as I "drew her out" on the subject, she said that every one felt "wehmüthig" before a Xmas tree.   I wish I cd. understand this feel-ing of theirs.   I dined yesterday with the Fischer family[8] to whom hosmer introduced me.   They belong to the elite, and in politeness to each other *as Fischers* leave the Sedgwicks no where.   I am sorry you were not interested in Hosmer.   I saw him but 2 hours & thought he might prove a "1st class mind."

I sent you about two mos. ago a letter containing photogs. of "Shakespeare's death mask" wh. Grimm gave me.   As you have said nothing about it I fear it may have been lost or detained like the other. I hope the latter only, for the mask is extremely interesting.

I have been trying blisters[9] on my back and they do undeniable good.   Get a number about the size of a 25 cents piece, or of a copper cent.   Apply one every night on alternate sides of the spine over the diseased muscles.   In the morning prick the bubbles, and cover them with a slip of rag with cerate, fastened down by cross straps of sticking plaster.   Try a dozen in this way at first.   Then wait two weeks and

try ½ dozen more,—two weeks, ½ doz more & so on.   If the blistering is done too *continuously* it loses its effect.   Between times sponge
back with cold water, (wrung out sponge) twice a day.   I think it does
good, the *Ice* is too powerful, the parts can't react against it.

I wrote Alice to send leaf for Frl. Bornemann for Frl. Thies.[10]   It
has not come in time.   Too bad.   I find reading slow work especially
in German and pine after some special practical work.   I hope next
summer to get it.   My attention is much distracted by a no. of stupid
mining students (americans) whom T.S.P. has brought to the room,
and who lounge all day talking with him about the way their pipes
colour.   It is getting to be a serious nuisance. But I have just made
the acquaintance of 2 german physiological students whom I hope to
gain s'thing fm.   I hope you are getting on better again.

Ever your loving bro.   Wm. James.

ALS: MH bMS Am 1092.9 (2557)

[1] Ernest Aimé Feydeau, *La Comtesse de Chalis* (Paris: Michel Lévy Frères, 1868), WJ, review in *Nation* 6 (23 January 1868): 73–74 (*ECR*).

[2] A British review of politics, literature, science, and art, founded in 1855.

[3] French satirical newspaper, a daily from 1866.

[4] *National Police Gazette*, a weekly published in New York from 1845, devoted to crime reporting to about 1875, afterwards to anything gory and bizarre.

[5] Neither Miss Adams nor Mrs. Hopkins is identified.

[6] HJ, "My Friend Bingham," *Atlantic Monthly* 19 (March 1867): 346–58.

[7] HJ, "Poor Richard."

[8] Not identified.

[9] Blisters were used as stimulants and counterirritants in the treatment of various physical and nervous disorders.

[10] In his letter to AJ, 19 November 1867 (bMS Am 1092.9 [1106]), WJ expresses the hope that his acquaintance with Frl. Bornemann will "ripen into familiarity."   Frl. Bornemann would like some leaves from the garden to surprise Frl. Thies for Christmas.

To Henry James

[Berlin January 1868]

Dear Harry

As T.S.P. is writing I will not till next week.   I got a letter fm. you
and one fm. Wilky last week, with the Nation and its contemptible
contexts.[1]   I perceived the tracks of your repairing hand, and thank
you for them.   I sent you another notice last week of 4fage's Anthro-
pology;[2] but feel so ashamed of merely writing against space without
having anything to say, that I think you had better either not give it or

cut it down to a mere page or two.   I really have no respect for this
unprincipled literary wash that floods the world and don't see why I
shd. be guilty of augmenting it.   No news.   I am sound of wind and
limb; but what would n't I give to have a good long talk with you all at
home, esp? Father & you.   I can hardly believe I ever shall.

Yours   W.J.

ALS: MH bMS Am 1092.9 (2558)

   [1] WJ, review of Grimm published 28 November 1867.   WJ may have meant 'contents' rather than 'contexts'.
   [2] WJ, review of Armand de Quatrefages de Bréau (1810–1892), French naturalist,
Rapport sur les progrès de l'anthropologie en France (Paris: L'Imprimerie Impériale [Hach-
ette], 1867), in *Nation* 6 (6 February 1868): 113–15 (*ECR*).

To Henry James

Teplitz Feby. 12. 68

My dear Harry
   I rec'd last week your letter of Jany 17, Aunt Kate's fm. Newport of
Jany[1] 15, & Mother's of Jany 20.   Father's of 10th the week before.
Many thanks to you all.   Baring[2] has advised me of Father's remittance.   I enclose with this another article for Charles Norton.[3]   I
rec'd while writing it Dr. Holmes's lecture from H. P. Bowditch & appended a few remarks suggested thereby, wh. are "gassy" enough as
far as they go.   The lecture tickled me to death by the perfection of
its style.   Have you read it?   If not, borrow it from Wendell.   I don't
know whether the Teplitz medium prevents me from appreciating
rightly the relative value of things, but it seems to me one of the best
things I know of Dr. Holmes's.   The "strange intensity of my feeling"
on the subject of article writing, of wh. you speak is to be explained
by the novelty of the exercise, & by the enormous difficulty I experience in turning out my clotted thought in a logical & grammatical
procession.   I find more freedom however in each successive attempt, and hope before long to write straight ahead as you do.   What
an activity by the bye you are displaying in the nation![4]   I like your
last articles very much indeed.   There is a vein of freedom about
them, greater than that which used to obtain in connection with your
earlier ones.   I don't think ephemeral newspaper articles ought to
appear too nice.   I was much pleased the other day by receiving from
Fräulein Bornemann some old Atlantic Monthlies, in wh. I found
parts II & III of your "Poor Richard."   I found it good much beyond
my expectations, story, characters, & way of telling excellent in fact.

And hardly a trace of that too diffuse explanation of the successive psychological steps wh. I remember attacking you for when you read it to me.   The Atlantics came in a Box which was sent me apparently fm. a party at the grimm's house, for it contained 3 sheets of allegorical contributions in German manuscript signed by seven or 8 of the grimm crowd.   The head-senders however were Mrs Grimm Miss Thies & Frl. Bornemann.   The contents varied from a big and bully liver sausage to a bottle of champagne—passing through some pots of the most india rubber like calves foot jelly, chocolate, meringues, cologne water, pin cushion, oranges, plaster statuary &c, forming with the allegory of the manuscript a most German mixture.   Luckily the allegory was in Prose, or it wd. have been even more insipid.   The sapidity of the sausage made amends—and there is in every phenomenon that takes place in the German female nature the most curious coexistence of sausage & what seems to us cold & moonshiny sentimentality.   It must be felt, for it cannot be analytically exhibited to a foreigner.   Mother's beloved letter contained an appeal couched in terms of that mellifluous persuasiveness with[5] the maternal heart alone can give utterance to, to come home & be nursed instead of remaining a lone outcast among the unfeeling foreigners.   I might simply content myself with pointing to the above box as a proof that I am kindly treated (Ay! Alice, well may you blush.   When did *you* ever feed me with sausage and jelly?)   But I will say in addition, that I live not only with every comfort I cd. possibly desire—(the "horrid german cookery" she speaks of being a mere myth evolved from the popular american consciousness) but I am convinced that I pass my time here on the whole much more profitably than I could possibly do so at present at home.   In fact I am just beginning to reap the harvest of my months of probation, just beginning to feel at home with the language & the people & to lose the sense of effort and strangeness with wh. the common processes of living have hitherto been conducted.   It wd. accordingly as a mere matter of self indulgence be foolish to go home at this moment.   But in addition to that, if I get enough improvement fm. this Cure this time to get into a laboratory, it will be a matter to affect the prosperity of my whole future life, and turn me from a nondescript loafer, into a respectable working man, with an honorable task before him.   I do not wish to run the risk of being disappointed by having immoderate expectations.   My cure is over at the beginning of next week (30 days) and the improvement will not begin till then.   At present I feel a good deal worse than when I came—but that is a good sign and the normal result of the

weakening effect of the baths.   I will let you know without any exageration how I am 3 weeks hence.—Life in this village is far more sociable than I expected.   There were actually three young englishmen
here for 8 days, Cambridge men & very good fellows, there is now an
Irishman at the Hotel with whom I dine every day, besides wh., I visit
my doctor (as a friend) and am hand in glove with the teacher of
languages of the town, than whom a more absolute rascal never
walked in the sun.   He visited me in his quality of an american citizen, & as he is a most entertaining beggar I have cultivated him.   He
is a pole, a red-republican, and his hand is against every gov'! in Europe.   He speaks french like a native and (without any exageration
on my part) lies worse than any character I ever heard of in a novel
or saw in a Farce.   He is a liar *absolute*, and tells a story with admirable
dramatic effect.   The 43 battles wh. he led in the last polish revolution, the immense hereditary wealth he has lost, his bearding the Czar
Nicholas[6] when a mere boy, his unnumerable escapes from death, &c.
are as good as a circulating library full of adventures.   There is
moreover in the house the charming Anna Adamowiz of whom I remember writing to Alice.[7]   But the jealous manners of the country,
wh. do not permit me to go a walking or a driving with her, but only
to way lay her in the entry, wh. is always crowded with children, domestics and workmen, have not allowed me an opportunity of revealing *les feux dont je brûle*.   Besides her, there is here for her rheumatism, an actress, a very handsome & agreeable jewess, who speaks
german beautifully.   I have in fact far more society than last summer.—The workmen mentioned above are re-opening a bath which
has been closed for several years, and to wh. hangs a slight tale.   The
late King of Prussia who came here for the gout, was sent to the Herrenhaus, a bath house below the Fürstenbad, and having inspected
(as Kings always do,) all the bath mechanism, he came to the conclusion that the water in wh. he bathed at the Herrenhaus came from a
spring wh boiled up in a public charity bath in this Fürstenbad, in wh.
12 rheumatic & paralysed beggars used to sit all day long.   This,
alltho' exceedingly swell for the beggars, did not please the King at
all, and he caused the bath to be sealed up.   I have not read anything
lately worth recording.   The bathing weakens one's brain so as to
almost prevent all study.   I took up Balzac's "Modeste Mignon"[8] the
other day.   I don't know whether you know it.   It must be one of the
very early ones, for the extraordinary research and effort in the style
is perfectly *cocasse*.   It is consoling to see a man overcome such difficulties.   But the story was so monstrously diseased morally that I cd.

not finish it, reading novels as I do for the sake of refreshment. It struck me as something inconceivable almost. Lots of love to every one at home. Excuse the egotism of this letter.

Ever yr | Wms.

ALS: MH bMS Am 1092.9 (2559)

[1] In the autograph letter, WJ took advantage of the fact that this 'Jany' fell on the line directly below the preceding 'Jany', and used ditto marks.

[2] Baring Brothers & Co., London bankers with offices in Boston and elsewhere, offering travelers checks and telegraphic transfers.

[3] Claude Bernard, *Rapport sur les progrès et la marche de la physiologie générale en France* (Paris: L'Imprimerie Imperiale [Hachette], 1867) (WJ 607.77). WJ's copy is signed Teplitz, February 1868. WJ, review in *North American Review* 107 (July 1868): 322–28 (*ECR*). The review contains some remarks about Oliver Wendell Holmes, *Teaching from the Chair and at the Bedside: An Introductory Lecture Delivered before the Medical Class of Harvard University, November 6, 1867* (Boston: David Clapp, 1867).

[4] From October 1867 to January 1868, HJ published six items in the *Nation*. The last two were "The Huguenots in England," 6 (9 January 1868): 32–33, and "Father Lacordaire," 6 (16 January 1868): 53–55.

[5] Probably a slip for 'which'.

[6] Nicholas I (1796–1855).

[7] Anna Adamowiz is not identified.

[8] Honoré de Balzac, *Modeste Mignon* (1844).

To Henry James

Fürstenbad, Teplitz, Bohemia March 4. 68

My dear H'ry

I rec'd last week a letter fm. Father, and the week before one fm. you & another fm. him.—You will be surprised to see that I am still in this place. I am very sorry to say that the Cure (as they call it here) wh. I finished two weeks ago, has had this time an effect exactly opposite to that of last summer, & has made me decidedly worse. It was a longer & a much more violent course of treatment than the first one, and I can only conceive of the result by supposing that it overstepped the bounds wh. in my case are salutary, & produced a permanent depression. This view seems to be countenanced too by the experience of both of us with the ice, & by what you said of that Irish youth's rubbing of you—at first great benefit and after passing a certain point a contrary effect. It shows that, whatever treatment is applied, there must be a very cautious adjustment of it. Being as I am I have judged it more prudent not to go back to Berlin for some time, as it is impossible for me to keep quiet there. Teplitz is as *safe* a place

as there is on the globe.   Nothing moves at this season save the heavenly bodies, & as one hardly feels tempted to arise & pursue them
around their orbits, one can keep very still.   In other respects, it is a
singularly blameless place, too.   This house is excellently kept and I
feel exactly like one of the family, and am on the most affectionate
terms with the domestics male and female, who in sooth are an excellent crowd.   The male, der alte Franz, resembles general Washington, both in form & feature & in moral character.   He walks at the
rate of about ½ a mile an hour, but never sits down and so in the
course of the day gets through a fabulous amount of the most heterogeneous work.   When spoken to, he always seems to count 25 before answering, and when angry (if that ever occurs) I have no doubt
he counts a full hundred.   I take my dinner at the one hotel wh. is
now open.   The bill of fare generally consists of veal in various
shapes, but now and then there is beefsteak, & even mutton, on wh.
days I lay in a large supply.   The liar[1] I wrote you about continues to
be attentive to me, but begins as you may imagine, to be a little of a
bore.   For the last 3 days there has been a roving young Englishman
here, named Shepherd,[2] whose gift of the gab, and power of quotation (I wonder if *all* Englishmen have this latter, all I've met have been
remarkable for it) were astounding.   He left this morning.   I was
very glad to have seen him, he's traveled in the Holy Land, in Iceland,
Egypt &c. &c, & will soon go to the U.S. where you may perhaps see
him.   He has written a short book on Iceland, & is a capital fellow.   I
have been admitted to the intimacy of a family here named Glaser,
who keep a hotel & restaurant.   Immense bulky garrulous kind-
hearted woman, Father with thick red face, little eyes & snow white
hair, two daughters of about twenty.   The whole conversation & tea
taking there reminded me so exactly of Erckmann Châtrian's stories,
that I wanted to get a stenographer & a photographer to take them
off.   The great thick remarks, all about housekeeping & domestic
economy of some sort or other, the jokes, the masses of eatables, fm.
the awful swine soup (tasting of nothing I cd. think of but the perspiration of the animal) and wh. the terrible mother forced me to gulp
down by accusing me, whenever I grew pale and faltered, of not rel-
ishing their food, through the sausages, (liver sausages, blood sausages) & more, to the beer & wine, then the masses of odoriferous
cheese, wh. I refused in spite of all attacks, entreaties and accusations,
& then heard, oh horrors! with some what the feeling I suppose with
which a criminal hears the judge pass sentence of death on him,—
then heard an order given for some more sausages to be brought in

to me instead, the air of religious earnestness with wh. the eating of the father was talked about, How the mother told the daughter not to give him so much wine, because he never enjoyed his beer so much after it, while he with his silver spectacles on pointing with his pudgy forefinger to the lines, read out of the newspaper half aloud to himself,—the immense long room with walls of dark wood, the big old fashioned china stove at each end of it &c, &c, all brought up the *Taverne du Jambon de Mayence* into my mind. There are lots of picturesque domestic architecture here in T. Nothing at all swell for Germany, but courts broken up into every possible combination by the irregularity of the buildings, stone arches, & stairs and galleries outside the houses, &c, &c, which break the light delightfully. And streets in the town wh. the sun never enters, (so that a deadly chill like that of a humid cellar strikes into your bones,) altho the whole open country in wh. to build lies close at hand. To tell the truth, Harry, I had a dream before the effects of my treatment were known, that if it did me a great deal of good, I shd. send home to have you sent here at any sacrifice, for it wd. be your only chance of salvation. You cd. have 3 spells of bathing by october & spend the meantimes in Dresden while I shd. be close at hand in Leipsic in Ludwig's laboratory,[3] and might perhaps go home in the Fall leaving you heare to enjoy your recovered strength. Foolish dream! Apart fm. the hypothetical benefit to your back, I infer fm. the tone of your letters that even a few months of change of scene wd. do your mind a great refreshment. It's a great pity it's fallen through. I think I shall stay however and take another course in April, strange as such logic may at first appear to you. For if this second course sinned only in excess, a 3rd. *milder* one wd. be as likely to repair its evil effects as those of any heterogeneous violence. It is a slight risk, perhaps, but its the best chance I see for myself. If I don't get better then I think I shall start for home, as I can't do anything profitable here, & its too lonely and expensive. My cost of living at this season here, without bathing, is but very little, if at all greater than in Berlin. I wrote you 3 weeks ago enclosing an article on Cl. Bernard for Chas. Norton. I was "struck all of a heap" by Chas.'s offering you the N.A.R.,[4] and though my idea of the duties are rather cloudy, I shd. think you did wisely in declining. I get the Nations reglar, including my 2 last articles.[5] Keepasending of them! I regard the Nation as the sole bulwark of our country's honour. If I were a rich man I wd. have 10,000 distributed gratis every week through the land, but I wd. keep *Godkin* poor & hungry, so that his "vein" might not be clogged and dulled by the

vapours of prosperity.   My schriftstellerisches Selbstgefühl was naturally rather mangled by the mutilations you had inflicted on my
keen article about Feydeau, for I had rather regarded those racy remarks on the french character wh. you left out as the brightest jewels
in my literary coronet & the rest merely as an illustration of them.
However, if you do not claim any of the money for your improve-
ments, I shall not complain.   Darwin's book[6] has just come to me.
As it is of course too late for the next N.A.R., I will send review of it
at my leisure.—I have rec'd the 2nd. Galaxy & Atlantic for Feby. with
yr. story of old Clothes.[7]   Both stories show a certain neatness & airy
grace of touch wh. is characteristic of your productions (I suppose
you want to hear in an unvarnished manner what is exactly the impression they make on me) and both show a greater suppleness &
freedom of movement in the composition; altho' the first was unsympathetic to me fm. being one of those male versus female subjects you
have so often treated, and besides there was something cold about it,
a want of heartiness or unction.   It seems to me that a story must
have rare picturesque elements of some sort, or much action, to compensate for the absence of heartiness, and the elements of yours were
those of every day life.   It can also escape by the exceeding "keen"-
ness of its analysis & thoroughness of its treatment as in some of Balzacs, (but even there the result is dis*agreeable*, if valuable) but in yours
the moral action was very lightly touched and rather indicated than
exhibited.   I fancy this rather dainty & disdainful treatment of yours
comes fm. a wholesome dread of being sloppy and gushing and over
abounding in power of expression like the most of your rivals in the
Atlantic,[8] (there was one in the same no. I've forgotten its name) and
that is excellent, in fact it is the instinct of truth against humbug &
twaddle, and when it governs the treatment of a rich material it produces 1st class works.   But the material in your stories (except Poor
Richard) has been *thin* (and even in P.R. relatively to its length) so that
they give a certain impression of the author clinging to his gentlemanlyness tho' all else be lost, and dying happy provided it be *sans
déroger*.   That to be sure is expressed rather violently, but you may
understand what I mean if I point to an article named Mrs. Johnson[9]
(I suppose by Howells) wh. was sent me in the Feby. Atlantic by T.S.P.
The quality of its humor is perfectly exquisite, and as far as I noticed
never *dérogér*s, but the article left on me (and I suspect on you) a certain feeling of dissatisfaction, as if the author were fit for better
things, as if this material were short measure and he had to coax &
cook it to make it fill even that sober form, as if it were at bottom a

trifling, for him.   Well, I feel something of a similar want of blood in your stories, as if you did not fully fit them, and I tell you so because I think the same thing wd. strike you if you read them as the work of another.   (For instance Charles Lambs essays are perfect because they are so short, and when De Quincey blames him for his want of continuity & his "refusing openings" continually, he seems quite wrong.[10]   Probably if Lamb had expanded his articles into the size of Mrs. Johnson a similar effect of inward dis-harmony wd. have arisen wh. wd. have been painful.)   If you see what I mean perhaps it may put you on the track of some useful discovery about yourself wh. is my excuse for talking to you thus unreservedly.   So far I think Poor R. the best of your stories because there is warmth in the material, and I shd. have read it and enjoyed it very much indeed had I met it anywhere.   The story of O. Clothes is in a different tone fm. any of yours, seems to have been written with the mind more unbent & careless, is very pleasantly done, but is, as the Nation said, "trifling" for you.[11]   I have read since I have been here "4 Neue Novellen" by Paul Heyse,[12] a small book, wh. if the German is not too great an obstacle wd. probably be useful to you.   The *genre* is just what you are engaged in & they are just about the length of magazine stories.   They are very conscientiously and firmly done, and thence satisfactory, tho' to me they had little magic.   But thoroughly respectable and good to have been written.   If you get the book, begin with das Mädchen von Treppi, wh. seemed to me the best.   I have uttered this long rigmarole in a dogmatic manner, as one speaks, to himself, but of course you will use it merely as a mass to react against in your own way, so that it may serve you some good purpose.   It must be almost impossible to get anyone's real whole feeling about what one has written.   I wish I cd. say it *viva voce*.   If I were you I'd select some particular problem, literary or historical to study on.   There's no comfort to the mind like having some special task, and then you cd. write stories by the way for pleasure & profit. I dont suppose *your* literarisches Selbstgefühl suffers fm. what I have said; for I really think my taste is rather incompetent in these matters, and as beforesaid, only *offer* these remarks as the impressions of an individual for you to philosophize upon yourself———

What will Cambridge do without the Nortons?   I have no time for more—my veal-time is long foreby.   But give lots of love to all, including Alice & Aunt Kate.   Send my love to the boys   Can't you send me occ.ᵞ one of Bob's letters.

Ever yours affect.ˡʸ | Wm. James

I found tinct. of Iodine sovran against the european chilblain or frostboil[13] as the G.'s call it, wh. s'evi——d[14] on my toes early this winter.   Paint on 2 times daily till skin begins to loosen.

Direct communications *here* till further orders.

ALS: MH bMS Am 1092.9 (2560)

[1] The Polish teacher described in the previous letter.

[2] Charles William Shepherd, *The North-West Peninsula of Iceland: Being the Journal of a Tour in Iceland in the Spring and Summer of 1862* (1867).

[3] Karl Friedrich Wilhelm Ludwig (1816–1895), German physiologist.   WJ studied in Leipzig in 1882.

[4] The *North American Review.*

[5] WJ, reviews of Feydeau and Armand Quatrefages de Bréau.

[6] Charles Darwin, *The Variation of Animals and Plants under Domestication* (1868).

[7] HJ, "The Romance of Certain Old Clothes," *Atlantic Monthly* 21 (February 1868): 209–20; "The Story of a Masterpiece," *Galaxy* 5 (January 1868): 5–21; (February 1868): 133–43.

[8] The description fits Harriet Elizabeth Prescott Spofford (1835–1921), American writer, "Flotsam and Jetsam," pt. 2, *Atlantic Monthly* 21 (February 1868): 186–98.   Reviewing an earlier novel by Spofford, HJ remarked: "To endeavor to fortify flimsy conceptions by the constant use of verbal superlatives is like painting the cheeks and pencilling the eyebrows of a corpse" ("Miss Prescott's Azarian," *North American Review* 100 [January 1865]: 276).

[9] William Dean Howells, "Mrs. Johnson," *Atlantic Monthly* 21 (January 1868): 97–106.

[10] Charles Lamb (1775–1834), British essayist, criticized by Thomas De Quincey (1785–1859), British essayist, "Charles Lamb" (1848), *The Collected Writings of Thomas De Quincey*, ed. David Masson, vol. 5 (London: A. & C. Black, 1897), 234.

[11] "A tantalizing story which, when the end turns out trivial, is seen to be trivial altogether," *Nation* 6 (30 January 1868): 94.

[12] Paul Johann Ludwig von Heyse (1830–1914), German author, "Das Mädchen von Treppi," in *Neue Novellen* (1858).

[13] Die Frostbeule in German.

[14] Evidenced itself.   WJ was comfortable in French and enjoyed playing with words.   In this instance, he combined the French reflexive with the English 'evidenced'.

To Henry James

[Dresden] March 9. [1868]

Dear H'ry

Here is the Darwin for Chas. Norton[1] wh. I spoke of in my letter of 3 days ago.   I slung it yesterday and breathe at last free.   Nothing new to tell you save that I have finished the Odyssey & been once to see the collection of casts in the Museum here.[2]   It is useless to deny that the Greeks had a certain cleverness.   Houp la la!—I have gone

& bought Renan's Questions Contemporaines.   Avis à toi de ne pas le faire, car je prévois que je te l'apporterai bientôt.   If there are any books that you & father want badly, you had better let me know, and I can import them cheaper.   Renan is—Renan, but abounds in felicitous sayings and suggestive aperçus.   E.g. Le barbare, représentant quelque chose d'inassouvi, est l'éternal trouble fête des sociétés trop satisfaites d'elles mêmes,[3] &c. strikes me as a good definition.—The more I think of Darwin's ideas the more weighty do they appear to me—tho' of course my opinion is worth very little—still I *believe* that that scoundrel Aggassiz is unworthy either intellectually or morally for him to wipe his shoes on, & I find a certain pleasure in yielding to the feeling.   I wish when you write you wd. say more about what you have been reading.   Love to Alice and all.   Adieu!   adieu!

Yrs. | Wm. James

I have entered into a platonic correspondance with *Mrs* Thies(!). She has some designs on me wh. I cannot as yet fathom, perhaps they relate to the house[4]

ALS: MH bMS AM 1092.9 (2561)

[1] Charles Darwin, *The Variation of Animals and Plants under Domestication*, 2 vols. (London: John Murray, 1868) (WJ 516.78), reviews by WJ in *North American Review* 107 (July 1868): 362–68 (*ECR*); *Atlantic Monthly* 22 (July 1868): 122–24 (*ECR*).

[2] The Zwinger Museum in Dresden had some 800 plaster casts of classical sculptures.

[3] Ernest Renan, *Les questions contemporaines* (1868), vol. 1 of *Œuvres complètes de Ernest Renan*, ed. Henriette Psichari (Paris: Calmann-Lévy, [n.d.]), 215.

[4] The Jameses were renting the Thies house in Cambridge and apparently were negotiating to buy.   Writing to his father, 3 July 1868 (bMS Am 1092.9 [2529]), WJ noted that he had heard about the "absurd demands" of the Thieses for the house.

To Henry James

Dresden Apl. 5. 68

My dear Harry

Since writing I have rec'd a letter fm. Aunt Kate (Mch. 4) fm. you (12th) & fm. Father (18th) the 2 latter came yesterday in Co. with one fm. M. Temple.   Much obliged to all concerned.—You see I am still in Dresden.   I have picked up a good deal in a dorsal point of view since leaving Teplitz & am rather better than I was at Berlin—I know I shd. be more so still if the uneasiness of my blood did not drive me to do so much running about—I have been more restless this time at Dresden than at all yet—I have been a number of times in the Gallery, you may imagine with what pleasure—like a bath from Heaven—for last summer when I was here I was only able to thrust my nose into it twice and look for a few minutes at some ½ dozen pictures.   I'd give a good deal to import you and hear how some of the things strike you.   I have been more absorbed this time in the general mental conception of the different schools & pictures than in their purely artistic qualities.   When you see together a nomber of different schools, each so evidently looking on the world with entirely different eyes, the result is very striking.   I have come to no conclusions of any sort, and see that to do so would require a study of all the galleries & antiquity cabinets of europe, & then you wd. very likely be unintelligible to any one but yourself.   Still the problems are fascinating.   One thing is certain, that the German blood is almost without a sense or a want of the beautiful.   The decadence of all schools shows in the same way a neglect of the beautiful, and a sea[r]ch of expression, spiciness, startling effects instead.   Some such pictures here by Ribera,[1] Guido Reni,[2] Rubens, & a lot of others whose names I cannot now think of show talent and ability wh. really *strike* you more than in the purer masters, but they are cold and heartless, and to one who stands out side of the race course of school-competition in wh. they were painted by men half unconscious of the peculiarity of their work, it seems a wonder how any one cd. have taken pleasure in such industry.   (Rubens is a bad example above, but I've not been for 10 days to the Gallery, & some other names escape me.   Rubens has a warmth & heat of his own—and the torrents of fat & rosy fleshed women wh. he pours out, the inexhaustible *verve* of the critter gives one a sympathy with him—though I think he is only to be classed with such men as Gustave Doré.) I've no doubt that the present school of novel-writing, I mean the french realistic school, will strike people hereafter just as the later Roman & Bolognese pictures strike us.   The painters were real strong men and their work was to them earnest, but they missed the one thing needful, & so do these novelists.   The old Germans seem nevertheless to have caught the beautiful very often, but I fancy it has been mostly incidentally.   They seem to have striven mainly after mere fact, truth of detail without choice in genre subjects, which are consequently generally really vulgar & hideous; and in religious subjects, truth of *ideal* detail, that is dressess ideally handsome, cheeks ideally smooth, light ideally pure, &c, &c, wh. of course makes the ensemble pleasing and accidentally carries many parts over into the territory of what other races call beautiful.   I think the real charm in nature which they *sought* to render will be found to be the *agreeable i.e.* that by wh. each separate sense is affected pleasantly, such as bright-

ness, velvetiness; and not at all that higher and more intellectual harmony, (consistent with far duller & inferior separate sensations) wh.
leaps at once to ones eyes out of the beginnings of the Italian schools,
(*e.g* Bellini &c)   With all this there is yet in the old Germans a repose,
wh. is analogous in some measure to that of the Greeks &c, inasmuch
as both seem to have conceived their subjects as simply *being*, and degenerate schools need to have the Being determined in some picturesque & expressive manner.   But the general mode of looking at the
Universe was as wide as East fm. West between the Greeks & Germans; and I fancy their agreeing in this point may possibly arise fm.
the fact that German *art* (and the repose I speak of is strongest in
ideal subjects) may have expressed only a small holy corner of what
the Germans call their "Weltanschauung," while to the Greek it expressed every thing.   The real brothers of the Greeks are the glorious Venetians—in both does the means of expression the artist is
able to dispose of seem to cover all he wants to say—the Artist is adequate to his universe.   Finiteness & serenity & perfection—tho' out
of the finiteness in both cases there steals a grace, wh. pierces the
moral hide of the observer, and lays hold of the "infinite" in some
mysterious way.—It is a touching thing in Titian & Paul Veronese,
who paint scenes wh. are a perfect charivari of splendor & luxury;
and manifold sensations as far removed fm. what we call simplicity as
anything well can be, that they preserve a tone of sober innocence, of
instinctive single heartedness, as natural as the breathing of a child.
The "blondness" of some Venetian things here!, as if the picture were
breathed on the canvass.   (That head "Isaac of York" by Allston[3] in
the Boston Atheneum will give you an idea of the kind of thing I
mean—only with Allston, you feel that the purity & unity comes
through a pretty deliberate choice & sacrifice, while it looks in the
Venetians as if it were effortless and instinctive[)]—I hope you will
excuse this vague tirade, of unripe & probably false impressions—
tho' by the blindness of the language in wh. I have expressed them,
their falsity or truth will probably neither strike you very plainly.—
Besides the Gallery, I have been enjoying that imperturbable old
heathen, Homus lately, and have read XX books of the Odyssey.
There are ½ doz. Germ. translations, all of wh. are esteemed to be far
ahead of Voss,[4] and in verity the thing reads just like a german
poem—no trace of an inversion or an awkward forced sentence such
as abound in translations generally, but a divine old marrowy homely
concrete unconscious-seeming language & narrative.   For my part,
I've no doubt its just as good as reading the original!?   The Odyssey

strikes me as very different in spirit from the Iliad, though whether such difference neccessarily implies a diff. of time of production I am too ignorant to have any idea. My S. Am indians keep rising before me now as I read the O., just as the Iliad rose before me as I went with the Indians.—But the health! the brightness, & the freshness! and yet "combined with a total absence" of almost all that we consider peculiarly valuable in ourselves. The very persons who wd. most writhe & wail at their surroundings if transported back into early Greece wd. I think be the neo-pagans,[5] & Hellas worshippers of to day—The cool acceptance by the bloody old heathens of every thing that happened around them, their indifference to evil in the abstract, their want of what we call sympathy, the essentially definite character of their joys, or at any rate of their sorrows (for their joy was perhaps coextensive with life itself,) wd. all make their society perfectly hateful to these over cultivated and vaguely sick complainers. But I don't blame them for being dazzled by the luminous harmony of the Greek productions. The Homeric Greeks "accepted the Universe"[6]—their only notion of evil was its perishability—We say the world in its very existence is evil—they say the only evil is that every thing in it in turn ceases to exist. To them existence was its own justification and the imperturbable tone of delight & admiration with wh. Homer speaks of every fact, is not in the least abated when the fact becomes to *our* eyes perfectly atrocious in character. As long as Ulysses is in the hands of the Cyclop, he abhors him, but when he is once out of danger, the chronic feeling of admiration or at least indifferent tolerance gains the upper hand. To the Greek a thing was evil only transiently & accidentally and with respect to those particular unfortunates whose bad luck happened to bring them under it. Bystanders cd. remain careless & untouched—no after-brooding, no disinterested hatred of it *in se*, & questioning of its right to darken the world, such as now prevail. No *vague* discontent—Are you free?—exult! Are you fettered or have you lost anything?—Lament your impediment or your loss, and that alone!—Or if a hero, accept it with sober sadness, and without making a fuss, for it is *ultimate*. There is no "reason" behind it, as our modern consciousness restlessly insists. This sad heroic acceptance (sans arrière pensée) of death seems to me the great tragic wind that blows through the Iliad, and comes out especially strong in Achilles. See a beautiful example in Il. XXI. 103 & following.[7] (Read the whole Book in Voss, it's worth the trouble.) It strikes us with a terrible impression of unapproachable greatness of character; but I can't help thinking that its *peculiarity* in our sight lies rather in an intellectual limitation than in any extraordinary moral tremendousness on the part of the hero. Take a modern man of vigorous will & great pride, and *give him the same conception of the world as Achilles had,*—a warm earth where every thing is good, a brazen Fate wh. is *really* inscrutable, and wh. is ever striking her big licks into the pleasant earth and finally cutting us off from it,—and I have no doubt he wd. live like Achilles, (firmly enjoying his earth & as firmly looking at the face of Fate,) without needing the introduction of any new & peculiar moral element of strength into his character. The trouble with the modern man wd. be intellectual; he wd. always be trying to get behind Fate, and discover some point of view fm wh. to reconcile his reason to it—either by denying the good of the world,— or inventing a better one on t'other side,—or something else. But this wd. neccessarily introduce a subtlety into his conception wh. wd be fatal to simplicity; and the seemingly super-human grandeur of Achilleus is due merely to the simplicity of the 2 elements wh. he seems to hold together by pure brute force of character.—9.30 P.M. At this pint I was interrupted by the thick-set-but-beaming-with moral-excellence-wench who said "Bitte Kommen Sie zu Tische!" So I went & devoured my portion of Kalbsbraten with the greater zest for having done you so much writing. I hope it boreth you not to read it. I write off my reflexions to you as they arise because it is the nearest intercourse of that pensive nature that I can have with my kind, & it is a satisfaction to make some definitions, however provi- sional, when you are reading. I don't know that I have anything more to say about the irrepressible Ulysses, at any rate on paper, but I advise you to try a Book or two in Voss's Iliad—I am pretty sure you'll get a bigger impression than from anything english. I am just in fm. the Theatre where has been a sacred concert to inaugurate passion week and the tones of Beethoven's 9th Symphony & Schiller's Hymn to Joy are ringing in my alas! too profane ears; and after a bowl of chocolate imbibed, and another mass of the Veal, very wet & cold as is the wont of the animal the first day in this country, en- gulphed, I sit down again in your society. I am enjoying here in Dresden the very best society of decayed gentlewomen which the city affords. All have a *von* to their name, some are widowed some not yet married, but all agree in having lost their money, and receiving pensions of 100 or 200 Thlrs. fm. the King or Queen. They are of course, all old Friends of Frau Spangenberg and every day some one of them dines with us or spends the evening in the Parlor. They are in general a lacklustre set, but I am getting more german out of them than ever before out of any one else.   Frau Sp. herself is a darling old lady, full of life and interest in every thing, with a great big warm heart and a great & good talker.   Most of her young boarders have been in the habit of calling her "Gross mutter" but altho' I have as yet evaded that form, I really have a filial feeling towards her, and shall be sorry to part with her.   There is another lady in the house, also of noble birth, Fräulein von Kracht[8] over whose blond head some 30 summers may have flown—but she has all the wayward ways of (and speaks of herself as) a naughty child.   She has hands of wondrous length & exquisite tenuity, to match her general frame, and a mode of speaking German so rich and beautiful that I cd. sit mute for hours (by spells) just to hear her.   Really with many little vain weaknesses, she is a very agreeable companion & I can't help feeling sorry for her. Without a penny, too proud of her birth &c to do any work, and in fact too weak in health to do much, she has got an appointment from the queen to a sort of genteel asylum for 6 spinsters of quality founded by someone in his will.   She gets a good room & 200 Thlrs a year, and is engaged to do nothing in return but wear clothes wh. shall be black or silver grey.   But her only friends that I can hear of seem to be these old tottering dowagers, and her path down life seems without any brighter spot ahead.   Poor girl, she was engaged 2 years ago to a Prussian officer who for unknown reasons shot himself during the campaign in Bohemia.[9]   I insert these details to interest alice.   Your last letters tell me she has been keeping her bed.   I have had no idea of her being so sick and it makes me feel very badly. Give her my true love, and a solid hug.   I think I may before long be home and then she'll get well.   She little knows what imaginary dialogues I keep having here with her, things to be said when we are once more together under the one roof, Bless her excellent little Soul!—I am very glad to hear fm. you my dear Harry that you are doing well.   The news of your sudden backsliding in the winter was very painful to me.   You have no idea how my sympathy with you has increased since I have had the same.   I am glad you can go out so much.   Keep it up.   I wrote you fm. Teplitz a long letter relative to your writings.   Exactly what escaped me in the ardor of composition I cannot now remember, but I have the impression I assumed a rather law-giving tone.   I hope it did not hurt you in any way, or mislead you as to the opinion I may have of you as a whole, for I feel as if you were one of the 2 or 3 sole intellectual & moral companions I have. If you cd. have known how I have ached at times to have you by and hear your opinion on different matters or see how things wd. strike you, you wd. not think I thought lightly of the evolutions of your mind.   But I have no doubt you understood rightly all I may have said.—One of the most fearful features of my being abroad it[10] this terrible fluency wh. is growing on me of writing letters—Last week I wrote 5 *sheets* to Arthur Sedgwick,[11] de Populo americano, wh. I wd. like you to read, so ask him for it.   My organ of perception-of-national-differences happened to be in a super-excited state that week and that letter was the consequence.   I don't know whether the "pints" raised, will seem to you just.—I was very much amused by Father's account of Emerson[12]—but I think Emerson probably has other "intellectual offspring" than those wretched imitators, and has truly stirred up honest men who are far fm. advertizing it by their mode of talking.—Good night! my dear old boy.   Once more, impress in some forcible way or other upon Alice the fact of my devotion to her—at any rate, smother her with kisses fm. me.   Thank A.K. heartily for her excellent letter—Give my love to F., M., Wilky & Bob, & believe me

Yours.   W.J.

Address until told not to: 2 Dohna Platz, Parterro

Dresden

Sachsen

I go in a week to Teplitz again for a month & Fr. Spangenb. will take care of my correspondence.

ALS: MH bMS Am 1092.9 (2562)

[1] José Ribera (1588–1656), Spanish painter.

[2] Guido Reni (1575–1642), Italian painter.

[3] For the painting see *A Man of Genius: The Art of Washington Allston (1779–1843)*, ed. William H. Gerdts and Theodore E. Stebbins, Jr. (Boston: Museum of Fine Arts, 1979), 79.

[4] Johann Heinrich Voss (1751–1826), translator of the *Odyssey* and the *Iliad*.

[5] For WJ's "The Neo-Pagans" (1875) see *ECR*.

[6] The phrase "I accept the universe" was reportedly a favorite of Sarah Margaret Fuller, Marchioness Ossoli (1810–1850), American critic and reformer; see *The Varieties of Religious Experience* (Cambridge: Harvard Univ. Press, 1985), 41.

[7] The slaying of Lycaon, whose pleas for mercy are rebuffed by Achilles to the effect that the same fate awaits everyone.

[8] Not identified.

[9] Apparently, during the Austro-Prussian War in summer 1866.

[10] A slip for 'is'.

[11] Letter of 23 March 1868 in the Sedgwick Collection, Massachusetts Historical Society.

[12] According to WJ, in his prefatory note to Henry James, "Emerson," *Atlantic Monthly* 94 (December 1904): 740–45, the essay was written in about 1868 and read to private audiences. His father, WJ adds, was working off his "mingled enchantment and irritation" with Emerson.

To Henry James

Dresden April 13. 68

My dear Harry

I am just in from the theatre and feel like dropping you a line to tell you I have got your last Atlantic story (Extraord? Case)[1] and read it with much satisfaction. It makes me think I may have partly misunderstood your aim heretofore, and that one of the objects you have had in view has been to give an impression like that we often get of people in life: Their orbits come out of space and lay themselves for a short time along of ours, and then off they whirl again into the unknown, leaving us with little more than an impression of their reality and a feeling of baffled curiosity as to the mystery of the beginning and end of their being, and of the intimate character of that segment of it wh. we have seen. Am I right in guessing that you had a conscious intention of this sort here? I think if so, you have succeeded quite well with the girl,[2] who gave me an impression of having roots spreading somewhere beyond your pages, and not failed with the men, though somehow they are thinner. Some expressions of feeling from the sick one did however "fetch," and had to me the mark of being drawn from experience. Of course the average reader feels at the end as if he had had a practical joke played upon him—and I myself after being let down suddenly from the pitch of curiosity excited by the title and the progress of the narrative felt rather as if you'd gone off sticking your thumb to your nose at my feelings. I chuckled fiendishly at the sell. But soon justified it on esthetic principles—You seem to acknowledge that you can't exhaust any character's feelings or thoughts by an articulate displaying of them—You shrink from the attempt to drag them all reeking and dripping & raw upon the stage, which most writers make and fail in, You expressly restrict yourself accordingly to showing a few external acts and speeches, and by the magic of your art making the reader *feel* back of these the existence of a body of being of which these are casual features. You wish to suggest a mysterious fullness which you do not lead the reader through. It seems to me this is a very legitimate method and has a great effect when it succeeds. (I only think at this moment of Mérimée[3] as an example—I read a story of his: "Arsène Guillot," last summer that struck me much by it.)   Only it must succeed.   The gushing system is better to fail in, since that admits of a warmth of feeling, and generosity of intention that may reconcile the reader.   I think in much of your previous productions you have failed through selecting characters uninteresting *per se*, and secondly in not indicating enough of them to make them stand out mysteriously.   (I except from all this Poor Richard wh. seems to belong to another type) e.g. The husband in your old clothes story[4] both the husband and the painter & the old lady in your Masterpiece story[5] under the first head.   Your young women seem to me all along to have been done in a very clean manner—they feel like women to me, and have always that atmosphere of loveliness and unapproachability, which the civilized women wears into the world, without seeming any the less fleshly for it.   This last one, although she is indicated by so few touches seems to me to stand out vividly.   I think a few plastically conceived situations help this effect very much: e.g where she smiles & takes a bite from her cake.   (Great oaks fm. little acorns grow!) Your style grows easier, firmer & more concise as you go on writing. The tendency to return on an idea and over-refine it becomes obsolete—you hit it, the first lick now.   The face of the whole story is bright & sparkling, no dead places, and on the whole the skepticism and as some people wd. say impudence implied in your giving a story which is no story at all is not only a rather *gentlemanly* thing, but has a deep justification in nature, for we know the beginning and end of nothing.   Still, while granting your success here, I must say that I think the thorough and passionate conception of a story is the highest, as of course you think yourself.   I haste to send you these remarks as I fancy in my previous ones I got exagerating in the unfavorable sense.—I have been hearing Devrient[6] play in Hamlet.   He was the 1st german actor—I believe Dawison[7] is considered to have got ahead of him now—is an old man but no one wd. believe it of him on the stage.   His hamlet is of the same Class as Booth's, and interesting in the same way, tho' by my recollection Booth goes ahead of him greatly in variety & subtlety.   What a thing the human voice is though!   The endless fullness of the play never struck me so before—It bursts & cracks at every seam—I may feel it the more for having been thinking of classical things lately—I was in the Cast collection[8] again yesterday.   The question what is the difference between the Classical conception of life & art & that of wh. Hamlet is an example besets me more & more, and I think by a long enough soaking in presence of examples of each, some light might dawn—And then the still bigger question is: what is the warrant for each? Is our present only a half way stage to another Classical era with a more complete conception of the Universe than the Greek, or is the difference between Classic & Romantic not one of intellect but of race & *temperament*. I was only thinking yesterday of the difference between the modern flower-on-a-dung hill (e.g. Victor Hugo[9] *passim*) poetry, where often the dirtier the dung the more touching the poetry of the flower, and the Greek idea, wh. cd. not possibly have conceived such a thing, but wd. have either made the flower leaven the heap or turned back on it altogether—harmony being the sine qua non; and here comes to add to my "realizing sense" of the chasm between them this awful Hamlet, which groans & aches so with the mystery of things, with the ineffable, that the *attempt* to express it is abandoned, one form of words seeming as irrelevant as another, and crazy conceits & counter senses slip and "whirl" around the vastness of the subject, as if the tongue were mocking itself. So too, action seems idle and to have nothing to do with the point; just as in a moral point of view it must have seemed vain to the author's of the Fantine-poetry[10] & to so many Christian sects. While the Greeks were far greater "Positivists" than any now.—But I fear you begin ere now to be in the same doubt about *my* sanity as most people are about Hamlets. Excuse the bosh wh. my pen has lately got into the habit of writing. In this matter I am prevented from expressing myself clearly by reason of the fogginess of my ideas—I think I could reach some analysis by keeping works of both sorts long enough before my eyes, but opportunity and skill are both lacking. And perhaps after all, such analyses are made by everyone more or less for himself and understood by no one else—witness all the german treatises on Aesthetiks; every one has written one here, just as every one has kept school once, in Mass.—I saw by the bye t'other day a German theory: Shakspere a homeopath! It waxes very late. Good night! Letter fm. mother (25 Mch.) rec'd. I'm very sorry Alice is so unwell. Heaps of love to her, I sent you two notices of Darwin last week. I see by 2 Nations rec'd yesterday that I am forestalled there—Perhaps the Round Table might pay for it, or the Atlantic. Do you know who wrote the Nation article?[11] Good night & my blessings to all

Yrs. W.J.

T.S.P. having asked me my opinion of your story I, to save trouble send him this to read and Post, at wh. I hope you will not be offended.[12]

ALS: MH BMS AM 1092.9 (2563)

[1] HJ, "A Most Extraordinary Case," *Atlantic Monthly* 21 (April 1868): 461–85.

[2] Ferdinand Mason, a Union officer wounded in the Civil War, falls in love with Caroline Hofmann. He becomes inexplicably ill and dies after Caroline becomes engaged to someone else. Her real feelings are never disclosed.

[3] Prosper Mérimée, *Arsène Guillot* (1844).

[4] Arthur Lloyd in HJ, "The Romance of Certain Old Clothes."

[5] John Lennox, Mrs. Denbigh, and Stephen Baxter in HJ, "The Story of a Master-piece."

[6] Emil Devrient (1803–1872), German actor.

[7] Bogumil Dawison (1818–1872), Polish-born actor, a member of the Dresden Court Theater from 1852 to 1864.

[8] Casts of classical sculptures in the Zwinger Museum.

[9] Victor-Marie Hugo (1802–1885), French poet and novelist.

[10] Perhaps a reference to Fantine, the heroine of Victor Hugo, *Les misérables* (1862), who in spite of her total degradation has the possibility of redemption.

[11] Asa Gray (1810–1888), American botanist, professor of natural history at Harvard, in *Nation* 6 (19 March 1868): 234–36.

[12] Thomas Sergeant Perry added the following note: 'Read ['&' *del.*] approved & respectfully forwarded. By the next steamer a letter fm. me. Yrs. recd'.

To Henry James

2 Dohna Platz, Dresden June 4. 68

My dear Harry—I am in rec! of a letter from you of May 4, & fm. Father of May 13. I sent you May 18 an article for Hammond's Quarterly[1] wh. I suppose you will have got, and wrote to Alice on the 14th. I have been leading a very quiet life for the 3 weeks I have been in Dresden, have avoided the Gallery entirely, & avoided walking very largely. If my patience only holds out long enough I think it will do me good. I cannot tell even yet if my last Teplitz fit has done me good. I think it pretty certain that it has done no harm, and it was decidedly my duty to try it. It has done me more harm in demoralizing me & getting me off my studies than in any other way. I have hardly yet got back to where I was. But now that I am all alone in the house with my old Grossmutter I shall be all right. There was a very nice young lady in the house fm. New York, an invalid, who went away a couple of days ago to Schwalbach much to my sorrow, for I took several Droschke rides with her and after tea we used to sit out on the garden steps gossiping in a life-like & american manner which brought back my youth again.[2] Of other society I see the Thieses. Miss Thies improves very much—but I'll write of her & society generally to alice—I have been reading up Goethe a little

lately—having finished to day vol ii of Eckermann's conversations
with him.[3]   Voll iii I cannot obtain.   I had read previously his and
Schiller's correspondence,[4] the perusal of wh. I strongly urge upon
you.   I believe it (or the important parts of it—much is of no interest
whatever to the public & I had to skip) is translated in Ripley's Collection.[5]   The spectacle of two such earnestly living & working men is
refreshing to the soul of any one, but in their aesthetic discussions
you will find a particular profit I fancy.   Goethe's ideas of the importance of the *subject-matter* in a work of poetry may perhaps cause you
to reflect.   I own that there was much in their talk about these matters, to wh., from the want of any technical experience, I could do no
justice, and which will all be alive to you.   Eckermann shows G. in a
much less agreeable light—Already old, conservative and occupied
more with reviewing his stores & turning them over than with increasing them.   Nevertheless, his dicta have great weight from the
load of experience one feels to lie behind them.   T.S.P. has the fr.
trans.[6] wh. is complete, and wh. you had certainly better read when
he gets home.   The revelation of the good Eckermann's character is
by no means the least merit of the book.   I have also read W. Meister's
Lehrjahre lately and wondered more than ever at the life & beauty of
the first part—To the latter part I am perhaps not yet *gewachsen*, as
they say here.   It seems to me too allegorical and coldly invented.
Read what Schiller writes about it to G.[7]   Altogether the old apparent
contradiction which bothered me so in Goethe, the seeming want of
humor, of that decisive glance in aesthetic and moral matters which
separates the wheat fm. the chaff, the essential fm. the accidental,
intuitively, has vanished, I can't say exactly how.   He used to bother
me by that incessant cataloguing of individual details, which you must
have noticed in whatever you have read of his; by his pitiless manner
of taking seriously *every thing* that came along, as if the world for the
time contained nothing else; by his noticing the binding of a copy of
Othello for instance with the same gravity as the poem itself, by his
literalness wh. used to remind me of that of the Emerson children,
&c. &c.   All these peculiarities suggest a want of humor and the
somewhat tennysonian character of the humor in Hermann &
Dorothy[8] & in those parts of Wahrheit & Dicht^g where he relates a
joke strenghened the impression. In spite of the humor shown in
"Egmont" & the abysses of "all is vanity" &c opened in Faust, he wd.
seem to me like a very serious man who fearing to lose *any*thing of
value & not having an immediate intuition saved up everything he
got, and put the important and the accessory in one sheaf.   Now as,

I say this foolish impression of mine is dissipated I know not exactly how.   In the first place his objectivity or literalness is to me now a merit in itself (altho it may be at times tedious to me to read), and does not offend me as it did in my raw youth.   At that time I remember I could not forgive him that he shd. describe the scenes of his childhood in Frankfort[9] in a dry light as they *were*.   I thought he ought to have lain back and given the public those subjective feelings, sentimental, musical, visceral, whatever you please to call them, with wh. he recalled them from the old past, in his late years.   I smile now to think of my unhealthiness & weakness.   And in the second place I have learned to distinguish between his general philosophic tendency, and his constitutional habit of *collecting*.   He was a born collector & cataloguer of facts and kept a regualar register in his mind or on paper of all his experience—he could not bear to *waste* or dishonor any item however small of that which struck his senses, and as he was alive at every pore of his skin, and received *every* impression in a sort of undistracted leisure which makes the movements of his mental machinery one of the most extraordinary exhibitions wh. this planet ever can have witnessed, his less healthily endowed reader is often made impatient by his minute seriousness.   But he *had* the intuitive glance beside, and the minutiae he gives you are only *thrown in* extra.   A little story of his called the "Novelle" contains him it seems to me in all his peculiarity & perfection.   You'd better read it in the original, for it is short.   Of his poems read all those in Elegiac meter. I tell you of them because they happen to be the ones I have just read. They are worth your trouble, Epigrams & all.   As a wielder of language he was a magician—there is no other word for it.   His verses grow fuller with every successive reading. Schiller's on the contrary seem most pregnant at first.   About G.'s "philosophy" I will say nothing now—it must be felt to be appreciated, and it can only be felt when it is seen applied in detail.   An abstract enunciation of it, (even could I make it, which I can't) wd. sound insignificant.   I feel pretty certain he did not exhaust human life, but he worked about as wide a stretch of it into an unity as most people have done, & I feel now like passively accepting all I can of positive in him before I begin to define his short-comings—Excuse this headlong scrawl.   By the bye, I'm sorry to mention it, but your own handwriting grows less legible with age—beware of the slippery slope you are on.   When does Father's Treatise appear?[10]   I expected it some time ago.—You can't tell how glad I am to hear from you that you are really better.   I trust there is no charitable exageration in your accounts.   I give you none now in mine.—I will close now and write to Alice to morrow. Lots of love to all & plenty fm.[11] yrself fm.

Yrs.   W.J.

ALS: MH bMS AM 1092.9 (2564)

[1] WJ, "Moral Medication," a review of Ambroise-Auguste Liébeault (1823–1904), French physician and hypnotist, *Du sommeil et des états analogues*, intended for *Quarterly Journal of Psychological Medicine and Medical Jurisprudence*, edited by William Alexander Hammond, appeared in *Nation* 7 (16 July 1868): 50–52 (*ECR*).   For WJ's reaction to the change in plans see his letter to HJ, 10 July 1868.

[2] Catherine E. Havens (1839–1939), a music teacher.   Copies of many letters from WJ, 1868–77, are at Houghton.

[3] Johann Peter Eckermann, *Gespräche mit Goethe in den letzten Jahren seines Lebens*, 3 vols.

[4] The correspondence is usually published in a separate volume of Goethe's works.

[5] *Correspondence between Schiller and Goethe from 1794–1805*, trans. George Henry Calvert, in *Specimens of Foreign Standard Literature*, ed. George Ripley.   Only vol. 1, covering 1794–97, was published.

[6] *Conversations de Goethe*, trans. Émile Délerot, 2 vols. (1863).

[7] Schiller commented on *Wilhelm Meister* extensively in his letters from December 1794 to July 1796.

[8] WJ mentions the following by Goethe: *Hermann und Dorothea* (1796); *Dichtung und Wahrheit* (1811–33); *Egmont* (1786); *Faust* (1808); "Novelle" (1828).

[9] At the beginning of the autobiographical *Dichtung und Wahrheit*.

[10] Henry James, *The Secret of Swedenborg* (Boston: Fields, Osgood and Co., 1869).

[11] WJ wrote 'fm.' instead of 'for', probably anticipating 'fm.' after 'yrself'.

To Henry James

Dresden July 10 [1868]

My dear H'ry

Your letter of the 21 is just to hand—also a galaxy with the story entitled Osbornes Revenge,[1] the which on a full stomach, and comfortably reclining on the sofa I have degustated with great satisfaction.   You grow in the variety of elements which you wield and the previous somewhat too great daintiness of your style is giving way to a mere "chastened"ness<.>   The richness of coloring of your story in the Atlantic (De Grey)[2] is quite remarkable, altho the "human<"> interest of the story is small.   In both stories the reader's curiosity to know what is coming is kept greatly stretched.   Go on—I trust your boarding house life this summer will enlarge your sphere of observation and give you some new characters.   I wish you could have seen a so-called Russian princess[3] whom I travelled with lately & who told me all about her conjugal troubles.   Her husband (the great Hanoverian statesman, Graf Münster) procured a divorce fm. her and married one Lady Harriet Sinclair (who wrote the book called dainty dishes wh. I believe mother has.)   Learning that I was a Doctor this lady gave me various interesting details about her divers *accouchements* (—or "enfantillages"—Mme. Grymes told me of a German who spoke French with great severity & precision, saying that his wife "est morte dans son second enfantillage")   Your article about Ste. Beuve[4] was recognized by me immediately.   I like your notice of Trolloppe's Novel[5] as well as anything you have done in that line.   The Galaxy containing "The Problem"[6] has not turned up.   I formally request it to be sent.   How much money have you made in the past year?   Answer this question.—About my sleep article[7] I am sorry, (as far as so trifling a matter admits of sorrow,) that you shd. have sent it to the Nation.   Even if Hammond's Quarterly[8] did not pay (wh. is doubtful, for it has started with great charivari, and costs a big price each number) I shd. rather have had it there, for the article dealt with a matter still in doubt and only fit for physicians to handle, and I wanted moreover to bring myself under Dr. Hammond's notice as one ready to do that kind of work for him, if neccessary.   It seems to me that the Nation has no concern with an article of that kind.   However, no harm is done.—I am very glad to hear of your "lifting cure."[9]   It is strange that when the contracting of those muscles in walking &c. should be deleterious, it should be advantageous in this other motion. What a dark business it all is, nit wahr?   I saw T.S.P. in Berlin in excellent condition & replete with German.   As he goes home in a month he will give you the latest news of me.   He is as good in quality as one need desire but it is a pity he so hates to take trouble of any sort.   It will keep him back all his life.   I suppose you are now somewhere in the mountains &, I hope, enjoying it there.   Macte virtute, valetudine, librorum notitiis, articulis fabulisque in magazinibus &c &c.   I have just read Tourguénieff "Smoke" and another short novelet "Faust."[10]   They are exceedingly brilliant and masterly, showing the artistic excellence of the French *school* with a wider range of ideas and a less provincial culture of the whole mind.   But, subjectively speaking, I have a sort of dislike to these lurid & suffocating love stories of which I have read so many which prevents the artistic excellence of them from receiving sympathetic justice at my hands.

Much love fm yours ever   W.J.

I wrote you June 4.   I suppose the letter has turned up sometime since your writing

ALS: MH bMS Am 1092.9 (2565)

[1] HJ, "Osborne's Revenge," *Galaxy* 6 (July 1868): 5–31.

[2] HJ, "De Grey: A Romance," *Atlantic Monthly* 22 (July 1868): 57–78.

[3] Alexandrine, Gräfin zu Münster, the widowed Princess Dolgoruki, originally Princess Galitzin, former wife of Georg Herbert, Graf zu Münster-Ledenburg (1820–1902), Hanoverian statesman. Münster's second wife was Harriet Elizabeth (St. Clair-Erskine), Gräfin zu Münster-Ledenburg (1831–1867), author of *Dainty Dishes. Receipts Collected by Lady Harriett St. Clair*, which in 1867 was in its sixth edition.

[4] HJ, review of Charles-Augustin Sainte-Beuve, *Portraits of Celebrated Women*, in *Nation* 6 (4 June 1868): 454–55.

[5] HJ, review of Anthony Trollope, *Linda Tressel*, in *Nation* 6 (18 June 1868): 494–95.

[6] HJ, "A Problem," *Galaxy* 5 (June 1868): 697–707.

[7] WJ, review of Liébeault.

[8] William Alexander Hammond (1828–1900), American neurologist, founder of *Quarterly Journal of Psychological Medicine and Medical Jurisprudence*.

[9] At various times both HJ and WJ lifted weights.

[10] Ivan Sergeevich Turgenev, *Fumée* (French translation 1867); *Smoke, or Life at Baden* (English translation 1868). The French translation of "Faust" appeared in *Scènes de la vie russe* (1858).

To Henry James

Divonne, Aug. 26 [1868]

My dear H'ry—You must have been envying me within the last few weeks, hearing that I was revisiting the sacred scenes of our youth,[1] the shores of Leman, the Hotel de l'Ecu de Genève, the Rue de la Corraterie, etc. The only pang I have felt has been caused by your absence, or rather by my presence instead of yours, for I think that your abstemious and poetic soul wd. have got infinitely more good out of the things I have seen than my hardening and definite growing nature. I wrote a few words about Nürnberg to Alice from Montreux. I think it was about as pleasant an impression as any I have got since being abroad. Perhaps because I did not expect it. All the Americans I saw at Dresden had told me it was totally uninteresting. I enclose you a few stereographs I got there, I know not why for they are totally irrelevant to the interest of the place. It wd. take Th. Gautier to describe it so I renounce.—I was astonished to find how little I remembered Geneva. I could not find the way I took every morning up to the academy. And the shops and houses visible in the rue du Rone from our windows left me quite uncertain whether they were the old ones or new ones. Kohler has set up a New Hotel on the Q. du Mt. Bl. but I went to the Ecu. The dining room was differently hung and the only thing in my whole 24 hours in the Place that stung me, so to speak with memory, was that kind of chinese patterned dessert service we used to have. So runs ye world away. I did not try to look up Ritter, Chantre[2] & Co, but started off here the next morning and have now been here a week.—The impression received on gradually coming from a german into a french atmosphere of things was unexpected and in many respects unpleasant. I have been in Germany half amused and half impatient with the slowness of execution, and the uncouthness of taste & expression that prevails there so largely in all things—but on exchanging it for the brightness and ship-shape-ness of these quasi-french arrangements of life, and for the somewhat tart, firecracker like speech of the french nation I found myself inclined to go backwards and for a few days had quite a homesickness for the easy ugly substantial ways I had left. The tarnal smartness in the way the R.R. depôt counters for example are dressed up, the narrowish waists and white caps of the female servants, the everlasting "monsieur" and "madame," and especially the rapidity and snappishness of enunciation suggesting such an inward impatience made me feel uncomfortable. I am getting used to it, and the french people who sit near me at table and who repelled me by the apparent artificialness with which they spoke to each other, now seem less heartless & inhuman. I am struck more than I ever was with the hopelessness of us english and with stronger reason the germans ever trg. to compete with the french in matters of form or finite taste of any sort. They are sensitive to things which do not exist for us. I notice it here in manners and speech—how can a people who speak with no tonic accents in their words help being cleaner and neater in expressing themselves?—On the other hand the limitations of *reach* in the french mind strike me more and more, their delight in rallying round an official standard in all matters, in counting and dating ever[y]thing from certain great names, their love of repeating catch words and current phrases and sacrificing their independance of mind for the mere sake of meeting their hearer or reader on common ground, their metaphysical incapacity not only to deal with questions but to know what the questions are, stand out plainer & plainer the more I read in German. One wonders where the "Versöhnung" or conciliation of all these rival national qualities is going to take place. I imagine we English stand between the French & the Germans both in taste and in intellectual[3] (or rather spiritual) intuition. In Germany while unable to avoid respecting that solidity of the national mind which causes such a mass of permanent work to be produced there annually, I could not help consoling myself by thinking that after all whatever they might *do* the Germans were a plebeian crowd and never could *be* such gentlemen as we were.   I now find myself getting over the french superiority by an exactly inverse process of thought.   The frenchman must sneer at us even more than we sneer at the germans—and which sneer is final, his at us two, or ours at him and the Germans at us?   It seems an insoluble question—at any rate for me—I have read several novels lately. Some of that irrepressible George Sand, Daniella, Beaux Mssrs. de Bois Doré[4] (by the bye was it thee that wrotest the Nation notices on her, on Morris's New Poem, and on the "Spanish Gypsey["]?[5]   The articles came to me unmarked.   The thoughts seemed such as you wd. write, and in some places the style, but elsewhere not.)   G.S. babbles her improvisations on so that I never begin to believe a word of what she says.   I also read the woman in white,[6] one or two Balzacs &c &c.   A volume of tales by Merimée which I bought & will try to engineer to you by Frank Washburn.   He is a big man.   But the things which have given me most pleasure have been some traveling sketches by Th. Gauthier.[7]   What an absolute thing genius is!   That this creature with no more soul than a healthy poodle dog, no morality, no knowledge (for I doubt exceedingly if his knowledge of architectural terms &c &c. is accurate) should give one a more perfect enjoyment than his betters in all these respects, by mere force of good nature, clear eyesight and fit use of language.   His style seems to me *perfect* and I shd. think it wd. pay you to study it over & over again, principally in the most trivial of his sketches of travel.   T.S.P. has a couple of them.   Another wh. I have read here is called Caprices & Zigzags[8] and is worth buying.   It contains a very amusing *french* (in the classical sense with all its associations) description of London.   I don't know whether you know G. at all except by the delicious Cap. Fracasse.[9]   These newspaper feuilletons are all of as good a quality and I shd. think wd. last as long as the language.———There are 70 or 80 people here in the house, no one of whom I have as yet particularly cottoned up to.   It is incredible how even so slight an obstacle as the foreignness of the french language, but still more the absence of past local & personal associations, gibes and other common ground to stand on, forms to your scraping an acquaintance with people.   Its disgusting and humiliating.   There is a lovely maiden of *etwa* 19 sits in sight of me at the table with whom I am falling deeply in love.   She has never looked at me yet, and I really believe I shd. be totally incapable of conversing with her if I were "introduced," from the above difficulties and because one does not know what subjects may be talked about with a *jeune fille*.   I suppose my life for the past year wd.

have furnished a good many subjects of observation & "motives" to the great american *nouvelliste* especially so in this place.   I wish I could pass them over to you.   Such as they are you wd. profit by them more than I.   I have noticed very few.   I shd. like full well an hour's (or even a longer) interview with you, and Father & Alice & Mother & A.K. and all; just so as to start afresh on a clean basis. Write a little oftener (to this place, until farther notice.)   Give my love to Wendell Holmes.   I have seen John Gray several times.   But what a cold blooded cuss he is.   Write me your impressions of T.S.P. who will probably reach you before this letter.   If Frank Washburn gets home, be friendly to him.   He is much aged by travel & experience and is a remarkably lovely character and generous mind.   Congratulate Gurney[10] on his engagement.   Remember me to A. Sedgwk & C. Atkinson.   Likewise to Ellen in the house.

Ever yours   W.J.

ALS: MH bMS Am 1092.9 (2566)

[1] In the course of their early wanderings, the Jameses stayed in Geneva several times.   According to HJ, *NSB*, 1, the family stayed at the Hôtel de l'Écu in 1859.   HJ describes their 1859–60 Geneva period in *NSB*, 1–16.

[2] Ernest Chantre (1843–1924), French anthropologist.

[3] WJ drew a line through 'intellectual' indicating deletion, but did not supply a substitute.   Nor did he underdot the deleted word for retention as was his custom. The editors have retained 'intellectual' since the sense of the sentence requires it.

[4] George Sand, *La Daniella* (1857) and *Les beaux messieurs de Bois-Doré* (1859).

[5] HJ, reviews in the *Nation*: George Eliot, *The Spanish Gypsy*, 7 (2 July 1868): 12–14; William Morris (1834–1896), English poet, *The Earthly Paradise*, 7 (9 July 1868): 33–34; George Sand, *Mademoiselle Merquem*, 7 (16 July 1868): 52–53.

[6] Wilkie Collins, *The Woman in White* (1860).

[7] Gautier published books about travels in Spain, Italy, Russia, and other countries.

[8] Théophile Gautier, *Caprices et zigzags* (1852).

[9] Théophile Gautier, *Le Capitaine Fracasse* (1863).

[10] Ephraim Whitman Gurney.

To Henry James

[Divonne September 22, 1868]
Dear H'ry,   Many thanks for your first class letter. I congratulate you on your $800 and on you're Pickering's Milton.[1]   Noble boy.—I wrote you some time since about blistering.   Fm you're not noticing it I suppose you've not tried it.   I urge you strongly to do so.   I tried it again this summer with an *excellent result* wh. however, an unwonted activity caused as usual to disappear.   Ergo.   Blister *& remain quiet.*

The application is uncomfortable *but will pay*.   Blisters (strong) the size of a 50 cent piece.   One every night on alternate sides of spine. Empty bubble in morning.   Dress with cloth covered with cerate kept in place by straps of adhesive plaster.   After each dozen blisters, omit a fortnight, and recommence.

—I went to town the other day and visited madame Desrogis whom I found sitting full blown as flush as May, with her daughter beside her, behind the same table to the right of the door, looking as if not one day had passed over either of their heads since we last saw them.[2] She said she remembered father very well.   Her manners, and her daughters, are perfect.   Adieu, for the nonce.   I am determined to get well by next Spring, if I die for it, so you may set your mind at rest on my score.   Give my love to Wendell H, to Atkinson and Arthur Sedgwick.   I'd give a good deal for a talk with Wendell as well as with you.   Ade!

                                                                 Yr.   W.J.

ALS: MH bMS Am 1092.9 (2567)

    [1] Several three-volume editions of the *Poetical Works of John Milton* were published in London by W. Pickering.
    [2] Not identified.

From Henry James

                                 London March 19th [1869] | 7 Half-Moon St W.
Dear Bill—

    As I have written three very long letters home without as yet anything like a sufficient equivalent, I wont trouble you this time with more than a few lines.   You must be very much startled, by the way, by my charming prolixity;   I suppose my impressions have been too many for me & that I shall gradually acquire greater self-control. You see I'm still in London but without a great deal of news beyond that simple fact—if simple it can in any sense be called.   Or rather I have a piece of news which ought to interest you very nearly as much as myself—which is two words that my experiment is turning out a perfect success & taking in all essentials the course that I had counted upon.   I go thro' everything that comes up, feeling the better & better for it; I feel every day less & less fatigue.   I made these long recitals of my adventures in my former letters only that you might appreciate how much I am able to do with impunity.   You mustn't think of course that I am literally on the gallop from morning till night: far

from it.   I mentioned all the people & things I saw, without speaking
of the corresponding intervals of rest, which of course have been numerous & salutary.   But I may say that I can do all that I care to—all
I should care to, if I were in perfect order.   I wouldn't go in if I could,
for perpetual & promiscuous pleasure.   It cheapens & vulgarizes enjoyment.   But when a man is able to breakfast out, to spend a couple
of hours at the British Museum & then to dine out & go to the play, &
feel none the worse for it, he may cease to be oppressed by a sense of
his physical wretchedness.   Such is my programme for to day—the
first item of which has been executed.   (You can interpolate this letter, by the way, into the list of my achievements.)   I have been break-
fasting with my neighbor Rutson,[1] of whom I have spoken, who
seems to take a most magnanimous view of his obligations towards
me.   He entertained me this morning with a certain Hon George
Broderick[2] (a son of Lord Middleton, you know)—an extremely
pleasant & intelligent man.   (Rutson has just stopped in to ask me
again for Sunday.   He is indeed as my landlord describes him—
"wrapped up in goodness & kindness.["])   The dinner this evening is
to be at the Stephen's.   It will have been however, except at the Nortons & Wilkinsons, the only house at wh. I've dined.   I've really of
course seen no people on my own basis.   I breakfasted yesterday at
the Nortons along with Frederic Harrison & Professor Beesly[3]—the
politico-economists of the Fortnightly Review.   It's very pleasant
meeting people at the N.'s as thanks to their large numbers, you are
lost in the crowd & can see & hear them without having to talk yourself.   The gents in question were very agreeable—altho' I felt of
course no special vocation for "meeting" political economists.   I shall
have gone off without seeing any literary folk, I suppose, save Leslie
Stephen—who in spite of his good nature seems mortally untalkative.
I was asked to dine to day at the N.'s with Ruskin & John Morley,
editor of the Fortnightly, but this dinner prevents.   Also to go with
C.N. to Lord Houghton's to see his collection of Blakes,[4] but for various reasons I have declined.   I spent a very pleasant morning the
other day by going out to Ruskin's at Denmark Hill, near Sydenham,
with C.N.   I didn't see the grand homme in person as he was shut up
with some very urgent writing; but I saw what was as good, his pictures—a splendid lot of Turners (the famous *Slaver*[5] among others) a
beautiful Tintoret & an ineffably handsome Titian—a portrait.   I
enjoyed very much too the sight of a quiet opulent long-established
suburban English home.   Tell Alice the house was (fundamentally)
just like Miss Austen's novels.[6]   I shall perhaps (or probably) dine

there next week.   I went out the other morning, by rail, to Dulwich[7] to see the gallery & spent an hour there very pleasantly.   One long gallery, lit from an old fashioned ceiling, paved with brick tiles & lined with very fair specimens of most of the great masters.   A pale English light from the rainy sky—a cold half-musty atmosphere & solitude complete save for a red nosed spinster at the end of the vista copying a Gainsborough[8]—the scene had quite a flavor of its own.   Only these indifferent Rubenses & Rembrandts make me long for the good ones.   The National Gallery is still closed.[9]—I dined yesterday with the Wilkinson's.   Mary is away.   Madame is agreeable & the Doctor excellent.   He is a great admirer of Swinburne & said some very good things about him.   In fact he said nothing but good things.   Father will know what I mean by his peculiar broad rich felicity of diction.   I doubt whether I should see in England a better talker in a certain way.   But my "few lines" are losing their fewness.   I leave as usual to the end to say that on Monday I received fathers little note of March 2 enclosing Nelly's,[10] wh. I have answered.   I was thankful for this small favor, but wofully disappointed at getting nothing else.   I live in the expectation of the next mail.   Next week I will have matured & will communicate my plans ahead.   I shall not outstay April 1st in this place.   Of course I shall go to Malvern, as I intended.   I needn't say how much I hope to get from you as good news as I have given.   I am in the most superior spirits—& very anxious to get some news fr. the boys or, at least, of them.

Beaucoup d'amour!   H.J.jr

ALS: MH bMS Am 1094 (1927)

[1] Albert Rutson, a friend of Charles Eliot Norton, HJ's "neighbor above stairs" (*HJL*, 1:91) on Half-Moon St.

[2] George Charles Brodrick (1831–1903), British journalist, later warden of Merton College, Oxford, son of William John Brodrick (1798–1870), 7th Viscount Middleton.

[3] Edward Spencer Beesly (1831–1915), British scholar and writer.

[4] William Blake (1757–1827), British poet and engraver.

[5] Turner's *The Slave Ship* was owned by Ruskin until 1872.   It is now in the Museum of Fine Arts, Boston.

[6] Jane Austen (1775–1817), British novelist.

[7] A district of London.   The gallery at Dulwich was noted for its collection of Dutch paintings.

[8] Thomas Gainsborough (1727–1788), British painter.

[9] Both the National Gallery and the Royal Academy were housed in the same building until 1869, when the academy was moved.   Perhaps HJ was in London at the time of the move.

[10] Mary Helen James Grymes.

To Henry James

Cambr. March 22. 69

Dear H'ry

On acc^{t} of my back I will write but one sheet though I fain wd. write more. I have missed your conversation bad, but not your services as errand boy, coal heaver &c at all.—We have got yr. letter fm. L'pol. & yr. first fm. London. Also a characteristically verbose one fm. Jane Norton about your arrival expressing affection for you & hopes that you wd. treat their family like your own.—Your photog^{s} were good. *Types* like that woman are far more valuable than *names* like that Matt. Arnold.—After you quit I put on 4 blisters, after wh. 4 days de suite of exercise and to my incalculable joy felt better after them than before. After ten days rest tried other 4 days exertion with result of throwing me away down & making me feel rather sick of life. That was ten days ago. I have been blistering since and am well on the rise again, with a good lesson in favor of beginning exercise gradually. The short taste of comparative wellness has given me new stomach however for the fight, and I find I don't get bored so much now as a couple of months ago by lying down a couple of hours a day doing nothing.—John La farge came in a few nights since. My affections gushed forth to meet him, but were soon coagulated by his invincible pretentiousness, that no one can teach him anything that he does not know already, you know what I mean—I suppose he happened to be in a particularly vicious mood that night, for it reminded me of old, rather than recent times with him. He goes abroad in Sept. Father & Mother get on well without you altho' M. & Alice give utterance to maudlin sighs & expressions of affection for you wh. I endeavor to discountenance. The scene when your letters arrived, the reading & re-reading &c wd. have done your heart good.—You will be glad to hear that Alice went to Newport last Saturday (day bef. yest.) escorted by John Bancroft. She will return in a few days, when Aunt K. does. Father was loath to let her go without him, but she said to me and mother that her main wish in going was to get rid of him & Mother, and I was very glad to find her understanding so clearly her position. She has seemed very well indeed since you left. I read recently Tourgeneff's Pères & Enfants,[1] wh. I thought had bigger defects than some others and began two eve^{gs} ago Browning R. & B.,[2] which is magnificent so far, and can be read for pure fun just like one of Charles Reade's novels,[3] without conscientious fear of missing fine points &c.—I wrote a notice of a book on Spiritualism "Planchette" for the Advertizer[4] and got $10.00!! Galaxy for April advertized this mng. with yr. dialogue.[5] No proof sent. It will be sent you next week. What is Bob Temple's address? All people here well that you know. Wendell H. unchanged. Chas. W. Eliot president[6]—I ween more bad about him than good, but we shall see. Wilky writes he is very busy about immigration and if they get 1000 Northerners into his county he will become a fixture. 1000!!! Much love. excuse conciseness

Yrs. W.J.

23rd. Aunt K. writes fm. Newport Alice not tired *a bit.* Galaxy got yest. & yr. thing reads very well.[7] better than when you read it to me. Father says "Harry has decidedly got a gift."

ALS: MH bMS AM 1092.9 (2568)

[1] The French translation, *Pères et enfants* (1863).

[2] Robert Browning, *The Ring and the Book* (1868–69).

[3] Charles Reade (1814–1884), English novelist and playwright, known for novels advocating reform and the historical romance *The Cloister and the Hearth* (1861).

[4] Epes Sargent (1813–1880), American journalist, *Planchette; Or, the Despair of Science* (Boston: Roberts Brothers, 1869) (WJ 479.75), WJ review in *Boston Daily Advertiser*, 10 March 1869, reprinted in *Essays in Psychical Research* (Cambridge: Harvard Univ. Press, 1986).

[5] HJ, "Pyramus and Thisbe," *Galaxy* 7 (April 1869): 538–49, a one-act play involving only two characters.

[6] Eliot's election by the Harvard Corporation was announced on 18 March 1869. The election had to be approved by the Board of Overseers. He was inaugurated on 19 October.

[7] "Pyramus and Thisbe."

From Henry James

Great Malvern April 8th [1869]

Dear Willy—

It was a great pleasure to receive at last your letter of March 23d, wh. came three days ago, together with a few lines from Mother, for which pray thank her. Of course I have been sorry to think that you have been unable to write before by reason of your back & I have greatly missed hearing from you. But I am glad to think that you're again on the rise & I accept your reflections as to the lesson you have learned by your misadventure. I likewise appreciate the joy you must have felt on finding yourself better: Fear nothing: it was a sign of the coming dawn. By this time I have no doubt you are once more soaring on the wings of confidence & hope.—I wrote only a week ago to day to father, but I nevertheless find it necessary to my comfort to write again. You mustn't let my letters bore you. Don't read them if you don't feel like it—but keep them nevertheless. They will serve me in the future as a series of notes or observations—the only ones I shall have written.—My last will have told you of my arrival & initiation at this place some ten days ago,[1]—since which there is not a great deal to add. I have got to feel quite at my ease here & am more or less able to pass judgement upon it. The first five or six days of my stay were very cold & bracing, which made the place appear at a decided advantage, thanks to which I quite lost my heart to it. But since then the mild rains of April have let in—the air is dead & muggy & there is decidedly too much water in one's life. Exactly how it is agreeing with me I know not. As far as I can judge, it is not exactly calculated to benefit my back. The baths seem exhausting & the life is monotonous. The place is unfortunately built up & down hill & whenever one goes out it is always (in some degree) a perpendicular trudge—which for a man with my trouble is a circumstance to be regretted. You get tired before you have been out half long enough. But (strange as it may appear) it was not precisely for my back that I came. I have been, I assure you, vastly well satisfied with my progress in that respect. (Here my letter becomes PRIVATE & unfit for the family circle.) It was to obtain relief & redress against my infernal constipation that I sought these precincts. Strange to say, all my travelling & knocking about have only seemed to rub the confounded thing in worse & worse—until during my last week in London I could stand it no longer. I must say however that the manner of my London life rather fostered it. Change of air & of habits gave me a vast appetite & my custom of dining almost habitually with the Nortons on rather a faint stomach, contributed to stuff me out considerably. I have no fear but that with time & steadily continued habits of temperate eating I shall obtain a sufficient regularity. The only thing is to tide over the trying period of getting into those habits. The diet here is good—both simple & palatable. But the only treatment for my complaint is the sitzbath. I was disappointed not to find here some such mechanism (i.e. that injection-douche) as you found at Divonne. I am curious to know whether you think its existence there is sufficient reason for my going on purpose to try it. A line on this point despatched immediately would greatly oblige me. I am rather at loss to say where it would find me. My ambition is to stay here a month—to May 1st. I shall stay as long as I don't find the systems

detrimental to my back.   The order of life is about as follows.   A
bath on rising (very cold of course) a walk to get up reaction.   Breakfast at 8.30.   Bath at noon.   Another reactionary walk.   Dinner at
2. "Running" sitz-bath at 5.   Walk number 3.   Tea at seven.   Bed
early.   I can't walk enough on these vertical slopes to fill out my time
& as I don't play billiards nor whist, I fall back on reading, with the
old results.   Nevertheless I *can* walk a great deal & I may be able to
be out of doors quite enough.   Unfortunately rain is the order of the
day just now.   Whither I shall turn when I leave this, I know not.
Before I left London C. E. Norton stirred up my imagination largely
on behalf of a tour in the North—that is up the West & down the East
side of England—thro' several of the great Cathedral towns.   Trim-
ming down his programme it would amount to a straight rush up to
Edinboro', wh. C.E.N. says is decidedly one of the places in Europe
best worth seeing; then strait down to Durham & York, Peterboro',
Ely & Oxford.   I could do it in between a fortnight & 3 weeks &
should allow myself sixty pounds.   On the one side I may not be
strong enough, & moreover not having come over for promiscuous
travelling, might be unwise in cutting into my resources at the outset.
On the other I feel at times as if a 3 weeks' tour would do me a world
of good.   My stay in England too has begotten within me a deep desire to see & know the land.   I should certainly be sorry to think that
I was leaving it forever without seeing more of it.   It's a most delightful place.   So if I should leave abruptly now it would be in the hope
of returning in the future.   I incline to think that I shall omit the
tour aforesaid as being beyond my mark generally.   There remain 3
things I should like to do.   One is to go over to Leamington (close to
this) & spend 3 or 4 days seeing Warwick, Stratford & Coventry.   The
next is to go for a few days to Oxford, where C.N. & Leslie Stephen
have offered me such letters as would enable me to see the place comfortably.   The last is to stop *en route* for France at Canterbury, which
by the way would compel me to choose Dover & Calais & cut poor old
Boulogne.   Besides, there are three or four old Cathedral towns (of
the second class) close to this, where I can spend a morning or afternoon—Worcester, Hereford & Gloucester.

9th   After writing the above yesterday I went off alone after dinner
by the train to the ancient city of Tewksbury in Gloucestershire where
I spent a long delicious afternoon.   Quaint old Elizabethan houses
(& older) a fine old Abbey—the whole set in elm-scattered meadows—*rien n'y manquait*.   I took tea in a dark little parlor in the old
Tun, by name the *Swan* & as I consumed my bread & butter & ale,

tried to sketch in the twilight one of the romantic, strangely timbered dwellings opposite. Altogether one of the best days yet—& a great tribute to my strength, as I spent a longer time on my feet than I should like to say. I hope to have some more afternoons of the same sort.—But ‹en›ough of this nauseous egotism. The great feature of your letter was Alice's visit to Newport & the news that she was none the worse. I'm desperately curious to hear the whole story, which if she's well enough, I hope she'll transmit to me on her return. Meanwhile give her a brother's love. I'm literally famished for news of you all & feel as if I'd literally heard *nothing* since my arrival. Do speak of Bob & Wilk. Tell more about the latter's immigration scheme & bid Bob answer my note of farewell. Command T. S. Perry to do the same. Give my love to Wendell Holmes & tell him I am maturing a little.—Pile in all the household gossip. Tell father that the oftener he writes the better. I haven't yet attempted to answer his three notes "in kind"—I dont know that I can better than by telling him that I haven't had a moment of deep satisfaction & enjoyment here (& I have had many) but I have immediately thought of him as being the real author of my pleasure—having placed it in my power to be here at all—& having taught me all my life to think & feel properly, so that my thoughts & feelings are possibly not idle. I have occasional spasms of nostalgia—in wh. I indulge in the most fulsome compliments to all of you; but on the whole I manage to keep comfortable.—Pourvu that you only do likewise. Thanks for the *Galaxy*. *Àpropos*, I wish you could—you & father between you remembering it—send me the *Nation*. I can't subscribe to it here as I meant, as it has ceased to publish any indication of an English agent. I miss it sadly. If you can find out whether there is an English agent, I will subscribe here. Send also the *Atlantic* including the last.[2] I find that here it has a real charm.—I send no more photos because you can have no idea of the fewness of faces worth sending to be found in London. I forgot to say that besides those 3 enterprises mentioned I think a bit of going into lodgings there for a week on my way to the Cont. I will then look up others. But my instinct has been to wait for the French ones.—Farewell, dear brother. Do send me next time unmitigated good news. Assure the best of parents of my deep affection, the sweetest of sisters of this brother's devotion—& all the rest of my cordial sentiments. Didn't A.K. get a note fr. me? I await an answer.—

Yours   H.

Remember to answer the Divonne inquiry.

ALS: MH bMS AM 1094 (1928)

Address: Wᵐ James esq | Cambridge | Mass. | United States America
Postmarks: MALVERN AP 9 69   LONDON AP 10 69   NEW Y< >

[1] HJ left London on 31 March.   Great Malvern is in an area of health resorts in the Malvern Hills in west central England.

[2] Nothing by HJ or WJ appeared in the *Atlantic Monthly* in spring 1869.

To Henry James

Cambr. Apr. 23. 69

Dear H'ry,   Yours of Malvern Apr 8 just got and read at bkfst. table. I will try concisely to give you advice, writing in pencil because it is Friday mng. and Ellen is revelling in my room in a carnaval of blood and dust, and Father is using the ink stand down here.   I'm sorry you keep so plugged up, and sorry that Malvern hills are unfavorable to the right kind of exercise.   You ask if the "douche rectale" of Divonne makes it worth while to go there.   It did me no good.   But it does good in some cases, and I shd. think that for walking &c, Divonne wd. be better for you than Malvern.   It sounds strange for you to say the baths are "weakening"; to me they were unspeakably invigorating.   But you cant expect much *solid* benefit fm. them in less than 2 months.—We are all alarmed at what you write of spending £60, in 2–3 weeks in a tour in England.   Father tells me to suggest that it seems a pity to let such a sum go bang in a single escapade when hereafter on the continent you may need it so much more.   I know if *I* were abroad now I shd. feel uncomfortable about staying a day in a land so expensive, without some definite sanitary hope such as Malvern affords.   I wd. postpone the enjoyment of E. to my back trip, when you hope to be better and perhaps to be in writing trim.   A pound with exchange & gold is worth now abt. 8 dols., and you can get so much more for it on the continent that it seems a pity not to. If you shd. make pretty straight for Divonne now and stay there 6 weeks I can't help thinking it would be worth while.   You cd. spend the rest of the summer (until you got tired) in Switzerland and then make up your mind where to settle for the winter.   If after Switzerland were done up, you still had inclination, a month at Wildbad in Wurtemberg *might* do yr. back much good. - - - - I have found myself realizing of late very intensely how much I had gained by the knowledge of German, more than I ever appreciated at the time.   It is a really classical & cosmopolitan literature, compared to which French

& Engl. both seem in very important respects provincial. I take back all I ever said to you about it being no matter if you never shd. learn it. I wd. give a good deal if I cd. have learned it 10 years ago—it wd. have saved me a great many lost steps and waste hours. The common currency of german thought is of a so much higher denomination than that of Engl. and Fr. that a mind of equal power playing the game of life with that coin for counters accomplishes far more with an equal exertion. So that if after Switzerland you feel like going Eastward instead of to Paris, you will be sure not to repent it in the End, however dull it may seem at the time.—With these contributions to your resolution I close. We are all well at home, Bob has a vacation in a day or two and is com^g back. Alice *decidedly* improved. Since March 11, I seem to have gone to Pot rather as to the back, and have been lying still and not making any applications to it. Strange to say, I feel quite indifferent to the damned thing—and have (any how for a time) cast off that slavish clinging to the hope of *doing* s'thing wh. has been the torment of my life hitherto, with a mental exhilaration I have been devoid of for a long time. Adieu,

Yours in haste | Wm. James

ALS: MH bMS Am 1092.9 (2569)

From Henry James

Oxford April 26<u>th</u> [1869] | Randolph Hotel.

Dearest Bill—

I found here to day on my arrival your letter of April 9<u>th</u> which I was mighty glad to get. It seemed strange, foul & unnatural to have heard from you only once in all these weeks. What you say of yourself & your prospects & humor interested me deeply & half pleased, half distressed me. I thoroughly agree with you that to exonerate your mind in the manner you speak of will of itself conduce to your recovery, & I fancy that the result of such a decision will be to smooth the way to convalescence in such a manner that much sooner than you seem inclined to believe you will be able to redeem your pledges & find that you had been even too much reconciled. For heaven's sake don't doubt of your recovery. It would seem that on this point I ought to need to say nothing. My example is proof enough of what a man can get over. Whenever you feel downish, think of me & my present adventures & spurn the azure demon from your side.—At all events I am heartily glad that your reflections have cleared up your

spirits & determined you to take things easy. *À la bonne heure!*—Altho' it lacks some days of mail-time I can't resist putting pen to paper
for a few minutes this evening & getting the start of any possible pressure of engagements or fatigue later in the week.   I feel as if I should
like to make a note of certain recent impressions before they quite
fade out of my mind.   You know, by the way, that I must economise
& concentrate my scribblements & write my diary & letters all in one.
You must take the evil with the good.   These same impressions date
from no earlier than this evening & from an hour & ½ stroll which I
took before dinner thro the streets of this incomparable town.   I
came hither from Leamington early this morng., after a decidedly
dull 3 days in the latter place.   I know not why—probably in a measure from a sort of reaction against the constant delight—the tension
of perception—during my 3 days run from Malvern—but the Leamington lions were decidedly tame.   I visited them all faithfully.   Warwick Castle is simply a showy modern house with nothing to interest
save a lot of admirable portraits, wh. I couldn't look at, owing to my
being dragged about by a hard alcoholic old housekeeper, in the train
of a dozen poking, prying, dowdy female visitants.   Kenilworth, for
situation & grandeur, reminded me forcibly of the old stone-mill, &
at Stratford, too, my enthusiasm hung fire in the most humiliating
manner.   Yesterday afternoon I drove over to Coventry.   I enjoyed
the drive but the place disappointed me.   It would seem decidedly
older if it didn't seem quite so new.   But I investigated a beautiful old
church, alone worth the price of the drive.   These English abbeys
have quite gone to my head.   They are quite the greatest works of art
I've ever seen.   I little knew what meaning & suggestion could reside
in the curve of an arch or the spring of a column,—in proportions &
relative sizes.   The Warwickshire scenery is incredibly rich & pastoral.   The land is one teeming garden.   It is in fact too monotonously sweet & smooth—too comfortable, too ovine, too bovine, too
English, in a word.   But in its way its the last word of human toil.   It
seems like a vast show region kept up at the expense of the poor.—
You know, as you pass along, you feel, that it's not poor man's property, but rich man's.   *Àpropos* of Leamington, tell Alice that I found
at the hotel her friend the late Julia Bryant & family.[1]   I called & had
a pleasant visit.   I don't find in myself as yet any tendency to flee the
society of Americans.   I never had enough of it in America to have
been satiated & indeed, from appearance, the only society I shall get
here will be theirs.—

27$\underline{th}$ a.m.   I turned in last evening without arriving at the famous "impressions."   Mrs. Norton gave me a letter to A. Vernon Harcourt esq. fellow of Christ-Church & at about five p.m. I strolled forth to deliver it.   Having left it at his college with my card I walked along, thro' the lovely Christ Church meadow, by the river side & back through the town.   It was a perfect evening & in the interminable British twilight the beauty of the whole place came forth with magical power.   There are no words for these colleges.   As I stood last eveg. within the precincts of mighty Magdalen, gazed at its great serene tower & uncapped my throbbing brow in the wild dimness of its courts, I thought that the heart of me would crack with the fulness of satisfied desire.   It is, as I say, satisfied desire that you feel here; it is your tribute to the place.   You ask nothing more; you have imagined only a quarter as much.   The whole place gives me a deeper sense of English life than anything yet.   As I walked along the river I saw hundreds of the mighty lads of England, clad in white flannel & blue, immense, fair-haired, magnificent in their youth, lounging down the stream in their punts or pulling in straining crews & rejoicing in their godlike strength.   When along with this you think of their haunts in the grey-green quadrangles, you esteem them as elect among men. I recd. last eveg. when I came in a note from Harcourt, telling me he would call this morg. & asking me to dine at his college commons in the eveg.   I have also from Jane Norton a note to Mrs. Pattison, rectoress of Lincoln College, wh. may shew me something good.   As this letter promises to become long, I will here interpolate a word about my physics, *en attendant* Harcourt, whose hour is up.   I gave you at Leamington, a list of my *haut faits* in Monmouthshire.   What I then said about my unblighted vigor is more true than ever.   I felt my improvement in the midst of my fatigue; I feel it doubly now.   There is no humbug nor illusion about it & no word for it but good honest *better*.   If my doings at Oxford have the same result I shall feel as if I have quite established a precedent.

29$\underline{th}$ Harcourt turns out to be simply angel no. 2.   He is tutor of chemistry in Ch.-Ch. & a very modest pleasant & thoroughly obliging fellow.   He came for me the other morning & we started together on our rounds.   It is certainly no small favor for a man to trudge about bodily for three hours in the noon-day sun with a creature thus rudely hurled into his existence from over the sea, whom he neither knows nor cares for.   His reward will be in heaven.   He took me first to Convocation—a lot of grizzled & toga'd old dons, debating of Uni-

versity matters in an ancient hall & concluding with much Latin from
one of them.   Thence to lunch with the rector of Lincoln's—Harcourt having kindly arranged with Mrs. Pattison before hand to bring
me there.   The Rector is a dessicated old scholar, torpid even to inci-
vility with too much learning; but his wife is of quite another fashion—very young (about 28) very pretty, very clever, very charming &
very conscious of it all.[2]   She is I believe highly "emancipated" & I
defy an English-woman to be emancipated except coldly & wantonly.
As a spectacle the thing had its points: the dark rich, scholastic old
dining room in the college court—the languid old rector & his pretty
little wife in a riding-habit, talking slang.   Otherwise it was slow.   I
then went about with Harcourt to various colleges, halls, & gardens—
he doing his duty most bravely—& I mine for that matter.   At four I
parted from him & at 6 rejoined him & dined with him in Hall at Ch.-
Ch.   This was a great adventure.   The hall is magnificent: an immense area, a great timbered & vaulted roof & a 100 former worthies
looking down from the walls, between the high stained windows.   I
sat at the tutors' table on a platform, at the upper end of the Hall, in
the place of honor, at the right of the Carver.   The students poured
in; I sat amid learned chat & quaffed strong ale from a silver tankard.
The dinner & the service, by the way, were quite elaborate & elegant.
On rising *we tutors* adjourned to the Common-room across the court,
to desert & precious wines.   In the eveg I went to a debating club, &
to a soirée at Dr. Acland's[3] (I've quite forgotten who & what he is)
where I saw your physiological friend Mr. Charles Robin.[4]   'Twas
mortal flat.   All this was well enough for one day.   Yesterday I kindly
left Harcourt alone & drove in the morng. out to Blenheim,[5] which
was highly satisfactory.   The palace is vast cold & pretentious but the
park is truly ducal.   As far as you can see, it encircles & fills the horizon—"immense, ombreux, seigneurial." (T. Gautier)   Enfin, I could
talk a week about the park.   But the great matter is the pictures.   It
was with the imperfect view at Warwick, the other day, my 1ˢᵗ glimpse
(save Ruskin's Titian & the poorish things at Dulwich) of the great
masters: thank the Lord it is not to be the last.   There is a single
magnificent Raphael & two great Rembrandts, but the strength of the
collection is in the Rubenses & Vandyks.   Seeing a mass of Rubenses
together commands you to believe that he was the 1ˢᵗ of painters—of
painters, in fact, I believe he was.   A lot of his pictures together is a
most healthy spectacle—fit to cure one of any woes.   And then the
noble, admirable modern Vandyk![6]   His great portrait of Chas. I on
horse-back is a thing of infinite beauty.—I strolled slowly away thro'

the park, watching the great groves & avenues murmuring & trembling in the sunny breeze & feeling very serious with it all.   On my return I went out alone & spent the afternoon in various college gardens.   These same gardens are the fairest things in Oxford. Locked in their own ancient verdure, behind their own ancient walls, filled with shade & music & perfumes & privacy—with lounging students & charming children—with the rich old college windows keeping guard from above—they are places to lie down on the grass in forever, in the happy belief the world is all an English garden & time a fine old English afternoon.   At 6 o'clock, I dined in Hall at Oriel with Mr. Pearson (the author of the early English History who was in America while you were away.)[7]   It was Ch.-Ch. over again on a reduced scale.   I stole away betimes to get a little walk in Magdalen Gardens—where by way of doing things handsomely they have, in the heart of the city—an immense old park or chase filled with deer—with deer, *pas davantage.   Ce détail*, it seems to me, gives, as well as anything, a notion of the scale of things here.   To day I am to lunch with Harcourt but shall take things quietly.   To morrow I shall depart.   I rec'd yesterday a note fr. Frank Washburn saying he had just arrived in England *en route* for home, May 11ᵗʰ.   We shall probably meet.   If I feel as well to morrow as to day I shall satisfy my desire for seeing a little more in the Cathedral line by going to London (roundabout) *via* Salisbury & Winchester.   My present notion is to stay a fortnight in London in lodgings & then make for Geneva. There is much in & about London that I want still to see.   My letter has been long & I fear, boresome.—Do in writing give more details gossip &c.   I'm glad you've been seeing Howells: give him my love & tell him to expect a letter.   Tell T.S.P. *I* expect one.   Do tell me something about Wendell Holmes.   One would think he was dead.   Give him my compliments & tell him I'm sadly afraid that one of these days I shall have to write to him.—I suppose all is well within doors, fr. your silence.   What demon prompts father to direct the letters he doesn't write?   It is really cruel.   If he only would write a few lines I'd as lief Isabella[8] should direct them.   You must have rec'd. my message about the *Nation*: I miss it sadly.   I repeat I heartily applaud your resolution to lie at your length & abolish study.   As one who has sounded the *replis* of the human back, I apprise that with such a course you cannot fail to amend.   Love to Mother & Alice, to Wilk & Bob.   Aunt Kate will have sailed.   Regards to Ellen & Isabella.   Is Eliza's successor a success?—Another piece of mine will have appeared in the *Galaxy*[9]—probably very ill printed.   You will of course

have sent it.   Howells will send father a proof to correct.   I am
haunted with the impression that it contains an imperfect quotation
of a scripture text to the effect that out of the lips of babes & sucklings
cometh knowledge.[10]   If there is such a text or anything like it ask
him to establish it; if not suppress it.   But farewell
                                                    —Your's   H.J.jr.

ALS: MH bMS AM 1094 (1929)

[1] Not identified.   Apparently HJ means that she has recently been married.
[2] HJ is referring to Mark Pattison and his wife.
[3] Henry Wentworth Acland (1815–1900), Regius Professor of Medicine at Oxford.
[4] Charles-Philippe Robin (1821–1885), French anatomist.
[5] Blenheim House, an 18th-century mansion near Oxford, noted for its art collection.   The two paintings by Rembrandt were *The Woman Taken in Adultery* and *Isaac
Blessing Jacob.*
[6] Anthony Van Dyck (or Vandyke) (1599–1641), Flemish painter.
[7] Charles Henry Pearson (1830–1894), British historian, fellow of Oriel College,
author of several works on early and medieval English history, later, a government
official in Australia.
[8] Isabella, Ellen, and Eliza were servants employed by the Jameses.
[9] "Pyramus and Thisbe."
[10] HJ, "Gabrielle de Bergerac," *Atlantic Monthly* 24 (July 1869): 55–71; (August
1869): 231–41; (September 1869): 352–61.   The quotation from Psalms 8:3 is found
in "Gabrielle de Bergerac," *The Complete Tales of Henry James*, ed. Leon Edel (Philadelphia: Lippincott, 1962), 2:117.

From Henry James

                                          23 Sackville St May 13. [1869]

Dearest Bill—
      I have just been writing to father but I can't help scrawling a short
note in response to yours of April 23ᵈ.   That your back shd. be at a
stand-still perplexes me sadly, tho' I can't too much applaud the noble
indifference of spirit with wh. you regard it.   Just keep along resting
& scorning it & some fine day before long, I'm sure you will discover
that all this dreary time you have been improving unawares.   Vous
allez voir.   The thing is *pro tempore* to throw all ambition to the winds
& pluck up all serious designs by the roots, to hurl them reeking &
bleeding in the face of fate.   Under this treatment she'll soon wear a
smoother visage.—Many thanks for your reply to my demand of advice.   Meanwhile I have been practicing violent measures.   You
know by this time the history of my little tour—*de force*, as I may call
it.   I cant help feeling as if you had gone back on me a little, in urging

me so emphatically to leave England with a short turn when I feel as if your discourse had in a measure put me up to coming.   However I regard my stay neither as time nor money wasted.   You must have fancied my undertaking a journey a rather exorbitant piece of expenditure, so long as it was on the basis of £60. in a fortnight.[1]   I am quite at loss now to understand how I came to write you that nonsense.   I was temporarily muddled & deluded.   My journey actually cost under 25£ & lasted nearly 3 weeks.   I may fairly claim that it was a sanitary measure & that it absorbed only such funds as would have been less easily & profitably spent on Malvern (prolonged) Divonne or Wildbad.   The result of it has been to convince me that my salvation is much more to be found in locomotion than in baths.   As regards my back I don't mean to say it has cured me, but it has effectively justified my impression that the more I knock about the better—taking it easy, that is, as knocking about, but letting it still be such, out & out.   At the last I felt rather over-tired owing to having compressed too much into a short space; but with short intervals of inaction to let my improvement accumulate, I honestly believe that a year's journeying would be a "sanitary measure" of the 1$\underline{st}$ excellence. I have *never* (since my trouble) felt so well as while at Oxford, after a week's *hard* sight seeing.   I came near telegraphing home about it.— As regards the other trouble, my adventures seem quite to have done for it & I have got a start of it which with care I don't think I need ever lose.   I have had a movement every day for a month—& at Oxford *two* daily!   It still keeps up; once the habit established it, it will last.   Under these circumstances & unless I relapse grievously, I think I needn't try Divonne & the *douche*.   I leave for Geneva tomorrow.   I have no idea of undertaking a tour of any sort, but it is a vast comfort to know that you have done the *worst* in the fatiguing process with an impunity shading exquisitely into a gain & destined to develop into it.   I can get the worth of a journey by generally brutalizing myself in Switzerland: you have no idea of the frenzy & weakness to which I was reduced at Malvern by the opposite process.   I have done little in London save go to the National Gallery.   I have been there daily for two or 3 hours & feel as if I knew it pretty well.   It is a capital collection, small, compact & choice. I admire Rafael: I enjoy Rubens; but I passionately love Titian.   His *Bacchus & Ariadne* in the N.G. is certainly one of the great facts of the Universe. Tell me not of Nature, in the presence of such Art.   Such painting extends the meaning of the word.—I went on Tuesday with C.N. to Rossetti's studio—a delightful antique house on the river at Chelsea. His pictures, as I saw them there, moved me to great respect. He is very much of a painter & even more of a poet. It's a pity that in each capacity he is so narrow & straitened. He paints nothing but Mrs. Morris—Mrs. M. in purple samite, on a very empty stomach.[2] But he is a great painter.—The Royal Academy is incredibly bad.—But I must cease. Lift up your heart & your back will follow.

In haste, thy brother | H.J.jr.

I forgot to thank father for his *Nations*. Send the *June* Atlantic.

ALS: MH bMS Am 1094 (1930)

[1] HJ to WJ, 8 April 1869.

[2] Jane Burden Morris, a model for several painters, wife of the English poet and artist William Morris. Rossetti was generally thought to be in love with her.

From Henry James

Geneva May 30th 69. (Sunday.)

Dear Brother Bill—

I wrote to Alice yesterday & remarked en passant that I meant soon to write to you. As I have just discovered that I forgot to enclose this photograph—as it's a dismal rainy day & I am confined within doors, the moment seems propitious for my design. Not that I have any wondrous things to tell; I was thinking more especially of the recommendation in your last note, with regard to studying German. Your words go to my heart. The thing on earth I should most like to do would be to make a bee-line for some agreeable German town & plunge into the speech & the literature of the land. I would give my head to be able to use it. But it's painfully evident that I can do nothing of the kind for many a month to come. I know that you didn't suggest it as an immediate project but that you chiefly wished to remind me of its intrinsic importance. I have no doubt whatever of the truth of what you say & and I hope one of these days to act upon your advice. But the day looks distant. I am no nearer being able to read with impunity than I was when I left home. The fact of my feeling the old familiar seediness owing to having tried it a little more than usual during these last days while confined to the house by the rain, shows me plainly enough that I must still interpose a little ease—as in other words a long interval of idleness. I have come to the conclusion that I must modify in a considerable degree the programme with which I came abroad. I remember that I wrote to father from London that I thought a year of travelling would go far towards making me a well man. If I felt any doubt then of the truth of the statement it has been removed by the experience of the last fortnight. Movement, & more movement & still movement—"du l'audace et encore du l'audace et toujours du l'audace"[1]—seems to be the best—the only prescription for my ills. It's the idea I came abroad with, only more so. Instead of a few long quiet sojourns I must make short sojourns & more of them; that is what I mean by "travelling." I can very well stay in a place until I have exhausted its material sights & resources & in some places of course this would imply a comparatively long stay (Paris & various Italian towns.) But when I have "done" the place so thoroughly that there is nothing left but to fall back upon my own society, it will be my best interest to leave it & take up with another. I feel that it is in my power to "do" any place, quietly, as thoroughly as it can be done. If this is not the case my condition & my destiny are a decidedly tough problem; for I have established it as an absolute certainty that I can't sit & read, & between sitting & standing I know of no middle state. These reflections have been forcibly suggested by my life in this place, in which there is so little external diversion that (in spite of considerable walking & two expeditions in particular wh. I described to Alice) I am reduced to the old *tête à tête* with my back—greatly to the detriment of both of us. I think it therefore necessary to face the situation & read it aright. Do communicate these views to father & mother & invoke their blessing on my theory. What I wish is firmly to establish it as a theory, even should my practice not diverge very widely from that which I originally contemplated. It will certainly not be extravagant & I shall be at best a very tame traveller. I was slightly disappointed at mother's reply in her last to my remarks about going to Scotland & at her apparent failure to suspect that it was not as a spree but as part of an *absolute remedy* that I thought of the journey. I doubtless neglected to give a hint of this, however, & my lovely mammy was further justified by my erroneous estimate of my expenses. That she should have thought it necessary to place a veto on my proposition, nevertheless proves the necessity of my thus defining my situation. I want to feel free to use my means to circulate as largely as necessity pure & simple seems to dictate. I have no desire to be restless or fanciful or wasteful. I wish simply to feel at liberty to spend my letter of credit rather more rapidly than I at first anticipated; & I shall by no means feel so blissfully commissioned until I have brought the sacred influences of home into harmony with my idea & ensured them against

being shocked by my apparent extravagance & inconstancy.   I want
father & mother to write & say that they understand & approve my
representations.   They cannot overestimate my perfect determination to spend my money only as wisely as it was generously given &
any future use I make of it will give me tenfold greater satisfaction
for receiving beforehand some slight propulsion from them.—In all
this I have no fixed plan whatever; it is not a matter of plans, but
simply of that one general tendency.   I may turn out after all, to have
done not very differently from what I should have done without all
this contortion of spirit.   I shall hang on to a place till it has yielded
me its last drop of life-blood.   I promise you, there shall be a method
in my madness.   In this way I hope to get a good deal for my money
& to make it last a long time.   How long I know not.   When it is gone
I shall come home a new man; I shall of course not ask for more.
But I incline to think that on this basis I shall get no regular study out
of my present residence in Europe, even if I stay, as I hope to do, two
years.   If I am ever to spend any time in Germany it will be later, on
my own responsibility.   On the other hand, tho' I get no study, I
think I shall absorb a good deal of "general culture."   I feel as if, in
this way, I have already made a good beginning.   I have enjoyed the
little I have seen in the way of pictures in a manner to suggest that, if
I take all I find, I may lay the basis of a serious interest in art & of
knowledge which may be of future use to me.   I embrace this idea
with a desperate grasp—tho' after all there may be nothing in it.   If
I knock two more years out of my life, as regards study, it will bring
me to 28—rather a late period to begin a course of reading—allowing even that I am then able to study.   If therefore I have made anything of a start in the knowledge of the history of art (& if I haven't
"reacted") it will be so much time gained.   But to do anything here at
present, implies infinite labor & research & this is but a passing vision.
Indeed I have no right to concern myself with what lies *au delà* this
season of idleness; my present business—strange destiny!—is simply
to be idle.   I shall have no plans but from month to month.   My
present notion is to remain here until I am irresistibly prompted to
depart; then to go to the hotel Byron at Villeneuve & stay as long as I
can; then to go to some other place & then to finish the summer if
possible at St. Moritz, where I hope to be fortified by the air.   In case
Switzerland proves too much for me or too little, rather, before the
summer is over I shall finish it elsewhere.   While in England I conceived the design of giving up Paris next winter & going to Italy instead, where I should have a better chance to circulate & carry out my

programme. In Paris, a year later, I may be in a condition to do something in the way of study—for which (that is for reading) making every allowance for all the practicable diversions of the place, I should have a deal of time left on my hands. With this view I made up my mind to secure 6 weeks of Paris at present by staying there to the 1ˢᵗ July. But I subsequently decided to come directly here & have perhaps thereby added to my summer at one end what I shall have to take off at the other. If I have had enough of Switzerland by the middle of August, I shall perhaps go to P. & stay till the middle of October & thence proceed *via* Marseilles & Leghorn² to Italy. But all this is black darkness & my prattle is superfluous. One would think that I wasn't to write to you every blessed week.—Pray tell father & mother for their satisfaction that I have in hand (i.e. my letter of credit represents) £867 & that upon this sum I build my adventures. It seems to me a good broad foundation. It will not be likely to diminish as rapidly as it has done in the last three months, owing both to lower prices & greater experience. 31ˢᵗ I have kept this over till to day but have little to add. I have told the long story because I felt a need of opening myself & taking hold of my situation. I don't forget that you too have a "situation" of your own. I wish I could prescribe for it as well. I wish I heard from you oftener, but don't write a line but when you feel like it. Give my love to father & mother & bid them be charitable to the egotism of my letter. I am fighting a very egotistical enemy. Farewell.

Tout à toi   H.J.jr

I don't know what you generally do with my letters—but read this to no one out of the family.

ALS: MH bMS Am 1094 (1931)

¹From a speech by Georges-Jacques Danton (1759–1794), French revolutionary, before the National Assembly.
²Leghorn is Livorno, Italy.

To Henry James

Cambridge June 1. 69

Dear H'ry. Your 2 of May 13 to me and the family were rec'd last week with the burst of joy wh. yʳ letters always call forth. Your accounts of your improved condition were real good news to all of us, as you may believe and fill us with a "deep peace" that you are in a way to get your deserts more or less. Alice raves about you as an "angel" and re-reads your letters so that I have for the sake of the family respectability to take the other tack and revile you, calling you "Ouida"[1] in allusion to your low novels, and use of french phrases in your letters, reminding them of "stuff" & "juice" &c,—all of wh. contributes to the family conversation or altercation.   Wilky is home and seems to have a great regard for you.   I find him much improved myself and aged in every way.   More considerate and moderate, willing to do favors and take reproof kindly, and brimming over with his extraordinary "geniality"—I find him quite a companion.   Alice is certainly much better, and is lively all day, visiting &c.   She never thinks now of lying down, and the slow steadiness of her improvement is a great thing in favor of its durability.   If it keeps on at the same rate this summer she'll be as good for social purposes next winter as any one.—I wrote you that my bottom rather fell out 2½ months ago. I have not picked up since much of any.   Though for the last few days, (owing I suppose to a couple of very painful boils on my loins, wh. have just subsided,—counter irritation!) my back has felt very comfortable.   My bowels have got as conservative as yours used to be—by the way your improvement in that respect is the best news yet.   *Never resist a motion to stool* no matter at what hour you may feel it.   That is a *hauptsache* in the discipline of the gut.   This summer, with *no* study and hardly any reading may start me up again. If not, I genuinely don't much care, for I have loosed the lockjaw grasp with wh. I clung to the hope of accomplishing external work, and transferred my interest in the game of life to the subjective attitude, *i.e.* become moralized, in some sort—In three weeks my medical exam. is over,[2] and I know I shall feel an enormous relief, for I'm oppressed now not so much by the anxiety and responsibility as by the *ennui* of the damned mass of stuff.—I've only seen Howells that once—A. G. Sedgwick grows a bore—*cul de plomb*—T.S.P. trails his lack lustre existence as of yore—Wendell Holmes[3] has skipped many saturdays often by my request, but comes pretty regular.   He is very affectionate *to* me and *of* you, and seemed to enjoy very much those of yr. letters I read to him.   I think he improves surely every year and has that in him which makes you sure his fire won't burn out before the age of 30, as 'most every one else's seems to.   But he's composed of at least 2½ distinct human beings and how they inhabit his one narrow skin without quarreling and trying to shove each other out of doors, I confess it's a mistory to me.   He says he will stay in Boston all summer.   He *may* be (tho' he hasn't said it) saving up money to go abroad in a year or so again.   T.S.P. thinks of going to Berlin this

vacation "taking my diner at Hanus's you know, and sitting at
Spagnarpani's smoking and reading the papers in the afternoon."[4]
You may consequently see him.   Franck Washb. has been home 10
days but has not got out here yet.—That's all the gossip I can think
of.   I think our senate has stultified itself tolerably well about the
Alabama business.[5]   Of course we shall back down.   The talk of the
few newspapers I have seen is characteristically american and mean—
not one (except the Nation) expresses a definite opinion on the subject—vague and absolutely meaningless phrases out of which crop
occasionally abusive epithets for England form the staple.   Of national *dignity* we have as yet no idea, and consider it far prouder to get
out of a scrape smartly that[6] not to get into one.   The rejection of the
treaty, or rather the endorsement of Sumner's speech[7] was a mere
example of the great american buoyant way of doing things, without
a thought of consequences, or of attaching any *definite* meaning to the
act.   Sufficient that Reverdy's dinner excesses were snubbed by it,[8]
and that its "general tone" was severe upon England.   Its a pity the
U. S. Senate shd. still be in this undeveloped state.—I wrote you in
my last s'thing about the advantage of securing German.   I return to
it, as I was then much hurried.—I have been reading for recreation
since you left a good many german books, Steffens's[9] and C. P.
Moritz's[10] autobiographies, some lyric poetry, W. Humboldts letters[11]
Schmidts hist. of germ. literature,[12] etc, which have brought to a head
the slowly maturing feeling of the importance of the german culture.
If you should go to Germany now you might not realize it for the first
18 months but then you wd. feel that the freedom of a great city (so
to speak) had been conferred upon you; and that (just as you probably have often thankfully found that the neccessity of reading certain books wh. you had once marked in your list of future duties, no
longer existed, other studies having raised you over them) the neccessity you once felt of more french culture had vanished, that you
had got to the goal in another way.—To me now the french mind
seems strangely monotonous—for *form*—*je ne dis pas!*, but for ideas I
don't feel as if I should ever find new ones in a french book,
not<hing> but a diffuse re-shuffling of the everlasting old stock.   In
Germany on the contrary there are *for us*, and there are (I imagine)
being produced all the while new *ideas*. Reading of the revival or
rather the birth of German literature, Kant, Schiller, Goethe, Jacobi,[13]
Fichte,[14] Schelling,[15] Schlegels,[16] Tieck,[17] Richter,[18] Herder,[19] Steffens, W. Humboldt, and a number of others, puts one into a real classical period.   These men were all interesting as *men*, each standing as

a type or representative of a certain way of taking life, and beginning at the bottom—taking nothing for *granted*.   In England the *only* parallel I can think of is Coleridge, and in France <Rou>sseau and Diderot.   If the heroes and heroines of all of Ste. Beuve's gossip, had had a tenth part the *significance* of these and their male and female friends, bad readers like myself wd. never think of growing impatient with him and regarding him as an old debauchee.   I shall, I know read with avidity whenever I can find it, any scrap of a letter dated from *that* society.   Its a question of how *significant* will one make his study—what shall be the denomination of the counters he plays with—in Germany they certainly are higher, so much so, as to make the *atmosphere* of french mental life seem quite fade & insipid.   From difference of mental constitution you might not have this result in the same degree as I but you'd be certain of it in some degree.   The upshot of it all is that I advise you to be prudent in adopting France for a residence now.   Trying Germany first will not cut you off frm. france later, and it *may* save you the neccessity of going to France at all.—By the way, Hosmer has gone to spend the summer in Brooklyn. He offers you introductions in Berlin.   His cheerfulness is beautiful. He says he improves steadily though slowly. Father has finished his book, wh. will be printed July 1st.[20]   He seems very well indeed. Adieu, adieu!   Letter fm. Aunt Kate this mng., day before arrival at Queenstown[21] good passage.   Be as economical as you can this summer.   You'll congratulate yourself on it next winter.   Of course my remarks on Germany are meant only as *data* for you to mix with others in drawing a conclusion.

Ever yours aff[y]   Wm. James.

ALS: MH bMS Am 1092.9 (2570)

   [1] Ouida, pen name of Louise De la Ramée (1839–1908), British novelist, who dealt with the disreputable side of military and fashionable life.   In a review, HJ called her a "charlatan" (*Nation* 21 [1 July 1875]: 11).

   [2] WJ passed his medical examination on 21 June 1869.

   [3] Among WJ's letters to Holmes in the Harvard Law School Library, there are a number of undated notes asking Holmes not to come.

   [4] Spagnarpani's was a *konditorei* on Unter den Linden, serving pastries, coffee, liqueurs, known for its reading room in which patrons could read foreign and local periodicals, a gathering place for journalists and politicians.

   [5] The *Alabama* was one of several Confederate cruisers built in Great Britain.   At the time, the United States was demanding compensation from Britain for damages inflicted by the cruisers.   The dispute was submitted to international arbitration in 1871.

   [6] A slip for 'than'.

[7] Charles Sumner, "Claims on England,—Individual and National," a speech before the United States Senate, 13 April 1869.

[8] Reverdy Johnson (1796–1876), American diplomat, represented the United States in the negotiations that produced the treaty attacked by Sumner.

[9] Heinrich Steffens, *Was Ich Erlebte*, 10 vols. (1840–44).

[10] Karl Philipp Moritz (1757–1793), German writer, *Anton Reiser: Ein psychologischer Roman* (1785–90).

[11] *Letters of William von Humboldt to a Female Friend*, Eng. trans. (1849).

[12] Julian Schmidt, *Geschichte der deutschen Literatur im neunzehnten Jahrhundert.* Several different editions were available.

[13] Friedrich Heinrich Jacobi (1743–1819), German philosopher.

[14] Johann Gottlieb Fichte (1762–1814), German philosopher.

[15] Friedrich Wilhelm Joseph von Schelling (1775–1854), German philosopher.

[16] August Wilhelm von Schlegel (1767–1845), and his brother Friedrich von Schlegel (1772–1829), German poets and critics.

[17] Ludwig Tieck (1773–1853), German writer.

[18] Johann Paul Friedrich Richter (1763–1825), German novelist, used the pseudonym Jean Paul.

[19] Johann Gottfried von Herder (1744–1803), German philosopher and writer.

[20] Henry James, *The Secret of Swedenborg*.

[21] A port in southern Ireland.

To Henry James

[Cambridge] Saturday mng. June 12. 69

My dear H'ry

O call my brother back to me,
I cannot play alone
The summer comes with flower & bee
Where is my brother gone?[1]

Your 2nd letter fm. Geneva (May 29) having just arrived has intensified the above familiar sentiment to the point of making me incontinently sit down & write ye a line.   To hear you call life at Geneva dull does not surprize me. It used to amuse me to hear you say after I got home that you felt a kind of yearning to get there again.   The life of Geneva seems to differ from that of most continental towns in being shut up within doors almost as much as our life here at home.   The stranger is out in the cold.   But is there not a grand sort of *style* about the respectable old city up a top the hill, and don't you get a proud sort of municipal flavor from the place, encamped as it were in the middle of all the newfangledness of its outskirts but superior to them like this grand Peace Jubilee "Coliseum"[2] they are just building in

Boston in the midst of the thousands of shanties & booths that have grown up about it.   I recollect being struck by a big placard last time I was in Geneva: "Bouffes Genevois."   The incongruity was at its maximum, but the term bouffes did not seem to get any hold on the term Genevois and was absolutely killed by it. - - What you wrote of your walks to Fernex & the Salève was the best thing I have heard from you yet.   The condition of your back is totally incomprehensible to me, and I have no opinion on the subject anyway.   My diagnosis of it now wd. be simply "dorsal insanity."—It wd. *seem* however that the general tonic effect of all this exercise and sight seeing you are now able to go through with must be gradually to revolutionize the old thing and through sympathy with the rest of your system bring it back to sanity.   So go ahead, but don't *over* fatigue yourself—The temptations thereto in Switzerland must be very great.—I should thing[3] that by loafing around at central places such as Interlaken etc. you could pass the 3 months very well and scrape a great many at least american acquaintances.   It seems to me that *the* way to become well acquainted with americans is to go to Europe.   Don't mind ennui, you've got to have it everywhere, I'm sure I had enough of it in Europe, but I now see that those heaviest days were full of instruction to me.

At any rate dont yield to homesickness.—I have seen Frank Washburn a couple of times.   He gives a good account of you but looks pretty shaky himself.—Next friday my clinical examination at the dispensary (wh. I tried to get exempted from but failed) takes place and the following monday[4] the big examination.   The tho't becomes more grisly every day, and I wish the thing were over.   My thesis was decent, and I suppose Dr. Holmes will veto my being plucked no matter how bad my examination may be, but the truth is I feel unprepared.   I've no doubt I'll éprouver a distinct bodily improvement when it's all over.   My feeling of unpreparedness has, so far from exciting me to study, given me a disgust for the subject—and this I account lucky for my head &c.   I made a discovery in sending in my credentials to the Dean which gratified me.   It was that adding in conscientiously every week in which I have had anything to do with medecine, I can't sum up more than 3 years and 2 or 3 months.   3 years is the minimum with wh. one can go up for examination; but as I began away back in '63 I have been considering myself as having studied about 5 years, and have felt much humiliated by the greater readiness of so many younger men, to answer questions and understand cases. My physical status is *quo*; but, as I say, I suppose the summer will make some difference. Meanwhile I am perfectly contented that the power which gave me these faculties should recall them partially or totally when and in what order it sees fit. I don't think I should "give a single damn" now if I were struck blind.—Tom Ward was here a few days ago—unpleasantly egotistical and ostentatious of his excentricity. If this be not in him a transient humor, I am sorry for him. He always had the germ of it, but a modesty and intellectual earnestness always kept it under. I have read nothing of late but Turgueneff's Nouv. scènes de la vie Russe[5] and your Onéguine of Pouchkine.[6] The latter even in its stiff french garb is charming, and in the pliant Russ, lapped in the magic of metre it must be *delirant*. I have glanced at Cherbuliez's Ladislas Bolski.[7] Quelle fougue! quel esprit! But it seems to me that as he becomes more astonishingly clever he becomes vulgar like the frenchmen, and less winningly interesting and distingué

Boston is to have her olympic games in the shape of the "jubilee" of which I dare say some news has been wafted to your ear. *Streng musikalisch genommen*, it may be poor enough, but as a grand imposing spectacle I feel sure it will be really worth having. I wd. give a good deal to get in to it. The outside of the building alone which is down opposite the institute of technology is very striking from its mere brute size. You have of course heard from mother of our going to Pomfret *Conn.* I believe Minny Temple is going there also for the month of July—Poor Aunt Kate & Cousin Helen! We have as yet had no letter from them since landing, but uncle R.[8] writes this morning that A.K. has written to him that they have decided to stay out their year.[9] We all feel delighted at Hel[e]n's showing so much sense.—John La f. wrote to ask for our different Taine works the other day. He is writing a review of him, for what periodical, I know not.[10] Your story is advertized in the July Atlantic[11] and will be sent to you as soon as got.—Henry Bowditch writes me fm. Bonn where he is to spend the summer, and hopes you may come there. He is an honest man.—You say you mean to write me about what I wrote to you of Germany. I wrote another letter on the same subject a few days ago. (care of Barings.) I hope the legislative tone of my advice don't offend you—it is for the sake of concision.—I shd. think, your physical state being of the kind it is, you wd. feel tempted to try *this* winter in Italy, where I suppose more & cheaper winter loafing is possible than elsewhere—*Whatever* time you spent in Italy wd. have to contain more of the loafing element in it than that spent elsewhere, and this year being peculiarly adapted for loafing for you, it wd. be the most economical division of time.

Alice, father, mother & Wilky all well.　I blush to say that detailed bulletins of your bowels, stomach &c as well as back are of the most enthralling interest to me.　A good plan is for you to write such on separate slips of paper marked private, so that I may then give freely the rest of the letter to Alice to carry about & re-read and wear in her bosom as she is wont to.　If you put it in the midst of other matter it prevents the whole letter from circulation.　Sur ce, Dieu vous garde.

Ever yrs aff⸞ | Wm. James

Charles Ritter, professeur a Morges or rue de la Machine, (en l'Ile) 5, Geneva wd. I know like to see you and is most *coulant* to meet.[12]　I wrote him but he has not answered me yet.

ALS: MH bMS AM 1092.9 (2571)

[1] Felicia Dorothea Hemans (1793–1835), British poet, "The Child's First Grief."

[2] The first concert in the new coliseum built for the National Peace Jubilee held to mark the return of peace after the Civil War was held on 15 June 1869.　Newspaper reports claim that the orchestra and chorus consisted of 10,000 performers.

[3] A slip for 'think'.

[4] 21 June 1869.

[5] Ivan Sergeevich Turgenev, *Scènes de la vie russe*, French trans. by Xavier Marmier (Paris: L. Hachette, 1858).

[6] Aleksandr Sergeevich Pushkin, *Eugène Onéguine*, French trans. by Paul Béesau (Paris: Franck, 1868).

[7] Victor Cherbuliez, *L'aventure de Ladislas Bolski* (Paris: L. Hachette, 1869).

[8] Alexander Robertson Walsh.

[9] The list of first class passengers on the *Siberia*, which left New York for Liverpool on 5 May 1869, includes Henry A. Wyckoff, Mr. and Mrs. L. Perkins (Helen Wyckoff and her husband), and Miss Helen Ripley.　Aunt Kate is not listed.　Since it is unlikely that she traveled second class, either her name was left off in error or she joined the group in Europe.

[10] The project was never completed; see WJ to HJ, 2 October 1869.

[11] HJ, "Gabrielle de Bergerac."

[12] Charles Ritter's letters bear the dateline "Morges."

From Henry James

Righi-Scheideck (Lucerne) | Monday July 12ᵗʰ '69.

My dear old Bill—

The unprecedented interval of nearly two weeks has elapsed since I last wrote from Glion.　Meanwhile your excellent letter of June 12ᵗʰ has added itself to that of June 1ˢᵗ & made it impossible that I should now address my remarks to any one but you. Meanwhile, too, adventures have piled themselves up & I am loth to let another day pass lest experience should outrun memory or memory strength of hand. My date informs you that I have at last torn myself away from the lake of Geneva & confined my frail existence to these unknown *parages*. Some twelve days ago I left the charming Glion, prepared to seek a spot which should combine economy with something more grand & novel in the way of scenery. First, however, I betook myself to Vevey to pay my duties to the Nortons in the shape of a four days' visit, lasting from Thursday to Monday. Four days I found as much as I could manage. I lodged in an extremely picturesque old farmhouse about ten minutes' walk from this place—a genuine old Vaudois concern, nestling among vineyards & orchards. The Nortons are living in great simplicity & great contentment. I hope the latter will not forsake them, for the former is a little excessive. Charles & his wife, are both poorly; the Swiss air seems not to agree with them. On my leaving the Nortons, began the famous "adventures," above mentioned, which have culminated in this mountain top. My plan as I quitted Vevey on the afternoon of July 5th, was to resort to Château d'Oeux a favored spot in the Canton de Vaud, back from the lake, behind the mountains, where living is cheap, nature beautiful & Americans abundant. With this laudable intention I betook myself to Aigle, in the Valley of the Rhone 1 & ½ hour from Vevey whence I proposed to proceed by coach next morning to Chateau d'Oeux. At Aigle I chanced to meet a respectable English lady, bound to the same spot who furnished me with information which led me to modify my views. The place was full, the pensions overflowing & the air not particularly mountainous. I slept on it & next morning decided to proceed only as far as Comballaz (4000 feet above the sea) halfway to C. d'Oeux, where the air is better & accommodation more plenteous. Meanwhile, in the watches of the night, I had interrogated my soul & inquired of it whether it was worth while to linger & hover so long in this comparatively familiar & secondary part of Switzerland while the splendid & famous regions lay blooming afar. Nevertheless I stuck to Comballaz, & having learned that it was but a three hours' walk & a very beautiful one, I despatched my luggage by the mail-coach, grasped my trusty staff & at 9. a.m. started away on foot. The morning was intensely hot—I absolutely rained perspiration; but I deeply enjoyed the walk. The road on leaving Aigle branches off from the Rhone valley & slowly winds & mounts, in splendid fashion, along the beautiful Gorge des Ormonts. Far below rushes & murmurs the usual torrent; above gleams the dusty macadamized band wandering among the green recesses.   A two hours' trudge brought me to the Village of Sepey, where at the inn I sat me down to rest.   Here, conversing with the post-mistress, I learned that there were as yet, at the hotel at Comballaz but three individuals—a circumstance which again led me to commune with my soul.   Further researches led me to commune more devoutly; half an hour's meditation led me to give it up.   It is needless to trace the process of thought which at this stage of my proceedings induced me to fix upon the Diablerets—a region about two hour's distant noted for the infernal grandeur of its scenery.   It contains a large pension, which was already well filled.   I communed awhile with the inestimable Bäddeker & found that when I wearied of the Diablerets I could make a direct journey to Thun & Interlaken, where I might abide permanently.   Behold me then awaiting the arrival of the coach at Sepey, transferring my luggage to the post-chaise for the Diablerets, dining & at two o'clock starting away.   I enjoyed in the chaise, by the way, the company of an elderly & ugly Miss Bradford of Chesnut St. Boston—a great botanist—a devotee of the "Flōwra" of America.[1] We reached the D. at about 5 o'clock—which left me a bit before dark to examine the scene.   Here occurred a new revelation of spirit.   Decidedly this was not a place to stop at: a vast amphitheatre, surrounded by bleak towering desolate walls of snow-crowned rock—grim, horrible & uninteresting.   The next morning, accordingly, I started on foot for Thun.   The first step was to cross the charming little Col de Pillon—a trudge of three hours.   You may imagine that the pass is of the mildest, inasmuch as I took with me a stout little car, for my luggage.   I don't mean I dragged it myself.   I have not yet come to that.   From the Col we descended into the lovely Simmenthal (Berne) by the little Village of Gesteig, where I stopped to rest & dine.   This walk to Gesteig was deeply delightful   Here, at the inn I met four lovely young Englishmen—the flower of the earth.—I am getting, by the way, absolutely to adore the English.   At this place, my brother, there came over me a rich & vivid recollection of the little foot-journey we made together years ago, when we had no aches & pains. As I sat in the little German-Swiss dining room, I could almost fancy you at my side & myself ten years younger.   From Gesteig in the afternoon I took a waggon to Zweisimmen—a three hours' ride & a very pretty one. Here, before dark, I still had time for an hour's walk in the "Environs" & spent the night at a very good inn.   Next morning at 5.45 I started in the coupé of the mail-coach for Thun, which we reached, thro' a most adorable country, at about 10.30. This gave me a chance for further meditating & communing—so that when we reached Thun & I had walked about for an hour & found it, thro'[2] extremely pretty, deplorably low & hot & reflected that Interlaken was in this respect identical & furthermore that it was a shame to come to Switzerland to bury one's self in Valleys when breezy steeps & summits were at one's disposal—when I had compressed these arduous cogitations & perambulations into the space of an hour, I was quite ready to proceed to the station & take my ticket for Lucerne *Via* Berne & depart at a quarter past twelve. The journey to Lucerne was of six hours—six of the hottest & grimiest I ever spent. I never enjoyed a wash so much as that in which I indulged at the gorgeous Schweizerhof. Here I dined, strolled a bit in the dark & retired to rest. Now during that busy hour at Thun I had fixed upon this Rigi-Scheideck as the goal of my future efforts. I had made a note of it in England at the urgent recommendation of a gentleman at Malvern & I found it qualified in Bädeker as the most frequented spot of the kind in Switzerland—bracing, comfortable, & "plein de calme & de repos." Having breakfasted therefore on Friday morning, I devoted &[3] hour & a half to perambulating the mysteries of Lucerne—a charming little old town, but given over body & soul to tourists. I then departed at 11.40. in the steamer for Gersau, at the further end of the lake. The mountains about the lake were all shrouded in a hot haze, but they loomed out in dim grandeur, out-crowding & overtopping each other. At Gersau I landed, dined & reposed a while previous to ascending the mountain. The Rigi as you probably know, rises directly above the lake, thus:

From the Kulm where people go to see the sunrise, it stretches a long undulating peak to this Scheideck, a second summit, to which you mount from Gersau. From Gersau, accordingly, having previously charged my luggage on the back of a sweating peasant, I began at 5. p.m. to trudge upwards. I reached the Scheideck in about 2 hrs. & ½ steady walk. Here I find a large rough-&-tumble sort of hotel, planted on the naked summit & crowded with Germans. Having telegraphed from Gersau I am fortunate enough to get a room—a little box of a place, but sufficient. I have as yet been here but 2 days & am unable to say how I shall like things. At any rate I shall give them a fair trial. The obvious drawback is the total absence of shade & the violent glare produced by the

"view" & by the clouds being as much below as above you. Nevertheless owing to the great elevation (I believe about 6,000 feet.) the air
even at noon-day is light & cool & stirring—it has a sort of flavor.
The house is conducted on strictly German principles—breakfast at
8; dinner at 12½; coffee at 5½ supper at 7½.   But the fare is very
good & plentiful.   As for the walks, I have as yet reconnoitred but
little.   They must be all rather stiff climbing.   But I assure you I am
not afraid of them; & by the time I write again, I hope to have some
high deeds to relate.   My sketch of my journey will shew you that a
considerable amount of fatigue & exertion has been my portion.   It
is the same story.   On each succeeding day I felt myself better & capable of more.   There were moments when I would have greeted
with enthusiasm the proposition of an amiable & intelligent youth to
undertake with him an extended walking-tour.   Indeed the chief
abatement of my pleasure was having to do it all alone.   So as I say, I
make⁴ have some startling performances to relate.   Your diagnosis of
my back in your last seems to me as good as another & I don't profess
to understand the matter any better than you.   I think however I
have a glimpse of the course it is to run before it returns to sanity.
Namely 3 stages.   1⁰ A stage in which exercise must go on increasing
until it entirely predominates & attains its maximum—even to not
sleeping, if necessary.   2⁰ A stage in which sitting, reading, writing
&c. may be gradually introduced & allowed to share its empire.   3⁰ A
stage in which they will hold their own against it & subsist on an equal
& finally a superior footing.   But I shall certainly never get beyond
having to be minutely cautious [Excuse the accidental irregularity of
my pages] in the distribution of my time & use of my strength.
When this last stage will come I know not.—But to return a moment
to actual plans.   I am already satisfied that I must not expect myself
to spend the summer on this spot.   It is so peculiar in its nature & the
exclusively German character of its habitués will afford me so little
society & conversation, that I must finish the season somewhere else.
In this emergency I have returned to St. Moritz, which I wrote you
that I had abandoned, chiefly on acct. of the cold.   The perpetual
confirmation of my belief that my powers of locomotion are steadily
on the increase, emboldens me to think that I may by constant movement de[s]pise the temperature.   So I wrote last evening to Leslie
Stephen, who is staying there to ask him to try & hire me a room for
three weeks hence.   He may be unsuccessful; but we shall see.—&
now enough of my own plans & my own doings.   I have unwound
this string of homely details in the belief that it may amuse mother &

Alice & gratify their feminine love of the minute & the petty.   I wish one of them would treat me to an equally keen analysis of your situation at Pomfret, which you must have already reached.   Since leaving Vevey I have been without my letters & am starving for news from home.   I actually *gloat* over the prospect of to-morrow's mail.   Meanwhile I have stayed my stomach by reading over your two inestimable letters, above mentioned.   There is much in them to respond to, but I am fagged by this long scribble   I deeply relish & enjoy all your remarks about German.   A little of your knowledge would stand me in very good stead up here. I hope to heaven your mind & body are both well rid of your examination.   I feel that in all I tell of my own amendment, I constantly anticipate as it were, & reply to any news of your continued suffering.   I feel as if every walk I take is a burning & shining light, for your encouragement, & I confess I don't understand how in the face of the phenomenon of my conduct you can feel any serious doubt or dejection.   All expression of such doubt I savagely resent.   But I shall suspend further judgement until the summer is over.   May you enjoy it calmly, lazily & selfishly!   I got a letter from H. Bowditch, assuming that I was coming to Bonn & that we might go to Switzerland together.   He comes Aug. 1ˢᵗ.   I hope I may meet him.   I have not heard in 2 weeks from Aunt K.   She is probably enjoying herself vastly.   She will lay up treasure for the rest of her life.   Is father's book yet out?[5]   I of course count in some way or other on a copy.   I hope to morrow to get letters from both Alice & him.   My blessings on them both!   I suppose mother is frisking & frolicking as usual, on being turned into the fields.   Imprint a kiss upon her lovely brow.   I am perpetually shedding tears over her patches in my night-shirts stockings &c.—Farewell!—

Thy brother | H.J.jr.

P.S.   My own intellectual feat is having read J. S. Mill on the subjection of women at Vevey.[6]———*Tuesday.* 13ᵗʰ   I can hardly put too strongly the good effect of my rovings of last week.   Yesterday afternoon I ascended with a young Englishman a very pretty little mountain near by, with a lovely view of the whole lake from the top: a matter of about 5 hours in all, including rest on the top.   To day I think of walking down to Gersau, taking boat to Lucerne, to make a purchase, & returning & walking back in the afternoon.   Goodbye!———Where is Wilky? how is he to spend the summer? make him write.———

ALS: MH bMS Am 1094 (1932)

[1] Boston directories do not show any Bradfords living on Chesnut St. at this time.
[2] A slip for 'tho''.
[3] HJ may have been anticipating the '&' after 'hour' when he wrote '&' instead of 'an'.
[4] HJ probably intended to write 'may'.
[5] Henry James, *The Secret of Swedenborg.*
[6] John Stuart Mill, *The Subjection of Women* (1869).

From Henry James

Gersau, Lucerne, Hotel Müller. | August 12th [1869] Dearest Bill—When I wrote to father a couple of days since from Interlaken I had no idea that I should so soon be writing again from this place. On the morning after my letter was written however, a slight change befell in my plans—caused by a variety of circumstances—the setting in of bad weather—the need of a little rest—the development of a slight affection in my right ankle (wh. immediate use might aggravate)—& finally a vague sort of collapse of physical enthusiasm. So instead of then & there pushing on over the Gemmi (wh. I had already done) I came immediately in one day over the *Brünig* to this place, to pick up my luggage & reorganize my programme. It seemed to me somewhat unwise to be pushing southward, without my effects only to give myself the labor of the upward journey again prior to starting afresh. Owing to my foot I thought it best not to try to walk the Brünig, but was fortunate enough to meet at Brienz with a frenchman & his wife with whom I went shares in the hire of a vehicle. We drove over yesterday comfortably in 8 hours— *plus* two more for me from Lucerne hither. I shall give my foot a day or two's rest & then, having forwarded my luggage to *Milan* start off again with my knapsack. It's quite as I expected: a few days interval brings out strongly the good effects of this doughty climbing. When I get home I shall tear your diploma in twain & prescribe to you a course of the same treatment. It ought to take rank among the regular stock remedies.—It takes something of an effort to get up steam to do the thing alone: but I shall find even this better than leaving it undone. I may not as I announced, cross the St. Gotthard, as that from here is a matter of only a couple of days. I *may* go down to the Simplon—& I may push on to Zermatt & scramble thence over the Monte Moro. I shall see when I get under way. But I shall make with great direction for the Italian Lakes, as I grudge spending any

more money on Switzerland.   I have been having quite a correspondence with H. P. Bowditch upon the possibility of our joining forces,
wh. I much wished: but am disappointed as he doesn't even enter
Switzerland till the twentieth.   I received to day most gratefully a
Nation of July 22ᵈ, but am still, thro' my cursed awkwardness, without
my recent letters.   I hope however to receive them in a day or two.—
The tenor of this & my last letters has been very dull—owing to the
fact that in walking you quite sweat the rhapsodical faculty out of you
& have no eloquence left for talk.   Mountain-climbing is an awfully
silent process.   I nevertheless should be very glad to be able to give
you some hint of one or two of my sensations—the great snow-&-ice-
world I gazed upon from the summit of the Titlis—& the spectacle
before me when, on the summit of the Wengern-Alp I sat on the
bench outside the inn & surveyed, directly opposite, the towering
gleaming pinnacles of the Silberhorn, the Eiger, the Mönch &c, both
views admirably favored by a cloudless air.   But you'll readily excuse
me.   Wait till I get into Italy—& then I'll dip my pen in purple &
gold.   I have been reading T. Gautier's *Italia.*[1]   *Le brave homme!*—
The only thing worth now putting into words is just what I can't—the
deep satisfaction in being able to do all this healthy trudging & climbing. It *is*—it *is* a pledge, a token of some future potency.   Amen!
What I especially wait for in my letters is some news of you—your
Pomfret life—habits, improvement.   I'm absolutely faint & sick for
home news.   From Aunt Kate I have heard nothing for a long time.
I'm afraid I have missed some letter she has sent.   It may yet turn
up.   She is not yet in Switzerland, inasmuch as her party were to be
in Paris on the Emperor's fete, 15ᵗʰ August. Farewell my brother.   I'd
give my right hand for an hour's talk with you—lying in some afternoon shade beneath a Connecticut sky.   I hope you & Alice get some
drives.   Ask her if the she[2] remembers that one she & I had last summer, that evening, at Littleton?[3]—at Littleton it used to be Switzerland,—& now it's Littleton!   Where & how is Wilky—fat & faithless
one!   Mother, I hope, is well & idle & free to roam where she likes.
I wish I could take her a sail down here into the Bay of Uri.   By this
time I suppose father's book is out.   Send any notices as well as the
vol.   Direct   as   I   wrote   a   fortnight   since: M.M. *Schielin frères,*
Banquiers
   Venice
      Italy.

Tout à toi | H. James jr.

ALS: MH bMS Am 1094 (1933)

¹ Théophile Gautier, *Italia* (1852).
² HJ probably intended to delete 'the' after changing his mind and writing 'she', but forgot to do so.
³ Apparently, Littleton, N.H., a resort region.

From Henry James

Venice Hotel Barbesi Sept. 25ᵗʰ [1869]
My dear Bill—I wrote to father as soon as I arrived here & mentioned my intention of sending you some copious account of my impressions of Venice.   I have since then written to J. La Farge (briefly) & to Howells & worked off in some degree the *éblouissement* of the 1ˢᵗ few days. I have a vague idea that I may write some notes for the *Atlantic* or the *Nation*; but at the risk of knocking the bottom out of them, I feel that I must despatch you a few choice remarks—although I'm too tired to plunge deeply into things.—Among the letters which I found here on my arrival was a most valuable one from you, of the last of July, which made me ache to my spirit's core for half an hour's talk with you.   I was unutterably gladdened by your statement of your improvement.   Three days since however came a letter from mother of Sept. 6ᵗʰ, speaking of a slight decline, hence your return home.   As she also mentions, however, your meaning to go to Newport & Lennox I trust you had not lost courage.   I hope next to hear that you have made your visits & are the better for them.   Give mother unutterable thanks for her letter: my only complaint is that I don't get one like it every day.   But I can't be at home & abroad both.   I have now been here nearly two weeks & have experienced that inevitable, reconciliation to things which six months of Europe cause to operate so rapidly & smoothly, no matter what the strangeness of things may be. A little stare—a little thrill—a little curiosity, & then all is over.   You subside into the plodding *blasé*, homesick "doer" of cities.   Venice is magnificently fair & quite, to my perception, the Venice of Romance & fancy.   Taine, I remember, somewhere speaks of "Venice & Oxford—the two most picturesque cities in Europe."   I personally prefer Oxford; it told me deeper & richer things &[c] than any I have learned here.   It's as if I had been born in Boston: I cant for my life frankly surrender myself to the Genius of Italy—or the Spirit of the South—or whatever one may call the confounded thing; but I nevertheless *feel* it in all my pulses.   If I could only write as I might talk I

should have no end of things to tell you about my last days in Switzerland & especially my descent of the Alps—that mighty summer's
day upon the Simplon when I communed with immensity & sniffed
Italy from afar.   This Italian tone of things which I then detected,
lies richly on my soul & gathers increasing weight, but it lies as a cold
& foreign mass—never to be absorbed & appropriated.   The meaning of this superb image is that I feel I shall never look at Italy—at
Venice for instance—but from without; whereas it seemed to me at
Oxford & in England generally that I was breathing the air of home.
Ruskin recommends the traveller to frequent & linger in a certain
glorious room at the Ducal Palace where P. Veronese revels on the
ceilings and Tintoret rages on the walls, because he "nowhere else will
enter so deeply into the heart of Venice."[1]   But I feel as if I might sit
there forever (as I sat there a long time this morning) & only feel
more & more my inexorable Yankeehood.   As a puling pining Yankee however, I enjoy things deeply.   What you will most care to hear
about is the painters; so I shall not feel bound to inflict upon you any
tall writing about the canals & palaces; the more especially as with
regard to them, photographs are worth something; but with regard
to the pictures comparatively nothing—*rapport à la couleur*—which is
quite half of Venetian painting.   The first thing that strikes you,
when you come to sum up after you [have] been to the D.P. & the
Academy is that you have not half so much been seeing paintings as
painters.   The accumulated mass of works by a few men drives each
man home to your senses with extraordinary force.   This is especially the case with the greatest of them all—Tintoretto—so much so
that he ends by becoming an immense perpetual moral presence,
brooding over the scene & worrying the mind into some species of
response & acknowledgement.   I have had more eyes & more
thoughts for him than for anything else in Venice; & in future, I
fancy, when I recall the place, I shall remember chiefly the full-
streaming dazzling light of the heavens & Tintoretto's dark range of
colour.   Ruskin truly says that it is well to devote yourself here solely
to three men—P. Veronese, Tintoretto and J. Bellini, inasmuch as you
can see sufficient specimens of the rest (including Titian—amply)
elsewhere but must come here for even a notion of these.   This is
true of the three, but especially of Tintoretto—whom I finally see
there is nothing for me to do but to admit (& have done with it) to be
the biggest genius (as far as I yet know) who ever wielded a brush.
Once do this & you can make your abatements; but if Shakspeare is
the greatest of poets Tintoretto is assuredly the greatest of painters.

He belongs to the same family & produces very much the same effect. He seems to me to have seen into painting to a distance unsuspected by any of his fellows. I don't mean into its sentimental virtues or didactic properties but into its simple pictorial capacity. Imagine Doré a 1000 times refined in quality & then as many times multiplied in quantity & you may have a sort of notion of him. But you must see him here at work like a great wholesale decorator to form an idea of his boundless invention & his passionate energy & the extraordinary possibilities of color—for he begins by striking you as the poorest & ends by impressing you as the greatest of colorists. Beside him the others are the simplest fellows in the world. For the present I give up Titian altogether. He is not adequately represented here. His *Assumption* strikes me as a magnificent second-rate picture; his presentation of the Virgin is utterly killed by another of Tintoretto's. I fancy you must see him in England, Madrid &c. P. Veronese is really great, in a very simple fashion. He seems to have had in his head a perfect realization of a world in which all things were interfused with a sort of silvery splendor delicious to look upon. He is thoroughly undramatic & "impersonal." A splendid scene in the concrete was enough for him & when he paints anything of a story the whole action seems to rest suspended in order to look handsome & *be* painted. If I weren't a base Anglo-Saxon & a coward slave, I should ask nothing better than his *Rape of Europa* in the D.P., where a great rosy blonde, gorgeous with brocade & pearls & bouncing with salubrity & a great mellow splendor of sea & sky & nymphs & flowers do their best to demoralize the world into a herd of Theophile Gautiers.[2] The great beauty of P. Veronese is the perfect unity & placidity of his talent. There is not a whit of struggle, nor fever, nor longing for the unattainable; simply a glorious sense of the look of things out of doors—of heads & columns against the sky, of the lustre of satin & of the beauty of looking up & seeing things lifted into the light above you. He is here chiefly found in the ceilings, where he is perfectly at home, & delights to force you to break your back to look at him—& wonder what sort of a back *he* must have had. John Bellini, a painter of whom I had no conception—one of the early Venetians—is equally great & simple in his own far different way. He has everything on a great scale—knowledge color & expression. He is the 1st "religious" painter I have yet seen who has made me understand that there can be—or that there once was at least, such a thing as pure religious art. I always fancied it more or less an illusion of the critics. But Bellini puts me to the blush. How to define his "religious" quality I know not; but he really makes you believe that his genius was essentially consecrated to heaven & that each of his pictures was a genuine act of worship. This is the more interesting because his piety prevails not the least against his science & his pictorial energy. There is not a ray in his works of debility or vagueness of conception. In vigor, breadth & richness he is a thorough Venetian. His best pictures here possess an extraordinary perfection. Everything is equal—the full deep beauty of the expression—the masterly—the more than masterly firmness & purity of the drawing—& the undimmed, unfathomed lucidity & richness of the coloring. And then over it all a sort of pious deference has passed & hushed & smoothed & polished it till the effect is one of unspeakable purity. He has hardly more than one subject—the Virgin & Child, alone, or enthroned & attended with Saints & cherubs; but you will be slow to tire of him, for long after you've had enough of his piety there is food for delight in the secret marvels of his handling. It gives one a strong sense of the vastness & strangeness of art, to compare these 2 men, Bellini & Tintoretto—to reflect upon their almost equal greatness & yet their immense dissimilarity, so that the great merit of each seems to have been that he possesses just those qualities the absence of which, apparently, ensures his high place to the other.—But to return to Tintoretto. I'd give a great deal to be able to fling down a dozen of his pictures into prose of corresponding force & color. I strongly urge you to look up in vol 3ᵈ of Ruskin's *Stones* (last appendix) a number of magnificent descriptive pages touching his principal pictures. (The whole appendix by the way, with all its exasperating points is invaluable to the visitor here & I have profited much by it.)[3] I should be sadly at a loss to make you understand in what his great power consists—the more especially as he offers a hundred superficial points of repulsion to the well-regulated mind. In a certain occasional imbecility & crudity & imperfection of drawing Delacroix is nothing to him. But then you see him at a vast disadvantage inasmuch as with hardly an exception his pictures are atrociously hung & lighted. When you reflect that he was willing to go on covering canvas to be hidden out of sight or falsely shown, you get some idea of the prodigality of his genius. Most of his pictures are immense & swarming with figures; All have suffered grievously from abuse & neglect. But there are all sorts; you can never feel that you have seen the last; & each new one throws a new light on his resources. Besides this, they are extremely unequal & it would be an easy task I fancy to collect a dozen pieces which would conclusively establish him an un-

mitigated bore.   His especial greatness, I should be tempted to say
lies in the fact that more than any painter yet, he habitually conceived
his subject as an *actual scene*, which could not possibly have happened
otherwise; not as a mere subject & fiction—but as a great fragment
wrenched out of life & history, with all its natural details clinging to it
& tes[t]ifying to its reality.   You seem not only to look *at* his pictures,
but *into* them—& this in spite of his not hesitating to open the clouds
& shower down the deities & mix up heaven & earth as freely as his
purpose demands.   His *Miracle of St. Mark* is a tremendous work,
with life enough in it to animate a planet.   But they can all paint a
crowd, & this is as much Venetian as individual.   A better specimen
of his peculiar power is a simple *Adam & Eve*, in the same room, as a
Cain & Abel, its mate, both atrociously hung—away aloft in the air.
Adam sits on a bank with his back to you; Eve facing you, with one
arm wound round a tree leans forward & holds out the apple.   The
composition is so simple that it hardly exists & yet the painting is so
rich & expressive that it seems as if the *natural* the real, could go no
further—unless indeed in the other, where Cain assaults Abel with
an intent to kill more murderous & tragical than words can describe
it.   One of his works that has much struck me is a large *Annunciation*,
immensely characteristic of this unlikeness to other painters. To the
right sits the Virgin, starting back from her angelic visitant with magnificent surprise & terror.   The Angel swoops down into the picture,
leading a swarm of cherubs, not as in most cases where the subject is
treated, as if he had come to pay her a pretty compliment but with a
fury characteristic of his tremendous message.   The greatest of all
though—the greatest picture it seemed to me as I looked at it I ever
saw—is a *crucifixion* in a small church.   (He has treated the same subject elsewhere on a stupendous scale; but on the whole I prefer this.)
Here as usual all is original & unconventional.   Ruskin describes it
far better than I can do. *Monday 26th*[4]   Having written so much last
evening, I succumbed to slumber, & this evening I hardly feel like
resuming the feeble thread of my discourse.   I have been abroad all
day bidding farewell to Venice, for I think of leaving tomorrow or
next day.   I began the day with several churches & saw two new &
magnificent Tintorets & a beautiful Titian.   Then I paid a farewell
visit to the Academy, which I have got pretty well by heart—& where
I saw Mr. & Mrs. Bronson of Newport who knew me not—the latter
very haggard & pale.   After wh. I took a gondola over to the Lido to
look my last at the Adriatic.   It was a glorious afternoon & I wan-
dered for nearly two hours by the side of the murmuring sea.   I was

more than ever struck with the resemblance of Venice—especially
that part of it—to Newport. The same atmosphere, the same lumi-
nosity. Standing looking out at the Adriatic with the low-lying linked
islands on the horizon was just like looking out to sea from one of the
Newport beaches, with Narragansett afar. I have seen the Atlantic
as blue & smooth & musical—almost! If words were not so stupid &
colorless, *fratello mio*, & sentences so interminable & chirography so
difficult, I should like to treat you to a dozen pages more about this
watery paradise. Read Theophile Gautier's *Italia*; its chiefly about
Venice. I'm curious to know how this enchanted fortnight will strike
me, in memory 11 years hence—for altho' I've got absurdly used to it
all, yet there is a palpable sub-current of deep delight. Gondolas
spoil you for a return to common life. To begin with, in themselves
they afford the perfection of indolent pleasure. The seat is so soft
and deep & slumberous & the motion so mild elastic & unbroken that
even if they bore you thro' miles of stupid darkness you'd think it
the most delectable fun. But when they lift you thro' this rosy air,
along these liquid paths, beneath the balconies of palaces as lovely in
design & fancy as they are pathetic in their loneliness & decay—you
may imagine that it's better than walking down Broadway. I should
never have forgiven myself had I come to Venice any later in the season. The mosquitoes are perfectly infernal—& you can't say more
for Venice than that you are willing, at this moment, for the sake of
the days she bestows to endure the nights she inflicts. But, bating
this, all else is in perfection—the weather, the temperature & the aspect of the canals. The Venetian population, on the water, is immensely picturesque. In the narrow streets, the people are far too
squalid & offensive to the nostrils, but with a good breadth of canal to
set them off & a heavy stream of sunshine to light them up, as they go
pushing & paddling & screaming—bare-chested, bare-legged, magnificently tanned & muscular—the men at least are a very effective
lot. Besides lolling in my gondola I have spent a good deal of time
in poking thro' the alleys which serve as streets & staring about in the
Campos—the little squares formed about every church—some of
them the most sunnily desolate, the most grass-grown, the most
cheerfully sad little reliquaries of a splendid past that you can imagine. Every one knows that the Grand Canal is a wonder; but really
to feel in your heart the ancient wealth of Venice, you must have frequented these canalettos & campos & seen the number & splendor of
the palaces that stand rotting & crumbling & abandoned to pau-
pers.—If I might talk of these things I would talk of more & tell you

in glowing accents how beautiful a thing this month in Italy has been
& how my brain swarms with pictures & my bosom aches with memories.   I should like in some neat formula to give you the *Italian feeling*—& tell you just how it is that one is conscious here of the aesthetic
pressure of the past.   But you'll learn one day for yourself. You'll go
to that admirable Verona & get your fill of it.—I wanted not only to
say a 100 things about Tintoretto which I've left unsaid (indeed I've
said nothing) but to gossip a bit about the other painters.   Whether
it is that the three great ones I've mentioned practically include all the
rest or not, I can't say; but (with the exception of two or three primitive members of the school, especially Carpaccio,[5] who seem to have
learned laboriously for themselves,) there flows from the great mass
of the secondary fellows no very powerful emanation of genius.   Immense aptitude & capital teaching—vigorous talent, in fine—seems
to be the amount of the matter.   In them the school trenches on Vulgarity.   Bonifazio,[6] Caligiari,[7] the two Palmas,[8] Paris Bordone[9] &c
have all an immense amount of ability, (often of a very exquisite kind)
to a comparatively small amount of originality.   Nevertheless I'm
very willing to believe—in fact I'm quite sure—that seen in other
places, in detached examples each of them would impress & charm
you very much as their betters do here.   All of them know endless
things about color: in this they are indeed exquisite.   Bonifazio is a
somewhat coarser Titian—a perfect Monarch of the mellow & glowing & richly darksome.   Paris Bordone equals him, on a slightly different range.   C. Caligiari (son of P. Veronese) is a very handsome
imitation of his father—& if the latter's works were destroyed, we'd
vote him a great master.   But what has fascinated me most here after
Tintoretto & Co. are the two great buildings—the Ducal Palace & St.
Mark's Church.   You have a general notion of what they amount to;
its all you can have, until you see them.   St. Mark's, within, is a great
hoary shadowy tabernacle of mosaic & marble, entrancing you with
its remoteness, its picturesqueness & its chiaroscuro—an immense
piece of Romanticism.   But the Ducal Palace is as pure & perpetual
as the façade of the Parthenon—& I think of all things in Venice, its
the one I should have been gladdest to achieve—the one most worthy
of civic affection & gratitude.   When you're heated & wearied to
death with Tintoretto & his feverish Bible Stories, you can come out
on the great Piazetta, between the marble columns, & grow comparatively cool & comfortable with gazing on this work of art which has so
little to do with *persons*!

    But I too am weary & hot—tho' I expect to find on my couch but little of coolness or comfort.   I have the delightful choice of sleeping with my window open & being *devoured*—maddened, poisoned—or closing it, in spite of the heat, & being stifled!—I have made no allusion to the contents of mother's letter, which I none the less prize.   I have written to Minny Temple about her sisters.   Elly's marriage strikes me as absolutely *sad.*[10]   I care not how good a fellow T. Emmet may be: Elly deserved a younger man.   Mother says nothing about Wilky's crops.[11]   I hope no news is good news.   I am not surprised to hear of Dr. Wilkinson's being at hand.   When I was in England he was evidently all ready for a chance to sail.   I'm very curious to know the impression he made.   I'm not to meet A.K.   They come at present no further S. than the Lakes.—But I *must* say good night.   I mean to write you again in a few days—*not* about painters.

À toi | H. James jr.

ALS: MH bMS Am 1094 (1934)

   [1] John Ruskin, *The Stones of Venice*, 3 vols. (1851–53), ending his description of the ducal palace in the "Venetian Index" at the end of vol. 3.

   [2] Edel, *HJL*, 1:144, interprets this as an allusion to Gautier's "love of the palpable and the visual."

   [3] Ruskin's *Stones of Venice* has a "Final Appendix" but after that there is the "Venetian Index."   There Ruskin describes Venetian buildings with emphasis on the works of Tintoretto which they house.

   [4] Monday was 27 September.

   [5] Vittore Carpaccio (c. 1450–c. 1522), Venetian painter.

   [6] Bonifazio de'Pitati (also Bonifazio Veronese) (c. 1487–c. 1553), Venetian painter.

   [7] Paolo Caliari was known as Paolo Veronese.

   [8] Jacopo Palma (c. 1480–1528) and his grandnephew Jacopo Palma (1544–1628), Venetian painters.

   [9] Paris Bordone (1500–1571), Venetian painter.

   [10] Ellen Temple married Christopher Temple Emmet on 15 September 1869. The young couple moved to California shortly thereafter.   For Mary Temple's view of the marriage see *NSB*, 492, 494–95.

   [11] To AJ on 28 April 1869 GWJ wrote that the cotton crop was never better (bMS Am 1095 [14]), but on 25 August 1869 he was notified that caterpillars had ravaged his estate (bMS Am 1095 [36]); see *BBF*, 107.

To Henry James

Cambr. Oct 2. 69

Dearest Harry—Within 10 days we have rec'd 2 letters fm. you—1 fm. Como, t'other fm. Brescia and most luscious epistles were they indeed.   It does one's heart good to think of you at last able to drink in full gulps the beautiful and the antique.   As mother said the other day, it seems as if your whole life had but been a preparation for this. Since I wrote you from Pomfret a couple of months since, so many things have happened and I have had so much to say to you of matters personal, moral, spiritual and practical that I hardly know how to begin this letter.   Some things will get crowded out anyhow.   First of my health.   It kept wonderful for about 6 weeks at Pomfret and I began to think that all was saved, but it suddenly caved in a week before I left without any assignable cause save perhaps the expiration of the "term of efficiency" of the last of 4 boils which I had been having on my back during that well time.   I do not however feel at all *confident* that my well being was solely due to the boils.   I kept pretty slim till 10 days ago when I suddenly & without known cause became better and risked a journey to Newport where I stayed 4 days subject to great fatigue but made none the worse for it.   Yesterday the old weakness (equally without cause) has partially returned. The result is that I find myself unable to predict my state as of yore; and I feel on the whole encouraged by it—for it shows that the condition, whatever it be, is mobile & not essential.   On Monday (this is Saturday) I am going to see Garratt and try the experiment of galvanism.   I am very much run down in nervous force and have resolved to read as little as I possibly can this winter and absolutely not study i.e. read nothing which I can get interested and *thinking* about.   There is plenty of biographical, historical & literary matter which I have always hoped to read some day, so this is just the time for it.   I cal'late likewise to pay a visit every evening when it is possible, and not to stick in the house as hitherto.   I cannot tell you my dear brother how my admiration of the silent pluck you exhibited during those long years has risen of late.   I never realized till within 3 or 4 months the full amount of endurance it must have needed to go through all that literary work and especially all that unshirking social activity which you accomplished.   I give up like a baby in comparison, tho' occasionnally I find my heart fired and my determination *retrempé'd* by a sudden wave of recollection of your behavior.—There was nobody at the Tweedies but Henrietta—a most uninteresting morsel.[1]   Edmund & Mary spitting at each other in a tiresome manner.   I spent a very pleasant 24 hrs. at Jno l. F.'s.   He had been in very good physical condition but a bad diarrhoea on the Hudson River had undone him again temporarily.   Of new things he had to show me *non multa* but on the whole *multum*.   I dont know whether you have seen them.

1 Portrait of Dick Hunt's son,[2] unfinished and very handsome in color

&c, but on the whole sentant trop la photographie, which I suspect played a good part in its production. 2 his big landscape of the gorge. A most honest, solid bit of study fm. nature, with less of his subjectivity than anything else of his I know. Full of light & splendor, and it kept "growing" on me all the time I was there. There is an immense amount of labor in it, and it must have taught him a great deal, which will be some consolation if it brings nothing to his pocket. It wants some man or animal in the foreground. 3 a vast green landscape of the fields near Paradise,[3] originally meant as background to a white figure but with the latter painted out. Also as big as all out doors and flooded with light even in its botchy state. He ought to repaint a figure in it no matter how "quaint" it will look to the vulgar. 4 A woman sleeping in a flowered (japanese) dress so cool in color & definite in treatment that I should hardly have suspected who painted it. The large, fat weighty figure is admirably drawn—rarely have I seen a better rendering of the way a supine person sinks into her chair. John seems very cheerful but the total impression of the visit was a sad one. I got an equally vivid impression of the depth of his talent (you've no idea of the pure splendor of some of those things) and of his destitution of that vulgar cleverness neccessary to make it available. It's really pitiful—the trouble he has to give himself to produce anything, and the shilly shally fumbling of his whole movement—made tenfold greater by his physical feebleness.—He wrote you lately to Venice. His prospects now of going abroad seem doubtful—His D.^r and wife don't like him to risk being sick there alone and there are great practical difficulties in the way of his taking his wife either with or without the children. Still, he may start alone before the winter and go pretty straight to Italy. He said there was no one he should so well like for a companion there as you, especially in Venice. I feel that he ought not to give up painting, and he ought some how to be yanked into a productive vein—instead of wasting all his little energy on detail and outside matters such as writing. He found it impossible to write on Taine after all, and is now writing a chapter on Japanese art for a book of travels there by one Pumpelly.[4] He has developed his ideas with admirable order & logic—but fm. that to the definite wording is a gulf, and the way he seems to be sweating over it is pitiful.—If I had money I wd. immediately buy his big landscape—Bob Temple was here a fortnight ago for 4 or 5 days. A lout positive & absolute. Whatever fleeting compunction or regret I may have felt in past times about his being left unaided in the army, is the last I shall ever feel. He is absolutely without a spark of ideal—

cares for nothing but his ease, systematically and consciously rejects every position, no matter what its privileges, if any voluntary effort is associated with them, gravitates consequently to the lowest level possible for him at any time and is happy there—says, and undoubtedly truly, that he prefers the company of low people to those of our "station," &c.   He will probably end by re-enlisting, and I doubt if out of the army it will be possible for him to lead a decent life.   He talked a great deal about his history & prospects, but indicated no shadow of regret (I don't mean moral regret or repentance but practical "it's a pity") at the chances he had thrown away in the past of making something of himself.   He made me feel certain that whatever future chance might be furnished him wd. be just as carelessly & cold bloodedly squandered.   He wrote you a letter to Venice wh. I suppose will amuse you—He was with all this lowness, more genial and less rancorous against what is successful through orderliness, than I ever remember him.   He was tall, thin, wiry looking, and has grown much like his father & Willy.—Kitty Prince was here[5]—decidedly distinguée—Wilkinson too—beautiful English—but rather sober, not to say dull, and would not commit himself at all on the subject of the country—it had struck him "just as he expected it wd." only more vividly.—Father's book is out "The Secret of Swedenborg" and is selling very fast, partly I suppose by virtue of the title to people who won't read it.   I read it, and am very much enlightened as to his ideas and as to his intellectual rank thereby.   I am going slowly through his other books.   I will write you more when I have read more.   Suffice it that many points which before were incomprehensible to me because doubtfully fallacious—I now definitely believe to be entirely fallacious—but as this pile accumulates on one side there is left a more and more definite residuum on the other of great & original ideas, so that my respect for him is on the whole increased rather than diminished.   But his ignorance of the way of thinking of other men, and his cool neglect of their difficulties is fabulous in a writer on such subjects.   It is pure theology and not philosophy commonly so called, that he deals with.—T.S.P. is back very well after his vacation up the St. Lawrence, Lake George, Newport &c.   I have spoken harshly of him of late, but after all, his true modesty, and unreserved kind feeling to everyone, together with his humour and enthusiasm ought not to let him be lightly estimated.   The more I live in the world the more the cold blooded conscious egotism & conceit of people afflict me— and T.S.P. is sweetly free of them.   All the noble qualities of Wendell Holmes for instance are poisoned by them—and friendly as I want to be towards him, as yet the good he has done me is more in presenting me something to kick away from or react against than to follow and embrace. I have seen him but sparingly since the spring—but expect he will be here to night. I will here stop—leaving mother & Alice to tell you of Wilky & Bob, and of Elly Temple's wedding &c.— I am forgetting your Gabrielle de B. Very exquisitely touched—but the denouement bad in that it did not end with Coquelin's death in that stormy meeting and her being sent to a nunnery.[6] At least Co ought to have had a lettre de cachet and she, resisting still the Vicount have ended in a nunnery. The end is both humdrum and improbable. I expect to write you more stiddy now. Get your belly full of enjoyment this winter. I hope your intestinal troubles will gradually improve.

Ever yr. loving   W.J.

Howell's comes to see father quite often & talks about religion but seems I know not why rather shy of me.

ALS: MH bMS AM 1092.9 (2572)

[1] Henrietta Temple.

[2] Richard Morris Hunt (1828–1895), American architect, brother of William Morris Hunt.

[3] A rocky promontory in Newport.

[4] Raphael Pumpelly, *Across America and Asia: Notes of a Five Years' Journey around the World* (New York: Leypoldt & Holt, 1870). Chapter 14, "An Essay on Japanese Art," is by John La Farge.

[5] Katharine Barber James (1834–1890), daughter of William James, WJ's and HJ's uncle, in and out of several mental hospitals, in fall 1861 married her psychiatrist, William Henry Prince. In a letter to her sister Elizabeth Tillman James, 1 August 1861, she described her visit to the Jameses at Newport. In her very enthusiastic account she notes that "Harry is not fond of cats" (William James Papers, Amherst College). WJ's letters to her survive from 1863 to 1888.

[6] In HJ's story, Pierre Coquelin elopes with and marries Gabrielle de Bergerac. Both die under the guillotine during the French Revolution. The vicomte Gaston de Treuil had been Gabrielle's suitor favored by Gabrielle's family.

From Henry James

Florence—Hotel de l'Europe | Thursday October 7$\underline{th}$ [1869]
Dear W$\underline{m}$.—

In writing to you some ten days since from Venice I mentioned intending to write shortly again on another topic; & as in a letter to Alice yesterday I threw out a hint on this topic, I had better come to the point without delay. I hoped to find here yesterday a letter from you, speaking of the receipt of a little note I sent you just before leaving Switzerland; it had not come however; but tho' it is probably not far distant I shall not wait for it. I feel too strongly the need of emitting some cry from the depths of my discomfort. I am sorry to have to put things so darkly; but truth compels me to state that I have none but the very worst news with regard to my old enemy no. 2—by which of course I mean *my* unhappy bowels. Things have reached that pass when I feel that *something must be done*—what I know not, but I have a vague hope that you may be able to throw some light on the subject. To begin with, it is of my *constipation* almost solely that I speak: those old attacks of pain have almost completely disappeared—tho' a very small error in diet is sufficient to start them up again. In spite of this I suffer so perpetually & so keenly from this hideous repletion of my belly that I feel as if my gain had been but small. That immense improvement which I felt in England ceased as soon as I touched the continent & tho' I have had fleeting moments of relief since the summer, my whole tendency, considering my uninterrupted & vehement efforts to combat it seems to have been to aggravation. When I reflect that after seven months of the active, wholesome open-air life I have been leading, I have no better tale to tell, I feel extremely miserable. During this last month in Italy my sufferings seem to have come to a climax. At Venice they came as near as possible to quite defeating the pleasure of my stay, & the week of busy sightseeing that I spent in the journey to this place has brought no amelioration. I had great hopes of Italy in this matter—I fancied I should get plenty of fruit & vegetables & that this effect would be highly laxative. Fruit is abundant but I can eat it only in small quantities; otherwise it produces pain. As for vegetables, *haricots verts* & spinach are obtainable, but invariably *fried in grease*—which quite robs them of their virtue. I have managed on the whole to feed reasonably enough, however,— which is only the more discouraging. I am compelled to eat a good amount of meat. Leading the life I do, this is essential—& meat is more nourishing & less crowding than other things. So I always breakfast on a beefsteak. At dinner I have more meat & a vegetable, which with a little fruit in the middle of the day is my regular diet. Potatoes I long since forswore, & I am now on the way to suppressing bread as nearly altogether as I can. Wine I never touch—the common sorts are too bad & the better too dear. At dinner I drink Vienna beer & at breakfast chocolate made with water. You must have been in Italy to appreciate the repugnance that one acquires for the *water* of the country as a beverage. Heaven knows what it passes thro' before it reaches you. My bowels yearn for the *cuisine* of my own happy land—& I think I should faint with joy at the sight [of] a leg of plain boiled mutton—a great mess of fresh vegetables—or a basin of cracked wheat, flanked by a loaf of stale brown bread. As regards diet however I might be worse off. The régime I follow would be kindly enough for a case less cruelly stubborn than mine. I may actually say that I *can't get a passage.* My "little squirt" has ceased to have more than a nominal use. The water either remains altogether or comes out as innocent as it entered. For the past ten days I have become quite demoralized & have been frantically dosing myself with pills. But they too are almost useless & I may take a dozen & hardly hear of them. In fact, I don't pretend to understand how I get on. When I reflect upon the utterly insignificant relation of what I get rid of to what I imbibe, I wonder that flesh & blood can stand it. I find it in every way a grievous trial & my wretched state alone prompts these outpourings. My condition affects alike my mind & my body: it tells upon my spirits & takes all the lightness & freedom out of them; & more & more as time goes by I feel what a drag it is upon my back. If I could get a daily passage, I am sure my back would improve as rapidly again, to say the least, as at present. To go about with this heavy burden weighing down my loins is the worst thing in the world for it. But this is quite a long enough recital of my miseries; I have made it only as a preliminary to the question of practical remedies. Somehow or other I *must* take the thing in hand. I have regretted very much of late (how wisely I know not) that I didn't get the opinion of some eminent London physician—or some big Paris Authority. The memory of my happy condition during my last month in England makes me feel as there I might again find some relief. It was Malvern that started me up & English cookery & English air that helped me along afterwards. It may surprise you to hear it—but here in this distant Italy I find myself hankering after Malvern. If I should return there I should submit to no treatment for my back, but simply take the running sitzbaths. As I think of it (as I have done many times) the idea assumes an enormous attraction—& the vision of the beef & mutton & the watery cauliflower of the Malvern table & of great walks across the Malvern hills causes my heart to beat & throb. I have good reason to believe that I should suffer very much less now than I did last spring from the monotony & dullness of the life. I can walk more & read more.—On the other hand it would break my heart to leave Italy a moment before I have had my fill. I fancy nevertheless that I shall be obliged to make a

very much shorter stay here than I originally intended.   If my condition remains as it is I shall go thro' the country rapidly & be ready
to leave it about three months hence, instead of six.   Long before
then I hope to have heard from you & if you suggest nothing more
practicable I shall think seriously of making straight for Malvern.
Mention if you are able to the names of a couple of the great Paris &
London doctors.   In the latter place I know of Sir W$^{\underline{m}}$ Ferguson &
Mr. Paget; but you may tell me something more to the purpose.—
Beloved brother, I hope you'll not let this dreary effusion weigh upon
your spirits.   I thought it best to be frank & copious.   My petty miseries seem but small when I think I have such a guide & friend as you,
to slap over to—& am so divinely blessed with means that I can freely
consider of remedies & methods.   I have written not in passion but
in patience.   Speak to father & mother of all this in such terms as you
think best.   I expect a letter from you tomorrow & shall keep this
over, so that I may add a word.   I say nothing of Florence nor of
yourself.   You can both wait.—*Friday.*   A letter from mother & one
from B. Temple (a most amusing one) but *none*, oh, my brother, from
you.   Mother, however, gives me your message—that you want awfully to write, but that you've so much to say you don't *dare* to begin.
Allons, du courage!   She says nothing more about your visits to Newport & Lenox—from wh. I infer that they were given up.   I was extremely interested, as you may suppose, in her mention of Dr. Wilkinson's diagnosis & prescription for you.   I *palpitate* to hear more &
invoke the next mail with tears in my eyes.   *Cut out* & send me your
articles in the N.A.R.[1]   *À propos*, I again receive the *Nation*.   It comes
apparently from the office & always thro' Lombard & Odier & thence
thro' my subsequent bankers.   As it is not well to have it pass thro' so
many hands & yet difficult to keep making them change my address
at the office, you had better make them send my copy thence to you,
so that you may mail it weekly, just as you do your letters.   *Pray act
upon this.*—I have been reading over what I wrote yesterday & am
half-dismayed at its dismal aspect.   But I shall not change it, as it
reflects fairly the facts of the case.—To day the Malvern plan seems
wild & unnatural: tomorrow it will again seem judicious.   So oscil-
lates the morbid human spirit.—Florence looks so promising & pleasant that I feel as if it would be a delightful thing to settle down here
for a winter & pass the time with pictures & books.   I mustn't think
of the books, in any serious way, but I hope during whatever stay I
make, to plunge deeply into the pictures.   I had a most interesting
journey here from Venice, tho' I have written Alice an extremely stu-

pid letter on the subject.   To tell the truth for some days past my peculiar affliction has developed the faculty of giving me an out & out *headache* & it was under this influence that I wrote.   But this is probably but temporary, "considering," my head has always been remarkably easy.   True, I have used it so little.   I hope to write you something satisfactory about the things here.   B. Cellini's *Perseus*, in the great square, quite deserves the fuss he makes about it in his book.[2] It kills M. Angelo's *David*.   But I must knock off.   Answer my question about the physicians & above all don't let this nasty effusion prey upon your spirits.

Tout à toi   H.Jjr

ALS: MH bMS Am 1094 (1935)

Address: Wm James esq | Quincy St. | Cambridge | Mass | Etats Unis d'Amerique

Postmarks: FIRENZE 9 OTT 69   MILANO STAZ. 10 OTT 69.   A third postmark is illegible.

¹WJ, review of Horace Bushnell, *Women's Suffrage; The Reform against Nature*   (New York: Charles Scribner, 1869), and John Stuart Mill, *The Subjection of Women* (New York: D. Appleton, 1869), in *North American Review* 109 (October 1869): 556–65 (*ECR*).

²Benvenuto Cellini (1500–1571), Italian sculptor.   He described his sculpture *Perseus with the Head of Medusa* in the Loggia dei Lanzi, Florence, in *The Life of Benvenuto Cellini*, trans. John Addington Symonds, 5th ed. (London: Macmillan, 1901), 409–11. The sculpture is pictured on p. 416.

From Henry James

Florence, Hotel de l'Europe | October 16th [1869] Sunday.[1] My dear Wm.   I wrote you a week ago a letter such as ought to be followed up, I feel, by some further communication.   I don't want to incur the charge of harrowing you up—without at least raking you over.   I hoped by this time to have got a letter from you; but I receive nothing but cold head-shakes from the *portier*.   Since, then, I've undertaken this "startling *exposé*" of my condition, I will proceed to draw the curtain altogether.   I felt very blue at having to write to you as I did; but I was glad I had done so; inasmuch as after I had sent my letter, matters came to a crisis which made me feel that they were truly serious & that if you were to give me any hints the sooner I got them the better.   I have just written to mother, without speaking of being unwell.   But you had better let father know that I am not quite all that I should be, since if I should be obliged (as I still hope not to be, however) to do anything or go anywhere for this special reason, so much of the tiresome story may be known.—I was feeling very badly when I wrote you: *je ne tardai pas* to feel worse.   For a week, owing to the state of my bowels, my head & stomach had been all out of order.   What I have called the "crisis" was brought on by taking 2 so-called "anti-bilious" pills, recommended me at the English druggist's.   They failed to relieve me & completely disagreed with me— bringing on a species of abortive diarrhoea.   That is I felt the most reiterated & most violent inclination to stool, without being able to effect anything save the passage of a little blood.   Meanwhile my head got much worse & this was accompanied by a gradual violent chill.   Whereupon I took to my bed, & here the chill began to merge into a fever, with cramps in my feet & legs—my bowels horribly stuffed & my head *infernal*.   Of course I sent for the English—(or rather, as he turned out the Irish) physician.   (I believe there are several here.)   He concentrated his energies upon getting me a stool as speedily as possible.   That is he made me take an injection, of some unknown elements, which completely failed to move me.   I repeated it largely—wholly in vain.   He left me late in the evening, apparently quite in despair; & between my abdomen & my head, I passed a very hard night & one such as I should be sorry to endure the repetition of.   Towards morning some pills wh. he had given me began to procure me comparative relief, tho' my head was slow to clear up.   Eventually however with reiterated pills I began to mend & that afternoon went out into the air.   Several days have now passed.   I have seen the doctor repeatedly, as he seems inclined (to what extent as a friend & to what as a doctor &[c] I ignore) to keep me in hand.   He has prescribed me a peculiar species of *aloetic* pill, to be taken an hour before dinner, wh. he hopes if kept up long enough will woo me into an habitual action.   *Je ne demande pas mieux,* so long as that in the interval, I can keep tolerably comfortable— which is the difficult point.   He says, what is doubtless true—that my bowels have been more injured by large injections in the past, than by the abuse of medicine.   He examined them (as far as he could) by the insertion of his finger (horrid tale!) & says there is no palpable obstruction.   He seemed surprised however that I haven't piles; you see we have always something to be grateful for.   On the whole nevertheless I find it hard to make him (as I should anyone who had'n't observed it) at all understand the stubbornness & extent—the length & breadth & depth, of my trouble.   He indulges in plenty of vague remarks about diet, exercise & not reading—which you will admit that I have earned the right to dispense with.—Of course all this business has left me uncomfortable in the present & apprehensive of the future. At this present moment of my writing, I know neither how I'm to do without a stool, nor how (in spite of the doctor's pills, as yet) I am to get one. The whole matter occupies perforce (how gracefully!) the foreground of my thoughts & oppresses equally my mind & my body. It seems hardly worth while to be in this great Italy on such a footing; but *enfin* circumstances are what they are; & mine might be very much worse. My trouble is a bad one, but the circumstances are very well: especially this of my sitting & scribbling to you. Of course I feel even more than when I last wrote that some change is imperative & that this state of things must discontinue *au plus tôt*. But as you see however I am not much nearer to finding an issue, & meanwhile my daily life becomes rather less than more, comfortable. Let me not however use too dark colors. I find the best restaurant here—the Café de Paris—very sufficient to my dietetic needs. I can get things done quite à l'anglais. I have entered into renewed engagements with myself with regard to eating & drinking, & by means of these, the doctor's pills & the same active life that I [have] been leading so long (tho' with only *this very* result against which I now appeal to it!) I hope to hold out till the dawning of some change.—But this matter of an active life suggests precisely the most serious point in these late developments. They have brought with them a rapidly growing sense of the relation between the state of my bowels & my *back*. My actual situation is complicated by the fact that this recent terrible constipation has made itself *directly* felt in my back (the lower part, across the base, loins & hips) to such a degree that it becomes an added effort to take that amount of exercise needful to combat this same constipation. I feel this heaviness of the bowels across my loins more palpably & unmistakably than I can express to you. I have always felt in a general way that if my bowels were regular, my back would be better; but it is only within the past few weeks that I have realized keenly the connection between the two & been able to measure the load of which my back would be lightened if I could keep my abdomen free. Formerly I had two distinct troubles—my constipation & my pain in my back. I now see that what I still retain of the latter is in a large degree but another phase of the former. I draw from this fact a stupendous hope—it shines to me as a light out of the darkness: & I depend upon it for drawing to your mind, by its cheering influence, the barbarity of this appeal to your sympathies. To put it in a word, I feel justified in believing that if, at the end of a month, (no matter how—by some miracle!) I had established a healthy action of my bowels, my back would by a corresponding movement have made a leap not of a *month*, but of a year—of two, three—what you please.   I should feel in other words IMMEDIATELY an improvement which I have been used to consider a thing of very distant days.   I dont mean to say that the relation between these two localities has always been the same: but there came a moment on the march of improvement when the one overtook & outstripped the other, & has ever since been dragged & held back by it. Disengaged from this fatal grasp it would at once advance to the end of its own chain—a longer one than than I have yet ventured to fancy.—These reflections fill me with a perfectly *passionate* desire for a reformation in my bowels.   I see in it not only the question of a special localized affection, but a large general change in my condition & a blissful renovation of my life—the reappearance above the horizon of pleasures which had well-nigh sunk forever behind that great murky pile of undiminishing contingencies to which my gaze has so long been accustomed.   It would result in the course of a comparatively short time, a return to repose—reading—hopes & ideas—an escape from this weary wor[l]d of idleness.   But I needn't descant further: a word to the wise is enough.—You may imagine that there's nothing I am not ready to do to compass my desire.   At present the prescription seems to be that hardest of all things—to wait.   Well— I'll even wait.   I shall remain in Florence until one way or the other I get some news of a change.   I shall do so almost *mechanically*, for I confess that in my present physical condition—with this perpetual oppression of the inner and outer man—to enjoy things keenly is difficult.   If I get no better, I shall not push on to Rome.   Such at least is my present disposition.   It would *spoil* Rome to see it under this perpetual drawback.   To go there simply as travelling & as therefore beneficial would moreover not be worthwhile, as here for some time to come I can get a sufficiency of movement.   If I leave Florence *not* for Rome, I don't see what is left for me but to go to *Malvern*—a matter on wh. I touched in my last.   I am not wrong I think, in attributing to Malvern my condition during the last part of my stay in England; & I feel now that once possessed of a similar *start*, I should not let it slip from me as before.   I should, however, deeply regret being forced to take this step & to turn my back upon Italy.   The thought is horrible.   Not only should I lose what may possibly be the most delightful & valuable part of this Italian experience; but I should find my subsequent plans grievously disarranged.   It is my dearest desire to get three months of England, in the fine season, before my return—to sail if possible thence. To take them now in midwinter would of course be a poor substitute.—On the other side, if I should make a solid gain by a couple of mos. at Malvern, it would reconcile me to everything. Such a start, I say, I would undertake to keep; & with my bowels thus regenerated I would laugh Italy to scorn. I should then feel comparatively small need of leading a life of sight-seeing & should not hesitate to claim from the days a fair allowance of reading. With this consolation—I should ask but for a moderate daily sitting—I should either remain in England (i.e. London) or re-sort to Paris & abide there till such a moment as I should feel pre-pared to venture on Germany. Thence, after a sojourn the duration of which I don't now pretend to fix—I should return to Cambridge & I devoutly trust to work.—

"The thought grows frightful, 'tis so wildly dear." [2] All this hangs as you see—on a feeble thread—but it *does* hang.—Meanwhile I eat beans & pease & grapes & figs & walk—walk—walk—in the hope of an *occasional* stool.—This is the end of my long story. I feel the bet-ter for having written it: I hope you will feel none the worse for read-ing it. Its because I know you not to be a maudlin & hysterical youth that I have let myself out. But dont think me a great fool if you should suddenly get a letter from me from England. I can imagine my being *forced* to fly, in desperation. For instance I don't think I could withstand the effects of another attack like that last—for tho' the "crisis" was accelerated by improper medicine I'm sure I felt all ripe for it. But I have good hopes of evading such miseries & re-maining here—at any rate. Having opened up the subject at such a rate, I shall of course keep you informed.—To shew you haven't taken this too ill, for heaven's sake make me a letter about your own health—poor modest flower!—Commend me most lovingly to my parents & sister. Write to me to as good purpose as (without worry-ing) you may & believe me your brother

H.J.jr

P.S. It's no more than just that the family should in some form repay themselves for your medical education. And what is a doctor meant for but to listen to old women's *doléances?*—Don't lose sight of that good news about my back.

———————

Give my love, when you see him to frank Washburn & tell him I long for news of him—& that if he should ever feel like sending me a line the gracious act would rank among benefits remembered. Let him remember Pisa & that Florence is but a larger sort of Pisa.

_____

I get no news at all of OWH.jr.—Tell him—I hate him most dam-nably; I never knew till the past few mos. how much; but that I yet think I shall write to him

19ᵗʰ I have kept my letter till to day, hoping I might have one from home to acknowledge.—But I close it, sick unto death of vain wait-ing.—I see in it nothing to alter—& nothing to add save the adjura-tion to TAKE IT EASY!—The Malvern plan is very thin: I don't see how I *can* leave Italy.—While there is life there is hope.—Address me as I wrote you: Mm. Em. Fenzi & Cie. Banquiers Florence, Italy. If I go to Rome they will forward & if I am likely to be there more than a mo. I will give you a new address. Pray stop the *Atlantic*, coming from the office. It keeps coming like the Nation whereof I wrote you, thro' Lombard Odier & Cie, & after them thro' a string of Bankers who each charge a commission I suppose. If you could have it sent you from the office & mail it yourselves as you do my letters I should prefer it. I made the same request about the Nation. If this is in-convenient, it would be better to suppress them.

ALS: MH bMS Am 1094 (1936)

¹ 16 October 1869 was a Saturday.

² Robert Browning, "Pictor Ignotus," in *Men and Women* (1855).

To Henry James

Cambr. Oct 25 [1869]

My dearest Harry—Your letter from Florence to Alice & me of Oct. 8th came this mng. I am truly distressed to hear of your condition. What you must do without delay is to see a physician—there must be a good foreign one in Florence—tell him your whole case and have him make a physical examination of you. My general advice can be of little use to you compared with that. It seems to me you must have somewhere in the gut an accumulation of old faeces wh. block the way. It must be thoroughly cleaned out & then the paralysed por-tion of gut reestablished in its functions. I can well understand how you should pine after Malvern & England; but wd. not give way to the longing until I became quite desperate—for the same result might not occur twice—your relief then may not have depended on the baths—it seems to me you took them too short a time to have got such an effect fm. them; and the subsequent "open" state may have de-pended on other conditions connected with your general change of life fm. that in america, wh. wd. not now be reproduced.   Go to the best doctor you can hear of in Florence, and follow his advice.— Rather than use any more of the "pills" you have found so ineffectual resort to croton oil (oleum tiglii).   The dose is 1 drop & a half, in an emulsion of mucilage or mixed with olive oil.   If it don't work in an hour take half a drop more but never go above 3½ drops as it is a dangerous remedy.   Senna taken at night, followed by Epsom salts in the morning is the next best thing, I suppose.   Inject in these cases as large & *hot* an enema as you can bear (not get it, *more tuo*, scalding) of soap suds & oil; the soap & oil mixed well by shaking in a bottle.— Electricity *some*times has a wonderful effect, applied not in the piddling way you recollect last winter but by a strong *galvanic* current from the spine to the abdominal muscles, or if the rectum be paralysed one pole put inside the rectum.   If I were you I wd. resort to it. I know of no Italian electro-therapeutist—though there probably is one in Florence.   *Benedikt* at Vienna is the first in Europe.[1]   Dr. Garratt told me it often failed, but often succeeded, & mentioned a gentlemen (president of some RR) who had told him recently he would not go back to his old condition for $10,000.   At Paris, *Onimus* is a good electrician,[2] in London *Althaus*.[3]   Your constipation is one of those things for wh. you had better not consult such big men as Ferguson & Paget, (who are surgeons besides.)   They will pay you too little attention. *Chambers* in London is a first rate man for the digestive canal, but also rather fashionable & busy.[4]   But this is not one of the subtle matters of medecine and any *sensible* physician can do as much for it as the greatest.   If you get no better with what treatment Florence or Rome afford, I wd. certainly *try* galvanism, and then see again what the English climate & Malvern can accomplish. It strikes me it must be a condition, which, once broken loose from, could be kept normal in you.   Tell the Dr all about your attacks of pain.   If you should go to Vienna you wd. get the most careful treatment probably that Europe affords.   You cd. easily find out fm. Pratt or some of the American medical students there, who best to go to. Remember that croton oil is to be taken only when the emergency becomes very severe—then don't delay it.—This is all I can think of to tell you.   It makes me sick to think of your life being blighted by this hideous affliction.   I will say nothing to the family about it, as they can do you no good, and it will only give them pain—but don't you hesitate hereafter to let me know minutely all about yourself.   I hope to God you will soon find a way to make it go better.   For what purpose we are thus tormented I know not,—I dont see that Father's philosophy explains it any more than any one else's.   But as Pascal says "malgré les misères qui nous tiennent par la gorge" there's a divine instinct in us, and at the end of life the good remains, and the evil sinks into darkness.[5]   If there is to be evil in the world at all, I don't see why you or I should not be its victims as well as any one else—the trouble is that there should be any.   My own costiveness gives me no inconvenience at all.   My back remains in statu quo—or if anything, better.   I'm going to start galvanism this week.   I find the days to pass easily and rapidly, altho' I do exceedingly little work of any sort.—Wilky raised a whopping big caterpiller crop this year, but writes that he will certainly pay all expenses.   Robeson[6] is going to become his partner, wh. will be an excellent thing.—You've no idea how we enjoyed your letters fm. Venice (to Howells & me)   Father is gone off to N.Y. this mng. to stay a week at Gertrude's & get a new leg.[7]   He is very well again.   Alice is very vigorous, goes in alone to the lifting cure 3 times a week, and walks & pays evening visits & "bees" on the off nights.[8]   No more this mng., but I'll write again soon.

Your loving bro.   W.J.

Elly Temple is gone overland to California with her husband. Minny is to follow by sea with another Emmett in 4 weeks.[9]   Mother has written for her to come here, but no answer yet.   I sent you my proof and the sheets of an article by Howells in the November Atlantic "A pedestrian tour."[10]

Bob Temple is in Florida, having gone down to sponge on Wilky who repulsed him.   This morn⁀ he writes to father for $50.   Father refused I think quite rightly.   He will probably end by re-enlisting.

Hosmer writes that he is better in all respects, and to a great extent leaves off his dark glasses.

ALS: MH bMS Am 1092.9 (2573)

[1] Moriz Benedikt (1835–1920), Austrian physician, author of *Elektrotherapie* (1868).

[2] Ernest Nicolas Joseph Onimus (b. 1840), French physician, wrote on medical uses of electricity.

[3] Julius Althaus (1833–1900), British physician, wrote on treatment by faradization.

[4] Thomas King Chambers (1818–1889), British physician, author of works on indigestion and obesity.

[5] A loose quotation and translation from Blaise Pascal (1623–1662), French philosopher, *Pensées*, no. 411 in most 19th-century editions.

[6] Identified as William R. Robeson in *BBF*, 108.

[7] Gertrude James Pendleton (d. 1889), daughter of Henry James's brother Augustus James, wife of James Pendleton of Virginia.   Henry James's leg had been amputated above the knee in 1828.

[8] For a history of the "Bee" see *AJB*, 132–35.

[9] For Mary Temple's plans to follow her sister to California see *NSB*, 497–502. She was to be escorted by a brother of Christopher Temple Emmet. The journey was not made.

[10] William Dean Howells, "A Pedestrian Tour," *Atlantic Monthly* 24 (November 1869): 591–603.

From Henry James

Florence Hotel de l'Europe | October 26ᵗʰ [1869]

Dear Bill—

I wrote you the enclosed long letter some ten days ago, but abstained from sending it, on account of its darksome purport & in the hope that by waiting I might have better news.[1]   But I haven't.   My condition has become so intolerable that I have well nigh made up my mind to leave Italy & fly to England—for the reasons & with the purpose mentioned in my letter.   For the past ten days I have been in the very depths of discomfort.   If it wasn't as great as it I can imagine it being, I should say it was getting worse.   I haven't the shadow of a reason left I think, after my long experience, for supposing that I shall encounter any change, on this footing.   Moreover, my back as I have related in my letter, is so chronically affected by my constipated state that there are times when I can hardly drag myself about.   Half the week I can eat but a single meal a day; I can't possibly find room for more—& this in spite of getting very tired & passably hungry with all my poking about.   I mean therefore to return to England in a very short time.   Just at the present moment, I am undecided as to whether I shall push on to Rome for a fortnight or depart straightway *via* Leghorn & Marseilles.   I shall advise you a couple of days hence. I have just written to father.   I have heard nothing from home in 3 weeks.   Excuse brutal brevity

Y⟨o⟩ur's in haste   H.J.jr.

ALS: MH bMS Am 1094 (1937)

[1] Letter of 16 October 1869.

From Henry James

Rome Hotel d'Angleterre, Oct. 30ᵗʰ [1869]

My dearest Wᵐ—

Some four days since I despatched to you & father respectively, from Florence, two very doleful epistles, which you will in course of time receive. No sooner had I posted them however than my spirits were revived by the arrival of a most blessed brotherly letter from you of October 8<u>th</u>, which had been detained either by my banker or the porter of the hotel & a little scrap from father of a later date, enclosing your review of Mill & a paper of Howells—as well as a couple of *Nations*.   Verily, it is worthwhile pining for letters for 3 weeks to know the exquisite joy of final relief.   I took yours with me to the theatre whither I went to see a comedy of Goldoni most delightfully played & read & re-read it between the acts.[1]—But of this anon.—I went as I proposed down to Pisa & spent two very pleasant days with the Nortons.   It is a very fine dull old town—& the great square with its four big treasures is quite the biggest thing I have seen in Italy—or rather was, until my arrival at this well-known locality.—I went about a whole morning with Chas. N. & profited vastly by his excellent knowledge of Italian history & art.   I wish I had a small fraction of it.   But my visit wouldn't have been complete unless I had got a ramble *solus*, which I did in perfection.   On my return to Florence I determined to start immediately for Rome.   The afternoon after I had posted those two letters I took a walk out of Florence to an enchanting old Chartreuse—an ancient monastery, perched up on top of a hill & turreted with little cells like a feudal castle.[2]   I attacked it & carried it by storm—*i.e.* obtained admission & went over it.   On coming out I swore to myself that while I had life in my body I wouldn't leave a country where adventures of that complexion are the common incidents of your daily constitutional: but that I would hurl myself upon Rome & fight it out on this line at the peril of my existence.   Here I am then in the Eternal city.   It was easy to leave Florence; the cold had become intolerable & the rain perpetual.   I started last night & at 10 & ½ o'clock & after a bleak & fatiguing journey of 12 hours found myself here with the morning light.   There are several places on the *route* I should have been glad to see; but the weather & my own condition made a direct journey imperative.   I rushed to this hotel (a very slow & obstructed rush it was I confess, thanks to the longueurs & lenteurs of the Papal dispensation) & after a wash & a breakfast let myself loose on the city.   From midday to dusk I have been roaming the streets.   Que vous en dirai-je?—At last—for the 1<u>st</u> time—I live! It beats everything: it leaves the Rome of your fancy—your education—nowhere.   It makes Venice—Florence—Oxford—London—seem like little cities of paste-board.   I went reeling & moaning thro' the streets, in a fever of enjoyment.   In the course of four or five hours I traversed almost the whole of Rome & got a glimpse of every-thing—the Forum, the Coliseum (stupendissimo!) the Pantheon—the Capitol—St. Peter's—the Column of Trajan—the Castle of St. Angelo—all the Piazzas & ruins & monuments. The effect is some-thing indescribable. For the 1ˢᵗ time I know what the picturesque is.—In St. Peter's I staid some time. It's even beyond it's reputation. It was filled with foreign ecclesiastics—great armies encamped in prayer on the marble plains of its pavement—an inexhaustible phys-iognomical study. To crown my day, on my way home, I met his Ho-liness in person—driving in prodigious purple state—sitting dim within the shadows of his coach with two uplifted benedictory fin-gers—like some dusky Hindoo idol in the depths of its shrine.[3] Even if I should leave Rome to night I should feel that I have caught the key-note of its operation on the senses. I have looked along the grassy vista of the Appian Way & seen the topmost stonework of the Coliseum sitting shrouded in the light of heaven, like the edge of an Alpine chain. I've trod the Forum & I have scaled the Capitol. I've seen the Tiber hurrying along, as swift & dirty as history! From the high tribune of a great chapel of St. Peter's I have heard in the papal choir a strange old man sing in a shrill unpleasant soprano. I've seen troops of little tonsured neophytes clad in scarlet, marching & countermarching & ducking & flopping, like poor little raw re-cruits for the heavenly host.—In fine I've seen Rome, & I shall go to bed a wiser man than I last rose—yesterday morning.—It was a great relief to me to have you at last give me some news of your health. Thank the Lord it's no worse. With all my I[4] heart I rejoice that you're going to try loafing & visiting. I discern the "inexorable logic" of the affair; courage, & you'll work out your redemption. I'm de-lighted with your good report of J.L.F.'s pictures. I've seen them all save the sleeping woman. I have given up expecting him here. If he does come, tant mieux. Your notice of Mill & Bushnell seemed to me (save the opening lines which savored faintly of Eugene Benson) very well & fluently written. Thank Father for his ten lines: may they increase & multiply!—Of course I don't know how long I shall be here. I would give my head to be able to remain 3 months: it would be a liberal education. As it is, I shall stay, if possible, simply from week to week. My "condition" remains the same. I am living on some medicine (aloes & sulphuric acid) given me by my Florentine doctor. I shall write again very shortly. Kisses to Alice & Mother. Blessings on yourself. Address me *Spada, Flamini* & Cie, Banquiers,

Rome.   Heaven grant I may be here when your letters come.   Love
to father.

$\qquad$ À toi   H.J.jr.

ALS: MH BMS AM 1094 (1938)

  [1] Carlo Goldoni (1707–1793), Italian dramatist.
  [2] The visit to the monastery is described by HJ in "Florentine Notes," *Transatlantic
Sketches* (Boston: James R. Osgood, 1875).
  [3] Pope Pius IX (1792–1878), pope in 1846–78, ruler of the Papal States to 1870.
  [4] It is not clear why HJ wrote 'I' after 'my', but he may have been anticipating the 'I'
after 'heart'.

To Henry James

$\qquad$ [Cambridge] Tuesday, Nov. 1. 69.[1]

My dearest Harry—I answered your constipation letter last monday
immediately on its reception.   I hope you will have got it and put
yourself in the hands of a Doctor before you get this.   I pity you from
the bottom of my heart.   I divined all along from the tone of your
letters that something was wrong with you though the rest of the family did not notice it.   It was more from what you did not say than
from anything you did.   I have no doubt this bowel trouble lies at the
root of your sleeplessless, which I imagine (also fm. what you don't
say) still to continue; and of your inability to do any study, which I
suppose (from your saying nothing to the contrary) to be as bad or
worse than ever.   It must also as you say pull down your back.   If it
continues 3 months longer in spite of what Doctors can do for you in
Italy and of the experiment (for 'tis nothing else) of galvanism, I
would post for Malvern again and see what England can do for me.
You have of course atony of the bowels, but that seems to me to be
consecutive to some old stoppage which must first be *déblayé* and the
place *kept déblayé*'d till the bowel acquire a healthy habit.   That, thank
heaven, is in man's power.   It is *possible* on the other hand that your
repeated colics may have produced inflammatory adhesions in parts
of the bowel & narrowed the passage so that the whole difficulty is
mechanical   But that seems to me counter indicated by the fact of
your having relief at times—A mechanical difficulty is of course absolutely permanent, and if your open condition in Malvern & summer before last in the M^{ts} here was not the result of diarrhoea, producing liquid stools, you may conclude pretty reasonably that the
difficulty, not being organic, is curable.   Anyhow the thing demands

active medical interference and you must not let it go any longer.
What you say of the difficulty of feeding well in Italy grieves me very
much, especially in that it debars you from a "pension" and so keeps
up your loneliness. You can eat but little fruit—you know of course
that before bkfst is the most potent time for such grapes and figs as
you *can* command. *Fried* oil don't agree with you. If butter, and fat
generally, agree with your *stomach*, the more of them you can take, the
better for your bowels, and eke for your nervous system. At the risk
of *rabachering* and repeating what your D: tells you I will press these
maxims once more. Go through the formality of a regular hour—
but never ignore an impulse to stool at any other hour. If you *have* to depend on purgatives it is better to take small doses daily than to run a
number of days and then take a large dose. Aloes in small quantities.
A small piece of rhubarb taken repeatedly during the day is often
efficacious. (though not to me) D: Flint says he has found cases
where a few drops of tincture of colchicum after each meal answered
perfectly.[2] Aloes (of which doses of 8 grains do all that can be done
by any dose, and repeated doses of 1 or two are the best) are said to
produce or aggravate *piles* when they do not succeed in evacuating
the rectum. So if you are troubled with tenesmus after any pills that
may be ordered you, and yet do not get relief, you may suspect that
you have had too much aloes. Most of these purgatives irritate the
stomach which makes it impossible for *me* to use them the remedy
being worse than the disease. The "peristalt. loz." you wot of, work
on my bowels perfectly if taken not 2 at night but one before each
meal and one at night, but they play the deuce with my stomach.
You must determine such things as this for yourself experimentally.
One last maxim. "If more than one small dose of purgative is required, it is better to divide it into 3 small doses to be taken through
the day.["] Less of it is needed than if given all at once. Aloes and
rhubarb may be given with meals, everything else so far as I know is
better on an empty stch. I hope you will get the better of this thing,
for life is a burden till you do. I don't wonder at your feeling
gloomy—for that trouble goes to the root of things and attacks first
of all the mind. I suspect more of your inability to do head work
depends on it than you have considered hitherto. I wish by the way
you wd. write me exactly how your back is. I hear of your doing all
this walking—but not that your *consciousness* of your back has a whit
diminished.—If after all, you go back to England after a couple of
months, I don't know that it shd. be considered by you in the light of

a collapse, even if you shd. *never* see Germany. One's powers of absorbing material are limited at best—and I don't see how you could hope in any event to do *justice* to England and Germany too. We all learn sooner or later that we must gather our selves up and more or less arbitrarily concentrate our interests, throw much overboard to save *any*. You have made a favorable start with England moreover, and will get more thorough cultivation fm. "living yourself still further *hinein*" (German idiom) than by doing both it and Germany superficially. Only what we truly appropriate helps us really, and England is evidently "sympathique" to you. *My* enthusiasm for Germany has been entirely on the basis of letting England slide. Your better plan wd. probably be the opposite; the more so as your business is to write English & the study of english writers can best help you therein. German wd, perhaps even hurt you. I came t'other day across an anecdote of Schiller—(by the bye 'twas in Crabb Robinson) Crabb saw a German Shakespeare in his library and asked him whether he did not read him in Engl. S. said he could, but did not, as his business was writing German and the habit of other tongues he thought hurt the delicacy of his feeling for what was good German.[3] You could not get even *started* in German fairly in less than 15 months. All this to be seriously thought of by you, not only as consolation after, but in deliberation before, your return to England. I wish now you'd write about your back, power of reading, and sleep. *I* sleep like a top. My "power of reading" however is gone to the dogs. I regret it the more now, as my mind was never in a more active, i.e. earnestly inquiring state and problems define themselves more sharply to me. I read lately Lecky's Hist. of Morals which is a fascinating work, though with a strange effect of amiability.[4] I was much satisfied by a new vol. of "Nouvelles Moscovites" of our old friend Turgeneff.[5] His mind is morbid but he is an artist through & through. His work is solid and will bear reading over and over. In other words *style* is there,—that mystery. I have been reading Moralism & X[ty] and Lect. & Miscel.[6] Father is a genius certainly—a religious genius. I feel it continually to be unfortunate that his discordance fm. me on other points in wh. I think the fault is really his—his want or indeed absence of *intellectual* sympathies of any sort—makes it so hard for me to make him feel how warmly I respond to the positive sides of him.—Minny has postponed her trip to Calif. for a month & we expect her here Thursday to say good bye to us.[7] T.S.P. femine to the last degree, but very good at bottom. Wendle Holmes ambitious and hard working. He took your Venice letter home to

read last week.   Alice first rate.   Mother & father ditto.   Clear frosty
weather.

Adieu.   Gute Besserung!

Yours ever   W.J.

ALS: MH bMS AM 1092.9 (2574)

[1] 1 November 1869 was a Monday.

[2] Either Austin Flint (1812–1886) or his son Austin Flint, Jr., American physicians.

[3] *Diary, Reminiscences, and Correspondence of Henry Crabb Robinson,* ed. Thomas Sadler, 3 vols. (London: Macmillan, 1869), 1:213.

[4] William Edward Hartpole Lecky, *History of European Morals from Augustus to Charlemagne* (1869).

[5] Ivan Sergeevich Turgenev, *Nouvelles moscovites,* trans. Prosper Mérimée (1869).

[6] Henry James, *Moralism and Christianity* (New York: Redfield, 1850), *Lectures and Miscellanies* (New York: Redfield, 1852).

[7] There was a change of plans and Mary Temple went to Cambridge several weeks later, 19 November 1869.

From Henry James

Rome, Monday Nov. 8th [1869] Hotel de Rome.
Dear W.—I have written Alice so long a letter[1] that I can only send
you 3 lines.—The purpose of them is to tell you that since coming to
Rome I have been immensely relieved of those woes concerning wh.
I sent you from Florence such copious bulletins.   Now that I feel
better I reproach myself that I broke silence on the subject.   But I
couldn't help it.   My improvement is owing to some pills which the
doctor gave me just as I left Florence.   Their effect has been so truly
remarkable that I enclose a copy of the prescription.   With a daily
pill (taken before dinner) I get a daily passage: not copious but sufficient—"And oh! the difference to me!"[2]   I needn't dilate upon it.
Whether they are a mere temporary aid or are destined to help me to
a cure I know not: as yet when I omit a pill, I miss the evacuation.
But this effect is so far cumulative & unattended with a reaction that
as yet I don't need to increase the dose.   Without this change I
couldn't possibly have staid in Rome.   It was quite unforseen; therefore I wrote you & probably distressed you as I did.   Their effect as
yet has been so magical that I have a horror of its coming to a sudden
explosion & leaving me as bad as before.   But at least I shall have
seen Rome.—The virtue seems to be in the sulfuric acid, for I
had quite come to an end of aloes.   Here it is—as well as I can decipher it.

aloes Barbad.   ʒii/s

Acidi Sulphur. fortissimi

Guttas XII & divide in pil XII—et. duas(?) mane nocteque si opus sit.

I can simply make a facsimile of the man's hieroglyphics: the thing has fewer details than I thought.—Do let me hear some good news of yourself—whether thro' Garratt or whatsoever.   Wait till I get home & I'll cheer & comfort you.—I have tried to give Alice a few of my impressions.—I spent yesterday a delightful day.   I went down to the Capitol & had a delicious long lazy stare at the Faun by Praxiteles & the Antinous.[3]   They are beyond everything.—They have a fault: they transcend the legitimate bounds of beauty.   To comprehend them becomes a delicious pain. Later I gazed at the glorious sculptures on the arch of Constantine.   *Manly!*

Thy brother | H.

ALS: MH bMS AM 1094 (1939)

[1] *HJL*, 1:161–71, dated 7 November 1869.

[2] From William Wordsworth, "She Dwelt among the Untrodden Ways."

[3] Praxiteles (c. 370–330 B.C.), Greek sculptor.   The satyr in the Capitoline Museum is generally considered a copy.   Antinous, a young Greek famed for his beauty, is often depicted in Roman sculpture.

From Henry James

Rome, Hotel de Rome, Nov. 30ᵗʰ [1869]

Beloved William—I have before me two excellent letters from you of Oct. 25ᵗʰ & Nov. 1ˢᵗ respectively, wh. I have been meaning for some days to answer.   Most welcome they have been to me & comforting to my spirit.   I have felt much better for letting you know out & out how I was & am very glad I did it, tho' at the time it seemed a brutal & senseless act.   You have had better news from me since those doleful letters from Florence wh. drew forth these answers of yours.   I wrote you a line telling you of the remedy finally given me by Doctor Duffy & of the blessed relief I have been getting from it.   I have now been a month in Rome & feel that I owe it quite to those little daily pills that I have had so great an experience.   The best things however must come to an end—*Surtout* the best!

The virtue of my pills has not quite departed but it is rapidly waning & unless I can keep afloat by some other means I fear I may again relapse into Florentine depths.   I went this morning to see Dr. Gould the chief American physician here, & he came to me this afternoon &

"examined" my bowels & abdomen. On the whole he was not very satisfactory—less so than Dr. Duffy. He says there is no apparent or palpable obstruction or organic disorder in the parts; & that as far as he can see I have only torpor &c. He recommended a certain Italian mineral water, a specific for this trouble, which I am to take before breakfast. He also spoke highly of the *Kissingen* waters, which he has taken himself, on the spot for two summers, for a similar complaint. I shall of course immediately try this Italian stuff & hope when I next write to let you hear that it works—tho' I have a fear that it succeeds only with lighter cases than mine. I suppose you are quite right in saying that I had better not attempt to consult any of the great medical swells; tho', if from these two men I get no permanent assistance I shall be rather at loss to know to whom to apply. I duly noted what you said about *electricity*. I shall be glad enough to try it, if there is any prospect of its helping me. I mentioned it to Dr. Gould, but he seemed sceptical on the subject. If you have started a battery yourself, you will perhaps have something to tell me from your own experience. Whether there is an electrician here or not, I haven't learned. I doubt it, so out of keeping is it with the general Roman tone of things. But at any rate I should try it not here but either in Florence or Paris. My stay here is almost at an end. I have (very wisely, I now think) abstained from fixing myself here & I feel less inclined to now than ever—(much—how much indeed—as I should like to.) If this confounded thing should settle down upon me again in the same way as at Florence, I feel as if it would be decidedly harder to bear & to contend with here than elsewhere. This heavy atmosphere is not a place to have troubles in. In view of a possible relapse I feel like using the last lingering traces of my *Besserung* to take a run down to Naples if only for a week. I know now what it would have been to lose Rome, & the knowledge gives me a horror of missing Naples. I should start to-morrow if I were not pledged to wait for A. Kate. She arrives however to morrow & after fairly seeing her, I suppose I can be off as soon as I please. In one way or another I hope to get a comfortable stay at Naples & to get back to Florence. There I shall reflect upon my further movements & make up my mind either to stick fast to the Continent or to go to Malvern. What I wrote you from Florence about the relation of this matter to my back has been amply borne out by experience here. That is, with my comparatively open condition, my back has been fifty per-cent more comfortable. You say that you hear of all this walking &c, but that you have yet to learn whether I am any the less conscious of my back.

Very much less so.   As much less so or as little (as you please to call it)
as is natural in one who expects at his final & ultimate best (whenever
that arrives) to stop a good bit short of perfect unconsciousness.   As
for being able to "study," that I have hardly tried.   I have found tho'
that little by little, in proportion as my bowels keep open, I am getting
back the power of reading with impunity.   I have read in the mornings of the past week with immense pleasure—pleasure in the simple
act of reading—a great thick French 8$\underline{^{vo}}$ on Italian history, & born it
far more easily & comfortably than I could have done it in those stupid months last winter before I left home.   I strongly suspect that a
prolonged "openness" would bring me up in this respect in a most
wonderful way.   Altogether I may decidedly say that with regard to
my back I have entered into a new stage or era.   All that walking,
walking & more walking can do for it, I think I have done; (& this is
equally true for my bowels.) Curious as it sounds, I think walking tires
me more—decidedly more—& resting—i.e. sitting, lying &c proportionately less than they did 3 months ago.   If I could reform my constipation I fancy I should find I could afford to be far more sedentary
now—& could afford equally to walk more for the simple pleasure of
change & not with the fierce monotony & feverish purpose that I have
done hitherto.   With regard to my sleep I am happy to say you are
quite mistaken.   All summer in Switzerland it was decidedly bad; but
since my coming to Italy it has been gradually improving & during
the past month has been particularly good.   My appetite is also excellent tho' (fortunately) in proportion as I tend to keep full, it diminishes.   It has become too a far more healthy & rational appetite than
the thing you knew of old.   I *like* everything now, without exception
(& am particularly fond of FAT!)—In what you said in your last about
England & Germany I was of course immensely interested.   I quite
incline to agree with you that if I were compelled a month hence to
go to England I needn't to look upon it as a misfortune.   In fact it
would quite solve the problem of my present destinies & heaven
knows it would crown all my longings & desires with bliss!   I have
been thinking a good deal about the possibility of going to Germany
for next summer but the plan offers many objections—or rather it is
subject to one-all-important: viz: that even putting things at their very
best, I have no business to assume in myself the capacity for real study
within the present year: & certainly to go to Germany & not to be able
to study fairly seems a false arrangement.   I confess I am surprised
however at your saying that 15 mos. is the *minimum* in wh. one could
get started there: I allude of course simply to reading.   T.S.P. I

should suppose at least very well "started," & he, if I'm not mistaken was there for considerably less than a year. But if one, with *work*, can do but little in 15 mos., one could hardly do much without it in 6. In truth I should be sorry at this time of day to sit down & forego all hope of my mastering German, but on the other hand I feel as if for some time to come there were things more important. Here I am at 26 with such a waste of lost time behind me & such an accumulated ignorance of so many of the elements & rudiments of my own tongue, literature &c piled up in my track—& with the practical needs of my "calling" facing me in the immediate future—with these things pressing on me to such a degree that to branch off into the awful chaos of that portentous tongue seems simply like an increase of care & responsibility without an increase of means. If I were to go to England a short time hence & remain till I go home (I am talking all the while on the basis of my return a year hence, when I shall have been absent about 20 mos.) I shall simply be getting in a different way a mass of impressions which, if I had hitherto been well & able to develop myself more freely & vigorously I should (probably) have got from study or at least from more liberal habits of reading. For mere pleasure alone, I can think of none greater than to spend a summer wandering thro' England with a certain freedom. It may be that the great impression England has left on my mind is owing in a measure to its being the 1st European country I saw—& saw just after that long monotonous period of home life; & that after Italy it will seem comparatively pale & colorless. But with all abatements, I am sure it will yield me great delights & rich instruction. The principal drawback I see to going there—to going anywhere in fact—is the possible—not to say probable dearth, of society. I feel as if "society" were yet destined to play a very large part in lifting me fairly onto my legs. It is an agent I have never fairly tried but I have great hopes of it. The only trouble is to get hold of it. If I were to settle here in Rome I should probably be able to see as much as I pleased of plenty of Americans. This one consideration almost outweighs several weighty objections. On the Continent alone is American society to be found; & the apparent inaccessibility of the natives is so great that save this there is little other. I get a strong feeling, while in England, of the degree to wh. to a lonely & unassisted man society must remain obstructed & closed & to go there & be left wholly to my own resources, tho it might be very pleasant for a couple of months would be rather dreary for six. To have any but really *Good* Society there, moreover, would be rather more intolerable than to have none at all.

If I go, I shall try & drum up a few introductions.—Meanwhile I still get the same heavy news of your immobility & continued wretchedness. And yet in spite of it I manage not to feel hopeless or even cheerless. I feel a conviction not to be shaken that your present condition is destined regularly to play itself out. Improvement will come to you as it came to me—with a lingering & stumbling tread—but still it will come. Little by little, inch by inch the divine messenger of relief will lay bare his countenance & when once you have seen it, you will be as one who has talked face to face with an angel. I hope you are carrying out that programme you hinted at some time since—visiting "evenings."[1] Go thro' it doggedly & mechanically when you can't otherwise & you will know your reward. Your days are composed but of hours, by taking each hour "empirically" & disposing of it as best you can, you can get thro' a month, & at the end of a month (probably) you find some appreciable result.—But I can't write to you about your back. The subject is to me too heavy—too sickening. All I can do is to remind you of my own career. Go thro' a certain course of combined rest & motion & meanwhile keep up a devil of a waiting! Now that I am better, my own waiting & watching seems as nothing—as a mere brief fitful fever—a bad dream, preceding a blissful awakening into serene reality.—Rome remains sublime to the end. My movements have been a good deal curtailed of late by rainy weather: still, no day has been empty.—I have also been going a little *dans le monde*—that is I dined recently twice at Mrs. Ward's[2] & met the second time Miss Story, daughter of the sculptor—a kind of Anglicized & highly imperious Helena De Kay.[3] Nay, really she only *looks* like H.D.K.—wh. she does very much: otherwise she is immensely *bon genre*. I went to Story's studio with Mrs. W. & saw S. in person. He was very civil & his statues very clever. I likewise received the card of George Ripley of the N. Y. *Tribune* & of course (feeling very grateful for his attention) immediately returned his visit. He was very kind & agreeable & asked lovingly about father. He is here as a species of reporter on the *Council*; but I fancy will get little satisfaction.[4]—I have seen nothing new in Rome—but have been repeatedly to old places. The Campagna is something tremendous—but it can only be seen on horseback. The *Vatican* is inexhaustible—& the general picturesqueness of Rome something not to be defined. I have seen it pretty well & despite many pangs, am fairly ready to go. The filth that is so remote from godliness & the dead weight of the moral & political atmosphere count for somewhat on the other scale. I have ceased to get the Atlantic & Nation. I suppose you have stopped them, in pursuance of my remarks.   I shall see them again at Florence.   After that I shall perhaps return to the subject.   Good night.   Love to all.   I shall write a week hence—probably from Naples.—If only I could be favored with an hour's conversation with you!—

Yours   H. James jr.

ALS: MH bMS Am 1094 (1940)

[1] See letter of 2 October 1869.

[2] Medora Grymes Ward (she changed her name from Marie Angéline), a famous New Orleans beauty, estranged wife of Sam Ward (1814–1884), author and influence peddler, known as "king of the lobbyists."   After her separation, Mrs. Ward lived lavishly and notoriously on the Riviera.   Sam Ward does not seem to be related to Thomas Wren Ward.

[3] Helena De Kay, an artist, sister of Katherine De Kay Bronson, in 1874 married Richard Watson Gilder.

[4] George Ripley was covering the First Vatican Council (1869–70) for the *New York Tribune*.

To Henry James

Cambr. Dec 5. 69[1]

Dear Harry   You can with difficulty conceive of the joy with which I received in your enclosed sheet from Rome of Nov 8 with the sulf. acid & aloes prescription the news of the temporary end of your moving intestinal drama. If I could believe it to be the beginning of *the* end, the happiness wd. be almost *too* great; it may be even that; but even if only a temporary respite, it comes at a moment which is important for your whole future, in deciding perhaps, whether you shall or shall not have Rome to furnish your consciousness with. Don't be too sanguine, nor count on escaping definitively the bore of Malvern.   The trouble with an habitual use of Aloes is that it tends to produce piles.   I spoke rather slightingly in one of my late letters (I have written you 2 long & one brief one, by the way since your first *complainte*, and hope you'll get them all) of your florence D.ͬ—but it seems you fell into good hands as this Sulfuric acid dodge is either a very late one not yet generally known or an ancestral secret of his. Stillé's materia med. says nothing of it,[2] and I find Tuck & Dwight never heard of it.   I have experimented on myself and find it very efficacious.   If having started yourself by it, you find symptoms of soreness about anus & rectum, slack up; it may then be that *small* doses of fluid extract of senna (say a third of a teaspoonful 3 times a day[)]—after meals if it will work so,—if not, on an empty stomach—

(or even a less dose,) will keep things open.   It is less trouble than the
confection with figs I wrote you about.   Nibbling a little solid Rhubarb, 3 times a day may also help.   But remember that you should in
no case get more than a *laxative* effect.   Real purging is always to be
avoided since its after-working is in the direction of increased torpor.
The minimum with which you can get a stool at all, is what you must
aim at, and a steady consumption of minute quantities of medecine is
far better than a rarer large dose.   I do hope you'll get on well after
this, as "something tells me" as it were, that it is your main trouble at
present.   But if you get bad again dont delay too long in Italy—and
above all don't be shy of consulting a Doctor again.   Remember that
there are purgatives & purgatives, and the undiscriminating advice
of druggists may be fatal.————I dare say you'll thank me at last for
dropping the subject.   Your letters from Italy are beyond praise.   It
is a great pity they should be born to blush unseen by the general
public, and that just the matter that they contain, in a little less ram-
bling style should not appear in the columns of the Nation.   They
are read partially to appreciative visitors and seem to cause "unfeigned delight."   Father took some to Emerson at Concord the
other day.[3]   He pleaded hard to keep them for study, but F. refused.
Meeting Edward in the Athenaeum the next day, the latter said his
father was doing nothing but talk of your letters.   That sample ought
to be enough for you.   As for my more humble self, your admirably
discriminating remarks on Art matters go to the right spot.   I can
well sympathize with what must be the turmoil of your feeling before
all this wealth—that strange impulse to exorcise it by extracting the
soul of it and throwing it off *in words*—which translation is in the nature of things impossible—but each attempt to storm its inaccessible
heights, produces, with the pang of failure, a keener sense of the reality of the ineffable subject, and a more welcome submission to its
yoke.   I had a touch of the fever at little Dresden; and I can't help
hoping that with your larger opportunities, there will be a distinct
intellectual precipitate from your experience, which may be commu-
nicable to others.   I'm sorry that your letter to me at Florence anent
these matters should have been stifled ere its birth.   It does not do to
trust to the matter remaining in the mind—Nothing can take the
place of notes struck off with the animal heat of the fever upon them,
and I hope you are making some for your own use all this time.—
What you say of the antique & of architecture touches a kindred
chord in me.   It seems as if the difference of classical & romantic had
some metaphysic parallel—and was but a symbol.   Soak yourself in

the symbol and perhaps the meaning will suddenly dawn upon you. You can't tell how *satisfied* I feel at your being able at last to see these things, or how I pray that you may finally attain the power to lead a working life and let your faculties bear their legitimate fruit. After all, even if you be cut short in Italy—what I said in a recent letter remains true, that one must have (nor try to escape it) but one intellectual *home*—if one tries to escape specialty, one misses being anything at all; and the more you get of England the better for you. I was struck yesterday in reading Sainte-Beuve's notice of Leopardi (Port. Contemp. t. iii) to find him asserting this so well of himself as critic. He apologizes for treating of a foreigner, persuaded as he is "que la critique litteraire n'a toute sa valeur et son originalité que lorsqu'elle s'applique à des sujets dont on possède de près & de longue main les fonds, les alentours, & toutes les circonstances." [4] In other words, we possess nothing well till we possess it to its remotest radicles. I sympathize fully with your wishing to spend some months in Paris. What I doubted was the propriety of your giving a year to it.———What can I tell you of our common home? M. Temple was here for a week a fortnight since. She was delightful in all respects, and although very thin, very cheerful. I am conscious of having done her a good deal of injustice for some years past, in nourishing a sort of unsympathetic hostility to her. She is after all a most honest little phenomenon, and there is a true respectability in the courage with which she keeps "true to her own instincts"—I mean it has a certain religious side with her. [5] Moreover she is more devoid of "meanness," of anything petty in her character than any one I know, perhaps either male or female. *Je tiens à* telling you this, as I recollect last winter abusing her to you rather virulently. She sails this bright cold day for Californy. I trust the voyage won't be too hard upon her. The thermom. fell to twelve last night, and to day the sky is brilliantissimo & the shadows blue on the thin snow. Jno l. f. has been contributing a chapter on Japanese art to a book of travels by one Pumpelly professor in the mining school here. [6] Excellent in matter, but I think fm. want of literary practice, without the important *points* being accented enough for the cursory reader.—T.S.P. seems to have genuinely buckled down to the study of philology, and is very well & happy. Its a pleasure to see him. O.W.H.jr. whom I've not seen for 3 weeks has accepted the $2000 (but 2 years of hard work) job, of annotating Kent's Commentaries. [7] C. S. Peirce gets now a salary of 2,500$ at the Observatory,—Bob Temple after a career of debauchery, has reenlisted at Savanna, and writes to father yesterday begging him to pawn out his chest from the hotel keeper who holds it for debt, and announcing that he will hereafter keep a silence of 5 years, "the world forgetting, by the world forgot."[8]   He says he rec'd your letter, which I forwarded to him there.—Indoors everything is lovely.   Our servants are a first class set—stylish in fact. The no. of periodicals taken has been swelled by the "Academy," and "Nature."   The A. is really worth taking, giving a thoroughly businesslike conspectus of the *whole* literature of the month, instead of the accidental fragments one gets elsewhere.   I find in my present condition that these periodicals are less odious than they have been. I have been reading Max Müller's "Chips" lately with much pleasure[9]—likewise a little of Leopardi, the italian of which is by no means insurmountable, and the matter & manner of wh. strangely attract me.   The extracts from a persion poet wh. C.E.N. sent to the last N.A.R. are mighty things.[10]   Borrow the book from him if you have a chance.   I have been galvanizing my back of late but so far ineffectually; or rather I suspect with a bad effect, the left side, which for the sake of comparison I have alone treated, being now more sensitive than the right.   Nevertheless I have been quite active the past 3 weeks or more, and though I dont assert anything on the subject, should not feel surprized if 3 months hence I realized that I had been gradually working into a more active condition—there seem so many days now on which my state surprizes me at not being as bad as I should from past experience have anticipated.   But as yet these days are sporadic, and among them abound days of equally unexpected collapse.   So I bide my time and even to my own heart say nothing encouraging.   Time passes with me like a whirlwind, however, and I am beginning to go regularly into the evening visit business.—To prove to you how well Alice is I may tell you that to day (Saturday) she started before eleven for town, where she is to go to the lifting cure, thence to lunch at a restaurant alone, then to be caught up by Mother & Annie Ashburner and to go to the Boston theatre to hear Maggie Mitchell in the Pearl of Savoy and then home to dinner.[11]   Last night she was at her bee.   They hoped to hear M.M. in her great new play "Lorlie, the tiny belle of the Canton" but the play has been changed. Such words as tiny, dainty, winsome, booklet, &c, &c, are growing ever more prevalent in our native literature.———Mother just bustles in with some clean shirts, and says I'd better tell "the dear boy" that we have every reason to suppose our offer of 20,000 for the house will be taken.[12]   You may be with A.K. when this gets you.   If so, give her lots of love say I got her letter & she may count on another fm. me

soon.   Sunday 6th.   Letter fm. Minny to Alice yest. saying Temple
Emmet had telegraphed her not to come to Cal. as he was coming
East in December.   Alice not tired a bit by her theatre.   I spent yest
eve§ at the Child's and am as well as ever this mng.   Billy Washburn's
story "Fair Harvard" is anonymously published.   Characters & action absolutely *nil*.   All his old jokes embalmed there without exception.   Much coarseness of allusion &c.   Nothing but drinking &
"going to Parker's" which are spoken of as if they were the highest
flights human freedom cd. soar to—in fact the tone of the 1st fresh-
man month throughout.   A strange objectivity of treatment wh. is
almost "weird," in that you hear and see the figures move & speak but
are furnished by the Author with no clue as to their motives or reasons; and half the time are uncertain whether he himself is writing of
them sarcastically or admiringly.   A style however almost classical in
its clearness and "terseness."   Write good news of yrself to your

W.

ALS: MH bMS Am 1092.9 (2575)

[1] The letter may be misdated because WJ says he is writing it on Saturday, but 5
December 1869 was a Sunday.

[2] Alfred Stillé (1813–1900), American physician, *Therapeutics and Materia Medica*
(1860).

[3] *Letters of Ellen Tucker Emerson*, ed. Edith E. W. Gregg, 2 vols. (Kent State: Kent
State Univ. Press, 1982).   For a description of the HJ reading see 1:537.   It was so
successful that a "lovely little plan of a letter dinner party" for 17 December 1869 was
made.   The letters were "even better the second time": "how well the James boys
understand the use of language."   WJ's letters had been read on 21 March 1868 (ibid.,
1:472).

[4] Charles-Augustin Sainte-Beuve, *Portraits contemporains*, 3 vols. (Paris: Didier,
1855), 3:72.

[5] For Mary Temple's religious side see her letter in *NSB*, 503–6.   She was sched-
uled to leave for California on 4 December and began her visit to Cambridge on 19
November.

[6] See letter of 2 October 1869.

[7] James Kent (1763–1847), *Commentaries on American Law* (1826–30).   The 12th
edition (1873) is edited by Holmes.

[8] From Alexander Pope, "Eloisa to Abelard" (1717).

[9] Friedrich Max Müller (1823–1900), German-born philologist, *Chips from a German
Workshop*, 5 vols. (1867–75).

[10] Charles Eliot Norton, review of *Les quatrains de Khèyam*, trans. J. B. Nicolas (1867),
and *Rubáiyát of Omar Khayyám, the Astronomer-Poet of Persia*, 2d ed. (1868), in *North
American Review* 109 (October 1869): 565–84.   Numerous verses are quoted.   The
latter translation is by Edward FitzGerald.

[11] WJ is confused either about the day or the play.   *The Pearl of Savoy* was performed at the Boston Theater on Monday, 6 December 1869, while other plays with
Maggie Mitchell (1832–1918), American actress, were performed on other nights.

Linda, the Pearl of Savoy: A Domestic Drama is an adaptation by Charles Zachary Barnett from the French. *Lorlie* is not identified.

[12] The house at 20 Quincy St., Cambridge, which the Jameses were renting from the Thies family.

To Henry James

[Cambridge] Dec 27. 69

Dear H'ry   Your letter to me of Nov. 31 got here this morning.   Last week came one for mother of first class contents written a week previous.   10000 thanks for the full & plain account of your condition which this one contains.   I am sorry to hear that your Aloes & sulf. ac. do not tone up your bowel but diminish in efficacy.   All you tell me makes me feel as if your bowel troubles were perhaps now all that stood in the way of your brain weakness.   That your brain should have been so much better during a month of comparative openness even when that openness was due to purgatives, the which themselves tend to produce dimness of mind and lowness of spirits, speaks strongly for this.   They be bad things to live on, and I *feel* as if the sooner you got to Malvern, the better for you; though of course that too is only an experiment, and my feeling is a matter of sentiment. Anyhow you've got Rome and it is evident that that is a gain to you for eternity.—Of course you can get *started* in German in 6 or 8 months; I meant it wd. be 15 ere you began to get *immediate* returns for the trouble and effort of reading.—My own condition is anything but satisfactory but I suppose you'll tell me it is the beginning of the end. Strong galvanism has done me no good (I haven't it strong enough to try on my bowels)   I have been wearing for a couple of months a galvanic disk of Garratt's, and it has enabled me to do a great deal more standing & walking than hitherto, more I suspect by its mechanical stiffening & support than by its electrical influence. The pain has spread within 3 months into my upper back & neck, giving me a realizing sense of all you must have suffered, and of what a tough nervous system you must have.—Moreover I find it to get along better by going into town every day or paying a visit than by keeping the house—not that I *improve* under it, but its a less evil than rest.   This may be a transition towards improvement.   Meanwhile my stomach, bowels, brain, temper & spirits are all at a pretty low ebb, and I don't think I'm a very pleasing addition to the family circle. Now I've told you sans disguise or alleviation everything in return for your confidence in me—and, I am inclined for a few months to consider my present state as a sort of turning point—in which belief I know very well you will encourage me. Xmas passed off here like any other day—Alice gave me a cravat & I to her the Golden Treasury,[1] but we rather shirked presents. Wendell Holmes spent the evening here and took your last letter home to read to John Gray. I have just been in to the Atheneum where I met Emerson who said he had enjoyed your letters extremely. No more to day. I shd not be sorry to hear of yr. turning up in Malvern; though I am pretty sure that England like every other place will seem pretty flat a[nd] ordinary on a second visit.

Ever your loving W.J.

ALS: MH bMS Am 1092.9 (2576)

[1] Francis Turner Palgrave (1824–1897), British poet, compiler of *Golden Treasury*, an anthology of songs and lyrics, available in numerous editions. The title varies somewhat from edition to edition.

From Henry James

Rome, Hotel de Rome | Nov. [December] 27th [1869]
Beloved Bill—

I have just found at my bankers a long letter from you (Dec. 5th) wh. has gratified me so inexpressibly that altho' I despatched home a document only a couple of days since, I feel powerfully moved to write to you directly—the more especially as my letter contained a promise that I would. Your letters fill me with a divine desire to occupy for an hour that old cane-bottomed chair before your bedroom fire. One of these days it will hold me for many hours. I am extremely glad you like my letters—& terrifically agitated by the thought that Emerson likes them. I never manage to write but a very small fraction of what has originally occurred to me. What you call the "animal heat" of contemplation is sure to evaporate within half an hour. I went this morning to bid farewell to M. Angelo's *Moses* at St. Pietro in Vincoli & was so tremendously impressed with its sublimity that on the spot my intellect gushed forth a torrent of wisdom & eloquence; but where is that torrent now? I *have* managed tolerably well however, wh. is the great thing to *soak* myself in the various scenes & phenomena. Conclusions occasionally leap full-armed from my Jovine brain, bringing with them an immensely restful sense of their finality. This mrng. I think I definitively settled the matter with re-

gard to M.A. I believe by the way I never explicitly assured you of
the greatness of the *Moses*—or of the vileness of that calumnious photograph. It is a work of magnificent beauty—beauty very nearly
equal to that of the statue of Lorenzo d'Medici. I now feel as if I
could judge of M.A.'s merits in tolerably complete *connaisance de cause*.
I have seen the Great Greek things; I have seen Raphael & I have seen
all his own works. He has something—he retains something, after
all experience—which belongs only to himself. This transcendent
"something" invested the *Moses* this morning with a more melting ex-
alting power than I have ever perceived in a work of art. It was a
great sensation—the greatest a work can give. I sat enthralled &
fascinated by that serene *Aristides* at Naples: but I stood agitated this
morng. by all the forces of my soul. The beauty of such a thing as
the *Aristides* is in the effect achieved; that of the *Moses*, the *Lorenzo*, the
figures on the Sistine roof in the absence of a limited effect. The
first take no account of the imagination; the others the largest. They
have a soul. Alack! 'tis poor work talking of them; je tenais seulement to work off something of the tremor in which they have left me,
& to gratify myself by writing down in black & white & if need be
taking my stand on it against the world, the assertion, that M.A. is the
greatest of artists. The question remained solely as between him &
the Greeks; but this morng. settled it. The *Moses* alone perhaps
would n't have done it; but it did it in combination with the vision of
Lorenzo's tomb—which I had it with the deepest distinctness. It's
the triumph of feeling: the Greeks deny it—poor stupid old Michael
proclaims it sovereign o'er a regenerated world:—& affords a magnificent pretext for making a stand against it *en suite*. It's the victo-
rious cause: the other will never be so well plead. It behoves therefore the generous mind to take up the latter. It was worth the
trouble going afterwards, as we did this morning, to San Agostino &
Sta. Maria della Pace to look upon Raphael's two wretchedly decayed
frescoes of Isaiah & the Sybils, in wh. *il a voulu faire du Michel Ange*.
There was in him none but the very smallest Michael Angelesque elements—I fancy that I have found after much fumbling & worrying—
much of the deepest enjoyment & of equal dissatisfaction—the secret
of his incontestable thinness & weakness. He was incapable of energy of statement. This may seem to be but another name for the
fault & not an explication of it. But, *enfin* this energy—positiveness—courage—call it what you will—is a simple fundamental primordial quality in the supremely superior genius. Alone it makes
the real man of action in art & disjoins him effectually from the critic.

I felt this morning irresistibly how that M. Angelo's greatness lay above all in the fact that he *was* this man of action—the greatest almost, considering the temptation he had to be otherwise—considering how his imagination embarrassed & charmed & bewildered him—the greatest perhaps, I say, that the race has produced.   So far from perfection, so finite, so full of errors, so broadly a target for criticism as it sits there, the *Moses* nevertheless by the vigor with which it utters its idea, the eloquence with which it tells the tale of the author's passionate abjuration of the inaction of fancy & contemplation—his willingness to let it stand, in the interest of life & health & movement as his *best* & his only possible,—by this high transcendent spirit it redeems itself from the subjection to its details & appeals most forcibly to the generosity & sympathy of the mind.   Raphael is undecided, slack & unconvinced.—I have seen little else since my return from Naples.   I have been staying on from day to day—partly from the general difficulty there is in leaving Rome, partly for the Xmas doings, & partly because it's a certain comfort to A.K. & Helen Ripley. My departure however is fixed for tomorrow.   You will have heard from A.K. of the steady hideousness of the weather.   It tells sadly upon her party & reduces to a very small amount the utmost that can be done in a day.   I have seen very little of the Xmas ceremonies.   I got my fill so completely at the Council of a crowd & a struggle that I made no attempt to go out on Xmas eve.   On Xmas day I roamed about St. Peter's.   I saw nothing of the Mass or the Pope—but the crowd there is immensely picturesque & well worth seeing.   A.K. & Helen R. (Cousin H. having been laid up for a week with a violent cold)[1] went with their Courier got beautiful places & saw to perfection.   I'm sick unto death of priests & churches.   Their "picturesqueness" ends by making you want to go strongly into political economy or the New England school system.   I conceived at Naples a tenfold deeper loathing than ever of the hideous heritage of the past—& felt for a moment as if I should like to devote my life to laying rail-roads & erecting blocks of stores on the most classic & romantic sites.   The age has a long row to hoe.—Your letter was full of delightful things.   I can't too heartily congratulate you on your plan of visiting.   Vous allez bien voir. You will live to do great things yet.

Assisi. *Tuesday Dec 28ᵗʰ* Since writing the above I have been taking a deep delicious bath of mediaevalism.   I left Rome this morning by the 6.40 a.m. train & under a villainous cloudy sky & came along in a mortally slow train (all the better to see from) thro the great romantic country which leads up to Florence.   Anything *more* romantic—more deeply & darkly dyed with the picturesque & all the happy chiaroscuro of song & story, it would be impossible to conceive.   Perpetual alternations of the landscape of Claude & that of Salvator Rosa—an unending repetition of old steel engravings—raised to the 100ᵗʰ power.   Oh NARNI—oh SPOLETO! who shall describe your unutterable picturesqueness?—what words can shadow forth your happy positions aloft on sinking mountain spurs—girt with your time-fretted crumbling bastions—incrusted with the rich deposit of history?   I've seen such passages of color & composition—such bits—such effects—as can only be reproduced by a moan of joy.   It's *dramatic* landscape.   The towns are all built alike perched on a mountain summit & huddled together within the dark-belted circuit of their walls.   At 2.30 after a long morning of delight (despite occasional grievous showers) I arrived at this famous little spot—famous as the birth-place of St. Francis & the seat of that vast wondrous double church of wh. you perhaps remember the description in Taine.   The town lies away up on the mountain & the church is built sheer upon its side.   I got the one little *carriole* at the station to convey me thither & found to my delight that I had time to see it tolerably well & get a hasty ramble thro' the terrific little city before dark.   I have made a magnificent afternoon of it and I am now scribbling this in the strangers' room of the *Leone d'Oro*, having just risen from an indigestibilissimo little repast.—The church is a vast & curious edifice of a great deal of beauty & even more picturesqueness—a dark cavernous solemn sanctuary below—& above it another, high, aspiring & filled with light—& with various sadly decayed frescoes of Giotto.[2] The position is glorious.   A great aerial portico winds about it & commands a tremendous view.   The whole thing is intensely mediaeval & the vocabulary of Michelet alone could furnish a proper characterization of it.   And if such is the church—what are the strange tortuous hill-scaling little streets of the city?   Never have I seen the local color laid on so thick.   They reek with antiquity.   The whole place is like a little miniature museum of the *genre*—a condensation of the elements of mediaevalism—or the effect it produces at least, a condensation of one's impressions of them.   I am to go on this eveg. by the 8.30 train to Perugia.   The man who brought me up has promised me to return with his vehicle & convey me down the mountain & across the plain to the station.   Meanwhile however, the wind howls wofully, the storm seems to be rousing itself & our transit may perhaps be uncomfortable.   But I am bent on reaching Florence to-morrow night & I wish to see Perugia in the morning.   I am haunted with the apprehension that the host has bribed the little driver *not* to return, so that I may be kept over night.—I have vilely calumniated the establishment: the *padrona*, with the loveliest & most beaming Italian face I have ever seen, has just come in, to herald the approach of the *vetturino*. Buona sera! I shall add a word at Florence.———*Florence.* Jan 1ˢᵗ 1870. A happy new-year! I have been here nearly three days but have been unable until now to get at my letter. I made with success the transit from Assisi to Perugia & now feel as if I had up a store of thrilling little memories wh. will last for many a year & witness many a recurrence of this would-be festive day. I spent at Perugia (which I found decorated with a snow-storm wh. would have done no discredit to the clime of obstructed horse-cars) a morning of unalloyed enjoyment. I put myself for the 1ˢᵗ time in Italy into the hands of a valet-de-place & found him a capital investment. So if there is one spot in Europe I know it's Perugia—Perugia the antique, the high-created—the Etruscan-walled, the nobly-palaced—the deeply darkly densely curious. It's the centre of that fine old Umbrian school of art of which Perugino[3] & he of Urbino[4] were the brightest efflorescence & I saw there a number of noble specimens of the former painter which almost reconciled me to his eternal monotony & insipid sweetness. What a summer could be spent in a long slow journey of long lingering days between Florence & Rome— every town stopped at—every landscape stared at—& lofty grim old Roman *Cortona* not whizzed by in the pitiless train near the Lake of Thrasymene barely glanced at thro a gust of cinders. With these reflections & under these annoyances I arrived in Florence. But the sweetness of Florence restores me to perfect equanimity. I feel once more its delicate charm—I find it the same rounded pearl of cities— cheerful, compact, complete—full of a delicious mixture of beauty & convenience. There is for the moment at least a return of fine weather, but the cold is simply devilish. The streets, the hotels, the churches & galleries all strive to out-freeze each other. I begin to appreciate now the mildness of Rome & Naples. Yesterday, however, the sun was glorious & I got a good warming up in a sweet lone walk all beside the rapid Arno to the uttermost end of the charming Cascine, where, sheltered from the North by a magnificent wall of perpetual verdure & basking full in the long-sealed smile of the South, all happy graceful Florence was watching the old year decline into its death-shroud of yellow & pink. I have spent a long day with the Nortons who are established in a cold capacious Villa not too far from one of the city gates, to their apparent perfect contentment. They made me as welcome as ever & we talked about Rome & Naples. Charles seems sufficiently well & is working in a way it does one good to see so many-burdened a man work, on Italian history and art. The rest are excellent & pleasant, comme toujours.   I took a turn yesterday thro' the Uffizi & the Pitti.   All my old friends there stood forth & greeted me with a splendid good-grace.   The lustrissimo Tiziano in especial gave me a glorious Venetian welcome.[5]   I spent half an hour too in Michael Angelo's chapel at San Lorenzo.   Great Lorenzo sits there none the less, above that weary Giantess who reclines at his feet, gazing at the future with affrighted eyes & revolving the destinies of humanity.   He has not yet guessed his riddle or broken his awful stillness.—Such lines were never conceived in other vision as Michael Angelo has there wrung out of his marble.   For the notion of real grandeur we must knock at that door.———But I am scribbling on without remembering that before I close I must thank you for your further counsel upon what you term so happily my moving intestinal drama.   I wrote you before I went to Naples that I had consulted Dr. Gould, the "popular" American physician at Rome. He recommended me a mineral water, wh. I tried without the least success.   Meanwhile however Dr. Duffy's pills began to resume their action & at Naples (owing I think to the concurrent influence of many oranges) became decidedly efficacious.   They are slacking up once more, but I continue to take them, wear a sort [of] bandage & get along very decently.   Dr. Gould recommended fluid extract of senna, of wh. I procured a supply but have as yet held off from going into it. I'm extremely glad to hear that you tested on yourself the Virtues of the sulfuric acid.   It has evidently an especial application to this matter.   I don't know where Dr. D. got hold of it.   I mean to see him again & will ask him.—Meanwhile I am gravitating northward.   You bid me not hope to escape wholly the bore of Malvern.   I don't in the least.   I'm determined to get rid of this thing before my return home, if not without Malvern, then with it.   I wish to put off my visit there till such a moment as that when I leave, the season will be advanced enough for me to remain in England without disadvantage. I shall try & hold off therefore till the 1ˢᵗ of March.   But you will be hearing from me again before I leave Florence.   I don't know that there's anything more to say upon this solemn theme.—In reading over what I have written it occurs to me that you will reproach me with brevity & paucity of *data* regarding A. Kate.   But there is nothing very startling to communicate.   The three ladies apparently found my presence a useful distraction from the unbroken scrutiny of each other's characters. I think they are a little bit tired of each other & owing partly to the presence of an insane[6] & partly to the absence of a sane, gentleman among them, have not introduced a "foreign element" into their circumstances to the degree they would have liked. A. Kate's energy, buoyancy & activity are magnificent. With a male companion & without a courier (a very stupefying as well as a very convenient appendage) she would have had a better chance to exercise them. Helen R. is very observant & very American (both for better & worse.) She regrets somewhat I fancy, the "good time" which she might have had under different circumstances. Cousin H. seems mild & gentle & patient of her adventures rather than actively interested in them.[7] I did what I could for them all but was very sorry I couldn't do more.—But I must bring this interminable scrawl to a close.—I am perpetually & deliciously preoccupied with home— as little as I can help to the detriment of European emotions—but to a degree wh. condemns me decidedly of being of being less in the intellect than the affections. But my intellect has a hand in it too. When you tell me of the noble working life that certain of our friends are leading in that clear American air, I hanker wofully to wind up these straggling threads of loafing & lounging & drifting & to toss my ball with the rest. But having waited so long I can wait a little longer.—I rejoice in the felicity of M. Temple's visit—& deplore her disappointment with regard to Cal[i]f[orni]a. But I mean to write to her. The *Nation* has ceased to come to me; but I felt a most refreshing blast of *paternity*, the other day in reading father's reply to a "Swedenborgian," in a number I saw at the bankers.[8] But was there ever so cruel a father? He writes to the newspapers but not to his exiled child. I have not yet got his letter to England. I saw Ripley & Mrs R. on my return to Rome. The former sent his love to father: the latter looked very pretty & related an "audience" she had had of the Queen of Wurtemburg, who was living at the same hotel.—But a truce to my gossip. Addio. A torrent of love & longing to my parents & sister.

Your brother   H.

P.S. Since T.S.P. is so hard at work on philology, ask him the Persian for a faithless & perjured friend!————

ALS: MH bMS Am 1094 (1941)

[1] Edel, *HJL*, 1:181, identifies H. as Cousin Henry Wyckoff. But it could be Helen Wyckoff Perkins.

[2] Giotto (c. 1266–c. 1337), Florentine painter and architect.

[3] Perugino (c. 1445–c. 1523), Umbrian painter.

[4] Raphael.

[5] Tiziano Vecellio was known as Titian.

[6] *HJL*, 1:186n notes that 'an insane' is written above the crossed out 'Henry' suggesting that it is a reference to Henry Wyckoff.

[7] Apparently Helen Wyckoff Perkins.

[8] A letter signed "A Swedenborgian" attacked Henry James for his criticisms of the Swedenborgian church (*Nation* 9 [25 November 1869]: 458). Henry James replied in a letter dated 26 November 1869 (9 [2 December 1869]: 482–83). Swedenborgian responded (9 [9 December 1869]: 505) while James ended the controversy with a second letter (9 [16 December 1869]: 534).

To Henry James

[Cambridge] Jany 19. 70

Dear Harry,   Your letter from Naples 21 Dec & Rome 23rd, arrove yesterday mng.   We were all heartily glad to have a tolerably cheerful report of your health, though it did not descend into details.   There was as usual the jaunty promise of a letter to me "in a day or two," which will as usual be kept I suppose in 3 or 4 weeks.   A letter was sent you by [*blank space for name*] three or 4 days ago to Fenzi & Co.   I write now a few words only (being impeded these days by an inflammation of the eyelids, produced in a remarkable way by an overdose of chloral (a new hypnotic remedy) which I took for the fun of it as an experiment, but whose effects are already on the wane).   I write mainly to undo the impression my last letter written about Christmas tide must have made on you.   Those days marked the turning point, and the unaccountable symptoms which have been bothering me for many months began to combine themselves about the new year in a way which gives me the strongest suspicion that they have formed but the transition to a second stage of the complaint.   The pain in the shoulders has abated of late although my exercise has been steadily increasing, and the days certainly are more frequent on which exercise does me more good than harm.   For the past week, to be sure I have been laid up, and without cause, but I have come to regard that as a periodical neccessity.   Had I the somewhat mystical faith of a Hosmer,[1] I suppose I should feel an inward conviction that I was from henceforth to rise; as it is, I only strongly suspect that it *may* be so.   It will need another month or two to make me feel sure; and meanwhile failure will not hurt my feelings as much as if my hopes had been more confident.—What a pity that the weather, which is I suppose the mainspring of Naples's power to charm, failed you when

there.   Your wanderings and sight seeings are beginning to foot up
to quite a respectable sum, and the tolerably simple conception that it
has been possible to frame of your life since you were reft from us, is
fading to a many hued chaos with a gradually widening gulf between
it and the grasping-power of our imagination.   But it doeth my very
gizzard good to think of you being able to lay all those meaty experiences to your soul.   Pourvu seulement que tes sacrés boyaux
s'arrangent!   I have nothing new to tell you of home matters, or of
myself, except the above.   Alice will have told you of our fandango[2]
a week or 10 days ago, which though hardly a success in point of
livelyness, escaped failure.   Father has been writing a couple of articles on "woman" & marriage in the Atlantic.[3]   I can't think he shows
himself to most advantage in this kind of speculation.   I will send you
to Bowle the Jany. no of the Atlantic,[4] with a long and good poem by
Lowell,[5] and also the other no. when it appears.   I won't send any
nations to Paris, as you can see them at the Bankers, and they are so
uninteresting of late.—I enjoyed last week the great pleasure of reading the "House of 7 Gables."[6]   I little expected so *great* a work.   It's
like a great symphony, with no touch alterable without injury to the
harmony.   It made a deep impression on me and I thank heaven that
H. was an American.   It also tickled my national feeling not a little to
note the resemble of H's style to yours & Howell's, even as I had earlier noted the converse.   That you & Howells with all the models in
English literature to follow, should needs involuntarily have imitated
(as it were) this American, seems to point to the existence of some real
American mental quality.   But I must spare my eyes & stop.

Ever your devoted   Wms.

—It's a burning shame that all the while you were in Italy you
should not have been able to write any "notes" for the Nation.   Is it
now too late? and how is your brain power on the whole?   It is rather
discouraging to think of it lagging behind so.

ALS: MH bMS Am 1092.9 (2577)

[1] In *TCWJ*, 1:315, Perry identifies him as Burr Griswold Hosmer, author of *Poems*
(Cambridge, Mass.: Riverside, 1868).

[2] No such letter was found.

[3] Henry James, "'The Woman Thou Gavest Me,'" *Atlantic Monthly* 25 (January
1870): 66–72; "Is Marriage Holy?" *Atlantic Monthly* 25 (March 1869): 360–68; "The
Logic of Marriage and Murder," *Atlantic Monthly* 25 (June 1870): 744–49.

[4] The word seems to be 'Bowle', but no such place was found.

[5] James Russell Lowell, "The Cathedral," *Atlantic Monthly* 25 (January 1870):
1–15.

[6] Nathaniel Hawthorne, *The House of the Seven Gables* (1851).

From Henry James

　　　　　　　　　　　Great Malvern. | Sunday—February 13ᵗʰ '70.
Beloved Brother—I have before me two letters from you—one of
Dec. 27ᵗʰ of that dead & gone old year which will have been so heavily
weighted a one in my mortal career (to say nothing of yours)—the
other of the 19ᵗʰ January in this lusty young '70.　They were both
received in Paris in those all too rich & rapid days that I tarried there
on that memorable—that tragical—pilgrimage from Florence—
from Naples, I may say—across the breadth of Europe, to this actual
British Malvern.　A week ago I wrote to mother from London & on
the following day, Monday last, came up to this place.　Here I am,
then, up to my neck in cold water & the old scenes & sensations of ten
months ago.　It's a horrible afternoon—a piercing blast, a driving
snow storm & my spirits *à l'avenant*.　I have had a cheery British fire
made up in my dingy British bedroom & have thus sate me down to
this ghastly mockery of a fraternal talk.　My heart reverts across the
awful leagues of wintry ocean to that blessed library in Quincy Street
& to the image of the gathering dusk the assembled family, the possible guest, the impending—oh the impending American *tea*!　In
fine, if I wanted I could be as homesick as you please.　All the conditions are present: *rien n'y manque*.　But I'll steep myself in action lest
I perish with despair.　I'll drive the heavy footed pen & brush away
the importunate tear.—Your last letter was a real blessing & a most
indispensable supplement to the previous one.　It contained, in your
statement of your slowly dawning capacity for increased action, just
the news that I had been expecting—that I had counted on as on the
rising of tomorrow's sun.　I have no doubt whatever that you have
really entered upon the "2ᵈ stage."　You'll find it a happier one than
the first.　Perhaps when I get home, six mos. hence (heaven forbid
that at the present moment I should entertain any other hypothesis)
I shall be able gently to usher you into the 3ᵈ & ultimate period of the
malady.　It does me good to think of you no longer leading that
dreary lonely prison-life. Before long I hope to hear of your trying
Dr. Butler.[1]　I can assure you, it will be a great day when, having
lifted, you find you're no worse, & then, having lifted again, you find
you are visibly better.　This experience sets the seal, in the very sanc-
tity of truth, to your still timid & shrinking assumption that you *can*
afford—that you must attempt, to indulge in action: & I almost think
(as I look back hence on those blessed two months that I practised it)
that the trouble is almost worth having for the joy of hugging to your

heart that deep & solid conviction which you wring from those iron weights. Yet, just as I did, possibly, you may find that having brought you to a certain point the lifting will take you no further. What I gained I gained in two mos. But the gain was immense. God speed you! I see you booked indelibly for the ringing grooves of change.[2]—I believe that I haven't written to you since my last days in Rome, & any reflections on my subsequent adventures will have reached you thro' father, mother & Alice. Nevertheless I have had many a fancy & feeling in the course of that extraordinary achievement—the deliberate cold-blooded conscious turning of my back on Italy—the gradual fatal relentless progression from Florence to Malvern—many a keen emotion & many a deep impression which I should have been glad to submit to your genial appreciation. Altogether, it has been a rather serious matter. I mean simply that you feel the interest of Italy with redoubled force when you begin to turn away from it & seek for the rare & beautiful in other lands. Brave old bonny England of ten short months ago—where are you now?—Where are the old thrills of fancy—the old heart-beats, the loving lingering gaze—the charm, the fever, the desire of those innocent days? Oh but I'll find them again. They lie nestling away with the blossoms of the hedges—they sit waiting in the lap of the longer twilights, & they'll burst forth once more in the green explosion of April. This I firmly count upon. Meanwhile I sit shuddering up to my chin in a "running sitz" & think of the olive groves at San Remo—of the view of Florence from San Miniato—of the Nortons at the Villa d'Elsi—of Aunt Kate looking across the Neapolitan bay to Capri. I got a letter from her yesterday. I haven't read it properly—I'm afraid to. I only know that it tells of a drive to Sorrento—of a drive to Baise—of a projected day at Perugia on the way to Florence. When Aunt Kate gets back make much of her! She's not the common clay you parted with. She has trod the perfumed meadows of Elysium—she has tasted of the magic of the South & listened to the echoes of the past!—I was very much disappointed in not being able to write to you at Florence, about which I fancied I had a good deal to say. Perhaps however that this was an illusion & that of definite statements I should not have found many rise to my pen. One definite statement however I do feel warranted in making—viz: that I became interested in the place & attached to it to a degree that makes me feel that it has really entered into my life & is destined to operate there as a motive, a prompter an inspirer of some sort.—By which I suppose I mean nothing more pregnant or sapient than that one of these days I shall be very glad to return there & spend a couple of years. I doubt that I shall ever undertake—shall ever care—to study Italian art—Italian history—for themselves or with a view to discoveries or contributions—or otherwise than as an irradiating focus of light on some other matter. *Ecco!* that I hope is sapient enough for one sitting!—I hope you managed to wring from my torpid pages some living hint of the luminous warmth & glory of my two days at Genoa & the following three days' journey to Nice. These latter were not surpassed by anything in my whole Italian record; for beside their own essential divineness of beauty & purity they borrowed a fine spiritual glow from the needful heroics of the occasion. They're a precious possession of memory, at all events & even Malvern douches can't wash them out. At Nice the charm of that happy journey began to fade: at Marseilles I found it dead in my bosom— dead of cold & inanition. I tried to stop & do a little sight-seeing in the South of France: but between being half paralysed by the *mistral* & half-sickened by the base insufficiency of the spectacle I was glad enough to push rapidly on to Paris.

At a first glance I found Paris strangely hollow & vulgar: but after the lapse of a few days, as soon as I had placed myself on a clean fresh basis I began to enjoy it—to admire it—& lo! before I left, to esteem it. I should be sorry to think that for a little paltry prettiness that confounded Italy had left me with a warped & shrunken mind. Let us be just to all men! (I'm coming to England presently.) From Nice to Boulogne I was deeply struck with the magnificent order & method & decency & prosperity of France—of the felicity of *manner* in all things—the completeness of form. There was a certain *table d'hôte* breakfast at Dijon where the whole cargo of the express train piled out & fed leisurely, comfortably, to perfection, *qui en disait* on the subject more than I can repeat. And the excellence of the little hotel de l'Amirauté where I spent a week—& the universal merit & sagacity of the cookery—& above all the splendors of arrangement— quite apart from the splendors of material—in the Louvre! The latter by the way are wondrous—a glorious synthesis of Italy. Altogether, as I say, I enjoyed Paris deeply. Beautiful weather came to my aid. A fortnight ago this afternoon—amazing thought!—I climbed the towers of Nôtre Dame. She is really great. Great too is the Théatre Français where I saw Molière & Emile Augier most rarely played. En voilà, de l'Art! We talk about it & write about it & criticize & dogmatize & analyse to the end of time: but those brave players stand forth & exemplify it & *act*—create—produce!

It's a most quickening & health giving spectacle!—with a strange expression of simplicity & breadth & dignity which I wouldn't have gone there to find.   I also went to the Palais Royal to see a famous four act Farce of the latest fashion: but I confess seeing Got as Sganarelle had spoiled me for it.[3]   Molière is every inch as droll & so much more beside!   I saw little else.   I needn't tell you how one feels & leaving Paris half-seen, half-felt. You have only to remember how you left it a year & ½ ago.   I have now been some ten days in England. In one of your last letters you very wisely assure me that England like every other place would seem very flat on a second visit.   For this contingency I made the most ample & providential preparation & in this way I have eluded serious disappointments.   But on the whole I don't much pretend or expect now, at best, to be ravished & charmed. I've been to my rope's length & had my great sensations.   In spite of decidedly unpropitious circumstances I find I like England still & I expect her (if I get better) to yield me many an hour of profit and many a visible delight.   I have come upon very fierce hard weather & of course I feel it keenly for this plunge into cold water.   We have had a week of grim winter that would do honor to Boston.   I find this house all that I remembered it—most comfortable—most admirably & irreproachably conducted.   There are some eighteen persons here at present—from whom however (without misanthropy) I expect little & gain less—such a group of worthy second rate Britons as invests with new meaning & illuminates with a supernatural glow— the term common-place.   But as if we Americans were any better!   I can't affirm it to my knowledge!   I find in Malvern itself even at this dark season all the promise of that beauty which delighted me last spring.   The winter indeed here strips the landscape far less than with us or in the South.   Literally (save for the orange trees) the country hereabouts looks less naked & out of season than that about Naples.   The fields are all vivid with their rain-deepened green—the hedges all dark & dense & damp with immediate possibilities of verdure—the trees so multitudinously twigged that as they rise against the watery sky a field's length away, you can fancy them touched with early leafage.   And ah! that watery sky—greatest of England's glories!—so high & vast & various, so many lighted & many-shadowed, so full of poetry & motion & of a strange affinity with the swarming detail of scenery beneath.   Indeed what I have most enjoyed in England since my return—what has most struck me—is the light—or rather, if you please, the darkness: that of Du Maurier's drawings. Elsewhere 'tis but a garish world.   If I can only get started to feeling better (of wh. I have good hopes) I shall get my fill of old England yet.   I have had a long walk every day of the past week.   The *detail* of the scenery is the great point.   Beside it even Italy is vague & general.   I walked this morning six miles—half of them in the teeth of the snow sharpened blast—down this Newlands to Maddersfield Court—a most delightful old moated manor-house, the seat of Earl Beauchamp.[4]   In spite of the snow it was still gentle England.   English mutton was grazing in the lee of the hedges & English smoke rolling from the chimneys in low-latticed, steep-thatched cottages.   *À propos* of mutton I wish I could enclose herewith one of those unutterable joints which daily figure on our board.   You don't *eat* it—you devoutly ecstatically appropriate it: you put a bit into your mouth & for the moment *il n'y a que ça*.   It beats the beef.   The beef varies—it has degrees, but the mutton is absolute, infallible, impeccable.   With plenty of mutton & a good many walks & a few books I hope to thrive & prosper.   I am able both to walk & read much more than when I was here before & I am quite amused at having then objected to the place on the ground of its giving you so much up-hill.   I shall probably do no very serious reading, but I hope at least to win back the habit.   I rec'd. your *Atlantic* with Lowell's poem,[5] which I enjoyed largely, tho' it seems to me lacking in the real poetic element thro' excess of cleverness—the old story.   I enjoyed unmitigatedly Howells' little paper.[6]   I have enjoyed all his things more even since being abroad than at home.   They are really American.   I'm glad you've been liking Hawthorne.   But I mean to write as good a novel one of these days (perhaps) as the H. of the 7 G.s.   *Monday 14ᵗʰ*.   With the above thrilling prophecy I last night laid down my pen.   I see nothing left but to close my letter.   When I began I had a vague intention of treating you to a grand summing up on the subject of Italy.   But it won't be summed up, happily for you.   I'm much obliged to you for your regret that I didn't achieve any notes for the *Nation*.   I have a vague dream, if I get started towards a cure, of attempting a few retrospective ones here.   Oh, no words can tell of the delicious romantic look it now suits my Italian journey to put on!—I have my heart constantly burdened with messages to all my friends at home which I never manage to discharge.   Keep me in the memories of my brothers.   Give my love to T.S.P. to whom I have the best will to write.   I wrote lately to A.G.S.[7]   Tell me anything that comes up about J.L.F. & O.W.H.   I am in daily hope of a letter from Howells.   A. Kate mentions that Mrs. Post has asked Minny to go abroad with her.[8]   Is it even so?   But I must be getting up a "pre-action" for that d——d running sitz. I calculate while here to walk from 8 to 10—or from 10 to 12 miles daily. Farewell. Think of me as most comfortable hopeful & happy. I *may* not write for a fortnight, until I have some results to announce. But I'll not promise silence. Farewell. Love to all—

Yours most fraternally | H James jr.

P.S. An Anecdote. You spoke recently of having read with pleasure Lecky's *Hist. of Morals*. I found at Florence that for a fortnight at Rome I had been sitting at breakfast opposite or next to the elegant author. We never spoke. He is very young & lanky & blond & soft-looking—but most pleasant of face: with quite the look of a better-class Cambridge Divinity student. I have been sorry ever since that I never addressed him: but he always came in to his breakfast about as I was finishing.—*À propos*—one of these days I'll tell you my little tale of "The Little Frenchman of Padua"—just such a one as F. J. Child likes to tell.

ALS: MH bMS Am 1094 (1942)

[1] There are several possible Dr. Butlers: John Simkins Butler (1803–1890), American physician, author of a book on the treatment of insanity, in 1864 treated WJ's cousin Katharine Prince at the Retreat, Hartford, Conn.; John Butler (1844–1885), homeopathic physician in New York, wrote on the uses of electricity in medicine; Samuel Wiswell Butler (1816–1881), practiced in Newport.

[2] Alfred, Lord Tennyson, *Locksley Hall* (1842), line 182.

[3] François-Jules-Edmond Got (1822–1901), French actor. Sganarelle is a farcical character in Molière's *Dom Juan*.

[4] Frederick Lygon (1830–1891), 6th Earl Beauchamp, at Madresfield Court, Worcestershire.

[5] See letter of 19 January 1870.

[6] William Dean Howells, "By Horse-Car to Boston," *Atlantic Monthly* 25 (January 1870): 114–22.

[7] Arthur George Sedgwick.

[8] Mary Ann King Post (1819–1892), daughter of Ellen James King, WJ's father's sister.

From Henry James

Great Malvern—| March 8th '70.

Beloved Bill—

You ask me in your last letter so "cordially" to write home every week, if its only a line, that altho' I have very little to say on this windy sunny March afternoon, I can't resist the homeward tendency of my thoughts. I wrote to Alice some eight days ago—raving largely about the beauty of Malvern, in the absence of a better theme: so I haven't even that topic to make talk of.   But as I say, my thoughts are facing squarely homeward & that is enough.   The fact that I have been here a month to day, I am sorry to say, doesn't even furnish me with a bundle of important tidings.   My stay as yet is attended with very slight results—powerful testimony to the obstinacy of my case. Nevertheless I have most unmistakeably made a beginning—or at least the beginning of one—& in this matter it is chiefly a premier pas qui coût.   On the whole I'm not disappointed, when I think from what a distance I have to return.   It is unfortunate here that the monotony & gross plainness of the diet (mutton potatoes & bread being its chief elements) are rather calculated in this particular trouble, to combat the effect of the baths.   Ye powers immortal! how I do find myself longing for a great succulent swash of American vegetables— for tomatoes & apples & Indian meal!   The narrowness of English diet is something absolutely ludicrous.   Breakfast cold mutton (or chop) toast & tea: dinner leg or shoulder, potatoes & rice pudding: tea cold mutton again (or chop) toast & tea.   I sometimes think that I shall never get well until I get a chance for a year at a pure vegetable diet—at unlimited tomatoes & beans & pease & squash & turnips & carrots & corn—I enjoy merely writing the words.   I have a deep delicious dream of some day uniting such a regimen with a daily ride on horseback—walking having proved inefficient.   So you see I have something ahead of me to live for.   But I have something better too than these vain impalpable dreams—the firm resolve to recover on my present basis—to fight it out on this line if it takes all summer— &c!   It would be too absurd not to!   A fortnight hence I count upon being able to give you some definite good news—to which period let us relegate the further discussion of the topic.   It constantly becomes more patent to me that the better I get of this—the more I shall be able to read—up to a certain point.   During the past month I have been tasting lightly of this pleasure—reading among other things Browning's Ring & Book, in honor of Italy, the President de Brosses's delightful letters,[1] Crabbe Robinsons Memoirs[2] & the new vol. of Ste Beuve.[3] Browning decidedly gains in interest tho' he loses in a certain mystery & (so to speak) infinitude, after a visit to Italy.   C. Robinson is disappointing I think—from the thinness of his individuality, the superficial character of his perceptions & his lack of descriptive power.   One of your letters contained something to make me think you have been reading him.   I have quite given up the idea of making a few retrospective sketches of Italy.   To begin with I shall not be

well enough (I foresee) while here; & in the second place I had far
rather let Italy slumber in my mind untouched as a perpetual capital,
whereof for my literary needs I shall draw simply the income—let it
lie warm & nutritive at the base of my mind, manuring & enriching
its roots.   I remember by the way that you recently expressed the
confident belief that I had made a series of notes for my own use.   I
am sorry to say that I did nothing of the sort.   Mere bald indications
(in this I was very wrong) seemed to me useless, & for copious mem-
oranda I was always too tired.   I expect however to find that I have
appropriated a good deal from mere "soaking": i.e. often when I
might have been scribbling in my room I was still sauntering & re-
sauntering & looking & "assimilating."—But now that I'm in England
you'd rather have me talk of the present than of pluperfect Italy.
But life furnishes so few incidents here that I cudgel my brains in
vain.   Plenty of gentle emotions from the scenery &c: but only man
is vile.   Among my fellow-patients here I find no intellectual companionship.   Never from a single Englishman of them all have I
heard the 1ˢᵗ word of appreciation or enjoyment of the things here
that I find delightful.   To a certain extent this is natural: but not to
the extent to wh. they carry it.   As for the women I give 'em up, in
advance.   I am tired of their plainness & stiffness & tastelessness—
their dowdy beads, their dirty collars & their linsey woolsey trains.
Nay, this is peevish & brutal.   Personally (with all their faults) they
are well enough.   I revolt from their dreary deathly want of—what
shall I call it?—Clover Hooper has it—intellectual grace[4]—Minny
Temple has it—moral spontaneity.[5]   They live wholly in the realm of
the cut & dried. "Have you ever been to Florence?"   "Oh yes."   "Isn't
it a most peculiarly interesting city?"   "Oh yes, I think its so very
nice."   "Have you read *Romola*?"[6]   "Oh yes."   "I suppose you admire
it."   "Oh yes I think it's so very clever."   The English have such a
mortal mistrust of anything like "criticism["] or "keen analysis" (wh.
they seem to regard as a kind of maudlin foreign flummery) that I
rarely remember to have heard on English lips any other intellectual
verdict (no matter under what provocation) than this broad synthesis—"So immensely clever."   What exasperates you is not that they
can't say more, but that they wouldn't if they could.   Ah, but they are
a great people, for all that.   Nevertheless I shd. vastly enjoy half an
hour's talk with an "intelligent American."   I find myself reflecting
with peculiar complacency on American women.   When I think of
their frequent beauty & grace & elegance & alertness, their cleverness
& self-assistance (if it be simply in the matter of toilet) & compare

them with English girls, living up to their necks among comforts &
influences & advantages wh. have no place with us, my bosom swells
with affection & pride.   Look at my lovely friend Mrs. Winslow.   To
find in England such beauty, such delicacy, such exquisite taste, such
graceful ease & laxity & freedom, you would have to look among the
duchesses—*et encore!*, judging from their photos. in the shop windows.   Not that Mrs. Winslow hasn't her little vulgarities, but taking
one thing with another they are so far more innocent than those of
common English women.   But it's a graceless task, abusing women of
any clime or country.   I can't help it tho', if American women have
something which gives them a lift!—Since my return here there is
one thing that I have often wished for strongly—*i.e.* that poor Jno.
La Farge were with me sharing my enjoyment of this English scenery—enjoying it that is, on his own hook, with an intensity beside
wh. I suppose, mine would be feeble indeed.   I never catch one of
the perpetual magical little "effects" of my walks without adverting to
him.   I feel sorry at moments that a couple of months ago I didn't
write to him proposing a rendezvous at Malvern, March 1ˢᵗ, where he
could stay & be doctored too, & whence we might subsequently roam
deliciously forth in search of the picturesque.   If I were at all sure of
my condition a couple of mos. hence & of the manner I shall spend
the spring & summer I would write to him & ask him if it is at all in
his power to take a three or four mos. holiday.   We might spend it
together & return together in the Autumn.   I feel sure that as a
painter he would enjoy England most intensely.   You may be a little
surprised at my thus embracing for a whole summer the prospect of
his undivided society.   But for one thing I feel as if I could endure
his peculiarities much better now than formerly; & then I feel too as
if in any further travelling I may do here—I should find it a great
gain to have a really good companion: & for observations what better
companion than he?   The lack of such a companion was in Italy a
serious loss.   I shall not write to him (if at all) with any such idea until
I see myself fairly on the way to be better; but meanwhile, you, if you
see him, might make some tentative inquiry & transmit me the result.
I have no doubt that he would vastly like the scheme; but little hope
of his finding it practicable.—Of Wendell Holmes I get very much
less news than I should like to have.   I heard recently from Arthur
Sedgwick who mentioned his being appointed at H.C. instructor in
Constitutional Law.   This has a very big sound; but I never doubted
of his having big destinies.—Do speak of him in your next.   Nor of
Gray do I hear anything.   Do you often see him & how does he wear?

I am very nervous about a letter from Howells which Mother some months ago mentioned his being on the point of sending. It hasn't yet turned up & I am utterly sickened at the idea of its being lost. Do ascertain from him whether it was ever sent. His letters are really things of value & I should find it a great feast to get one. Heaven speed it & guard it!—I rec'd. a few days since thro' father a letter from Bob: very pleasant but with a strangely quaint & formal tone about it. But I was very glad to hear from him. It fills me with wonder & sadness that he should be off in that Western desolation[7] while I am revelling in England & Italy. I should like extremely to get a line out of Wilky: but fate seems adverse. I very much wish by the way, that some one would let me know *who & what* is W̲m̲ Robeson, his partner. I simply know that he is not Andrew R.[8] À propos of the family property, you've bought the house—an event I don't quarrel with. Since I began my letter the afternoon has waned into dusk & by my firelight & candles Cambridge looks like the sweetest place on earth. And it's a good old house too & I'm not ashamed of it. This reminds me of what you said in yr. last about getting photos. & books. I some time since sent home a statement of my complete non-purchase of the former save 4 very handsome statues I got for Alice in Rome which A.K. will bring her (viz. the great Augustus, the boy Augustus, the Demosthenes & the so called "Genius of the Vatican" (Praxiteles.)) As soon as I arrived in Italy I saw that I must either buy more than I believed I had means for or leave them quite alone. The mere going into the shops to buy an occasional one would have been fatal: besides you can't carry a few; if you get many, you provide a particular receptacle. Oh then! the delicious things I left unbought! If I return to the Continent I will do what I can to repair discreetly my abstinence. I very much regret now that I didn't immediately demand of father & mother a commission of purchase. But I seem condemned to do things in a small way. I am sure that as notes for future reference photos. are unapproached & indispensable.—As for books you rather amuse me by your assumption that in Italy I went in for a certain number of *vellum bindings*. Not for one. To get books seemed to me at that stage of my adventures to needlessly multiply my cares: & I felt like waiting till I had read a few of the vast accumulation on my hands before swelling the number. I shall probably pick up a few before going home; I fancy not many. If you want any particular ones you'll of course let me know. A very good way to get books in England—modern ones—is to buy them off Mudie's Surplus Catalogue—frequently great bargains.[9]—But I must put an end to my stupid letter.   I have been shut up all day & the greater part of yesterday with a bad sore-throat & feel rather muddled & stultified.   In a couple of days or so I hope again to be hearing from home.   I look very soon for a letter from you correcting that last account of your relapse.   I re-echo with all my heart your impatience for the moment of our meeting again.   I should despair of ever making you know how your conversation m'a manqué or how when regained, I shall enjoy it.   All I ask for is that I may spend the interval to the best advantage—& you too.   The more we shall have to say to each other the better. Your last letter spoke of father & mother having "shocking colds."   I hope they have melted away. Among the things I have recently read is father's *Marriage* paper in the *Atlantic*—with great enjoyment of its manner & approval of its matter.   I see he is becoming one of our prominent magazinists.   He will send me the thing from *Old & New*.[10]   A young scotchman here gets the *Nation*, sent him by his brother from N.Y.   Whose are the three female papers on Woman?   They are "so very clever."[11]   À propos—I retract all those brutalities about the Engländerinnen. They are the mellow mothers & daughters of a mighty race.—I expect daily a letter from A.K. announcing her arrival in Paris.   She has been having the inappreciable sorrow of a rainy fortnight in Florence.   I hope very much to hear, tho', that she has had a journey along the Riviera divinely fair enough to make up for it.   But I *must* pull in.   I have still lots of unsatisfied curiosity & unexpressed affection, but they must stand over.   I never hear anything about the Tweedies.   Give them my love when you see them.   T.S.P. I suppose grows in wisdom & virtue.   Tell him I would give a great deal for a humorous line from him.   Farewell.   Salute my parents & sister & believe me your brother of brothers

H. James jr.

P.S.   Tuesday, 9th.[12]   Don't be discouraged by what I said above of the slowness of my progress here.   I have made an impression & I mean to deepen it.—

ALS: MH bMS Am 1094 (1943)

[1] Charles de Brosses, *Lettres familières écrites d'Italie en 1739 et 1740*.
[2] See letter of 1 November 1869.
[3] Several different works appeared at about this time.
[4] Marian (Clover) Hooper, married Henry Adams on 27 June 1872.
[5] Mary Temple died on 8 March 1870.
[6] George Eliot, *Romola* (1863).
[7] RJ moved to Milwaukee in September 1868.
[8] Not identified.

[9]Charles Edward Mudie (1818–1890), British bookseller, founder of Mudie's Lending Library.

[10]*Old and New* appeared in 1870–75, edited by Edward Everett Hale. Nothing by Henry James in this publication is known.

[11]Lulu Gray Noble, "Notes on the Woman's Rights Agitation," *Nation* 10 (20 January 1870): 38–39; 10 (10 February 1870): 88–89; 10 (17 February 1870): 101–4.

[12]9 March was a Wednesday.

From Henry James

Malvern March 29th [1870]

Dear Willy—

My mind is so full of poor Minny's death that altho' I immediately wrote in answer to mother's letter, I find it easier to take up my pen again than to leave it alone.   A few short hours have amply sufficed to more than reconcile me to the event & to make it seem the most natural—the happiest, fact, almost in her whole career.   So it seems, at least, on reflection: to the eye of feeling there is something immensely moving in the sudden & complete extinction of a vitality so exquisite & so apparently infinite as Minny's.   But what most occupies me, as it will have done all of you at home, is the thought of how her whole life seemed to tend & hasten, visibly, audibly, sensibly, to this consummation.   Her character may be almost literally said to have been without practical application to life.   She seems a sort of experiment of nature—an attempt, a specimen or example—a mere subject without an object.   She was at any rate the helpless victim & toy of her own intelligence—so that there is positive relief in thinking of her being removed from her own heroic treatment & placed in kinder hands.   What a vast amount of truth appears now in all the common-places that she used to provoke—that she was restless—that she was helpless—that she was unpractical.   How far she may have been considered up to the time of her illness to have achieved a tolerable happiness, I don't know: hardly at all, I should say, for her happiness like her unhappiness remained wholly incomplete: but what strikes me above all is how great & rare a benefit her life has been to those with whom she was associated.   I feel as if a very fair portion of my sense of the reach & quality & capacity of human nature rested upon my experience of her character: certainly a large portion of my admiration of it. She was a case of pure generosity— she had more even than she ever had use for—inasmuch as she could hardly have suffered at the hands of others nearly as keenly as she

did at her own.   Upon her limitations, now, it seems idle to dwell; the
list of her virtues is so much longer than her life.   My own personal
relations with her were always of the happiest.   Every one was supposed I believe to be more or less in love with her: others may answer
for themselves: I never was, & yet I had the great satisfaction that I
enjoyed *pleasing* her almost as much as if I had been.   I cared more
to please her perhaps than she ever cared to be pleased.   Looking
back upon the past half-dozen years, it seems as if she *represented*, in a
manner, in my life several of the elements or phases of life at large—
her own sex, to begin with, but even more *Youth*, with which ow⟨in⟩g
to my invalidism, I always fel⟨t⟩ in rather indirect relation.   Poor
Minny—what a cold thankless part it seems for her to have played—
an actor & setter-forth of things in which she had so little permanent
interest!   Among the sad reflections that her death provokes, for me,
there is none sadder than this view of the gradual change & reversal
of our relations: I slowly crawling from weakness & inaction & suffering into strength & health & hope: she sinking out of brightness &
youth into decline & death.   It's almost as if she had passed away—as
far as I am concerned,—from having served her purpose—that of
standing well within the world, inviting & inviting me onward by all
the bright intensity of her example.   She never knew how sick & dis-
ordered a creature I was & I always felt that she knew me at my worst.
I always looked forward with a certain eagerness to the day when I
should have regained my natural lead, and our friendship on my
part, at least might become more active & masculine.   This I have
especially felt during the powerful experience of the past year.   In a
measure I had worked away from the old ground of my relations with
her, without having quite taken possession of the new: but I had it
constantly in my eyes.   But here I am, plucking all the sweetest fruits
of this Europe which was a dream among her many dreams—while
she has "gone abroad" in another sense!   Every thought of her is a
singular mixture of pleasure and pain.   The thought of what either
she has lost or we, comes to one as if only to enforce the idea of *her*
gain in eternal freedom & rest & our's in the sense of it.   Freedom &
rest! one must have known poor Minny to feel their value—to know
what they may contain—if one can measure, that is, the balm by the
ache.—I have been hearing all my life of the sense of loss wh. death
leaves behind it:—now for the first time I have a chance to learn what
it amounts to.   The whole past—all times & places—seems full of
her.   Newport especially—to my mind—she seems the very genius
of the place.   I could shed tears of joy far more copious than any

tears of sorrow when I think of her feverish earthly lot exchanged for this serene promotion into pure fellowship with our memories, thoughts and fancies.   I had imagined many a happy talk with her in years to come—many a cunning device for cheering & consoling her illness, & many a feast on the ripened fruits of our friendship: but this on the whole surpasses anything I had conceived.   You will all have felt by this time the novel delight of thinking of Minny without the lurking impulse of fond regret & uneasy conjecture so familiar to the minds of her friends.   She has gone where there is neither marrying nor giving in marriage! no illusions & no disillusions—no sleepless nights & no ebbing strength.   The more I think of her the more perfectly satisfied I am to have her translated from this changing realm of fact to the steady realm of thought.   There she may bloom into a beauty more radiant than our dull eyes will avail to contemplate.—My first feeling was an immense regret that I had been separated from her last days by so great a distance of time & space; but this has been of brief duration.   I'm really not sorry not to have seen her materially changed & thoroughly thankful to have been spared the sight of her suffering.   Of this you must all have had a keen realization.   There is nevertheless something so appealing in the pathos of her final weakness and decline that my heart keeps returning again & again to the scene, regardless of its pain.   When I went to bid Minny farewell at Pelham before I sailed I asked her about her sleep. "Sleep," she said: "Oh, I don't sleep. *I've given it up.*"   And I well remember the laugh with which she made this sad attempt at humor. And so she went on, sleeping less & less, waking wider & wider, until she awaked absolutely!   I asked mother to tell me what she could about her last weeks & to repeat me any of her talk or any chance incidents, no matter how trivial.   This is a request easier to make than to comply with, & really to talk about Minny we must wait till we meet.   But I *should* like one of her last photos., if you can get one. You will have felt for yourself I suppose how little is the utmost one can *do*, in a positive sense, as regards her memory.   Her presence was so much, so intent—so strenuous—so full of human exaction: her absence is so modest, content with so little.   A little decent passionless grief—a little rummage in our little store of wisdom—a sigh of relief—and we begin to live for ourselves again.   If we can imagine the departed spirit cognizant of our action in the matter, we may suppose it much better pleased by our perfect acceptance of the void it has left than by our quarreling with it and wishing it filled up again.   What once was life is always life, in one form or another, & speaking simply of this world I feel as if in effect and influence Minny had lost very little by her change of state.   She lives as a steady unfaltering luminary in the mind rather than as a flickering wasting earth-stifled lamp.   Among all my thoughts & conceptions I am sure I shall never have one of greater sereneness & purity: her image will preside in my intellect, in fact, as a sort of measure and standard of brightness and repose.   But I have scribbled enough.   While I sit spinning my sentences she is *dead*: and I suppose it is partly to defend myself from too direct a sense of her death that I indulge in this fruitless attempt to transmute it from a hard fact into a soft idea.   Time of course will bring almost even-handedly the inevitable pain & the inexorable cure.   I am willing to leave life to answer for life: but meanwhile, thinking how small at greatest, is our change as compared with her change & how vast an apathy goes to our little murmur of sympathy, I take a certain satisfaction in having simply written twelve pages.—I have been reading over the three or four letters I have got from her since I have been abroad: they are full of herself—or at least of a fraction of herself: they would say little to strangers.   Poor living Minny!   No letters would hold you.   It's the *living* ones that die; the writing ones that survive.—One thought there is that moves me much—that I should be here delving into this alien England in which it was one of her fancies that she had a kind of property.   It was not, I think one of the happiest.   Every time that I have been out during the last three days, the aspect of things has perpetually seemed to enforce her image by simple contrast & difference.   The landscape assents stolidly enough to her death: it would have ministered but scantily to her life.   She was a breathing protest against English grossness, English compromises & conventions—a plant of pure American growth.   None the less, tho', I had a dream of telling her of England & of her immensely enjoying my stories.   But it's only a half change: instead of my discoursing to her I shall have her forever talking to me.   Amen, Amen to all she may say!   Farewell to all that she was!   How much this was, & how sweet it was!   How it comes back to one, the charm & essential grace of her early years.   We shall all have known something!   How it teaches, absolutely, tenderness & wonder to the mind.—But it's all locked away, incorruptibly, within the crystal walls of the past.   And there is my youth—& anything of yours you please & welcome!—turning to gold in her bright keeping. In exchange, for you, dearest Minny we'll all keep your future. Don't fancy that your task is done. Twenty years hence we shall be loving with your love & longing with your eagerness—suffering with your patience.

30ᵗʰ p.m.   So much I wrote last evening; but it has left me little to add, incomplete as it is.   In fact it is too soon to talk of Minny's death or to pretend to feel it.   This I shall not do till I get home.   Every now & then the thought of it stops me short but it's from the life of home that I shall really miss her.   With this European world of associations & art & studies, she has nothing to do: she belongs to the deep domestic moral affectional realm.   I can't put away the thought that just as I am beginning life she has ended it.   But her very death is an answer to all the regrets it provokes.   You remember how largely she dealt in the future—how she considered & planned & arranged.   Now it's to haunt & trouble her no longer—she has her present & future in one.—To you I suppose her death must have been an unmitigated relief—you must have suffered keenly from the knowledge of her suffer⟨ings.⟩ Thank heaven they lasted n⟨o⟩ longer.   When I first hear⟨d of⟩ her death I could think ⟨only⟩ of them: now I can't think of them even when I try.———I have not heard from you for a long time: I am impatiently expecting a letter from you.   With this long effusion you will all have been getting of late an ample share *de mes nouvelles.*   From Alice too I daily expect to hear.   Yesterday came to me a very welcome & pleasantly turned note from Mr. Boott.—I hope I haven't hitherto expressed myself in a way to leave room for excursive disappointment when I say that after now nearly 8 weeks of this place, I have made materially less progress than I hoped.   I shall be here about ten days longer.   In town, I shall immediately go ⟨to s⟩ee a couple of as good & *special* ⟨physi⟩cians as I can hear of.   Unhappily ⟨my sou⟩rces of knowledge are few. [*end of letter missing*]

AL incomplete: MH bMS Am 1094 (1944)

To Henry James

Cambr. May 7. 70

Dear Harry,   T'is Saturday eveᵍ 10 minutes past 6 of the clock and a cold & rainy day (Indian winter as T.S.P. calls such)   I had a fire lighted in my grate this afternoon.   There is nevertheless a broken blue spot in the Eastern clouds as I look out, and the grass and buds have started visibly since the morning.   The trees are about ½ way out—(you of course have long had them in full leaf)—and the early green is like a bath to the eye.   Father is gone to Newport for a day & is expected back within the hour.   My jaw is aching badly in consequence of a tooth I had out 2 days ago the which refused to be pulled, was broken but finally extracted, and has left its neighbors prone to ache since.   I hope it won't last much longer.   I spent the morning— part of it at least—in fishing the revues germaniques up fm. cellar, looking over their contents, and placing them volume wise, and flat, in the two top shelves of the big library bookcase, *vice* Thies's good old books, just removed; the shelves being too low to take any of our books upright.   I feel melancholy as a whip-poor-will and took up pen and paper to sigh melodiously to you.   But sighs are hard to express in words.   We have been three weeks now without hearing from you, and if a letter don't come to morrow or Monday, I dont know what will become of us.   Howells' bro't a week ago a long letter you had written to him on the eve of leaving Malvern so our next will be from London and I hope will contain a word to me of definite news about your health & plans.   It's a mean business this constipa- tion of yours.   In fact I dont feel as if I knew anything about your health at all, not from any reticence of yours, but from the want of my own eyes' testimony.   That you should not yet be able to work shows you still to be pretty badly off, in spite of your activity.   And apropos of that, haven't you perhaps overdone walking &c?   You speak to howells' of nightly exhaustion—and your habit is you know to know no bounds in anything of that sort wh. you undertake.   If you go to switzerland this summer I conjure you to bear that possibil- ity in mind, you may *drain* all strength from yourselfe.   Certainly for the bowels after 6 miles a day, I should suppose nothing would tell. And probably any amount of walking which led to general physical exhaustion & fatigue wd. tend rather to paralyse than to stimulate them.   Sedentary life is bad, but it does not follow that the *more* ex- ercise the better, absolutely, any more than if an ounce of salts are a purge, a pound is a better one.   Mother wrote advising your return in September.   I am impatient to hear your answer.   Of course if you should be able to stay and work there, one wd. gladly think of your staying; but if not, my sympathies too will be with your return.   My! how I long to see you and feel of you & talk things over.—I have I think at last begun to rise out of the slough of the past 3 months, and I mean to try not to fall back again.   I think I at last see a certain order in the state I'm in.   I'm better now than at the same date last year, and I don't despair consequently of getting even more good out of this summer than I did out of that. The difficulty will be to regulate my exercise, but I'll bend all my energies to it. I intend to be almost absolutely idle—no easy work as you know. In a fortnight I hope to go to the lifting cure. What a blessing this change of seasons is, as you used to say especially the spring. The winter is man's enemy he must exert himself against it to live, or it will squeeze him in one night out of existence. So it is hateful to a sick man—and all the greater is the peace of the latter when it yields to a time when nature seems to cooperate with life & float one passively on. But I hear father arriving & must go down to hear his usual compte rendu

(Sunday 3. P.M) No letter fm you this mng but one fm. A.K. just after her arrival in London speaking of a violent pain in your back and a reference of it to your kidneys by Dr Reynolds,[1] moving a load off your mind. What new horror is this? and is the catalogue to be absolutely endless? She speaks of a letter you wrote me "a fortnight ago." The last letter we have got fm. you was one to me about M.T., but written 3½ weeks before aunt Kate's, so a subsequent one may have been lost. I am more than ever anxious to see Aunt Kate and hear some full account of your condition. Perhaps the kidney trouble, whatever it is, may be a winding up crisis, one likes until forced not to, to indulge in such poetical interpretations.—It seems to me that all a man has to depend on in this world, is in the last resort, mere brute power of resistance. I can't bring myself as so many men seem able to, to blink the evil out of sight, and gloss it over. It's as real as the good, and if it is denied, good must be denied too. It must be accepted and hated and resisted while there's breath in our bodies I will write no more now. There's no news to tell you that I think of except poor Salter's death on board the steamer going to Europe, fm. heart disease.[2] It was wholly unexpected. He was a manly fellow. I hope to God this new trouble of yours wont amount to anything. You don't know what a good inspiration it was for you to write those letters about Minny to me—I can say—they were a solid gift—

Yours affty Wm. James.

Monday morn. Your letter of Apl. 24th lay on my plate this mng. The letter fm. Oxford you speak of in it has never come—a providential occurrence as it must needs have given us great anxiety. Probably it was in the Siberia which put back. It seems queer you should be so out of order after your weeks of Water Cure, but it may be a crisis bro't on by the Water Cure.   Low spirits is a concomitant of oxaluria—so remember that, if you feel too blue, and pick up heart. Wilkinsons advice about Karlsbad is doubtless good; but I'd rather have the advice of some German D.r—unless indeed W. have specially studied the subject of bath places in Germany.   Each of them fills some special indications, and to prescribe the right one is quite a German specialty. However Karlsbad is perhaps the most *potent* of all in abdominal disorders—and is a delightful abode, they say.—But it is quite a long journey to get there.   If I were in your place I would consult some good physician in one of the nearest large German towns—perhaps you can hear of such a one in London—as to the best waters for my case.   Very likely he too will say Karlsbad; but its best to make sure.   I believe 30 days is the term of sojourn there.   I shall be glad to think of your having enjoyed a spell of German watering place life 'ere your return.   I cant help thinking you'll find it delightful.

And I hope to God it will do you good.   You've had by this time your fair share of earth's misery.   As to your coming home—there is one advantage about bremen besides the cheapness, namely that the stoppage at southampton gives the stomach time to recover itself and start afresh wh. must be, judging by my St. Thomas experience, a considerable advantage.   We are all counting the hours until Aunt Kate's arrival.   I hope her passage will have been an easy one.   The last 4 days here have been drearily cold and rainy, but with little wind. If you go to Karlsbad, you will be near Teplitz.   You may feel like going there for a day for my sake.   If so go to the "Stadt London" hotel, and try to get a bath in the Fürstenbad in remembrance of me, and take the drive to Doppelburg.   In passing through Dresden, Frau Spangenberg's new address is "Walpurgis Strasse 8, parterre." We have just decided to go to pomfret again with the bootts, for 4 weeks in July, father & A.K. staying at home together.   I have nothing else to tell you.   Never say die

Ever your loving | Wm. James

Mother tells me to add that they heartily agree to this new plan of yours—viz. Karlsbad &c.

ALS: MH bMS AM 1092.9 (2578)

[1] John Russell Reynolds (1828–1896), British physician, often consulted by patients with nervous disorders.

[2] Salter is not identified.

From Henry James

Grindelwald, Aigle Noir. | July 24th [1872]

My dear Wm.

I have not hitherto written you an especial letter of your own, because I have been plying a rather active pen for the family in general & have believed that you were getting your fill of my penmanship. You have followed our fortunes hitherto with interest—possibly with envy, I suppose; & have learned that, for all practical purposes our journey has been a constant success. Father & mother have kept us informed of your movements & occupations & given us an impression that you manage to get on tolerably without us—thanks to Chauncey Wright, Ch. Atkinson *e tutti quanti*. We have heard the tale of your visit to Stamford[1] & Alice has just got a letter from Sara Sedgwick, saying you were expected at Mt. Desert.[2] I am very glad to think of you out of the little back-room, the two green chairs & all their old, not especially cheerful associations. I myself am far enough away from them now—though possibly not as far as you might think. The romance of travel—of *tables d'hôtes*, strange figures & faces, & even of Alps—soon rubs off & the throb of admiration & surprise soon subsides into a tolerably jog trot sort of pulsation. I nevertheless very largely enjoy my life, get a great deal out of it & feel as if very little of the time were wasted. The great satisfaction of it all, of course, has been the sight of Alice's immense improvement.[3] We have written home such copious accounts of all this that by this time you have become familiar with the idea. You will probably see a great change in her when she gets home—if the second half of our journey is as propitious as the first—as it can hardly fail to be. The Bootts as you know, are with us for the present & we shall probably be together as long as we remain here. Lizzie is quite unchanged, save in her singing, which is very improved. Her voice seems to me to have almost doubled in volume & power, so that she is now not merely a pleasing, but quite a moving, Vocalist. She has learned a number of new songs & sings them all well. Her painting seems to have remained about the same, & her amiability & sweetness are, if possible, even greater. Those of her father seem *in statu quo*. They are very good company for us, as this hotel is rather a *lieu de passage* & the passers are mainly German. We shall perhaps have to separate however as Mr. Boott doesn't like the place, & we on our side, are a little disappointed in the air, which in spite of 3000 feet above the sea, proves on further acquaintance rather less "bracing" than we had hoped. The Bootts incline to the Rigi; & we, if we move, shall go in for the genuine article & march upon the Engadine. The genuine article was one of the chief things Alice came for & it would be a pity she shouldn't get. This Grindelwald Valley is wonderfully hand-some & I wish you could have a look at it, at some of its best moments. Two superb mountains—the Matterhorn & the Eiger, keep us com-pany on either hand, & from our windows we stare straight up the ice-paved glittering gorge of the lower glacier, which seems to tumble out of the common lap of the two white pyramids of the Fischerhör-ner. The other day, I got the whole view of which this forms a part, by a delightful walk up the Faulhorn, a moderate mountain, directly facing the Oberland chain. It shows you every jagged white peak of the ranges—marshalled in a long row, like a regiment of ice-giants & glaring & flashing in the light in the most magnificent way. The Faulhorn gave me about eight hours' walk, for which I was the better; so that you see my old Swiss legs, such as they are, haven't lost their cunning. An interesting feature of Grindelwald is the presence of various thin-flanked Englishmen with par-boiled faces, fresh (if fresh it can be called) from the Wetterhorn & the Eiger, & meditating the Shreckhorn & the Monk. They excite my envy, & I wish I had their *physiques*—to say nothing of their *morales*. *Àpropos* of *physiques* mine has been doing very well since I came abroad; or had been at least till we came to Switzerland, which seems somehow to be unfriendly to it. Still, I get on very comfortably. I made a vow this time, not to hurt myself with overwalking, & the weather at this place has been so hot that it is easy to keep it.—I have had no very distinct acct. of your own health & the state of your eyes. Your letter to us a month ago, and your recent one to Lizzie Boott seem to indicate a progress. I needn't say how much I hope it will continue & increase. I have spent various loose hours in manufacturing four long letters to the *Nation*, all on English subjects.[4] I have received very little news of them yet; but the 1st at least, you have perhaps by this time seen in print. My way of life hasn't been of course, altogether favorable to this sort of work; but with practice, it comes easier & I hope to do considerably more of it.—I incline more & more to decide to remain abroad & shall try and manage it. But it is yet early to talk of this.— I have left Wilky's engagement as the *pièce de résistance* among topics of interest.[5] You have doubtless discussed it with father & mother in all its phases & we, knowing nothing of Miss C., have no light to throw upon it. We are very anxious to receive light, & to hear more about her, as remembered by father & mother.

Meyringen July 28<u>th</u> My letter was interrupted four days since, & this morning finds [us] afloat again. We determined suddenly to leave Grindelwald, which on the essential point of climate had proved distinctly unsatisfactory. We are now on our way to the Engadine— a rather long journey but one of sort to do Alice good as it will be performed altogether in driving. We tried the experiment of coming hither over the Sheideck pass—Alice & A.K. on horses, with a possible afterthought of the Grimsel. The Sheideck is a lovely pass & Alice enjoyed it much, but the weather is too intensely hot to admit of the Grimsel; so that we shall go tomorrow over the Brünig, in a carriage to Lucerne, thence down the lake to Flüelen & thence drive up to Andermatt on the St. Gothard, whence we shall wend along towards the Engadine, keeping as much as possible in the high places. These geographical details can have little interest to you, but they may stir a sympathetic thrill in your soul.—I felt the other day when I began my letter, as if I had a good deal to say; but I don't know that it amounts to much, after all. I find my feelings, this time, as to Europe considerably less elastic than before, & am conscious mentally, of the wholesome hand of time. Switzerland I enjoy about as I expected to—not so much but that I would be willing at any moment to leave it for a more humanly interesting land.—Since I began my letter there has come a trio of notes from home—3 from father for Alice & me & 1 fr. mother to A.K. The account they give of your heat is very appalling, and makes us draw a long breath, in spite of our being in the midst of a good warm spell here. You have got through it, I hope, without leaving your vitality behind & the horrible thing is probably some time since at an end.—I interrupted myself above in speaking of Wilkie's engagement, in which I feel deeply interested. Poor excellent Wilk! to this has the world come with him! But he has been proving himself of late certainly a solid enough man to become a husband & father. We are exceedingly inquisitive about Miss C., (whom it now appears father & mother did *not* see), & we have all written to both parties. Farewell. My letter is dull & empty; I shall write you a better one before long. May the Summer sit lightly on you! Father mentions your having begun a notice of Taine, which of course you will send us, when it appears![6]

Yours ever | H.

We left the Bootts at Grindelwald, which Mr. B. doesn't like. They think of joining the Harry Lees somewhere.

ALS: MH bMS Am 1094 (1946)

¹ WJ's uncle Robertson Walsh lived in Stamford, Conn.

² Mount Desert Island, Maine, site of Bar Harbor.

³ AJ, HJ, and Aunt Kate sailed for Europe 11 May 1872; the two women began the return trip 15 October.

⁴ The series by HJ titled "A European Summer" in the *Nation*, consists of seven pieces: 15 (4 July 1872): 7–9; 15 (25 July 1872): 57–58; 15 (8 August 1872): 86–87; 15 (22 August 1872): 117–19; 15 (19 September 1872): 183–84; 15 (21 November 1872): 332–34; 16 (6 March 1873): 163–65, reprinted in *Transatlantic Sketches*. The last three describe travels on the Continent.

⁵ GWJ became engaged to Caroline Eames Cary in summer 1872. The marriage was delayed because GWJ was not earning enough to support a family.

⁶ Hippolyte-Adolphe Taine, *On Intelligence*, trans. T. D. Haye (New York: Holt & Williams, 1871), review in *Nation* 15 (29 August 1872): 139–41 (*ECR*).

To Henry James

Atlantic House, Scarboro | Saturday Aug. 24. 72

Beloved H'ry

I got yᵉ letter fm. Grindelwald and Meyringen some 10 days ago just as I was starting for the second time for Mᵗ Desert. I meant to have written you immediately fm. there, but circumstances prevented, and in the interests of local color, 'tis as well I should be here. I drove down here yesterday evening from Portland where I arrived with Grace Ashburner after 24 hours on the Steamboat. She went on to Boston. I could not resist the temptation of stopping and getting 3 sea baths.¹ I shall return on Monday. The beach shines as of yore—it is really superb, and the wood is delightful even after Mᵗ D. None of the Can[a]dians, not even the McDonalds, of last year have been here, but the first man I saw was old Uncle Hartshorne writing a letter in the office. Mrs. H. is bulkier, and has a coating more of sunburn than she had. Mrs. Clifford is here—her accomplished spouse being off stumping the state in favor of Greeley!² The Gennets are here, the Toffies, Mᵗ Smith, &c. The Clarks, Mrs. C. fatter, whiter & more sonorous than ever, Mr. Guanison is the same, and his graceless & mysterious sister seems to be as fond as ever of mrs hartshorne, and as determined as ever to die without having been in bathing.³ Freedom is still in the stable, having dyed his moustache, to keep up with the progress of the age, Ida & Jenny in the dining room. But the other "personnel" is changed. Every one has been cordial in questions about you all, & about Wilky, and Mrs. Gennett confided to me that she and several other ladies had always tho't Aunt Kate "the fainest lady" they had ever had in the house here. Don't tell A.K. if

you think it will make her arrogant.   I write in the little parlor opposite the Office—4.30 P.M—the steady heavy roaring of the surf comes
through the open window borne by the delicious salt breeze over the
great bank of stooping willows, field and fence.   The little horse
chestnut trees are as big, the cow with the board face still crops the
grass.   The broad sky & sea are whanging with the mellow light.   All
is as it was & will be.   Alice's words in a late letter, "What a joke poor
dear scarboro' seems from here!" (grindelwald) words which I keenly
enjoyed as having felicitously come to her pen to express all the distance fm. Europe & Cathay, rise again in my memory—but I spurn.
Scarboro, which I myself despised at m! Desert, is real, and in such
glorious weather as this capable of yielding solid and lasting joy even
to a European.   My lounge in the wood this AM. and my bath this
noon were in their kind perfect—So now conjure up one last picture
of the place—and say good bye to it.—Your own letters, especially
Alice's[—]Aunt Kate has written not so often—have given me great
delight.   I have tried feebly to imagine the scenes you have lived
through.   Alice must be tired ere now of the epithet of M$\underline{me}$ de Se-
vigné, so I won't repeat it.[4]   I expect to find her on her return sprung
into full possession & exercise of faculties of mind and I trust heart,
hitherto undreamt of by any of us, & only drempt of by herself.   She
will be the lioness of the next season.   I will sniff up some of the
incense, and live on that, her photograph book, and the 300 dollars a
year of my instructorship.   I do envy you very much what you are
going to see in Italy, and a good deal what you are and have been
seeing in Switzerland.   Though Nature as to its *essence* is the same
anywhere, and many nervous puckers which were in my mind when
I left Cambridge in July have been smoothed out gently & fairly by
the sweet influences of many a lie on a hill top at mt. Desert with sky
& sea & Islands before me, by many a row, and a couple of sails, and
by my bath and siesta on the blazing sand this morn.   But I envy ye
the world of Art.   Away from it, as we live, we sink into a flatter
blanker kind of consciousness, and indulge in an ostrichlike forget-
fulness of all our richest potentialities—and they startle us now and
then when by accident some rich human product, pictorial, literary,
or architectural slaps us with its tail.   I feel more and more as if I
ought to try to learn to sketch in water-colours, but am too lazy to
begin.   Perhaps I will at Mrs. Tappans.   Your letters to the Nation of
wh. I have as yet seen three, have been very exquisite, & both I and
others especially Sara Sedgwick have got great refreshment fm.
them.[5]   But as one gets more appreciative one's self for fineness of

perception & fineness of literary touch either in poetry or prose, one also finds how few there are to sympathize with one. I suppose moreover that descriptive writing is on the whole not a popular kind. Your own tendency is more and more to over-refinement, and elaboration. Recollect that for Newspaporial purposes, a broader treatment hits a broader mark; and keep bearing that way as much as you can with comfort. I suppose traits of human nature & character wd. also agreeably speckle the columns.

(24th.[6] After Episcopal service in the old parlor, wh. is unchanged—& still has "they're saved! they're saved!" upon the wall.)— I have passed a summer on the whole profitable at M! Desert and certainly pleasant, tho' it was somewhat marred by wakeful nights. The society there is *too* numerous & good for creatures no tougher in nerve than myself, but the last time I managed to confine myself to the inmates of the house—(except Miss Minturn) & got on better.[7] I am absolutely ashamed of not falling in love with Sara Sedgwick—so fully does my judgment commend her. Tell Alice this to offset certain remonstrances I erst made against her engouement, but don't let it be repeated. Poor Theodora fell sick & spoilt her fun.[8] She is very ladylike, both in her propensities and aversions, but has too few of the former, and rolls her eyes so interrogatively upon you whenever your glances meet, that you don't know what to do for her. But she's a very amiable girl. Grace Ashburner's *ways* have a good deal of the catlike stealthiness which I suppose old maidhood breeds—I mean her way of eating, of silent suffering & the like—but she's a charming companion, & was I think a great social success. Miss Minturn is a regular phoenix and no mistake, her acquirements wd. be extraordinary in a man of her age—and she is full of feminine timidity & sensibility beside. But one suspects a certain dryness to accompany so firm & hard an understanding. She condescended to say she liked *you*, about the only creature or institution in favor of wh. she made a like confession. But my chief delig[h]t in the way of human nature was Miss Greene, who was chock full of it, & whom I hope Alice may get to know sometime. The Sedgwicks have warmly taken her up. She is the only woman I have met who can be classified with Minny Temple, for originality and inexhaustible good nature. Her interests too are mainly moral, but her temperament is very different, being singularly devoid of the coquettish impulse. I like her extremely and am the better for having known her. My first impression, which I think I communicated to alice, was very wrong, Let it never be repeated.   Arthur arrived at M! D, the day before I left, well & in good spirits, & fond of his work.

You will like an account of my own condition.   My eyes serve fm 3 to 4 hrs. daily.   I dont wish in this vacation to use them more—seldom as much, but feel sure they will respond whenever I make the demand.   My other symptoms are gradually modifying themselves—I can hardly say for the better, except that all change is of good omen, and suggests a possible turn of the wheel into the track of soundness.   The fits of languor have become somewhat rarer, but what were the healthy intervals have been assuming since your departure more and more of a morbid character, namely just the opposite, nervousness, wakefulness, uneasiness.   Perhaps the whole thing will soon smooth itself out.   The appointment to teach physiology is a perfect godsend to me just now.   An external motive to work, which yet does not strain me—a dealing with men instead of my own mind, & a diversion from those introspective studies which had bred a sort of philosophical hypochondria in me of late & which it will certainly do me good to drop for a year.—I have just read Babolain— so unsatisfactory in its ability—but the rascal is growing more & more into a serious writer.[9]   I should like to hear you talk about it. McCobb and Looney, two names I saw in Portland, are good for Novills.[10]   It is one o'clock—I now go down to take a plunge in the surf, & close this epistle with lots of love to you, Alice & dear old Aunt Kate.   Good bye

ever y! W.J.

Home, Monday Aug. 27.[11]   I find Camb! not looking at all wan or seedy, as it has looked to me in past years, and F. & M. perfectly comfortable & happy.   F. says it is the pleasantest summer he ever spent—and mother has experienced no ennui, tho' she confesses to an occasional pant for the sea wind, or a wider foliage than Quincy St. affords.   I write before bkfst in our study with the crickets filling the air with their stridulation and the sky muffled in mist.   I hear Maria setting the table   mother has read me your three letters (one apiece) the last yrs. of Aug 4. from the entrance to Via Mala.   What a gorgeous time you must be having, and how I envy you.   I see y! 4th letter in the Nation & shall read it after bkfst.[12]   Anderson told me a good hawthornian plot for a story.   It is the property of Billy Everett, so you may not use it, but it may suggest s'thing to you.   A man while murdering some one perceives the flash of a dark lantern thrown upon him—no more; and ever through life is accompanied by the

dread uncertainty thence arising. Adieu once more. Heaps of love
to Alice, Aunt Kate & yrself fm. your ever affect[ionate]

W.J.

I go now to the P.O.

ALS: MH bMS Am 1092.9 (2579)

[1] Scarboro is a coastal town in southern Maine.

[2] Horace Greeley was a candidate for president of the Liberal Republican party in
1872.

[3] Summer friends are usually too much out of context for purposes of identification
and none in this group has been identified.

[4] Marie de Rabutin-Chantal, marquise de Sévigné (1626–1696), is known primarily
for her letters.

[5] See letter of 24 July 1872.

[6] Probably 25 August, which was a Sunday.

[7] A Miss E. T. Minturn contributed several items to the *Nation* after 1876, but no
information about her was found.

[8] Theodora Sedgwick.

[9] Gustave Droz (1832–1895), French writer, *Babolain* (1872).

[10] McCobb and Looney appear to be names that struck WJ as useful for literary
purposes.

[11] Monday was 26 August.

[12] See letter of 24 July 1872.

From Henry James

Paris, Hotel Rastadt | Rue Nue. St. Augustin. | Sept 22$^{\underline{d}}$ [1872]
Dear W$^{\underline{m}}$.

I found awaiting me at Munroe's a couple of days since your de-
lightful & excellent letter of Aug. 24$^{\underline{th}}$ from Scarboro;[1] & I must let
my usual Sunday letter, to day, serve as an answer to it. It found us
arriving in Paris rather sated with travel & pleased at the prospect of
a three weeks' rest. These weeks will slip rapidly by & then I shall
find myself turning away from the ship's side, at Liverpool and (if I
remain of the same mind that I am of now) leaving my companions
to take home such account of me as may seem to them veracious.
The five months that we were looking forward to such a short time
since, now lie behind us, having changed their blank vacuity for the
rich complexion of a mingled experience. They have done more for
us, I suppose, than we yet can measure, & I have gathered impressions which tho' now wofully scattered & confused by incessant travel,
I hope never altogether to lose. We have really seen a great deal; &
I think Alice, in the tranquil leisures of home will find that her mind

is richly stocked with delightful pictures and memories. As regards her health, I don't see how the journey could have been a more distinct success; but it is needless to talk of this now, for you will soon see her & make the same judgment. *Sept. 28ᵗʰ* I wrote the above a week ago, was interrupted, & have lacked time since to resume—having devoted my mornings to doing something for the *Nation* about our Italian journey[2]—which there was no chance for at the time & yet is a sort of thing very difficult after the immediate glow of experience is past.—The week has gone pleasantly albeit for Paris, quietly. I already feel so much at home here that I lack the spur of curiosity to drive me into the streets. Alice & A.K., even with their moderate demands, find plenty of occupation with milliners & dressmakers—& have even now sallied forth on an expedition to the Bon Marché. A.K's energy & capacity in this as in everything else, shine forth most powerfully. A letter has just come in from father, enclosing a piece from the Tribune about my new story.[3] The critic is very polite & makes me curious to see the piece, which I have rather forgotten, so long ago was it written. Father also says that you have not come back with J. Gray from Conway & leaves me wondering how you found it there & what you did. It was just then, last year, that I was there & somehow wasn't charmed with it. I hope at any rate you have found some impetus to your physique—& may perhaps have sounded the mysteries of J. Gray's *morale.* You, too, will have had a somewhat diversified summer & will have seen more of human nature, at any rate, than we, who have seen none worth mentioning. Lately we have been spectators of the familiar virtues & vices of the Tweedies, who live here below us & dine with us every day. The Nortons too are here, & J. R. Lowell & wife, & Chauncey Wright & Rowse.[4] C.W. seems in Paris just as he did in Cambridge—serenely purpurine. He lives at the Grand Hotel, & I frequently see him trundling on tip-toes along the Boulevard, as he did at home along the Main Street. The Nortons are excellent, but I feel less & less at home with them, owing to a high moral *je ne sais quoi* which passes quite above my head. I went with Charles the other day to the Louvre, where he made some exellent criticisms, but he takes art altogether too hard for me to follow him—if not in his likings, at least in his dislikes. I daily pray *not* to grow in discrimination & to be suffered to aim at superficial pleasure. Otherwise, I shudder to think of my state of mind ten years hence. Paris continues to seem very pleasant, but doesn't become interesting. You get tired of a place which you can call nothing but *charmant.* Besides, I read the Figaro every day, religiously & it leaves a bad taste in my mouth. Hereabouts, moreover, the place is totally americanized—the Boulevard des Capucines & the Rue de la Paix are a perfect reproduction of Broadway. The want of comprehension of the real moral situation of France leaves one unsatisfied, too. Beneath all this neatness & coquetry, you seem to smell the Commune suppressed, but seething.[5] Alice, Grace Norton & I went the other night to the Comédie Francaise to see Musset's *Il ne faut pas badiner* &c. Perdican was beautifully played, but the piece is too exquisite not to suffer by acting.[6] The only other noteworthy things I have seen were two pictures of Henri Regnault, yesterday, at the Luxembourg, the *Exécution Mauresque* & the Portrait of General Prim. They are very juvenile works, but they make one feel that their author if he had lived & kept his promise, would have been the first of all modern painters, with much of the easy power which marks the great Italians. He seems to have thought, so to speak, in color. You have learned, by my recent letters, that I mean to try my luck at remaining abroad. I have little doubt that I shall be able to pull through. I want to spend a quiet winter, with a chance to read a good deal & to write enough. I shall be able to write enough & well enough, I think: my only question is how to dispose of my wares. But in this, too, I shall not fail. Your criticism of my *Nation* letters was welcome & just: their tendency is certainly to over-refinement. Howells wrote to me to the same effect & you are both right. But I am not afraid of not being able, on the whole, & in so far as this is deeply desirable, to work it off with practise. Beyond a certain point, this would not be desirable I think—for me at least, who must give up the ambition of ever being a free-going & light-paced enough writer to please the multitude. The multitude, I am more & more convinced, has absolutely no taste—none at least that a thinking man is bound to defer to. To write for the few who have is doubtless to lose money—but I am not afraid of starving. *Au point où nous en sommes* all writing not really leavened with thought—of some sort or other—is terribly unprofitable, and to try & work one's material closely is the only way to form a manner on which one can keep afloat—without intellectual bankruptcy at least. I have a mortal horror of seeming to write thin—& if I ever feel my pen beginning to scratch, shall consider that my death-knell has rung. I should prefer to spend the winter in Florence or Rome—rather the latter, in spite of its being, I imagine, pretty distracting. But it would pay me best, I think, & the *Nation* would value letters thence. But enough of my own affairs. All we

hear of Wilk & Bob & their prospective mates is very interesting—
especially father's mention this morning of Bob's possible marriage in
November.   I hope he knows what he is about.   If so 'tis excellent.
I read your Taine & admired, thought[7] but imperfectly understood
it.[8] Charles Norton praised it to me the other day.—Proceed, & all
blessings attend you!   Howells lately wrote me that there was a
chance of T.S.P. getting, subordinately, the *N.A.R.*   Good luck to
him?   From allusions in letters, he seems to be still in Cambⁱriⁱdge.
Is he then keeping his place?[9]   Give him my love & tell him that I
have a constant design of writing to him.   You sometimes see Wendell H., I suppose, of whose matrimonial fate I should be glad to hear
something.[10]   Farewell.   I have another letter to write & the morning is ebbing.   Alice & A.K. are counting the days.—It seemed to me
that I had much more to say—& I have: but I must keep it for another day.—

Yours ever—H. James jr

ALS: MH bMS Am 1094 (1947)

[1] In a letter to his parents of 9 September 1872, HJ writes that in about a week he
will claim "the letters even now piling up for us at Munroe's in Paris" (*HJL*, 1:298).
Munroe's seems to be an agency.

[2] HJ, "From Chambéry to Milan," final segment of "A European Summer"; see letter of 24 July 1872.

[3] Nothing in HJ's bibliography fits the description "new story," unless the *New York
Tribune* reviewer obtained an advance copy of the "Guest's Confession," *Atlantic
Monthly* 30 (October 1872): 385–403; 30 (November 1872): 566–83.   The 1872 dat-
ing of the letter is confirmed by the presence of the Lowells in Europe.

[4] Samuel Worcester Rowse (1822–1901), American artist, illustrator.

[5] The Commune of Paris was suppressed in May 1871.

[6] Perdican is a character in Alfred de Musset, *On ne badine pas avec l'amour*.   HJ
appears to combine this title and that of another play, *Il ne faut jurer de rien*.

[7] Probably a slip for 'though'.

[8] See letter of 24 July 1872.

[9] Perry resigned from Harvard.

[10] The engagement of Holmes and Fanny Dixwell was announced on 13 March
1872; the wedding was on 17 June 1872.

To Henry James

Cambr. Oct. [10] 72

My dear Harry

On returning yesterday from Lenox I found that 2 letters from
Alice & 1 fm you had been rec'd since your arrival in Paris.   This of
course will get you after you have been left alone to the enjoyment of

freedom and the occasional *unheimlichkeit* of solitude.   Where you
will be I know not.   I write to you so seldom that I have a terrible
amount of stuff to communicate & probably the most important part
of the items wh. I have fm. time to time tucked up on a shelf in my
mind for you will have evaporated.   I begin by saying how good &
full of information, (except perhaps about Aunt Kate) your letters
home have been, leaving, in fact, nothing to be desired.   Your letters
to the Nation have been rather too few, and very much enjoyed by
me, and by a number of other people so large that I confess it has
rather surprised me; as I thought the style ran a little more to *curliness*
than suited the average mind, or in general the newspaper reader.
In my opinion what you should *cultivate* is directness of style.   Delicacy, subtlety and ingenuity will take care of themselves.   The one
that pleased me best was the first. (Chester)   Wendell Holmes said he
was delighted with the Haddon Hall one, and his wife had had great
pleasure fm. them.   He preferred that, because in it you seemed to
him to give more immediately yr. first impression, whereas your usual
fault was to be looking too much for yr. 2nd imp:ⁿ[1]   Mrs Perry at the
white Mᵗˢ spoke with unfeigned or affected pleasure in them and yʳ
stories.[2]   John Ropes said he had been reading the letters with success to "people at Newport" & had enjoyed them greatly himself.
Gray said he liked them much, and thought they were simpler than
most of your writing—the reverse of my impression.—Mother or Father will have told you of Arthur's collapse in the Post and of his new
scheme of raising money for a daily Nation.   He has 5000 subscribed.   I should fear Godkin wd. not be good enough "caterer" or
as he wd. called it, panderer, to make a daily paper sell, though, if well
edited I shd. think a paper of those principles wd. now command the
support of the public.[3]   Arthur has found that the editorial life suits
him.   He considers himself somewhat as a martyr to principle, and
has a rather amusing way of talking about his past now, as if he felt
that he had a record to stand on.   Anyway I hope if this fails, that he
won't go to Europe but wait for a new engagement here.   Europe
wd. break him in the back entirely, as regards a career.   He shows no
desire to enlarge his mind by reading at all.   T.S.P.'s relation to the
N.A.R. will also have been announced to you.   He was on here to day
from Newport, tallowy with health and calm innervation.   He says
he has another engagement in N.Y. on his hook—[On looking this
minute out of the window of mother's bedroom—where I write in the
clear yellow October sunset, I see him striding past with two short
young ladies unknown to me][4]—and will not close with the N.A.R.

for a week.   He did not say what the engagement was, but it probably
has to do with the Godkin, Sedgwick Scheme.[5]   He bro't me a drawing fm. J.L.F. wh. I enclose to you.[6]   The same was recently on here,
about the same in health he says, and unchanged in morale.   He has
made 7 good drawings for a selection of "Songs fm the Old Dramatists" to which he had a pretty poor cover in his pocket designed by
Fanny Holmes.   He has an order for twelve drawings for a handsome edition of the Gospels by Hurd & Houghton to wh. he has as
yet done nought but but read the book & "saturate himself with its
spirit."[7]—The Art Critic in the Atlantic now is Clarence Cook,[8] & he
in the nation Earl Shin.(!)—I never so much as this summer felt the
soothing and hygienic effects of nature upon the human spirit.   Before when I enjoyed it, it has been as a luxury, but this time t'was as a
vital food, or medecine.   I have regretted extremely letting my drawing die out.   A man needs to keep open all his channels of activity;
for the day may always come when his mind needs to change its attitude for the sake of its health.   Simply getting absorbed in the look
of nature is after abstract study like standing on one's feet after having been on one's head, and next summer I will if it is at all possible
make an effort to begin painting in water colors.   I have been of late
so sickened & skeptical of philosophic activity as to regret much that
I did not stick to painting, and to envy those like you to whom the
aesthetic relations of things were the real world.   Surely they reveal
a deeper part of the universal life than all the mechanical and logical
abstractions do, and if I were you I wd. never repine that my life had
got cast among them rather than elsewhere.—I had a very pleasant
visit to Conway with John Gray.   A lot of pretty and lady-like Phila-
delpianesses in the house made me realize how pleasant it is to talk to
people whose minds were slack—and who did not expect you to
make such fearfully knowing discriminations.   To say that so-and-so
was a good fellow, or disagreeable, was to them to exhaust the subject.
Gray seemed cheerful enough there but I fancy he is quite under-
mined by depression of spirits. Poor fellow!   I like him very much in
spite of everything.   But a shining day in the woods half way up a
mountain there was worth all the other experiences put together.
Since then I have been to Mrs Tappans, and had a rather dullish
week, confined a good deal to the house by dull weather.   Mrs Tappan struck me as a stronger battery than ever so far as independence
and positiveness go, and the girls are the same muffled unresonant
forms of life.—We have been having the Gourlays in the house for a
fortnight, Jeannette having been taken sick wh. prolonged their stay.

They too are sufficiently unresonant, but very good & simple.   They
have absolutely no talk in them.   Mother has been heroic in her in-
defatigable companionship of them.   Father reads excerpts fm. the
paper aloud at bkfst. and "nights," and to morrow they leave.   They
look very little affected by hoary eld, and are very good & simple.
But if they've had as dull a time with us as we with them, they won't
soon want to come again. John Fiske expressed to day to Father his
great regret that you were to stay away.   His trip to lecture in Milwaukie was a great success.   He is Librarian now, as I suppose you know.[9]
If I were well enough now wd. be my chance to strike at Harvard
college, for Peterson has just resigned his sub professorship of Philosophy, and I know of no very formidable opponent.[10]   But its impossible.   I keep up a small daily pegging at my Physiology whose duties
don't begin till January, & which I shall find easy, I think.[11]—Adieu,
where this gets you & how, I know not, but suppose you'll feel like
making a short stay in England before returning to the South.
Happy wretch!   I hope you appreciate your lot, to spend the winter
in an environment whose impression thickly assail your every sense &
interest, instead of this naked vacuous america; and in a climate
which in spite of its quantum of chill, on the whole lets you alone in a
way that ours never thinks of, and has no NW winds.

Ever yr. affect.   Wm. James.

Gertrude Pendleton is suddenly engaged to a Virginian named
Jones.[12]

Date: Oct 10

forgot to enclose J.L.F's photog.   Will do it next time.

ALS: MH bMS Am 1092.9 (2580)
Address: Henry James jr Esq | Care of Brown, Shipley & Co | London | England
Postmarks: CAMBRIDG⟨E⟩ OCT 10   B⟨OS⟩TON OCT 11   AA OCT 23 1872.   One other
postmark is illegible and another was excised.

[1] See letter of 24 July 1872.   HJ's first piece was called "Chester," the second, "Lich-
field and Warwick," describing Haddon Hall.

[2] Frances Sergeant Perry, Thomas Sergeant Perry's mother.

[3] In a memorandum to Arthur Sedgwick, Godkin insisted that "not less than
$75,000 capital be raised" (*The Gilded Age Letters of E. L. Godkin*, ed. William M. Arm-
strong [Albany: State Univ. of New York Press, 1974], 192).

[4] Thomas Sergeant Perry added the following note to the letter: 'Dear Harry: I left
them at the lower gate & came in here to find myself turned to ridicule as W. has done
it.   When, if ever, I get settled I'll write you a line, I have always intended to, I still
intend to but———The main objection to letter writing is its uselessness.   You don't
care, no one cares, for dreary biographical records, but I'll write soon when I shall
have settled on a port for the winter. | Yrs. | T.S.P.'

[5] Perry was interested in joining the staff of the *Nation*.

[6] Included with this letter in the Harvard collection is a photograph of a painting by La Farge. According to his postscript, WJ forgot to enclose the photograph and there are no references to it in subsequent letters. It is possible that when the papers were being sorted for storage at Harvard, the present photograph was included, although there is no way of verifying whether this is the photograph referred to by WJ. For a similar painting by La Farge, see William H. Gerdts, *Painters of the Humble Truth: Masterpieces of American Still Life, 1801–1939* (Tulsa: Philbrook Art Center, 1981), figure 7.1.

[7] Abby Richardson, *Songs from the Old Dramatists* (New York: Hurd & Houghton, 1873). No edition of the gospels published by Hurd & Houghton was found.

[8] Clarence Chatham Cook (1828–1900), American art critic.

[9] John Fiske served as assistant librarian at Harvard in 1872–79.

[10] Ralph Barton Perry, *TCWJ*, 1:330, states that 1871–72 was the last year in which Ellis Peterson taught at Harvard. George Herbert Palmer (1842–1933), American philosopher, began teaching at Harvard in 1872–73. No information about Peterson was found.

[11] WJ's first course at Harvard was "Natural History 3: Comparative Anatomy and Physiology." WJ was responsible for physiology; Thomas Dwight, for anatomy.

[12] Gertrude James Pendleton (1834–1889), daughter of Augustus James, brother of WJ's father, married McKendrie Wise Jones. It was her second marriage.

To Henry James

Cambr Nov 24. 72

Dear H'ry

On this saintly Sabbath morn I take up my long unwonted pen to make you a report of progress at home ensheathed in other gossip. I sit at your old table facing the Lowell's empty house which has grown to look more tumble down than ever during the absence of the family in the country—(they are still there, old Mrs L. being sick)— the double sashes just put up in front and a sickly mist-swathed November sunshine pouring through the back window on the right. Thermometer 32°. Frm. the library comes the din of cheerful voices, those of Bob & Mary Holton among them. Mary has won the hearts of all of us by her combination of prettiness, amiability, vivacity, & modesty with a certain dash of pluckiness wh. is very charming— and even the fastidious Alice is loud in praise of her native "refinement." Bob's good fortune is certainly great. There is not much to be said of him save that he seems in very good condition mentally, and his physique has become even broader & stronger looking than it was. Alice seems perfectly delighted with Mary. They spend a good part of the day rapt in each other's arms or with arms round waists and cheek to cheek &c &c. Father also is very lively with her and I fancy the rather trying ordeal of coming to us will pass off very pleasantly to her. Alice's condition we found of course greatly changed for the better both in "flesh" and in spirit. She has shown no languor since her return, and evidently is in every respect more elastic and toned up. Her journey was a great thing for her in every way and her talk about things & people seen has been very abundant & good. Mother will have told you of A.K's visit to Derby who reassured her about the cataract & told her to wear glasses & use her eyes.[1] Her irritation continuing I found this morning a rough growth inside of her upper eyelid wh. D. did not see and wh. she will have to consult him about to morrow. her spirits seem excellent, and it's a great shame she did not consult an oculist abroad immediately. I send you to day the last Nation with your letter about Chambiery &c &c, a very delightful light bit of work, and perhaps the best of all for commercial newspaporial purposes.[2] I must however still protest against your constant use of french phrases. There is an order of taste—and certainly a respectable one—to which they are simply maddening. I have said nothing to you about Guest's Confession(!) which I read and enjoyed, admiring its cleverness though not loving it exactly. I noted at the time a couple of blemishes, one the french phrase "*les indifférents*" at the end of one of her sentences which suddenly chills one's very marrow. The other the expression: "to whom I had dedicated a sentiment," earlier in the story—I cannot well look up the page, but you will doubtless identify it.[3] Of the people who experience a personal dislike so to speak of your stories, the most I think will be repelled by the element wh. gets expression in these two phrases, something cold, thin blooded & priggish suddenly popping in and freezing the genial current. And I think that is the principal defect you have now to guard against. In flexibility, ease, & light power of style you clearly continue to gain, Guest's Conf. & this last letter in the Nation are proofs of it, but I think you shd. fight shy of that note of literary reminiscence in the midst of what ought to be pure imagination absorbed in the Object, which keeps every now & then betraying itself as in these french phrases. I criticize you so much as perhaps to seem a mere caviller, but I think it ought to be of use to you to have any detailed criticism fm even a wrong judge, and you don't get much fm. any one else. I meanwhile say nothing of the great delight which all your pieces give me by their insight into the shades of being, and their exquisite diction & sense of beauty and expression in the sights of the world. I still believe in your greatness as a critic and hope you will send home s'thing good of that kind.

Alice said you were going to do Middlemarch.[4]   If you spread yrself on it, I've no doubt, either Howells' or T.S.P. will be glad to print it in the "Body" part of their respective periodicals.   I have been reading with deep pleasure though not *pure* pleasure, 3 chaps. fm. Morley's forthcoming life of Rousseau wh. have appeared in the Fortnightly.[5] I shd. advise you by all means to get it & read it, paying for it by a notice for the N.A.R. wh. I will now bespeak with Perry, subject to your ulterior refusal.   I think I'll try to sling a notice of it for Howells', and keep the book.[6]   I gave him a rather ill-considered notice of M's Voltaire contrasting M. favorably with Tyndall & Huxley & in the heat of composition calling T. a coxcomb wh. Howells did not alter and wh. seemed rather uncourteous as T. & the magazine made their appearance at the same moment, and the Boston Globe said it made one despair of the future of American letters to find such criticisms in the Atlantic.[7]   But Morley is I think a very great moralist, and if he wd. only be less redundant a very great writer.   Your letter describing yr. intimacy with J. R. Lowell and your dinner with the irascible frenchmen at the Hotel de Lorraine was rec'd a few days ago & was very entertaining.   But can't you find out a way of knowing any good french people?   It seems preposterous that a man like you shd be condemned to the society of washer women and café waiters.   I envy you however even the sight of such.

Massive & teeming Paris with its sights sounds & smells is so huge & real in the world that fm. this insubstantial america one longs occasionally for it with a mighty yearn.   Just about nightfall at this season with drizzle above & mud paste beneath and gas blazing streets and restaurants is the time that particularly appeals to me with thick wafted associations—Poor Shaler, who, with a little less bombast about him wd. be about the most charming man I know, has had a sort of break down with his head.   I trust & think it is superficial but he knocks off work & with his family starts now for the Malvern water cure.   Wendell H. spent an eveᵍ here this week.   He grows more & more concentrated upon his law.   His mind resembles a stiff spring, which has to be abducted violently from it, and which every instant it is left to itself flies tight back.   He works less since his marriage and feels the better for it.   His wife is getting well and he seems now quite cheerful about her. Chas. Peirce & wife are going to washington again for the winter and perhaps for good.[8]   He says he is appreciated there, & only tolerated here and wd. be a fool not to go there.   He read us an admirable introductory chapter to his book on logic the other day.[9]   I go in to the Med. Sch. nearly every morn. to hear Bowditch lecture or paddle round in his lab. It is a noble thing for one's spirits to have some responsible work to do. I enjoy my revived physiological reading greatly, and have in a corporeal sense been better for the past 4 or 5 weeks than I have been at all since you left.— You may be surprized that I have as yet not mentioned the fire. But it was so snug & circumscribed an affair that one has felt no *horror* at all about it. Rich men suffered, but upon the community at large I shd. say its effect had been rather exhilarating than otherwise. Boston feels rather proud that the fire of youth & prodigality yet smoulders in her.[10] Harvard Col. has lost nearly ¼ million but last night the subscriptions to aid her footed 80 odd thousand so that she may lose nothing in the end. And I am convinced now that each occasion for giving in charity strenghthens the habit and makes it easier. No one that we know intimately seems to have lost much. But mother will have told you already the "personalities" connected with the affair, so I hush up. Adieu. adieu! I am glad to hear that you are so well, and hope it will last. I have found a homeopathic remedy, *hydrastis*, to be of decided efficacy for constip? and will send you a bottle. If you have chilblains Iodine ointment is better than the tincture, & is *the* thing. The coat you sent me is very satisfactory. Ditto the cravats of wh. I have one on now. Sedgwicks and Anderson dined here yest.ᵈʸ I go there now—i.e. to Sedgw.? Arthur is writing on N.Y. His daily Nation scheme depends now on one capitalist who is in N.Y. But I mistrust Godkin as editor. Howells says he wd have no difficulty at all in getting more articles for the weekly N. The length of time your letters are kept unprinted and the fact that they have kept a book notice of mine back nearly 3 mos. shows I think that the poverty of the paper is due to the editors and not to their resources. The Evening Post wd. I know be glad to print any letter fm. you I don't know how they pay. Once more farewell. Write more now about what you read and think. You will be able to, now that you have no bulletins to write about Alice.

Ever yr. affec? | W.J.

Mrs R. James modestly refuses my proposal that she shd. add a P.S. to this letter, but "wishes to be affectionatly remembered to you"[11]

ALS: MH bMS Am 1092.9 (2581)

[1] Hasket Derby (1835–1914), American physician, in 1871 gave a lecture at Harvard on cataract surgery.

[2] See letter of 24 July 1872. HJ's sixth piece in the series was titled "From Chambéry to Milan."

[3] Laura Guest, the heroine of "Guest's Confession" concludes one of her remarks

with *"les indifférents"* (*Atlantic Monthly* 17 [November 1872]: 571); the objectionable phrase occurs in the first installment, 17 (October 1872): 397.

[4] HJ, review of George Eliot, *Middlemarch*, in *Galaxy* 15 (March 1873): 424–28.

[5] John Morley, *Rousseau*, 2 vols. (London: Chapman and Hall, 1873); excerpts appeared in *Fortnightly Review* 18 (1 September 1872): 287–308; 18 (1 October 1872): 438–57; 18 (1 November 1872): 572–94.

[6] Neither brother reviewed the book.

[7] John Morley, *Voltaire*, 2d ed. (London: Chapman and Hall, 1872), review in *Atlantic Monthly* 30 (November 1872): 624–25 (*ECR*). John Tyndall (1820–1893), British physicist, was lecturing in the United States in December 1872.

[8] In November 1872 Peirce was put in charge of pendulum experiments for the United States Coast and Geodesic Survey. The proposed move may have been connected with this.

[9] The material that Peirce intended for the first chapter of the planned book appears in his "Fixation of Belief" (1877); see Max H. Fisch, *Peirce, Semeiotic, and Pragmatism* (Bloomington: Indiana Univ. Press, 1986), 123.

[10] The Boston fire on 9 November 1872 destroyed some sixty-seven acres of the city.

[11] RJ added the following note: 'Dr. Harry. I am home with my wife for a week. The only detraction from our pleasure is your absence—The family all seem unusually well. Willy never looked so fine to me—in health before—and Alice is an Amazon. I have to thank you for the scarf you sent me by Alice and which I wore on my marriage day. Wilky is talking somewhat of being wedded in the Spring—When I get leisure—I hope to write you a long letter—about your Milwaukee interests which are growing and flourishing | Always Aff | RJ.'

From Henry James

Paris 44 Rue Nue. St. Augustin. | Nov. 31st. [December 1] '72.[1]
Dear Brother:—

I have not written home for nearly a fortnight. I suppose the domestic circle has begun to wonder &[2] my silence. But it has not been caused by calamity of any kind. I am well, active & joyous & have been kept from writing only by a series of accidental interruptions & delays—humiliatingly trivial now that I look back on them. Meanwhile I have rec'd. an excellent letter both from A. Kate & Alice. That of my sister which was extremely satisfactory, shall be answered within a reasonable period. Aunt Kate's contained such blessed good news about her eye that I am surprised at myself for not having immediately despatched her a note of congratulation. I enclose her a few lines in this.—I have from yourself a letter a month old which I have read over several times since getting it & should be unjust to leave longer unanswered. Aunt Kate & Alice both expatiate glee-

fully on that threadbare topic, as I believe you consider it, the remarkable salubrity of your appearance & I have ventured to reflect
upon it with some complacency.   If you are but half as well as they
make out that you look I shall be perfectly satisfied.   I hope, in spite
of your improvement that you did nothing in the way of putting out
the great Fire.   A.K.'s & Alice's letter contained the 1ˢᵗ details on the
subject that had reached me, but as they wrote on the following day,
these were still scanty.   Anything more of especial interest I suppose
some of you will transmit.   There are some "views" of the burnt district in the last *Illustrated London News* which give the *débris* a grandly
romantic appearance & make them look like the ruins of Palmyra.
If they are as good as that I might as well be enjoying the picturesque
at home.—The picturesque at any rate, has been with you & departed again, I suppose, in the shape of Bob & his plump little
spouse.   Mother & father can hardly fail to write me all about them
& the impression they produced singly and unitedly.   I hope everything seemed propitious for their happiness & prosperity.—With me
the weeks chase each other along at a steady pace, none of them
bringing as yet any great amount of grist to the Mill.   I have been
busy the last fortnight writing a little story, which now that it is finished I hardly know what to do with—having other designs on the
Atlantic I shall probably send it to the Magazine (*Wood's Household*—
degrading connection!) for which Gail Hamilton lately appealed to
me.³   My life is not composed of many elements, but they have
seemed hitherto quite sufficient.   Mornings & very often evenings in
my Room; afternoons in the streets, walking, strolling, *flânant*,
prying, staring, lingering at Bookstalls & shop-windows; six o'clock
dinner at a restaurant (generally Hill's, on the Bvd. des Capucines,
where I get a *rosbif saignant* & a *pinte*—a pot of prime English ale.)
De temps en temps the theatre, which I don't enjoy quite as wildly as
I expected; but quite enough to be thankful for.   I've enjoyed nothing more than a night of Molière recently at the Odéon: the Pré-
cieuses Ridicules & the Malade Imaginaire.   He was certainly the
heartiest & most heroic of humorists.   The *M.I.* is a broad farce with
a vengeance, but, acted as they do it at the Odéon, it's the sublime of
the comic and a thousand times more wholesome than anything now
going in Paris.   I walked over to the Odéon in the rain (it hasn't
stopped in three weeks) & enjoyed through the flaring dripping
darkness from the Pont du Carrousel the great spectacle of the moment, the enormous *crue* of the Seine.   The endless rains of the last
six weeks have swelled it prodigiously & it stretched out from quay to

quay, rushing tremendously & flashing back the myriad lights from
its vast black bosom like a sort of civilized Missi[ssi]ppi. Not so very
civilized either; if the rain keeps up, it will soon be in the streets.
The weather is a great trial & makes of one's walks a rather dreary
pother in the mud & wet. But one gets used to everything—even to
seeing the sun but once a month. The rain too has kept away the
cold & I haven't suffered at all from that bugbear. I cross the river
once or twice a week to see Lowell, with whom I haven't exactly sworn
an eternal friendship—but we have at any rate struck a truce to the
mutual indifference in which we dwelt in Cambridge. He is very
friendly, entertaining & full of knowledge, but his weak point will always be his *opinions.* Poor little Mr. John Holmes, the most *unassimilable,* in Europe, of New Englanders, lives with him & they make a little
Cambridge together.[4] Of other society I have had that of Chas. H.
Dorr, who called on me & chirped away as usual for half an hour;[5] of
Mr. & Mrs. Theo. Lyman & Miss G. Russell (with whom I dined the
other day)[6] & of the Dixwell family, whom I lately met at Munroe's &
was invited to call upon. They live a good bit off, near the Parc Mon-
ceau & are at housekeeping. Mrs. Dixwell is extremely handsome—
her eye bluer & her complexion fresher than ever—& most emancipated & delighted with Europe.—Most of my social intercourse however consists of looking at people in the streets, theatres & restaurants. I find they excite my curiosity far more than at home—often
doubtless *à tort* and always vainly. The Americans in Paris (as observed at Munroe's the Grand Hotel &c) excite nothing but antipa-
thy.—I enjoy very much in a sort of chronic way which has every now
& then a deeper throb, the sense of being in a denser civilization than
our own. Life at home has the compensation that there you are a
part of the civilization, such as it is, whereas here you are outside of
it. It's a choice of advantages. I have the same feeling as you in
coming to write, that I have made a note of a hundred things to say,
but can't say them because they are a hundred at[7] not two or three.
I have made serious reflections about the French; but they are a
threadbare topic and I'm tired of them. I've done them justice,
mentally & arrived at a sort of ultimate feeling about them. I doubt
if they are ever again a 1$^{\underline{st}}$ class influence in the world; though they
can't fail to be a precious 2$^{\underline{d}}$ class one.—Politics are just now very lively
& quite interesting & comprehensible even to politically stupid me.
There has been a prolonged battle between Thiers & the majority
(monarchical) in the chamber, ending or tending to end in the discomfiture, well-deserved, of the latter.[8] Thiers is really a sublime

little creature, in his way, & since listening to that row at Lowell's table that I wrote you of, I can believe anything of monarchical blindness & folly.   But every crisis, like the present, this republic outweathers & worries through in the regular parliamentary way, the less hope for either Bonapartists or Orleanists.

Monday a.m. Dec 1ˢᵗ   It struck midnight as I wrote the above sentence, & I suddenly discovered that I was sleepy and went to bed. The morning brings nothing new but rain—which isn't at all new, & a letter from Lizzie Boott, from Rome.   À propos of this, I have pretty well decided to repair thither a fortnight hence.   A fortnight ago I thought of sticking it out in Paris two or three months more & letting Rome pass for the present.   But I have come to the conclusion that this would be a tolerably—in fact an extremely—unremunerative course, & that if I have a chance to nail Rome I ought to do it without delay.   I expect therefore to start about the 15ᵗʰ & beg you to address your letters till I give you a permanent address Care of *Spada, Flamini & Co. Bankers.*   If anything comes to me here after I leave I can trust Mme. Thuillier[9] to forward it.   Lizzie B. is enchanted with Rome & seems to be in the midst of a nest of Americans—who, I can't say form an unmitigated attraction.   Still, I shall brave them.   Aunt Mary Tweedy has just written me a second time, at great length, reviling the place as a "nest of abominations," & I am afraid from what Lizzie B. says, that in spite of her coupé with a "snowy stud," she is unhappy there.   She offers me a room in their apartment, which I shall discreetly, & I hope, unoffendingly, decline.   It would make one feel that the world was terribly small.————There were several things in your letter which I had at heart to reply to, categorically; but I must leave them till another time   For the present, farewell.

Yours ever   H. James jr

Was your overcoat satisfactory—& the Wordsworth.

ALS: MH bMS AM 1094 (1948)

[1] An error in dating.   Apparently the letter was begun on 1 December and continued on 2 December, a Monday.

[2] Although HJ clearly wrote '&', the phrase should read 'at my silence'.

[3] Gail Hamilton, pseudonym of Mary Abigail Dodge (1833–1896), editor of *Wood's Household Magazine* in 1872–73.   HJ's story was "The Sweetheart of M. Briseux," published in *Galaxy* 15 (June 1873): 760–79; see *HJL*, 1:334.

[4] John Holmes (1812–1899), brother of Oliver Wendell Holmes, Sr.   John Holmes had no special occupation and it is not clear why he made several trips to Europe.   In any case, he found very few European places that compared favorably with Brattle St., Cambridge.

[5]Nothing concerning Charles H. Dorr was found, except that he was somewhat older than HJ. Dorr's wife is occasionally mentioned as a Boston hostess.

[6]Theodore Lyman (1833–1897), American zoologist, married Elizabeth Russell. Miss G. Russell is not identified.

[7]HJ probably intended to write 'and'.

[8]Louis-Adolphe Thiers (1797–1877), French statesman, head of the government after the Franco-Prussian War.

[9]Apparently, HJ's Parisian landlady.

To Henry James

Cambr. Dec [8, 1872]

My dear Harry

I can write you but a few lines to day. Your letter of Nov 12, complaining of no news fm. A. & A.K. came to day. Some days ago came a later letter in wh. you had heard. Your questions about the fire will have been answered by Father. There is no news here to tell you. I wrote you (before—?) last Sunday I think, and sent a bottle of hydrastis canadensis to the banker's for you. The Nation containing yr. letter fm. Milan &c was sent you.[1] I think you will have got it by this time. It was kept a long while by them. Dennett wrote me the other day that they were always frightfully overcrowded. Perry says that D. wants badly to enlarge the paper, but Godkin resists till they have got 10,000 subscribers, showing I shd. think poor editorial tact, if the thing can possibly be afforded at present. I enclose a request fm. P. wh. I hope you will feel like complying with. I shd. enjoy nothing myself more than an article bristling with plums fm. Gautier. The prurience of the human mind never seemed to me better shown than by the fact that all the notices of G. which I have seen since his death have dwelt upon Mlle. Maupin with great emphasis as if it were *the* book of the author—I hope you'll ignore it altogether if you write— he is sufficiently big for an article on the basis of the "balance" of his works.[2] I can send you his books by Post if you want them to refer to. Thos. told me he shd. like you very much to review Morley's Rousseau for him. He seems uncommon well & genial, and is going to write a long notice of Middlemarch for his April No.[3] I am in the 4th vol of that wonderful work & stand perfectly aghast at the tremenj'us intellectual power displayed. Surely 'tis the *biggest* novel ever writ. I can make no critical estimate of it without reading more, and I wish that you when you get through with your copy wd. send it home by mail.   That wd. probably be cheaper for us considerably than buying even, Harper's bad edition here.

Aunt Kate has gone to N.Y. yielding again the first floor bedroom to me, wh. feels now like a great luxury.   Many is the pang of simpathy I have felt of late up in that roof room, with you during these past dreary winters.   This one has been delicious so far.   A steady temperature of about 30 – 34 with but one cold day to break it, and the winter sticking as persistently to the SW, as it did last year to the NW. I have just come fm. seeing Wright, whom I find unmodified by Europe, except that he's fatter.   Father read his paper on Carlyle yesterday at the Radical Club very successfully.[4]   He is writing now what I think will be a much better presentment of his views on "Creation" than the former ones.[5]   Alice keeps wonderfully well & cheerful.   I hope that your bwls are in decent order, and that altogether you feel alive & vigorous.   I shd. think you'd ought ter after your summer and being in Paris.   Farewell.

Ever affect.ly yours   W.J.

ALS: MH bMS AM 1092.9 (2582)

[1] Reference is to the sixth installment of HJ, "A European Summer"; see letter of 24 July 1872.

[2] HJ wrote a review article on Gautier, "Théâtre de Théophile Gautier: Mystères, Comédies, et Ballets," *North American Review* 116 (April 1873): 310–29.

[3] Thomas Sergeant Perry, review of George Eliot, *Middlemarch* (New York: Harper & Brothers, 1872), in *North American Review* 116 (April 1873): 432–40.

[4] The reading is not mentioned in *Sketches and Reminiscences of the Radical Club*, ed. Mrs. John T. Sergeant (Boston: James R. Osgood and Co., 1880).   Henry James later published "Some Personal Recollections of Carlyle," *Atlantic Monthly* 47 (May 1881): 593–609.

[5] Perhaps Henry James, *Society the Redeemed Form of Man* (Boston: Houghton, Osgood and Co., 1879).

From Henry James

Rome, Hotel de Rome | Jan 8th [1873]
Dearest Wm.   I am so heavily in your debt for letters that I despair of discharging my obligations at a single sitting.   Nevertheless, I must make a beginning.   Shortly before I left Paris came to me your large & delightful communication of Nov. 24th, & since my arrival here I have been overtaken by your note of Dec. 8, enclosing T. S. Perry's petition to write on Théophile Gautier.   I have had the beginning of a letter on my pen's end many times these last ten days, when Rome has been peculiarly suggestive & it has seemed a pity to swallow my

impressions like a greedy feeder without offering some one a taste of it. You will know through my letter to mother of my having been here a fortnight how I got here &c. I am taking Rome much more quietly & prosaically than before (—to this complexion do we come at last!)—but a certain restlessless was inevitable during the first days. This I have well worked off and now really feel at home. But I ought to tell you without delay of Mr. Tweedy, whom I found tolerably ill. He has been mending steadily ever since my arrival & it seems to me that his smooth recovery proves more in favor of the Roman climate than against it. His trouble was in no degree "Roman fever"—he is confident he would have had it anywhere, as he had been for many weeks gastrically deranged. For the past day or two he has been a little less well; but the interruption is transient & I think he expects very soon to drive out. Aunt Mary, somewhat mellowed by tribulation, has been very hospitable & gracious to me: indeed I feel, dining, & driving with her, as if during poor Tweedy's eclipse, I were enacting a sort of *caro sposo*. Her dinners are of course good—& her drives (when she doesn't use up too much sunshine in a preliminary round at the butcher's & baker's) must be taken to be appreciated. She has a most affable coachman who talks, not Italian, but Roman—delicious stately, full-lipped *Latin*, which adds greatly to the local color of a drive on the Appian way.—I rec'd. a couple of days since a blessed letter from mother, full of all goodness and especially of tender injunctions as to the care of my health. They are not superfluous, but I am incapable of being imprudent. I have made an excellent *début* in Rome, in this respect. In Paris, I may say, I was not especially well for some five or six weeks before leaving; but since my arrival here all is changed & I am better than ever, almost. I don't know whether it is Paris's fault or Rome's virtue; but so it is and so may it remain! It is hard to think any ill of a climate in which on the 8th of January, you sit as I am doing now, fireless and coatless at your open window, with your room more than warmed—heated, by the strong sunshine. It is a blessed change from drenched & draggled Paris. The flies are irritating my nose, I have just killed a mosquito on my window curtain, & in half an hour I am going (by invitation) to drive with Miss Cleveland & Lizzie Boott in the Villa Wolkonski.—Mother's letter spoke cheerfully of most things at home save of father's health. I am very sorry to hear of his having again those strange visitations (as I infer the case to be) of last winter. Give him my love & my wishes for their leaving him as suddenly as, if I remember right, they did before. I have had lately a good batch of home news, in the shape of a letter from A.K. and one from mother (as well my own) to A.M.T., which the latter gave me.[1]   A. Kate mentions uncle James's death, of which I hadn't heard;[2] a relief of course to every one.   Yesterday came an *Atlantic*, with my *Bethnal Green* Notice & its other rare treasures.[3] The B.G.N. doesn't figure very solidly as a "Lady-article"; it was meant as a notice.   But it is as good as the rest, which, save Howells' two pieces, which his genius saves, read rather queerly in Rome.[4]   As I ought to be decently punctual for Miss Cleveland, I postpone further utterance to this evening which I shall devote to you.—Calling last evening, by the way, on Miss C. to tell her in answer to a note that I would drive with her, I found her mother in *tête à tête* with Mrs. Kemble, of whom I had thus half an hours contemplation.   She is very magnificent, & was very gracious, & being draped (for an evening call) in lavender satin lavishly *décolleté*, reminded me strangely, in her talk and manner, of the time when as infants, in St. John's Wood, we heard her read the Midsummer night's dream.[5]   It was very singular how the smallest details of her physiognomy come back to me. *Evening.*   The Wolkonski is of course charming, but the visit was one of those party affairs which are (to me, at least) so deadly unprofitable.   Miss Cleveland had invited the two Miss Greenoughs & Lizzie Boott & I stood round holding their shawls & listening to their prattle & grinning & wishing them at the deuce—& resolving I would go there before I got entrapped again.—I dined at the Tweedies' (an occasional privilege which bad Roman tratterias makes most valuable) and sat for an hour conversing by Tweedy's bedside.—I have been reading over your fine long letter to me in Paris, & find it contains a bewildering amount of answerable matter.   Often in Paris I felt as if I had a hundred things to say to you, but I came away before the best of them got written, & now such of them as will keep must wait for future days.—It was a very pleasant & profitable couple of months I had there, & though to be at one's ease in Paris probably seemed to you in Quincy Street a more rich and wonderful fortune than it did as a regular thing to me, yet at certain hours I enjoyed it all keenly & gathered a host of impressions.   Every thing Italian & especially everything Roman, that is not a ruin, a landscape or a Museum, has such a deadly provinciality & more than American dreariness, that in coming here with a mindful of Parisian memories, one seems to have turned one's back on modern civilization.   I regretted much in Paris, however, never having the chance to exchange a word with a typical Frenchman, & there grew to be something irritating at last in this perpetual humiliating sense of ungratified curiosity.

There came enclosed yesterday in mother's letter a note from T.S.P. offering me (if I would write back & ask for it!) an introduction from J.L.F. to Paul de Saint Victor.[6]   If it had come while I was there, I should have been very glad to use it; but if I had had to wait till John had heard from me & brought himself to send it out, I should, short of a miracle, have waited six months.   But the mere daily & hourly spectacle of human life in Paris is greatly suggestive & remunerative.—*À propos* of all this, I thank you for the trouble of writing to sustain T. S. Perry's request to do something for the N.A.R. about Gautier.   I immediately wrote to him that I couldn't undertake anything on the large scale you recommend, having just now neither the inclination nor the opportunity (lacking his volumes) to re-read him all, *plume en main*: but I shall do something shorter which I hope he may make serve.[7]—I am far from surprised at the admiration you express in your last for *Middlemarch*.   I read it all in Paris & sent a review of it to the dilatory *Nation*.[8]   (The *N*. has now *five* unprinted things of mine: of course I shan't add to the number till they begin to disgorge.)   I admired & relished *Middlemarch* hugely, & yet I am afraid you will think I have spoken of it stingily.   I necessarily judged it I suppose, more critically than you.   Nevertheless, I didn't make perhaps, a sufficiently succinct statement of its rare intellectual power.   This is amazing.—You ask me to tell you what I am reading & thinking.   I have been thinking (if thinking it may be called) almost too many things and reading too few.   No new books—cropping simply on the few old volumes I brought with me.   (About sending you *Middlemarch* by post—I left my set of it in Paris, to be kept at the Rastadt with a small pile of other books.   It would have cost more than you seem to think—certainly more than Harper's cheap reprint.)—What I find Rome and am likely to find it, it is hard to say in few words.   Much less simply & sensuously & satisfyingly picturesque than before, but on the whole immensely interesting.   It is a strange jumble now of its old inalterable self and its new Italian assumptions—a most disturbing one for sentimentalists, such as generally all educated strangers are, here.   It is an impossible modern city &. will be a lugubrious modern capital, such as Victor Emanuel is trying to make it.[9]   It has for this purpose both too many virtues and too many vices.   It is too picturesque to spoil & too inconvenient to remedy.   Of course in living here one isn't perpetually wound-up to the seventh heaven of "appreciation" & sensation, but every now & then there come to you great gusts of largely-mingled delight such as no other place can give.   Generally, what one feels and inhales, nat-

urally & easily, with every breath, is the importunate presence of tradition of every kind—the influence of an atmosphere electrically
charged with historic intimations and whisperings.   Practical profit
from so huge an influence as this must disengage itself shortly, but I
hope eventually to get much.   I shall stay on here as late as possible
into the lovely spring & give myself a chance to react.—American "Society" here as far as I can judge of it, is a rather meagre affair, & the
Bootts & Tweedies stand up in familiar shape like dusky terminal
stones along the social horizon.   However I am invited to dine on
Sunday by Mrs. Terry (née Crawford,)—or rather made Crawford, &
née a sister of Mrs. Howe.   She lives in great state in the Odescalchi
palace & has a very agreeable and clever daughter.   I am also bidden
on Saturday evening by Mrs. Wister whom I have before mentioned
& whom every one greatly admires.   She is at moments, in certain
lights & with her hat on, a startling likeness to Minny Temple; but the
likeness is all in the face.—The "artist" society in Rome I have as yet
seen nothing of.   As far as it is American, I doubt that it amounts to
much. I hear of no interesting men.   I see the Bootts occasionally &
find them of course unchanged.   Lizzie is as sweet & good as ever, &
is greatly enjoying Rome.   She has a little studio, where she paints
little tatterdemalion Checcos & Ninas—with decidedly increasing
ability.   She also rides three or four times a week with Miss Cleveland
& a groom—& that would be enough to make misery smile.   Lizzie
has still the attribute of making you fancy from her deadly languid
passivity at times, that she is acutely miserable.   But she is evidently
very happy & has plenty of society.   Boott also greatly relishes
Rome—that is his daily half-dozen walks with his overcoat on his arm.
But they are fixed, I believe, to return in July.—I am writing such a
letter as will ruin me in postage, & yet I haven't said any of the things
which I have had it in my mind to say.—You suppose me of course to
be growing all the while in wisdom & skill from association with those
objects which you keenly feel the absence of.   I grow more slowly
than it must seem in Cambridge, that I ought to; but that I do grow, I
hope continually to prove.   I find I can work quite enough: but that
I have everything to learn in the way of *how* to work.—I would write a
short notice of Morley's Rousseau if I could have the book: but I can't
get it here in Rome without great expense.   I am now doing something for the *Atlantic*.—By this time I suppose you have begun to lecture or teach or preach, or whatever it is.   Amen!   This letter is for
Alice as well as you: so that I send her no vain message but my love.

This also to my parents.   Farewell.—What a poor business is writing after all!   Answer my letter nevertheless.

Ever yours   H.

ALS: MH bMS AM 1094 (1949)

[1] Mary Tweedy.

[2] James Walsh, youngest brother of WJ's mother.

[3] HJ, "The Bethnal Green Museum," *Atlantic Monthly* 31 (January 1873): 69–75.

[4] William Dean Howells, "A Chance Acquaintance," part 1, *Atlantic Monthly* 31 (January 1873): 17–28; "Among the Ruins," 31 (January 1873): 97–101.

[5] Saint John's Wood is a district in northwest London where the Jameses lived in 1855–56.

[6] Paul-Jacques-Raymond Binsee, comte de Saint Victor (1827–1881), French essayist and critic.

[7] See letter of 8 December 1872.

[8] A review of *Middlemarch* by HJ appeared in *Galaxy*; see letters of 24 November 1872 and 13 February 1873.

[9] Victor Emmanuel II (1820–1878), first king of unified Italy.

To Henry James

Cambr. Feb. 13. 73

Dear Harry.

Your letter to me fm. Rome of Jany(?) came to hand some 3 or 4 days agone, & most welcome it was.   I have been prevented fm. writing you the many letters lately I have felt like emitting, by having my hands too full of other business.   To hear of your dolce far niente under a summer sky, and enthroned among such high sounding, yet familiar names, both of places and of women, is like unto a dream, in white skied Cambridge.   That you speak so soundly of health and capacity for work is indeed a subject for rejoicing.   And I hope that Roman impressions will some day surprise you by summating themselves suddenly into conscious increment of wisdom, as such things do surely enough, whether you worry about them or not.   To day Advertizer & Tribune are out with notices of your tale, which I clip out & enclose.   Father decided to squeeze it into one no. by docking its two episodes, I think with advantage, tho' the first one might have had its sense preserved, with the loss of its some what cold & repulsive details had anyone here had the art to abridge it into a short and poetically vague statement that he had once broken with an iconoclastic love.   On a 3rd reading I quite agreed with Howells that the story was transparent enough without the 2nd episode, which then became

an excrescence.   Altogether the story is a masterpiece.[1]   Your Bethnal green article, notice of Regnault & Paris theatres, were all admirably easy in touch.[2]   What a slow and mysterious thing the growth
of skill is, and how it must cheer one to be convinced that it still takes
place in him!   Osgood sent $60 for Bethnal Green.[3]   T.S.P. said he
thought you might make better terms for yourself now by asking, and
ought to look out for yourself with them, as they are a mean house.
The nation is quite the reverse of mean, sending me e.g. $5.00 for a
"*note*" on Renouvier's philosophy in last week's no, for wh. I never
expected a cent.[4]   T'is a great pity they have crowded out your things
so.   I hope your last Summer in Europe letter may be used again or
elsewhere, but have heard nothing of its Fate.   Perry dined here yesterday, saying he had got your Gautier and wd put it into the April
no.[5]   He liked it.   He is growing to have the calm breadth and san-
guineness of middle life.   His Editorial work agrees with him very
well, and I should think he probably did it pretty well, altho his original writing seems pretty ineffectual, at least he gave me a very lame
abstract of a notice he had written of Middlemarch.[6]   He was very
sorry Dennett had sent yours to the Galaxy instead of to him.[7]   What
a blasted artistic failure Middlemarch is but what a well of wisdom.
It may be a case of not seeing the forest for the trees, it may be that
her "purpose" did not work out clear in her own mind, but the obscu-
rity of the ending disappoints everybody.   Her perpetual tendency
to criticise and preach a propos of every detail make you expect some
rather distinct doctrine or conclusion to emerge from the ensemble,
and its being sandwiched between those two St. Theresa covers, still
further stimulates you to look for it.[8]   Unsheathe the Lydgate-Rosa-
mund episode fm. the rest, and you have in it a pure artistic study,
perfectly successful and being an end in itself, but Ladislaw-Dorothea
suggest too much & solve too little.   And again the cold blooded construction and firm working out of that miserable old mechanical *ficelle*
of Bulstrode-Ladislaw-Raffles-Casaubon—which she adopted fm. the
common novelists property-room but which was never born in her
private imagination, and which she can't possibly have had any glow
about—her crafty skill in the use of this old rubbish, I say, forbids one
to excuse her constructive short comings where there *is* a moral matter involved, on the plea of an innate incapacity for plan and *use* of
material.

Feb. 14.   My pen rushed headlong into this diatribe on middlemarch yesterday without the least premeditation, leaving me just time
to dress for a dinner party at the Morses in town.   Alice was seized in

the midst of her toilet by an intensely acute colic (caused no doubt by inhaling sewer gas wh. came pouring out of all our waste pipes this mng. esp^ly in the pantry where she in the lack of a "parlor girl" was washing the bkfst. things.) and cd. not go, wh. was a pity, as the party was given in her name. I packed off in a carriage with Mr. & Mrs Child, thermometer at 10°, they going to a dinner at the Bangs's,[9] & Child cursing and swearing all the way in. At the Morses sat between Mrs M. & the beauteous and adorably naive miss Mary M. Opposite were Jim Putnam Miss Bessie Lee & Edwd Emerson who has returned more charming than ever,[10] and beyond me Chas. Jackson,[11] & Theodora Sedgwick while Mr. Morse sat silently blushing, squinting & showing his dazzling teeth in a lady like manner at the head of the table. I enjoyed it extremely, as it was my first & probably last dinner party of the season. Coming home found that Alice had soon been relieved "copieusement" (proving cause of trouble) and was all right. This morning arose went to Brewer's to get two partridge's to garnish our cod fish dinner.[12] Bought at Richardson's an Appleton's Journal containing part i of "Bressant" a novel by Julian Hawthorne[13] to send Bob Temple. At 10.30 arrived your letter of Jany. 26th wh. was a very pleasant continuation of your Aufenthalt in Rome. At 12.30 after reading an hour in Flints physiology,[14] I went to town paid a bill of Randidge's[15] looked in to the Atheneum reading room, got 1 doz. raw oysters at Higgins's saloon in Court Street, came out again, thermometer having risen to near thawing point, dozed ½ an hour before the fire, and am now writing this to you.—I am enjoying a two weeks respite from tuition the boys being condemned to pass examinations, in which I luckily take no part at present. I find the work very interesting and stimulating. It presents two problems, the intellectual one—how best to state your matter to them, and the practical one, how to govern them, stir them up, not bore them, yet make them work &c. I should think it not unpleasant as a permanent thing. The authority is at first rather flattering to one. So far, I seem to have succeeded in interesting them, for they are admirably attentive, and I hear of expressions of satisfaction on their part. Whether it will go on next year cant at this hour, for many reasons, be decided. I have done almost absolutely no visiting this winter, and seen hardly any one or heard any thing till last week when a sort of frenzy took possession of me and I went to a symphony concert & thrice to the theatre. A most lovely English actress, young, innocent, refined, has been playing Juliet, which play I enjoyed most intensley, tho' it was at the Boston theatre and her support almost as poor as it could have been. Neilson is she hight. I ne'er heard of her before.[16]   A rival american beauty has been playing a stinking thing of Sardou's (Agnes) at the Globe, which disgusted me with cleverness.   Her name is Miss Ethel, and she is a lady like but depressing phenomenon, all made up of nerves & american insubstantiality.[17]   I have read hardly anything of late, some of the immortal Wordsworth's excursion having been the best.[18]   I have simply shaken hands with Gray since his engagement, and have only seen holmes 2ce this winter.   I fear he is at last feeling the effects of his overwork.   I wish he and his wife wd. go abroad for 6 mos. after he gets his Kent out in the Spring. It might be the salvation of him physically and of her mentally.— Freund returned to Breslau this week with wife & brats.[19]   Letter fm. Wilky this A.M. saying he may take a new place on the R.R. at "Watertown," lonely but active & more instructive than his present office. Carrie can't leave her Father or Milwaukie.[20]

Poor Mr. Tweedy.   I'm very glad to hear of his definitive recovery. He must have had a dismal time of it when sick.   But I envied you your run of the house, and your drives in the Coupé.—I enclose one of Bob's recent notes.

—No jokes, no anything to tell you.   My own spirits are very good, as I have got some things rather straitened out in my mind lately, and this external responsibility and college work agree with human nature better than lonely self culture.

Adieu! Adieu!   Enjoy & produce.   If you are still with Tweedies & Bootts when you get this give them my love.   I got a week ago a letter & some photogs. fm. Miss Lizzie Boott wh. I will soon reply to.   She seems to have missed one letter I wrote her.

Yrs.   W.J.

ALS: MH bMS Am 1092.9 (2583)

[1] WJ is describing the editing of "The Madonna of the Future," *Atlantic Monthly* 31 (March 1873): 276–97.   For HJ's reaction and a fuller account of Howells's qualms, see HJ's letter to his father, 1 February 1873, *HJL*, 1:333–36.

[2] See letter of 8 January 1873 for "The Bethnal Green Museum"; "Henri Regnault," *Nation* 16 (2 January 1873): 13–15; "The Parisian Stage," *Nation* 16 (9 January 1873): 23–24.

[3] James R. Osgood & Co., publishers of the *Atlantic Monthly*.

[4] WJ, note on Renouvier's contribution to *La Critique Philosophique*, in *Nation* 16 (6 February 1873): 94 (*ECR*).

[5] See letter of 8 December 1872.

[6] See letter of 8 December 1872.

[7] See letter of 24 November 1872.

[8] *Middlemarch* begins and ends with allusions to St. Theresa, while Dorothea, the heroine, is described as a later-born Theresa.

[9] Not identified.

[10] Edward Emerson, his sister Ellen Tucker Emerson, and their father were in Europe in fall 1872. Edward returned home, while the other two traveled to Egypt, returning to Concord in May 1873.

[11] Charles Loring Jackson (1847–1935), American chemist, taught at Harvard from 1871.

[12] There were two provision dealers with that name on Brattle St., Cambridge.

[13] Julian Hawthorne, *Bressant* (New York: D. Appleton, 1873). Benjamin Richardson sold books and stationery at 5 Harvard Square, Cambridge.

[14] Austin Flint, Jr., *The Physiology of Man*, 5 vols. (1866–75).

[15] George L. Randidge, a tailor, 6 Tremont St., Boston.

[16] Adelaide Neilson (1846–1880), English actress, performing in *Romeo and Juliet* at the Boston Theater.

[17] Agnes Ethel (1852–1903), American actress, appeared in *Agnes* at the Globe Theater. This appears to be an adaptation from Victorien Sardou (1831–1908), French playwright.

[18] William Wordsworth, *The Excursion* (1814).

[19] Wilhelm Alexander Freund (1833–1918), German physician.

[20] Both GWJ and RJ were then working for the Chicago, Milwaukee and St. Paul Railway. For an account of the tensions between the Jameses and Joseph Cary, GWJ's wife's father, see *BBF*, 116.

To Henry James

Cambr. April 6th 1873

My dear Harry

I take up my pen once more after this long interval to converse with my in many respects twin bro. We have not heard from you in a fortnight and eagerly expect a letter to day, describing new sensual delights and luxuries in wh. your body & soul shall have alike been wallowing. Alice & I keep up a rather constant fire of badinage &c of which you furnish the material; she never speaking of you except as "that angel"—and I sarcastically calling you the "angel-hero-martyr." Usually towards bed-time I wander into the parlor where the three are sitting and say "I suppose that angel is now in such and such an attitude,["] drawing on my imagination for something very "oriental," to which alice generally finds no better reply than a tirade upon the petty jealousies of *men*. Long may you have the power of enjoying what luxuries you can get!—Of home news the chief is that Wilky has been promoted to be ass! paymaster on his road, a place of no greater salary but of more honour & responsability. 6,000,000 pass through his hands yearly, his headquarters are in Milwaukee, but he has a great deal of traveling to do, and comes into contact with

men.   He seems quite set up by the change and says—but hold—I'll
enclose his letter!—Alice has been for 10 days in N.Y. & returns to
morrow with A.K.   She writes as if she had enjoyed herself.—I have
just got through 3 months of tuition, and have 4 weeks holiday before
taking them up again for a final month.   It has turned out a solider
job than I anticipated, both in respect of the effort it has taken to put
it through and in respect of the information I have imparted.   Altogether I look back on it with some satisfaction, while feeling all the
time how much better & easier I could do it another year.   Whether
I shall be asked to is doubtful.   Eliot offered me the other day the
whole department (i.e this physiology + Dwight's anatomy) for next
year.¹   But I told him I had resolved to fight it out on the line of
mental science, & with such arrears of lost time behind me & such
curtailed power of work now, could not afford to make such an expedition into anatomy.   It cost me some perplexity to make the decision, for had I accepted, it might easily grow into a permanent biolog-
ical appointment, to succeed Wyman perhaps;² and that study, tho'
less native to my taste, has many things in its favor.   But I am satisfied
the decision I made was a wise one, and I shall bide my time, they
looking out for some one man to take the work that Dwight & I have
shared between us.   I have done enough now to show me that the
duty of teaching comes kindly to me, and that I probably should become a good instructor with practice.   From what I hear reported
the boys have been satisfied so far.—Another event for us has been
the reception of a proof (minus the first 3 or 4 pages) of your article
on Gautier.³   It is admirable, delightful, as good as G. himself at his
best, & when one considers that it was written impromptu, i.e. from
memory, it shows after all that the power one contains in his skin at a
given moment does accumalate insensibly by years and experience.
When one sees you doing that sort of thing so well, it makes one curse
every day that passes without your trying your hand on Tourguenief,
Balzac, G. Sand, Dumas fils & others.   Collected, they would make a
standard book.   You must come to it some day, for no talent can escape its destiny. And my dying words to you are, therefore: Keep that
in mind as one of your ends, and take notes with reference to it as you
read.   The book would be d'autant plus valuable, if a string of gener-
alisation about the french character went through it, that is, if the
special studies were but chapters of a general study of the french
mind in certain of its aspects.   I have been, or rather still am, reading
a very vigorous & important book, Frankreich u. die Franzosen by
Hillebrand, which has stirred me up a good deal.⁴   I'd give much to

talk it over with you in the light of your recent experience. He, though seeing wondrously into the french mind, is yet so little sympathetic with it, *condemns* it so from the thoroughly German Weltanschauung in which plunged to the armpits he rests gleefully planted, that it arouses a spirit of antagonism in one. Disbelief in invisible ends, or even in any visible ends so complex that they can't be clearly analysed & formulated, whence their rationalizing radicalism, their vanity, & their worldly prudence, timidity & intellectual gregariousness, are the the burden of his complaint. But you will of course read the book in french, as it can't fail of being translated soon, and ought to do great good to those frenchmen strong minded enough to appropriate its criticism. The mans soul is not nearly so cosmopolitan as his intellect.—'Tis a dull gray windless weeping Sunday morn. I shall now pretermit this exercise, do a job or two about the house and go to pay my usual Sunday call on Sara Sedgwick.—The poor thing seems very poorly & gets little society—and finish my letter on returning. In your last by the bye you said nothing of having got one from me which should have been due. I hope it went not astray.—12.30 P.M. I am just back from the sedgwicks via the P.O. in wh. no letter from you was found. [Let me say ere I forget it that both your last letter and Wilky's have been sent to A.K., so that I can't give you date of former, nor enclose the latter. This shall be done in the next that is written, if A.K. brings it back to morrow. Both M. & F. say they have written to you since your last arrived. I hope nothing of yours has been lost in that fearful wreck of the Atlantic.[5] I should almost feel if I had habitually to mail manuscripts like you that I had better keep a copy, wh. cd. be done by writing with copying ink, and either getting a small press or using some tradesman's or banker's to take off the impression. Every business man takes in that way a duplicate of his letters.] I sat with Theodora & Sara for an hour—conversation largely consisting of us chaffing Theodora. That amiable but narrow sympathied creature is fretting for a larger sphere than Cambridge affords tho' I doubt if she knows what's the matter with her. To all her complaints the black-draped females of the house have no remedy to offer but that she should read some instructive book, and it is quite refreshing to hear her kick out occasionally. To day she confessed that she ought to "keep up" her German, if only there were anything decent to read. Sara suggested Goethe's Wahrheit u. D. when she broke out "Oh! I can n't STAND a third life of Goethe in 6 months" with a genuine impulsiveness that was quite amusing. She ought to be in a brilliant moving social medium, with continual novelties, and plenty of men to see, and I don't wonder that she *morfonds* herself here with never a man but Child & myself, and all those grimly conscientious women.   Anne Ashb. grows in character and expression more & more like unto Lachesis, Atropos, or what dye call the other of the Parcae I know not which.[6]—Sara is lovely to the core, and it seems truly deplorable that she should be growing so delicate.   If you could sling her a letter I think it would make her feel good.—I have been cut off this winter from the men with whom I used to gossip on *generalities* Holmes, Putnam, Peirce, Shaler & John Gray, and last not least yourself.   I rather hanker after it, Bowditch being almost the only man I have seen any thing of this winter, and that at his laboratory.   Anderson has fallen sick and gone home for the rest of the academic year.   Child & I have struck up quite an intimacy.   The poor man is stifled beneath his themes, his babies, his helpless wife & his poverty.   To add to the horrors of his situation Mrs. Channing is coming to live in the house!!!![7]   After that his sun may be considered set.   He wants fearfully to go abroad this summer both for his health & for his ballads of which a new edition is to be published, but he can't raise the money.[8]   I wish I could give it to him, for with all his intellectual shortcomings er ist und bleibt the cleanest & best man I know.   I have struck up quite an intimacy with him.   Last night strolling out in the twilight after dinner I dropped in upon him.   Mrs Child was in N.Y. with her dying brother.[9]   he was giving the beautiful faced Helen & the complacently-finite Susy their tea.   And he went on talking in his old erotic vein, saying he was in despair about Arthur[10] & me, that a man ought to go in at a venture, not grow gray with waiting and so forth—that love's pains were superior to all the other pleasures in the world &c &c. T.S.P. is my only surviving crony.   He dines pretty regular once a week here, and is acquiring some thing of the amplitude & settled calmness of middle life.   His work & life perfectly suit him now.   His review will be published to morrow & a copy shall be mailed to you forthwith.   The notice of Middlemarch is by him, he sweat more over it and expresses himself less [s]atisfied with it than he has ever done before, so I'm curious to see it.[11]   Adieu, I must not write forever.   Give much love to the Bootts & Tweedies, if you see them.   I rather envy you riding on the Campagna with the wonderful miss Bartlett, but I hope you'll continue to enjoy it.   Henry Higginson goes as "Commissioner" to Vienna[12] & Chas Atkinson to Europe generally on a vacation tour of a couple of months.   He sorely needs it, but does not yet know his itinerary.   Father has just slung a very readable article for Howells, in the form of a review of a book on Spiritualism.[13]

Ever yr. affect^nte   W.J.

ALS: MH bMS Am 1092.9 (2584)

[1] WJ did not teach in 1873–74.   When he returned in 1874–75, he was responsible for the whole of Natural History 3, including both anatomy and physiology.

[2] Jeffries Wyman (1814–1874), American anatomist and physician, one of WJ's major teachers at Harvard.

[3] See letter of 8 December 1872.

[4] Karl Hillebrand, *Frankreich und die Franzosen in der zweiten hälfte der XIX Jahrhunderts* (1873).

[5] The steamship *Atlantic* of the White Star Line was wrecked off Halifax, Nova Scotia, 1 April 1873.   Newspaper reports claim that more than 700 lives were lost, including all of the women and children on board.

[6] The fates in Greek and Roman mythology.

[7] Child's predecessor at Harvard was Edward Tyrrell Channing (1790–1856), professor of rhetoric and oratory.   Perhaps Mrs. Channing was his widow, Henrietta Ellery Channing.

[8] Francis James Child, *English and Scottish Ballads*, 8 vols. (1857–58).   There were several later editions, with slight variations in the title.   The earliest edition later than the date of this letter appeared in 1877.

[9] Elizabeth Sedgwick Child had one brother, Charles Sedgwick.

[10] Arthur George Sedgwick.

[11] See letter of 8 December 1872.

[12] Henry Lee Higginson was a member of a commission established by the Massachusetts legislature to visit and report on the Vienna Exposition. According to Higginson's biographer, the trip was a junket and the commissioners spent most of their time shopping in Paris (Bliss Perry, *The Life and Letters of Henry Lee Higginson* [Boston: Atlantic Monthly Press, 1921], 279).

[13] Henry James, review of M. J. Williamson, *Modern Diabolism* (New York: James Miller, 1873), in *Atlantic Monthly* 32 (August 1873): 219–24.

From Henry James

Rome 101 Corso | April 9th 73.

Dear W^m:—

I have had in hand from you for some time a letter of Feb. 13th, which gave me great pleasure on its arrival & of which I have just been refreshing my memory.   Three days since too came a letter from father of March 18, which I shall answer at my next writing. Many thanks to him meanwhile.   As always, when I write, I feel that in some mood a week or two before, I would have had a good deal more to say & that the full stream of utterance is not turned on at this particular hour.　But we must say what we can—and read it.　From all my letters as they come, you get, I suppose, a certain impression of my life, if not of my soul.　In fact, my soul has not been quite as active as a well regulated soul should be.　(By soul, here, I mean especially brain.)　The winter is at last fairly over, & I can look at it as a whole & decide that though under the circumstances I am fairly satisfied with it, I shouldn't care to spend another just like it.　All of it that has been of pure Rome (with the exception of one point) has been delightful: but there is little left here now of which that can be said & the mark of the fiend—the American fiend—is on everything.　I surrendered myself with malice prepense when I came, to whatever "social" entanglements should come up.　They multiplied actively & took up my evenings pretty well for three months; but on retrospect they don't seem to have been very remunerative.　I have seen few new people & no new types, & met not a single man, old or young, of any interest.　There have been several interesting women "round"— Mrs. Wister being the one I saw most of—but none of the men have fait époque in my existence.　Mrs. Wister has gone, to bury her regrets in Germantown Penn., & I have of late been seeing a good deal of Mrs. Sumner & Miss Bartlett, who live together, are now my neighbors, & since I have given up my horse have amiably invited me several times to ride one of theirs—having three.　They are both superior & very natural women, & Mrs. Sumner a very charming one (to Miss B. I feel very much as if she were a boy—an excellent fellow)— but they are limited by a kind of characteristic American want of culture.　(Mrs. W. has much more of this—a good deal in fact, & a very literary mind, if not a powerful one.)　For the rest society (for Americans) is very thin and such at home as we would dream of coming somewhere else to get something superior to.　Storys and Terrys soon pall, & such is our fatal capacity for getting *blasé* that it soon ceased to be for me, what it was at first, a kind of pretty spectacle to go to their houses.　At the S.'s however, the other night I met & conversed for a few minutes with Matthew Arnold, whom, if I had more ingenuity, I suppose I might have managed to see more of.　He is handsome but not as handsome as his fame or his poetry & (to me) he said nothing momentous.　But I think I mentioned all this in my last.　This in parenthesis.　I suppose there are interesting individuals to know in Rome, but I doubt that there is any very edifying society.　And I doubt that one meets interesting—generally interesting—individuals anywhere by going round & hungering for them. If you have some active prosperous speciality, it introduces you to fellow-workers, & the interest of such is the one, I suppose that wears best.—My own speciality has suffered a good deal, for the immediate hour, by my still unformed and childish habits of application having been much at the mercy of the distractions & preoccupations of my daily goings & comings, innocent as they have been. I have written less than I had supposed I should & read not at all. But in the long run I have gained for it has all after all been "quite an experience" & I have gathered more impressions I am sure than I suppose—impressions I shall find a value in when I come to use them. And for the actual writing now that life is growing quieter, I shall sufficiently overtake myself. The point at which, above, I took exception to Rome in itself is one I have only gradually made up my mind about—namely, the influence of the climate. (This has had much to do with my intellectual idleness.) When I first came & the winter gave it a certain freshness, I felt nothing but its lovely mildness; but for the past eight or ten weeks I have been in a state of ineffable languefaction. The want of "tone" in the air is altogether indescribable: it makes it mortally flat and dead and relaxing. The great point is that it is all excessively pleasant & you succumb to languor with a perfectly demoralized conscience. But it is languor (for me at least)—languor perpetual and irresistible. My struggles with sleep have been heroic, but utterly vain, & to sit down with a book after 8 p.m. (& after a rousing cup of caffé nero) & not snore the evening ignobly away has been a dream never realized. It seems to me that I have slept in these three months more than in my whole life beside. The soft divine, enchanting days of spring have of course made matters worse & I feel as if, for six weeks past, I had been looking at the world from under half-meeting eyelids. But I am going to fight it out to the end, for I don't know when I shall ever be here again. Nothing of all this means that I find the air unwholesome: on the contrary. It makes me thick-headed and a little head-achy; but the languor & the "fever" are two very different matters, & I have been steadily living & still live, in the most salubrious conditions.—Of Rome itself, otherwise, I have grown very fond, in spite of the inevitable fits of distaste that one has here. You feel altogether out of the current of modern civilization and in so far, very provincial, but (as I believe I have more than once said) I often hanker for the high culture & high finish of Paris—the theatres & newspapers & booksellers & restaurants & boulevards. But the atmosphere is nevertheless weighted—to infinitude—with a something that forever stirs and feeds and fills the mind and makes the sentient being feel that on the whole he can lead as complete a life

here as elsewhere.—Then there is the something—the myriad some-
things—that one grows irresistibly and tenderly fond of—the unan-
alysable *loveableness* of Italy.   This fills my spirit mightily on occasions
& seems a sort of intimation of my learning how to be and do something here.   These last—or first—weeks of spring have been
strangely delicious, & it has seemed a sort of crime to be keeping
them to myself.   The weather has been perfect; as it [h]as been constantly since my arrival, & perfect Roman weather seems somehow,
beyond all others, the weather for the *mind*.   My riding has put me in
the way of supremely enjoying it & of course has doubled the horizon
of Rome. Physically, I doubt that it will ever do wonders for me; but
morally & intellectually, it is wondrous good.   Life here (after one
has known it) would be very tame without it and to try it is to make it
an essential.   Like every thing that is worth doing, riding well is difficult; but I have learned to sit a well-disposed horse decently
enough—the Campagna, with its great stretches of turf, its slopes
and holes and ditches, being a capital place to acquire vigilance &
firmness.   I wish *fratello mio*, that you might come & take a turn at
it.—But you'll soon be thinking that my only mission in life is to
preach amusement.—Of Italian, *per se*, I have learned much less than
I had dreamed of doing—not having (with so many other things to
do) hired the intelligent young Roman of my vision to come daily &
converse with me.   But I read it fairly well & to speak it after the
fashion of a rank foreigner is not hard. I lately formed a contract with
Miss Bartlett to come twice a week and read *Tasso* with her (delicious
stuff!)[1] & this I hope will progress as finely as my inevitably falling
into a three hours' dead sleep over my dictionary will allow.   I have
been now for a fortnight in these rooms on the Corso (extremely
good ones) where I have more observation of moeurs Italiennes than
at my hotel.   The *padrone* keeps a little shop of Catholic images in the
basement and lives with all his family (wife, three children, sister in
law, maid servant & various female hangers-on) behind a curtain, in
an alcove off the vestibule to my two rooms, which being on the front,
with a balcony, are the main source of his subsistence.   It's a pathetic
old-world situation & I feel as if (if I were not a brute) I would invite
them in to air themselves in my apartment.—Your letter was full of
points of great interest.   Your criticism on *Middlemarch* was excellent
& I have duly transcribed it into that *note-book* which it will be a relief
to your mind to know I have at last set up.[2]   Better still was your
expression of interest in your lectures & of their good effect on
you.—Without flattery, I don't see how you could fail to please and

stimulate your students, & hope the thing will develop and bring you larger opportunities.   That your health, too, should keep pace with them is my cordial wish.   Your praise of my articles was of great value.   I feel, myself, that I constantly improve, & I have only now to strive & to let myself go to prosper & improve indefinitely.   So I think!   I mean to spend a not idle summer.   Our friends here are in eclipse.   The Tweedies, with Mrs. Temple have gone to Albano, for a change of air, poor Mr. T. having lately been suffering acutely from rheumatism.   Rome doesn't agree with him & I should think he would be glad to get away.   His brother (John T.) has had his daughter ill at Albano for many weeks with typhus fever (brought from Naples,); so that the whole family has been roughly used.[3]   Aunt Mary is on the whole rather tragical (not to call it comical) & I pity their want of a central influence or guiding principle (such as their children would have been.)   They don't know where to go, what to do, or why to do it.   They have been full of hospitality to me.—The Bootts after a few days at Albano, are gone to Naples, prior to a month at Bellosguardo again.   I have seen a good deal of them all winter; & miss them now.   Lizzie wears better than her father, whose dryness & coldness & tendency to spring back to calling you *Mr.* again like a bent twig, is ineffable.   But still, if you get him laughing (as you so easily can) you forgive him everything.   Lizzie still makes one pity her—though I don't know why.   Her painting has developed into a resource that most girls would feel very thankful to possess, & she has had a very entertaining winter.   Her work will always lack the last delicacy, but if she would only paint a little less *helplessly*, she would still go far—as women go.   But with her want of *initiative*, it is remarkable that she does as well.   I should think she might make very successful little drawings for books.   She has made a lot of excellent sketches.—In the way of old friends we have been having Henry Adams & his wife, back from Egypt & (last) from Naples, each with what the doctor pronounced the germs of typhus fever.   But he dosed them and they mended & asked me to dinner, with Miss Lowe, (beautiful & sad)[4] & came to Mrs. Sumners, where I dined with them again, & shewed me specimens of their (of course) crop of bric-à-brac & Adams's Egyptian photos. (by himself—very pretty)—& were very pleasant, friendly & (as to A.) improved.   Mrs. Clover has had her wit clipped a little I think—but I suppose has expanded in the "affections."—I have been meeting lately at dinner for ten days young *Ireland* (Miss I.'s brother) who used to dine with us on Sundays.[5]   He is travelling hereabouts & spending a month in Rome & seems rather helpless & listless & lonely & thankful for chance company.   He has a more amiable air than in former days.—There have been hordes of other people here, before-seen, most of whom I have contrived to elude.   The Andrews have gone to Florence, having much enjoyed Rome.   I surrendered lately an evening to the Dixwells—who were very wholesome & lively, especially Mrs. D., whom Europe animates & beautifies.   I have first or last seen in a cab in the Corso every one I ever saw anywhere before—including (tell Alice) Ella Eustis & mamma—the latter, apparently, with the same ink stain on her nose she had at Oxford![6]   Also the Dr. Kings & in fine, every one!—But my letter is eternal.   Continue to say all you can about the boys.   Bob evidently will thrive, & our blessings & hopes must go with Wilky. I'm glad Alice was to have been in N.Y., & hope it will have tuned her up to writing me a line.   My blessings on her.   Did A.K. come back with her?   If so, a line from her again, when she can, will be welcome.—Love to every one else.   There were some things in father's letter I wanted to answer, but I must wait.   Kisses in profusion to my inestimable mammy.   I am wearing all my old undergarments, though in rags, because they have her needlework.—Farewell, dear Bill.   I haven't said twenty things I meant but it must serve.

Ever your | H.J.jr.

ALS: MH bMS Am 1094 (1950)

[1] Torquato Tasso (1544–1595), Italian poet.

[2] According to Edel, the notebook has not survived; see *HJL*, 1:369n.

[3] In *HJL*, 1:346, HJ calls her Mrs. William Temple, while in *HJL*, 1:352, he describes her as "Mrs. Captain Temple (Mrs. T's sister in law)." A John H. Tweedy from Danbury, Conn., a legislator and railroad pioneer, died in Milwaukee in 1891. Another John Tweedy, postmaster at Danbury, died in 1912. No evidence was found showing that either of the two is the brother in question.

[4] Elena Lowe, daughter of Francis Lowe, of Boston, married Gerald Perry; see Leon Edel, *Henry James: The Conquest of London (1870–1881)* (Philadelphia: Lippincott, 1962), 112.

[5] Apparently Frederick Guion Ireland (1846–1915), graduate of Harvard in 1868, compiler of a dictionary and author of several children's books, later a civil servant in New York.   He could have been a brother of Miss Ireland, AJ's teacher and friend (see *AJB*, 91).

[6] Writing to AJ, 25 April 1873, HJ makes clear that Ella Eustis is a friend of AJ's (*HJL*, 1:373).   She seems related to the family of George Eustis (1796–1858), American jurist.   His widow died in France in 1876, while a son and his family were also living in France.

Henry James at Geneva, 1859–60. (*By permission of the Houghton Library, Harvard University*)

Henry James, 1882. (*By permission of the Houghton Library, Harvard University*)

William James, ca. 1869. (*By permission of the Houghton Library, Harvard University*)

William James, ca. 1873. (*By permission of the Houghton Library, Harvard University*)

Henry James, Sr. (*By permission of the Houghton Library, Harvard University*)

Mary Temple. (*By permission of the Houghton Library, Harvard University*)

Alice Gibbens before her marriage. (*By permission of the Houghton Library, Harvard University*)

Alice Gibbens James and son Henry James. (*By permission of the Houghton Library, Harvard University*)

Galleries of the Boston Athenaeum at about the time William James and Henry James were frequent visitors. *Top:* Picture gallery. *Bottom:* Sculpture gallery. (*Courtesy of the Boston Athenaeum*)

Artist's rendering of the *Great Eastern*. (From Jules Verne, *A Floating City* [London, 1876])

Thomas Sergeant Perry. *(By permission of the Hough- ton Library, Harvard Uni- versity)*

Oliver Wendell Holmes. *(By permission of the Hough- ton Library, Harvard Uni- versity)*

Louis Agassiz. *(By permis- sion of the Houghton Library, Harvard University)*

William James to Henry James, 8 December 1872. (*By permission of the Houghton Library, Harvard University*)

Henry James to William James, 15 June 1879. (*By permission of the Houghton Library, Harvard University*)

To Henry James

Cambr. May 11. 73

My dear Harry

I was delighted to get your letter of April 9th, which despite your complaints of sleepiness & inability to do work, seemed to reveal a great physical bienêtre—I hope not untruthfully. I am only sorry you should say that you have met not a single man of any account during the winter. I am afraid of an exclusive diet of women. I write this time no letter but only a line to accompany the enclosed letter from Bob which is so beautiful that I think you ought to see it before it gets many months older. In a subsequent one he says that Mary is in the family way.—No news to tell you. You miss chances in the book reviewing line by being out of the country; e.g. Pater's studies in the renaissance,[1] & Morley's Rousseau. Do you see the fortnightly Review in Rome. If so you will have read a big little article by Morley on Pater, whose book Alice has been reading & pronounces exquisite.[2]

Morley's self, I'm sorry to say, has chosen the worser of the two paths that a while ago seemed open to him. He has grown more and more lavish & gushing in style, and french in idiom, instead of more clean & chaste; more emotional instead of more rational, and I doubt not will develop a thorough going mannerism in ten years, which one will be able to quarrel with no one for physiologically loathing. Gurney & Alex. Agassiz are the last two brain collapsers. By the way I believe I told you in my last that I had determined to stick to psychology or die. I have changed my mind & for the present give myself to biology. i.e accept the tuition here for next year with its 600 dollars, & this is virtually tantamount to my clinging to those subjects for the next 10 or 12 years if I linger so long.[3] On the whole this is the wiser, if the tamer decision—the fact is, I'm not a strong enough man to choose the other and nobler lot in life, but I can in a less penetrating way work out a philosophy in the midst of the other duties.—It's a pity you have stopped you[r] nation letters entirely. I've heard a great many people lately say how much they had been delighted by them.

Ever yours affect^ly   Wm. James

ALS: MH bMS Am 1092.9 (2585)

[1] Walter Horatio Pater, *Studies in the History of the Renaissance* (London: Macmillan, 1873).

[2]John Morley, "Mr. Pater's Essays," *Fortnightly Review*, n.s. 13 (1 April 1873): 469–77.
[3]WJ changed his mind once more.

From Henry James

Perugia. May 19ᵗʰ [1873]

Dearest Wᵐ: I haven't written home for two long weeks, & my conscience gnaws me accordingly. I hasten (now) to put it to rest & beg
you all to forgive my silence which will not have again the same effi-
cient cause. The cause was simply that my last week in Rome was
extremely occupied with doing twenty things (chiefly sight-seeing)
which I had been purposely leaving all winter 'till the foreigners had
cleared out & left a free field; & then that the *scirocco* was blowing
vigorously & producing a lassitude not favorable to an even very light
use of one's brain. The atmosphere didn't at all suit me; but I staid
on from day to day, to get certain impressions which I should have
been sorry to miss. Then, (yesterday,) I clutched my traps together
& departed. I reached this lovely Perugia in the afternoon, after a
six hour's journey through a landscape of surpassing fascinations &
rejoice greatly in the delightful change of air I find here. I mean to
pause two or three days & enjoy it.—I forget whether it was before I
last wrote (to father & mother) that your letter of April 6ᵗʰ had come.
I think so, & that I acknowledged it. Many thanks for everything in it.
Alice's letter of the 13ᵗʰ is still unacknowledged, which I hereby do,
embracing her in the lovingest manner, *en attendant* that I answer it.
The enclosed scrap from the Advertiser about my *Gautier* was very
agreeable. À propos of which, do you know the authorship of the
Nation notice? The general style of the article didn't read like Dennett, though the phrases about my thing were obscure enough for
him. Whoever he is, he is very silly.[1]—I hardly know what to tell
about my last days in Rome. It had become very empty & very fascinating & I would gladly have staid there till July 1ˢᵗ. The weather
was beautiful & the heat not intense: but with the peculiar quality of
the air I grew visibly on worse & worse terms & I continued to breathe
it only for the sake of everything else & of my growing doubt that (on
this very account) I should soon behold Rome again. All the last
weeks I was there I found it almost impossible to read or write; but
the enchanting experience of Rome in April and May was too valuable to be sacrificed: so I said to myself: "Get your impressions now;
you may never have another chance; & *use* them afterward." In-

deed, now that I look back at my five months there (almost) from an external standpoint, I see that they were languid months & that I enjoyed but the half of my moderate capacity for work. I had always an incipient headache. But for all that the episode has been immensely profitable. My impressions will abide, & in this breezy Perugia the headache has already past away. As for the work, that I shall easily overtake. I go into all this, because I must have seemed to you for a long time very unproductive. But I am a great deal wiser.—The Tweedies had left Rome a day or two before me, & poor Mr. T. certainly needed it. You will think I have found out Aunt M.'s soft spot when I tell you that *a couple of hours* after her arrival in Florence, after twelve spent in the railway train, on a hot day, she wrote me a copious & affectionate note. They are still in Florence, where I may possibly overtake them. They go thence to the lakes where they hope to meet Lady Rose, & thence to Kissingen. I saw no one else in the last days of Rome, save the ladies of the Via della Croce (Mrs. S. & Miss B.)[2] who were both rather wilted, & preparing to depart for the chateau at Dinant in Brittany which Mrs. S. has taken for the summer. The Terrys & Storys were thriving & I spent my last evening in the most affectionate manner with the latter, for whom I don't care an inordinate number of straws. Story is too much occupied with himself, & Madam with the Duchess of Northumberland.[3] Mlle. is on the whole the most satisfactory as well as the handsomest. I dined a day or two before at the Terrys *en famille*, & had a better time there than ever before. The two Miss C.'s[4] had just come back from a wonderful ten days tour through a dozen old Sabine & Etruscan cities with Hare, the author of the *Walks*,[5] & Miss A. was *intarissable* with characteristic cleverness—although she did intimate at table that poor Terry was a *beast.*—You may despise these trivial personalities, but they will interest mother & Alice: the latter too will be glad to hear that the poor pallid Von Hoffmanns are to spend the summer at a pension at *Berne*: a change from the Villa Mattei. But a personality in which you will be interested is one (or rather two) I encountered this morning, in the breakfast room of this inn. A German & his wife were drinking their tea with a great reverberation, but with an amiable air which led me to make overtures (in French) to conversation. The husband replied with alacrity & we conversed long & agreeably, chiefly about the contrasted characteristics of Rome & Florence, where (at F.) he had been spending three months, "dans un but scientifique." His wife seemed to speak no French, but took a kind of tacit part, by play of feature, in the talk. After we had parted, it

was borne in upon me that they were the H. Grimms; & so in truth
they are.   I hope they will be round at dinner time, & I will introduce
myself over you.—An individual I shall certainly see in Florence is
Hillebrand who lives there & whom Boott has introduced me to.   He
& Gryzanowski are two very good social elements in Florence—&
such as I have greatly missed the like of during the past winter.   An
intelligent male brain to communicate with occasionally would be a
practical blessing.   I have encountered none for so long that I don't
even know how to address your's & find it impossible to express a
hundred ideas which at various times I have laid aside, to be pro-
pounded to you.—Looking over your letter, I perceive your adjura-
tion to prepare articles &c on the French, G. Sand, Balzac &c.   I may
come to it, some day, but there are various things I want to do first.
Just at present I shall write a few more notes of travel: for two reasons: 1° that a few more joined with those already published & written
will make a decent little volume;[6] & 2° that now or never (I think) is
my time.   The *keen* love & observation of the picturesque is ebbing
away from me as I grow older, & I doubt whether a year or two hence,
I shall have it in me to describe houses and mountains, or even cathe-
drals & pictures.   I don't know whether I shall do anything better,
but I shall have spoiled for this.   The real, natural time,—if I *could*—
would have been when I was abroad before.   Mysterious & incon-
trollable (even to one's self) is the growth of one's mind.   Little by
little, I trust, my abilities will catch up with my ambitions.—I am glad
to hear you have decided on the Physiolog. & Anatomy place for next
year.   Father mentioned it [in] a letter rec'd. about the same time
with A.s, whether before or after I can't remember, & can't verify, as
it is in a trunk down stairs.   I hope you will go on from success to
success.   But I shall be interested to hear how you have compromised
with the desire to give time and strength to other things.—Your account of Child & his tribulations was very touching.   The poor little
man looms up to me like a perfect Colossus of domestic heroism.   In
Theod. Sedgwick too I am interested; but short of marrying her, I
can't give her a social start.   (Not that I could by this.)   Is anything
more heard from Wilky & does this man ahead show any signs of
making room?—*Later. Evening.*   They *are* the Grimms & I have just
had a most effusive meeting with them in the dining room.   They
weren't at dinner but I caught them over their beefsteak-tea, a moment before they went to the little theatre at which for 3 frs. they had
taken a box holding four persons.   They asked me to go with them;
but I preferred finishing my letter to you.   I reintroduced myself &

they exclaimed greatly & delightedly, asked much about you & said sie liebten Sie sehr &c. I shall probably see them again tomorrow. Why is Mrs. G. the only German woman of condition who don't speak French? There is something extremely taking about her—a wondrous frankness & sweetness. She of course asked me if I too loved die Kunst & painted; & addressed me for some moments in faster German than I could comprehend.—I interrupted my letter this a.m. & went forth, because there was a menace of rain which I wished to anticipate. Perugia is a most enchantingly picturesque little city perched on a mountain & sweeping over the most wonderful panorama of tender blue undulations that you can imagine. The prospect is really transcendent & far more than human eyes can manage in one day. I shall be here two or three more. At the Pinacoteca, rich in lovely Peruginos, I met little Richard Staigg (whom I had seen several times in Rome) with his nice wife; & she gave me news of C. Atkinson, to whom through her I sent a message. I should like to see that good creature.—But I mustn't write forever. You shall have more about Perugia in print. I hope to make excursions to Assisi & Cortona & combine the three.[7]—There are by this time, I trust, letters forwarded to Florence for me—letters full of home & all I long to hear. I wrote last that you were to address *Fenzi (Emile)* Florence. Love, love, love.

Your's ever   H. James jr

ALS: MH bMS Am 1094 (1951)

[1] *Nation* 16 (24 April 1873): 289, has several comments about HJ in a review of the *North American Review*. The writer is not identified.

[2] Mrs. Sumner and Miss Bartlett.

[3] Henrietta Percy (1813–1899), wife of Algernon Percy, duke of Northumberland.

[4] Annie Crawford and Mimoli Crawford, daughters of Louisa Crawford Terry.

[5] Augustus John Cuthbert Hare, *Walks in Rome* (1871).

[6] HJ, *Transatlantic Sketches* (Boston: James R. Osgood and Co., 1875), containing the sketches of "A European Summer" and numerous others.

[7] HJ, "A Chain of Italian Cities," *Atlantic Monthly* 33 (February 1874): 158–64, reprinted in *Transatlantic Sketches*.

To Henry James

Cambr. May 25th. 73

My dear Harry

Your letter to Alice after your return to rome from albano arrived about a week ago and was received with the usual enthusiasm, and *attendrissement* on Alice's part. I take up the pen to day mainly on a matter of business, that is to get at as early a date as possible certain renseignements which may affect my choice of how to spend next winter.   This is my situation: I have succeeded in doing my college work this half year without losing ground so far as I know in health but also without gaining an inch.   I don't know whether you still consider my ailments to be imagination & humbug or not, but I know myself that they are as real as any one's ailments ever were, and that with the exception of my eyes which can now be used 4 hours a day the improvement I have made in 12 months is very slight.   The college work although as so much business, it has been of great moral service to me, is I am convinced, a draw back on the rate of my wished for improvement.   I get utterly collapsed & exhausted with the experimental preparations, and the regular triweekly recurrence of the feverish sort of erethism in which the lecture or recitation hour leaves me cannot be good for one whose trouble seems mainly to be a nervous weakness, and who craves for sedation all the while.   I told Eliot some time ago in accepting the place for the whole of next year that the acceptance was subject to the right to back out by the middle of August if I feel so inclined.   Of course my deep active desire is to go on working uninterruptedly now that after all this delay I have begun, and the benefits of this weigh heavy in the balance against the non-hygienic effects of the 3 hours a week course next year, in fact they preponderate, even without the thought of the $600 wh. in my I confess somewhat loathsome condition of dependence make them altogether prevail.   But lo, so easy and attractive has the study proved to the already too large division of 45 students that have taken it this year that it seems certain that about 100 will elect it for next year.   To make two divisions and double my working hours is simply impossible.   The only alternatives are: to back out, and letting Dwight take them for next year, hope that I shall be *gewachsen* to the task for the year following; or else to implore that on a plea of the teacher's invalidism my students be forcibly pruned down to a manageable number. Now in the really most doubtful condition of my future I don't like to be pledged to the college by receiving such unusual favors as this last. The former alternative commends itself to me as part of a plan for which I would ask your advice: Namely to advertize for a pupil or ward to pay my travelling expenses, (in Wilk's and Bob's present condition I have no right to ask father for a cent for any such purpose) and spent the winter 6 months in Italy or elsewhere in the South of Europe with you.   This would give me a sedative mild winter, one which I think now might make a good deal of difference in my progress; it wd. deprive me of the ever recurring strain and fever of lecturing and the great fret of pressing against and always overstepping my working powers which during the past 6 months has so unstrung me; it wd. also in a scientific point of view not be so very bad, since I could carry on with advantage a certain line of study there which I should some day have to do, and might as well then as ever, and the appeal to the senses and so forth would prevent my postponement of "business" from affecting my spirits as unpleasantly as would be the case were the winter so spent in Cambridge. The only doubtful points are these. I should probably not be able, at any rate should not count beforehand on reading more than four hours a day, and my pedestrian powers, vary from some day almost nil, to a maximum of 3 miles a day all little goings and comings told. Now are the resources of Italy & so forth such that I might not suffer under these circumstances from excessive loneliness & ennui. Here at home there are various modes of killing time, the ride to boston and back destroys one hour, there are constantly visitors in the house to me or to the others who cheer one up, and one can lounge over meals and in the parlor or look in upon the Gurney's & Ashburner's &c, in short escape being shut up face to face with ones impotence to do anything, that I should think a lonely invalid might find rather desperate in Europe. I remember how bad this loneliness was often in Dresden & Teplitz, although I could read there more than twice as long as I can now. This is the point I want you to answer; from your experience of killing time in Rome & elsewhere, should you think the experiment would be a safe one for a man in my state to try? Your being there and with me, (if you are willing) would of course help it through amazingly—Answer as soon as you can so as to let me have the datum to help my decision. I confess its not an easy one to make anyhow. On the one hand the everlasting postponement of active life, on the other the reality of my sickness, and the misery of being ever knocked back by it from the work I burn to do from each day to the morrow— and which wd. partly disappear with the outward requirement to work.———

You will have been informed of T.S.P.'s engagement to Miss Cabot. I don't know what they'll live on, for I believe she's not rich. Wendell Holmes spoke tenderly of you t'other day, saying it was simply impossible for him to write, but he sent his love. The Nortons are being expected to day or to morrow. Arthur is on to meet them, as fat as Wilky, & looking like Ben Butler.[1] He says he makes from 3000 to 4000 a year by his articles. Your story in the Galaxy has been published, and read by me, without, I must say the delight I have so often got from your things.[2]

Ever yours affet.[ly]   Wm. James

ALS: MH bMS Am 1092.9 (2586)

[1] Benjamin Franklin Butler (1818–1893), a military officer, a candidate for governor of Massachusetts in 1872, was balding and had prominent jowls.

[2] HJ, "The Sweetheart of M. Briseux," *Galaxy* 15 (June 1873): 760–69.

From Henry James

Florence May 31st [1873]

Dear W[m]

I got this morning with pleasure your note of May 11th, enclosing Bob's.   The latter I greatly thank you for.   It is most wonderful & beautiful.   What a marvellous child he is.   One may certainly hear with pleasure that, with such feelings & views, he is going to become a father.   Your note was otherwise equally welcome—& a voice (unheard by me for many months in the profitless society which is the dark feature of one's expatriation here) from the world of serious things.—There seems something half tragic in the tone with which you speak of having averted yourself from psychology.   But I hope you have settled down calmly to it & will have no irritating regrets. You know best, & one must do not what one plans, but what one can. For the chance I miss to review books by being absent, I suppose there is something in it: but not overmuch, for I am struggling through long delays to get at something better than book reviewing. Mine is a slow progression, but a progression, I believe, it is.   I saw Pater's *Studies*, just after getting your letter, in the English bookseller's window: and was inflamed to think of buying it & trying a notice. But I see it treats of several things I know nothing about.—I wrote less than a week ago to mother, just after my arrival in Florence & as well as I can remember, my letter must have been rather plaintive. There is no need to *piangere*, even tho' I probably *shall* shuffle off from Florence to-morrow.   I am confirmed in my impression that I had better be moving out of Italy.   Though as yet we have had no heat to speak of, I find the Italian spring atmosphere curiously & obstinately relaxing. [*Private*.   You will be interested to know just how; & probably guess that I mean in its effect on my well-known idiosyncrasy.   Even so.   Ten weeks ago (after an excellent winter) I began to break down & ever since have suffered from perfect torpor

& inaction of the bowels; I suppose too of the liver as I am as yellow as an orange.   I see every reason to believe it's the climate.   Places in which I am very sleepy immediately tell on this point (I verified this distinctly twice last summer in Switzerland) & here I am always soporific & heavy headed.   It makes me sick & seedy & unable to work & it's too great a loss of time to see it out further.   I hope, reasonably enough, that as my improvement becomes confirmed by time I can stand Italian springs.   But it's better to knock under now and depart.   Besides, of the whole spring I have drunk deep: & this is the summer, which makes many exiles, & I am not a lonely victim.   This for your interested ear: but don't let it trouble you.   I'm a vastly better man than a year ago.]   I shall make straight from here to Lago Maggiore & station myself on the Simplon road—at Bavino or Pallanza.   I shall try a few days there & if I find them propitious a few more; so as to eat as much off as possible from the cope of THREE MONTHS in Switzerland.   Alice will envy me!   But I am very content & look forward to a healthy, tranquil, somewhat productive summer.   I had my jocund summering all winter in Rome.   I shall go straight either to Lausanne or Glion (Montreux), according to the the moment at which I arrive.   Please therefore begin & address Poste Restante, Montreux, as I shall probably be there at the right moment to get your letters & will advise you of new addresses proportionately.   Two or three will probably suffice for the whole summer.—I have been strolling about gently & looking at Florence, but finding in her I blush to say how little of her old magic.   Rome has murdered her— Rome a hundred times more wondrous in retrospect.   Her great smiting hands have snapt the tender cords of perception to which Florence appeals.   I should vainly try to tell you how one looks back on Rome & hungers for her again.   How I envy the people—lethargic Terry & tough Story—who thrive there till July 1st!—I have seen no one here but Gryzanowski whom I shall probably see again.   I have been shy of calling on Hillebrand as I meant, *an* my short stay.   Gryzanowski isn't, in talk, quite as "masterly" as in writing, but he is very superior every way, & delightfully bland as a companion.—You say nothing of the family summer.   Is it fixed?   Let me hear, oh beloved ones all.—I send to father by this mail, in another package, the M.S. I last wrote about: & wish it a safe journey.[1]   Please mention also to T.S.P. that I sent him yesterday a review of Cherbuliez's novel.[2]   It, also, heaven speed.—My blessings dear brother on all your renunciations & undertakings.   Love to all.

Your's ever   H. James jr.

ALS: MH bMS AM 1094 (1952)
    [1] See letter of 19 May 1873.
    [2] HJ, review of Victor Cherbuliez, *Meta Holdenis* (Paris: Hachette, 1873), in *North American Review* 117 (October 1873): 461–68.

From Henry James

Glion—June 18$\underline{th}$ 73.

Dear W$\underline{m}$:

I received last evening your letter of May 25$\underline{th}$ & mother's of the same date (for which please thank her.)   I wrote a week ago to Alice, so that you will already know of my having migrated to these parts. Your letters were forwarded from Florence, which involved some delay: but now that I have got your's I lose no time.—I am very sorry to hear that your strength has increased less during the past winter than I supposed & that your work is so much of an effort to you.   If this is the case, I well understand why you should be indisposed to deal with your augmented class, & that some such plan as you ask my advice about, should have its attractions.   I am strongly inclined to think that you might subsist very comfortably *in Rome* on the footing you set forth.   The place has more resources in one way & another than any in Europe & is peculiarly adapted to help one get through time. I found for myself that it stole away many hours—quite too many— in which I would have preferred being shut up to myself.   Of course I was more active than you could be: but even the difference would, I should think, leave enough in your favor to make your idle hours tolerable.   You would find a good many people to drop in upon: sitting round in the villas & churches is in itself a great resource, & hack hire is extremely cheap.   This without counting the galleries.   Wishing a sedative climate you might not (probably would not) find that of Rome too relaxing: & if the winter were reasonably fine, you would be able to spend much of it in the open air.   Altogether counting up all the various chances of Roman life I can hardly doubt that they would serve your need.   Of course my society would fill up a great many crevices.—These things I can undertake to say of Rome alone. Florence would be less favorable, for though there are a good many people there, there are vastly fewer resorts & lounging places & a much harsher climate.   In Naples you would get a warm but exciting atmosphere & a belle nature, but very little society.   Rome in short is quite apart.   My own plans for next winter have been vague, & I have been divided about Rome: partly because of the (for me) *too* sedative climate, & partly because of the importunate demands of the American village (which is a proof that you could kill time.) But if you were to come to Rome, I would willingly & joyfully decide to go back, because I enormously want to. I could avoid over-relaxation by leaving early in the spring. My plan otherwise had been to spend the autumn & spring in Florence & the midwinter in Naples. But Rome has such a hold on my affections that I only want a pretext for going back. Another winter I should know how too[1] play my cards (both physically & socially) more profitably.—This is the whole story, I think, as far as it may be told. I hope you will find the *data* sufficient to help you to a tolerably easy decision. It can't be very easy I know; & for me to *advise* is impossible. But this I can say: that with my high opinion of Rome, I don't see how to an observant & reflective man even a loafing winter there could fail to be profitable. You will have Lizzie Boott to interrogate: I imagine she would confirm my impression. It is a pity they are gone, as their house would help you to loaf.—If you come I will do all in my power to help you through. We should certainly have much profitable talk.———

I rec'd. several days ago father's letter, telling me of T.S.P.'s engagement. Thank him (father) & tell him I shall very soon answer it. The engagement surprised me somewhat, but not altogether. I always fancied T.S.P. would never marry: but if he does it seems to me in character that he should marry a Miss L.C. I suppose they will have to wait. Meanwhile I shall write him a note. I'm very glad Silvia Watson is provided for.[2] She will be a providence to her provider. I was interested in A Sedgwick's $4000 a year. I wish you would tell me by what papers he makes it & how much they pay him. Does it all come from the *Nation* & the *Atlantic?* For what else does he write?—I'm sorry you didn't like my *Galaxy* tale, which I haven't seen.[3] Has it been sent? I hoped it was sufficiently pleasing. But one can't know. I wrote you what I remember as a rather plaintive letter from Florence a fortnight ago, which I hope you'll not let afflict you. I did well to come to Switzerland, though I haven't chosen just here a very happy resting place. I had a curious experience last summer of the influence of this immediate region. I hoped it was confined to Villeneuve, but it has removed itself here—as is but natural as the places are hardly more than ¾ of an hour apart. I shall leave this as soon as the present rainy spell is over & go *via* Berne (where I shall stop awhile) to Thusis which took my fancy greatly last summer & suited me apparently though it didn't suit Alice. It will be rather a dull *séjour* for two months, so I shall try and break the back of the summer at Berne which I also greatly liked last year. Your letters for a while will have concentrated at Montreux: but direct them henceforth: *Poste Restante—Thusis, Grisons, Switzld.* It would have been wiser to give you this address from the 1ˢᵗ: but I was uncertain.—Don't bother a jot about my ailment. I am wondrous well & content & shall be much better for this Swiss summer. I was at 1ˢᵗ indisposed to come here: but it was the thing to do. My winter in Rome was a poor working winter & I have done less than I hoped: but it was very "educative" & will tell before long. Mother tells me you are going to see the boys. All prosperity to your journey. Write me something about it, if only a few words.——I have said nothing about the Boston fire! What can one say? I hope the suffering isn't great. Love to W. Holmes: I don't expect him to write to me, but hope (that is mean) some day to write to him. I think there is nothing more to say about the subject of your letter. I can only give you the *data* on this side. Let me hear in due time of your conclusion.

Yours ever   H. James jr

Excuse misfolding of letter

ALS: MH bMS Am 1094 (1953)

[1] A slip for 'to'.

[2] Sylvia Watson and William Ralph Emerson became engaged in the fall of 1872 and married in the summer of 1873. He was a distant relative of Ralph Waldo Emerson.

[3] See letter of 25 May 1873.

To Henry James

Isles of Shoals | July 14, [1873]

Beginning

Dear H.—It occurs to me as I wait this July 14 6 P.M. on board the little steamer Major going to the Isles of Shoals for her to start,[1] that I may as well begin a letter to you in pencil, and be so much advanced on my way towards finishing that impending task. I left home 4 hours ago, where I had spent 3 days with F. & M. after my visit to the Coast at "Magnolia,"[2] and am now off again till August, propos̲g̲ to touch at various points. To day F. got your 2nd fm. Berne, I getting at Magnolia your answer to my prudential inquiry. Your account of Rome was more satisfactory than anything I anticipated. I earnestly hope however not to have to verify it next winter—as such a step wd. be about equivalent to desperation of any continuous professional development, and wd. leave my future quite adrift again. I shall let July & August shape my decision and bear whatever comes with as equal a mind as I can. What weighs on me perhaps as much as anything now is the ignominy of my parasitic life on the family in view of the sweating existence of Bob & Wilky and their need of money as married men. Every hundred dollars I take or don't earn is so much less that Father can give them. The only thing with me now is my health; my ideas, my plans of study are all straightened out. But I have no clue to the future of my strength, nor can I be *sure* what course is safest for that. I alternate between fits lasting from 4 or 5 days to three weeks of the most extreme languor & depression, weakness of body & head & pain in back,—during wh. however I sleep well—and fits of equally uneven duration of great exhilaration of spirits, restlessness, comparative bodily & mental activity—coupled however with wakefulness of the most distressing sort that makes me absolutely sick—But the boat begins to move & I stop—I went home fm. Magnolia to try to break up the wakefulness that seized upon me there after the first 3 or 4 days—

Next day noon. The far famed Isles of Shoals are absolutely barren rocks with a great & first class hotel on two of them. This one, Appledore, the biggest, may be walked round in half an hour. I performed the feat after bkfst. The piazzas and different rooms are perfection, but the place does not yet tempt me to settle upon it for a long time. I have found Miss Bessie Greene & Mary Parkman among the guests. The former has some of the finest traits I ever knew in Woman, but I fear she will never be a perfectly adult & serious being. The ocean is a flat calm, absolutely no sign of swell, although a pleasant breeze ruffles the surface of the water. I suppose the island becomes really interesting when clouds are abundant and the breakers are thundering round about it.

I have enjoyed this vacation intensely so far. I got to magnolia feeling pretty seedy. After 5 days there I had revived the spirits I used to possess at Newport. I did not know such a deep revulsion of mind was possible in so short a time. Von allen Wissensqualm entladen, I just lay around drinking the air and the light & the sounds. I succeeded in reading no word for three days and then took Goethe's Gedichte out on my walks, and with them in my memory the smell of the laurels & pines in my nose, and the rythmic pounding of the surf upon my ear I was free and happy again. How people can pass years without a week of that *Normal* life I can't imagine. Life in which your cares responsibilities and thoughts for the morrow become a far off dream, and you *are* simply, floating on fm. from day to day, and "boarded" you don't know how, by what Providence, washed clean, without & within, by the light and the tender air. It ought to do me good. Unluckily I can only enjoy its plenitude for ten days more. I must then do a little daily task of study, as I have to deliver about 30 new lectures next year and have hardly yet made a stroke of preparation. No joke<.>—There were two nice girls, Miss Wards, at Magn. who have spent much time in Europe & were "cultivated," and at the same time jolly and not devoid of the principle of sexual fascination.[3] The day before I left Mrs Ernest Longfellow lay on the beach backed by a rock reading your Roman Holiday to her Mamma aloud.[4] Her looks lose their magic by being seen in conjunction with her family, whose faces are so many half way houses, gropings as it were after hers, and awful failures, her sister being pollywog faced & her mother *unique dans son genre*. Mrs E.L. is flat as dish water mentally. Ernest himself is a well bred little nonentity, whose painting is probably hopeless as regards mental interest, but good in facility and accuracy, and ability to stick in a crowd of details and facts. The Bootts' steamer arrived 5 days ago but we had not heard fm. them when (16th July) left home. Another night—good sleep, and another shining day. The world recedes; and I can begin to understand Mrs Celia Thaxter's ravings about the beauty of these rocks.[5] Yesterday afternoon I took a long sail with a fresh breeze which quite recalled the Newport days 10 years ago, as I sailed the boat myself.—I will close this letter here, you perceive I have not *multa* to say. I have read nothing of late except a few of Goethe's poems wh. make me feel like living entirely on poetry for the rest of my days. I hope your derangements will give over soon. I have found the *hydrastis* canadensis I sent you, homeopathic, mother tincture, sufficient to keep me going whenever an obstruction took place. Good bye! Perhaps, in case I should go abroad, you had better send me a list of books or other furniture you wd. like me to bring you.

Affectionately yours Wm. James

I forgot to say that that moon faced but excellent Myers of the law school, (haply you remember him) spoke with great rapture of your Guest's Confession especially of the exquisiteness of the female character.[6]

ALS: MH bMS AM 1092.9 (2587)

[1] Resort islands off the coast of Maine.

[2] A coastal town south of Gloucester, Mass.

[3] The Miss Wards are not sisters of Thomas Wren Ward. In a letter to his parents

of about the same date (bMS Am 1092.9 [2325]), WJ says that the Magnolia Miss Wards once lived in Cambridge.

[4] HJ, "A Roman Holiday," *Atlantic Monthly* 32 (July 1873): 1–11, reprinted in *Transatlantic Sketches*.

[5] Celia Laighton Thaxter (1835–1894), daughter of the lighthouse keeper and owner of one of the islands, *Among the Isles of Shoals* (1873). After buying it, her father renamed the island Appledore.

[6] James Jefferson Myers (1842–1915), graduated from Harvard College in 1869, Harvard Law School in 1872.

From Henry James

Bad Homburg, Aug 5$\underline{^{th}}$ [1873]

Dear W$\underline{^{m}}$—I don't mean to write you a letter—(I wrote yesterday to F & M. & a few days before to A.K.;) I want simply to thank you for your letters fr. the Steamboat & the Isle of Shoals. I am glad my report of Rome struck you as favorable—I have seen no reason since to think it was too high colored.—Your decision for the winter I can of course say nothing to illuminate; & I am so anxious to have you decide the matter on simply discretionary grounds that I even hesitate to express the muchness of my desire to see you.—It was a pleasure at any rate to read of the happy influences of your holiday and your loafings by the sea. Limited as they were I hope they have substantially helped you. Every word you say about Nature & the "normal life" has an echo in my soul. I enjoy them more the older I grow & acquire a fatal facility in sitting under trees & letting the hours expire without *particular* fruits. Homburg is excellent for this & for much else beside—a lovely little place which is insidiously reconciling me to Germany, which I have been hating ever since I came abroad, on the evidence of travelling Germans. I have been taking the waters with indifferent results, & feel better for stopping them. I have touched bottom I think in this particular episode of insalubrity & shall gradually rise to the surface again, & after that I think I can almost pledge myself to keep afloat. Meanwhile I am very well "located" for being either better or worse. I have for two years (up to May 1$\underline{^{st}}$ last) been so well & have now in spite of everything such a standing fund of vigor, that I am sure time will see me through. I have no especial ideas or anecdotes to communicate. I am re-reading Turgenieff in German & beginning a review for T.S.P. The German goes very easily. I lately sent a Homburg letter to the Nation by which you will judge me a Teutomaniac. I'm not—but what's the good of writing except imaginatively; Here, at any rate, one feels as if one lived in an Atmosphere with a present living force playing into it—which you don't in sweet Italy, smiling in her sleep.—The Tweedies are here, very well & preferring Homburg to anything in Europe.   I see no one else except (in my hotel) Dr. Parkes, the persecutor of the Boston homopaths & a good Englishman, the partner of my loafings, "afflicted" like myself, but "benefitted" by the waters.[1] A "gentlemanly" English mind wears well for daily companionship.— You offer, if you come, to bring books & "furniture."   I should like 2 or 3 boxes of Harrison's Lozenges.   I brought with me a box & ½, & in 14 mos. have only used the ½, which testifies to my hitherto well being—this being the only med. I have taken.   Also 3 or 4 cakes Davis's tooth soap, & in the way of books, *chiefly* Ferrari's *Revolution*[2] & Valery's Voyage in Italie.[3]—I am with you all in spirit & desire.   I trust your subsequent summer has been useful & happy.   I shall be here till Sept 1st, but write always to B & S.

Ever yours   H.J.jr.

ALS: MH bMS Am 1094 (1955)

   [1] Probably Edmund Alexander Parkes (1819–1876), British physician, author of books on practical hygiene.

   [2] Giuseppe Ferrari published several works on revolutions, *Filosofia della rivoluzione* (1851) and *Storia della rivoluzioni d'Italia* (1870–72).

   [3] Antoine-Claude-Pasquin Valery, pseudonym, *Voyages historiques et littéraires en Italie* (1831–33).

To Henry James

Cambr. Aug 25. [1873] Monday

My dear H—I arrived home last night but one prematurely from the Catskills, and found father arriving at the same time prematurely fm. St. J.[1]   To day we have a teleg. fm. Mother &c Co who were left at Kittery saying they will come this eveᵍ so we are once more united again.[2]   I write you these few lines to let you know of my plans so far. I am distinctly tho' slightly better for my vacation—that is though I have been more than ever troubled with wakefulness this summer, I feel in the past fortnight that I am tougher, and rendered much less seedy by it than at any time last year.   It has also occurred to me that instead of adopting the risky method of advertizing for a pupil (which as the whole decision is based on *chances* wd. largely increase the no. of them against going) I might borrow $1000 capital fm. A.K. This wd. be for her as good an investment as any she cd. make, for it wd. go hard with me but I could hereafter pay her the $75 per annum interest, out of my earnings.   So I have written to Eliot this A.M. telling him to find a substitute.   If he cannot, I will stay.   I more than fear he cannot, so don't be too sure of seeing me.   Nevertheless be prepared for the event.   I wish I might join you.   It will be throwing the heavier risk for the heavier gain.   If it succeeds in putting me on a moderately working basis I know it will be the wisest move of my life, and the $1000 will have been well invested.   If it fails, 'twill be that I am a failure anyway, and between one or another mode of failing there is little choice, save that in that case one will regret more the $1000.   I shall certainly know of Eliot's success in a fortnight and tell you forthwith.   If I go I shall sail probably for England about the middle of October.   You had better let me know in your next letter home where you judge best to meet me, for between my telling you I'm coming & my sailing there may not be time to get an answer fm. you.—Letters fm. you fm Hmbg. to me, Father & A.K.   I am sorry you are no better, but I have no end of faith in your toughness and tenacity to worry down anything.   I bring the books lozenges, &c of wh. you speak. I'm glad you are writing abᵗ Turgenjew,[3] and reading German.   I'm curious to hear yr. letter from Homburg.

Yrs affᵗˡʸ | W.

ALS: MH bMS Am 1092.9 (2588)

[1] Saint John's, Newfoundland.

[2] A town in southern Maine.

[3] HJ's review of two works by Turgenev appeared in *North American Review* 108 (April 1874): 326–56.   Turgenjew is the German transliteration.

To Henry James

Cambr. Sept 2. 73

My dear H.—the die is cast!   The 600 dollars salary fall into the pocket of another!   And for a year I am adrift again & free.   I feel the solemnity of the moment, & that I *must* get well now or give up. It seems as if I should too—for nothing remains but this g—— d——d weakness of nerve now.

So you may expect me to rejoin you about Nov 1.   I do not yet know how to sail—wait in fact a week to consult Boott about the cheapest overland journey to Italy.   Wd. prefer sailing for England because so get the biggest least seasick vessel.   Suppose now the french land journey wd. be cheaper than the German.   If you are in

Paris for your teeth and feel like staying on there till I come we might pass a pleasant 10 days there & go southward together.   Of course I can't wait to take passage till I hear from you, it wd. give me too bad a choice of berths.   I only write this word to tell you the decision, to say that I rejoice in the prospect of so soon communing with you and to enclose the appended letter which came yesterday from Dennett. The writer is a cousin of father's!   Your H——bg letter was first class.[1]

Ever your aff<u>te</u> | W.J.

I send the Homburg nation with this

ALS: MH bMS Am 1092.9 (2589)

[1] HJ, "Homburg Reformed," *Nation* 17 (28 August 1873): 142–44, reprinted in *Transatlantic Sketches.*

From Henry James

Homburg. Monday Sept. 15. [1873]

Dear W<u>m</u>.   I have been some three or four days in recipt of your letter of Aug. 28<u>th</u>, but I have been waiting to answer it till I had made up my mind about my movements.   I am very glad to hear you have determined to come abroad & sincerely hope you may make the arrangements which will enable you to do so.   It will seem an immense pity that you should be kept, against your will, by Eliot's not finding a successor for you.   I thought your successor stood ready in *Dwight.* I suppose he has backed out.   Your decision seems to me a wise one; I should think the results of your summer would convince you that it is the thing for you to do and I shall be surprised if, having got under way with it, you don't get great help from it.   If you can't come I shall be much disappointed, as your letter has greatly quickened my desire to see you.   I wait impatiently for your next.   My first impulse was to write to you that I would go and meet you & wait for you in Paris, but I have decided that I had better go down to Florence & wait for you there.   You will probably not wish to remain in Paris longer than to rest from your journey from England & will be able to make the journey to Florence alone.   Arrange it as I would, the journey & the stay in Paris would consume more money than it is now convenient to get rid of and one doesn't want to begin a Roman winter with diminished funds.   My present intention, therefore, is to go to Florence by October 1<u>st</u>.   May you promptly and safely join me!   If you shouldn't hear from me before sailing (after this) you will of course ask for a letter at Brown & Shipley's.   I had thought of going to Paris to see a dentist, but I learn of there being a good one in Rome, beside the one in Florence.—You see I'm still at Homburg, lingering on after almost every other soul has departed.   I have been here nearly ten weeks. But my days too are numbered.   I shall start in a day or two for Switzerland wait at Berne for your letter, which I hope to receive by the 25th, and then proceed to Italy.   Homburg is very cold and wet just now & I am being frozen out.   The Tweedies lately departed for the Tyrol and Vienna, in good health and spirits; but their place in my affections has been taken by Mrs. Ward & Bessie who are lodging in this house next door to me.   Bessie is making a cure & her mother has recently joined her.   Sam, thank the Lord, is in England; he gave us a taste of his presence for a day.   I see them rather much as I am their only friend here & as far as Bessie is concerned, I don't complain.   She is very lovely.   Mrs. W. is the same old *discoureuse*, yet with the tatters & remnants of a charm too.—There come to me no other home letters but yours.   Others I trust, from Canada, have arrived since & are awaiting my orders in the Bankers hands; for my last (from father, St. John's Aug. 8th) is now of very old date.   You speak of your all getting home "prematurely."   I hope this implies nothing amiss with you.   Of your excursion to the Catskills I had heard nothing.—Let me not forget to say apropos of your bringing books &c. that you had better leave the Ferrari, as I can get a cheap Italian edition of it,[1] & I had rather fill the space in your trunks with other things.   If[2] have undertaken to write for the N.A.R. a series of French articles & I mean to put them through.   I should therefore like such volumes as you can stuff in of Ste. Beuve, A. de Musset & Stendhal.[3]   Also if you can manage it, with the Valery & with my *Letters*, if possible of the P. de Brosses, my *bound* volumes of Balzac. If to these you will add a supply of Harrison's lozenges & of Davis's tooth-soap, I will be greatly thankful.—I continue to be much better in health and each day confirms my belief that it is a progressive & permanent gain.   I hope so.—I trust you found the family well and happy after their absence.   I have never heard so little of them & felt so detached, as this summer.—I read with great pleasure your *Vacations*.[4]   It was all very well worth saying & was very well said.   It must have been much noticed, & I hope they paid you decently for it.   Of Bob & Wilk I hear little, & expect soon to learn more about Wilky's marriage.   Have you seen the Boott's?   They will miss you.—Address your next to Brown and Shipley.   Indeed all please continue for the present to write to them.   Farewell.   Come, & I promise to send you home a better man.   I have been thinking so so much of talks we might have that I shall *miss* you if you don't.

Yours,   H.J.jr.

ALS: MH bMS Am 1094 (1956)

¹See letter of 5 August 1873.

²Although HJ clearly wrote 'If', the reading should be 'I'.

³Stendhal, pseudonym of Marie-Henri Beyle (1783–1842), French writer. The series was not published.

⁴WJ, "Vacations," *Nation* 17 (7 August 1873): 90–91 (*ECR*).

From Henry James

Berne, Friday, Sept. 26th [1873]

Dear Willy—

I yesterday received mother's letter of Sept. 12th, telling me that you had taken passage for October 11th.¹   She tells me also that you had already written to me, announcing your decision, but strange to say, I haven't received your letter nor one of Alice's written about the same time.   I can't bear to think they are lost—& they are probably not, for they are the first I have ever missed.   They may, carelessly have been sent to Homburg & forwarded thence amiss.   I have written to have them looked for, & hope when I next write to be able to tell you they have turned up.   Alice's letter I should intensely regret not getting, as I have long looked for it.   Give her my love & thank her for it & tell her I ardently hope to recover it.—I am greatly relieved to hear that you have not been prevented from coming & that your way is smooth.   I wrote you a week ago, telling you that I could meet you only at Florence, & I send this further information hoping it may catch you just before you sail.   At the date of mother's letter you still expected I would be in Paris, & I hope you won't be too much disappointed not to find me there.   Since I'm not obliged to go there, it suits me better to make straight for Florence, where I hope you will overtake me without trouble or fatigue.   I should greatly enjoy spending a few days there with you, & making the journey southward in your company; but tother thing can be done on half the money & this must decide it.   I shall of course have a letter for you at the Adelphi, giving you full instructions for your journey.   I hope your voyage will be fair & not too trying; I am most happy to hear from mother that your doings this summer give you faith in your travelling-powers.   May they increase with each succeeding mile.   This will only just catch you I'm afraid, & to make it do so I must catch the now departing English mail. I have no last requests—save not to forget the Davis's tooth soap, & the Harrison's Lozenges. Also a package or so, if you have room, of Star-mills paper.—I suppose, making your journey (via Mt. Cenis) comfortably, you can reach Florence by the first days in November. Buy a through ticket to Rome (good for ten days) (or at least to Florence) at the office in Alta Italia railway co, back side of the Grand Hotel. This makes it very reasonable.—But all this I will set forth in the Adelphi Letter. My address is Fenzi, Florence. Farewell, à bientôt. Buonissimo viaggio.—I was delighted to hear of Wilky's good marrying basis. Love to all.

Yours ever | H. James jr.

I leave tomorrow or next day for Milan, *via* St. Gotthard. It is very cold & I pine for Italy.

ALS: MH bMS Am 1094 (1957)

[1] On 11 October 1873, WJ departed on the *Spain* for Liverpool. The steamer was off Queenstown, Ireland, 21 October 1873.

To Henry James

Dresden Friday [February 27, 1874]

Dear H.

I'm off at noon to day for Bremen—will post this on board ship.[1]— Enclose the letter you sent me this A.M.—Will drop her a line—Took my berth to[o] late to notify F. & M. so that they will be spared anxiety about me during the voyage. Frau Sp. will forward me any letters fm. you. I am awful glad I'm off.—Bremen 9 A.M. I am bkfst꙼ & washing at Hotel, as the train for the Steamer don't leave till eleven. Weather mild & still. My own thought of a steamer chair reminds me that the one I used on the Spain is being kept by the Porter of the Adelphi hotel (clasped in a loving embrace with Miss Kellogg's—both marked distinctly,) and he will surrender it to you for a slight fee.[2] I now go out to see the town—I got in dresden 2 beautiful coats and cd. not at the last moment resist a fur overcoat for 60 thalers—not having had time to order another one made.

Beautiful ship & fine weather—Will write again at Southampton

Yrs W.J.

ALS: MH bMS Am 1092.9 (2590)

[1] According to HJ, WJ reached New York on 13 March (see HJ's letter of 22 March 1874), which means that he had to move up his 4 March departure date (see letter of 28 February 1874). Since he sailed on a Saturday, he was a passenger on the *Mosel*,

which left Bremen on 28 February 1874, a Saturday, was off Southampton on 3 March and reached New York on 14 March. A ship from Bremen reached New York on 13 March, which fits HJ's remark, but it did not leave Bremen on a Saturday. The dating of the letter depends on the sailing date. WJ received HJ's letter of 28 February 1874 after reaching Cambridge. WJ's reference in his letter of 22 March 1874 to HJ's letter of 27 February indicates either a lost letter or an error made by WJ in trying to assign a date to HJ's "Saturday."

² WJ's fellow passenger on the *Spain* had been Julia Antoinette Kellogg (1830–1914), a Swedenborgian writer and reformer, author of *The Philosophy of Henry James* (1883).

From Henry James

Florence. Saturday. [February 28, 1874]

Dear W<u>m</u>—I received last night your letter from Dresden, & thanked the Lord for all your comfortable & agreeable impressions—especially for the good bread & butter. I hasten to reply however to its more practical portions. I am very sorry you should feel bothered & trammeled in your decision as to sailing by any thoughts of me. I beg you to cast them off instantly & decide simply w⟨ith a⟩ view to your own comf⟨ort.⟩ I hope for your own sake you don't overwhelmingly incline to hurry off by March 4<u>th</u>: & I should think that to wait along a while & take a Bremener at your ease would be the better thing or best of all take the Russia, Apr. 4<u>th</u>. I should think that with the T.s,¹ in your sympathetic Germany you might spend the interval with out being too much harried by impatience. Or in April couldn't you take a Bremener? I say this because—(as I was going to hasten to write you even if your letter hadn't come)—even by April 4<u>th</u> I think I should be reluctant to sail fr. England. In fact, to tell the truth, there has been germinating in my mind within the last days & in proportion as I feel (as I do daily) better & stronger, a most overwhelming desire to hang on here for three or four months longer. A project ha⟨s no⟩w taken shape of remaining till July or August 1<u>st</u> & sailing from Leghorn for N.Y. The boats are said to be large & good & cheap and a south Atlantic passage at midsummer mightn't to be so very trying. The voyage is 18 days, but the first 5 or 6 are taken up with dawdling about the Mediterranean & stopping at Naples, Messina & other picturesque places. But leaving this question quite aside, I feel as I say, a daily-growing desire, now that I'm here to stick here a while longer. I don't know when I may come again; & when I do it will be in an older & colder mood, when I shan't relish it as I do now nor get what I can now out of it. Four or five years hence I shall feel like you, about Italy, probably & be sorry that I didn't squeeze the orange tighter before the sensibilities of youth were quite extinct. I have got back to writing again & feel as if I might in the next 3 or 4 months do some things (dependent on being here) which are worth doing & which if I leave I shall never do. In short it's a healthy & vigorous longing that I feel & I think I shall entertain it a week (or even a fortnight longer) & then decide. Now that I feel well enough to write very sufficiently again, I can from appearances keep very reasonably abreast of father's financial advances—the more as my life here won't be dear, & I shall be spared the expense of the northward journey &c & the Cunard voyage. I have no desire whatever to "see" Paris or London again at present: on the contrary I have an aversion to it & a desire to concentrate myself on Italy similar to yours to keep yourself down to your own studies. In fine I incline to make up my mind to stay—especially as I shall be pledged to nothing & can leave if it become advisable. The moral of all this is that you are to drop me from your mind & decide upon your own course freely. I only hope you will not have lost a chance you wished to take by waiting to hear from me. But I hope Dresden will hold you a while. When I go up to post this I shall telegraph to you, if the telegr. is not too dear. My intestines remain the same. A week's rain, but to day clear, tho' unsettled. Florence is getting a more normal atmosphere & under the shadow of departure I am getting to adore it. The days pass easily—tho' a trifle lonelily. I sent you yesterday a letter from M. & one fr. A.K. Thank A.M. much for her's & love to both. Write as soon again as possible

Yours   H. James jr

ALS: MH bMS Am 1094 (1958)

[1] Tweedies.

To Henry James

Cambridge March 22. 74
Dear H.—Your letter of Feby 27 cum to hand the other day and all its painstaking details about me were read aloud in my presence, much to the amusement of all—You will already have got a line from me telling of the voyage. Now for impressions of home. Things look surprisingly mean and flimsy here after my short absence. I'm glad on that account that I made it no longer. How they will appear to

you I dare not venture to guess.   But I'm glad to observe that even one week begins to give a worthy look again to the scence, and one gets accustomed to the diminished scale of interest.   Alice says it struck here very much on her return, but soon passed off again.   I find her in prime condition much better than she ever was—and father and mother extremely well.   My meeting with the Sedgwick's— at least my enjoyment of them, has been of a rather milder character than I anticipated when I had that fit of homesickness.   Perry & Atkinson came out here yesterday.   T.S.P. did nothing but rummage among the books, said nothing, but looked very well.   He is to be married next month and to spend the summer in the Cabot's town house.   Miss C. is not very well, and he is doing nothing but write for Atlantic & Nation.   Alice says he tried to get up a class in literature but it fell through.   I lunched at Parker's with Wendell H. yesterday, and found him uncongenial as I have always found him of late.   He says he is doing very well in his business and that his Kent annotations got great praise.[1]—Wendell expressed great affection for you & desire to see you.   Howells ditto.   I expressed to him my newly quickened sense of the aridity of american life, but he replied that it was teeming with suggestions to his imagination.   H. looks magnificently. The bootts are jolly.   They had a german club party 2 nights ago to which I went, and saw a play very prettily *mis en scène* and (by a Miss Howe) very well acted.[2]   But the whole party was rather of the old Newport order of drearyness & countrifaction.   So once more I sympathized with your aversion to your native soil, and you can be sure that when you come home I will not badger you as I did in Italy about your want of piety.   I repent me of having interfered so then with your free mental inclination.   I also loathe myself for my divided interest in things while I was in Italy.   I was too weak for my circumstances.   But now I am more satisfied than ever with my promised career at home if only I get strength enough to pursue it.—Chas. Norton came in the other morning and was genial—though I could n't help treading on his toes about Munich &c—I find that what one regrets on his return as much as anything is not having spent more money on presents & photogs &c.   Instead of praising you, they revile you for your economy.   So don't be afraid to go in if you're tempted.—Your Madame de Mauve gets great praise from all quarters.[3]   I think it is one of your very best things.   Father sent the first corrected proof of your Adina back to Scribner yesterday.[4]   The Galaxy sent $65 for your Swiss Italian article,[5] and Howells says he will print your last story about the ingenuous youth in Baden & the Coquette in one number.[6] He says its your best thing.—I will now cease and drop a line to the Tweedies. I have begun to study with much pleasure & may perhaps [*lower half of page missing*]

AL incomplete: MH bMS AM 1092.9 (2591)

[1] See letter of 5 December 1869.

[2] A performance by the German Club of Harvard College.

[3] HJ, "Mme. de Mauves," *Galaxy* 17 (February 1874): 216–33; 17 (March 1874): 354–74.

[4] HJ, "Adina," *Scribner's Monthly* 8 (May 1874): 33–43; 8 (June 1874): 181–91.

[5] HJ, "An Autumn Journey," *Galaxy* 17 (April 1874): 536–44, reprinted in *Transatlantic Sketches*.

[6] HJ, "Eugene Pickering," *Atlantic Monthly* 34 (October 1874): 397–410; 34 (November 1874): 513–26.

From Henry James

Florence, Corona d'Italia | March 22ᵈ [1874]
Dearest Wᵐ: After looking vainly for many days I at last discovered in the *Times* a couple of days since the arrival of your ship on the 13ᵗʰ I shudder at the thought of your 14 day passage, which implies that you were terribly tossed and afflicted. You wrote me a line, I trust, as soon as you landed, for I am anxiously expecting one. Till I receive it, *taceo* & don't indulge in vain conjectures as to what you have endured & survived. Youre at home and lapped in familiar joys, that at least is secure. I suppose Florence & Rome are already beginning to seem dim & visionary. Solid & sensible I hope will prove, however, such increase of strength as you have gained from them! You must have found at home letters with news no later than you had got before sailing: for you missed at least *one* from me, sent at the last to Mᵐᵉ Spangenberg. I got from A.M.T.[1] after you left Dresden a letter speaking of you as seeming to be below par while there but as this was opposite to the impression I received from your own letters, I try to explain it away by her somewhat crooked way of seeing things. She spoke at any rate as if they had greatly enjoyed your visit.—I wrote home some ten days since, in a manner which I trust will give general satisfaction. Father will take charge of my notes to Dr. Holland,[2] & send one or the other according to the news he gets from Howells to whom he wrote by the same mail. If the thing falls thro' on the question of payment, it little matters, as I can make quite as much in the same time by short pieces.—You will infer from this remark that I am doing well in health & work. I am in truth better every day—decid-

edly better than before my illness & even than I was while you were
with me here, before my visit to Rome.   My fever has really done me
a service & been a blessing in disguise.—I am here at the Corona still,
as you see, in your old room, & sandwiched daily between the Heidekopers & Mrs. Mallet.³   My relations with the former are genial &
active: but I shall soon change my residence probably, somehow.   I
lead the same quiet life & have made no new acquaintances save that
of a young Roman who comes 3 or 4 times a week to act as a crutch to
my hobbling Italian.   He's a *bravo giovane* (recommended by a friend
of Hillebrands) & I think I shall learn something.   In another way
there is a very good fellow here with his sister, by name Bancroft of
Boston, with whom I often walk & talk.⁴   He is indeed quite a resource.   Lizzie Boott will tell you about him, tho' probably, remembering Rome, she will think that if I *he*⁵ is my mainstay, Florence has
indeed brought me low.   I see Hillebrand once in a while, & dined
there lately, very pleasantly: one of those polyglot dinners which excite the imagination.   Gryzanowski I don't often see.   I'm afraid I
offended him the other night (from his manner) by offering him payment for those visits he made me.   I insisted on his taking it—perhaps infelicitously. Àpropos—I attribute great benefit to Davis's remedy *Calcaria carbonica* which I have been taking regularly since you
left.—Florence is of course lively & the spring fairly on us.   The air
is more relaxing than I strictly care for; but I think I shall do very
well.   Mrs. Huntington⁶ gave 'tother night a large party (I didn't get
home till 3) at which I talked long with Miss Whitwell—not about you.
Farewell, dear Bro.   I have ordered the trunk to be sent from L. &
<by> Boston Curnarder & you will receive the Bill of Lading & the
key—by my sending which latter to L. the box will go much more
cheaply.   Love—love love to all & all blessings on yourself

                                          Your's ever   H.Jjr

ALS: MH bMS Am 1094 (1959)

¹ Mary Tweedy.

² Josiah Gilbert Holland (1819–1881), American novelist, editor of *Scribner's
Monthly*, asked HJ to write a novel for *Scribner's*.   HJ was interested but thought that
loyalty required him to offer first choice to the *Atlantic*.   He sent two notes to his
father, one accepting and the other rejecting Holland's offer.   If the *Atlantic* agreed
to meet the asking price of $1,200, Henry James was to send Holland the rejection
note (*HJL*, 1:436–37). The novel, as yet unwritten, was *Roderick Hudson*, serialized in
the *Atlantic Monthly* in 1875.

³ Neither the Heidekopers nor Mrs. Mallet is identified.   The latter could be Mary
Elizabeth Ormond Mallet (d. 1886), wife of John William Mallet (1832–1912), Irish-
born chemist.

⁴Not identified.

⁵HJ may have intended to write a verb after 'I', or more likely, he began a thought with 'I', then changed his mind and wrote '*he*', forgetting to delete the 'I'.

⁶Ellen Greenough Huntington (d. 1893), sister of the Greenoughs, living in Florence.

To Henry James

Cambr. April 18. 74

Dear H.

Yours of the 22nd to me cum to hand about a week ago and much pleasure did it give by its good news of your health.   May it last!   I'm sorry you should have struck on a "morbid" vein in Gryz'——sky—its too bad.   It's also too bad you shd. have "conversed long with Miss Whitwell, *not* about me." Where's the messages I charged you to give her about my wanting to take her to that restored castle?   Is it true she's not coming home for another year?   Alack the day!   Any gossip about florence you can still communicate will be greedily sucked in by me, who feel towards it as I do towards the old Albany of our childhood with afternoon shadows of trees &c. &c.—Not but that I am happy here—more so than I ever was there because I'm in a permanent path, and it shows me how for our type of character the thought of the *whole* dominates the particular moments.   All my moments here are inferior to those in Italy, but they are parts of a long plan which is good, so they content me more than the Italian ones wh. only existed for themselves.   I have been feeling uncommonly strong for almost three weeks, (having been pretty miserable for the six preceding) and done a good deal of work in Bowditch's laboratory.   I am engaged to go to spend this Saturday night & to morrow with him at Jamaica Plains.¹   He is worthy—Yesterday was a cold NEster, which left two good inches of snow on the ground for to day's glittering sun to clear away.   A different spring from yours—but on the whole not intolerable to me for you know that each day may be the last.   Terrible weather at sea.   I'm glad our joint voyage in April fell through.   No news yet of the trunk.—I went yesterday to dine with mrs Tappan & 'did not get out till midnight through the snow storm   She lives on Beacon St. looking down Dartmouth, and Emerson & Ellen Dr Holmes, and Miss Georgina Putnam were the guests.²   None oped the mouth save holmes at table.   Emerson looks in magnificent health, but the refined idiocy of his manner seems as if it must be affectation.   After dinner I had a long and drastic dose of Miss Put-nam then was relieved by the incoming of Miss Bessie Lee who is very "nice."   The Tappan girls are improved.   Ellen longs for Europe, Boston being so "tame"(!) and they probably will go next fall.   After all Mrs Tappans eagerness for intellectual sensations, her *passion*, more than atone for all her crimes, and make her the most nutritious person I have yet struck here.   I confess that we seem a poor lot on the whole.   My short stay abroad has given me quite a new sense of what you used to call the provinciality of Boston, but that is no harm. What displeases me is the want of stoutness & squareness in the people, their ultra quietness, prudence, slyness, intellectualness of gait.   Not that their intellects amount to anything, either.   You will be discouraged, I remain happy! but this brings me to the subject of your return, of which I have thought much.   It is evident that you will have to eat your bread in sorrow for a time here—it is equally evident that time (but it may take years) will prove a remedy for a great deal of the trouble and you will attune your at present coarse senses to snatch a fearful joy from wooden fences and commercial faces, a joy the more thrilling for being so subtly extracted.   Are you ready to make the heroic effort?   It is a fork in the path of your life and upon your decision hangs your whole future.   If you are not persuaded enough of the importance of living at home to wade through perhaps three years slough of despond, I see no particular reason why you should come at all just now—and its extravagance is against it.   This is your dilemma: The congeniality of europe on the one hand + the difficulty of making an entire living out of original writing, and its abnormality as a matter of mental hygiene, on the one hand;—the dreariness of american conditions of life + a mechanical routine occupation possibly to be obtained, which from day to day is *done* when 'tis done, mixed up with the writing into which you distil your essence.   Alice tells me that since you have been away she has received but $1800 for your writing (this week 25 for your '93, and 20 for your excellent Merimée have come in)[3]   You see to *live* by the pen is what very few people can do unless they "prostitute" them-selves like [*blank space for name*]

As for better health at home I'm not sure we did not exaggerate that. My bowels were very lively till I sailed from Bremen.   I hardly passed anything the two weeks I was on board, and they have been very tight ever since in spite of home diet.   In short don't come unless with a *resolute* intention.   If you come, your worst years will be the first,   If you stay, the bad years may be the later ones, when moreover you *cant* change.   And I have a suspicion that if you come too and *can* get once acclimated the quality of what you write will be higher than it wd. be in Europe.   The rest of the family concur in thinking that if it is probable that you are to return in a year, you had better for econo- my's sake not come.   Of course you can correct proofs of your books by mail, without any trouble.   It seems to me a very critical moment in your history.   But you have several months to decide.

Goodbye.   Bill of lading & key of trunk have just come.

AL: MH bMS Am 1092.9 (2592)

[1] Bowditch lived in Jamaica Plain, an area of Boston.

[2] Ellen Tucker Emerson's version of the same evening: "Father and I stayed one night at Mrs. Tappan's last week, and Dr. Holmes dined there with us.   It was the first time I ever heard him talk, it was worth while.   William James was there too.   I can imagine how he made you feel.   The intellectual always makes me feel so.   But at Mrs. Tappan's he didn't soar, was only very pleasant" (*The Letters of Ellen Tucker Emerson*, 2:128).   Georgina Lowell Putnam was the daughter of Mary Lowell Putnam, sis- ter of James Russell Lowell.

[3] HJ, "Ninety-Three," review of Victor Hugo, *Quatrevingt-treize* and its English translation, in *Nation* 18 (9 April 1874): 238–39; "The Letters of Prosper Mérimée," in *Independent* (9 April 1874): 9–10.   HJ also published a review of Mérimée's *Der- nières nouvelles*, in *Nation* 18 (12 February 1874): 111.

From Henry James

Florence, May 3ᵈ [1874]

Dear Wᵐ.   I wrote some ten days ago to Alice, & I am not sure whether I then had received your letter of April 5ᵗʰ.   Since then, at all events, has come to me father's note containing my notice of Meri- mée & also the N.A.R. (2ᵈ number,) for which I am greatly obliged. I have sent the Review to Turgeneff through Hetzel the Paris pub- lisher, as I could find no other address.[1]—I was glad to get from you any new expression of impressions of home—& was much enter- tained by your thermometrical record.   But I could send you one almost as entertaining.   After ten days a short time since, of very hot—of really July & August—weather, some thing very like winter has set in again & cold & rain are the order of the day.   To day is a raw, rainy Sunday of anything but an exhilarating kind.   The Piazza di Sta Maria Novella, before my windows is a wide glittering flood, with here and there two legs picking their steps beneath an umbrella. I have already written you of my being established at housekeeping—

or something very like it.   It wears very well & my rooms are delightful; if I came back to Florence again, I should certainly take them for the winter.   The way of life is rather solitudinous—especially the lonely feeding: but I have found a very good dining-place, where I can at least converse with the flower-girl who comes every day to distribute rosebuds for the button-hole.   (The place is Victor's, Via Rondinelli, whose window, like those in the palais Royal you must remember.)   The days go on with me monotonously enough & I make no new friends.   I spend my time very much as when you were here, save that when the warm weather fairly set in, I took to going out in the morning & working during the hot hours from lunch to dinner. There is nothing especial to tell you of your acquaintances here, tho' I continue to see most of them occasionally.   I pay frequent short visits to the Lombards, & though long since mortally tired of their nature & conversation am reduced to accepting their parlor gratefully for half an hour as the nearest approach to a domestic *foyer*.   In fact I shall miss them, uncomfortably, when they go.   Mrs. L. is better & worse, & lately much pleased to hear that Essie was coming out to join her.   But E. will not find her anywhere in Italy, as she is constantly on the point of leaving.   But she can't imagine where to go.— I have had great pleasure lately in seeing Mrs. Effie Lowell, who is a most lovely being surely.[2]   I have seen her only in the evening, however, & haven't undertaken to "go round" with her.   She says she doesn't care for "art," & the other day was going to visit the poorhouse in company with a colored doctoress established here!   Gryzanowski came in just as I was reading your last letter & told me to tell you that he had received the books you lately sent him & prized them greatly, but that your generosity made him uncomfortable.   He is "simpatico" as ever.   Hillebrand becomes to me less & less so; he is an unmistakeable snob.   I went the other evening to a large & very wearisome party given by Mrs. Taylor (M$\underline{me}$ Lannsot's mother,)[3] filled with very ordinary folk, Italian, German & English.—James Lowell & his wife spent a few days here on their return from Rome & have left for Paris—without revealing any new traits of mind or character.   I feel as if I knew Lowell now very well; but don't feel as I should ever get anything very valuable out of him.   They (the Lowells) were very frankly critical of the Storys with whom they staid a while in Rome & seem to have been chiefly busy after the 1$\underline{st}$ day in inventing subterfuges for getting away.   The Andrews are here, back from Rome, Edith ill (slightly I believe) with fever, as you were.—Let me say, without more loss of time, that my letter of credit expires (the date, not the sum) on May 27th, & that I should like father to please ask Uncle R. to have it renewed for June, July & August.[4]   The last was for £500; this had better be (nominally) for £250.   I shall draw no such sum, probably; but I had better be able to draw all that I need for my expenses in getting home & making any purchases for you.   If this can be done without delay, it will be a convenience to me; as I have left too long speaking of it.   I keep your various lists of commissions; though they imply as a *certainty* my sailing *via* England.   I have given up all idea of taking an Italian steamer: but if I leave Italy in the early part of June, I may be reduced to going to Homburg as the best place to spend the interval of the 7 weeks of July & August.   In that case I shall hesitate to think it worth while to go to England, expensively, when I can make the journey from Bremen; & I suppose you won't want me to go there on purpose to buy your things.   But there is time to decide on this. Father sent me a rather puzzling request in his last: *i.e.* to buy $75 worth of virtù for the tops of the bookcases.   I can't very well buy it here, as to send it would be (I'm told) very expensive—costing as much, almost, as the thing itself.   Then to carry it about with me would be equally so, & not very convenient.   I think therefore I had better let my getting it depend on my being in Paris; where the choice of things is probably better also.   I see no reason here to suppose it remarkable.   Thank father *àpropos* of his last, for his care of the proof's of my last story.   I suppose it has been sent me, though it has not yet arrived.—I have fairly settled down to work upon my long story for the *Atlantic* & hope to bring it home finished or nearly so.[5]   Except therefore for two or three more Italian sketches (if opportunity offers) I shall send home no short things before I leave, & shall have to draw more money than, for the present, I cause to flow in.   But if I am paid down, even in part, for my MS. I shall be able to offer full reimbursement.   I lately sent a tale to the Galaxy[6] & a couple more reviews to the *Nation*:[7] but I want henceforth to give all my time & attention to my novel.   I am determined it shall be a very good piece of work.   Farewell, dear brother.   Would that you were here for an hour, this dreary day, at my solitary side. I'm sorry Waterman doesn't give you your place since you are disposed to resume it.[8]   But such is life.   Farewell.   My being aches with unsatisfied domestic affection, & just now I could howl with homesickness

Ever yours   H.J.jr

ALS: MH bMS Am 1094 (1960)

[1] J. Hetzel, publisher of French translation of Turgenev.

[2] Josephine Shaw Lowell, widow of Charles Russell Lowell.   He was a nephew of James Russell Lowell and was killed in battle in 1864.

[3] Neither Mrs. Taylor nor Mme Lannsot is identified.   The latter name could be a misreading since HJ's always difficult hand is even more mysterious at this point.

[4] Alexander Robertson Walsh.

[5] HJ, *Roderick Hudson.*

[6] HJ, "Professor Fargo," *Galaxy* 18 (August 1874): 233–53.

[7] Fitting best the date of the letter are reviews of Gustave Flaubert, *Temptation of St. Anthony,* in *Nation* 18 (4 June 1874): 365–66; and Émile Montégut, *Souvenirs de Bourgogne,* in *Nation* 19 (23 July 1874): 62.

[8] Thomas Waterman (1842–1901), American physician.   After WJ decided not to teach in 1873–74, Waterman taught the course in anatomy and physiology.

From Henry James

Monte Generoso | Near Como. June 13ᵗʰ [1874]

Dear Wᵐ.   I am sitting under a sort of little shed, on a sort of terrace, overlooking a sort of view—writing this at a rustic table, the rusty nails of which lacerate my wrists as I drive the pen.   Opposite are established Mrs. Lombard & Fanny!!   But of them anon.—I wrote home last from Florence—speaking then, if I remember, as if I expected to remain there till the 20ᵗʰ.   I absconded at a day's notice, just a week ago, under pressure of the terrific heat which suddenly descended upon all Italy a few days before & sent all travellers spinning northward.   I was greatly contrarié to leave, but the atmosphere was intolerable & work had become impossible.   I came on to Milan, grasping on the way a most scorching but most delightful day at Ravenna.   Of this I shall write to the *Nation.*[1]   At Milan I met the Lombards flung from Venice & much distracted to know where to go.   I being minded to come up here to await, if possible July 1ˢᵗ, they decided to come as well: so we ascended together last evening, in a thunder storm which caused them much discomfiture.   But this morning we are rested & dried; & though I confess to a certain sinking of the heart at finding myself fixed on a mountain top, with the old too, too familiar Swiss pension life going on about me, & a dozen English clergymen in "puggaries" kicking their enormous heels on the front steps—yet I am inclined to take a cheerful view of things.   A small closet 5 feet square isn't favorable to literary labor, but I shall give myself a chance to get used to it, & doubtless succeed.   The air is delicious—Alpine freshness tempered by Italian softness—the views enchanting, the food eatable & the company apparently estimable. There are agreeable strolls & shady hillsides & I shall perch till I can perch no longer. (Your letters, meanwhile, must come to Brown & Shipley.) The heat in Italy for the past fortnight has been extraordinary & for a week in especial, intolerable. The journey from Florence & the couple of days at Milan were spent in a mere demoralized *soak* of perspiration. The Lombards say Venice was fatally uncomfortable & seem to have come away with an indifferent opinion of it. I am more than satiated with their society, but they are too feeble for criticism; & they make no exactions. They will probably depart in a few days for Geneva to join Essie.—I have not heard from home in some time, & am expecting letters to be sent from Florence. Just before starting I got a *nation* with my letter from Pisa &c.[2] What do you think of this for a misprint:—"idle vistas & melancholy nooks" = "*idle sisters & melancholy monks!!*" In the article on *Siena* the sense of two or three good sentences was also ruined.[3]—But this is not a letter—but only a notification of my whereabouts & I must not embark on details. I am rather stiff & sore with my climb yesterday & must lie off, horizontally. I am afraid you are all struggling painfully with the summer question, & I wish I had a bosky-flanked Monte G. to offer you. The opal-tinted view, the drowsy breeze, the stillness & the tinkling cow-bells are gradually sinking into my soul.—I had been wondrous well in Florence, until the great heat began, & that rather undid me: but on this higher plane I shall doubtless mend. Much love to all: I shall write again speedily. In spite of the temperature, I have been lacerated at leaving Italy. Ravenna is remarkable: I wish I had given a 2ᵈ day to it. I trust you are prospering & that the summer will pass well with you. I have not yet answered directly your letter about my coming home; but I answered it through mother. I shall certainly come.

Yours ever   H. James jr

ALS: MH bMS Am 1094 (1961)

[1] HJ, "Ravenna," *Nation* 19 (9 July 1874): 23–25.

[2] HJ, "Tuscan Cities," *Nation* 18 (21 May 1874): 329–30, reprinted in *Transatlantic Sketches*.

[3] HJ, "Siena," *Atlantic Monthly* 33 (June 1874): 664–69, reprinted in *Transatlantic Sketches*.

To Henry James

Cambr. June 25. 74

Dear H.

A few days ago came your letter from florence of June 3, speaking of the glare on the piazza and the coolness and space of your rooms, of your late dinners & your solitude, and of the progress of your novel, and finally of your expected departure about the 20th so that I suppose you are to day percolating the cool arcades of Bologna or the faded beauties of Verona, or haply at Venice. Since I last wrote you several events have occurred the which as they passed prompted communication with you; but now the visit I made to Concord a fortnight or more ago seems rather too stale for description, Class day has been eclipsed by "Dedication" day, and to day at Noon ΦBK crowns the edifice. My dip into Concord simplicity, rural prettiness, and intellectual and moral worth was most refreshing. Ellen & Edwd. Emerson were delightful, and Miss May Alcott showed me her copies of Turner, the result of a year of hard work alone in London, & quite a fine thing for a poor yankee girl to have done.[1] F., M., & A go there to morrow, and Ellen writes this A.M. for me to come too, as the Alcotts are going to have Miss Bartlett whom I had expressed curiosity to see. But I don't think I shall go. The dedication of M.H (which has become the great consoling feature in Cambridge) was rather a failure owing to the great heat, immense crowd & inaudibility of the speeches.[2] Three or four nights ago the Longfellows gave a fête champêtre—about 100 young couples—a dry hot half mooned evening which made it possible to the girls to lie around on the grass without extra covering—the house all wide open with its many noble rooms and innumerable piazzas & halls, beauties by the score, and the delicious grounds all made it the loveliest scene of the kind I had ever seen.[3] And I think even your high fed sensualism wd. not have been untouched by the charm of it, and wd. have said that there are elements in american life wh. may grow into something handsome. I am sorry you think you are not likely to meet with O.W.H for I think it would do you both good. F. J. Child sails in 3 days and will probably be in Switzerland. I hardly know what to advise about your return. The big English steamers are so much more comfortable that I cd. wish you on that account to return that way. But on the other hand I wish you might sail in Augst. instead of Sept. A month more of pleasant weather at home wd. ease you into the winter, and you are not staying for any particular reason. Why don't you sail in August from England?—My own plans for the summer will be decided on the 1st of July. Duty to the boys, and pity for poor Bob's outcast state, stranded as he is in P. du Ch., lead me West, but in that case I should get no vacation, for the journey there wd. hardly count as refreshment, and wd. cost too much to allow me to go elsewhere after it.[4] 9 months vacation this year already ou[gh]t to have fitted me to do without any this summer, and it is a little disappointing after but 3 months work at home to find myself panting again for sea side idleness and cool salubrity as much as I do. I fear it will come to my turning my back on the boys.—Last night I supped with the Gurneys, the Godkins being there. The latter asked after you—Father just comes in from town with a New Fortnightly review containing an article by Hillebrand on Winckelmann, wh. I shall read with interest.[5] I am sorry Hillebrand has ended by decidedly displeasing you, but can easily imagine it of him. Did you never get to see his young sculptor?—As the weeks glide by, my present life and my last year's life at home seem to glide together across the 5 months breach that Italy made in them and to become continuous; while those months step out of the line and become a sort of side decoration or picture hanging vaguely in my memory. As this happens more and more I take the greater pleasure in it. Especially does the utter *friendliness* of Florence, Rome &c grow dear to me, and get strangely mixed up with still earlier and more faded impressions derived I know not whence, which infused in to the places when I first saw them that strange thread of familiarity. The thought of the florentine places you name in your letters like "leiser Nachhall längst verklungner Lieder, Zieht mit Erinnerungsschauer durch die Brust."—I hope you'll pass through Dresden if you sail from Germany. I forgot to say that the Eagle line from Hamburg has now the largest and finest ships, and the newest.[6]—6.30 P.M I am just in from the Phi Beta K. festivities. The oration by Chas Carroll Everett was good.[7] The poem by C. P Cranch, a Glorification of Our Century was in very good verses, though somewhat too long.[8] The dinner speeches were somewhat poor owing to the wretched trick of Dana, the president, not warning anyone that he is to be called on.[9] But the College yard with its rustling trees & moving sunshine, looked delicious and so did the cool chapel. Altogether this annual week of celebrations is one of the things that thicken the air about Cambridge and make one not averse to living here. Ive no doubt one year more will quite reinstate me in harmony with the place. Your last paper in the Independent, on florentine architecture was first rate.[10] $15 came for it this AM.—

I send you with this a copy of the Advertizer containing the Commencement speeches yesterday.   Every one said General Bartlett's was first rate.[11]   He is living now in Richmond (Va.)   Also Beecher's misdoings with the wife of Theodore Tilton wh all the papers have been licking their lips over for the past year.[12]   I think Parisian lewdness is purity itself compared with this Puritanic pruriency.   Bob's baby enclosed.

                                        Adieu.   Your | W.J.

ALS: MH bMS Am 1092.9 (2593)

    [1] May Alcott (1840–1879), American painter, noted for her copies of Turner, daughter of Amos Bronson Alcott (1799–1888), American reformer, and sister of Louisa May Alcott (1832–1888), American novelist.

    [2] Memorial Hall, built in honor of the Harvard dead in the Civil War, was completed in 1878.   Dedicated on 24 June 1874 were Alumni Hall and the Memorial Transept.   A plaque in memory of William James Temple hangs on one of the walls.

    [3] Probably the Cambridge home of Henry Wadsworth Longfellow (1807–1882), American poet.

    [4] Prairie du Chien, Wis., where RJ had moved from Milwaukee.   WJ did not make the trip in summer 1874.

    [5] Karl Hillebrand, "Winckelmann," *North American Review* 118 (June 1874): 760–84, about Johann Joachim Winckelmann (1717–1768), German archaeologist and art historian.

    [6] No mention of an Eagle Line was found.   Perhaps he means the Hamburg-Amerika Line.

    [7] Charles Carroll Everett (1829–1900), American theologian.

    [8] Christopher Pearse Cranch, "The Century and the Nation," published in *The Bird and the Bell, with Other Poems* (1875).

    [9] Richard Henry Dana (1851–1931), American lawyer.

    [10] HJ, "Florentine Architecture," *Independent* (18 June 1874): 3–4.

    [11] William Francis Bartlett (1840–1876), American military officer, made a general in 1864.

    [12] Contemporary journalists dubbed the summer of 1874 "scandal summer." The affair involved Henry Ward Beecher (1813–1887), a popular clergyman, advocate of the "gospel of love," and Elizabeth Richards Tilton, wife of Theodore Tilton (1835–1907), American journalist.   Advocates of free love claimed that Beecher really agreed with them but being a hypocrite hid behind the vague notion of "gospel of love."

From Henry James

                          Baden Baden July 6th [1874] | Hotel Royal
Beloved Brother:
    I wrote some ten days ago, while I was still waiting for your letters to be sent from Florence: They came a day or two later—one from

you of June 1ˢᵗ, one from father of the 11ᵗʰ, & one forwarded from Wilky.   Also a number of the Independent.[1]   The time has come round again for a new arrival, but I won't wait to acknowledge it. Your letter was most welcome & satisfactory, but I am afraid I can give you nothing of equal value in return.   I am sorry your eyes had been bothering you, but I trust you have worked them up by this time to their normal level.   What chiefly preoccupies me is my wonderment as to what your are going to do with the summer.   I saw in one of the papers an allusion to some late terrific heat in New-Y⟨or⟩k.   I hope it was not as bad as reported or that if so, it stopped mercifully short of Cambridge.   Alice & A.K. are of course by this time packed off to the Green Mountains & I hope you have salubrious retreat in prospect, for at least a part of the summer.—Writing from out of these shady blue forests of Baden, I feel as if it shamed me even to allude to your possibilities of discomfort.   Heaven bless you (or rather *fan* you, all!)   My last letter will have told you of my coming here straight from Italy, of my having lost my heart my heart to the loveliness of the place & fixed myself here for an indefinite period.   I shall probably remain undisturbedly till Sept. 1ˢᵗ, unless induced to adjourn to Homburg about Aug. 1ˢᵗ by the Tweedies, who are probably coming back from England to go there.   But I hope, for a little conversation's sake, to make them c⟨ome⟩ here.—I have been ⟨here⟩ passing a very tranquil & uneventful ten days.   I scribble in the morning, walk in the woods in the afternoon & sit listening to the music on the promenade & eating an ice in the evening.   Baden is a wonderfully pretty place & exactly arranged by nature for its rôle.   It is embowered in Forests & these are singularly handsome; I never knew to the same extent the fascination of trees.   The walks & strolls are multitudinous & wherever you go you want to lie down on the grass in verden shade and look at the blue hills.   Socially, the beaux jours of Baden are over & the life of the place is very dull.   I have seen no one I know, & converse with nature more than with man.   Turgenieff, alas, has just sold his villa & departed.   I am told that in former years he was constantly "round."—You will have learned by this time by my late lett⟨er my⟩ intentions as to coming home, promulgated in reply to your letter received in Florence.   You will have observed that I don't consider my return now equivalent to the design of fixing myself there for ever, as you seemed to imply.   But we can talk of this when I arrive, which will probably be in October *via* England.   I regret that I cannot echo your satisfaction on leaving Italy for Germany. I don't think a residence of years would modify materially my joyless attitude toward this people, their physiognomy, & and their manners. I didn't know, until coming back here now, how wedded I was to my preference for a life in Italy to any other, & indeed if I couldn't live there I think I would rather not live in Europe at all.   Either Italy or downright Yankeedom!   The hitch in the matter is that I'm wrong in not caring for the horrible G.'s, as Mrs. Lombard ⟨woul⟩d say, more: but when I ⟨want⟩ a justification, I find it in their atrocious passion for foul air.   Reserve your opinion until you have had to sit down with fifteen persons to a 1 o'clock dinner in a low-ceiled dining room, on a July day, with the thermometer at 86° & every crack & cranny hermetically sealed.   We have been having very great heat & I'm afraid Baden isn't particularly cool.   The nights however, have been delicious.   I don't know what to tell you.   I note your injunction if I stay in Europe to "get married" & if I write you that I have changed my mind & mean to pass the winter, you may expect to hear of my *matrimonio* by the next steamer.   Perhaps the chambermaid here, the large-waisted Anna, will have me.   I got, apropos, a letter from Wilky in which, speaking of his marriage, he says *more suo*: "The former condition is as happy a one as any I ever made for myself!"   Father's letter contained an extract from Bob, about his baby ⟨which⟩ made me feel unmi⟨s⟩t⟨a⟩kably the bowels of an uncle.   It was a charming sketch and must make mother and Alice hanker terribly after the babe.   Tell Alice & A.K. that they must write me about their inn.   Do you see Lowell, if as, I suppose, he has returned?   I parted from him in Florence most affectionately & promised him to dine with him at home, every Sunday: but I confess I don't look forward with absolute enthusiasm to a life in which the chief recreation should be a weekly dinner with L.   I wish you had given me more gossip about certain people at home. How is T.S.P. in matrimony?   Do you see La Farge, & what was the history, and what the results of his time abroad?   The result, I see by the *Nation*, was his getting his pictures refused at the academy.[2]   I have written to W.H.[3] but hear nothing from him: I trust he will come here.   Are there any more facts about the Nortons?   I heard from A. M. Tweedy lately, from England, that they thought of coming to Homburg for August & wanted me to meet them there: but this I have mentioned.   I also shortly since heard from Mrs. Lombard, very desperate for a refuge in Switzerland & wanting to come here.   I wrote her a report of prices, & as they are not high, she may arrive.   I received *one* Independent, with a notice of the Pitti P⟨alace⟩.[4]   Father speaks as if two had been sent⟨.   I sent⟩ the Indpt. the other day a sketch of my journey out of Italy: but

of meagre value, as the subject was not rich.[5]   Farewell, dear Bill:
excuse this insipid scrawl.   It is the best I have just now.   Thank father for his letter & blessings on him & mother.   Peace & comfort to
you all—

Yours ever   H. James jr

ALS: MH bMS Am 1094 (1954)

[1] The *Independent* was publishing nearly every week a piece by HJ on Italy or Italian
art.   These were reprinted in *Transatlantic Sketches*.

[2] *Nation* 18 (4 June 1874): 363, a note on the policies of the hanging committee of
the National Academy of Design.   The committee rejected La Farge, hung a landscape by James Abbott McNeill Whistler where it could not be seen, and used the space
gained for works by members of the committee.

[3] Oliver Wendell Holmes, Jr.

[4] HJ, "Florentine Notes," *Independent* (21 May 1874): 1–2, reprinted in *Transatlantic
Sketches*.

[5] HJ, "A Northward Journey," *Independent* (20 August 1874): 6; (27 August
1874): 4.

To Henry James

Cambr. July 26. 74

Dear H.   I have been at home a day or two and only got yesterday
your letter from Baden wh. was sent unopened to Scarboro' for me
and had to be sent back as I did not turn up there.   I'm glad you find
Baden so pleasant, tho' its a pity Turg. is not there.   You will by this
time have heard from both Mother & me urging a speedier return
than that October 4 which you now announce, (—Father yells out to
me fm. the Library "tell him not to let Mrs Lombard return to him!"
which I do with a good will.   To have her on you at B. wd. be too
much.—) so I hope you'll start a good while earlier and in passing
through England execute the little commission I requested.   I had a
very pleasant fortnight down the coast and am well nigh reinstated in
my last years good humor with things American.   The yankee common people are so excellent, kindly, talkative, & honest.   The defects
of the Yankee character show most in the highest examples, its cool
bloodedness, caution, want of human nature in short.   I went to
Newcastle, York Harbor & the Shoals all close to Portsmouth, then to
Saco Pool, where the Russells, and 3 Cambridge fellows were, and
then home instead of going for a week to Scarboro' as I had intended.
I took a great deal of exercise and felt very well but found that the
bathing started up a wakeful spell only to be broken by a return to my
own bed.   This disappointed me as I have had nothing of the sort

since leaving rome.   I am all right again now.   At the Pool I just escaped falling in love with Miss Sally Russell of the smile.   5 minutes longer and nothing wd. have been left of me to tell the tale.   She is so still and has such an unspeakable decency in all her ways, her smile is so ravishing, and her reputation for erudition so vast, that your imagination can, and does, work furiously upon her.   You say such are the only ones that interest you.   Come & try her!   Only I don't know that the cloister like imaginings she prompts are such as you care for. I have settled down to work for a week more at home.   Then I go to Henry Higginson's for a couple of days, then to Bowditch's after that I know not.—I have not read your story in the Galaxy Prof. Fargo yet, but soon shall.   Father says it is not one of your genuine ergo good ones.   I sent you Nations with your Ravenna & Montégut.[1] Adams has rec'd your Feydeau, and will "probably" print it.[2]   He and wife asked me to go for 3 weeks to the Adirondacks and live in a shanty.   I yearn to do it, but have refused.   The party wd be composed of L. Boott, and 2 as yet unknown others making in all 6.— The great—and truly very great—excitement here has been the Beecher Tilton affair.[3]   Tilton's testimony which was printed in full was so staggering a document, and so well written, as to be very impressive.   But it wd. seem more probable now that he is either insanely deluded or the most malicious villain ever created.   One is glad for human natures sake that Beecher will go free; but from the point of view of Art one would have preferred his guilt, so colossally dramatic wd. his figure of hypocrisy have been.—Cambridge is delightfully cool & pleasant.   I saw Chas. Norton yestreen at the sedgwicks, Theodora being at home.   He stays alternate weeks here.   I spent a couple of hours this A.M. with Fiske who is drowsy and heavy. I hope you may yet meet O.W.H.jr.   The Gurneys are here too, and very comfortable folk to know.   Lafarge is very well in health and says he is working (Gurney & Perry being my informers)   He worked not in Europe, and I imagine is too set now in his mould to ever take a new departure in the painting line, tho' he may grow more industrious in his old way.   Lowell is well pleased to be back, Father says. I have not yet seen him.   T.S.P. and wife seem very affectionate.   His article on Schmidt in the last Atlantic was a very readable magazine article, tho' not valuable as criticism.[4]

Leb' recht wohl.

Your affectionate | W.J.

I shd. think now that the Tweedies have a cottage on the Thames, you wd. feel like passing a while with them.

ALS: MH bMS Am 1092.9 (2594)

[1] See letters of 3 May 1874 and 13 June 1874.

[2] HJ, review of Ernest Feydeau, *Théophile Gautier,* and Théophile Gautier, *Histoire du romantisme,* in *North American Review* 119 (October 1874): 416–23. Henry Adams at the time was an editor of the *North American Review.*

[3] See letter of 25 June 1874.

[4] Thomas Sergeant Perry, "Julian Schmidt: A German Critic," *Atlantic Monthly* 34 (August 1874): 207–14.

To Henry James

Cambr. Nov 14. 75

My dear H.

We have been disappointed at not getting a letter from you with our English papers this week. You have of course heard of the thick sown *events* that have occurred in the family since you left. A.K's sickness—(she is sitting up writing a letter now) F. & M.'s return fm Milwaukee with Bob's retirement from the R.R. (He has just bo't a farm 2 hours by Rail fm. M.) Dido's diarrhea & mange (she is now well of both) Alice's great vigor, my poisoned finger (now well,) Chas Norton's head collapse, Trowbridge's engagement to the widow Gray &c &c.[1] Things are now running peaceably in the house. We have decided to Alice's great grief and resentment to send Dido to Bob. She is getting too big and noisome for a house dog, barks too loudly and ferociously, ranges too far, can't be kept from swill debauches & consequent nocturnal "attacks," and has moreover developed an extremely strong smell of soup about the abdomen which is really quite suffocating. I shall get Alice a terrier to take her place. *Sic transit!* Just now as she lies on the floor, (she has visited some swill pail since bkfst.) she emits a *crepitus* and bathes me with its pungent intestinal perfume. My busy-ness at the Museum has begun to slacken a little of late owing to my decision not to sweat so hard at making osteological preparations which after all are to go before long to another man's professorship.[2] I have never felt so well and have never on the whole been so busy as since your departure, though I've read absolutely nothing of a "general" sort. We have had another club dinner (at the Union Club this time) fuller & pleasanter than the last, though I confess I fear the thing is hopelessly swamped in its buttoned up Boston respectable character.[3] I was more struck than ever by the middle aged tone of the thing—the irresponsible confidingness of boyhood all evaporated. The other club of naturalists to which I belong, al-

though they are men of much inferior "culture" yet have this element—which I suppose lawyers and men of society and business *über-
haupt*, must neccessarily lose.   I have tho't several times with envy of
you lately, in the Paris twilight hour.   That is decidedly *the* hour for a
romancer in a city to get suggestions.   I experienced it twice lately in
Boston.—A.K. has borne her sickness with great sweetness & patience.   It has done Alice good to have her to attend to.   I am going
to be able to give Alice some work at the Museum probably.   I have
seen no one of your friends except Fiske about whom nought to say.
I look with great impatience for the conclusion of Christina's fate; for
Roderick is of course ended—nothing but a physical disposal of him
seems now possible.   I forget that I had read Sardou's Haine.[4]
Splendid subject & splendid mechanism—the background of war so
incessant &c.   But how much better wd. Dumas have made the dia-
loge in the last scenes.   Good luck

Yrs. ever   W.J.

ALS: MH bMS Am 1092.9 (2595)

[1] John Trowbridge (1843–1923), American physicist, professor at Harvard, on 20
June 1877 married Louise Thayer Gray.

[2] The Museum of Comparative Zoology at Harvard, founded by Louis Agassiz and
at the time directed by Alexander Agassiz.

[3] The history of the Union Club is given in a letter by Thomas Sergeant Perry to
WJ's son, Henry James, 11 July 1920 (bMS Am 1092.10 [134]).   The club was formed
in 1870 and included among the original members WJ, HJ, Henry Adams, Dennett,
Fiske, Gray, Holmes, Howells, Perry, and others.

[4] Victorien Sardou, *La haine* (1875).

From Henry James

Rue de Luxembourg 29. | Dec. 3ᵈ. [1875]
Dear Wᵐ.   I have safely rec'd. your letter of Nov. 14ᵗʰ.   My own from
London must have come immediately after it left.   Since then I have
written three times (including letter just sent to A.K.)   This last,
which if she has left Quincy St. you had better open and read will give
you some gossip about myself.   I am very comfortable & have every
ground for contentment & as Uncle Robertson would say, for "gratitude."   I am very well lodged, & bating the dismal prospect of the
Paris winter weather & the in-door cold, have nothing but good to say
of everything.   The improvement in my physical condition which I
hoped would ensue upon a return to this climate, gave from the 1ˢᵗ of
my arrival, very marked symptoms of setting in.   The difficulty of

keeping warm is against me, but if they continue I will let you know more about it.   In such of your news as was good—your own good condition &c—I much rejoiced. May it daily increase!   Thanks also for the note from Bob, about his farm.   I hope he will thrive mightily; but from the point of view of the Rue de Luxembourg it is hard to enter into his situation.   I have seen few people—chiefly Turgénieff, of whom I descanted to A.K.   He is a most attractive man & I took a great shine to him.   I saw a couple of times J. Crafts who had heard from you & has gone to Cannes.   His countenance seemed healthy & his conversation cheerful, but he said he was poorly.   Also Chas Peirce, who wears beautiful clothes &c.   He is busy swinging pendulums at the Observatory & thinks himself indifferently treated by the Paris scientists.   We meet every two or three days to dine together; but tho' we get on very well, our sympathy is economical rather than intellectual.—I have plenty of work here, & shall be able to do it comfortably.   I can think of nothing in life to put into the *Tribune*: it is quite appalling.   But I suppose it will come.   I see *Roderick Hudson* is out; send me any notices you see of it.   You will of course allow for all the misprints in the *Balzac*; in one quotation there is a whole line left out.[1]   That is the bane of my present situation.   I suppose you will have twigged the translation of my tale in the *Revue* of Nov. 15th.   I don't know by whom it was done—I suppose by Mme. Bentzon; whom, if it was, I shall know.   It was copied into the *Independance Belge*![2]   Write me what you (& others) think of the close of *R.H.*   I shall speedily begin, in the *Galaxy*, another novel: it is the best I can do.[3]   Thank you for sending Shephard's letter, about my bill.[4] You don't mention what the amount was; & I am glad on the whole not to know.   It must have been hideously large.   Father will know all I feel about his paying it.   Please to tell him also that I have been obliged to use my letter of credit rather more than I expected.   My 10 days in London, purchases of clothes, &c, journey, & 1st expenses of installation here made it necessary.   But before very long this will stop, I trust.   Meanwhile I hope Osgood has paid him the money he owes me & concerning which I solemnly enjoined him.   I also make over to the family the full profits, such as they may be, of *R.H.*, in return for its advances.   May they be something decent!   Farewell. (The call upon Laugel has just been followed by an introduction[5] to dinner)   Love to all, & especial compliments to Alice on her heroics as a nurse.

Yours always   H.J.jr

ALS: MH bMS Am 1094 (1962)

[1] HJ, "Honoré de Balzac," *Galaxy* 20 (December 1875): 814–36.

[2] HJ, "Le dernier des Valerius," *Revue des Deux Mondes*, n.s. 12 (15 November 1875): 431–55, reprinted in *Indépendance Belge*, 21–27 November 1875. Translator was Lucien Biart. Bentzon is the pseudonym of Marie-Thérèse Blanc (de Solms) (1840–1907), French writer who had published about HJ.

[3] The plan was not carried out. *The American* was not serialized in the *Galaxy* but in the *Atlantic Monthly* in 1876–77.

[4] HJ departed for Europe on 17 October 1875. Apparently he had extensive dental work done before departure, leaving his father to worry about bills. Shephard is probably Luther Dimmick Shepard, a dentist teaching at Harvard.

[5] Although HJ clearly wrote 'introduction', he probably meant to write 'invitation'.

To Henry James

Cambr. Dec 12. 75

My dear Harry

We have rec'd your first letter from Paris and last night the Tribune arrived with your first official one blazoned forth as you will no doubt see before you get this.[1]   I am amused that you should have fallen into the arms of C. S. Peirce, whom I imagine you find a rather uncomfortable bedfellow, thorny & spinous, but the way to treat him is after the fabled "nettle" receipt: grasp firmly, contradict, push hard, make fun of him, and he is as pleasant as any one; but be overawed by his sententious manner and his paradoxical & obscure statements, wait upon them as it were, for light to dawn, and you will never get a feeling of ease with him any more than I did for years, until I changed my course & treated him more or less chaffingly.   I confess I like him very much in spite of all his peculiarities, for he is a man of genius and there's always something in that to compel one's sympathy. I got a letter from him about Chauncey Wright in which he said he had just seen you.   Miss Ammy fay paid me a long visit the other night[2]—Alice, father & mother having gone to hear Mr Thaxter read a translation of the Agamennon by Fitzgerald (of Omar Khayam notoriety) at the Thayers[3]—she being chaperoned by here bro' in law, one stone, who sat speechless one hour & a half listening to our gabble—and said that you were C. S. Peirce's particular admiration. How long does he stay in Paris & when does he return?   I may feel like asking him to bring me back an instrument or two when he comes.   Please tell him I got his letter, and enjoyed it, and that a subscription paper is now passing round to defray the cost of publishing Wright's remains—40 names at $20 each are what is hoped for.[4]

Norton will be editor, & if it is decided to have any extended introductory notice, I will tell him that Peirce is willing to write an account of his philosophical ideas. Norton did intend giving it to Fiske, who wd. make a very inferior thing of it.

Roderick Hudson seems to be a very common theme of conversation, to be in fact a great success, though I can give you no saying about which is memorable for its matter or its source. Every one praises the end, including myself. You have seen the excellent review in the world, wh. father sent you.[5] In looking through the volume it seems to me even better than it did, but I must tell you that I am again struck unfavorably by the tendency of the personages to reflect on themselves and give an acute critical scientific introspective classification of their own natures & states of mind, à la G. Sand. Take warning once more!

Yesterday Howells & wife & Godkin & aunt dined here. Plenty of laughter, but not much else. 2 nights ago I took the Adirondack M.D.'s to see Caste at the Globe. Mr G. Honey a very broad & able but not delicate comedian in the chief part.[6] A few nights previous to that our club at the Union Club. 6 men—a rather pot bellied conservative affair—decidedly the price must come down, or some men of genius get put in, or something or other. The last parker house bill was $7.00 which is simply ridiculous. The only other thing I have done except mind my anatomy is the Squib in the Nation which I enclose. In the interval between sending it and seeing it appear in print, I have dipped into B., & am reluctantly obliged to confess that Schérer is quite as wrong as Saintsbury. It is a pity that every writer in france is bound to do injustice to the opposite "camp." B. is really in his fleurs du mal original & in a certain sense elevated, & on the whole I can bear no rancor against him, altho at times he writes like a person half awake & groping for words. The most amusing thing about it all is the impression one gets of the innocence of a generation in wh. the fleurs du mal should have made a *scandal*. It is a mild & spiritualistic book to day. Get it and write about it in the Nation or atlantic if you like, and esp? read a letter of Ste Beuve's at the end of it, which is the ne plus ultra of his diabolic subtlety & *malice*.[7]

I had an interview with C. W. Eliot the other day, who smiles on me & lets me expect $1200 this year and possibly hope for $2000 next, which will be a sweet boon if it occurs. As the term advances I become sensible that I am really better than I was last year in almost every way; which gives me still better prospects for the future. Alice has got her historical professorship which will no doubt be an immense thing for her.[8]   Bob writes must[9] contentedly about his farm, Wilky sanguinely about his business, so that altogether the family has not for a long time been in so flourishing a condition.

We have been having a perfectly steady thermometer fm. 25° to 34 degrees for 10 days past and you can imagine how I've enjoyed it— altogether the season has been must humane so far.   I called on T.S.P. a few days ago but he was out.   I saw a recent envelope fm. you on his table.   I am told that he has resumed his work for the Nation. I'm glad of it.   His wife has had I believe a relapse, poor thing. Good bye!   Heaven bless you—get as much society as you can.   Your first letter was a very good beginning, tho' one sees that you are to a certain extent fishing for the proper tone or level.   I shd like to accompany you to some of the theatres.

Adieu! | W.J

Latest american humor, quoted last night by Godkin: Child lost at a fair. "Where's my mother?   I told the darned thing she'd lose me.["]

ALS: MH bMS Am 1092.9 (2596)

[1] HJ, "Paris Revisited," *New York Tribune*, 11 December 1875 (dated 22 November), reprinted in *Parisian Sketches* (1957).

[2] Amy (Amelia Muller) Fay (1844–1928), American pianist.

[3] James Bradley Thayer (1831–1902), American lawyer.   No translation of the *Agamemnon* by Edward FitzGerald (1809–1883), English writer, published at the time of the reading was found.   Thaxter could be Levi Lincoln Thaxter, husband of Celia Laighton Thaxter.

[4] Chauncey Wright died on 12 September 1875.   His papers were published, *Philosophical Discussions*, ed. Charles Eliot Norton (New York: Henry Holt, 1877).

[5] Apparently the *New York World*.

[6] George Honey (1822–1880), British actor, appeared at the Globe Theater as Old Eccles in *Caste* by Thomas William Robertson (1829–1871), American-born playwright.

[7] WJ, "The Neo-Pagans and an Editorial Reply," *Nation* 21 (2 December 1875): 355 (*ECR*), a discussion of the conflicting views of Baudelaire offered by George Edward Bateman Saintsbury (1845–1933), English critic, and Edmond-Henri-Adolphe Scherer (1815–1889), French critic.   No edition of Baudelaire's *Les fleurs du mal* (1857) appeared with comments by Sainte-Beuve.   Perhaps WJ has in mind a note by Sainte-Beuve explaining why he has kept silent about *Les fleurs du mal*, "Des prochaines élections de l'academie," *Nouveaux lundis*, vol. 1 (Paris: Michel Lévy Frères, 1863).

[8] AJ had agreed to teach history by correspondence to young women for the Society to Encourage Studies at Home; see *AJB*, 174.

[9] Probably a slip for 'most', both here and in the following sentence.

To Henry James

Cambr. Jany 1. 76

My dear H.   T''is ½ past 11 P.M. & I have just returned from a small
gathering at Mrs. Mary Parkman's in honor of Miss Agnes Irwin—an
average sort of affair.[1]   I have been cooling off in the moist & tepid
air, & I think as good a thing as I can do is to write to you before going
to bed.   I have inherited your habit now of sitting up alone & reading
till between 11 & 12 o'clock & find it enlarges very much the day.
You can judge from it too how much more "capable" I am than I have
been.   In fact I am enjoying my excellent condition enormously.   I
think the extremely steady dampish weather we have had since the
middle of November probably has something to do with it—at least
with my immunity from nervous feelings.   We have had but one
break in all that time—(a severe one in which the thermometer rose
fm. 15 below o to 50 above in 30 hours.   To day and yesterday have
been just like summer—the thermometer at 65 & every thing afloat
with mud!   I have been enjoying my first week of Christmas holiday
amazingly, visiting & reading metaphysics.   I spent yesterday afternoon with Miss Peabody in Longwood.   She is a most demoralizing
person to deal with, but I can't help liking her very much.   No other
girl that I know has anything like her eagerness and constant scraping against moral problems.   I suppose she wd. be happier if she
were married, but regret my inability to help her to that consummation.—[Sunday morning]—Sleep bade me desist last night.   Alice
has been suffering with an ulcerated tooth for 3 days past, the result
of one of Dr Shepard's fillings.   It was wearing her out so that last
night he came out & extracted it, she bearing the operation with stoic
fortitude, and finding herself immediately relieved.   Your letter no 2
speaking of your visit to Turguenieff was received by me duly and
greatly enjoyed.   I never heard you speak so enthusiastically of any
human being.   It is too bad he is to leave Paris.   But if he gives you
the "run" of Flaubert & eke G. Sand it will be so much gained.   I
don't think you know Miss Alice Parkman but if you did you wd.
thank me for pointing out to you the parallelism between her & G.S.
which overwhelmed me the other day when I was calling on her, and
she (who has just lost her sister Bertha & had her father go through
an attack of insanity) was snuggling down so hyper-comfortably into
garrulity about Bertha & poor dead theodore and her dead mother
that I was fairly suffocated just as I am by the *comfort* G.S. takes in in

telling you of the loves of servant men for ladies, & other things *contra naturam*.—Christmas passed off here in a rather wan & sallow manner. I got a gold scarf ring from mother & a gold watch chain from A.K. Let me by the way advise you to get a scarf ring—'t is one of the greatest inventions of modern times, in saving labor, silk & shirt fronts. Alice got a desk and from me a scotch terrier pup only 7 weeks old whom we call Bunch, who has almost doubled his size in a week, who is a perfect lion in determination & courage, & who don't seem to care a jot for any human society but that of Jane in the kitchen whose person is I suppose pervaded by a greasy & smoky smell agreeable to his nostrils. He has a perfect passion for the dining room; whenever he is left to himself he travels thither and lies down under the table & takes no notice of you when you go to call him. He does not sleep half as much as Dido, never utters a sound when shut up for the night in the kitchen & altogether fills us with a sort of awe for the roman firmness and independence of his character. He is "animated" by a colliquative diarrhoea or cholera which keeps us all sponging over his tracks but which don't affect his strength or spirits a bit. He is in short a very queer substitute for poor dear Dido.—You have heard of wilky's new female baby of course, likewise of his inflammatory rheumatism, wh. seems to be a mild attack. Poor Bob writes that his back has broken down. I don't know how long it is going to last but it is a fearful trial for him, poor boy. I am sure though that he will get well before long. I am just going to put up a large box of books for him to furnish his house with. The family income will be reduced hereafter by the interest of the $7000 father has put into his farm, and likewise by the fall of rents. One of father's tenants in Syracuse has just become insolvent.[2] *Verbum sap.!* I told you I believe that I shd. probably make 1200 this year & *possibly* 2000 next. From all accounts Roderick Hudson seems to be a great success, and much is expected from its author. Prof. F. J. Child has been reading it aloud to his wife & speaks with great enthusiasm of it. He says however that you misuse your shalls & wills &c, and use the word sympathetic too often. Next week we have a french theatre here at Beethoven Hall and have nothing to envy you.[3] Good bye

Yours ever   W.J.

ALS: MH bMS Am 1092.9 (2597)

[1] Agnes Irwin (1841–1914), American educator, later dean of Radcliffe College.

[2] At some time in the mid-1870s RJ bought a farm at Whitewater, Wis.; see *BBF*,

129. Some of the dates given by Maher in this connection cannot be correct. The James family owned several stores, and perhaps other property, in Syracuse, N.Y.

[3] A number of French plays were performed at Beethoven Hall by the Parisian Company from the Lyceum Theater, New York.

To Henry James

Cambridge Jany 22. 76

My dear Harry

We have been spending an unusually long time without hearing fm. you. Last night in the Tribune came your letter about Meissonier &c,[1] but no letter in MS. I hope with all your other writing to do that you will never write home fm. a feeling of duty but wait till the mood comes. We have had a good dose of you this week in the shape of the Galaxy with your Bernard & Flaubert and your notice of the Inn Album in the nation.[2] That last was done in a masterly manner— experience tells. The Flaubert part of the Galaxy article was also first rate, and so was the Bernard part, save for a tendency to repeat essentially the same thing in different connections, & with different words which I have s'times noticed in your more hastily written things. I can tell you no particular news about home. I have been working as usual & doing more than my usual share of visiting and so forth. Last night I went of all places in the world to mrs. Sargent's esthetic tea in Chesnut street.[3] Certain individuals read poetry, whilst others sat and longed for them to stop so that they might begin to talk. The room was full of a decidedly good looking set of people especially women—but new england all over! Give me a human race with some *guts* to them, no matter if they do belch at you now and then. On coming home, by the way, I read in the Galaxy the article on Emerson by John Burroughs, (disfigured itself by the jerkiness &c &c he speaks of, new england itself) but what first rate perceptions the man has.—I shall buy his book and hope to find in it the article on england I told you I had read in the hotel on Lake Champlain.[4] The chief reason why I went, after having gone once to escape the importunities of Mrs Sargent is that on that first occasion I had found a most particularly delightful young woman whom I also found again on the second occasion with a still more lovely sister. But I don't think even their charms can take me a third time.—Roderick Hudson has been praised to me by Miss Sally Russell and by Wm. Everett, who went out of his way in the library to do it, & who especially rejoiced in

your having escaped the temptation to make a guide book of Italy out
of it.   Mother's Receptions are over, all but one, which I suppose will
be the fullest of the lot.   I think it has been a pretty good thing to do.
[*end of letter missing*]

AL incomplete: MH bMS Am 1092.9 (2598)

¹HJ, "Parisian Sketches," *New York Tribune*, 22 January 1876 (dated 28 December
1875), reprinted in *Parisian Sketches*, a discussion of the painting *Battle of Friedland*, by
Jean-Louis-Ernest Meissonier (1815–1891), French painter of military subjects.

²HJ, "The Minor French Novelists," *Galaxy* 21 (February 1876): 219–33, discussion
of Charles de Bernard (1804–1850), French novelist, and Gustave Flaubert; review of
Robert Browning, *The Inn Album* (Boston: James R. Osgood and Co., 1875; London:
Smith, Elder and Co., 1875), in *Nation* 22 (20 January 1876): 49–50.

³Apparently the widow of Howard Sergeant (1811?–1872), Boston physician.

⁴John Burroughs (1837–1921), American naturalist and nature writer, "A Word or
Two on Emerson," *Galaxy* 21 (February 1876): 254–59.   He had published a number
of books by then, the most recent being *Winter Sunshine* (New York: Hurd & Houghton, 1875).   It does not include a paper on England.

From Henry James

29 Rue de Luxembourg. | Feb. 8ᵗʰ. [1876]
Dear Wᵐ.—I am in your debt for many letters—for all of which I
have been devoutly grateful.   The last, arrived yesterday, was of Feb.¹
22ᵈ.   I wrote home, last, I think, about a fortnight ago.   To day I
could believe I am at home.   The snow is falling from a leaden sky, &
the opposite house tops are piled thick with it.   But the winter is
drifting rapidly away & the European spring is not very far off.   The
days bring me nothing much to relate, & I am ashamed of myself
that, living in Paris, I have not more rich and rare things to tell you.
I do my best to collect such material, & it is not my fault if I haven't
more of it.—I keep seeing a little of the few people I know.   I dined
awhile since at the Laugels with Renan & his wife, & am invited there
tomorrow eveg. to encounter the Duc d'Aumale, who is their great
social card.²   Renan is hideous and charming—more hideous even
than his photos. & more charming even than his writing.   His talk at
table was really exquisite for urbanity, fineness & wit—all quite without show-off.   I talked with him for three quarters of an hour, in the
corner, after dinner, told him that I couldn't measure his writings on
the side of erudition, but that they had always been for me (& all my
family!!) "la plus haute perfection de l'expression," & he treated me
as if I were a distinguished savant.—I saw Tourguéneff the other day,
again—he having written me a charming note (I enclose it, if I can

find it, for Alice,) telling me he was still ill, & asking me to come & see him. So I went & passed almost the whole of a rainy afternoon with him. He is an *amour d'homme*. He talked more about his own writings &c than before, & said he had never *invented* anything or any one. Every thing in his stories comes from some figure he has seen—tho' often the figure from whom the story has started may turn out to be a secondary figure. He said moreover that he never consciously *puts anything into* his people and things. To his sense all the interest, the beauty, the poetry, the strangeness &c, are there, *in* the people & things (the definite ones, whom he has seen) in much larger measure than he can get out; & that (what strikes him himself as a limitation of his genius,) touches that are too *raffiné*, words and phrases that are too striking, or too complete, inspire him with an instinctive *méfiance*; it seems to him that they *can't* be true—for to be true to a given, individual type is the utmost he is able to strive for. In short he gave me a sort of definition of his own mental process, which was admirably intelligent & limpidly honest. This last is the whole man; and it is written in his face. He also talked much about Flaubert, with regard to whom he thinks that the great trouble is that he has never known a decent woman—or even a woman who was a little interesting. He has passed his life exclusively "avec des courtisanes & des rien-du-tout." In poor old Flaubert there is something almost tragic: his big intellectual temperament, machinery &c, & his vainly colossal attempts to press out the least little drop of *passion*. So much talent, and so much naïveté and honesty, and yet so much dryness & coldness.—I have seen a little of the Lee Childes, the Nortons' friends, who seem agreeable & kindly people, tho' a trifle superfine & *poseurs*. I dined there the other day with a large & gorgeous party— all American; & I call in the afternoon & find Mme L.C. in black velvet by her fire (she is a very graceful, elegant & clever Frenchwoman,) with old decor[a]ted counts & generals leaning against the mantlepiece. Mme Viardot has invited me to a bal costumé on the 19th, to which I shall probably go, if I find a domino doesn't cost too much. There are some amiable Boston people here, the Harrison Ritchies by name, with whom I dined a couple of days since, & took in Mme Bonaparte—an American with beautiful eyes. She was a Mrs. Edgar, I believe, & is now wife of the American-born grandson of old Gérome. He is now recognised by the Empress & Prince Imperial as against Prince Napoleon; & the ci-devant Mrs. Edgar (she is a granddaughter of Danl. Webster,[3] whom she strikingly resembles,) is moving heaven & earth in the Bonapartist cause, as if it ever comes up again she will be a princess, or a great swell.   She is very charming, very clever, and quite capable of playing a part.   Bonaparte is a *bel homme*, but stupid.⁴—Que vous dirai-je encore?   I keep on scribbling—sending stuff to the Nation & the Tribune (whose headings & editorial remarks over my letters sicken me to the soul,) & working at the novel I have begun for the *Galaxy*.⁵   The G.'s printing is as usual. I write (in that last thing) "a quiet & peaceful *nun*"—& it stands "a quiet & peaceful *man!*"⁶   Little Henry Mason ("Sonny") came the other day to see me—a very nice, gentle, sweet-faced youth of 22— living in the Latin quarter & working at painting in Gérome's studio.⁷ I believe he has just been summoned home by his father.—It was true, in Laugel's letter, that the Right and Left combined to exclude the Right Centre (the Orleanists.)   But this was only after the O's had refused with much arrogance to admit a single Left or Extreme Right name to their Senatorial list.   "It must be all ours or nothing!" they said.   "It shall be nothing, then!" said the others, & clubbed together to make it so.   It was a regular chopping off of their own head by the O's.   But they have lost nothing, because they have nothing to lose; they have no hold on the country—partly because they are too good for it.   "Ils n'ont pas de prestige" I heard a Frenchman say the other day—& they haven't—a grain.   And yet they are the only party in France who hasn't proscribed, murdered, burnt &c.   That is "prestige."—But I think [there] is a very fair chance now for the conservative republicans.   In the elections, just over, the Bonapartists have been heavily beaten.

—Love to all, & blessings on yourself.

Yours ever | H. James jr.

ALS: MH bMS Am 1094 (1963)

¹ 'Feb.' is an error.   The letter referred to is the preceding one of 22 January.

² Henri-Eugène-Philippe-Louis d'Orléans, duc d'Aumale (1822–1897), French writer.

³ Daniel Webster (1782–1852), American statesman and orator.

⁴ Jérôme Bonaparte (1784–1860), Napoleon's brother, had an American grandson, Jerome Napoleon Bonaparte (1830–1893), who married Caroline Le Roy Appleton Edgar, a widow.

⁵ No novel by HJ appeared in *Galaxy* over the next several years.   *The American* was serialized in the *Atlantic Monthly* from June 1876 to May 1877 (vols. 37–39).   See also letter of 14 March 1876.

⁶ HJ, "The Minor French Novelists."

⁷ Henry Mason (1853–1879), an art student, was the son of Lydia Lush James Mason, who was a daughter of Robert James, WJ's father's half-brother. His father was Henry Mason.   He studied with Jean-Léon Gérôme (1824–1904), French painter.

From Henry James

         29 Rue de Luxembourg. | March 14$\underline{th}$ [1876]
Dear W$\underline{m}$. I am afraid that I have neglected writing home longer than has been agreeable to you: but the delay has been inevitable. When I last wrote I was unwell, & this may have increased your impatience of my silence. I have nothing but good news however, & it is not illness that has kept me from writing. I was pretty poorly for upwards of a fortnight, but since then I have been quite myself. Since then, too have come two letters from mother (of Feb 12$\underline{th}$ & 13$\underline{th}$) & yours of Feb. 21$\underline{st}$. I can't say how much I thank you for the frequency of your letters. They are a balm & blessing, & I beg you to persevere, so far as you can, in your noble work. I write to you, rather than to mother; but tell her that I was overcome by the loveliness of hers of Feb. 13$\underline{th}$, & am most grieved for any pain she had in writing it.

    I have not much to show for my silence, nothing of moment having befallen me. It has been a month of detestable weather, but I am expecting a great charm when the spring really shows itself. Already, when the wind & rain stop the air is soft and lovely. There is something very amiable in Paris in these coming weeks, & I expect to enjoy them. I keep along seeing a little of a few people, but I form no intimacies & never have a visitor. Apropos of "intimacies," Charles Peirce departed a week since for Berlin—my intimacy with whom mother says "greatly amuses" you. It was no intimacy, for during the last two months of his stay I saw almost nothing of him. He is a very good fellow, & one must appreciate his mental ability; but he has too little social talent, too little art of making himself agreeable. He had however a very lonely & dreary winter here & I should think would detest Paris. I did what I could to give him society—introduced him to Mrs. Von Hoffmann (who was very civil to him & to whom he took a fancy,) & to Mrs. Harrison Ritchie; but I think I believed I could have done more. I couldn't! I have seen no one very new or strange. I had another talk with Renan at M$\underline{me}$ Tourguéneff's the widow of the Russian emancipationist (the W$\underline{m}$ L. Garrison of Russia) who lived here in exile for so many years.[1] (She had given a party to keep the anniversary of the emancipation & Renan & I were the only non-Muscovites.) He is a most *ameno* little man, & essentially good & gentle, but I of course am too entirely profane, as regards his interests & occupations, to go very far with him. His conversation, equally of course, has a perfume of the highest

intelligence.   He thinks very ill of the prospects of France.   "Je voy-
ais tout en noir avant les élections, je vois tout en noir depuis."   I
don't think *that* is thoroughly intelligent, but enfin I like Renan—bien
qu'il soit d'une laideur vraiment repoussante.   His wife is a plain &
excellent person, niece of Ary Scheffer[2] & initiated into all his work,
in which she assists him.   The Tourguéneffs are of a virtue worthy of
Cambridge—especially the plain high-shouldered Mlle. T.—le dé-
vouement même.   I am sorry to say I have seen nothing, of late, of
Ivan Sergeitch, nor of Flaubert; but I expect to see them both soon.—
The Childes continue civil to me & I dined there the other day in
company with Dr. Guéneau de Mussy, the great Orleanist medical
man (who shared the exile of the princes)—a very pleasant fellow[3]—
& a certain Mrs. Mansfield, an Englishwoman steeped in diplomacy,
& the most extraordinary, clever & entertaining woman I ever met.[4]
I can't describe her, but some day I shall clap her into a novel.   Trollope, with a finer genius, might have invented her.   Mrs. Childe is a
very charming woman—charming to look at too, & extremely intelligent.   Childe strikes me as taking himself rather more au sérieux
than one sees warrant for; but he is a good fellow.   I have seen something of late of one Baron Holstein,[5] German secrétaire d'ambas-
sade—one of the most acute & intelligent men I have ever met.   We
occasionally dine together—he being the only detached male that I
know.   (He is by the way the gentleman whose attentions to Mrs.
Sumner—he was then secretary in Washington—were the prime
cause of the explosion of the Hon Charles, & the consequent separation.)—I went the other evening with Mrs. Von Hoffmann, who
shows to much better advantage in Paris, as a Frenchwoman, than in
N.Y., to the salon of an old Marquise de Blocqville—the daughter of
Marshal Davoust.[6]   She is a literary dowager, & the patroness of Emile Montégut, who is her *commensal* or pensioner, like the literati of the
last century.   C'est un type très curieux & a very gracious & caressing
woman.   She is a great invalid, very corpulent, never leaves the house
and has her head swathed in long veils & laces à la sultane—but with
the remains of beauty.   She had a lot of people about her, none of
whom of course I knew, & as I was not introduced of course it was not
exhilarating.   But I shall go again (she receives every Monday) & by
keeping it up long enough shall perhaps get something out of it.—I
have found as yet poor old Mme Mohl more remunerative.[7]   She is
much flattened out by the recent deaths of her husband & of her best
friend Lady Augusta Stanley,[8] but she is a little battered old stoic, &
she is still entertaining. Imagine a little old woman of ninety with her

grey hair in her eyes, precisely like a Skye terrier, a grotesque cap & a shabby black dress. It is hard to imagine her as the quondam rival of Mme Récamier[9] & the intimate friend of the Queen of Holland & other potentates. She was very kind & friendly with me, & I shall have no trouble in seeing her as often as I wish. Unfortunately she appears somewhat to have lost her memory.

These are all my anecdotes, & I have no more *intimes* experiences to relate. I scribble along week by week—though I am afraid I don't appear to you at home to accomplish much. I would do more for the *Nation* but I have no English books. This however, I don't regret, as I am weary of reviewing. I sent some time since the beginning of a novel to the *Galaxy*; but there is a hitch thro' their threatening delay of publication.[10] In case they delay, I have given straight orders to have it sent to father, who, if he receives it, will make it straight over to Howells. I don't know how it will turn out & meanwhile it annoys me.—I hope your short vacation passed agreeably away & that you are working comfortably again. My heart goes forth to you all & I wish you every blessing. I have just got a letter from Wilky, speaking sadly of his foot. Is it true that there is peril of his losing it? What a strange & sad consummation. I depend upon its being his loose way of talking. *Tell Alice to send me (what she believes to be) Carrie's number in gloves.* I want to send her a pair or two. *Pray attend to this.* I hope that by the time you get this the softness of spring will rest on you. Infinite love to parents & sister; Exhort father to write—he hasn't in an age. I have heard nothing about A.K. in an age. *Send her this.* Is she keeping well in N.Y? Farewell, sweet brother.

Your faithful   H. James jr.

ALS: MH bMS Am 1094 (1964)

[1] William Lloyd Garrison (1805–1879), American abolitionist.

[2] Arry Scheffer (1823–1892), Dutch-born painter.

[3] Henri-François Guéneau de Mussy (1814–1892), French physician, went into exile with Louis-Philippe (1773–1850) and his family in 1848.

[4] Perhaps Margaret Fellowes Mansfield (d. 1892), wife of Sir William Rose Mansfield (1819–1876), British military officer.

[5] Baron Friedrich von Holstein (1837–1909), German diplomat.

[6] Louis-Nicolas Davout (1770–1823), marshall of France.

[7] Mary Clarke Mohl (1793–1883), wife of Jules Mohl, an orientalist, had a salon in Paris.

[8] Lady Augusta Frederica Elizabeth Stanley (1822–1876), a lady in waiting at the British court.

[9] Jeanne-Françoise-Julie-Adélaïde Bernard Récamier (1777–1849), known for her literary and political salon in Paris.

[10] See letter of 8 February 1876.

From Henry James

29 Rue de Luxembourg. | April 25ᵗʰ [1876]
My dear Wᵐ. I received a letter from you some little time ago, which
I acknowledged thro' father, in my last letter. It was peculiarly welcome, as all your letters are. Yesterday came one from mother without a date, which was was peculiarly lovely, as all *hers* are.—Let me say
immediately that I have just (½ an hour since) received the two *coupes
de Brücke* which you asked me some time ago to get.[1] I delayed going
for them for a little while, because I was for the moment short of
money. Then I received a handsome cheque for the Tribune for my
winter's letters, & felt rich. I ordered them but they have been some
time sending them. (The address is *1 Rue Bonaparte*.) They are very
heavy to send by post but I will try it.—In my last letter written not
long since I gave you all possible news & gossip & I have little of interest to day. The spring is now quite settled & very lovely. It makes
me feel extremely fond of Paris & confirms my feeling of being at
home here. My life runs on in an even current, very rapidly, but
brings forth nothing very important. I scribble along with a good
deal of regularity, (tho' I imagine I don't seem to you to be very productive.) But I don't aspire to do more, in quantity, than I am forced
to. What I am doing gives me enough money to live comfortably &
I rest content with that. The Tribune publishes my letters at longer
intervals than it bargained to, though I send them regularly enough.
I am rather sick of them, but I shall keep it up. Politics now are very
quiet & not nearly so interesting as they were earlier in the winter.
The most interesting thing is to watch the gradual extreme conserva-
tization of Gambetta.[2]—I have heard of late a quantity of music—
Music at Mᵐᵉ Viardot's, music at Mᵐᵉ de Blocqville's, music at the Baronne de Hoffmann's (late Mrs. L.H. of New York) music a couple of
nights since at Miss Reid's (the American singer whom you saw in
Rome)[3] where I heard a certain Mᵐᵉ Conneau, wife of the late Emper-
or's doctor,[4] whose singing was the finest thing possible. On this
same occasion I sat in a corner all the evening with the very handsome
Mrs. Wadsworth, (once famous, I believe, as Miss Peters,) of whom I
had heard a great deal & whose conversation disappointed me somewhat. Mais elle est diablement belle—especially as she is rather ugly.
In the little American crowd that I see something of here no figures
detach themselves with any relief. Those that come nearest to it are
two very amiable women—Mrs. C. Strong, whom I like much & have
seen lately pretty often. She has a spark of feu sacré, an ability to

interest herself & s'enthousiasmer which is sincere & pleasing. The other is a certain Miss Reubell, who has lived here always, is 27 or 28 years old & extremely ugly, but with something very frank, intelligent & agreeable about her.[5]   If I wanted to desire to marry an ugly Parisian-American, with money & toutes les élégances, & a very considerable capacity for development if transported into a favoring medium, Miss R. would be a very good objective.   But I don't—j'en suis à 1000 lieues.—These are the only women—except poor Miss Julia Tucker[6]—& the men are complete nullities.   I have been several times of late to the Tourgéneff's, who are very friendly & of a literally more than Bostonian virtue.   They are an oasis of purity & goodness in the midst of this Parisian Babylon, & I like much to be with them. They and Ivan Sergeitch, and a young man whose acquaintance I have lately made, give me a high idea of the Russian nature—at least in some of its forms.   The young man, Paul Joukofski, is a great friend of Ivan S.'s, & has told me some interesting things about him. He says his absolute goodness & tenderness cannot be exaggerated, but that also neither can his *mollesse* & want of will.   He can't even choose a pair of trousers for himself. (Don't repeat this promiscuously.)   He also told me that Ivan Sergeitch spoke to him of me with an appreciation "qui alla jusqu'à l'attendrissement" & in a way that he had rarely spoken to him of any one!!   At the risk of seeming fatuous I repeat this for the entertainment of the family.—Joukofski himself is a very amiable fellow, of about my own age, & we have quite sworn an eternal friendship.   He is a painter (amateurish, as he has money) has lived many years in Italy, adores it &c, & tho' endowed I suspect also with a great deal of mollesse & want of will, has something very sweet & distingué about him.   He was brought up at court as an orphan by the Empress (wife of Nicholas,) his father having been tutor of the present Emperor;[7] so you see that I don't love beneath my station.   He is to dine with me tomorrow, & I will make him tell me something more about Ivan Sergeitch.   The latter I have not seen myself, I think, since I last wrote.   I *have* however seen the divine Smalley (of the Tribune.)   He was in Paris some time since & called upon me, & now is here again.   He is a singular specimen of a successfully Anglicised Yankee, &, to me, very civil & friendly.   His letters seem to me the one redeeming feature of the Tribune, when I see it.—I sometimes see Huntington—the most amiable, loosely-knit optimist on the planet; a very good creature, but an extreme Bohemian.[8]—These are about all the stories I can tell you.   Your own remarks about Cabot Lodge, & the frequency of the type here were excellent.[9]   I can fancy that if one were much in society here it would often be very exasperating.   Indeed its mere physiognomy which one recognises, is often annoying.   I hope your fatigue is ebbing away.   Guard yourself on your return to health, against expecting to be without fatigue. When it comes one regards it as belonging to one's old invalidism, but often it is quite normal & one would have had it if one had never been ill.   These reflections, at least, I have often made for myself.   I am very sorry to hear from mother of Uncle Robertson's troubles; I hope they will remain within reasonable bounds. Please give father a message *en attendant* that I can write to him Osgood is to send him (May 1ˢᵗ) the acct. of the sales of R.H., with the money he owes me.   Tell him that he is not to forward to me, but to keep it.   I will write him.   I have almost finished reading one or two books which I will send to Alice.   I sent her one some weeks ago.   I am very curious to see the notice of *R.H* in the N.A.R.   Send it, & tell me who wrote it.   I know who did the Nation's.[10]   Farewell, sweet brother

Yours ever   H. James jr.

ALS: MH bMS Am 1094 (1965)

[1] Optic lenses made by Ernst Wilhelm, Ritter von Brücke (1819–1892), German physiologist.

[2] Léon Gambetta (1838–1882), French statesman.

[3] Not identified.

[4] Joséphine Conneau, wife of François-Alexandre-Henri Conneau (1803–1877), physician at the court of Napoleon III following the restoration of the Empire.

[5] Henrietta Reubell, a wealthy American, had a famous salon in Paris.

[6] Not identified.

[7] Nicholas I and his son Alexander II (1818–1881), tsar of Russia.

[8] William Henry Huntington (1820–1885), European correspondent for the *New York Tribune*.

[9] Henry Cabot Lodge (1850–1924), American politician and author, assistant editor of the *North American Review*.

[10] Sarah Butler Wister, unsigned review of *Roderick Hudson*, in *North American Review* 122 (April 1876): 420–25; Grace Norton, unsigned review, *Nation* 22 (9 March 1876): 164–65.

To Henry James

Newport, June 3rd. 76

My dear H,   I write you after a considerable interval filled with too much work & weariness to make letter writing convenient.   Father's condition is of course the great news.   He improves, but slowly and one cant tell when he will be entirely well, if he ever is again. His docile passivity is very pathetic & so is the devotion of Mother Alice & A.K. to him. I ran away 3 days ago, the recitations being over for the year in order to break from the studious associations of home. I have been staying at the Tweedies with Mrs Chapman,[1] & James Sturgis and his wife,[2] and enjoying extremely, not the conversation indoors but, but the lovely lying on the grass on the cliffs at Lily pond, and 4 or 5 hours yesterday at the Dumplings, feeling the moving air and the gentle living sea. There is a purity and mildness about the elements here which purges the soul of one, and I have been as if I had taken opium, not wanting to do anything else than the particular thing I happened to be doing at the moment, and feeling equally good whether I stood or walked or lay, or spoke or was silent. It's a splendid relief from the overstrain and stimulus of the past few scholastic months. I go the day after to morrow (Monday) with the Tweedies to N.Y., assist at Henrietta Temple's wedding on Tuesday[3] & then pass on to the Centennial for a couple of days.[4] I suppose it will be pretty tiresome, but I want to see the english pictures, which they say are a good show. Our summer plans are all contingent on poor father's condition. I hardly think they will any of them leave home, and I fancy my vacationing will be confined to visits of a week at a time to different points, perhaps the pleasantest way after all of spending it.—Newport as to its villas and all that is most repulsive to me. I really didn't know how little charm and how much shabbiness there was about the place. There are not more than 3 or 4 houses out of the whole lot that are not offensive in some way externally. But the mild nature grows on one every day. This afternoon God willing I shall spend on Paradise.[5] The Tweedies keep no horses which makes one walk more or pay more than one wd. wish. The younger Seabury told me yesterday that he was just reading your Roderick Hudson, but offered no [*page ends*][6] Colonel Waring said of your "American" to me: "Im not a blind admirer of H. James jr., but I said to my wife after reading that first number: By Jove, I think he's hit it this time!"[7] I think myself the thing opens very well indeed, you have a first rate datum to work up, and I hope you'll do it well.—Your last few letters home have breathed a tone of contentment and domestication in Paris wh. was very agreeable to get. I'm afraid though that your native snobbery will wax wanton on your intimacy with crowned heads and that you'll be more intolerably supercilious than ever if you do return home. I suppose you think of us now in Cambridge as we think of Bob out on his wild cattle farm in

Wisconsin.   Your accounts of Ivan Sergeitch are delightful, and I
envy you the possession of the young russian painter's intimacy.[8]
Give my best love to Ivan.   I read his book which you sent home
(Foreign books sent by mail pay duty now though, so send none but
good ones) and although the vein of "morbidness" was so pronounced in the stories, yet the mysterious depths which his plummet
sounds atone for all.   It is the amount of life which a man feels that
makes you value his mind, and Turguenieff has a sense of worlds
within worlds whose existence is unsuspected by the vulgar.   It
amuses me to recommend his books to people who mention them as
they would the novels of a Wilkie Collins: You say we don't notice D.
Deronda.   I find it extremely interesting.   Gwendolen & her spouse
are masterpieces of conception and delineation.   Her ideal figures
are much vaguer & thinner—but her "sapience" as you excellently
call it passes all decent bounds.   There is something essentially wom-
anish in the irrepressible garrulity of her moral reflexions.   Why is it
that it makes women feel so good to moralize?   Man philosophizes as
a matter of business, because he must—he does it to a purpose and
then lets it rest; but women don't seem to get over being tickled at the
discovery that they have the faculty, hence the tedious iteration and
restlessness of G. Eliots commentary on life.

The Lafarges are absent.   I hope you have sent the bill for Brucke
lenses.[9]

Yours always   W.J.

P.S

I am forgetting to tell you that the Johnstons whom you will recollect as the companions of Miss Darlington in Rome are about to pass
through Paris for Switzerland soon.   I gave them your address and
if he calls on you you must do whatever you can for his sister who is
really remarkably fine and attractive girl.   I never pitied any one
more.   He[r] eldest brother a sweet young fellow died the other day
of combined mania & diphtheria, and she is almost alone in the
world, with an almost impossibility of sleeping.   I charge you not to
neglect her.

ALS: MH bMS Am 1092.9 (2599)

   [1] Perhaps the mother of Elizabeth Bates Chapman Laugel.

   [2] Perhaps James Sturgis (1822–1888), Boston merchant, brother-in-law of George
Santayana's mother.

   [3] Henrietta Temple married Leslie Pell-Clarke of Newport on 6 June 1876 in Pelham, N.Y.

   [4] The Centenary of American Independence.   The exposition was held in Philadelphia.

5 A rocky promontory in Newport.

6 In *The Letters of William James*, ed. Henry James, 2 vols. (Boston: Atlantic Monthly Press, 1920), 1:184, the editor inserts 'comment' at this point. Seabury is not identified. Several persons of that name of about the right age lived in Providence, R.I.

7 George Edwin Waring (1833–1898), a cavalry officer in the Civil War, an engineer, living in Newport at the time.

8 Paul Joukofski.

9 See letter of 25 April 1876.

From Henry James

Paris 29 Rue Luxbg. | June 22ᵈ [1876]

Dear Wᵐ—Your letter from Newport came safe to hand (with a couple of very brief notes from Alice & Mother) and gave me great pleasure, 1° By its good account of Father's convalescence; 2ᵈ by its cheerful report of your beginning of your vacation. I trust both of these things have been going on well Give all my love to father & tell him that I wish greatly I too were there to glide about his couch & chair, in offices of tenderness. But with such ministrants as he has he can lack nothing, & I hope he will very soon cease to need the ministrations of any one. Your picture of Newport filled me with a gentle melancholy, but did not make me wish to be there; I hope greatly to hear of your subsequent adventures. Tell me about Philadelphia[1] & H. Temple's marriage. Apropos of the latter I received also Bob Temple's letter at last—a most extraordinary interesting, &, to me, touching, performance. I answered it immediately, but I fear that the address he gave me being so old my letter will not reach him.—This must be but a hasty scrawl, dear Wᵐ; as I am very busy. I have had a very idle & demoralized month, & must make up for lost time. A great lot of people I know have been assembling in Paris & infringing upon my once quiet hours. But it has not been without its agreeable & even profitable side. The Bootts have departed for Villiers-le-Bel, in very good spirits. The day before they went I bade them to a modest repast, & had my friend Joukowsky to meet them. As he found Boott "extrêmement sympathique" & thought he looked like one of Titian's men & as Lizzie, among her unsuspected accomplishments, reveals a complete mastery of the French tongue, I suppose it was a success. A few days afterward I went out with my Russian to dine &c at the good & patriarchal Tourgéneffs (Nicholas) who have a most enchanting place about ¾ of an hour from Paris, adjoining the Malmaison, the Empress Josephine's old place.   The T.'s are all kindness, naiveté & mutually doting family life.   I also spent a day (rather drearily) at Fontainebleau with a "party"—a sort of thing I loathe—the Kings, M<u>mes</u> Wadsworth & Strong & so forth.   But F. is enchanting.   Then M<u>me</u> Laugel drove me very kindly to the annual review at Longchamps, where I stood for 4 hours in the sun on a rickety straw-bottomed chair, craning my neck over the crowd toward the glittering squadrons.   Then she invited me to a party (dull) where I was introduced to the Duc de Broglie, the Comte Duchatel,[2] the famous M<u>me</u> de Villeneuve &c.[3]   So much for base gossip.   Your remarks about G. Eliot were excellent—but *D.D.* strikes me as (in proportion to its elaborate ability) a great failure compared with her other books.   Gwendolen, to me, *lives* a little; but not the others: D.D. least of all.   But the episode with Mordecai is fine.   I send Alice Fromentin's book, "Les Maitres d'autrefois," worth reading for its charm, even tho' it is rather special.[4]   I don't send her the 2 big volumes of M. Doudan wh. I have noticed in the Tribune, because they are so heavy & on the whole not worth it, in spite of my praise of them.[5]   I remember not at all your Darlington-Johnson friends in Rome—je ne les remets pas: but I will none the less, should they appear, treat them with all possible civility.—It is summer here, en plein, & at moments, very hot.   But Paris is still charming.   I shall be (I have just been interrupted by a young woman from M. Julian Klaczko (of the "2 Chancellors,") to know whether I didn't steal his overcoat the other night at the Laugel's.[6]   I didn't.)—I shall be here to July 15<u>th</u>, & shall between then & Aug 1<u>st</u> pay a short visit to the Childes, at Montargis.   In August & Sept, I don't know what I shall do.   I trust you will arrange your Summer comfortably, & the rest of them too.   I infer from your letter that A.K. is returned to C.[7]   Give her much love, & embrace every one.   What is thought (outside of the Nation) of the nomination of Hayes?[8]   Je n'y comprends rein.   What is heard from Bob & Wilk?   *What is B's address?* I wish you rest & joy.

Yours | H.J.jr.

ALS: MH bMS Am 1094 (1966)

[1] The Centenary of American Independence Exposition.

[2] Charles-Jacques-Marie Tanneguy, Comte Duchatel (b. 1838), French politician.

[3] Perhaps Marie-Amèlie Guyot de Villeneuve, wife of François-Gustave-Adolphe Guyot de Villeneuve (1825–1899), French diplomat, served in the French legation in Washington.

[4] Eugène Fromentin (1820–1876), French painter and writer, *Les maîtres d'autrefois; Belgique-Hollande* (1876).

[5] Ximénès Doudan, *Mélanges et lettres*, noticed by HJ in "Parisian Topics," *New York Tribune*, 1 July 1876 (dated 9 June 1876).

[6] Julian Klaczko (1825–1906), Polish historian, *The Two Chancellors: Gortchakof and Prince Bismarck* (1876).

[7] Cambridge.

[8] The *Nation* argued that while Rutherford B. Hayes was a "sober man," he was not suited for the crises of the day.

From Henry James

29 Rue de Luxembourg | July 4th [1876]

Dear Wm—Yesterday came your note (undated) about the lens & about Renan: & a few days before had come a letter from mother (also undated,) telling me of father's prosperous convalescence, & of your return from Phila. &c. Your note seems to have been detained & to be anterior to her's: this at any rate is an answer to both of you— I will get the lens (or order it) to morrow, & send it to you in the same way as the others. The others cost 20 frs. apiece & 8 frs. postage for the two. This will cost in all 24 frs. & you will therefore owe me 72 *frs.* which you can pay me at your convenience. I am very happy to hear that father continues to thrive—& I wish I were there to see it. By this time, I trust that his recovery is complete. Give him my blessing.—Your remarks on Renan were most refreshing & (strange as it may appear to you after my worthless acct. of his book in the Tribune) quite in accordance with my own sentiments.[1] I suspected what you say, but as it was only a vague feeling, (mingled with a great admiration of his artistry,) I attempted to make nothing of it (since I could make so little) & chose the tack of rather wholesale & general praise. But I am ready to believe anything bad of him. The longer I live in France the better I like the French personally, but the more convinced I am for their bottomless superficiality. No particular news. I went out a couple of days since & spent an afternoon & evening with the Bootts, at Villiers le Bel. They are living in quarters so primitive as to test their devotion to their errand but they seem very happy. I paid with them a long visit to Couture, who is an amusing but a vulgar little fat & dirty old man—en somme (to me) peu sympathique. But Lizzie says he is an admirable teacher, & he praised her much to me— "de très-grandes dispositions—plus que des dispositions, du talent. Une élève excellente. On ne peut pas lui dire un mot dont elle ne profite." He seems very fond of her, & I suspect that with him she

will make long strides.   The place, tho' near Paris, is most rural &
prettily French; I believe Ernest Longfellow & Cady are about to
arrive[2] & the B.'s think of taking a villa with them.   Frank is most
faultless.   Nelly Grymes & her poor, sick husband are here (since a
week) at M$\underline{me}$ de Hoffmann's.   Grymes is about, but I am afraid is
seriously ill; he is to be operated in a few days for stone.   Poor Nelly
is troubled, but very nice & affectionate.   I believe they expect to be
for the summer at Vichy.   Old Mrs. G. (your friend) is there also (at
her daughter's)—a cantankerous old barbarian; & young Mabel
Grymes Nelly's step-child, a very nice little creature, of dwarfish stat-
ure.   There have been in Paris for the last month a great many
people I know, & I have incurred a good deal of time-wasting & *trim-*
ballage.   But it is quieting down.   C. S. Peirce passed through here a
short time since, & spent three or four days, during which I saw him
several times, & enjoyed, by way of a change, his profound 1$\underline{st}$ class
intellect, reflected in his ardent eyes.   It will amuse you to hear that
he is an *extreme* admirer of *R. Hudson*: a conquest which flatters me.
He wrote me a few days since from the Kew Observatory, Richmond,
where he seems to be dwelling—a charming berth.[3]   Your Darlington-Johnson friends have not turned up, & I suspect have passed
thro' without calling on me—which I regret as I should have liked to
see Miss J.   I have of late had some queer observations of Americans—one young woman, *e.g.* (quite unknown to me, & knowing me
only by *R.H.*) calling on me to interpose in a duel about to be fought
on her behalf between an American & an Englishman.   But while
she was with me they had had it out with fisticuffs.   I send Alice photos. of Dubois's admirable statues.[4]   I had to cut the margin, but it
doesn't spoil it, when trimmed, for framing.   Farewell, sweet brother.
No one ever tells me a word about Wilk & Bob—especially B.   *Give*
me the latter's address, & tell me how he is succeeding.   Continue to
address me here: my precious portier will take care of my letters.
Farewell.   Je vous embrasse bien, I renew my assurances to father &
include mother Alice, & A. Kate.   Tell the last to write to me.

Yours ever,   H. James jr

ALS: MH bMS Am 1094 (1967)

[1] HJ noticed Renan's *Dialogues et fragments philosophiques* (1876) in "Parisian Topics,"
New York Tribune, 17 June 1876 (dated 27 May 1876).

[2] Cady is not identified.

[3] Kew Observatory was founded by Edward Sabine (1788–1883) for making mag-
netic and metereological observations.

[4] Paul Dubois (1829–1905), French painter and sculptor.

To Henry James

Cambr. July 5. [1876][1]

My dear H.   Your letters breathe more and more a spirit of domestication in the modern Babylon, which is very pleasant to me to receive.
I suppose from your gilded & snobbish heights you think of us here
with great pity, but for my part I hurl it back at you, being on the
whole contented with my outward lot.   I got back last night from a
week on the South Shore, including Nantucket, Martha's Vineyard &
Wendell Holmes' at Mattapoisett.   There is a strange naked and
lonely poetry about clean pure little Nantucket under its tender sky.
The settlement at Martha's vineyard, "oak bluffs" is probably the most
audacious paradise of "caddish"ness which has ever flaunted itself in
the eye of day.   A flat insipid sand bank.   The building company in
advertising it perpetrates the most charming instance of the american
defiant style of advertisement I ever met.   "No vegetation to breed
disease by its decay"—!!! I wish Renan & Matt. Arnold might be confined there for a season.   They would write s'thing worth reading
afterwards.   *July 7th.*   I was interrupted by a visitor and resume after
2 days during which your letter to me of June 22nd has arrived.   Alice also had one from Lizzie Boott (enclosed characteristically in one
to the Greenough's) in which she speaks of your blooming appearance.   You say nothing of your bodily condition lately & I let myself
suppose that it is good.   Your spiritual condition is evidently felicitous, with your Tourguenieffs, your de Broglies, your Montargis &
your Longchamps.   Long may you enjoy them, only keep watch and
ward lest in your style you become too Parisian and lose your hold on
the pulse of the great american public to which after all you must
pander for support.   In your last Tribune letter (about the Doudan
letters,) there were too many traces of gallicism in manner.[2]   It will
be a good thing for you to resolve never to use the word "supreme,"
and to get great care not to use "delicate" in the french sense of a
"cultured & fastidious" person.   I hear several persons speak well of
your letters in the Trib. & I suppose there can be little doubt of their
being a success.   The two on the Salon I enjoyed very much.[3]   I wish
you were home to do the Centennial pictures, for, well as Shin writes,
he lacks a certain discretion, heats himself & becomes too emphatic.
They ought never again in a universal Exhibition to make the mistake
they have made in Phila. of admitting such a lot of trashy works of
art.   They spoil your eye & mind for the enjoyment of the good

things.   France has nothing good to show.   The Makart decorative pieces Shin has written about, *struck* me more than anything.[4]   And an unexpected thing that much pleased me was the high average of the american pieces.   It is obvious that we are a people of artistic sensibility—Not that there were there any very great american works, but there was almost nothing vile, such as every foreign school gives you in its degenerate pupils who without a grain of inward decency or cleverness of their own, manufacture a far off echo of some one else's chic or ability.   An immense preponderance of the american work was landscape, and in almost every case the animus was a perfectly sincere effort to reproduce a natural aspect which had affected in some particular way the painter's sensibility.   There was little schooling through it all, but genuine native refinement and speaking in a broad way, intelligence of purpose.   The English school was a most curious study, being so good in its best works, but so utterly preposterous and inartistic in some of its worst things of 30 or 40 years ago; the *saugrenu* comic shakespeare scenes, the platitude of the book of beauty portraits, and a general tendency to go wholly off the track, showing a real want of artistic intelligence in the race, which we, with all our present feebleness, do not approach.   Lafarges Paradise landscape looked admirably well   The Saint Paul was ruined by indecision of drawing.   Lizzie Boott will have told you of his last landscape. It is now at Doll's, and is, it seems to me, as distingué a work as has *ever* been produced.[5]   Unfortunately the subject is really arid, so the picture remains somewhat of a *tour de force*, which is always a matter for regret.—Your second instalment of the American is prime. The morbid little clergyman is worthy of Ivan Sergeitch.   I was not a little amused to find some of my own attributes in him—I think you found my "moral reaction" excessive when I was abroad.   But I do detest the monthly part way of publication except in Geo. Eliot.   The feminine gush and weakness she has begun to show in D.D. are adorable after her big show of cynicism hitherto.   Daniel's preaching is so schoolgirl like that [one] has a sort of tender pity for the inconsistency of the authoress.   I hope in addition to what you say of G. Sand in the Tribune you'll set to and give us a good long N.A.R. article, with lots of short extracts.[6]   I read at Nantucket the Dilemma, by Col. Chesney, a novel of the Indian Mutiny just published which I strongly urge you to read.[7]   It left a impression of reality on me which I can't shake off—it is a strange, gloomy, manly book, and intensely english. I have also read "Cometh up as a flower" with deep pleasure for its heavy english atmosphere, the wh. I more & more grow attached to

in imagination.[8]—I spent three very pleasant days with the Holmes',
at Mattappoissett. I fell quite in love with she; & he exemplified in
the most ridiculous way Michelet's "marriage de l'homme et de la
terre."[9] I told him that he looked like Millets peasant figures as he
stooped over his little plants in his flannel shirt & trowsers.[10] He is a
powerful battery, formed like a planing machine to gouge a deep self-
beneficial groove through life, & his virtues and faults were thrown
into singular relief by the lonesomeness of the shore, which as it
makes every object rock or shrub, stand out so vividly, seemed also to
put him and his wife under a sort of lens for you. (Excuse the uncouthness of my epistolary style, I find I don't outgrow it.[)] Poor
father is very feeble and his improvement is latterly almost insensible.
To day he has added to his troubles an attack of lumbago, not bad but
very disagreeable, and this afternoon I sit and write in the big green
chair in the N.W. bedroom while A.K. is polishing his bed ridden back
with a towel. Alice, thank heaven, has consented to go to Gloucester
for a week, where she is with the Childs. Otherwise no news. You ask
about Hayes. There is no doubt that both his & Tilden's candidacies
are victories for the reform cause.[11] Hayes seems to be a "high
toned" man, and the catch words of the election (which are the step-
ping stones of the people's political education) will lie in virtuousness
with each other. There is no doubt there will be progress effected,
whoever gets in.—You have again failed to let me know the cost of the
lenses you supplied.[12] Send the third one as soon as you conve-
niently can & I will remit as soon as I know how much. Farewell.
Mother is more virtuous than ever since father's illness, & aunt Kate
and Alice are considerateness incarnate. Next week I go for a couple
of days to the Morses, later to Bowditchs, but I shall be here off and
on till August 15 when I shall probably start for a month to the Adirondacks.

Yours ever | W.J

Send Joukowsky's Portrait.

ALS: MH bMS Am 1092.9 (2600)

[1] WJ's letters to HJ from July 1876 to October 1882 are lost.

[2] See letter of 22 June 1876.

[3] HJ, two notes on the Paris salon of 1876 in *Nation* 22 (22 June 1876): 397–98;
Nation 22 (29 June 1876): 415–16.

[4] No essay by Earl Shinn about Hans Makart (1840–1884), Austrian painter, was
found.

[5] Doll & Richards, an art gallery on Park St., Boston.

[6] HJ, "George Sand," *New York Tribune*, 22 July 1876 (dated 28 June 1876).

[7] George Tomkyns Chesney (1830–1895), *The Dilemma: A Tale of the Mutiny* (1876).

[8] Rhoda Broughton, *Cometh Up as a Flower: An Autobiography* (1867).

[9] Jules Michelet (1798–1874), French historian and writer, *Le peuple* (1846). "Marriage de l'homme et de la terre" is the title of the first section of chapter 1, "Servitudes de paysan."

[10] Jean-François Millet (1814–1875), French painter.

[11] Samuel Jones Tilden (1814–1886), American politician, a presidential candidate in 1876.

[12] See letter of 25 April 1876.

From Henry James

Etretat. July 29th. [1876]

Dear W[m].   Your long & charming letter of July 5th came to me just before I left Paris—some ten days since.   Since then, directly after my arrival here, I wrote a few words to Alice by which you will know where I am "located." Your letter, with its superior criticism of so many things, the Philadelphia Exhibition especially, interested me extremely & quickened my frequent desire to converse with you.   What you said of the good effect of the American pictures there gave me great pleasure; & I have no doubt you are right about our artistic spontaneity & sensibility.   My chief impression of the Salon was that $4/5$[ths] of it were purely mechanical, & *de plus*, vile.   I bolted from Paris on the 20th, feeling a real need of a change of air.   I found it with a vengeance here, where as I write I have just had to shut my window, for the cold.   I made a mistake in not getting a room with sun, strange, & even loathsome, as it may appear to you!   The quality of the air is delicious—the only trouble is indeed that it has too shipboard & midocean a savor.   The little place is picturesque, with noble cliffs, a little Casino, & your French bathing going on all day long on the little pebbly beach.   But as I am to do it in the Tribune, I won't steal my own thunder.[1]   The company is rather low, & I know no one save Edward Boit & his wife (of Boston & Rome) who have taken a most charming old country house for the Summer.[2]   Before I left Paris, I spent an afternoon with the Bootts, who are in Paradise— though with Ernest Longfellow & lady as fellow-seraphs.   They have a delightful old villa, with immense garden & all sorts of picturesque qualities, & their place is (as I found by taking a walk with Boott) much prettier than I supposed—in fact very charming, & with the air of being 500 miles from Paris.   Lizzie & Longfellow are working with *acharnement*, & both, I ween, much improving.   I have little to tell you of myself.   I shall be here till August 15 – 20, & shall then go & spend the rest of the month with the Childes, near Orléans (an ugly country I believe,) & after that try & devise some frugal scheme for keeping out of Paris till as late as possible in the Autumn. The winter there always begins soon enough. I am much obliged to you for your literary encouragement & advice—glad especially you like my novel. I can't judge it. Your remarks on my French tricks in my letters are doubtless most just, & shall be heeded. But it's an odd thing that such tricks should grow at a time when my last layer of resistance to a long-encroaching weariness & satiety with the French mind & its utterance has fallen from me like a garment. I have done with 'em, forever, & am turning English all over. I desire only to feed on English life & the contact of English minds—I wish greatly I knew some. Easy & smooth-flowing as life is in Paris, I would throw it over to morrow for an even very small chance to plant myself for a while in England. If I had but a single good friend in London I would go thither. I have got nothing important out of P. nor am likely to. My life there makes a much more succulent figure in your letters, as my mention of its thin ingredients comes back to me than in my own consciousness. A good deal of Boulevard & 3ᵈ rate Americanism: few retributive relations otherwise. I know the Théâtre Francais by heart!—Daniel Deronda (Dan'l. himself) is indeed a dead, though amiable failure. But the book is a large affair; I shall write an article of some sort about it.[3] All desire is dead within me to produce something on George Sand; though perhaps I shall, all the same, mercenarily & mechanically— though only if I am forced.[4] *Please make a point of mentioning*, by the way, whether a letter of mine, upon her, exclusively, *did* appear lately in the Tribune. I don't see the T. regularly & have missed it. They misprint sadly. I never said, e.g., in announcing her death, that she was "*fearfully* shy": I used no such vile adverb, but another—I forget which.[5]—I am hoping, from day to day for another letter from home, as the period has come round. I hope father is getting on smoothly & growing able to enjoy life a little more. I am afraid the extreme heat does not help him and I fear also that your common sufferings from it have been great—though you, in your letter didn't speak of it. I hope Alice will have invented some plan of going out of town. Is there any one left in Cambridge whom the family sees?—I am glad you went to Mattapoisett, which I remember kindly, tho' its meagre nature seems in memory doubly meagre beside the rich picturesqueness of this fine old Normandy. What you say of nature putting Wendell H. & his wife under a lens there is very true. I see no one here; a common & lowish lot; & the American institution of "ringing in" is as regards the French impossible.   I hope your own plans for the summer will prosper, & health & happiness be your portion. Give much love to father, & to the ladies.

—Yours always—H. James jr.

ALS: MH bMS Am 1094 (1968)

   [1] HJ, "A French Watering Place," *New York Tribune*, 26 August 1876 (dated 4 August 1876).

   [2] Edward Darley Boit (1840–1915), American artist, and his wife, Mary Louisa Cushing Boit.   Boit established studios in Paris and Rome.

   [3] HJ, "Daniel Deronda: A Conversation," *Atlantic Monthly* 38 (December 1876): 684–94.

   [4] HJ, "George Sand," *Galaxy* 24 (July 1877): 45–61.

   [5] HJ mentioned the death of George Sand in "Parisian Topics," *New York Tribune*, 1 July 1876 (dated 9 June 1876).   For HJ's letter on her see letter of 5 July 1876.

From Henry James

                    29 Rue de Luxembourg. | Oct 13ᵗʰ [1876]
Dear Wᵐ.   I have been most sorry to learn by your two letters that you came home from the country so well and strong only to become a prey to dsyentery,[1] & that the weakness resulting therefrom still continued.   You had really pas de chanceux & I lament your sufferings, tempered as I ween they were, by loving female care.   But I hope that long 'ere this you have begun to bloom again. Your second letter came yesterday, & this a.m. I went over to Vasseur's (Rue de l'Ecole de Méd.), the best place in Paris, & demanded an *os sphénoide*.[2]   He absolutely refused to give me one & said it was impossible to obtain one detached from the head.   I might find an old one in a bric-a-brac shop, but it would be certain in the nature of things to be broken and not what you want—that no perfect sphénoid was ever found for sale independent of the head.   He would give me a très-belle tête for 35 or 40 francs.   As I had not your authority to buy this I thought it better to write & ask your leave.   If you wish it I will instantly purchase & send one.   I am very sorry not to find your old bone; but I will go over to that region tomorrow a.m. & try again at some other place.   I did not go farther to day for good reason.

   I can't write you a regular letter, as I am busy, this a.m. & wrote three days since, at length, to father.   I am extremely gratified by your approval of my novel; but you reiterate so the Blondin metaphor that I am afraid you will deem, before the end, that I have toppled off the rope.[3]   But if I haven't, *tant mieux*. T.S.P. on George

Sand was indeed most pitiful.[4] I have just rec'd. a most childlike letter from him. I shall in all probability write something on G.S. The obstacle, as regards the "extracts" you clamor for, is that I find it impossible to re-read her. I send you the Doudan in vols. by Mrs. Winslow, who sails immediately. I am thinking seriously of going to England, but *please say nothing about it until I decide.* I will write you more properly anon. Love to all.

Yours ever | H. James jr

ALS: MH bMS Am 1094 (1969)

[1] A slip for 'dysentery.'

[2] Maison Vasseur, supplier of anatomical models.

[3] The term 'Blondin', meaning a rope, a cableway, is derived from the name Blondin, pseudonym of a French tightrope walker. The discussion concerns *Roderick Hudson.*

[4] Thomas Sergeant Perry, "George Sand," *Atlantic Monthly* 38 (October 1876): 444–51.

From Henry James

29 Rue de Luxembourg | Oct. 23ᵈ [1876]
Dear Wᵐ. I am sorry to say that the wretched Talrich has disappointed me about the sphenoids.[1] After promising me that he would procure them he has just informed me that he has tried in vain—that it is impossible to get a good & perfect sphenoid, detached. He repeat the statements of Vasseur, & offered me a head, for 40 francs. But as he says it would make a parcel as large as a hat, I suppose that, should I get it, the carriage to America would make it cost as much as a cranium would cost you there. But I will do whatever you say. I am sorry to disappoint you.—I have lately received two or three notes from you. Many thanks for the Mark Aurelius, which I am very happy to have, & for E. Temple's letter, which bro't tears to my eyes. I wish you had told me something about her. I shall do everything possible for Miss May Whitwell, whom I commiserate if she has before her a *winter* at Ecouen. She has not yet turned up. Pray acknowledge to mother her letter of Oct. 9ᵗʰ, just rec'd., & very welcome. I hope your strength has quite come back to you, & that you are as if your malady had never been. It must have been a grievous blow. But you have ere this, I trust, risen phoenix-like. Tell father I rejoice in mother's account of his salubrious doings; but I am still afraid to ask him to write to me.

I suppose you will think me a model of inconstancy if I tell you that I have about decided to remove to London on Dec. 1ˢᵗ. Six weeks of Paris have lately been depriving the enterprise of its terrors, for I have realized here that the winter holds out no very elevated prospects to me. My fleeing compatriots are back & the idea of beginning again to play at "society" with *them* is intolerable. There is nothing else, for me personally, on the horizon, & it is rather ignoble to stay in Paris simply for the restaurants—which is really what it would amount to—that & ½ a dozen visits to the Théatre Français. In short since I have begun to think seriously of London, my impatience to get there & try it, & get through with whatever dreariness the stage of initiation may have, has become extreme. So, D.V., I shall leave this place in about 5 weeks. I shall make bold to apply to a few persons, (I have not yet decided whom,) for introductions. I am much obliged to Henry Adams for his kind offer, & shall write to him. You had better address me, *after Nov. 15ᵗʰ*, Care of Brown & Shipley, Founder's Court, Lothbury: till then here. I will write you from London my permanent address. I shall feel as if I had given Paris not only a fair, but a generous, trial. The air is full of War & the whole continent sniffing at England—those who wish to stand up for whom have no easy task. Indeed they have to fall back quite on general principles—her conduct, in detail, is not graceful. Her discovering now, suddenly, that the Turks are not worth fighting for is *un peu fort*. If she doesn't fight, before long, for some one or something, I am afraid we can order our mourning for English glory. But this will make it a very interesting time to be in London; & if the "Decadence of England" has really set in, the breaking-up will be a big spectacle—may I be there to see! My friend Joukowsky tells me that Ivan Sergéitch whom I haven't seen (he is still in the country) is vomiting *feu & flammes* for War, & that he represents the enthusiasm of the Russian people for the same as something tremendous & contagious. They regard it as a religious crusade—they have never been so stirred-up.[2]

I went out to dine the other day with the Nicolas Tourgéneffs but they are always virtuous & pacific—de bonnes gens s'il en fait. The lovely Mrs. Mason[3] is here for the winter, & her I shall regret to leave. I dined with her a couple of days since in comp'y. with the much-whiskered Sturgis Bigelow—a Viennese medical student.[4] I sent you the *Doudan* thro' Mrs. Winslow (70 Boylston St.) She sails to day. You had better send for the book. I will send Balzac's letters as soon as I have reviewed them.[5] Farewell blessings on your health. Tell

Alice I sent s'thing by Mrs. Winslow to her.   Mrs. W. will send it, but she had better call afterwards.   'Tis of *real chantilly*, tell her.

Love to all from your   H. James jr

ALS: MH bMS AM 1094 (1970)

[1] Jules Talrich, a supplier of anatomical models in Paris.

[2] The Russo-Turkish War, 1877–78.

[3] Alice Mason.

[4] Probably William Sturgis Bigelow, a physician, who in 1871–74 attended Harvard Medical School.

[5] HJ, "The Letters of Honoré de Balzac," *Galaxy* 23 (February 1877): 183–95.

From Henry James

3 Bolton St. Piccadilly. | Jan 12<u>th</u> [1877]
Dear W<u>m</u>.   I have lately received 3 letters from home—1. from you, with Sheldon's 1<u>st</u> cheque;[1] 1 from father, with 2<u>d</u> cheque; & 1 from Alice.   I will answer yours first, as it came first, but you may share your joy with the others, to whom give also my thanks & blessing. Tell Alice that her lost letter was some time since returned from Baltimore, & that her precious words are not squandered.   I have also rec'd. a couple of notes from you, & have paid your *Medical Record* bill, & subscribed for another year.[2]   I have deferred scandalously sending you gloves; but I now enclose a couple of pair (I hope they are not too ornamental) on the sole condition (since you countermanded the original order) that you accept them as presents.   Mind you that.   They are in different envelopes.—I am by this time an established Londoner, tho' I have I have no particular adventures to relate.   I have passed these five weeks in profound tranquillity & seen no one.   The one or two persons I saw on first coming I have not since beheld, & my only view of the "world" has been in dining once at the Smalley's—a very savoury interruption to the lugubrious fare of one's London ordinary.   Or rather, I forget: a lady whom I met at the S.'s, a great friend of theirs, very amiably bade me to a banquet of her own; & not being proud I went, & sat thro' a heavy London dinner, composed of fearful viands & people I didn't know. But I took in a very nice, ugly woman, Mrs. Hill, wife of the *Daily News*, & on the other side of me sat a great beauty, Lady Gordon, daughter of Sir W<u>m</u> Herschel[3]—& on the other side of her, Sir Charles Dilke.   I have also been bidden by Lady Pollock (thro' the Smalleys) to call upon her, she being an *admiress* of my literature(!)—tho' who she is I haven't an idea.   So, doubtless, my London horizon is open-

ing.   I have no doubt it will, gradually, & that the day will come when all my endeavor will be to contract it.   The weather has been uninterruptedly atrocious.   It has rained here for 3 months in torrents; half England is under water, & there is gt. consternation & misery.   It is a great depression & a gt. inconvenience, as walking just now is my principal pastime, & it has been almost impossible.   In spite of this I like London better & better & am very glad I didn't delay another hour to come here.   For the practical convenience of life (except *fires*,) living as I live, it is immeasurably inferior to Paris—no cafés, no restaurants, no Boulevards, no kiosks, no theatres, (that one can go to) no evening visits &c.   But it is more interesting—much; & the incommodities & drearinesses are of a sort that I shall feel less as time goes on, while other resources will grow, that would never grow on the Continent.   Ce n'est pas, pourtant, que je lâche cette bonne vieille France.   I am tired to death of her, but England, & all its uglinesses & hypocrisies, make one think not worse of her but better.   I have just called in my landlady to pay my bill, & her deadly woodenfaced "respectability," with an avidity, beneath, every whit as grasping as the French, & not a grace to glaze it over, makes me feel as if, beside such a type as that, the most impudent Paris *cocotte* were a divinity. But this is foggy "spleen."   London *is* agreeable to me, as well as interesting, & I am in excellent humor with it.   My lodgings are excellent, the service perfection, & the situation *ditto*. Physically I am (as always,) much better since being in England.   In Paris, indoors, I had always two physical ennuis—cold feet & sore throat.   Since being here I have not had a trace of them.   I have also done a good deal of work—(sent a lot of stuff to the Nation, wh. you will probably recognise.)[4] I shall be able to work much more here than in Paris.—So much for myself.   I am very sorry that your own work has exhausted you so much, & I trust that in vacation you will lay in a sufficient stock of strength for future contingencies.   Tell father it was a great pleasure to see his handwriting again, & I perceive in it no trace of shakiness—a great improvement on the note he wrote me some time since. But I was much distressed by your mention of mother's sanitary eccentricities.   Kiss the lovely creature all over for me, & repeat the process as often as necessary until she is completely cured. Make her write to me & tell me all about it.   Your letter enclosed one from Bob, written just after his return from Cambridge, which filled me with an extreme sense of the grimness of his lot, & made Bolton St, & my existence here, seem like a festering sore on the bosom of Justice. But I can't help it, any more than he can!   Your suggestion to send him *Punch* was a blessed one, & was instantly acted upon.[5] TELL ME THIS. Does father, as he used, mail the *Graphic* to him from home?[6] If not, I will post it to him weekly—the expense is nothing; & if he *does*, I will send him something else. *(Please see that this question is answered).* Apropos of which I will send father (tell him) the *weekly* edition of the *Times* which they have just begun (Jan. 1ˢᵗ) to issue. I am sure the *Mail*, with its ponderous mass of local news, twice a week, would sicken him. (I will begin to morrow.) I am extremely sorry to hear of the way father is losing money, as well as of Aunt Kate's reverses. Is it is[7] a serious discomfort? Whatever it is I hope it will stop there, & go no further. Isn't it true that prices have, on the other hand, fallen very low?[8] The way gold is going down (105.) is a great advantage to me, as to the drafts I receive.—I am sorry Godkin's course strikes you as so vicious—I had been wondering much what you thought of it. Seeing no American paper but the *Nation*, I had supposed not exactly that its tone was the correct thing, but that there was much reason in it. From here it all looks shocking bad, & I give up trying to discriminate. Over here things have reached the farcical stage. The Turks are making fools of assembled Europe, & Russia backing down. But every one nevertheless, expects war in the spring.[9] Your remarks on *D.D.* were most sagacious.[10] The book is a great *exposé* of the female mind. Tell Lathrop, particularly, from me, of my interest in his troubles, good wishes &c.[11] And T.S.P. a father! He writes me the letters of a child! I will write as things unfold. Meantime I bless you all, particularly my poor suffering Mammy.

Yours ever   H.J.jr

ALS: MH bMS Am 1094 (1971)

[1] *Galaxy* was published by Sheldon & Company, managed by Colonel Alexander E. Sheldon.

[2] Also called the *London Medical Record*.

[3] Caroline Emilia Mary Gordon was the daughter of John Frederick William Herschel (1792–1871), British astronomer, and the granddaughter of William Herschel (1738–1822), British astronomer.

[4] HJ published ten items in the *Nation* in January and February 1877.

[5] *Punch, or the London Charivari*.

[6] *The Graphic: An Illustrated Weekly Magazine* published in London.

[7] This second 'is' appears to be an error.

[8] The panic of 1873 was followed by a period of falling prices. It was an especially difficult time for railroads and investors in railroad stocks, both because of general economic decline and because of frauds.

[9] The last of the Russo-Turkish wars was in 1877–78.

[10] *Daniel Deronda*.

[11] George Parsons Lathrop (1851–1898), American author, associate editor of *Atlantic Monthly* in 1875–77. He resigned as of 1 September 1877 in a controversy.

From Henry James

3 Bolton St. Piccadilly | Feb. 2ᵈ [1877]

Dear Wᵐ. I enclose herewith a letter, in pencil, from Bob Temple; & with it I enclose another which I rec'd. a short time since. The former came last night; it speaks for himself. It seems a sad story, & I suppose it is not unveracious. I enclose it to you because I don't want to trouble father, at present, with it; tho' you will of course show it to him. It is hard to know what is to be done for him—seeing the probability of his drinking up any money that is sent him to start him when he leaves the army. Nevertheless I send you—I *must* send—something for you to forward to him by P.O. order, or otherwise, from home: viz. a P.O. order for 7£ (seven pounds) which you will find herein. You will probably be able to add a little more to it at home, & will send the money in a lump. With the $30 which he speaks of in his letter he will have therefore 80 or 90 dollars, which *ought* to be enough to keep him till he obtains work: tho' of course it will be at the mercy of his squandering it. There is something most tragi-comical in the idea of his seeking work as a *teacher*! I recommend your writing a line to his Captain, asking if his story is *literally* true—if he is indeed forced to leave the Army: & even sending the money, if possible, to the former, to be put into his hands when he *does* leave. I delegate this trouble to you because you can communicate in so much shorter a time. Bob's letters are very "touching"; but what can one do or say? The long one is well worth reading, throughout: I have been meaning to send it to you. Whether any money is sent to him from home or not, be sure & send him mine, which is no loss to me. I have written to him that I have sent it to you for him. (Be sure & address him Robt. Travis[1]—& have order made out to that name.)—I have no time to write more; but I despatched to mother a *long* budget 3 days since. I rec'd. last night her note with B's letter & verses—which he had already sent me.[2] What a wonderful phenomenon he is!

Yours ever   H.J.jr.

The P.O. order will be sent you by the P.O. *here*.

ALS: MH bMS Am 1094 (1972)

[1] The name under which Robert Temple enlisted.

[2] In bMS Am 1095.2 (22–24) there are several undated poems by RJ.

From Henry James

ATHENÆUM CLUB | PALL MALL London Feb 9th [1877]
Dear Wm.

I drop you a line to add to my note of a few days since, enclosing Bob Temple's letter. If you have not already sent him the money which I despatched at the same time (the P.O. order for which will have already reached you, please add to the sum a certain $12. which Osgood has been directed to send you (or father, rather) a cheque for. If you *have* sent it, keep the $12.00 for future contingencies of the same sort.

This is not meant to be a letter, & I must not prolong it, as I have a head weary with letter-writing, & other writing, at which I have been busy all the morning. London goes on very well, as the headpiece of my note paper will show you. The favor of being put down on the honorary list of this club I owe to the extreme kindness of Mr. Motley, who, barely knowing me & quite unsolicited, called upon me a few days since & told me he had had this done for me. It will be an extreme convenience. He brought me here, showed me the ropes, & introduced me to the Duke of Argyll! The place is the last word of a high civilization—I wish you could see the great library in which I am writing this. Such bookshelves—such stands of "Mudie,"[1] such lounges & easy chairs! The only drawback is having to drop it after 2 or 3 months!—I have made (through Mrs. Wister) a charming acquaintance in the person of George Howard, to whom I have taken a great fancy, & with whom I spent last Sunday afternoon at Burne Jones's studio.[2] B.J.'s things very able & interesting. I haven't any anecdotes, as I have lately not been dining out.

Blessings on all, from your fond   H.J.jr

ALS: MH bMS Am 1094 (1973)

[1] See letter of 8 March 1870.
[2] Sir Edward Coley Burne-Jones (1833–1898), British artist.

From Henry James

3 Bolton St. Piccadilly | Feb. 28th [1877]
Dear Wm. Since last writing home I have rec'd. two letters from you: the 1st on general topics & very welcome; the 2d a request to get you a *Maudsley*, which I immediately did.[1] I hope it has safely reached you. Meanwhile, the wheel of London life, for me, has been steadily revolving, turning up no great prizes, but no disappointing blanks

either.   I go on seeing a good many people, & yet I seem to myself to be leading a very tranquil life.   I suppose it is because my relations with the people I see are very superficial & momentary, & that I encounter no one of whom I hanker to see more.   All the Englishmen I meet are of the "useful-information" prosaic sort, & I don't think that in an equal lot of people I ever rec'd. such an impression of a want of imagination.   Some times I feel as if this process of "making acquaintances" in a strange country were very dreary work: it is so empirical & experimental, & you have to try one by one so many uninteresting people to hit upon even the *possibly* interesting ones.   I hope it won't be often repeated, & that I shall be able to settle down in England long enough to keep, & profit by, any sense of domestication that I may acquire.—I have dined out a few times lately; but not so often as a while ago.   I think I mentioned that Ld. Houghton had asked me to breakfast—where I met half a dozen men, all terribly "useful-information," & whose names & faces I have forgotten.   But he has invited me again, for a few days hence, & sent me, very kindly, for the season, a card for the *Cosmopolitan*—a sort of talking-club, extremely select, which meets on Wednesdays & Sunday nights.[2]   I was taken there a while ago by Frederick Locker, Boott's friend (B. gave me a note to him) (a very nice fellow,)[3] &, amid a little knot of Parliamentary swells, conversed chiefly with Anthony Trollope—"all gobble & glare," as he was described by someone who heard him make a speech.—I lunched the other day with Andrew Lang to meet J. Addington Symonds—a mild, cultured man, with the Oxford perfume, who invited me to visit him at Clifton, where he lives.[4]   Also, Albert Dicey (he who is America with Bryce[5] & who is a very good fellow in spite of his physique) asked me to lunch with Henry Sidgwick. About Sidgwick there is something exceptionally pleasant (in spite of a painful stammer.)   He had read Roderick Hudson(!) & asked me to stop with him at Cambridge.[6]   Further, as to lunches, I lunched yesterday with poor Leslie Stephen, whom, however, rendered more inarticulate than ever by his wife's death, I find an impossible companion, in spite of the moral & intellectual confidence that he inspires.   I had but a glimpse of Miss Thackeray, who has likewise been greatly knocked up by her sister's death, & is ill & little visible.[7]   She inspired me with a kindly feeling.   All this in spite of the fact that, theoretically, I don't lunch out at all; as it spoils a morning's work.   I dined 'tother day with one Robarts, at his club; he having made up to me I know not why.[8]   Tho' civil, he belongs to the type of Englishman one least endures—the big Englishman who looks like a superior footman, with a turn up nose & an indented chin. At his dinner were several unmemorable men—very legal: he is a practising barrister. I also dined some days since with Mrs. Rogerson—I think I have told you who she is; a clever, liberal woman who invites me to dinner every four or five days. This was a sort of theatrical banquet, with the whole Bateman family, who are patronized here socially. They sat however below the salt & I at the summit with Lady Hamilton Gordon who is on the whole, though almost upwards of fifty, the handsomest woman I have ever seen.[9] She has the head of an antique cameo. I dined yesterday with Boughton, the painter, (an American—Londonized;) a good plain man; & with two other painters who happened to be remarkably pleasant fellows.—When I add that I lately feasted also with Mrs. Pakenham, an American married to a British general, to whom Mrs. Wister sent me a letter, (a very nice woman with a very nice husband) I shall have exhausted the list of my adventures. I must have told you that I have for the present the frequentation of the Athenaeum Club (thro' Motley,) & that I find it a little heaven here below.[10] It transfigures the face of material existence for me: & alas! I already find it indispensable. I also have a temporary membership of another club—the small & modest Savile.[11] It is very respectably composed—supposed, I believe, to be particularly so; but after the Athenaeum it seems dreadfully caddish, & I shall resort to it only when the latter fails me. When that melancholy day comes I shall feel at 1ˢᵗ as if London had become impossible: the having it makes such a difference. The Athenaeum is a place it takes 16 years for a Briton to become a member of!—if things go very smoothly.—I am more & more content to have come to England, & only desire to be left soaking here for an indefinite period. I positively *suck* the atmosphere of its intimations & edifications.—This is a very personal letter, as I suppose you desire; & I trust you will answer questions without waiting for them to be asked. What is your "Herbert Spencer elective"?—to which you have alluded, but without explaining its sudden genesis.[12] Whatever it is I am glad you like it. I often take an afternoon nap beside H.S. at the Athenaeum, & feel as if I were robbing *you* of the privilege. A good speech of Matthew Arnold's, which seems to be classical here: "Oh, yes, my wife is a delightful woman; she has all my sweetness, & none of my airs." I hope the family circle prospers. Tell Alice to get from the Athenaeum Lord George Campbell's *Log letters fr. the Challenger*: a delightful book.[13] Tell her also I saw the Ashburners the other evening & they struck me as more lively. I rec'd. yesterday a long call from F. T.

Palgrave, who is not *sympathique*, but apparently well-intentioned. He said G. Eliot's picture of English country house life in *D.D.* might have been written by a housemaid! DON'T REPEAT THIS, FOR PARTICULAR REASONS. In fact F.T.P. stuck in pins, right & left. Write all you can; bless you all.

H. James jr.

ALS: MH bMS AM 1094 (1974)

[1] Henry Maudsley (1835–1918), British physiologist and psychologist. The book could be *Body and Mind* (1869).

[2] The Cosmopolitan Club met in Charles St., Berkeley Square.

[3] Frederick Locker-Lampson (1821–1895), British poet. He was Frederick Locker before his marriage to Jane Lampson in 1874.

[4] John Addington Symonds (1840–1893), British author.

[5] Bryce and Albert Dicey visited the United States in 1870 and acquired lifelong interests in America. In 1888 Bryce published his *American Commonwealth*.

[6] Henry Sidgwick (1838–1900), British philosopher.

[7] Lady Anne Isabella Ritchie (1837–1919), a writer, daughter of William Makepeace Thackeray. Her sister Harriet Marian Stephen died 28 November 1875. Leslie Stephen remarried 26 March 1878. His letters up to the time of his second marriage emphasize his great loss.

[8] Henry Adams met Charles Henry Robarts (b. 1840), probably the same individual, while in England. Adams found him something of a bore but "decidedly a gentleman in manners and talk" (*The Letters of Henry Adams*, ed. J. C. Levenson et al., 6 vols. [Cambridge: Belknap Press of Harvard Univ. Press, 1982–88], 2:47).

[9] Hamilton Gordon is an unusual combination of names in the British nobility, not used after 1900. Lady Hamilton Gordon could be Mary Baillie Hamilton Gordon, wife of George John James Hamilton Gordon, earl of Aberdeen (1816–1864). She was eighty-five when she died in 1900 and thus somewhat older than HJ thought her to be. She is not to be confused with Lady Gordon, Herschel's daughter.

[10] The Athenaeum Club, a literary club established in 1824.

[11] A small literary club in Piccadilly.

[12] Natural History 2: Physiological Psychology, in which WJ used Herbert Spencer's *Principles of Psychology* as a text.

[13] Lord George Granville Campbell (1850–1915), British traveler, *Log Letters from the "Challenger"* (1876).

From Henry James

ATHENÆUM CLUB | PALL MALL March 29th [1877]

Dear W^m—I will write you a few lines before I leave this place this evening. I thanked you for your last letter thro' mother a few days since—a letter of wh. I forget the exact date; (you described your brain-lecture &c.)   I have been dining here, & then sitting awhile to read the last no of the 19th Cent'y.   (I won't send it you as I send it to

Mrs. Lockwood, who can't afford to buy it & would never see it otherwise.)[1] Vide in the same Prof. Clifford's thing at the end.[2]—London life jogs along with me, pausing every now & then at some more or less succulent patch of herbage. I was almost ashamed to tell you thro' mother that I, unworthy, was seeing a bit of Huxley. I went to his house again last Sunday evening—a pleasant easy, no-dress-coat sort of house (in our old Marlboro' Place, by the way.)[3] Huxley is a very genial, comfortable being—yet with none of the noisy & windy geniality of some folks here, whom you find with their backs turned when you are responding to the remarks that they have very offensively made you. But of course my talk with him is mere amiable generalities. These, however, he likes to cultivate for recreation's sake, of a Sunday evening. (The slumbering Spencer I have not lately seen here: I am told he is terribly "nervous".) Some mornings since, I breakfasted with Lord Houghton again—he invites me most dotingly. Present: John Morley, Goldwin Smith (pleasanter than my prejudice agt. him)[4] Henry Cowper,[5] Frederick Wedmore & a monstrous cleverly & agreeably-talking M.P., Mr. Otway.[6] John Morley has a most agreeable face, but he hardly opened his mouth. (He is, like so many of the men who have done much here, very young looking.) Yesterday I dined with Lord Houghton—with Gladstone, Tennyson, Dr. Schliemann (the excavator of old Mycenae &c)[7] & half a dozen other men of "high culture." I sat next but one to the Bard, & heard most of his talk which was all about port-wine & tobacco: he seems to know much about them, & can drink a whole bottle of port at a sitting with no incommodity. He is very swarthy & scraggy & strikes one at first as much less handsome than his photos.: but gradually you see that it's a face of genius. He had I know not what simplicity, speaks with a strange rustic accent & seemed altogether like a creature of some primordial English stock, a 1000 miles away from American manufacture.—Behold me after dinner conversing affably with Mr. Gladstone—not by my own seeking, but by the almost importunate affection of Lord H. But I was glad of a chance to feel the "personality" of a great political leader—or as G. is now thought here even, I think, by his partisans, ex-leader. That of Gladstone is very fascinating—his urbanity extreme—his eye that of a man of genius—& his apparent self surrender to what he is talking of, without a flaw. He made a great impression on me—greater than any one I have seen here: tho' 'tis perhaps owing to my naïveté, & unfamiliarity with statesmen. Dr. Schliemann told me 2 or 3 curious things. 1° he is an American citizen having lived some years in America in business.

2° though he is now a great Hellenist he knew no word of Greek till he was 34 years old, when he learned it in 6 weeks(!!) at St. Petersburg. *Ce que c'est d'être Allemand!* The other men at Houghton's dinner were all special notabilities. Next me sat a very amiable Lord Zouche—noted as the unhappy young peer who a short time since married a young wife who three or four months after her marriage eloped *bel et bien* with a guardsman.[8]—Did I tell you that I some time since spent an evening with F. T. Palgrave? Strictly between ourselves—i.e. as regards H. Adams, & every one else,—I dont particularly like him: but he is evidently very respectable. He is a tremendous case of culture, & a "beggar for talk" such as you never faintly dreamed of. But *all* his talk is kicks & thrusts at every one going, & I suspect that, in the last, analysis, "invidious mediocrity" would be the scientific appellation of his temper. His absence of the *simpatico* is only surpassed by that of his wife. (This sounds pretty scornful: & I hasten to add that I imagine he very much improves on acquaintance. I shall take a chance to see.) Did I tell you too that I had been to the Oxford & Cam. boat-race? But I have paragraphed it in the *Nation*, to wh. I refer you.[9] It was for about 2 minutes a supremely beautiful sight; but for those 2 minutes I had to wait a horribly bleak hour & a ½, shivering, in mid-Thames, the sour March-wind. I can't think of any other adventures: save that I dined 2 or 3 days since at Mrs. Godfrey Lushington's (they are very nice, *blushing* people) with a parcel of quiet folk: but next to a divine little Miss Lushington (so pretty English girls can be!) who told me that she lived in the depths of the City, at Guy's Hospital, whereof her father is administrator.[10] Guy's Hospital, of which I have read in all old English novels. So does one move all the while here on identified ground. This is the eve. of Good Friday, a most lugubrious day here—& all the world (save 4000,000 or so) are out of London for the 10 day's Easter holiday. I think of making two or three excursions of a few hours apiece, to places near London whence I can come back to sleep: Canterbury, Chichester &c (but as I shall commemorate them for lucre I won't talk of them thus.) Farewell dear brother, I won't prattle further. Thank father for the 2 cuts from the *Galaxy*—tho' I wish he had sent a line with them. I enclose $2.00 I accidentally possess. Add them to that $12.00 & expend them for any cost I may put you to. Have you rec'd. your *Maudsley*?[11] Don't you think very well of Hayes, & are not things in a brightening way? Encourage Alice to write to me.

My blessings on yourself from your fraternal   H.J.jr.

Ask Alice to keep these London scrawls of mine: I may be glad to refer to them later.

ALS: MH bMS AM 1094 (1975)

[1] Florence Bayard Lockwood (1842–1898), American-born author.

[2] William Kingdon Clifford (1845–1879), British mathematician and philosopher, his contribution to "A Modern Symposium," on "The Influence upon Morality of a Decline in Religious Belief," *Nineteenth Century* 1 (April 1877): 353–58.

[3] In 1855–56 the Jameses lived at 10 Marlborough Place, St. John's Wood, London.

[4] Goldwin Smith (1823–1910), British controversialist, journalist, historian.

[5] Henry Cowper (1836–1887), member of parliament.

[6] Sir Arthur John Otway (1822–1912), British politician.

[7] Heinrich Schliemann (1822–1890), German archaeologist. He acquired American citizenship because he was in California when the United States annexed it.

[8] Robert Nathaniel Cecil George, Lord Zouche of Haryngworth (1851–1914), on 15 July 1875 married Annie Mary Eleanor Fraser (b. 1857), daughter of 18th Lord Saltoun of Abernethy. She left his house after three months.

[9] HJ, note on the Oxford-Cambridge Boat Race, *Nation* 24 (12 April 1877): 221–22.

[10] Guy's Hospital in London was founded in 1721. Probably Godfrey Lushington (1832–1907), British lawyer.

[11] See letter of 28 February 1877.

From Henry James

SAVILE CLUB, | 15, SAVILE ROW. W. April 19ᵗʰ [1877]

Dear Wᵐ

I received yesterday your postal card about the MS. I sent you, & am much obliged to you for your trouble. I am not surprised that Howells refused it; I feared he would find it too "painful." Nor am I surprised that you found it disagreeable, for I rather went back on it mentally after sending it. Je m'étais battu un peu les flancs to like it myself, in order to oblige Leslie Stephen who had sent it to me, with the request to try & get it into the *Atlantic.* You were right in sending it to Church, & I will immediately write to him.[1] This is all—I wrote to mother yesterday & to Alice shortly before. I hope you are getting reassuring news from Wilky & that you are not unhappy. I do very well, settle down more & more in London & have (mentally at least) many irons on the fire. This is a chance to tell you that my health (constipation &c) continues to hold, thro' a variety of ups & downs, a marked course upward. In the long run, I do very well— though sometimes discouraged (even greatly) by my small powers of head work—by the damnable nausea (as I call it for want of a better word) that continuous reading & writing bring on. But I can work as much as I need, & if one can do that one should be thankful. I hope that, *en somme*, you can do as much.   I have no news save what I wrote yesterday to M.   Farewell; with blessings

Yours ever | H. James jr

N.B.   If a letter for my annual dues to the *Century* should come, please send it straight out to me, as it is, in envelope.   I will settle then.   I desire by no means to break my connection.

ALS: MH bMS AM 1094 (1976)

[1] William Conant Church (1836–1917), editor of *Galaxy*, or his brother Francis Pharcellus Church.

From Henry James

3 Bolton St. W. June 28. [1877]

Dear Brother—

It is a good while ago now since I received your letter of May 27$\underline{\text{th}}$; since when also I got a note from father, in which he spoke of sending me a p.o. order from Osgood, & the German translation of my novel.[1] Both of these have come; for which many thanks.   Did you ever see such vile impudence as the translator's performance on the dénoue-ment of the tale? and the "cheek" of the man in sending it to me with his "compliments"!   If those are your Germans I give them up.—I *do* congratulate you on arriving at your holiday, & I hope it will yield you the most priceless satisfaction, of every kind.   By the time this reaches you you will probably be lying along side of one of those small cedars, with your head on a neatly-massed stone, wrapped in the en-chantments of Paradise.[2]   For you, as for all the others, I trust these may prove infinite.—It is so long since I have written to you that you will expect me to have many wonders to relate: but in fact I have very few.   The season has brought me—thank the Lord!—no increase of diversions; it would be absurd to pretend or attempt to work if it had done so.   In fact I have been little in the world, as the world goes here.   Just after I last wrote, I went for 24 hrs. down to Oxford to "Commemoration"—James Bryce, who as Regius Professor of Civil Law, presents, in a gorgeous crimson robe, the honorary D.C.L.s hav-ing invited me, very kindly, to stay at his college, (Oriel.)   I occupied there some pleasant rooms & found the thing very jolly.   I have writ-ten of it, however, somewhere & won't say much here.[3]   In the a.m. I breakfasted with little Chas. Wyman of America (Mrs. Whitman's

brother) who is studying "History" at Oriel. Then I went to commemoration—then I lunched at All-Souls with Montagu Bernard—a
big feast & a charming affair:[4] then I went to a beautiful garden fête
at Worcester College: then I dined with the little Oriel Dons, in the
common-room. After which I took the late train, with Bryce, back
to London. I have dined out hardly at all. Two or three unmemorable dinners at the frequently-inviting Mrs. Rogerson's: a pleasant
one, with good people, at Mrs. Edward Dicey's: a most amusing one
at Greenwich with Woolner:[5] the annual Greenwich dinner of a sort
of Bohemianish-literary-artist-club; composed, however, not of 1st
class men, but of persons somewhat of the Hepworth-Dixon calibre:[6]
he looking like a 3[d] rate Bulwer,[7] making the principal speech. The
dinner was wondrous for fish & champagne, & the occasion most entertaining. A lot of hard-working London professional men frankly
taking a holiday are not such a bad lot—if for nothing else than the
handsome share of the individual (even if he himself is not remarkable) in the magnificent temperament of the race, which comes out so
strongly, & on the whole so estimably, at such an affair.—I got another
day in the country by going down to lunch with my old friend Coulson near Richmond.[8] It was a lovely day & a lovely region & we
walked & lounged for a while delightfully, in Richmond & Sudbrook
Parks. I have also been to 2 garden-parties at the Duchess of Argyll's—she having invited me at the friendly prompting of Geo. Howard. They are very pretty & full of fine folks, some few of whom I
knew, & could talk to. But my intercourse with the family did not
get further than shaking hands with the poor dropsical (or paralytic)
Duchess & the Marquis of Lorne.[9] I didn't even have a chance of
falling on my face before the Prince of Wales,[10] as yesterday (the last
party) most of the people managed to do.—I dined one day this week
at Mrs. Dugdale's—a niece of Ld. Macaulay (daughter of Lady Trevelyan) & a nice friendly little woman.[11] The next day I feasted with
M[me] du Quaire[12] whom I used to see in Paris at M[me] de Blocqville's—
a big, fashionable blonde, English widow of a Frenchman of some
position, I believe, who lives ½ in London, ½ in Paris, & gives dinners
& is liked, in both places. I took in a queer very clever, old woman,
Mrs. Alfred Wigan, an ex-actress, who, with her husband, appears to
be much in circulation in London society.[13] Indeed all her talk was—
"Yes, as the Queen said to me the other day at Osborne;" and "the
dear Prss. Beatrice is so deliciously *naïve*." I dine to day at Charles
Rose's (Lady R.'s son) who seems a very nice fellow, lives like a lord, &
invited me a month ago.—The only other "outing" I have had—but

'twas rather an *inning*—was taking Julia Ward Howe & daughter over St. Bartholomew's hospital.[14]   This sounds like a queer errand for me; as indeed it was.   But a very good young fellow, the Warden of the Hptl. had asked me to come & see it; & as Mrs. Howe had demanded of me to show her some of London, I've killed 2 birds with one stone, & got credit with both parties.   But the mission would have been for you; the hospital is most ancient & interesting—with nothing in it—but the patients later than the 12th century, & one of the most beautiful old Norman chapels you can see.—I must break as I have got to go & see your—excuse me but I must say, accursed friend Miss Hillard,[15] who has turned up here & writes me a note every three days, appointing an interview.   I do what I can; but she will certainly tell you that I neglect her horribly.   Do you admire her, particularly?   She is, I suppose, a very honorable specimen of her type; but the type—the literary spinster, sailing-into-your intimacy-American-hotel piazza type—doesnt bear somehow, the mellow light of the old world.   Miss H. announced her arrival here to me by writing to ask me to take her to the Grosvenor Gallery[16] & Rembrandt etchings[17] & then go out & dine with her—at Hammersmith miles away!—at the Conway's.[18]   And this a maid whom I had never seen!—I have in the interval of my two sentences driven over to the remote region of Paddington & back, at an expense of 3/, to see Miss H., whom I did not find.   But she will nevertheless deem that I have neglected her.—Excuse the freedom of my speech, which I have not stinted, as I have no reason to suppose that you are "soft" upon her. (Of course I went immediately to see her, after the Grosvenor Gallery proposition, which I was utterly unable to accept.   I spent a large part of a Sunday afternoon with her.)   Tell mother I also instantly called upon Mrs. Van Buren, who sent me a note, just as she was leaving town. I saw only her 2 little daughters—2 amiable little sprigs of Fishkill.   I have just heard from Baron Osten Sacken that he is here, & hope to see him tomorrow, & get news of you.[19]   Lawrence Walsh & his Uncle called upon me yesterday, & seemed in good spirits: but as they are living at an inn in the City, & seem much disposed, & very competent, to take care of themselves, I don't suppose I shall see much of them; especially as I believe they spend but 5 or 6 days.[20] Sara Sedgwick has just gone back to the country, suddenly, after a short stay in town during which I saw less of her than I should have liked.   She was exhausted with London, & gave up a visit to the A. Dicey's, during which I was expecting to approach her more, as she was to be much nearer.   But I did 2 or 3 things for her, & went to see

her when I could.   She seemed in good spirits & very lovely & pleasant to be with.—I went (2 days since) to see the Ashburners the last
thing before they sailed & sent you all my blessings by them.   Unfortunately I had nothing else to send—save to A., a small tribute, which
I hope will reach her safely, & which she is not to sneer at because it
doesn't bear the mark of the *fabricant* with whom she is familiar.   It is
by the most correct artist here—the cream of the cream—who leaves
her old friend far behind.   I informed myself carefully, at the highest sources: wrote to the Princess of Wales.—I got yesterday a note
from Lord Houghton, who had had a fall from his horse in the Park
& was slightly crippled, asking me to come in (he lives near) & sit with
him.   I of course responded.   He is a queer, but most kind & human
old fellow, & is getting better.—Also I had another call from Lady
Selina Bidwell, whom I think I have mentioned.[21]   This time she had
not the pretext of Joukowsky's picture, which I have sent away; but
being in town (from Brighton) for the day & near my lodging, she
comes up *en bonne camarade* for a little chat.   And talk after that of
the coldness & stiffness of the English aristocracy.   And Lady S. is the
best of women—not at all adventurous or "fast."   I had also a visit
yesterday from Frederick Wedmore, an amiable weakling of the aesthetic school, who writes in the Academy.   (He is noted for the close
of one of his articles: he was speaking of Dutch painting.   "Then—
Cuyp."   That was all the sentence.)[22]   I enclose a notice of the American from the *Daily News*.   I esteem it a considerable compliment that
Frank Hill, the editor, a fiercely busy man, should have found time to
read it, & write me a very good, appreciative little note about it; which
I should enclose if I hadn't lost it.   (He didn't write the notice.)   The
American will be reviewed (I learn) in the *Saturday Rev.*; probably, indifferently well, as 'tis by Walter Pollock, a very amiable mediocrity.[23]
Apropos of this matter, I forgot to thank father for enclosing poor
T.S.P.'s note of distress to you about the treatment of *his* article in the
Nation.   I am very sorry for his distress, & wrote to him.   The notice
was respectable; but it was helpless & unperceptive in poor Garrison
(*as* regards *me*) to cut out his comments.[24]—Behold all the base gossip
I can invent.   When I next write to you I probably shall have taken
flight to some rural retreat.   I shall certainly not stop in London to
the end of July, as I until lately purposed, or supposed I purposed.
It is too hot & noisy & I find it impossible (especially living where I
do—in Mayfair) to fix my attention upon work, & I must without delay get to work at my novel for next year, the beginnings of which
must be ready by the autumn.[25]   I have besides no people I care for

to stay here for, & no invitations ahead. I don't know where I shall go; but I shall go somewhere. I am afraid of the dullness of the English watering place—afraid of the lonely chop, for breakfast, for lunch & for dinner, in a lodging on some genteel, cockneyfied Crescent or Terrace. But I shall try it, as soon as possible; & if I break down I shall go abroad, where I hope, in any event, to go in September. (Of course I expect to be back here for the winter.) (Address always *here*, for I shall keep a lien on my rooms.) I wish you all every joy, & (especially father) complete invigoration. Little Jim Putnam came again to see me 'tother day, & I have asked him to dine with me somewhere in the country, day & place yet to be fixed.—Mrs. Kemble has left town for Switzerland; & I miss her as we had become very good friends. Write me all about Newport & about everything— about your *philosophical* prospects. Tell A.K. with infinite love, that I will answer her two letters directly I get out of this dusty, noisy, headachy Babylon, where, in spite of having decked my 2 balconies with flowers & awnings, the turbid atmosphere palls upon me.

Ever dear Bro. your fond   H.Jjr.

ALS: MH bMS Am 1094 (1977)

[1] Two translations of *The American* appeared in 1877, one by Heichen-Abenheim and the other by Moritz Busch. A third translation of *The American* appeared the following year. Edel, *HJL*, 2:121n, says that HJ has in mind Heichen-Abenheim, who supplied the novel with a happy ending.

[2] A rocky promontory in Newport.

[3] HJ, "Three Excursions," *Galaxy* 24 (September 1877): 346–56.

[4] Montague Bernard (1820–1882), British jurist, professor at Oxford.

[5] Thomas Woolner (1825–1892), British sculptor.

[6] William Hepworth Dixon (1821–1879), British editor and author.

[7] Sir Henry Bulwer (1801–1872), British diplomat and writer, or his brother, Edward George Earle Lytton Bulwer-Lytton, 1st baron (1803–1873), British novelist.

[8] In a letter to his parents of 9 November 1875, HJ mentions "my old friend Coulson of Hamburg" who is married to a Miss Unwin, the great-granddaughter of Mrs. Mary Unwin who sheltered William Cowper (1731–1800), British poet (*HJL*, 2:4–5).

[9] John Douglas Sutherland Campbell (1845–1914), marquess of Lorn, later 9th duke of Argyll. His wife was Princess Louise Caroline Alberta (b. 1848), daughter of Queen Victoria.

[10] Albert Edward, Prince of Wales (1841–1910), succeeded his mother, Queen Victoria, in 1901.

[11] Thomas Babington Macaulay, 1st baron (1800–1859), British historian and statesman. His nephew was Sir George Otto Trevelyan, whose wife was Caroline Philips Trevelyan. Trevelyan's sister Alice Frances Trevelyan married William Stratford Dugdale (1828–1882).

[12] Not identified.

[13] Leonora Wigan (1805–1884), British actress, wife of Alfred Wigan.

[14] St. Bartholomew's Hospital was founded in 1123.

[15] On the back of the letter's last page WJ wrote: 'Do you notice the demoniac way in which he speaks of the sweet Miss Hillard? [*short rule*] I have sent the times last week—and will promptly send father's corresp. with Abbot. W.J.' WJ is referring to a series of letters Henry James contributed to *The Index* in 1876 (7:26, 52, 74–75, 134–35, 172–73, 230–31). *The Index* was edited by Francis Ellingwood Abbot (1836–1903), American philosopher.

[16] Grosvenor Gallery opened on 1 May 1877 and emphasized works by Burne-Jones.

[17] The Burlington Fine Arts' Club sponsored an exhibition of some 200 Rembrandt etchings.

[18] Moncure Daniel Conway (1832–1907), American clergyman and biographer, was then living at Hamlet House, Hammersmith, a borough of London.

[19] Nicolai Dmitrievich, count von der Osten-Sacken (d. 1912), Russian diplomat.

[20] John Lawrence Walsh (1847–1879), son of James William Walsh, WJ's mother's brother. The uncle was not identified.

[21] Not identified.

[22] The article was not found in *Academy and Literature* (London).

[23] Walter Herries Pollock (1850–1926), British lawyer and critic. The review of *The American* in *Saturday Review* 44 (18 August 1877): 214–15, is unsigned.

[24] A review of *The American* by Thomas Sergeant Perry, *Nation* 24 (31 May 1877): 325–26. The editor of the *Nation* was Wendell Phillips Garrison (1840–1907).

[25] HJ's next novel to appear as a serial was *The Europeans*, in *Atlantic Monthly*, July 1878–October 1878 (vol. 42).

From Henry James

3 Bolton St. July 10th [1877]

Dear W^{m}—Yesterday came your letter of June 24th, (having taken a most extraordinary time for its journey—15 days—) containing your excellent photog., Alice's note about her hat (which I will comply with) & last, but not least, the startling news of Lowell's application for me to be his Secretary in Spain.[1] This is altogether news to me, Lowell not having written to me a word on the subject. I know not what to think of it, & in the complete absence of data, almost wish either that I knew much more, or knew not the fact, as yet, at all. If the appointment comes to me I suppose I shall decide to accept it, tho' the rose will not seem to me to be altogether without thorns. It will cost me something to give up London, which I have thoroughly taken up with, & to forfeit for three or four years the opportunity of work. I suppose a secretary of legation cannot with dignity and propriety contribute light articles to periodical literature; & yet I have an idea also that without writing occasionally, the salary is not sufficient to maintain one in gt. ease. On this & on other points I am quite in the air & in the dark. I am sufficiently excited by the prospect to feel a sensible disappointment if it comes to nothing, & am quite ignorant of how far Lowell's choice of me carries with it the presumption of my getting the place. At moments it seems too good to be true: for a salaried post enabling me to do a small amount of 1ˢᵗ class work at leisure & remit this constant mercenary scribbling, has long been my delightful dream. I am also, as you may suppose, inflamed at the idea of seeing & knowing Spain. To Lowell himself I am of course most devoutly grateful. But I seriously dread the climate—especially the confinement at Madrid during the summer heats. There are likewise other things. But I won't, for good or for ill, count my chickens before they are hatched; I will only wait patiently for the event & above all for further information. If the event hangs fire, (as the suspense to me is, as regards my personal plans & arrangements, materially awkward) I wish you would write me such information as you can gather, as regards probability, salary &c. I don't like to write to Lowell until he has written to me about the matter.————

You see I am still in London, tho' a week ago I hoped to have got off by by to day or tomorrow. But London is not a place where, after 7 months residence, one can pull up stakes abruptly; & as the weather has lately (until to day) been extremely cool, I have lingered on. What has kept me last has been an invitation from Charles Gaskell, (H. Adams's friend) or from his wife, Lady Catherine G., to go down for 3 days to Wenlock Abbey, their place, or one of their places, in Shropshire. I was on the point of declining it as I was deadly desirous to get away from London, when, by an odd chance, came a letter fr. H. Adams saying—"If Gaskell asks you to Wenlock don't for the world fail to go";² & adding other remarks, of a most attractive kind: the upshot of wh. has been that I have accepted the invitation, & go on the 12ᵗʰ, to stay to the 16ᵗʰ. It is, according to Murray's *Shropshire*,³ a very exquisite place: a medieval Abbey, half ruined, ½ preserved & restored.—For the rest, I have in these latter days neither seen nor done much in London: though somehow, in the simple paying of farewell calls, &c., the days have melted away without remunerative occupation. I am aching to get into some quiet rural spot & at work: for the last fortnight here, I have been utterly unable to fix my attention. Until this Spanish news came I had meant directly after my return from Wenlock, to take boat, by night, straight from Newhaven to Dieppe, & settle down there (or at some place near it on the Norman coast) for the next 6 weeks. But if I am really to go before long to Madrid, I would rather remain in England until I start. I hope by the time I return from Wenlock I shall hear something definite; for I don't even know whether to begin work upon a novel I have projected for next year. If I go to Madrid I shall postpone it; & if I don't must begin without more than an already extreme delay.—I have scarcely dined out. Once at Mrs. Rogerson's, to meet Eugene Schuyler (with whom, & Mackenzie Wallace I 2 days later breakfasted.)[4] Once at Smalley's, in comp'y. with Huxley, Senator Conkling of N.Y. (a most extraordinary specimen!)[5] the Edward Diceys, Mr. Eliot (the "house-hold" man, of Boston) &c:[6] a most singular medley: Conkling "orat-ing" softly & longwindedly the whole dinner-time, with a kind of baleful fascination. On Sunday (2 days since) I dined *en famille* at the Huxley's. I wish you knew H., himself. I lunched once at Lord Houghtons at one of his great medleys—Miss Rhoda Broughton ("Cometh up as a Flower"), W$\underline{m}$ Black, a little red-faced cad of a Scotchman who says "aboot", "doobt" &c.:[7] Capt. Burnaby ("Ride to Khina,")[8] poor little Frederick Wedmore & others. To day I had dear Benson (whom I haven't seen in months) to breakfast: I lunched at the Andrew Langs, & I dine at M$\underline{me}$ Van de Weyer's for which last I must now swiftly dress.[9]—11½ p.m. I have just come in from dinner at M$\underline{me}$ de Van Weyer's, a big luscious & ponderous banquet, where I sat between the fat M$\underline{me}$ V. de W. & the fatter Miss *do*; but was re-warded by the presence & by some talk with, the adorable Mrs. Lyulph Stanley.[10] I can think of no other gayeties or gossip. I went the other night to a musical party at M$\underline{me}$ du Quaire's, where I saw the once famous Mrs. Ronalds, of America, who has lately turned up here again, & who though somewhat "gone off," as they say here, is still as pretty as an angel. I also lunched at the Greek chargé d'af-faires, a very nice fellow, whom I knew at the Athenaeum (which I still frequent & prize) & who entertained Mrs. Howe & daughter, & the Baker family.[11] I also lunched at Mrs. Pakenham's & ate strawberries (3) as big as my fist.—I did what I could further about Miss Hillard, who has left London: called again upon her & saw her, & went to a party at the Boughtons' in order to meet her, where, having found her I quitted Mrs. Mark Pattison for her & adhered to her for the rest of the evening. She is a good girl: her faults are that she is herself too adhesive, too interrogative & too epistolary. I have rec'd. (I think) 7 notes & letters from her, for 2 or 3 that I have written her.—

Your acct. of Class-day sounded very pretty;[12] but prettier still was the announcement of yr. speedy departure for Newport; which I hope will be fraught with rarest charm. Many thanks for your criticisms on my articles (G.S. &c.) which are much to the point & very useful. Farewell; love to all—from yr. fond brother

H. James jr.

Tell A that I will myself attend to her *hat*, when it comes.

ALS: MH bMS AM 1094 (1978)

[1] James Russell Lowell, appointed American minister to Spain, wanted HJ to serve as a secretary. Edel, *HJL*, 2:125n, comments: "Nothing came of his request for HJ, the State Department taking the sensible view that one inexperienced diplomat in a legation sufficed."

[2] The letter is not published in *The Letters of Henry Adams*.

[3] *Handbook for Shropshire, Cheshire, and Lancashire* (1870), published by John Murray.

[4] Eugene Schuyler (1840–1890), American traveler, diplomat, and author; Donald Mackenzie Wallace (1841–1919), Scottish-born journalist and editor.

[5] Roscoe Conkling (1829–1888), American politician.

[6] Samuel Eliot (1821–1898), Boston philanthropist. A household man is a male servant.

[7] William Black (1841–1898), Scottish journalist and biographer.

[8] Frederick Gustavus Burnaby (1842–1885), British soldier and adventurer, *A Ride to Khiva: Travels and Adventures in Central Asia* (1876).

[9] Sylvain Van de Weyer (d. 1874), Belgian ambassador to Great Britain. His wife was an American, the daughter of Joshua Bates, a banker. Their daughter is referred to in the following sentence as 'Miss *do*' [i.e., 'Miss *ditto*'].

[10] Mary Katharine Bell Stanley, wife of Edward Lyulph Stanley, 4th Baron Stanley of Alderley (1839–1925), British lawyer and politician.

[11] Probably Sir Samuel White Baker (1821–1893), British traveler, and his wife Florence Baker.

[12] A part of Harvard graduation ceremonies.

From Henry James

3 Bolton St. Picc. Jan 28. [1878]

Dear W<u>m</u>. Your letter, dictated to mother & accompanied with a note from herself, arrived some two days since; & more lately came another little letter from dear mammy. It was a great satisfaction to hear from you at last; but I was sorry to find that you were still obliged to borrow other people's eyes. I hope that by this time you have got pretty well master of your own. It is a pleasure to hear however, that apart from your eyes you are robust & elastic & able to do your needful work without scamping. You go into no especial detail about anything: but your allusion to your possible visit to Baltimore & its results was highly interesting.[1] May the visit, if you make it, be delightful & the results *solidissimi*. I subscribed to the two periodicals instantly (with the missing *Mind*,) & I enclose the two bills.   Please, when you send the amount of these, do so by P.O. order.   I have, also, just rec'd. the volume of Chauncey Wright which I am very glad to possess & am much obliged for.[2]   I have had no time to look at it.—In the way of news, the most recent is that I returned 2 hours since from spending Sunday (yesterday) with Sara Sedgwick, at Basset: (I went on Saturday in time for dinner.)   The visit was very pleasant, although it poured with rain from the moment of my arrival.   Sara seems utterly unchanged by matrimony—neither exhilarated nor depressed: very sweet, soft, gentle & without initiative.   She is in a densely English *milieu* & has a densely English husband.   Both, however, are excellent in their way.   Darwin is a very gentle, kindly, reasonable, liberal, bald-headed, dull-eyed, British-featured, sandy-haired little *insulaire*, who will to a certainty never fail of goodness & carefulness towards his wife & who must have merit, & a great deal of it, to have appreciated merit so retiring, appealing & delicate as Sara's.   He is fond of conversation & laughter, of books & etchings, & was particularly nice in his manner to Theodora.   The latter struck me as the brilliant feature of the affair.   Whether or no it is from juxtaposition with the British Female, but at all events Theodora appeared a miracle of beauty, elegance grace & intellectual sparkle.   She strikes me as greatly improved—probably by the influence of Chas. Norton. Sara, as I say, is wholly unmodified.   But I have no doubt she will be reasonably happy, & she certainly did a wise thing (so far as one can tell) in marrying.   Her house is a very pretty roomy villa, with charming grounds & views, completely in the country, though in the midst of a very agreeable residential suburb of Southampton.   She is surrounded by plenty of solid British comfort, & judged by American habits would appear to be mistress of an opulent home.   She had on Saturday a couple of genteel people (very pleasant ones) to dinner & apparently may have as much as she desires of the society of the "upper middle class:" the more so as she keeps a very pretty brougham! Altogether, she struck me as very happy & comfortable, & I should have great confidence in Darwin & his prosaic virtues.—As regards other matters my London life flows evenly along, making, I think in various ways more & more of a Londoner of me.   If I keep along here patiently for a certain time I rather think I shall become a (sufficiently) great man.   I have got back to work with great zest after my autumnal loafings, & mean to do some this year which will make a mark.   I am, as you suppose, weary of writing articles about places, & mere potboilers of all kinds; but shall probably, after the next six months, be able to forswear it altogether, & give myself up seriously to "creative" writing.   Then, & not till then, my real career will begin. After that, *Gare à vous!*—I find here to day a note from Wilky enclosing 2 very pretty photos. of his children, who seem, especially the boy, very handsome & solid & make me desire much to be near them. But poor W. gives a sorry account of his present business & says he means to leave it & look for a clerkship, in March.   He seems to have a rude career; but I hope his wife eases him down.   Please send me (the next who writes) Bob's Milwaukee address.   I wish to send him the illustrated papers &c for this year—as I did last.   *So please make a point of this.*

Under the usual heading of my dinings-out there is very little to relate. I feasted some time ago (just as I was last writing, I think) with Augustus Hare (or rather an old aunt of his a genteel high Tory old lady.)   There I took out Lady Eastlake, widow of the painter; one of those dense, positive, accomplished, specialising old London gentle-women whom one so often meets.[3]   I dined also (as a contrast) with Henrietta Temple & consort.   Her husband seems a very charming & attractive boy, & Henrietta was less undeveloped than I supposed. But they seem, in this huge metropolis, to be people of barely appreciable magnitude or maturity.—I also dined one day at Sir Garnet Wolseley's—amid the usual collection of rich accessories (it is a beautiful old house in Portman Square, filled with Queen Anne bric à brac to a degree that quite flattens one out) plain women, gentlemanly men &c.   After dinner I was entertained of course (the men were all, I think, army men) with plenty of the densest war talk.   Sir Garnet is a very handsome, well-mannered & fascinating little man—with rosy dimples and an eye of steel: an excellent specimen of the *cultivated* British soldier.   But my slight acquaintance is chiefly with his wife, who is pretty, & has the air, the manners, the toilets & the taste, of an American.—I went one night to a very pretty musical party at Hamilton Aidé's,[4] full of actors, actresses & artists, where Mrs. Ronalds (the American) who has appeared again, in a miraculous way on the surface of London society, sang, very strikingly.   Another night I went with Lady Gordon & Lady Wade (her sister)[5] to see Henry Irving in "Chas. I"; an occasion on which the combined wretchedness of the performance & satisfaction of the full-dressed audience *en* suggested to me *plus long* regarding the British mind than I can attempt to give a notion of here.   From the continental point of view it made one think more basely of human nature.   But of British artistry one cannot think too basely.   I am going, in another hour, to dine with my friend of last winter Mrs. Rogerson, who has but just returned from Scotland. Between her & the Smalleys, who were formerly near & dear to each other, there now reigns a mysterious "madness." I don't know the reason of it—& am simply sure in a general way that the fault (something bad has happened) cannot be with the Smalleys, who are generically irreproachable: but though it was they who introduced me to Mrs. R. I haven't dropped her; as to me she continues to be extremely *gentille.* I see little of the Smalleys, who are very *mondains* & dine out three times a day. They are a good example of the way that people always (or almost always) make up for the extremes of their destiny. Reared in New England Abolitionism & asceticism they never had any "society" in the early part of their career, & in consequence they go in for it now, tooth & nail. It is curious to see the Londonization of Mrs. S., a perfect & very pretty, product of Watertown. But an end to this idle gossip, which I give you for local color's sake, & to gratify the intellectual femininity of mother & Alice. It is 7 o'clock & I must dress for dinner.—Nothing, of course, is talked of here but the War & the possible share of England in it. Three days since, this appeared great, but now that an armistice has been made, the excitement (for a moment it was intense) has diminished.[6] The military & aristocratic Turcophiles are certainly detestable (it was interesting to see them *en famille* at Sir G. Wolseley's) but one would detest them more if one did not want to keep one's skirts clear of the equally odious peace-at-any price, "Manchester"-minded party.[7] An empire so artificial as that of Great Britain must be vigilant & jealous, not to begin to crack & crumble, & one has a feeling that from the day the vigilance & jealousy let "Manchester" get the upper hand, the ancient greatness of Britain has begun to decay. It may be that the ancient greatness of Britain has been an iniquity, an "hypocrisy" & an insolence: but to live here is (for me) to feel a kindness for the products of those energetic qualities of the race that are the compensation for its want of charm. At any rate I believe England will keep out of war for the reason that up to this stage of her relation to events in the East, her going to war would be simply for the sake of her "prestige," & that the nation as a whole, looking at the matter deliberately, have decided that mere prestige is not sufficient ground for a huge amount of bloodshed. This seems to me to indicate a high pitch of civilization—a pitch which England alone, of all the European nations, has reached. It has been curious to see that all the French republican papers have lately been denouncing her fiercely for not pitching into Russia—the defense of prestige being a perfectly valid *casus belli* to the French mind.—It certainly remains to be seen whether in material respects England can afford to abdicate even such a privilege as that.   I have a sort of feeling that if we are to see the déchéance of England it is inevitable, & will come to pass somewhat in this way.   She will push further & further her non-fighting & keeping-out-of-scrapes-policy, until contemptuous Europe, growing audacious with impunity, shall put upon her some supreme & unendurable affront.   Then—too late—she will rise ferociously & plunge clumsily & unpreparedly into war.   She will be worsted & laid on her back—& when she is laid on her back will exhibit—in her colossal wealth & pluck—an unprecedented power of resistance.   But she will never really recover, as a European power, & will find that there is no chance in the armed-to-the-teeth Europe of our time for a country whose stubbornly aristocratic social arrangements make compulsory military service—the standing together in the ranks of peasants, "cads" & gentlemen—fatally impossible! Such is the vision I sometimes entertain, & which events, doubtless, will consummately bring to naught.

Midnight.   I have come in from dinner & will close this interminable scrawl before I go to bed.   I dined, as I think I mentioned, with Mrs. Rogerson, with her usual little set of intimates: Sir Frederick & Lady Pollock, the Hills, Lady Gordon &c.   But the dinner, I am sorry to say, was dullish, & I have nothing particular to relate of it.   I am also tired, with a busy day & a walk down from Queen's Gate.—I hope everything is smooth at home & am very glad you are having so "glorious" (as mother says,) a winter.   Here it is very much better than last, & with nothing in the world to call cold. Thank mother for her letters; I hope father thrives in the fine weather.   If you do go to Baltimore let me hear as much as possible about it.   Goodnight!

Your faithful | H.J.jr

ALS: MH bMS Am 1094 (1979)

[1] From 11 February 1878 to 22 February, WJ lectured at Johns Hopkins University in Baltimore on "The Senses and the Brain and Their Relation to Thought" (for his notes see WJ, *Manuscript Lectures* [Cambridge: Harvard Univ. Press, 1988]).   At the same time he was discussing with Daniel Coit Gilman, president of Johns Hopkins, the possibility of an appointment.   Many of the details are recorded in WJ's correspondence with Gilman.

[2] Wright, *Philosophical Discussions.*

[3] Lady Elizabeth Rigby Eastlake (1809–1893), British author, widow of Sir Charles Lock Eastlake (1793–1865), British painter.

[4] Charles Hamilton Aïdé (1826–1906), French-born composer and playwright.

[5] Amelia Herschel Wade, daughter of John Frederick William Herschel, wife of Sir Thomas Francis Wade (1818–1895), British diplomat.

[6] An armistice in the Russo-Turkish War was arranged as of 31 January 1878.

[7] A liberal movement associated with the city of Manchester led by Richard Cobden (1804–1865), British statesman, and John Bright (1811–1889), British orator. Their position was that Britain should not interfere in the long-standing conflict between Russia and Turkey.

From Henry James

3 Bolton St. W. May 1st [1878]

Dear William—Since I last wrote home two good letters have come to me—your's of April 7th, & Mother's of the 15th do. I will answer you 1st, as I have written more lately to mother. It was very agreeable to see your definite handwriting again, & I hope it is a sign of real eye-betterment. Your letter was forwarded to me more than a week since, while I was down in Herefordshire spending a couple of days with Florence Wilkinson. This had been a very perfunctory performance; but it proved to be, for that short period, very comfortable. I am far from meaning, however, to go back for a fortnight, as I got off only by falsely promising to do. It is a picturesque, ancient house, of the Tudor days (much modernized) with nothing to speak of in the way of grounds, but standing in a very charming & what they call here "wild" country, close to the Welsh border. Mary W. & spouse were also there, & she & her sister are both very nice, gentle, ladylike women. Their respective husbands are also very good men. St. John Matthews, (Florence's) is a very handsome, distinguished well-dressed personage, with very proper, polite manners & no perceptible aroma of his native Birmingham. His cousin, Mary's consort, is a hardworking London solicitor, much less distingué, but very sharp & clever, & a Cambridge Wrangler. I walked with him one morning up a very pretty little Welsh mountain, & greatly enjoyed it. Mary W. is very sweet & innocent (though chronically depressed by having no children) &, by way of conversation, says to me, àpropos of nothing—"Is Mrs. James *very* fond of London?" Is she? Ask mother. Mary is in fact lovely; but the dullness, small provinciality, & "lower middle class" quality of the conversation & the *milieu* are incompatible with close relations. St. John Matthews is a "lower middle-class" Tory (of the type of Sara Sedgwick's famous cousin)[1] & one can't live or pretend to attempt to live, with such people—especially when their only other outlook on the universe consists of fly-fishing. The Wilkinson family are, I opine, in adoration & subservience before St.J.M., whom they consider a Phoenix of gentility &

pecuniosity. (He seems, in fact, very pecunious<.>)—Coming back to London I dined at the Oxford & Cambridge Club with Alexr. Carter, who had asked two or three other men—Sir David Wedderburn, who has been much in America,[2] &c; & this is the only dinner party I have lately attended. It is still Eastertide, "every one" is out of town, & there are no invitations. I profited by the stillness to run down for a couple of days to the Isle of Wight & call upon our little friend Miss Peabody—a design I had entertained more or less ever since she came to England. I had proceeded on the hypothesis that she was in solitude & desolation; but I found her *très-entourée*, having with her 4 other American women beside her mother, who is much better. But I enjoyed the wonderful prettiness of Ventnor & Boncherch, as well as seeing Miss P., with whom I walked on the downs & conversed, quite in the Boston manner. In spite of her 5 American women I think my visit was a benefaction to her & I am very glad to have made it. She was very nice, intelligent & charming; & it is a pleasure, immersed in Britishness as I am, to come in contact with the native *finesse* & animation of the American female mind; accompanied though it strike me as being with a certain thinness of nature & with much circumstantial crudity. The Isle of Wight is charming; but I shall probably "do" my impressions of it and of the Wilkinsonian country, in an article; so I won't expatiate here.[3]—There were, many interesting allusions in your letter which I shld. like to take up one by one. I should like to see the fair Hellenists of Baltimore;[4] & I greatly regret that, living over here, my person cannot profit by my American reputation. It is a great loss to have one's person in one country & one's glory in another, especially when there are lovely young women in the case. Neither can one's glory, then, profit by one's person—as I flatter myself, even in your jealous teeth, that mine might, in Baltimore!! Also about my going to Washington & its being my "duty," &c. I think there is much in that; but I can't whisk about the world quite so actively as you seem to recommend. It would be great folly for me, à peine established in London & getting a footing here, to break it all off for the sake of going to spend 4 or 5 mos. in Washington. I expect to spend many a year in London—I have submitted myself without reserve to that Londonizing process of which the effect is to convince you that, having lived here, you may, if need be, abjure civilization and bury yourself in the country; but may not, in pursuit of civilization, live in any smaller town. I am still completely an outsider here, and my only chance for becoming a little of an insider (in that limited sense in which an American can ever do so) is to remain

here for the present.   After that—a couple of years hence—I shall
go home for a year, embrace you all, & see everything of the country
I can, including Washington.   Meanwhile, if one will take what
comes, one is by no means cut off from getting American impressions
here.   I got ever so many, the other day, from my visit to the six Boston ladies at Ventnor.   I know what I am about, & I have always my
eyes on my native land.—I am very glad that Howells's play seemed
so pretty, on the stage.   Much of the dialogue, as it read, was certainly
charming; but I should have been afraid of the slimness & un-scenic
quality of the plot.[5]   For myself (in answer to your adjuration) it has
long been my most earnest & definite intention to commence at play-
wrighting as soon as I can.   This will now be soon, & then I shall
astound the world!   My inspection of the French theatre will fructify.
I have thoroughly mastered Dumas, Augier & Sardou (whom it is
greatly lacking to Howells—by the way—to have studied;) & I know
all they know & a great deal more besides.   Seriously speaking, I
have a great many ideas on this subject, & I sometimes feel tempted
to retire to some frugal village, for 12 months, where, my current
expenses being inconsiderable, I might have leisure to work them off.
Even I could only find some manager or publisher sufficiently devoted to believe in this and make me an allowance for such a period,
I would afterwards make a compact and sign it with my blood, to
reimburse him in thousands.   But I shall not have to come to this, or
to depend upon it.—I rec'd. a few days since your article on H. Spencer, but I have not yet had time to read it.[6]   I shall very presently
attack—I won't say understand, it.   Mother speaks to me of your articles in Renouvier's magazine—& why have you not sent me these?[7]
I wish you would do so, punctually.   I met Herbert Spencer the other
Sunday at George Eliot's, whither I had at last bent my steps.   G. H.
Lewes introduced me to him as an American; & it seemed to me that
at this fact, coupled with my name, his attention was aroused & he
was on the point of asking me if I were related to you.   But something instantly happened to separate me from him, & soon afterwards he went away.   The Leweses were very urbane & friendly & I
think that I shall have the right *dorénavant* to consider myself a Sunday *habitué*.   The great G.E. herself is both sweet and superior, & has
a delightful expression in her large, long, pale equine face.   I had
my turn at sitting beside her & being conversed with in a low, but most
harmonious tone; & bating a tendency to *aborder* only the highest
themes I have no fault to find with her.   Lewes told some of his usual
stories, chiefly French—the Frenchman who, coming out of a Berlin

salon, said "C'est un peuple froid, sec et disgracieux," &c.[8]   There were various other people there; the Du Mauriers, Sir James Paget &c.—But enough of London.—I hope your Easter vacation tuned you up & that you find comforting qualities in the advance of the spring.   Mother said more than it made me happy to hear about Alice's having been of late a good deal enfeebled; but as she also mentioned a promising *régime* she had entered upon, I hope the news is better now.   She also told me "all about" Miss Catherine Loring, whose strength of wind and limb, to say nothing of her nobler qualities, must make her a valuable addition to the Quincy St. circle.   Tell Alice I delight in the thought of her & she must send me her photo. I asked Miss Peabody about her, who said she greatly admired her, & had always timidly aspired to know her, but thought herself unworthy.   I had shuffled your note, now so old, about the cravats & toothbrushes away under some papers, where as it remained unseen, I completely & characteristically forgot it.   A 1000 regrets.   Just now, being rather low in pocket, I am only awaiting some money which must arrive from day to day, before *de me défaire* of the little sum needful for the purchase of your articles, which I will immediately send you.—We expect to hear any hour that war has broken out; & yet it may not.   It will be a good deal of a scandal if it does—especially if the English find themselves fighting side by side with the bloody, filthy Turks & their own Indian sepoys.   And to think that a clever Jew should have juggled old England into it![9]   The papers are full of the Paris exhibition, which opens to day; but it leaves me perfectly incurious.[10]

Blessings on all from your's fraternally   H. James jr
  P.S. to letter to W⍛.   I enclose, though I suppose you have seen it, a notice of my book from the *Saturday Rev.*   The shabbiness of its tone is such as really—n'est ce pas?—to make one think more meanly of human nature.   It is evidently, by intrinsic indication, by Walter Pollock.[11]   I rec'd. the notice in the *Evening Post*; & hope you will send me any more that you see.—I am sorry Lizzie B.'s pictures are a *fiasco*, but understand the impression they must make.   I am afraid both she & her father will feel it; & I hope it will at least have the effect of keeping her from returning to her detestable Couture.

ALS: MH bMS Am 1094 (1980)

[1] Since the remark is made after Sara Sedgwick's marriage to William Darwin, it is possible that HJ means a cousin by marriage.   This would point in the direction of Francis Galton, Charles Darwin's cousin, and, if the term is used loosely, a cousin of Sara Sedgwick's husband.   But Galton's biographers claim that he was a good social

companion, a good conversationalist, and nothing was found indicating HJ's view of Galton.

[2] Sir David Wedderburn (1836–1882), British politician and lawyer.

[3] Apparently not written.

[4] Nothing was found to cast light upon this obscure allusion. In February 1879 WJ delivered a course of lectures at Johns Hopkins University. In the lost letter to which HJ is replying, WJ must have reported some Baltimore gossip. The classicist at Johns Hopkins was Basil Laneau Gildersleeve (1831–1924) and it is said that Emma Louise Gildersleeve, his wife, was strikingly beautiful. It is possible that Emma Gildersleeve admired HJ, but no evidence of this or of meetings with WJ was found.

[5] *A Counterfeit Presentiment*, by William Dean Howells, was performed on 1 April 1878 at the Boston Museum.

[6] WJ, "Remarks on Spencer's Definition of Mind as Correspondence," *Journal of Speculative Philosophy* 12 (January 1878): 1–18.

[7] WJ, "Quelques considérations sur la méthode subjective," *Critique Philosophique*, 6th year, vol. 2 (24 January 1878): 407–13.

[8] George Henry Lewes (1817–1878), English philosopher and writer. He and George Eliot considered themselves married.

[9] Benjamin Disraeli (1804–1881) was prime minister of Great Britain.

[10] The Paris Universal Exposition.

[11] For the reference to a review of HJ by Pollock see letter of 28 June 1877. It is not clear whether the same review is meant in both cases.

From Henry James

THE REFORM CLUB[1] May 29th [1878]

Dear W^m.

You have my blessing indeed, & Miss Gibbens also; or rather Miss Gibbens particularly, as she will need it most. (I wish to pay her a compliment at your expense & to intimate that she gives more than she receives; yet I wish not to sacrifice you too much.)[2] Your letter came to me yesterday, giving me great joy, but less surprise than you might think. In fact, I was not surprised at all, for I had been expecting to get some such news as this from you. And yet of Miss Gibbens & your attentions I had heard almost nothing—a slight mention a year ago, in a letter of mother's, which had never been repeated. The wish, perhaps, was father to the thought. I had long wished to see you married; I believe almost as much in matrimony for most other people as I believe in it little for myself—which is saying a good deal. What you say of Miss Gibbens (even after I have made due allowance for natural partiality) inflames my imagination & crowns my wishes. I have great faith in the wisdom of your choice &

am prepared to believe everything good & delightful of its object.   I
am sure she has neither flaw nor failing.   Give her then my cordial—
my already fraternal—benediction.   I look forward to knowing her
as to one of the consolations of the future.   Very soon I will write to
her—in a few days.   Her photograph is indispensable to me—please
remember this; & also that a sketch of her from another hand than
your's—father's, mother's & Alice's—would be eminently satisfactory.
This must be a very pleasant moment to you—& I envy you your
actualities & futurities.   May they all minister to your prosperity &
nourish your genius! I don't believe you capable of making a marriage of which one must expect less than this.   Farewell, dear
brother, I will write before long again, & meanwhile I shall welcome
all contributions to an image of Miss Gibbens.

Always yours   H.J.jr

ALS: MH bMS Am 1094 (1981)

[1] The Reform Club was established in 1830–32 by liberal members of Parliament
as a way of supporting the Reform Bill.   It had numerous apartments for members
and was known for its splendor.

[2] WJ and AGJ became engaged on 10 May 1878.

From Henry James

REFORM CLUB, | PALL MALL. S.W. July 15th [1878]

Dear William:

I have just heard from mother that you had decided to be married
on the 10th ult., & as I was divorced from you by an untimely fate on
this unique occasion, let me at least repair the injury by giving you, in
the most earnest words that my clumsy pen can shape, a tender bridal
benediction.   I am very glad indeed to hear that you have ceased to
find occasion for delay, & that you were to repair to the happy Adirondacks under hymeneal influences.[1]   I should think you would
look look forward, in effect, to next winter's work more freely & fruit-
fully by getting your matrimonial start thus much earlier. May you
keep along at a pace of steady felicity!   The abruptness of your union
has prevented me from a becoming punctuality in sending Alice a
small material emblem of my good wishes; & now I shall wait till next
autumn & the beginning of your winter life.   I thank her meanwhile
extremely for the little note—the charming note—that she sent me
in answer to my own—& I feel most agreeably conscious of my inten-
sification of kinship.   I envy you your mountains & lakes—your

deep, free nature.   May it do you both—weary workers—all the good you deserve.

Ever your fond & faithful brother   H.J.jr

ALS: MH bMS Am 1094 (1982)

¹WJ and AGJ were married 10 July 1878 at the home of AGJ's grandmother, 153 Boylston St., Boston, by the Rev. Rufus Ellis.   For their honeymoon they went to Keene Valley in the Adirondacks.

From Henry James

REFORM CLUB, | PALL MALL. S.W. July 23ᵈ [1878]

Dear Wᵐ.

I just find your letter of July 8ᵗʰ, enclosing your wife's lovely photograph (which, having carefully, & as Ruskin says, "reverently," studied it, I re-enclose here, with a 1000 thanks.)   You tell me that you were to be married 2 days later, but you are painfully silent as to details— saying not a word as to the hour, or place, or manner of the ceremony—the officiating functionary, or any of those things which in such a case one likes to be told of.   I should not forgive you for this if it were not that I count upon mother, after the event, writing to me in a manner to supply deficiencies.   I wrote you briefly the other day, on 1ˢᵗ hearing that your marriage was coming off immediately—so that you know my sentiments about it.   I can best repeat them by saying that I rejoice in it as if it were my own; or rather much more. I wish I could pay you a visit in your romantic shanty, among those mountains with which you must now be so familiar & which I have never seen.   It will surely be the beginning of a beautiful era for you. You have only to go about your work, & health & happiness will take care of themselves.—Yes, I know that it must be a sad summer in Cambridge, & my thoughts are constantly in Quincy St.   But I note what you say about the amelioration of poor Alice's symptoms.¹   She must have been having a tragic time; but I hope most earnestly it is melting away.   I am much interested in the prospect of the Baltimore professorship, of which you speak, & surely hope that, since you desire it, you will quietly come into it.   But I shall regret, on grounds of "general culture," &c that you should detach yourself from Harvard College.   It must, however, conduce to "general culture" to have Baltimore winters instead of Massachusetts ones.   Bravo also for the Holt psychology & its coincidence with your labors.²   May it go along triumphantly.   I am very glad indeed that you were pleased with

"Daisy Miller," who appears (*literally*) to have made a great hit here.[3] "Every one is talking about it" &c, & it has been much noticed in the papers.   Its success has encouraged me as regards the faculty of appreciation of the English public; for the thing is sufficiently subtle, yet people appear to have comprehended it.   It has given me a capital start here, & in future I shall publish all my things in English magazines (at least all the *good* ones) & sell advance sheets in America; thereby doubling my profits.   I am much obliged to you for your economical advice; such advice is never amiss, but I don't think I specifically need it.   I think I am decently careful, & have no fear but that, after a little, I shall be able at once to live very comfortably, to "put by," & to make an allowance to each member of the family.   This is my dream.   I am very impatient to get at work writing for the stage—a project I have long had.   I am morally certain I should succeed, & it would be an open gate to money-making.   The "great novel" you ask about is only begun; I am doing other things just now. It is the history of an *Americana*—a female counterpart to Newman.[4] I have the option of publishing it in *Macmillan* or in the *Cornhill* (with preference given to the former), & I hope to be able to get at work upon it this autumn; though I am not sure.—As regards the *Europeans* I am very sorry, & it is a great injustice to it, that it should have been advertised or talked of as a *novel*.   It is only a sketch—very brief & with no space for much action; in fact it is a "study," like Daisy Miller.   (I am just completing, by the way, a counterpart to *D.M.*, for the *Cornhill*.)[5]   I have no personal news of any value.   It is very hot indeed, at last—though not so terrible as I see by the papers it has been at home, as I am afraid F. & M. & Alice & A.K. must have felt to their cost.   I shall be in London all summer, as I have plenty of occupation here.   I have rec'd. several invitations to pay short visits, but have declined them all, save one for a week at Wenlock Abbey (Charles Gaskell's) on August 10th.   I have just telegraphed a refusal to Wm Spottiswoode, the new Presdt. of the Royal Society, who has a very charming place down in Kent.   I shall, however, probably go to spend next Sunday with Sara Darwin.   I rejoice in your rejoicings in my fat, & would gladly cut off fifty lbs. or so and send them to you as a wedding-gift.   I am extremely well, & though London heat is rather a vile compound, I, strange to say, like it.   I was sure I had acknowledged the P.O. order for 15$: a thousand pardons.   I sent home the toothbrushes and cravats by Theodora S.,[6] & took the liberty of joining to them the present of a pair of hair brushes, for travelling, in a leather case.   I got only SIX cravats; & could not get them of the maker you designated.   But I will send another six by a near opportunity.   Read all this to Alice: it is a great pleasure to me to be writing to her too, as I always shall in writing to you.   Here I sit with the uproar of Charing X in my ears,[7] & envy you your strange wood-land life.   May it be excellent for you this summer.   You had better forward this to Cambridge; it will eke out my correspondence there. Farewell; all my love to your wife.   Seeing her photo. & getting an image of her beautiful face has made all the difference.

Yours,   H.J.jr

ALS: MH bMS Am 1094 (1983)

[1] Strouse argues that WJ's marriage worsened AJ's condition; see *AJB*, 183–90.

[2] WJ signed a contract with Henry Holt & Co. to write *The Principles of Psychology* in 1878.

[3] HJ, *Daisy Miller: A Study* appeared in the *Cornhill Magazine* 37 (June 1878): 678–98; 38 (July 1878): 44–67.

[4] Christopher Newman is the central character of *The American*.   His projected female counterpart is not identified.

[5] HJ, *An International Episode*, published in the *Cornhill Magazine* 38 (December 1878): 687–713; 39 (January 1879): 61–90.

[6] Theodora Sedgwick.

[7] Charing Cross.

From Henry James

DEVONSHIRE CLUB, | ST JAMES'S, S.W. Nov. 14th [1878]

My dear William—

I have only just now—by an extraordinary accident—rec'd. your note, from Keene Valley, of Sept. 12th.   (The Reform Club is closed for repairs & meanwhile the members come here, where the servants, not knowing them & getting confused, play all kinds of devilish tricks with the letters.)   This incident is perhaps all the pleasanter for the long delay; but I fear I must have seemed brutal in not acknowledg-ing your letter & not mentioning in writing to the others.   I can't do more than simply acknowledge it now—I can't write you a worthy reply.   With it were handed me three other (English) notes, equally delayed, to which I have had to write answers, apologies & explana-tions (one of them was from Wm Spottiswoode the President of the Royal Society asking me to go down—a month ago—& stay at his place in Kent!) & as I have been working all the morning, particularly long, I am too tired for a regular letter.   But I must congratulate you on your interesting & delightful remarks upon an "inside view" of matrimony.   They fill me with satisfaction, & I would declare, if it were not superfluous, that I hope you may never take it into your head to take another tone.   You evidently won't!   I am as well pleased as if I had made your match & protected your courtship.   I am hardly less gratified by your statement of your psychological development & prospects.   May they daily expand & brighten & may your book, for Henry Holt, sweep through many an edition.   (You had better have it published also here.   I will put this through for you, if you like, when the time comes, with ardor.)   With your letter was handed me the Journal of Spec. Science with your article on the brain in animals & man, which I shall read;[1] & this a.m. came a letter from mother telling me how well you were going through your Lowell lectures.[2]   Please tell mother I have rec'd. her letter (it's of October 30th) & that I will very soon write to her.   Give them this, meanwhile, to read, in Quincy St., as a stopgap.   I am delighted with the manner in which mother speaks of Alice's continued improvement—what a blessing it must be!   I will say nothing of father's loss of money, of which I have written, & will again write, to mother.—I was much depressed on reading your letter by your painful reflections on the *Europeans*: but now, an hour having elapsed, I am beginning to hold up my head a little; the more so as I think I myself estimate the book very justly & am aware of its extreme slightness.   I think you take these things too rigidly & unimaginatively—too much as if an artistic experiment were a piece of conduct, to which one's life were somehow committed; but I think also that you're quite right in pronouncing the book "thin," & empty.   I don't at all despair, yet, of doing something fat.   Meanwhile I hope you will continue to give me, when you can, your free impression of my performances.   It is a great thing to have some one write to one of one's things as if one were a 3d person, & you are the only individual who will do this.   I don't think however you are always right, by any means.   As for instance in your objection to the closing paragraph of *Daisy Miller*, which seems to me queer & narrow, & as regards which I don't seize your point of view.   J'en appelle to the sentiment of any other storyteller whomsoever; I am sure none such would wish the paragraph away.   You may say—"Ah, but other *readers* would."   But that is the same; for the teller is but a more developed reader.   I don't trust your judgment altogether (if you will permit me to say so) about *details*; but I think you are altogether right in returning always to the importance of subject.   I hold to this, strongly; & if I don't as yet, seem to proceed upon it more, it is because being "very artistic" I have a constant impulse to try experiments of form, in which I wish to not run the risk of wasting or gratuitously using big situations.   But to these I am coming now. It is something to have learned how to write, & when I look round me & see how few people (doing my sort of work) know how, (to my sense) I don't regret my step by step evolution.   I don't advise you however to read the 2 last things I have written—one a thing in the Dec. & Jan *Cornhill*, which I will send home;[3] & the other, a piece I am just sending to Howells.[4]   They are each quite in the same manner as the *Europeans*.—I *have* written you a letter, after all.   I am tired & must stop. I went into the country the other day to stay with a friend a couple of days (Mrs. Greville)[5] & went with her to lunch with Tennyson, who, after lunch, read us Locksley Hall.[6]   The next day went to Geo. Eliot's.   Blessings on Alice.

Ever your   H.J.jr

ALS: MH bMS Am 1094 (1984)

[1] WJ, "Brute and Human Intellect," *Journal of Speculative Philosophy* 12 (July 1878): 236–76.

[2] WJ lectured before the Lowell Institute, Boston, on "The Brain and the Mind" from 15 October 1878 to 1 November 1878; for the lectures see *Manuscript Lectures*.

[3] See letter of 23 July 1878.

[4] HJ, "The Pension Beaurepas," *Atlantic Monthly* 43 (April 1879): 388–92.

[5] There are two well-known diarists of that name, brothers, Charles Cavendish Fulke Greville (1794–1865) and Henry William Greville (1801–1872). Mrs. Greville is probably related to them.

[6] Alfred, Lord Tennyson, "Locksley Hall" (1842).

From Henry James

3, BOLTON STREET, | PICCADILLY. W. Tuesday March 4ᵗʰ [1879]
Dear Wᵐ

I regret with a sense of personal misery the continuation of your trouble with your eyes.   I was in hopes it was passing away; & I can well imagine the restrictions it lays upon you.   It was all the more noble of you, therefore, to have written me your note of Feb. 15, which came to me 2 days since.   I had not very lately heard from Quincy St, & had begun to hanker for a line.   Thank you for your commendation of the "I.E."[1] which, here, has been, though successful, less so than "Daisy Miller."   The book, with the 3 tales, has already been out a fortnight; so you see it was too late for me to act upon your advice to include "Longstaff's Marriage."[2]   This latter surprised me, by the way; inasmuch as I had an idea this little tale had seemed but a poor affair.   But if it has any virtue I shall still have plenty of chance to reprint it, as a few months hence, I shall have material for another collection of short things.[3]   I shall before very long gratify your "pining" for a "big novel"—or a bigger one at least than these last little things.   I have just lately answered in the affirmative an appeal of Scribner's for a serial tale about a ⅓ longer than the Europeans.[4]   I am immediately getting to work upon it, & having a good idea in my head, I shall put it forward rapidly.   They apparently stand ready to publish as rapidly.   I was just getting under way with my little book upon Hawthorne when Scribner's proposal came; & as there was no imperative hurry about the Hawthorne, I have put it off two or three months.[5]   I had gone down to Hastings just before this, to spend 36 hours & have some talk with Julian Hawthorne, who is spending the winter there.   He gave me little satisfaction or information about his father; but I enjoyed my day by the sea, & also got on very well with him.   He has something personally attractive & likeable, though he is by no means cultivated or in any way illuminated.   He detests England & the English, & reminds me so a dozen times a day.   I can make allowance for his feelings, but I can't for a man in that state of mind continuing to live here.   It is very unfair all round.—This is the only incident that has lately befallen me.   I continue to dabble a little, as usual, in "London life," but I don't land any very big fish from its waters.—I like London more & more as a big city & a regular basis of mundane existence; but sometimes I get wofully tired of its people & their talk.   There seems something awfully stale & stupid about the whole business & I long to take a plunge in something different.   I feel as if it were only necessary to insert the small end of the wedge to begin and be as inimical as J. Hawthorne. But these emotions are of course mainly subjective, & appertain to one's feelings about any human society, in any big agglomeration of people.   As things go in this world I am inclined to think that London is as good as anything, & to agree with Dr. Johnson that he who is tired of it is simply tired of life.[6]   I dined last night at the New University Club with Ernest Myers[7] & four or five ci-devant Oxford men who are supposed to be choice spirits—Andrew Lang—a leader-writer for the *Times* &c.   I suppose this strikes you as an attractive occasion & in the stillness of Harvard St. excites your envy & speculation.[8]   But it failed to give me a sense of rare privilege—owing partly, I think, to the *ungemüthlich* associations I have, humanly, with Oxford—dreary, ill-favored men, with local conversation & dirty hands.   (All the men in London, however, have dirty hands.)   The other night, at Charles Godfrey Leland's—a queer literary party, composed of the ex-King of Oude[9] and various 3ᵈ rate magazinists, just like something in Dickens or Thackeray, I was roped into a certain "Rabelais Club," which Leland has it greatly at heart to found, to resist the encroachments of effeminacy & the joyless element in literature. Leland is a very good fellow but a big half-Germanized Philadelphia boy, & I am afraid his club will evaporate, as his Rabelaisians seem to me all very feeble & beneath the level of the rôle.[10] He is trying to get Lord Houghton as president or figure-head—also Gustave Doré &c. I have been looking to see where I have dined lately, but though I see various names none of them recall any particularly memorable occasions. If you dine out a good deal in London, you forget your dinner the next morning—or rather, if you walk home, as I always do, you forget it by the time you have turned the corner of the street. Familiarity with such occasions breeds contempt, & my impressions evaporate with the fumes of the champagne. I met James Bryce out at dinner somewhere the other night, & he walked home with me & sat & talked an hour. He is a distinctly able fellow, but he gives one the impression of being on the whole a failure. He has had three conflicting dispositions—to literature (History)—to the law—& to politics—& he has not made a complete thing of any of them. He is now however trying to throw himself into politics—to stand for the Tower Hamlets. I am afraid he won't succeed—he belongs to the class of young doctrinaire Radicals (they are all growing old in it) who don't take the "popular heart" & seem booked to remain out of affairs. They are all tainted with priggishness—though Bryce less so than some of the others The man who is shooting ahead much faster than any one else is Charles Dilke. His ability is not at all rare, but he is very skilful and very ambitious, & though he is only 35 years old, he would almost certainly, if the Liberals should come into power tomorrow, be a cabinet minister. I heard the other evening an interesting parallel drawn between him & George Trevelyan, who has fallen off, since his start, as much as Dilke has gained—thanks to "priggishness." This is very instructive, & if one has been living here awhile these comparisons are interesting. I must say, however, that, so far as my observation goes, pure political ability, such as Dilke's, doesn't appear a very elevated form of genius.—Tell Alice (sister) that I went to Annie Ashburner's wedding, & meant to write to her about it, but this virtuous intention was crowded out. Tell her Annie A. looked extremely pretty (in yellow satin, with a yellow veil) & appeared to great advantage.[11] The breakfast was very sumptuous & agreeable & the whole affair pleasant, save that at the end, her angry father, coming with me to the door, broke out into a torrent of protestations & imprecations.   I am afraid she has had no easy time—but S.A. is a selfish old Turk.   Farewell, I must close my letter.   I hope you are beginning to breathe the spring, as we are, after the vilest of possible winters.   Tender greetings to Alice, & to you earnest hopes of amelioration.

Ever dear W^m your devoted brother   H. James jr

ALS: MH bMS Am 1094 (1985)

[1] HJ, *An International Episode.*

[2] HJ, "Longstaff's Marriage," *Scribner's Monthly* 16 (August 1878): 537–50. The two volumes containing *Daisy Miller, An International Episode,* and *Four Meetings* were published on 15 February 1879 by Macmillan and Co.

[3] In October HJ published *The Madonna of the Future and Other Tales,* 2 vols. (London: Macmillan, 1879).

[4] HJ, *Confidence* appeared in *Scribner's Monthly* from August 1879 to January 1880 (vols. 18–19).

[5] On 12 December 1879 HJ published *Hawthorne* (London: Macmillan and Co., 1879).

[6] Samuel Johnson (1709–1784), English author, quoted in James Boswell, *Life of Samuel Johnson* (remarks of 20 September 1777).

[7] The University Club was established in 1824 for members of Parliament with university degrees.   Whether the New University Club is a continuation of the older club is not clear.

[8] WJ was then living at 387 Harvard St.

[9] Oudh (also Oude) is a province of India annexed by the British in 1856 when the king was deposed.

[10] Charles Godfrey Leland (1824–1903), American-born poet and author, founder of the Rabelais Club, a literary club.   In a letter concerning club membership, Leland writes: "James is unobjectionable, but he was proposed and elected, I may say, without my knowing anything about it" (Elizabeth Robins Pennell, *Charles Godfrey Leland: A Biography,* 2 vols. [Boston and New York: Houghton, Mifflin and Company, 1906], 2:55).

[11] Annie Ashburner married Francis Gardiner Richards.

From Henry James

3, BOLTON STREET, | PICCADILLY. W. June 15th [1879]

Dear William—I have been balancing for some moments between addressing this letter to our common (or rather, uncommon) mother, or to you; I have decided for you on the general ground of having long intended & desired to write to you,—as well as the special one of having received a letter from you (accompanying one from your Alice) some fortnight ago.   But please give mother very tenderly to understand that I adore her none the less, & that I have before me now two good letters from her—one received some ten days since, & the other last night, the latter enclosing a most charming letter from Bob, & also an extract from the Springfield Republican which in its crude & brutal vulgarity strikes me as anything but charming.[1]   The American newspaper tone strikes one over here, where certain reticences & ménagements, a certain varnish of good manners & respectful way of saying things, still hold their own, as of too glaring, too scorching, an indecency.   But never mind that.—I wrote to Alice just a week ago— much more briefly than I could have desired, but I hope my letter will have reached her safely, as it contained a little document which constituted its only value.   I gather from father's *p.s.* to mother's letter of last night that your wife is so well on the way to her normal condition again that you have no longer any cause for anxiety.[2]   I delight in the image, indiscinctly as I yet perceive it, of your infantine Henry & cordially hope he will be a fund of comfort & entertainment to you. He will be for many a day the flower of Quincy St. & I hope he will bloom with dazzling brilliancy.   I can fancy the interest you will take (as a psychologist) in watching his growth, & can trust you to give him a superior education.—Let me say before I go any further that I have *not* yet heard definitely from Knowles about your MS.[3]—He told me the other day that he was *greatly* crowded with philosophic & psychologic papers (I don't know whose) but that he shld. (though he thought on this ground the presumption was against yours) be sorry to decide not to take it till he had looked at it more closely.   He is keeping it for this purpose, but I hope soon to hear from him.   If he doesn't take it I have hopes of being able to get it printed somewhere—I will try everything I can.—Mother has lately given me a good deal of information about you—e.g. with regard to your plan of building a house upon father's "grounds."[4]   It seems a bright particular idea, & I deeply regret that delays & difficulties interpose themselves.   It is an odious thought that you should have so small an income, & I am very sorry to hear that the inconsiderate Bowen shows the reverse of a tendency to resign.[5]   But patience will see any game out, & yours I trust will brighten materially before your supply of this commodity is exhausted.   A curse indeed must your deficient eye-sight be!—I wonder greatly at the work you manage to do.——— Bob's letter, enclosed by mother, was very delightful, & has helped to dispel the impression of the rather dark account of him & of his possible future contained in your letter.   It is strange that with his intelligence & ability—as one seems to perceive it in his letters—he shouldn't arrive at more successful occupations.   I am very sorry for him, & I wish I were nearer to him & able to see him sometimes & perhaps help him along a little. His account of Wilkie's manière d'être is quite to the life & is on the whole favorable as regards the amenity of existence for poor W. But into what a queer, social *milieu* he must have planted himself. Some months ago he sent me a friend of his from Milwaukee, with a letter of introduction, describing him as his most beloved intimate & requesting me to make him *mine*! The friend was a French-teacher—an old Frenchman who appeared to have been in Milwaukee for many years & to have quite unlearned his native tongue, which he pronounced & spoke in the most barbaric & incomprehensible fashion. He seemed very stupid & common & had nothing at all to say (even about Wilkie) but that he desired I should try to find him *pupils* for the few weeks that he was to remain in London—or failing this, that I should do the same in Edinburgh, whither, I believe, he afterwards betook himself. He was in every way a most curious apparition (he appeared to speak no English, & his French was atrocious) & not an encouraging specimen of the social resources of Milwaukee. Wilkie wrote—"Show him London, & above all show him yourself!" I was as tender as possible with him, but I was not sorry when he vanished. (N.B. Never report this to Wilky—who had evidently been very kind & humane to the poor old man.)—I feel at moments as if I could write you 50 pages of general & particular reflections upon my own manner of life, occupations, observations, impressions &c—but when it comes to the point, in giving my account of London days & London doings, one hardly knows where to begin. I suppose this is a proof that such days are full, such doings numerous, & that if one could, by a strong effort detach one's self from them & look at them as objectively as a person living quite out of it & far away from it, (like yourself) would do—there would be many more things worth dwelling upon than one falls here into the way of seeing. To dwell on *nothing*, indeed, comes to be here one's desire as well as one's habit—& half the facts of London life are tolerable only because they exist to you just for the moment of your personal contact with them. Heaven have mercy on you if you were obliged to drag them about in memory or, in esteem! I am sinking also rapidly into that condition of accepted & accepting Londonism when impressions lose their sharpness & the idiosyncrasies of the place cease to be salient. To see them, to feel them, I have to lash my flanks & assume a point of view. The confession is doubtless a low one, but I have certainly become a hopeless, helpless, shameless (and

you will add, a *bloated,*) cockney. No, I am not bloated—morally; I
am philosophic to lean-ness—to stringiness. Physically, it's another
affair, & I am bloated *tout que vous voudrez.* I am as broad as I am
long, as fat as a butter-tub & as red as a British materfamilias. On
the other hand, as a compensation, I am excellently well! I am working along very quietly & steadily, & consider no reasonable share of
fame & no decent literary competence out of my reach. Apropos of
such matters, mother expresses in her last night's letter the hope that
I have derived much gold from the large sale (upwards of 20000 copies) of my two little Harper stories. I am sorry to say I have done
nothing of the sort. Having in advance no prevision of their success
I made a very poor bargain. The *Episode* I sold outright (copyright
& all!) for a very moderate sum of ready money—so I have had no
percentage at all on its sale! For Daisy Miller I have rec'd. simply the
usual 10%—which, as it sells for twenty cents, brings me but 2 cents a
copy.[6] This has a beggarly sound, but the Harpers sent me the other
day a cheque for 200$. This represents but meanly so great a
vogue—but you may be sure that I shall clinch the Harpers in future;
as having now taught them my value I shall be able to do. A man's
1st successes are those, always, by which he makes least. I am not a
grasping business-man—on the contrary, and I sometimes—or
rather, often—strike myself as gaining wofully less money than fame.
My reputation in England seems (considering what it is based on) lu-
dicrously larger than any cash payments that I have yet received for
it. The Macmillans are everything that's friendly—caressing—old
Macmillan physically *hugs* me; but the delicious ring of the sovereign
is conspicuous in our intercourse by its absence.[7] However, I am
sure of the future—that is the great thing—& it is something to be-
have like a gentleman even when other people don't. I shall have
made by the end of this year very much more money than I have ever
made before; & next year I shall make as much as that again. As for
the years after that,—nous verrons bien. The other night, at a "literary gathering," the excellent Cotter Morison came at the "urgent
request" of *celui-ci* to introduce me to Edmond About, who is here in
a sort of 2d rate "International Literary Congress" which appears to
have made a foolish *fiasco.*[8] About seized me by both hands & told
me that what he wished of me (beyond the pleasure of making my
acquaintance) was that I should promise to give him a translation of
my next novel for the feuilleton of his paper, the XIXe Siècle. "Voy-
ons, cher Monsieur James, je tiens à cela très-seriousement—je tiens

à ce [que] vous me donnez la parole.   Mettez la main sur un traduc-
teur qui vous satisfasse—envoyez moi le manuscrit—je vous donne
ma parole qu'il n'attendra pas.   Je sais que vous êtes tres-puissant,
très-original que vous êtes en train de vous poser ici comme personne: etc, etc."   I gave him my promise, & I shall probably send him
"Confidence";[9] but what strikes me in everything of this kind is the
absurd, the grotesque, facility of success.   What have I done, juste
ciel?   It humiliates me to the earth, & I can only right myself by
thinking of all the excellent things I mean to do in the future.—The
other night John Fiske rose, moon-like, above my horizon—apparently very well & happy, & I immediately invited him to dine with me
to meet Turgenieff next week—the latter coming over by invitation to
receive the D.C.L. degree at Oxford—a very pretty attention to pay
him (to which I imagine James Bryce chiefly put them up.)   He has
promised solemnly (by letter from Paris) to dine with me on the 20ᵗʰ;
& it is quite on the cards that he shld. play me false; but I trust he
wont.   I wish you were here to share & adorn the feast—Fiske on his
return will tell you about it.—Henry Adams & his wife arrived a few
days since & are staying at the Milnes Gaskell's.   I have seen them but
once or twice & find them rather compressed & depressed by being
kept from getting into quarters of their own.   Gaskell has taken a
great house in London on purpose to entertain them, & this seems to
weigh upon their spirits.   Henry A. can never be in the nature of
things a very gracious or sympathetic companion, & Mrs. A. strikes
me as toned down & bedimmed from her ancient brilliancy; but they
are both very pleasant, & doubtless when they get into lodgings will
be more animated.   I have had as yet very little talk with them.—I
have scrawled you a great many pages—but it seems to me I have told
you none the things I meant to in sitting down.   But I must pause—
I have already written two letters before this.   I hope you will get all
possible good of your vacation—that your eyes will heal—and that
your bride & babe will flourish in emulation.—Every now & then (ir-
relevantly) I meet Mallock & have a little talk with him.[10]   He has
promised to come & see me; but he never does—to my regret.   I
think he wants to, but is defeated by a mixture of English shame-
facedness & London accidents.   I regret it much for I have a strong
impression I should like him & we should get on.   But I shall probably see more of him some time—his face expresses his intelligence.
Farewell.   My blessings on mother, father, sister, &—if she is there,
God bless her!, as they say here,—upon the aunt.   Many greetings to

your Alice—I suppose you will get into the country with her and the infant.   I take much interest in the latter, & if ever you shld. get tired of him, shall be very glad to adopt him.

Fraternally yrs. | H. James jr

I enclose to Alice (single) a very pleasant letter from Lowell, which I beg her to keep for me.—

ALS: MH bMS Am 1094 (1986)

[1] A newspaper published in Springfield, Mass.

[2] WJ's first son, Henry James, was born on 18 May 1879.

[3] Probably WJ's "Rationality, Activity, and Faith," *Princeton Review* 2 (July 1882): 58–86, reprinted in *The Will to Believe* (1897).

[4] WJ considered several possibilities until 1889 when the house at 95 Irving St. was built.   The plan mentioned involved a lot owned by his father on Quincy St.

[5] Francis Bowen (1811–1890), American philosopher, a professor at Harvard, often WJ's critic especially concerning the theory of evolution.

[6] American book editions of *Daisy Miller* and *An International Episode* were published by Harper & Brothers, the former 1 November 1878, the latter, 24 January 1879.

[7] Alexander Macmillan (1813–1896), British publisher.   For HJ's dealings with the firm during this period see *HJL*, vol. 2.

[8] James Augustus Cotter Morison (1832–1888), British biographer and author; Edmond-François-Valentin About (1828–1885), French writer, editor of *Le XIXe Siècle*. The first session of the Congrès Littéraire International was held at the Paris Universal Exposition; the second session, in London, beginning on 9 June 1879.   Edmond About presided.

[9] See letter of 4 March 1879.   The French version was not published.

[10] William Hurrell Mallock (1849–1923), British author, published *Is Life Worth Living?* (1879).

From Henry James

REFORM CLUB, | PALL MALL. S.W. Aug. 19th [1879]

Dear William—

I have only just heard definitively from Knowles that he can't print your article, owing to having other philosophic things, accepted, on his hands.   I shall immediately send it to Morley; but I am afraid that its chances with him will hardly be better.   However, I shall see—as he is less of an editor pure & simple, than the very commercial & humbugging little Knowles.   There would probably not be *any* use in trying any of the popular magazines; but if Morley will none of it, I shall try the *Contemporary*.   I am afraid Knowles's refusal will be a disappointment to you; & I devoutly trust your noble labour won't be wasted.———I wrote to Alice this morning & don't feel equal to pro-

ducing another letter—especially as at the same time I wrote three or
four epistles.   But I must give you my fraternal, as well as to your
wife & babe.   They tell me your in the White Mounts. & I hope you
are having a genial summer.   You are having a different one at any
rate from your poor cockney brother, who is spending it on the London paving-stones.   But the season here is so cold & dark & damnable—day after day of ceaseless & torrential rain—that it is good to
be absolved from the need of pretending to enjoy the country.   But
as I was saying to Alice, I pine for the woods & fields.   I shall go &
spend the autumn in Paris.   I long to get out of England for a while,
& this is the easiest & most convenient resort.   London is now perfectly dead, & I see nothing & no one.   The Henry Adamses were
near me for a while, but have now gone to the Lakes.   I have accepted no invitations & paid no visits, designedly, this year; though if
I chose I might have gone to Scotland.   But that is better for an occasion than for a regularity.   Your young friend Zenos Clark (why
Zenos?) turned up & seemed very innocent & rustic; but withal intelligent & interesting.[1]   I had him to dine at this place & did all I could
for him (which was little;) but I am afraid he was depressed & disappointed at his helplessness here & at his finding the people he wished
to see all out of town.   Also by my telling him (as it was my duty, in
reply to his question) that it would *not* be a normal thing for him to
call upon the principal philosophers unintroduced, & ask them to
interest themselves in him.   "You know," he said, "I should be quite
at liberty to do it in America."   He appears to have gone off to Germany—he was a touching specimen of a young American son of the
soil, & of the local purity of nature.   My heart warmed to him for his
virtue & native refinement, but I am afraid he found me rather useless.   Apropos of such matters, I am just taking the liberty of giving
(at his urgent request) of giving a line of introduction to you, to a
young Englishman, J. L. Whitman.   He is the English cousin of the
husband of Mrs. Whitman of Boston (the artist) who took her poor
crazy brother off my hands (that is, relieved me of the trouble concerning myself further about him) last autumn.   He is a young Oxford man, a chemist, & has lately gone to Boston & Cambridge, to
take, as he writes me, "high class pupils."   (He has been in America
before.)   He asks me for introductions to such people as would help
him to find such; & the only thing I can do for him is to give him a
line to you.   He wishes to be a coach, &c.   He is quite unavailable for
social purposes, & won't come to you on a social basis, so you needn't
in the least bother about him in that way.   I was mixed up with him

in the tiresome Wyman episode, & he was so obliging in helping me to have nothing more to do with it that I feel as if I ought to respond to his appeal.   The only thing you can do is to tell him you will mention him to possible pupils.—But I must close, with many blessings. I send much love to Alice, & to the precocious babe.   I hope they flourish & that you are well.

Ever yrs.   H. James jr

ALS: MH bMS Am 1094 (1987)

[1] Xenos Clark, a student of philosophy.   Two letters to him from WJ have survived (1880, 1886).

From Henry James

3, BOLTON STREET, | PICCADILLY. W. Aug 30<u>th</u> [1879]

Dear William—

Your post-card & pamphlet have just come.   I am very sorry to say that Morley declined your article some days since in the note which I enclose.[1]   (His use of the word "friend," by the way, is not a sign I didn't tell him you were my brother.   On the contrary, I told him all about you & blew your trumpet loudly.)   I am afraid you will be much disappointed.   I immediately sent the MS. to the *Contemporary*, with another note, & shall have to wait for an answer to that.   If it is declined there, I will then return it you, in much sorrow & shame at British unappreciativeness.   Knowles cares only for lively actuality; but I had hoped for better things from Morley.—I wrote you but a few days since, & have no news now.   London is an absolute desert— & the summer has been so terrible (rain absolutely uninterrupted & the whole country a perfect bog) that one feels as if one had been shut up on shipboard during a long tempest.   I have not slept out of London the whole time, or indeed been out, & I hanker for a change & a touch of nature.   I can't afford to travel, & so to get the change, if not the touch of nature, I shall go over to Paris for the autumn (as I must have told you the other day.)   I hope to have in a day or two, & will give you *de mes nouvelles* from there.   I hope you are settled & domesticated in your house, & that your Infant is getting used to the trouble of living.   Also that both Alice & you have got some good of your summer.   Give her much love—

Ever yours   H.J.jr

ALS: MH bMS Am 1094 (1988)

[1] See letter of 15 June 1879.

From Henry James

        Paris. 51 Rue Nue. St. Augustin. | 10 November [1879]
My dear William—

The enclosed note with your MS. is all the satisfaction which I have at last succeeded in extracting from the *Contemporary*. I deeply regret it, & I return the MS. by this post, not knowing what else I can attempt. I am much ashamed that my frivolous efforts shld. be acclaimed while your much more valuable lucubrations go a-begging; but such, apparently, is the taste of a light-minded generation. But keep up your courage & try again; you have for you like Wordsworth's Toussaint, "man's unconquerable mind."[1] I suppose you will have no difficulty in getting this piece inserted in the *Princeton Review*.[2] I won't conceal from you that I have not read it in manuscript; but I long greatly to peruse it in print, as I have become greatly interested in it. What the English periodicals do to you, the American do to me. The vulgarly-edited *North American* has had for the last seven months a paper (very good) of mine on Ste. Beuve's Correspondence, & another, inferior, on that of Eugène Delacroix, concerning which it will give me no satisfaction whatever, not even that of returning them.[3] I don't wish to say it in a tone of brutal triumph, but if I *could* get them back, I would *easily* introduce them into the Fortnightly or the 19th Cent'y. But the N.A.R. will take no notice of my letters, & I don't know what to do about it. I have sent a last summons, from which I am awaiting results.—You will, ere this, from my Quincy St. letters,[4] have learned all about my being in Paris, which has been my abode since the last of August. It has been a lovely autumn (which still lasts, very tolerably,) & Paris has been to me, I think, more quietly and comfortably pleasant than ever before. It has still a great charm, in spite of everything that is being done from year to year, to transform it into a mere big bazaar; & when one comes from London French civilization certainly strikes one as high. I have enjoyed being away from England, but I am beginning to want to get back. I shall probably go down to Florence for three weeks before I return to Bolton St; but I keep putting it off from week to week. You may have heard from the Bootts, that Lizzie has brought Duveneck (her Munich instructor,) to settle there, with all his pupils, & having done this, means to remain there this winter, to work with him. The natural & logical thing now seems to me to be for Lizzie to marry Duveneck.—I have seen almost no one of interest here. The American circle is of the poorest, & altogether composed of women. The only "personality" I have seen is my old friend the Prss. Ourousoff,[5] whose open, philosophic Russian mind, with its absence of Gallicisms, & its German & English culture, make her a most agreeable change from the others.   Laugel I have seen two or three times, & he is very kind & friendly, but his tone depresses & irritates me, & I agree with him in nothing.   As they say here, C'est un dégommé.   I am however, at this moment, expecting Turgenieff to come in from the country to breakfast with me—I enclose his autograph, for Alice. (Show it also in Quincy St.)   I wish you—& Alice also,—could sit down with us & mingle in the conversation.   I have only seen him once, owing to his being out of town, & am longing for a talk with him—his own share in it is always so good.   Farewell, dear brother; I hope your winter s'annonce bien, & that your work is smoothing its self out.   Blessings on your wife & child.   Much love to Alice.

Ever yours—H. James jr

ALS: MH bMS Am 1094 (1989)

[1] From Wordsworth's poem "To Toussaint l'Ouverture" (1803).

[2] See letter of 15 June 1879.

[3] HJ's review of *Correspondance de C. A. Sainte-Beuve, 1822–1869* appeared in *North American Review* 130 (January 1880): 51–68; his review of *Lettres d'Eugène Delacroix (1815 à 1863)* appeared in *International Review* 8 (April 1880): 357–71.

[4] In 1879–80 WJ lived at 4 Arrow St., Cambridge.   The parents were living on Quincy St.

[5] Marie Ourousoff, Russian princess, hostess of a literary salon in Paris.

From Henry James

3, BOLTON STREET, | PICCADILLY. W. Dec. 16th [1879]

My dear William—

Only a line to acknowledge your note of Nov. 27th acknowledging my return of your MS., & containing strictures on *Confidence* &c. The latter were I think just (as regards the lightness of the tale;) but I also think that, read as a whole, the thing will appear more grave.   I have got (heaven knows!) plenty of gravity within me, & I don't know why I can't put it more into the things I write.   It comes from modesty & delicacy (to drop those qualities for the moment;) or at least from the high state of development of my artistic conscience, which is so greatly attached to *form* that it shrinks from believing that it can supply it properly for *big* subjects, & yet is constantly studying the way to do so; so that at last, I am sure, it will arrive.   I am determined that the novel I write this next year shall be "big."—I am sorry you "out-

grow" so, & hardly know what remedy to suggest—as I can't like
Joshua, bid Science to stand still.   But keep up your heart, & sometime you will have your year or so of leisure in Europe—which I will
endeavour, in the future, to further.   I trust your eyes continue to
improve.   I have just written to father—& refer you to the Quincy
St. letter.   I am returned as you see, from Paris, & am settled down
again in this darksome but satisfactory town.   I gave up Italy, *rapport
au* cold.   I am full of work, projects, &c; & save for an occasional big
head-ache (tea or no tea) am in very good health.   I brought a dozen
pr. gloves from Paris for Alice, to post here, as more safe; but shall
have to send them pair by pair, till the dozen is told.   Bid her receive
them with my love, (I address them to you) but not acknowledge them
till they have all arrived.   A comfortable Xmas!   Your picture of the
"squab-like" babe went to *mon coeur d'oncle*!

ever yr.   H.J.jr

ALS: MH bMS Am 1094 (1990)

From Henry James

Florence. May 9th 1880

My dear William—
I received some days ago your short note, telling me that you had
lost the prospect of coming abroad, & enclosing the list of ancient
books which you wish me to get & the wood-cut of the new Harvard
building.[1]   I deplore your decision with regard to giving up Europe,
for I had hoped that something pleasant (for both of us) would come
of your plan.   I should have been very happy to do the honours of
London for you!   This however will be but a pleasure postponed—
to a time, I trust, when Alice will be able to share it.   At present I
should, I confess, have been but half satisfied to see you without
seeing her—to say nothing of the little Henri Trois.   I deplore still
more the condition of your eyes, which must indeed be an unmitigated curse.   Having heard nothing of them for some time I hoped
they were better; I wonder how you get on, & I suppose it often seems
to you that you don't get on at all.   But you do, for all that, I ween, &
better days, I equally ween, will not be denied you.   I will make a
point of looking up Voltaire, Diderot, Condillac &c, in Paris.   Here,
one finds nothing good, in the way of books.   Having obtained the
above works in Paris, I will present them to you in elegant bindings,
gratis.   I am glad you have so good a reason for not coming abroad

as that you are going to plant your roof-tree. I hope that Richardson's genius of which you speak, will not be cramped by the conditions in which he will have to work & that your cottage will be a veritable "bijou."[2] I would offer to stock it for you with a collection of the charming Cantagalli pottery, which one gets here now; but unfortunately, as these charming things are very cheap, it would cost much more than their value to transport them to Boston, besides almost certainty of breakage.[3] If you have any design or sketch of your house, other than mere ground-plan &c, I should like very much to see it.———I am spending this month of May in Florence, & am chiefly engaged in pegging away, day after day, at my next novel, for which by the way I have obtained a postponement (which I hope will not disappoint the impatience of the family—they will have another, in the *Cornhill*, to beguile the interval) from *August* to *October*.[4] I find Florence, for which all my old affection has completely revived, a blissfully better place to work just now than London. The extent to which I enjoy the free use of my time gives me the measure of the social pressure which in London had become chronic. I get here some time to read as well as write—which in London had long been painfully impossible. I would fain remain absent from England till July 1st; but I am not sure that I shall be able to do so. I have always my rooms in Bolton St. on my hands, &c. But I shall stay away as long as possible, & on my return shall, during the quieter months, stick fast till I go home.—Florence is most amiable, in spite of the fact that it rains from morning till night—unseasonable weather, making up for a winter abnormally dry. But the rain keeps the temperature low & will probably do so for another month. You never did justice to this place, if I remember rightly, during your short & gloomy sojourn here, & you almost succeeded in making me believe that it was a mockery & a snare. But I don't believe so now; & I enjoy Italy more reasonably & profitably since I have become more productive, more posé dans le monde, &c. Long may it survive as a land of rest & loveliness, a refuge from the Londons & Parises, the hardness & haste, of the Northern world. It wouldn't do, alone, without the northern world; but this, in turn, would be too much of a poor thing without Italy. Of course I see the Bootts tolerably often, & find their society agreeable, if not exciting. Save in growing older, they haven't changed in the least. B.'s childishness of mind is often oppressive, but his honesty & consistency make up for it, & though he has turned from a young man into an old, on the whole he laughs as much as ever and as heartily. Lizzie is just the same, except that she is if pos-

sible more gentle.   She is trying to form herself upon Duveneck, &
produces dozens of canvases & panels, many of which show a zealous
effort.   But the quality of her powers has not radically altered.—I
have also seen a good deal of the Hillebrands, both of whom are very
friendly and are also apparently very happy in the realization of their
long-deferred union.   M<u>me</u> H. is deafer than ever, but a fine nature,
& Hillebrand une intelligence assouplie.   Do you remember old Mrs.
Taylor, the mother, now paralytic & imbecile?[5]   Amid the ruin of her
faculties *your* image stands erect, & though she has forgotten everything else, she always presents me her ear-trumpet & mumbles an
inquiry as to whether my brother is not coming.   I must close, to go
& call on some people who two days since brought me a letter of introduction (from Lady Musgrave.)[6]   To this pitch have I come, that such
advances are frequently made me—alternating with requests for my
autograph.   The penalties of the glory of your none the less (with
love to wife & babe) devoted

H. James jr

ALS: MH bMS Am 1094 (1991)

[1] Sever Hall was completed in 1880.   Henry Hobson Richardson was the architect.

[2] Henry Hobson Richardson (1838–1886), American architect, a member with WJ
of the Saturday Club, designed homes for a number of Harvard faculty.   For the
design of WJ's house see Jeffrey Karl Ochsner, *H. H. Richardson, Complete Architectural
Works* (Cambridge: MIT Press, 1982), 277.   The house was not built.

[3] Ulisse Cantagalli (d. 1901), Italian potter.   His firm was located near Florence.

[4] HJ, *Washington Square* appeared in *Cornhill Magazine* in June–November 1880
(vols. 41–42).

[5] Not identified.   A Mrs. Henry A. Tayler lived on Bellevue Avenue, Newport,
when the Jameses lived there.

[6] Perhaps Frances Mary Musgrave (d. 1895), wife of Richard Musgrave, 4th baron.
But there are other possibilities.   HJ's Lady Musgrave was a friend of Sarah Butler
Wister.

To Henry James

        Reichenau Monday night | Aug 2nd. [1880] 9 oclock
Dear H.—I am getting on splendidly.   Have walked from Grindelwald over the Scheideck, Grimsel & Furka, and took stage this A.M
from Andermatt and had a most unforgettable day in the Banquette
through the Vorder Rhein Thal.   Stage to morrow to Thusis from
whence shall walk to Splügen.   Hurried away from Interlaken region missing much in order to get that foul fiend Davidson at Andermatt, but he's off for Venice.   Have not sent for my Berne letters yet.

Shall make very short work of the Italian lakes & return via Simplon to Brieg & Zermatt where I may possibly stay a week. The effect of these mountains on body and soul is indescribable. My enjoyment of them is only embittered by the tho't of their being so unhandy to Cambridge.

I have for a variety of reasons about made up my mind that it will be expedient for me to return earlier than Sept 16. So hang on to your Gallia berth until you hear from me again.[1] In case I leave in her I shall probably not spend more than a day in London and Paris respectively. Keep sending letters & Nations to Banque Cantonale Bern.

Affectly yrs | Wm James

ALS: MH bMS Am 1092.9 (2724)

[1] Writing to AJ on 15 August 1880, WJ noted that he would not return on 21 August because the *Gallia* was to be replaced by two "old tubs." Apparently the *Gallia* was undergoing repairs (bMS Am 1092.9 [1249]).

From Henry James

THE SPRING. | KENILWORTH. Aug. 31ˢᵗ [1880]
Dear William—

I enclose you herewith a letter that has just come for you, & which may be of importance. You are at the present moment on the lonely deep, but so near home, I hope that you will begin to take an interest in the post again.[1] The weather, in England, has been so lovely since you left that I pray you may have had something like it on the Atlantic: if so, you must have had the pleasantest of voyages. But of this you will tell me. Your letter enclosing the £15 came with extreme punctuality. I am much obliged to you for them, but sorry that you should have troubled yourself about them in the stress of getting afloat. The remainder I particularly hope you will completely ignore for the present. I hope you have found your wife & infant well, & send many blessings to both of them. Also to those of Quincy St. to whom I shall soon be writing again. I have been spending three charming days at this place with my amiable friend Mrs. Carter—who has just greatly surprised me by announcing her engagement to E. L. Trevillian—a pleasant Englishman who was a while ago in America.[2] She lost her first husband, a charming fellow, less than 2 years ago, & has been plunged in the most desolate & morbid grief up to within a few days ago, from which she has abruptly emerged, to marry Trevillian, an old & intimate friend of her husband, who is now staying here.   The weather is perfect, & anything more charming cannot be conceived than this rich, ripe Warwickshire scenery, laden with golden grain & studded with ancient oaks.   I go back to town tomorrow, & after that shall invent some scheme for being absent for the month of September.   I hope you will find more & more that your journey has been a good thing for you, as it was for me.   Renewed greetings.

Yours   H. James jr

ALS: MH bMS Am 1094 (1992)

[1] WJ sailed from Liverpool for Boston on 25 August 1880 on the *Parthia*.

[2] Neither Mrs. Carter nor E. L. Trevillian is identified.

From Henry James

3, BOLTON STREET, | PICCADILLY. W. Nov. 13ᵗʰ. [1880]

Dear William.

I have a short letter of yours long unanswered—it is of the date of Sept. 30ᵗʰ.   I have not written to you partly because the tone of your letter was rather low & I didn't know in what fashion to respond. You appear not to have been exhilarated on your return by renewed contact with American life, or by the aspect of the American individual, & I am obviously not in a situation to reassure you on those points.   Doubtless the feeling you expressed has melted down a good deal since you have got into your work again & ceased to see Boston & London in immediate juxtaposition.   I hope you are physically comfortable, & that Louisburg Square stands the test of time.[1]   Of me there is little to tell you.   The weeks that have elapsed since you left me have been very quiet ones; but profitable; inasmuch as I have both written & read a good deal.   I am afraid that if you found me basely naturalised here when you came out, I am not less so these few months later.   I feel more & more at home here, & find London more & more, on the whole, the best point of view.   Though one gets sick of it at times & tired to death of the flatness of much—though, fortunately, by no means of *all*—of one's social life, yet there is a daily sustenance in the huge, multitudinous place.   It has been a very fine autumn—clear, bright & american-like; & is only now turning to soft darkness & mild moisture—an element I like.   The fogs are as yet (after a false alarm early in the season) mercifully absent.   The town is still quiet & society not reconstituted; so I have seen but few people—though I dined yesterday at Andrew Lang's (the vaguely-glancing,) in company with Lionel Tennyson (the much-stammering) & his wife.[2]—I got a letter a few days since from Alice (sister)—long, bright & delightful, which I beg you to thank her for while I wait to acknowledge it. I hope your own wife & babe do not languish in the air of the town, & send a tender remembrance to each. I dined a few days ago (on the 9ᵗʰ) with the Lord Mayor—the big banquet which he gives annually at the Guildhall to the Cabinet Ministers & a couple of 1000 others, & at which the head of the Government usually makes a more or less sensational speech. It is a huge, scrambling, pompous & picturesque affair, well to see once; but I should care little to go again—even to hear Gladstone speak—as the rank & file of the guests are squeezed to death & fed only (or almost only) with alder-manic Turtle.[3] I dont know what else I can tell you. Edwin Booth is acting here, with but indifferent success; people find him very inferior to Irving. To me they are both so bad there is little to choose. I embrace them in Quincy St, & also in Louisburg Square. God bless & sustain you.

Ever yours | H. James jr

P.S. Your article in the Atlantic a couple of months ago, gave me extreme pleasure.[4]

ALS: MH bMS Am 1094 (1993)

[1] WJ spent the summer of 1880 in Europe, stopping in London before his departure for home in late August. Louisburg Square is in Boston, off Mount Vernon St.

[2] Lionel Tennyson (1854–1886), son of the poet, married Eleanor Locker.

[3] Sir William McArthur (1809–1887), newly elected Lord Mayor of London, held his inaugural banquet on 9 November 1880. Gladstone, the prime minister, was present and spoke. The report in the *Times* says nothing about the menu and it is not clear whether "aldermanic Turtle" is meant to describe the fare or the speeches.

[4] WJ, "Great Men, Great Thoughts, and the Environment," *Atlantic Monthly* 46 (October 1880): 441–59; reprinted in *The Will to Believe* (1897).

From Henry James

REFORM CLUB, | PALL MALL. S.W. Nov. 27ᵗʰ [1880]

Dear William.

I sent you last p.m. the two vols. of Rosmini, done up separately & registered; & I hope they will arrive safely.[1] Don't talk of refunding.—A few days before, I had received a very welcome letter from you, in Alice's hand;[2] & should have addressed this answer to her if I had not begun merely with the intention of notifying you about the

book.   As it is, I can now hardly do more.   This is a Saturday afternoon, & I go very presently down to spend Sunday at Lord Rosebery's—so I have only a moment.   (If the party at Mentmore proves
interesting I will write of it to Quincy St.,[3] whence I received, the same
day as your, a dear letter from mother.)   It gives me great pleasure to
hear that your work this year leaves you leisure for reading & study,
which must be a great satisfaction.   It is the position I desire more &
more to arrive at—which I am happy to say I tend to do.   Thank you
for what you say about my two novels.   The young man in *Washington
Square* is not a portrait—he is sketched from the outside merely & not
fouillé.   The only good thing in the story is the girl.   The other book
increases, I think, in merit & interest as it goes on, & being told in a
more spacious, expansive way than its predecessors, is inevitably
more human, more sociable.[4]   It was the constant effort at *condensation* (which you used always to drum into my head—àpropos of Mérimée &c—when I was young & you bullied me,) that has deprived my
former things of these qualities.   I shall read what G. Allen & Fiske
reply to you in the *Atlantic*, but shall be sure not to enter into what
they say as I did into your article, which I greatly appreciated.[5]—I
spent last Sunday at Wm Darwin's, very pleasantly, owing to beautiful
cold, crisp weather & to Sara seeming very well & happy.   I am very
sorry your lodgings smell of soup, especially as I have lately wholly
abjured it by the advice of Dr. Andrew Clark, whom I had to consult
for matutinal nausea, which has vanished by the suppression for the
pottage.[6]   Tell them in Quincy St. that I will speedily respond to
Mother's letter.   Say to Alice (sister) that I send her a new hat a week
or two hence by Mrs. Mason, who has kindly offered (taking a great
interest in the episode) to carry it.   It came home this a.m. & is much
superior to the other.   Love to your own Alice & baby.   I will send
them some benefits the 1st chance I get.

Tout à toi   H. James jr

ALS: MH bMS Am 1094 (1994)

[1] Antonio Rosmini-Serbati (1797–1855), Italian philosopher.

[2] For several years after their marriage, AGJ served as WJ's amanuensis.

[3] Mentmore was Lord Rosebery's estate.

[4] HJ, *Portrait of a Lady* was serialized in *Macmillan's Magazine*, October 1880–
November 1881 (vols. 42–45) and in *Atlantic Monthly*, November 1880–December
1881 (vols. 46–48).

[5] Charles Grant Blairfindie Allen (1848–1899), Canadian-born naturalist and
writer, "The Genesis of Genius," *Atlantic Monthly* 47 (March 1881): 371–81; John
Fiske, "Sociology and Hero-Worship: An Evolutionist's Reply to Dr. James," *Atlantic*

Monthly 47 (January 1881): 75–84. Both papers are responses to criticisms made by WJ in "Great Men, Great Thoughts, and the Environment."
⁶Andrew Clark (1826–1893), British physician.

From Henry James

Milan. Hotel de la Ville. | March. 21ˢᵗ, 1881.

Dear William.

Your letter of the 3ᵈ ult. dictated to Bob,¹ has (after an apparently long voyage) just reached me here, & I lose no time in replying to it.———I am very glad to hear you have the prospect of being able to come abroad for a year's study, but I confess that I don't feel able to "advise" you very definitely.   What strikes me first is that from the point of view of economy, the *nearest* place (the one reached with least frais de voyage) ought to have most to recommend it.   This would put a residence in England first on the list.   A winter in Florence would have many charms, but there would be within a few months the journey there & back to be paid for, & from the moment one begins with hotels & railways . . . . !   It might be that you would live there cheaply enough to make up for this, but of that I can't judge, having no experience of Florence from the house-keeping point of view.   As regards London, I don't at all know the price of lodgings in Bloomsbury &c;² I only know that they are considerably cheaper than in my part of the town.   If I were in London I would immediately make inquiries for you—but you see I am far away.   It is my belief that you could get good lodgings in the neighborhood of the British Museum or in some other unfashionable but respectable part of London, for a sum within your means.   I pay 2½ guineas a week for my second floor in Bolton St.; which, however, has always struck me as, for the situation, cheap.³   On the other hand the extra-expenses of living in London are larger than they would be in some other places; the single item of cab fares is in itself a thing to be considered.   It is useless to say you wouldn't use cabs.   In fact, you would, & Alice would have to: that is, more or less.   You would need human intercourse after your work (as you say;) & human intercourse in a *big* place inevitably entails certain expenses—especially when a woman is concerned.   In Paris you would perhaps have a cheaper rent—but I can't think Paris would be really cheap for you unless at the price of too sordid efforts.   You would have little chance for human intercourse there, & there would be nothing left for you, in the way of recreation, but venal pleasures—i.e. the theatres, dining at restaurants &c. These are all more or less costly, & the general situation of living in a city like Paris *for economy*, sums me to a contradiction & a discomfort. There are temptations at every turn to spend money, & it is better to be where there are fewer. Paris strikes me in a word as having the drawbacks of London without the compensations—the same scale of prices (about) & none of the social advantages. In London you might see some interesting men (those you already know, & others;) whereas in Paris you would see none; (for I put the American colony out of the question.) (You would have nothing to do with it.) Your suggestion of *Cambridge* seems to me the best in your letter; though I should need to know more about the place to venture to *recommend* you to go there. If I were in England I would make inquiries for you—but now can only offer to do so when I go back. It must be cheaper than London, & I have no doubt that you could get good rooms there, & be decently nourished, on terms that from the American point of view would appear moderate. My own disposition is to urge you to choose *England*, as being so much more filling at the price than any foreign land. Your impressions there would sink into you, & nourish you more, than any you would have in Paris or Florence; & besides, you would know some people. In Florence there is no one but Hillebrand. Assuming that England is the best country, Cambridge appears better than London as having a sufficient life of its own & yet being smaller, more concentrated & easy to deal with. It is true that if you come abroad this summer I shouldn't recommend you to begin with Cambridge then, or before October. Your summer would therefore have to be spent somewhere, & you suggest Wales. Wales would probably do beautifully if you knew (or I knew) before hand just the sequestered nook to go to: but Wales, roughly speaking, means crowds of tourists, dear hotels, &c. Scotland the same. Nevertheless, if you don't insist on the *fine fleur* of scenery, I think you would have no trouble in finding reasonable & wholesome (also pleasant) country lodgings *somewhere* in England for the summer—especially in the North. Behold then the general contention of my letter. 1° That England is intrinsically the best residence for you, as a year there would enrich your mind humanly &c; & extrinsically as being the nearest. 2° That if you come abroad for the summer you may pass it comfortably if you will be content to go to some small & quiet (unfashionable) English watering place, & STICK THERE. 3° That for the winter (or the part of it you speak of especially—

October to February) Cambridge would be decidedly worth trying & has presumptions in its favour. 4º That Paris & Florence are, one too dear & superfluously rich; & the other too far away to go to *except for a long stay*.—I may add that I assume with regard to an English residence that your having your wife & child with you makes all the difference; & that you can support the "insularity" &c. of English life infinitely better with them than you could alone—in which latter case I shld. never recommend it.—I won't add more, except to hope very much that your plans won't take such a form as that I shall miss you both here & in the U.S., to which I return as you know, either in the late summer or in October. That is, I hope you will either arrive some little time before I leave or some little time after. I won't write about myself—I am on my way to Rome, & wrote to Mother very few days since. Love & blessing to Alice & the Babe. Shouldn't she like to try England?

Ever yours | H James jr

ALS: MH bMS AM 1094 (1995)

[1] RJ was from time to time estranged from his wife and living in Cambridge.
[2] A district of London.
[3] Bolton Street is in Westminster, in central London.

From Henry James

Milan, March 22ᵈ. [1881]
Dear William & Alice.

Your letter of the 3ᵈ, dictated to Bob, *did* arrive safely, without taint of mud, & was answered by me yesterday; & was on the point of being posted when your supplementary communication of the 6ᵗʰ came in. As I had given some time & thought to my answer, I didn't change it but posted it all the same. Your second letter, however, suggests some revisions & amendments. I perhaps put the case too strongly in favour of England, & did not sufficiently take into account your need for *informal* relaxation. There are fewer chances for this in England, certainly (especially in winter—in summer country walks & excursions supply to a certain extent the want) than on the Continent; & it is true that your relaxation in Cambridge would probably be mainly *formal*—or at least have a formal element in it. Bating this, however, the case for England stands about as I put it. I don't think Paris more desirable than London. The Paris winter is not believed by me to be sufficiently superior to the London one, the Paris prices sufficiently lower, & the opportunities for inexpensive recreation sufficiently greater (always in *winter*) to make up for the absence of the social richness which might be to a certain extent an attribute (or an incident) of a residence in Bloomsbury.   The Tyrol-Florence-Paris plan strikes me as picturesque but not sound economically.   It seems to me a pity to launch yourself at the very outset in Continental adventures.   The journey from Liverpool to Salzburg (or wherever you might go) is a very long one.   The journey thence to Florence is the same &c; and ditto the journey from Florence to Paris.   All this travelling in a few months would probably rather take it out of you; the more as you would probably go to the Tyrol rather in the dark.   If you had friends at a particular spot there who would write: "*This* is the place—we take rooms for you; come here & *stick*;" you might go *de confiance* & make a long summer of it, which would be economical. A Florence winter would certainly be very pleasant & would have many merits; Florence has after all many resources.   It seems to me however, a pity to conclude against England from the 1$\underline{st}$.   I therefore recommend that if you come abroad this summer you pass it in England as an experiment, & decide meanwhile (ie. during the summer) about your winter.   You ought to be able to spend ten weeks in the country somewhere sans trop souffrir.   Or you might cross by the short & inexpensive sea-route (New Haven to Dieppe or Southampton to Havre,) to the Normandy coast & have a cheap & healthy (also pleasant,) summer at Etretat.   If at the end of this time you you shld. feel like trying England for the winter, you would still be near enough to do it easily.   If you *don't* come this summer, there will be time before the autumn to counsel you further.   You write as if you supposed me still in England, though I have done nothing but announce my Italiänische Reise.   I can't therefore give you statistics, prices &c. By *somewhere* in England (your summer) I mean at some Seacoast place, in the North, which I shld. recommend your going straight to without coming to London.   Of course, to go straight (or crooked) to it, you must know it first, & I will undertake to obtain some information for you if you announce your coming.

Ever yours of the both of you—H. James jr

P.S.—I find I have accidentally left this page blank, so I add a line to say that your supposition that "mother has told me all about Bob" is erroneous.   She has told me nothing but that he was at home for rest, & had a temperament that was "a trial both to himself & to others." This is the only sort of information I ever get about him; but it is tormentingly mysterious & I beg for more.

ALS: MH bMS Am 1094 (1996)

To Henry James

Address me: | Hotel d'Angleterre | Venezia, Oct 2. 82[1]
My dear Harry

Yours of 29th ult. fm. Tours rec'd just now.   I got here yesterday A.M. to find for the first time in a Month beautiful weather.   It has but just begun here.   I enjoyed Vienna sufficiently but not extremely, my capacity for enjoyment being a good deal impaired by the entirely unexpected condition of my sleep, my eyes, & my back, which have rather turned traitors.   It may be merely the effect of the toneless air of Europe, and lead gradually into its contrary.   But while it lasts it is very "contrary" to me & all my immediate interests.   I think I wrote you of my decision to give up Berlin altogether and come to Paris about Nov 1st.   I'll give you the reasons later.   Spent last evening in the company of Jas. Bryce M.P., his brother, & two sisters, very pleasantly.   He left this A.M. for the south and returns to London end of October.   I enclose you a hasty letter from Alice, wh. keep.   Containing less sentiment than her other letters, it is fitter for your cold & fishy eye.   It has just this minute arrived.   I also enclose one from Kate Gourlay, and likewise part of Alice's former letter.   The Royces are my substitutes in the College.[2]   I'm sorry they're not more promising.   I must cut short, as I've read nothing for a week past but Renan, Cherbuliez & Pasteur, (—poor Pasteur! how Renan chaffs him!—Renan is really deliquescent with putrefaction,—but who can putrefy with such a fine old flavor as he?) and have no end of letters to write.   Breathe not a word of my complaints homeward.   They *must* be transient.   Venice is delicious, the very air of lotus eating.   To day every thing is filled with music, tolling, cannonading and every sort of tintinnabulation.   "Viva l'esercito," posted on every wall, because forsooth, the army did s'thing towards lending a hand in the inundations.

Goodbye | W.J.

ALS: MH bMS Am 1092.9 (2601)

[1] WJ sailed for Europe, leaving his wife and child behind, on 2 September 1882 from Quebec City, Canada, on the *Parisian*.

²Josiah Royce (1855–1916), American philosopher, replaced WJ during his sabbatical in 1882–83.   Correspondence survives for 1878–1910.   Royce's wife was Katharine Head Royce, who did some translating.   AGJ did not like the Royces and complained about them to HJ; see *HJL*, 2:385.   WJ is commenting from a social point of view.

From Henry James

Bordeaux. Oct 15<u>th</u>. [1882]

My dear William

Yours of the 10<u>th</u> via London, reached me here yesterday, & I reenclose to you the fragment from Alice, which it contained.   I also send you one from Howells, just received, which will show you where he is. I don't know when he thinks of starting for Venice.   I have heard no more from home since that last of Father's, which I sent you.   I am delighted to hear that you feel some symptoms of betterment & trust they will increase till they surround you with joy.   My mind is relieved to hear that you have company "nights," as I feared you perhaps lacked this element of recreation.   I am especially glad you have fallen upon James Bryce, who must be an agreeable change from Mrs. McKaye¹ & Mrs. Smith Van Buren!   I trust Venice will in every way succeed to you, as I think it can't fail to do if you give it time. There's a church I want to tell you to go to, to see a John Bellini & a Sebastian del Piombo—the latter especially—but I can't remember its name!²—I pursue my pilgrimage through these rather dull French towns & through a good deal of bad weather, & all my desire now is to bring it to a prompt conclusion.   It is rather dreary work, for most of the places, I am sorry to say, are much less rich in the picturesque than I had supposed they would be.   I don't despair, however, of being able to do something with them.   Tomorrow I start for Toulouse, Carcassonne &c; after which I begin to travel northward.   As soon as I reach Paris I shall go to the Grand Hotel, where I have left some luggage.———Alice's letters seem to point to a sufficiently comfortable existence, & I should think would make you rather homesick. I, for some mysterious reason, am more so in this *poco simpatico* French pilgrimage than I have been for years.   I haven't spoken to a soul for a fortnight & see nothing but commis voyageurs.   But I shall soon make an end.

Ever yours   H. James jr

ALS: MH bMS Am 1094 (1997)

[1] Maria Ellery McKaye (b. 1830), American author. Two letters by WJ to her are known (1900, 1902).

[2] Sebastian del Piombo (Sebastiano Luciani) (1485–1547), Italian painter.

To Henry James

Pension Anglaise, Venice | Oct 16. 82

Dear Harry

Your letter from Tours of the 7th did not get to me till this morning. I supposed I had told you to address the Banca di Credito Veneto, and only went quasi accidentally to look at the Hotel d'Anglterre where it must have been lying 4 days. Stick to the B. di C. V. hereafter. This house, next door but one to Mrs Bronson's is very comfortable, and especially very clean. I have a room on the canal, with board, for 7.25 fr. a day, and there are very nice people at the table. It did me good to get a sight of father's hand which certainly shows no symptoms of old age. Neither does his style; but I think his disinclination to "private" writing is a symptom. I'm glad you've got a bigger job, if it only interests you, and if the weather holds good. You say nothing about it, so I hope it's improved. To day for the second time in a fortnight we have had sunshine. It makes a tremendous difference. As for myself, my eyes are much better for a few days past, as well as they've been for a long time. I think my weakness has been due to the toneless air and will slowly wear off. I enjoy V. thoroughly, am reading some books about it & shall doubtless not wish to leave till the month is out. I wrote you about Sicily—but merely to probe possibilities. I don't think I ought to go. What I may do will be to return by way of florence; which as my mind begins to vibrate in unison with the world of art, takes the shape of an immensely rich and large city, & lures me on considerably. I have had some ideas, of which an article might possibly be made, relatively to the evolution of schools of painting, and Florence would help me out.[1] But I think I shall arrive in Paris at the latest by the middle of Nov. I renounce Berlin for the simple reason that my great trouble in Europe will be to pass the evenings. They will there be very long, with no open fires, few friends to visit etc. Moreover the Psychology is the one thing that justifies my trip,[2] and what I should find philosophically in Berlin wd. rather take the form of rival & conflicting interests than of helps. I find the Curtis's and their house here great helps.[3] Of Mrs Bronson's I don't make much—she takes her cigarette from her mouth to swear that she "loves" you & has written you an introduction to some castle owning friends of hers. Martin Brimmer & wife,[4] Mrs Smith Van Buren & daughters also are here. Also Sargent the painter, a charming young fellow. But I felt at the Bronson's last night how I was too old to have anything to do with the Van B. jeune fille type, with its fierce appetite for young male conversation, coupled with as fierce a hostility to the conversation containing any intellectual element whatever. I enclose a letter rec'd to day. Send it back. Little Harry has been having dysentery.

Yrs   W.J.

ALS: MH bMS Am 1092.9 (2602)

[1] Scattered notes of this project are published in WJ, *Manuscript Essays and Notes* (Cambridge: Harvard Univ. Press, 1988), 294–96.

[2] WJ was then working on *The Principles of Psychology* (1890).

[3] Ariana Randolph Wormeley Curtis (1833–1922), American author, and her husband, Daniel S. Curtis, residents of Venice.

[4] Martin Brimmer (1829–1896), traveler and philanthropist.

To Henry James

GRAND HOTEL Paris, Nov 22nd [1882]
Dear H.   Found at Hottingners this A.M. your letter with all the enclosures you add—& a wail you had sent to Berlin.   Also 6 letters from my wife & 7 or 8 others, not counting papers & magazines.   I will mail you back yours and father's letter to me.   Alice speaks of father's indubitable improvement in strength, but our sister Alice apparently is somewhat run down.—Paris looks delicious—I shall try to get settled as soon as possible and meanwhile feel as if the confusion of life was recommencing.   I saw in Germany all the men I cared to see and talked with most of them.   With 3 or 4 I had a really nutritious time.   The trip has amply paid for itself—I found 3rd Class, "nichtraucher" almost always empty and perfectly comfortable.   The great use of such experiences is less the definite information you gain from anyone, than a sort of solidification of your own foothold on life.   No where did I see a university which seems to do for *all* its students anything like what Harvard does.   Our methods throughout are better.   It is only in the select "seminaria" (private classes) that a few German students making researches with the professor gain something from him personally which his genius alone can give. I certainly got a most distinct impression of my own *information* in regard to *modern* philosophic matters being broader than that of any-

one I met, and of our Harvard post of observation being more cosmopolitan. Delboeuf in Liege was an angel & much the best *teacher*
Ive seen.[1]—I wanted to ask you here whether I should n't repay your
loan now. I can do it with a stroke of the pen, and I hope you will
write me yes, if it is the slightest convenience. "The Century" with
your very good portrait etc, was at Hottingners this A.M., sent by my
wife.[2] I shall read it presently. I'm off now to see if I can get your
leather trunk, sent from London, arrested by inundations & ordered
to be returned to Paris. I never needed its contents a second. And
in your little american valise & my flabby black hand bag & shawl
straps & a small satchel, I carried not only everything I used, but collected a whole library of books in Leipzig, some pieces of Venetian
glass in their bulky bolsters of sea weed, a quart bottle of eau de Cologne, and a lot of other acquisitions   I feel remarkably tough now
and fairly ravenous for my psychologic work.
    Address Hottingner

W.J.

ALS: MH bMS Am 1092.9 (2603)

    [1] Joseph Remi Léopold Delbœuf (1831–1896), Belgian philosopher and psycholo-
gist. Correspondence with WJ survives for 1882–91.
    [2] HJ, "Venice," *Century Magazine* 25 (November 1882): 3–23; reprinted in *Portraits
of Places* (1883). Also in the issue were a portrait of HJ (p. 24) and William Dean
Howells, "Henry James Jr.," *Century Magazine* 25 (November 1882): 25–29.

To Henry James

Bolton St[1] | Wdsdy. Dec 20. 82 | 8 P.M.

My dear Harry
    All is over! as I learn by the Standard this P.M.[2]   Poor Father!   It
saddens me more, much more than I expected.   I wish I had been
there, & I cannot cease to regret that you should be arriving, perhaps
even *now*, too late.   I wrote to Alice.   You will write me a full account
of everything.   Were Wilky & Bob there?[3]   My last news is only to
Dec. 4th, when alice says he was "decidedly recovering."   I feel like
leaving for home—not for any definite reason—but because when
such changes are happening it seems the place.   But I will of course
wait a fortnight till I hear more of how the details are going.   Pray
write fully & promptly.   Best of love to A, A.K. & the boys.   I have
been lapped in comfort here in your quarters—I feel in fact too much
at home & wish it were more foreign.

Yours | W.J.

ALS: MH bMS Am 1092.9 (2604)

¹ WJ was staying in HJ's rooms in London.
² The *Standard,* a London newspaper.
³ RJ was present.

From Henry James

131 Mount Vernon St. | Dec. 26ᵗʰ [1882]

My dear William.

You will already have heard the circumstances under which I arrived at New York on Thursday 21ˢᵗ, at noon, after a very rapid & prosperous, but painful passage.   Letters from Alice & Katherine L. were awaiting me at the dock, telling me that dear Father was to be buried that morning.   I reached Boston at 11 that night; there was so much delay in getting up-town.   I found Bob at the station here; he had come on for the funeral only, & returned to Milwaukee the next morning.   Alice, who was in bed, was very quiet & A.K. was perfect.   They told me everything—or at least they told me a great deal—before we parted that night, & what they told me was deeply touching, & yet not at all literally painful.   Father had been so tranquil, so painless, had died so easily &, as it were, deliberately, & there had been none—not the least—of that anguish & confusion which we imagined in London.—The next morning Alice was ill, & went to Beverley—for complete change, absence from the house &c.—with Miss Loring.   Meanwhile I had become conscious of a very bad head, which was rapidly getting worse.   I had disembarked with it, & hoped it would pass away, but on Friday p.m. I had to take to my bed, after having seen your Alice in the afternoon & definitely learned from her that you had *not* been telegraphed to.   This had been judged best, but I regretted it so much that on Saturday a.m. which was the earliest time possible, I got A.K. to go out & do it.   Alice's letters will however already explained to you this episode.   Their not telegraphing you was not neglect, but simply a miscalculation of the advisable.   My head got much worse, I sent for Dr. Beach, & have been for 3 days in bed, with one of the sharpest attacks of that damnable sort that I have ever had.   To-day, however, I am much better, but my still seedy condition must explain the poverty of this letter. Alice is still absent, & I have spent these days wholly with A.K., who quite unexhausted by her devotion to Father, has been, as always, the perfection of a nurse.   She has now told me much about all his last days—about everything that followed that news which was the last to come before I sailed. Your wife tells me that since then she has written to you every day or two—so that you will have had, by the time this reaches you, a sort of history, in detail, of his illness. It appears to have been most strange, most characteristic, above all, & as full of beauty as it was void of suffering. There was none of what we feared—no paralysis, no dementia, no violence. He simply after the "improvement" of which we were written before I sailed, had a sudden relapse—a series of swoons—after which he took to his bed not to rise again. He had no visible malady—strange as it may seem. The "softening of the brain" was simply a gradual refusal of food, because he *wished* to die. There was no dementia except a sort of exaltation of belief that he had entered into "the spiritual life." Nothing could persuade him to eat, & yet he never suffered, or gave the least sign of suffering, from inanition. All this will seem strange & incredible to you—but told with all the details, as Aunt Kate has told it to me, it becomes real—taking father as he was—almost natural. He prayed & longed to die. He ebbed & faded away—though in spite of his strength becoming continually less, he was able to see people & to talk. He wished to see as many people as he could, & he talked with them without effort. He saw F. Boott, & talked much 2 or 3 days before he died. Alice says he said the most picturesque & humorous things! He knew I was coming & was glad, but not impatient. He was delighted when he was told that you would stay in my rooms in my absence, & seemed much interested in the idea. He had no belief apparently that he should live to see me, but was perfectly cheerful about it. He slept a great deal, &, as A.K. says there was "so little of the sick-room" about him. He lay facing the windows, which he would never have darkened—never pained by the light. I sit writing this in his room upstairs, & a cast which Alice had taken from his head but which is very unsatisfactory & represents him as terribly emaciated, stands behind me on that high chest of drawers. It is late in the evening, & I have been down into the parlour—I broke off ½ an hour ago—to talk again with Aunt Kate, who sits there alone. She & the nurse alone were with him at the last—Alice was in her room with your Alice & K. Loring, & had not seen him since the night before. She saw him very little for a good many days before his death—she was too ill, & K.L. looked after her entirely. This left Father to Aunt Kate & the nurse, & the quiet simple character of his illness made them perfectly able to do everything—so that, as I said just now, there was no confusion, no embarrassment. He spoke of everything—the disposition of his things, made all his arrangements of every kind. Aunt Kate repeats again & again, that he *yearned unspeakably* to die. I am too tired to write more, & my head is beginning to ache; I must either finish this in the morning, or send it as it is. In the latter case I will write again immediately, as I have many more things to say. The house is so *empty*—I scarcely know myself. Yesterday was such a Xmas as you may imagine—with Alice at K. Loring's, me ill in bed here, & A.K. sitting alone downstairs, not only without a Xmas dinner but without any dinner, as she doesn't eat according to her wont!—27ᵗʰ a.m. Will send this now & write again tonight. All our wish here is that you should remain abroad the next six months.

Ever your   H. James jr

ALS: MH bMS Am 1094 (1998)

From Henry James

131 Mount Vernon St. | Dec. 28ᵗʰ [1882]

Dear William.

I was not able yesterday to write you a second letter, as I hoped, as I was still suffering rather too much from my head; but this evening I am pretty well myself again, & shall endeavour to go on with my story. I have seen your wife yesterday & to-day, & she tells me again that she wrote you so minutely & so constantly during the progress of Father's illness that my very imperfect record gathered from hearsay will have little value for you. Mainly, I can only repeat that the whole thing was tranquil & happy—almost, as it were, comfortable. The wanderings of his mind which were never great, were always of a joyous description, & his determination not to eat was cheerful & reasonable. That is, he was always prepared to explain why he wouldn't eat—i.e. because he had entered upon the "spiritual life,["] & didn't wish to keep up the mere form of living in the body. During the last 10 or 15 hours only his speech became thick & inarticulate: he had an accumulation of phlegm in his throat which he was too weak to get rid of. The doctor gave him a little opium, to help him, as I understand A.K., to clear his larynx, which had to some extent this effect, but which also made him sink into a gentle unconsciousness, in which, however, he still continued vaguely to talk. He spoke then several times of mother—uttering (intelligibly) her name: "Mary—my

Mary." Somewhat before this A.K. says he murmured—"Oh, I have such good boys—*such* good boys!" The efforts that he made to speak toward the last were, the Dr. (Ahlborn) assured A.K., quite mechanical & unconscious.[1] I have had (with as little delay, myself, as possible) to learn as executor. Father's property is roughly estimated at $95000; of which $75000 are in the three Syracuse houses, the rest in railway (B.C. & Q.)[2] bonds & shares.—I wish I could be assured that you have banished all thoughts of coming home, & that you find London habitable & profitable. If not, go back to Paris, but stay abroad & get all possible good, so long as I stay here, which will be till the summer. This is what we all wish. (Don't tell this to people in London, however,—or to Miss Balls, to whom I shall soon be writing.)[3] (If you are asked about my stay, say you don't know—it is uncertain.) Alice was here yesterday with the two children,[4] whom she had been having photographed—all very lovely. Farewell, dear William.

Ever yours   H James

ALS: MH bMS Am 1094 (1999)

[1] *AJB*, 207, indicates that Dr. Ahlborn was a homeopathic physician, but provides no further information.

[2] John Murray Forbes (1813–1898), a family friend, was a major railroad developer of the period. His group built the Chicago, Burlington & Quincy Line and the bonds may be associated with that company. But in the period there were numerous small railway companies with similar names and many mergers.

[3] *HJL*, 1:397, identifies Miss Balls as HJ's London landlady.

[4] Henry James and William James.

From Henry James

131 Mt. Vernon St. | Jan 1st 1883.

Dear William

I receive this a.m. your note of the 20th, written after you had seen the news of Father's death in the *Standard*. I can imagine how sadly it must have presented itself, as you sit alone in those dark, far-away rooms of mine. But it would have been sadder still if you also had arrived only to hear that after those miserable eight days at sea he was lost forever & forever to our eyes. Thank God we haven't another parent to lose;[1] though all Aunt Kate's sweetness & devotion makes me feel, in advance, that it will be scarcely less a pang when *she* goes! Such is the consequence of cherishing our "natural ties!" After a little, Father's departure will begin to seem a simple & natural fact, however, as it has begun to appear to us here.   I went out yesterday (Sunday) morning, to the Cambridge cemetery (I had not been able to start early enough on Saturday afternoon, as I wrote you I meant to do)—& stood beside his grave a long time & read him your letter of farewell—which I am sure he heard somewhere out of the depths of the still, bright winter air.[2]   He lies extraordinarily close to Mother, & as I stood there and looked at this last expression of so many years of mortal union, it was difficult not to believe that they were not united again in some consciousness of my belief.   On my way back I stopped to see Alice & sat with her for an hour & admired the lovely babe, who is a most loving little mortal.[3]   Then I went to see F. J. Child, because I had been told that he has been beyond every one full of kindness & sympathy since the first of father's illness, & had appeared to feel his death more than any one outside the family.   Every one, however, has been full of kindness—absolutely *tender* does this good old Boston appear to have shown itself.   Among others Wendell Holmes (who is now a Judge of the Supreme Court) has shone— perhaps a little unexpectedly,[4] in this respect.   Alice has been ill this last 24 hours—but not with any nervousness; only from nausea produced apparently from the doses of salvic soda that Beach has been giving her.   She is at present much better   Your letter makes me nervous in regard to your dispositions of coming home.   *Don't for the world think of this, I beseech you*—it would be a very idle step.   There is *nothing* here for you to do, not a place even for you to live, & there is every reason why you should remain abroad till the summer.   Your wishing to come is a mere vague, uneasy sentiment, not unnatural under the circumstances, but corresponding to no real fitness.   Let it subside as soon as possible, we all beg you.   I wrote you two days ago everything that there is to be told you as yet as regards Father's will. Wait quietly till you hear more from me.   I am going as soon as I can get away, to Milwaukee, & I will write you more as soon as I have been there.   A.K. is still here.   Make the most of London.

Ever yours   H. James jr

I receive all your enclosures.

ALS: MH bMS Am 1094 (2000)

   [1] WJ's mother died on 29 January 1882.

   [2] WJ's farewell letter is dated 14 December 1882 (bMS Am 1092.9 [2545]).

   [3] WJ's second son, William, in later years a painter, was born on 17 June 1882.

   [4] Oliver Wendell Holmes served as a justice on the Supreme Judicial Court of Massachusetts in 1883–1902, when he was appointed to the United States Supreme Court.

From Henry James

131 Mt. Vernon St. | Jan 8ᵗʰ [1883]

Dear William.

I wrote you two days ago, & I add a few lines to-day to make that letter complete. It is simply to let you know that I spoke to Alice this a.m. on the subject of an equal re-division of the estate, & that she gives her complete & cordial assent to the plan. It has not been possible for me to talk with her about it before, but I now find that the will has made her very unhappy from the first, & that she had placed her hopes on this arrangement. As soon as I hear from you, therefore, it will be made. I tell you this that you may know that your own voice alone is now wanting.[1] I would tell you more (about the circumstances in which the will was made—the considerations which led Father to omit Wilky &c) if I were not to[o] pressed with writing at present. This must wait till we meet. There are such a multitude of letters here to be answered. I haven't seen your Alice for a week & am therefore without any news I may have received from you. I have been very busy (back at my work, thank heaven,) & I can't leave Alice much. She is very much better, & I feel pretty sure will go on. I shall see your wife in a day or two. The redivision will be a perfectly simple transaction—not demanding in the faintest degree your presence, &c. I hope your situation is fair.

Ever faithfully yours   H. James

ALS: MH bMS Am 1094 (2001)

[1] Henry James proposed to disinherit GWJ. For the discussions within the family concerning this, see the Introduction, pp. xxxix–xli, and *BBF*, 147–56.

To Henry James

Bolton St. Jan. 9th. '83

My dear Harry,

Your eagerly awaited letter came yesterday. I was truly grieved to hear of your tumbling immediately into such a bad headache. But I hope it may have cleared you up & left you all the better for a time. Your details of the illness were very touching, but in no essential points altered the impression Alice's letters have given me. I still regret extremely that you could not have got there in time. What would I not give myself if I could have seen the dear old man lying there as you describe him, culminating his life by this drama of complete detachment from it.   I must now make amends for my rather hard non-receptivity of his doctrines as he urged them so absolutely during his life, by trying to get a little more public justice done them now.   As life closes, all a man has done seems like one cry or sentence. Father's cry was the single one that religion is real.   The thing is so to "voice" it that other ears shall hear,—no easy task, but a worthy one, which in some shape I shall attempt.[1]

I should have written you earlier, but knowing you would get my news, I concluded to wait till I should receive your letter.   You speak of a "prosperous but *painful*" voyage, a singular epithet, whose significance awakens my curiosity, as it hardly seems to betoken sea-sickness.   Alice writes no details about the will, but implies that Wilky has been cut off, to my great regret.

His diminutions of the estate in Florida were done when he was a mere boy, doing the best he knew how, too, & father was as much responsible for them as he, &c.[2]   His sickness now will make him need more money than ever, & the Cary estate, whatever its potential value may be, does not, as far as I know, bring in any considerable revenue at present.[3]   I wait for more details; but my present impression is that, however it may be with the principal, I shall make over to Wilky whatever turns out to be his natural portion of the income of my share.   With Bob & Alice the case may be somewhat different.   I hope I shall hear from you in a few days just what the details of the will are.

Of course I am anxious to know how Alice's plans & yours are shaping themselves; but that will probably be a gradual thing.   Tell her to count on my co-operation & help in any thing she thinks best for herself.

And now I suppose you would like to hear a little about the life of me in this habitat of yours.   It has been dull decidedly; & more than once I have found myself tempted to cut it all & run back to Paris where I was feeling so well, & beginning so to enjoy the expressiveness of the place.   There has been no bad fog since the week you left, but almost steady mildness & darkness, so that my eyes have got quite used up, & of late I have hired a reader for a couple of hours a day. I found the difference of light between the two floors so inconsiderable that I have stuck to the lower one as the most luxurious.   The service runs like clock-work, of course, & I feel as if I had never lived anywhere else all my life.   That is one objection to London, that its sights & sounds so soon fail to call out your observing faculties.   My social existence has been rather languid too   The rhythm of London life is so slow that I see that if one wishes to lay social "siege" to the place he must be prepared to spend many patient months of waiting till his turn come round.   Hodgson & Robertson are good friends, with whom I am always at home.[4]   Leslie Stephen has called & asked me to dinner twice, so that is all right.   Fred. Pollock asked me to dinner one Sunday noon, but has shown no subsequent thirst for my acquaintance, not calling or speaking to me in the club, &c.   Of course I have done my duty in the way of calling on the ladies of all the houses that have fed me.   I went to the Smalleys, but S. hasn't even left a card.   I've called twice on Lady Rose, & found her friendly enough, but no further notice.   Mrs. Stanley Clark the same.[5]   Hodgson has been out of town, & so has Sully.[6] Gurney, whom I should most have liked to know, has taken no notice of me, &c, &c, &c.[7]   Dont think for heaven's sake that I enumerate all this by way of complaint!   I know perfectly well that were I to stay here long enough I should get as familiar with all these people as I am with my friends at home. But meanwhile, with intense homesickness gnawing at my vitals, with no literary work being accomplished, with the darkness & with bad sleep, it need not surprise you to hear that I sometimes felt as if what I wanted to gain in London were hardly likely to be worth, when it should come, the time spent in earning it.[8]

What is the difference of outward *expressiveness* between our Anglo-Saxon civilizations & those of the continent?   The complete absence of any aggregate & outward expression of pure & direct intelligence is what is so striking here.   After Paris, London seems like a mediaeval village, with nothing but its blanket of golden dirt to take the place of style, beauty, & rationality.   At times one feels as if the former were a poor substitute.   & then one does grow impatient at times with the universal expression of aggregate stupidity, stupidity heavy & massive with a sort of voluntary self corroboration, the like whereof exist nowhere else under the sun.   Germany is the abode of the purest grace & lucency compared with this life, clogged with every kind of senseless unneccessariness, & moving down the centuries under its thick swathings, all unconscious of its load.   It appeals to me as a physical image,—with which doubtless the meteorological conditions of my stay here have s'thing to do,—England under a filthy, smeary, smoky, fog, lusty & happy, hale & hearty, with the eternal sunlit ether outside, & she not suspecting, or not caring, to think that with a puff of her breath she might rend the veil & be there.   You ought to have seen the Rossetti exhibition,—the work of a boarding school girl, no color, no drawing, no cleverness of any sort, nothing but feebleness incarnate, & a sort of refined intention of an extremely narrow sort, with no technical power to carry it out.   Yet such expressions of admiration as I heard from the bystanders!   Then the theatres & the hippopotamus-like satisfaction of their audiences!   Bad as our theatres are, they are not so massively hopeless as that.   It makes Paris seem like a sort of Athens.   Then the determination on the part of all who write now to do it as amateurs, & never to use the airs & language of a professional, to be first of all a layman & a gentleman, & to pretend that your ideas came to you accidentally as it were, & are things you care nothing about.   As I said, it makes one impatient at times; & one finds himself wondering whether England can afford forever, when her rivals are living by the light of pure rationality to so great an extent, to go blundering thus unsystematically along, & trusting to mere luck to help her to find what is good, a fragment at a time.   It's a queer mystery!   She never *has* failed to find it hitherto in perhaps richer measure than they, by her method of blundering into it.   But will it always last? & can she *always* fight without stripping?   Won't the general clearness & keenness of a rational age force her to throw some of her nonsense away, or to fall behind the rest?   I thus vomit out my bile into your probably in part sympathizing, in part indifferent ear.

But I must now stop.   I have faithfully sent all letters.   Give my warmest love to Aunt Kate, & to Alice, who of course is ere this back in Mount Vernon Street.

Ever your affectionate brother | Wm James

You might, after letting my Alice see this, send it to Wilky, to whom however I will write in a day or two.

Your "Siege of London" begins capitally.[9]

TLS: MH bMS Am 1092.9 (2605)

[1] WJ edited *The Literary Remains of the Late Henry James* (Boston: James R. Osgood, 1884).

[2] In a letter to RJ, 26 December 1882, GWJ claims that he operated the Florida enterprise for his father and that after leaving Florida he has burdened himself "for life with indebtedness to other people" in order to save the property for the family; see *BBF*, 149.

[3] GWJ's father-in-law, Joseph Cary, owned a clothing store in Milwaukee and was wealthy; see *BBF*, 116.

[4] George Croom Robertson (1842–1892), British philosopher, editor of *Mind*. Correspondence with WJ survives from 1878 to 1892.

[5] Mary Temple Rose, daughter of Lady Rose, married Sir Stanley de Astel Clarke (1837–1911), British military officer.

[6] James Sully (1842–1923), British psychologist and philosopher.

[7] Edmund Gurney.

[8] While in Europe, WJ intended to work on *The Principles of Psychology* and had brought a typewriter for that purpose.

[9] HJ, "The Siege of London," *Cornhill Magazine* 47 (January 1883): 1–34; 47 (February 1883): 225–56.

To Henry James

Bolton St Jan. 8th [9, 1883] 5 P.M.

Since mailing my letter this A.M. yours of the 28th. has arrived, containing copy of will explanations, &c. I send off this line to say that in no event should I have written to Wilky about this till I had heard something more from you. What you say relieves my mind considerably, especially as regards the size of his childrens expectations. But as regards his getting no additional income himself now that he needs it more than ever I don't think it right & will do what I can myself to obviate it. I am not sure that Alice will have enough. My share & yours from your estimate of 95,000 dollars, is very much larger than I had any idea of. The most I expected was some 5 or 6 thousand, & this makes over 20,000 a piece.

I hope you will soon go to Milwaukee. You ll find Wilky's brothers in law a poor lot, & Carry very shy, in a queer way. Be as American & homely as you can in your ways, & it will go off best. You can afterwards base a novel on it!

In great haste, yours ever, | Wm. J.

I've just had a very good time with Francis Galton at the club— asked to the Royal Society by him &c.[1]

P.S. I have spent all the afternoon trying to decide upon & expound to Bob Holton the right way of treating our revenue,[2] and such is the complicated nature of my mind that only after two good hours or more did I hit upon the true solution, which is perfectly simple. Divide estate into sixteenths, of these give wilky 3, each of us 4, and treat the rest as a separate entity. Then *we* each get $4/16 = 1/4$ of the rents and pay $1/4$ of the taxes & of the insurance. Wilky ditto, $3/16$ The odd $1/16$ pays all the interest on Wilky's mortgage, plus $1/16$ of the taxes, & $1/16$ of the insurance, and it gets $1/16$ of the rents. This gives for *our* shares this month $31.25 each, and not what I wrote you. Wilky's share is 23.46. & that of the "entity" is 7.82. Here is the balance

Wm's	31.25
H's	31.25
R's	31.25

Wk's	23.46	
Odd $\frac{1}{16}$'s	7.82	
Insurance	75 00	to be paid by me out of this remittance
	$200.03	

$200.00 being what Munroe remitted.—I think, if I am to send Holton a minute account every month that my back can't stand the burden, and for that, as well as for other reasons, it will be far best to sell store 47. Then if Holton[3] refuses to guarantee Bob life interest and we abide by terms of Will, it will oblige us only to pay him about $13,000. With the rest, we can pay off both mortgages, and have a surplus to invest, or hand over to Carrie as a still further instalment of her share. Write me immediately whether you agree to sale. I think it ought to take place, anyhow if Mary keeps the property.[4]

W.J.

TLS: MH bMS Am 1092.9 (2606)

[1] Francis Galton (1822–1911), British scientist. Correspondence with WJ survives from 1883 to 1884.

[2] Perhaps some relative of Mary Holton James, RJ's wife.

[3] Edward Holton, RJ's father-in-law.

[4] Mary Holton James.

From Henry James

131 Mt. Vernon St. | Jan. 11$\underline{th}$ [1883]

Dear William.

I wrote you two letters within these last days, & I telegraphed you to day—so that you will not have been without news of me. My telegram was the result of Alice sending me your last from London this a.m. & of my going out to see her & talking with her of your apparent plans of return. These plans were so definitely announced in the letter she had sent me, (I forget of what date,) that I was moved on my return to town to go straight to the telegraph office & send you the despatch which you will almost have received as I write this. You speak of being "determined to sail at latest in Servia of Feb. 11$\underline{th}$." This determination makes me really so sad—& Alice as well, I think—that I must do what I can to keep you from breaking loose from Europe & giving up your stay there as a failure, prematurely. The *pity* of it almost brings tears to my eyes; & when I look upon the barren scene (bating your wife & babes) that awaits you here, I feel as if I were justified in doing almost anything to keep you on the other side. I left you so comfortably established in London, with such promise of

improvement & stability (as far as the fundamentals or rather, materials of life could give it) that it seems a kind of "irony of fate" that will
bring you back, in the midst of this harsh & rasping winter, to narrow
&, as it were, accidental accommodation in Mrs. Gibbons's[1] small
house, where I think that for these coming months you would greatly
lack space & quiet.   For you to return before the summer seems a
melancholy confession of failure (as regards your projects of absence,) & sort of proclamation of want of continuity of purpose.   I
am afraid my three last letters (in relation to Father's will) will have
ministered to your unrest & anxiety, & therefore have made it more
difficult to persuade you to remain.   But I wish I could convince you
how entirely such emotions are "subjective" & without foundation in
any necessities or opportunities that exist here.   I am assuming that
you will agree to a redivision of the estate, & once that is agreed to
everything will go on as simply smoothly & easily as possible.   I go to
Milwaukee on the 15th.   Our Alice is improving every day, & fills me
with the conviction that in six months time she will have reached a
comparatively normal level.   There is every prospect of her being
able to (afford to) keep this house.[2]   We have it (the estate has it) for
the next two years & ½, & she has almost made up her mind to take it
to herself; so that she will have no anxiety, fatigue or general trouble
of change.   Your wife strikes me as distinctly *distressed* at the prospect
of your return, & she could not restrain her tears as she spoke of it to
me today.   She sees you back here by the end of February (if not
before) in a house where no provision has been made for having you
& where you cannot live as it will be well for you to live; & with a long
stretch of time to be provided for before the end of next summer; the
whole question of *what to do* forced upon her early in the season (or as
soon as you return indeed) while she hoped it would sleep on for
some months to come.   It is of course very disappointing that you
have not been able to get well at work—that you continue to feel
seedy—that the London winter should not be more helpful.   But
there is the general fact that your being in Europe is a valuable thing
& that your undertaking there oughtn't to be abandoned—to set
against these things.   It *is a long, long change for you* & as that, even as
that alone, it seems to me you would do well to hold on to it.   It is a
chance, an opportunity, which may not come to you again for years.
All this came over me much as this morning I went out to poor nudi-
fied & staring Cambridge & thought that *that* & your life there is what
you are in such a hurry to get back to!   At furthest you will take up
that life soon enough—*interpose* therefore as much as you can before

that day—continue to interpose the Europe that you are already in possession of.   Do this even at the cost of sacrifices.   You thought it well to make a great point of going there, & you were surely not altogether wrong.   You don't know when it will be possible for you to go again—therefore don't drop the occasion from your grasp.   Even if you don't do your psychology, you will do something else that it is good (being there & with strong reasons at any rate against your return) to do; & you will escape the depressing effect of seeing yourself (& being seen by others) simply *retomber* here, to domestic worries & interruptions & into circumstances from which you had undertaken to abstract yourself.   It seems to Alice of course (as well as to me) that your idea of going to live in some other house (i.e. take a room somewhere in Garden St.)³ would give a dreary & tragic completeness to such a collapse & have the air of your having committed yourselves to inconstant & accidental (not to say shiftless) ways.   Therefore I say, stick to Europe till the summer, in spite of everything, in the faith that you are getting a great deal out of it & that it is a good & valuable thing.   My rooms shall you have for an *indefinite period*, without *the cost of a penny*.   After Feb 1ˢᵗ your circumstances will improve—the air will be much more fogless, the days longer, the light abundant.   If you are lonely, I will send you as many introductions as you can desire.   Take the money that is necessary, for the reason that you are doing a thing that you will not do again for a long time.   As soon as the estate is settled you will begin to receive your share of the income from the houses in Syracuse, which (if the redivision takes place,) will then be owned by you, Wilky, Bob, & me; Alice's share residing wholly in the railway securities into which the money of the Quincy St. house was put.   These houses are of the value of $75000, & Mr. Munroe writes a very favourable account of the property.   It yields *ten percent*, which however is reduced to *seven* by taxes, repairs & other expenses (his salary, which he has now begun to take.)   The houses in question are to be greatly improved by the creation, close to them, of the new public offices of the city—post-office, city hall, court house, &c. There is nothing to be done, that I know of, to delay the settlement of the estate after the re-distribution (to include Wilky) is made.   The more promptly therefore as well as the more definitely, I hear from you about this the sooner the whole business will be brought to a conclusion.   Of course on your assent being given to the re-division, a document, which we are all to sign, must be sent out to you; so that there will be delay to that extent.   My last three letters must have seemed to you very dry & sordid—especially the first, in which I enclosed you a copy of Father's Will; but the whole subject is one I have had to *aborder* without loss of time.   I think it very possible that you wrote to Wilky after you had got that first letter of mine & if so, told him that you desired, in your degree, to make up to him for his having been excluded by Father.   In this case you will have done what the rest of us have done.   Don't judge that exclusion of Wilky harshly, as regards Father; *don't judge at all*, in fact, for the present. Eventually when you have been home & we have talked about it, & you know the circumstances, you will see it all in a just light.   I wish to warn you once for all, in advance, most solemnly, against letting anything I may write to you, by accident or necessity, add in any degree to your restlessness, foster your anxiety or your homesickness or make you believe in the least that there is a reason for your being here.   There is & can be no such reason, & it is only the agitation of sentiment (very natural, of course) that will make you feel so.   I must close my letter, lest you think I say too much.   Excuse me if I have been indiscreet or violent; I have only tried to translate the impression that is strong within me—the fear that after you should get back, finding yourself face to face with the long stretch of time which you would have to dispose of in uncomfortable ways before begining your college work next autumn, you would curse your folly in having let go of your simpler existence in Europe.   Send postcards to the people (e.g. Miss Hilliard)[4] who write to you, telling them that you can't answer them at length.   Alice tells me that she has spoken to you of a plan of going out to you for the summer, to spend it in some quiet place in England.   I think it would be feasible, for, as she says, you & she have no present home & you must arrange yourselves somewhere & somehow, from June to September.   Ask Mrs Leslie Stephen about St. Ives, Cornwall, where she & her husband have a house & go every summer.   I should think that would suit you—& you would have the Stephens' society.   I told Alice I would write you a "strong" letter on the subject of your return; she gave her full assent, & you will probably think I have succeeded.—Aunt Kate who has been ten days in Newport, will by this time have returned to N.Y.   Poor old Tweedy appears to be failing.   Father's absence has become a natural fact—it seems (to me at least) as if he had been gone for a long time.   But that comes of course partly from my own absence.   I write this in the parlour, late in the evening, after Alice has gone to bed; Duveneck's picture, which is opposite to me, grows unexpectedly in value.[5]   It seems so odd that *he* should have translated, perpetuated Father! There has been a week of snowstorms, & the earth is buried deep. Does the Athenaeum comfort you?

Ever your brother   H. James jr

P.S.   Much as I have said I feel as I had not said enough: expressed my sense of the (as it were) painful want of *form* there would be in your coming back—a few weeks after Father's death—after having been away at that time, & through all his illness—to live in a homeless & nondescript way in Cambridge, where you have ceded your place— and where, for the time, you would be neither in the college nor out of it.   And I can't bear to see you *lâcher* Europe! Lastly, I think it would be a great disappointment to your wife!—

ALS: MH bMS Am 1094 (2002)

[1] Eliza Gibbens.

[2] The house at 131 Mount Vernon St., Boston.

[3] WJ lived at 15 Appian Way in 1883–85 and then moved to 18 Garden St.

[4] Mary Hillard.

[5] The portrait of Henry James by Frank Duveneck is in the Brooklyn Museum.   It is reproduced as a frontispiece in Frederic Harold Young, *The Philosophy of Henry James, Sr.* (New York: Bookman Associates, 1951).

To Henry James

London Jan. 22 [1883]

Dear Harry,

Yours of the 8th. is just in, telling of Alice's consent, &c.   I suppose my alternative proposition has arrived too late.   I confess I'm a little sorry for it, as it seems to me to have a certain number of merits, & I should think Wilky himself might prefer it to a simple division.   It saves the *principle* of father's will, which was no doubt dictated by a sort of undiscriminating justice that made no exact calculations of consequences,—when did father ever calculate a consequence?—& it practically results in giving Alice a larger sum than she would other- wise have, without seeming directly to rob you and me, and at a cost to Wilky of at the outside less than $2000.   I remember perfectly how troubled father was by the repeated money demands to stave off Wilky's business failure, & how Wilky urged those demands by beg- ging that the money advanced be considered as a discounting of his inheritance.   Father made no legal bargain of that kind with him for the simple reason that legal bargains were foreign to his nature; but I know that he kept the feeling that Wilky in some way ought to remain responsible for the money thus lost, & this foolish wholesale will was the expression of that feeling. I feel quite sure myself that Wilky would rather be responsible. For us absolutely to ignore that element in father's will would be to cast rather a dishonourable slur on *him*, would it not? Just as absolutely to carry it out would cast too dishonorable a slur on Wilky. The compromise I suggest would thus be a harmonious thing all round on which we could with cordiality combine.

I meant to have written anyhow to Wilky to day to assure him of my undying love &c.; but four notes come in to answer, in addition to your letter, & I've been awake since half past four, & *must* get at my psychology. Thick yellow fog to day, I dined two nights ago at Mrs Frederic Harrison's between her & a very vivacious Mrs. Cookson, who spoke very affectionately of you, & invites me to dine on Friday.[1] But I'm engaged, & must on Saturday save my life by escaping to Paris. Ne'er did place seem to agree with me less than London, strange to say. I like the people more & more; of all the *kunstproducte* of this globe, the exquisitely & far-fetchédly fashioned structure called the English race & temperament, is the most precious. I should think a poor Frenchman would behold with a kind of frenzy the easy & genial way in which it solves, or achieves without needing to solve, all those things which are for his unfortunate people the impossible.

Pray let Wilky see both my letters,—they will serve as letters to him, & if he likes, he can pass them on to Bob with the same intent. Give my warmest love to Alice. I'm delighted your report of her is better.

Yours ever, | Wm. J.

TLS: MH bMS AM 1092.9 (2607)

[1] In an 1880 letter to his father, HJ mentions a Montagu Cookson (*HJL*, 2:273). Since during his stay in London WJ took over HJ's social circle, it is likely that the same Cooksons are involved. Perhaps he is the Montague Hughes Cookson who in 1866 published a book on law.

To Henry James

Bolton St. Jan 23 [1883]

My dear Harry,

On my return from a little dinner party at Hodgsons half an hour ago, I found your long letter of the day of the "stay" telegram (Jan. 11) waiting for me. I shall owe you the price of that telegram, plus I dont know what for literary work spent on me. It makes my heart bleed that the relation of brother should entail such sacrifices. & I know now just how one's half-crazy relations feel when they get letters of good counsel.   Your solicitude is natural enough, but it certainly flows from a great misconception of all the premises that are operative in the case,—it is true that you are not to blame for that, since I alone can know them.   In the first place, I hesitated long whether to take my leave of absence at all; doubting whether anything material was to be gained by it.   What decided me was the Psychology alone. Then I long doubted whether the better way would not be to finish that in Cambridge, & not come away; & finally decided that the chance of hygienic benefit & refreshment for me, & undisturbed possession of its mother by the baby, spoke in favor of departure.   But as far as the opinion of outsiders & their exclamations of "failure" (which you seem so much to dread,) go, I took great pains to say to every one that I did not think I could stay the winter, & I heard many, President Eliot among the rest, echo that they should not think I could, away from my wife.   The horror you seem to feel at Cambridge is something with which I have no sympathy, preferring it as I do to any place in the known world.   Quite as little do I feel the infinite blessing of simply being in London, or in Europe ueberhaupt. The truth is, we each of us speak from the point of view of his own work; the place where a man's work is best done seems & ought to seem the place of places to him.   I feel tempted to go back now just to show you how happy a man can be in the wretched circumstances that so distress your imagination.   A room outside of my wife's house, with the privilege of seeing her twice a day, is luxury itself compared with *this* mode of being outside of her house.   A quiet evening with sleep at ten, is heaven, to this obligatory Punchinello-existence every night in the week, a thing I never could stand at home & which threatens completely to undo my sleep here.   Of course, feeling as I did about my possible return, it was a terrible practical mistake to have let my house to Toy.   I did it in a moment of economic impulsiveness & hope, repented it loudly the next instant, and every instant afterwards,—last summer hardly less than now.   But it is folly because you can't have everything to take nothing.   If Cambridge out of my wife's house appears better for work & sleep than Europe, I ought to go there; even tho Cambridge *in* my wife's house would be better still.   I have already gained much from Europe in the way of seeing philosophers & races of men; but all that is secondary to my main purpose.   I have *apparently* gained nothing at this date in the way of health, but that can't be fully known till next winter when I shall see if I bear the year's strain better for this rest. I certainly believe, since I have *begun* the experiment, in prolonging it as long as possible, short of the point of absolutely losing the year, which would happen if if the non-psychologising weeks of hitherto extend into the future. I also believe in leaving Alice as long as possible to the baby undisturbed. When I decided on returning, a few weeks ago, things seemed less hopeful here than they do now. The stress of my correspondence is now over, not to be renewed. (To poor Miss Hillard I have not even sent the post-card you recommend). The last two days I have written some psychology; & since yesterday noon a dry east wind & cold air has made me feel like a different man,—I should not have supposed that change of weather could effect such a revolution. Dr. Ferreir[1] told me last night he had never seen such weather as that of the last month for aggravating nervous diseases, all his patients, & himself, worse than they ever had been. Having a reader occasionally helps matters very much too, & I accordingly thought this morning it would be safe to write to Alice that it would not be neccessary for me to return on the 10th. The fact is that although from a moral point of view your sympathy commands my warmest thanks; from the intellectual point of view, it seems first to suppose that I am a bachelor, & second that I am one who suffers intensely from the skinniness & aridity of America. I should perhaps suffer were I not at work there, but as it is I dont; & being a married man, any place near *her* is a good bit better than any place where she is not.

If the Psychology only keeps on as it has now started, & more than all, if the air either of Paris or of an improved London,—they tell me that never in the memory of man has there been so uninterruptedly depressing a winter here,—starts up my eyes & sleep again, I certainly shall not think of coming home for a good many weeks to come.

I suppose you will be sorry to get so elaborate a self "vindication". I might have simply sent you a line of light reassurance. But really there was something distressing about so painful a solicitude on your part, resulting from so imperfect an apprehension of the facts of my *status* in Cambridge. There is not a man in the College who knows me, to whom my return now would not seem the most natural & proper of acts. I should only have to make the best of the joke of having let my house to Toy, surely a very easy thing to do. (24th A.M.) I have half a mind to tear up this over solemn reply & write you a single page. But I can't do any more writing on the subject. It was drawn from me in the first flush of indignation at being treated like a small child who didn't know what his own motives or interests were. Your feeling evidently comes from comparing Cambridge at large with Europe at large, & then supposing that any given human being must be worse off in the one than in the other. Whereas it all depends on which place the human being has *business* in. I'm sure I've heard you complain enough of having to live where all your time went in futilities and your serious affairs went irreparably lost. Your working power is about three times mine; & what is lost this year on my psychology can perhaps never, or not for 8 years to come, be made up. *All* that I see & do here is futility compared to that.—I'm glad you intimate that the Syracuse property is not to be sold yet. I must go out & see it, as soon as I return. I'm especially glad that you give so encouraging an account of Alice. Please give her my best love & with many thanks to yourself for your sympathy and trouble believe me always your loving bro.

Wm.

My Alice can tell you all about our doubts relative to Europe. Just the things we realized as dangers beforehand are what have come to pass,—and the remedy of return was always present to our minds<.> Of course if Syracuse is not to be sold, division by simple fifths is by far better than my proposal.

What is our Alices glove number   I'll send her some from Paris.

TLS: MH bMS AM 1092.9 (2608)

¹David Ferrier (1843–1928), Scottish neurologist and physiologist. One letter from WJ is known, dated 1881.

From Henry James

Globe Hotel | Syracuse. Jan 23ᵈ [1883]
Dear William.

I wrote you a long letter upwards of a fortnight ago—& you will perhaps at the present moment be staggering under the receipt of it. I trust that the purity of my intentions may have served as an excuse for the exaggerated zeal—possibly—with wh. I entered into the question of your coming home. It seemed to me such a pity you should do so at this dreary season, & in the present situation of your wife, that, seeing she also thought it an equal pity, I couldn't restrain the violence of my feeling on the subject. It seemed to me—& it strikes me so still—very melancholy, & wanting in the proper dignity of your station, that you should come back to spend these next months in Cambridge without a home of your own & without your normal position in the College. However, I won't return to all that now, for by the time this reaches you, you will have made up your mind in pursuance of your own reasons. Perhaps—I certainly hope so—that the problem of life in London will have put on a fairer face. I hope at any rate that you are physically better, whether you come or stay. If you do come back the right place—i.e. habitation—for you will be the 3ᵈ bed-room in the Mt. Vernon St. House. That will be better than living at Mrs. Gibbens's. I occupy Father's room, & Alice her old room; but there is an excellent 3ᵈ story front bedroom, which used to be A. Kate's I won't offer to give you up Father's room, because I lately made you a present of my rooms in London. But peace to all this—which is not àpropos as I sit at the window of the principal hotel at Syracuse, looking out at our "property" here, which returns my gaze from its eminently eligible position across the way.—I am on my way back from a visit of about four days to Wilky & Bob. We are in the midst of a period of terrific cold—the thermometer at Milwaukee was 20° below zero. This of course did not conduce to the cheerfulness of an episode intrinsically rather sad. The three letters I have written you as executor of the estate will have put you into possession of all that has lately passed with regard to it. It has been an immense load off my mind in seeing Wilky & Bob that before I did so I should have written you my proposal for your assent to an equal redivision of the estate. If I made you that proposal *then* with eagerness, I should have made it now with an even greater desire that it be realized. I wrote you last of Alice's entire assent to it—& Bob of course is only too glad. That Father's will should have been made just as it was, has been a source of the greatest unhappiness to all of us here—an unhappiness but faintly reflected in the first letters I wrote you on the subject, for reasons which I shall be able to explain to you better some other day. Time—each succeeding day—has only made the thing more regrettable. I have so far presumed on your seeing it in this light that I asked Joe Warner, before leaving Boston, to send you a paper of agreement to a redivision, to sign—before waiting to hear from you definitely. I did this simply to save time—though I now see that it makes very little practical difference, as it will take three or four months longer to settle the estate. It will however be a great pleasure to me to write to Wilky & Bob on the earliest day that you *do* assent to the redivision. You probably will yourself have written to them to this effect.　I staid with Wilky at Milwaukee, & found him, I am sorry to say, a sadly broken & changed person.　I am afraid he is pretty well finished, for his spirits have gone a good deal, as well as his health, though all his old gentleness & softness remains.　When I got there he was in the grip of a rheumatic attack, but it left him 36 hours after my arrival, & then he was very much better.　I think he might, in spite of his double malady, get on decently well in the future if he had some small idea of taking care of himself, or if his wife had some idea of taking care of him.　But they have absolutely none—as is shown in their whole manner of life, & Carry's imbecility is especially deplorable.　I lectured & preached them much; I hope with some effect.　Bob strikes me as a good deal better than he used to be; he has become a landed proprietor.　That is, he & Mary have by her father's advice, invested $7000 (of hers) in the purchase of a country residence or rural retreat about 5 miles from Milwaukee & about 2 from Holton's own residence.　It is a small but solid brick house, with a Grecian portico, & a really very charming domain of 35 acres.　It needs to have a little money spent on it—but it is, says Holton, a very wise investment.—I have spent a large part of to-day with Munroe, our agent here.　The "property" is very good; much better than I supposed—in the very best position in town, in good order, & occupied by prosperous 1$\underline{st}$ class tenants. It yields, after all charges are paid, $5,250. per annum—which makes for each of the four of us $1312 income.　(As I told you, Alice's share is to be taken from the other property.)　Munroe strongly advises its being kept together about 4 years longer, as it is constantly increasing in value.　He is sure that at the end of that time the property would sell for about $87000.　Of all this however I will write you later.　I scribble this while I wait for the train which tonight bears me away— I reach Boston tomorrow night.　Munroe drove me this afternoon, in spite of the cold, along *James St.* the 5$\underline{th}$ Avenue of Syracuse, one of the handsomest American strts. I have ever seen—named after our poor Grandfather![1]　I must close this, pack my bag, & eat my "supper."　I shall probably find news from you in Boston.

Yours ever | H. James jr

ALS: MH bMS Am 1094 (2003)

[1] William James (of Albany) (1771–1832).

From Henry James

Boston, Jan. 25, 1883

My dear William,—

. . . I got home last evening and found the letters . . . of January 9th and of later the same day; acknowledging my first two letters, the copy of Father's will, etc. The first contains two or three pages of remark and reflection upon England and the English, which, although rather gloomy and splenetic, are so admirably felt and admirably expressed that they have given me extraordinary pleasure. They put into much more vigorous form than I have ever been able to give them, the thoughts and impressions which have again and again arisen within me during all these years that I have lived in London, and which have finally landed me in the consciousness that if it is good to have one foot in England, it is still better, or at least as good, to have the other out of it. I have n't time to answer all you say at present, but of course you know, true as it all is, it is only part of the statement. There is more beside, and it is this *more beside* that I have been living on in London. Every now and then you will feel it (though as you are not a "story writer" you will feel it less than I) much as you have felt the stupidity, the dowdiness and darkness. England always seems to me like a man swimming with his clothes on his head. . . .

Your social solitude, I confess, is what I feared—but I hope that the days will bring forth some social incidents of an easy type, as well as more light, more cheerfulness, and more of the sense that underneath, as it were, you *are* getting good. I offered you introductions (letters) in my last, but don't know how, where, or whether, to begin with them,—and doubt even that the simple dinner-party-producing-invitation-letter is just the alleviation you want. This alleviation will come from *general* causes,—partly from London brightening and improving, and partly from your getting used to it.

Ever yours, | H. James

TCWJ, 1:390–91

From Henry James

131 Mt. Vernon St. | Feb. 5th [1883]

Dear William.

Your letter of Jan. 20th in which you acknowledge my first (of Jan 6th) with regard to a re-division of Father's estate, has just come in, &

I hastily acknowledge it.   You will have heard from me *since then* about that matter, & I hope will have since made up your mind to agree to a re-division *pure & simple*.   I think that if you were here, you would do so.   What you say about deducting $5000 (the amount furnished Wilky on the eve of his failure,) has something to be said for it, but my *strong* feeling is now, & it is in a high degree Bob's & Alice's, that as things are at present this had better not be insisted upon. What Wilky owes Bob to-day is only a $1000; & this amount *is* to be deducted from his share & made over to Bob.   This done, it will be better not to attempt to take acct. of his debt to the estate.   If we did so, the money gained would make only a little more than $1000 for each of the rest of us, which is not enough to set against the satisfaction of having let the thing go, in deference to Wilky's broken down condition.   He strikes me so much (& so pitiably) not having long to live, that it doesn't seem well, in these last *months* (perhaps) to attempt to give him a lesson.   So, I say, Alice feels, & so does Bob, & I therefore (as it is my own earnest feeling) again express the sincere hope that you will by this time have signified to me your assent to the division *pure & simple* (as I say,) making no differences between us on account of money supplied in the past.   I have already given Wilky an assurance that this would be the arrangement & I feel as if I could not now take upon myself to undeceive him.   What you say about our making over certain fractions (obtained through the execution of Wilky's forfeit) to Alice & to Bob, would be admitted by you to be nugatory if you were here.   Bob will have—(we each will have) $21000 or $22000 from the estate, & though he has embraced a life of leisure, the prospects of his children, with their solidly well-off grandfather, (I judged of all this at Milwaukee) are much better than those of any other members of the family.   And, as I say, Bob himself desires the redistribution more than any of us.   Of course the forfeiture by him of $7000 was a thing never to be for a moment entertained.   Alice will with her own well-invested property be *perfectly well off*—she will have (with the letting of her Manchester house) an income of about $3,500.   She is very apparently to let the house this year for $1000 (to Mrs. Pratt & Mrs. Bell. To do so she is to build a stable—which she can easily do by getting a mortgage of $1000 on the house, which she can easily pay off *moyennant* $50 a year.)[1]   I have so counted on your assenting to the simple re-division that as I told you the other day I authorized J. Warner to send you a paper to sign, (before I should hear from you) to save time.   It now appears that he will have to send you another, inasmuch as the former didn't embody the fact that I intend to take upon myself to put Wilky's share *in trust* for him (to J. Warner himself, who says he will be very glad to be his trustee & in whom we can surely have perfect confidence.) This I regard as my bounden duty. Therefore I shall settle Wilky's share upon his children, with a life-interest for him & for Carry; the money to revert to Father's heirs in case the children die childless. I CANNOT go into the question of Wilky's debts, though I fear they are many. I can only go by what I see—Wilky broken down, dying, on the point of giving up his office & salary (he must do so in any &[2] event & notably now, to come to Alice & me here, for the long stay we have urged upon him,) & none but the most vague, indefinite & impalpable expectations for his children. (Don't allude to all this if you write him.) If therefore, by the time you get this, you have not assented to the literal redivision, let me—I beseech you—hear from you that you have thought better of it & will do so. This will refresh, revive & rest me more than I can say. I can't now go into what you say further about coming home. I can only express my gladness that you have (for your own sake) been away all this time, & that you are still away. The interruptions—(the family life & famy questions) here—would have been *bien autre* for you than any you can have suffered from all alone in London. *I am hoping exceedingly that you will have gone to Paris.* If this simple & easy expedient will help you to remain longer in Europe, it seems to me your bounden duty to embrace it.

Bien à toi   H. James jr

ALS: MH bMS Am 1094 (2004)

[1] In 1881 AJ bought some land in Manchester, a coastal town in Massachusetts north of Boston. She had a house built in 1882. The two renters are not identified.

[2] HJ may have been anticipating the '&' after 'event' when he wrote this unnecessary '&'.

To Henry James

Bolton St. Feb. 6th 1883

My dear Harry,

Two letters from you, one from Syracuse, & the other of the 25th from Boston just after your return. Your account of poor Wilky is pathetic enough; I hope the plan of his spending some weeks or months in Boston will prove a feasible one. What you say of the Syracuse property is good to hear,—I had thought it might be a good thing to get rid of it, having heard nothing for years past but delays of rent, & taxes & repairs eating up so much of what came at last.

You say you enjoyed the outpouring of my bile upon England: you will ere this have learned from my other letters that I see "the other side" as well.　They are a delectable brood, & only the slow considerings of a Goethe could do them plenary justice.　The great point about them seems their good-humour & *cheerfulness*; but their civilization is *stuffy*.　In spite of that, *it* is, & their whole nature is, one of the most exquisite *Kunstwerke* that the womb of time has ever brought forth.　It might have failed to ripen so smoothly, but fortune seconded them without a break, & they grew into the set of customs & traditions & balancing of rights that now rolls so elastically along.

However, I can't write a proper letter & must refer you to my bride for gossip.　Your allusions to my return, continue by their solemn tone to amuse me extremely.　Especially are the expressions "confession of failure" & "appearance of vacillation" comical.　The only possible "failure" would be to stay here longer than the refreshment, which was the only motive, either tacit or avowed, of my coming, lasted.　& there can be no appearance of vacillation where there was no plan announced beyond that of staying on from week to week as long as I found it to pay.　However, my reply to your first letter will have opened your eyes to all that; meanwhile the strength of your sympathy does equal credit to your head & heart.　For some reason or other London does thoroughly disagree with me.　I am in a state of acute brain-fag, although I've done a mere minimum of work.　I am only staying out the week on account of a philosophical dinner which takes place on Friday, this being Monday.[1]　I feel as if the darkness of your quarters must have something to do with it; & I can't bear to think of you yourself being permanently here.　I'm sure any man of your temperament needs the direct light of the sky, if not of the sun, in his rooms, bed-room as well as sitting room.　I am glad to hear from my wife that Alice is doing well.　This letter is for her as well as for you.　Give her lots of affection & sympathy, & believe me ever yours,

Wm. James

How your letter writing must destroy you.　Don't feel any call to write to me when inconvenient.　You know my Alice tells me everything, & will tell me any messages you send.

TL: MH bMS Am 1092.9 (2609)

[1] 6 February 1883 was a Tuesday.　The dinner was that of an informal philosophical group called the "Scratch Eight," with Edmund Gurney, George Croom Robertson, Frederick Pollock, Leslie Stephen, James Sully, Shadworth Hodgson, and Frederic William Maitland (1850–1906), British legal historian, as members.　The

talk WJ gave that evening became "On Some Omissions of Introspective Psychology."

From Henry James

131 Mt. Vernon St. | Feb. 7th [1883]

Dear William.

I receive this a.m. your letter of Jan 23^{d} written on the receipt of *my* letter (accompanying telegram) urging you to remain in Europe. I quite expected that you would be irritated by my long argument on the subject of your not coming home, & you may imagine how much I wished to put it before you that I should have written to you in the face of this conviction—& have also recurred to the matter more than once in writing to you since—with touches which will have revived your irritation. Of course I didn't pretend or attempt to treat of the reasons that presented themselves to you on behalf of your coming back—for you could be amply trusted to look after these yourself. Such reasons there were, I know—but all I could afford to do was to talk of the opposite ones. It *did* seem a part of my duty to put these latter before you as they presented themselves here, especially as I saw that Alice was so full of them; & I even thought you might after all be glad to know how your return would look—superficially at least from the point of view of standing here. I have no doubt that you *have* been glad, since you wrote. But all this is over & done with by this time, & I only write to acknowledge your letter though I wrote you yesterday (Don't of course answer my letters any more than is absolutely necessary). There has also come this a.m. your other note of Jan. 23^{d}, making it all right about the equal re-division—which, if I had waited till to-day, would have spared me my letter of yester-day.—I enter fully into all your reasons for coming back, as set forth in your to-day's letter—but I *still* hope you will have gone to Paris, & will be better enough for the change to remain there some weeks. I am bound to say, however, that I still don't see how in your lonely life in London (for though you speak now of seeing more people) you had written me at the time I telegraphed that your social solitude was complete, your time is not more your own than in Cambridge, sur-rounded by so many relatives, & so much family, all in so little room. You speak of a "Punchinello-life" in the evenings—but I don't know what you mean by this—& you must allude to something quite differ-ent from the state you were in a month ago. Different, & if you survive it, I venture to believe better!   I stick to the doctrine of the "skin-niness" of Cambridge, even for you, enough to be sure that [there] is nothing Punchinello-like that may have happened to you in London, even at the cost of your sleep, that you will not be glad of after you get back here.   Let me add that so far from writing to you as a bachelor, my letter was the direct product of much talk with your wife about your return & much sympathy with the distress that the prospect caused her—distress I mean, on acct. of your homeless condition & the failure of your attempt.   Now, I shall be equally satisfied, which-ever you do.   Don't use your eyes upon me, any more than simple business may require.

Ever your   H. James

ALS: MH bMS Am 1094 (2005)

From Henry James

131 Mt. Vernon St. | Feb. 11<u>th</u> [1883]

Dear W<u>m</u>

I feel as if I ought to write to you again to-day on acct. of your letter of Jan. 22<u>d</u> (just rec'd.) although I have written you so much of late. My last, two or three days since, was a rather (perhaps) heated reply to the letter in which you acknowledge the arrival of mine (sent at the same time as the telegram) urging you not to return home.   If this has seemed to you nasty or ill-tempered, please don't mind it.   It *was* rather meddlesom in me to have so much to say about the question of your coming back—but I repeat that it was a case in which to meddle seemed the *safest* thing, & to trot out all the reasons against your re-turn (leaving you to do justice to the others) seemed the only way to treat the subject from this side (if treated at all.)   I even persist in meddling, so far as to be glad that you have not yet come & that ac-cording to your last (of the 25<u>th</u> Jan.) to Alice you are probably now in Paris.   (Alice reads me & sends me everything possible.)   I write this with a clear understanding that you won't answer it, & that you will write to me after this as little, & as briefly, as possible.   This is only to return, very briefly on my side, to the question of the redivision of the estate with regard to Wilky, as to which I have already written you so much & to which you again return, yourself, in this letter of Jan 22<u>d</u> (I have just been for three days to Newport, & I find it on my return.) I agree in all you say as to the *principle* of Father's holding Wilky re-sponsible for the $5000 advanced to him before his failure, & I can only repeat that if the circumstances were now more favourable to our cutting down his allowance it should certainly be done. But they are as little so as possible. I have now decided to assent to his *own* request to except $5000 from the amount I am to put into trust for him (*i.e.* the rest of his equal share,) to enable him to pay his debt to Bob & two or three other "debts of honour." (His debt to Bob, it now appears, amounts, not as I told you last, to $1000 but to about $1500) To cut off more than this would be rather grievous—& his state of mind & of health together are such that I shrink from carrying out such a plan. Just now both his children are ill with scarlet fever (it appears to be light) & in the midst of this addition to his other troubles I feel like letting him off easily. You may think that I am rather weak about this; & I am, I admit. But I put it all on the ground of Wilky's generally collapsed condition. If it were a palpable injury to any of us, I should not urge my own project in preference to yours. But as the difference between the two is so small, in favour of yourself, of Alice & of me, & as Bob moreover is to be paid in this way, as well as in yours, I think we had better abide by the fact that having Wilky equal with us & not insisting on the forfeit in order to justify Father, will be the thing which satisfies most of the proprieties of the case. The will was unfortunate, in its wholesale character, & the best way to justify Father is simply to assume that he expected us, (as he *did* expect us) to rearrange equally. No need to go over all this though, as I believe that I said in my last, you will have assented to my way of doing the thing, before this reaches you. What I have, after all, mainly wished to tell you is that I have judged it best *not* to forward him your letters recommending this modification of my proposal. I shall let him suppose that you have simply assented to it, & shall leave it to your confidence that I am acting for the best as the circumstances appear to me here, to justify me.

Yours ever | H. James

Our Alice gets on very well.

ALS: MH bMS Am 1094 (2006)

To Henry James

Paris, Feb. 22. 83

My poor Harry

Yesterday two letters from you one about Wilky & Bob & the property business which it is too bad you had to write; another about my letter in reply to yours urging me not to come home. As that matter seems to be solving itself by my taking your advice, I need say no more about it, except to tell you that I was not "irritated" or if so, but for a moment and in the gentlest degree, by your talk about public confession of failure & vacillating purpose etc, which seemed to me rather a misunderstanding of the facts. I don't know how it was, but for three or 4 weeks in London I did *nothing* literally *nothing*, but write letters, day after day. Naturally that was a most excellent reason, added to the rest for thinking I had made a mistake. But fortunately the need of it has all passed away, and except my letters to Alice, I have none to speak of to write. I think it highly probable now that I shall go to Florence about the 4th or 5th of March to have a few days of interview with Davidson for philosophic purposes, and that this accession of variety will enable me to stay on into April without sacrificing any thing besides money. As for that I rather shut my eyes. I would give any thing to see you, and to see Alice & Wilky, and talk over all that has been gone through. But the time will come. For other news & gossip I must refer you to the letters I write to my bride. I envy you the privilege of conversation with her, as I envy her hers with you. I have just written to poor Wilky on whom the hand of the Lord seems to lie pretty heavy in these days. Your arrangement about trust and reversion if his children have no children of their own seems to me hardly a good thing. I dislike the idea of the principle of father's will being absolutely set aside. But the dangers of controlling property beyond two lives seem not only to pertain to cases where the last beneficiary has natural heirs. Witness Nelly Grymes & Cousin Helen.[1] Our children's children may be like Albert Wyckoff or R. Temple, who can say? I think it is a dangerous principle. But if you've already taken steps, go ahead. The danger is only potential, and it saves the principle of the will. Best love to Alice, who, I hope, is doing well.

Ever yours   W.J.

ALS: MH bMS Am 1092.9 (2610)

[1] Apparently Helen Wyckoff Perkins.

To Henry James

Paris Feb. 26. [1883]

Dear H.

Here is a letter from Aunt Josey, which has sufficient real grounds, apart from any possible desire on her part to open communications with us now that father's estate is divided.[1] I wrote her a long answer this A.M. and said (what is true enough) that I have always thought it a pity we should not know the girls, but that it went on from month to month so without systematic intention. I told her you were summoned away from Washington by telegram after two weeks, & I felt sure that you would have looked up Florence earlier had you expected your stay to be so short. My eyes are very bad so I will say no more. I wrote you a post-card yesterday. I hope you won't have to write any more details about the estate—all can be made clear when we see each other, which I don't believe is far hence.

Please give my best love to Alice. I bought her a few gloves this A.M. which I will send by mail.

Adieu! | W.J.

28th

This letter from Wilky comes this morning—I send it on account of the feeling allusion to your self, which will undoubtedly do good to your heart. You are rapidly becoming the "rich bachelor uncle" of fiction & the drama, and surely could n't have a better *emploi*. I have at last decided to go home in the Servia of the 17 or in some big ship thereabouts.[2] Staying longer is overstaying the good of the trip. I shall do twice as much work & be twice as happy now at home, and a wonderful peace has stolen over me since I made the decision. I get tired of the theatre here except the francais etc. and so many nights of it are bad for me. On friday I accompany Mrs Perry & Mrs Wister to Judic in "Nitouche."[3]

Affect^{ly} yours Wm.

I shall be glad enough to see you all face to face after all you've been through.

WJ

I enclose a pair of gloves for Alice, & will soon send some more.

ALS: MH bMS Am 1092.9 (2611)

[1] Apparently Josephine James.

[2] The *Servia* with WJ aboard left Liverpool 17 March 1883 and arrived in New York on 26 March 1883.

[3] Perhaps Frances Sergeant Perry, Thomas Sergeant Perry's mother. Anna-Marie-

Louise Judic (1849–1911), French actress, in *Mam'zelle Nitouche*, by Henri Meilhac (1831–1897) and Albert Millaud (1844–1892), French playwrights.

To Henry James

Care of Smith Beede | Keene Valley, Essex Co, N.Y. | Aug. 1. 83
Dear Harry

I re-enclose Munroe's letter which came last night. I wish you'd tie up all your correspondence with him separate, for me to inherit when you go. You don't seem, judging by the $122 you call my share this month, to have deducted anything from the rents for the mortgage expenses,—perhaps, however they were very small. The valley here looks more beautiful than ever, & the Putnams have made great improvements about the place.[1] William is a transformed being, hardly having whimpered for 4 days, and Harry is perfectly intoxicated with all he can do here, and with the attractions of a female companion aged 11 & named Berthy.[2] So everything looks rosy for our summer, and t'is a solid comfort to have so unexpectedly got off an article for Mind before leaving.[3] You'll probably be off to M̰ Desert when this reaches Boston, so I won't say more. The nights have been quite cold here—Love to Bob, who, I hope, is prospering.

Yrs. always | Wm James

I have been reading your two Atlantic contributions. You treat Renan very well in his own tone, and the pictures, especially of Chambord & Loche, I think are extremely pleasant reading.[4]

ALS: MH bMS Am 1092.9 (2612)

[1] The so-called Putnam Shanty, Keene Valley, in the Adirondacks.

[2] WJ's sons William James and Henry James.

[3] WJ, "On Some Omissions of Introspective Psychology," *Mind* 9 (January 1884): 1–26.

[4] HJ, "The Reminiscences of Ernest Renan," *Atlantic Monthly* 52 (August 1883): 274–81; "En Provence," *Atlantic Monthly* 52 (August 1883): 169–86, one of eight installments, reprinted in *A Little Tour in France* (1884). Chambord and Loches are two French towns described by HJ.

To Henry James

Care of Smith Beede | Keene Valley, Essex Co | N.Y. Aug 12 [1883]
My dear Harry,

I am going to leave tomorrow for a week probably in the woods, in company with several first-class Hebrews of N.Y.—Felix Adler being one[1]—so I may not have a chance of exchanging words with you again on this side the water,—Appalling thought! The shrinkage of our family life makes one feel rather solemn. I am doing no head work here at all, and am consequently in excellent physical condition. The weather has been excellent but for a little too much cold at first. Wife & young well. Let Bob write me how he is getting on and what doing. I suppose you have already settled the financial matters, trusteeship, etc, with Warner & got his bill. Pray tell me the details of this. Tell me also, to guide my writing to Munroe, whether you have told him distinctly that the sale was stopped; or only told him to do nothing more at present. Your advance to me will of course have swallowed up my rents due August 1st. If by miracle not, send me a cheque here; send me your *bill* in the contrary event. Miss Sever & Miss Amy White are our only companions in the settlement.[2] Alice wrote me you had much enjoyed Mount Desert, for which I was glad. Miss S. has much enjoyed your "En Provence" having been there herself, and quotes other enjoyers. Alice will from her account be with you in a few days. I hope she'll have good weather, and find first then how much really better she is. Of course I—and Alice who has just come into the charming little "hog-house" in which I write—send the most heartfelt wishes for your good journey & your pleasant settlement after you get back. I like to think of you in Macmillan's house & hope you'll get it, and get the reward which a good conscience should give you, after your irksome and beneficent sojourn here.[3] Love to Alice & Bob—send me anything you may get from Wilky. Once more Adieu, & bon voyage! It would have amused you to hear Harry yesterday, pretending he was a guide pointing out the mountains, solemnly & deliberately tell the whole company that a certain one he pointed at was "*Diarrhoea-mountain* very hard to climb." When examined by me afterwards it appeared he had no understanding of the name and used it only because I had "told him he must name all the mountains."

W.J.

ALS: MH bMS Am 1092.9 (2613)

[1] Felix Adler (1851–1933), German-born educator, advocate of ethical culture.

[2] Not identified.

[3] Macmillan and Co. for a number of years had been HJ's English publishers, and HJ knew socially Frederick Orridge Macmillan (1851–1936), a partner in the firm. No information bearing on WJ's remark was found.

From Henry James

131 Mount Vernon St. | Aug. 17ᵗʰ [1883]

Dear William.

Your letter & your postcard have just come in. (I will not fail to write to Mary Gibbens on arriving in London.)[1] I wrote to you & sent a cheque (or rather two cheques) on Monday, & am surprised that your postcard at least didn't acknowledge the receipt of them. But they probably came just after. I suppose you have now started into the woods with your German Jews, & hope that one of them will be your Moses on such an enterprise. I am winding up everything & am infinitely pressed with the innumerable different items I have to attend to. Warner's papers cannot be made ready in time, & will have to be sent to me in London to sign. It makes, however, little practical difference. I have written to Munroe to send you all cheques & communications in future. I will give his past letters, tied up in a bundle, to Bob to give to you when you return. He will of course send you by the 10ᵗʰ (I suppose) of next month, the August rents. After that, in October & November, there will be little, as the letter I enclosed to you notified us, on account of the city taxes. I told Munroe that the sale was *indefinitely postponed*. In dividing the rents please send my share to Alice; this I desire always to be its regular destination. She assures me that she will have no occasion to use it—will save & invest it for my benefit &c. But I wish her to have it, to cover all the contingencies of her new existence. If she does put it by, it is understood between us that it is to go to paying off the Syracuse mortgages, &c. This, on my own side, I shall make my aim. As regards the division of the rents among us, you must take account of Wilkie's diminution of capital by $5000. I have done so by assuming each share to be *about* $20,000 & giving him therefore ¾'s of a portion of the remittance, instead of a whole portion, & dividing the remaining 4ᵗʰ among the other three of us. I enclose you the two last letters I have got from him. His case since his return appears pretty poor; yet in regard to his plan of coming east, I have been able to reply to him nothing but generalities. I have told him to plan for it & look forward to it, but I don't see how he can execute it, without some extraordinary assistance which he is not likely to receive, & which neither you nor Alice are in the least able to give him. In addition to carrying his own poor suffering body hither, he would have also to carry his absolutely inert & helpless wife & children. She neither can nor will lift a finger to help him. The case therefore seems to me hopeless. It is impossible to tell him so—one must appear to encourage him; but that is the state of affairs. All *I* can do is to send him money. He will get from me about $1200 a year. I say to myself that this will ease him off a good deal, & perhaps help him to exist at Milwaukee.—Alice came to town yesterday, to spend this last couple of days with me; & is markedly & encouragingly better. She had been at Beverley a week or more, & returns there tomorrow; but after Sept 1ˢᵗ will be in some lodgings, taking Mary with her.[2] Bob is doing very well, sticks to his studio, is much interested &c, & seems to thrive physically. He seems 50 percent better than when he came. I will adjure him to write to you.—I am delighted to hear you are so well, & send tender love to Alice & the young. I embrace them in farewell.—I don't know that there is anything more to say about the property. The manner in which Warner has arranged the papers you will learn from himself; there is too much of this to describe. But I think it is all very wise, & he is a most excellent fellow to deal with. I am writing to Hanchett, the Insurance man, at Syracuse to send you a definite account of the expiration of policies &c.[3] Farewell, dear Brother. I spend 24 hours with A.K. I feel as if my departure were a great disintegration; but we will reintegrate.

Ever your affectionate H James

ALS: MH bMS Am 1094 (2007)

[1] Mary Sherwin Gibbens (1851–1933), WJ's sister-in-law, later the wife of William M. Salter.

[2] AJ had spent most of the summer of 1883 at the Adams Nervine Asylum near Boston. In early August she went to Beverly, Mass., to stay with Katharine Loring. She returned to Boston to see HJ off and returned to Beverly. Mary apparently is a servant.

[3] Not identified.

From Henry James

3 Bolton St. W. | Nov. 24ᵗʰ [1883]

Dear William.

I return without delay Bob's letter enclosed to me this a.m. I rejoice in his apparently reasonable state of mind, & hope the trusteeship can be settled satisfactorily. It seems to me a hundred times better that you shldn't. be saddled with it. At the same time it must be also arranged that *you* do not have to send elaborate monthly reports—a burden under which you will perish if it be kept up. Never, I again beg you, take the trouble to tell ME anything at all about my

Syracuse dividend.   I have made my income entirely over to Alice &
take no further interest in it.———A telegram from Carrie about
poor Wilkie's blessed liberation came to me two hours before yours,
which arrived at 2.30 a.m.[1]   I instantly wrote to Carrie, & afterwards
to Alice, who will have forwarded you my letter.   It is a great weight
off my spirit—not to see him lying there in that interminable suffering.   Meanwhile your letter comes to me, forwarding Carrie's & Bob's
notes & speaking of the days before his death—just as they came to
you here, last winter, after you had heard that Father had gone.   You
will, I hope, have had news to send me about his last hours.   May
they have been easy—I suppose they were unconscious.   I like to
think that somewhere in the mysterious infinite of the universe, Father & Mother may exist together as pure, individual spirits—& that
poor Wilkie, lightened of all his woes, may come to them & tell them
of us, their poor *empêtrés* children on earth.—This post brings me also
a letter from Katherine Loring from which I gather, though she tries
to dissimulate it, that on the whole, since I have been away, Alice has
been pretty poorly.   I try to hope, however, that now she is in her
own house, independent & surrounded with her own arrangements,
she may pull herself together, if she doesn't languish from loneliness.[2]
I am very sorry to hear of Miss Webb's condition—& fear it must
make a sad house in Garden St.[3]   Much love to your Alice.—You will
have rec'd. my letter expressing my anxious hope for an *early* execution of the division.

Ever your   Henry

P.S.—As I must always worry about something, I worry now, as regards Wilkie, about his burial-place.   It will be a great regret to me if
he doesn't lie beside Father & Mother, where we must all lie.[4]   I hope,
at any rate, you have had no trouble—that is no discussion & no excessive correspondence or fatigue about it—& above all no expense.
I have sent Carry £42, to contribute to Wilkie's funeral (& other last
expenses.)

Yours ever | H.J.

ALS: MH bMS Am 1094 (2008)

   [1] GWJ died on 15 November 1883.
   [2] After staying with Katharine Loring at Beverly, Mass., AJ returned to 131 Mount
Vernon St., Boston.
   [3] An unidentified relative of AGJ.
   [4] GWJ was buried in Milwaukee.

From Henry James

3 Bolton St. W. | Jan. 25th [1884]

Dear William.

I have your note of the 10th, enclosing Bob's two letters, & your own to Carrie. The latter I return you. There is nothing more for me to say about the discussion save what I have already said—i.e. that my desire that Carrie shld. have the property in as free & unreserved a manner as possible. I, having no children, have nothing to gain by attaching a condition to her tenure of it; & I hope the matter may by this time have ended in the manner you describe—by Bob's showing her the correspondence & her *offering* to make a will such as you designate.[1]—I am afraid I have no news, no impressions, nor accidents to relate. The winter passes swiftly, mildly & brightly, & the London routine imparts its tinge to everything. I think of going on Feb. 1st to Paris, for 15 days, but have not yet positively decided. I think I can get you through Bain, Bradley's *Ethical Studies*;[2] he is looking for father's 2 volumes that you asked for.[3] I shall be glad to do what I can for you in regard to the nurse; though your plan of importing one strikes me as rather bold. A modest, unaccomplished one (a "nursery-maid" as they call it here) would perhaps not be worth that cost & danger; & on the other hand, I fear, from what I am told, that a ripe, finished one (a Nurse, as distinguished from a n.m.,) might be rather a Tartar. She would be likely to have the exactingness of English upper-servants, be discontent with a small establishment, expect a nursery-maid under her, as is always the custom here. Should you decide to risk it I shall be happy to help you, though I confess I shld. greatly feel the responsibility. Why don't you try for a good German?—or a German nursery-governess?—I went the other night to a *soirée* of Gurney & Myers's Psychical Society; & found it very dull & even repulsive, owing to the fearful verdigreased human & social types congregated there.[4] I have sent Gurney a narrative of a "presentiment" that lately occurred to a friend—"lady-friend," of mine, in connection with myself, but, though the story is very good of its kind, repent of having done so, as I discover that they wish to print these things with names. I embrace your wife & children & give Alice my tender good wishes.—I shall write soon to Mt. Vernon St.[5]

Ever your brotherly | Henry

ALS: MH bMS Am 1094 (2009)

[1] For GWJ's financial affairs see *BBF*, 165–67.

[2] Alexander Bain (1818–1903), Scottish philosopher and psychologist; Francis

Herbert Bradley (1846–1924), British philosopher, *Ethical Studies* (London: H. S. King, 1876).

³ WJ was then editing *The Literary Remains of the Late Henry James*.

⁴ Edmund Gurney and Frederic William Henry Myers were the leading figures in the Society for Psychical Research in England.

⁵ After her father's death, AJ continued to live at 131 Mount Vernon St.

From Henry James

Hotel de Hollande. | Paris. Feb. 20ᵗʰ [1884]

My dear William.

I owe you an answer to two letters—especially to the one in which you announce to me the birth of your little Israelite.¹ I bid him the most affectionate welcome into this world of care & I hope that by this time he has begun to get used to it. I am to[o] delighted to hear of Alice's well-being, & trust it has now merged into complete recovery. Apropos of the Babe, allow me to express an earnest hope that you will give him some handsome & pictorial name (within discreet limits.) Most of our names are rather colourless—collez-lui dessus, therefore, a little patch of wightness. And don't call him *after* any one—give him a name quite to himself. And let it be only one.— Your 2ᵈ note came to me just as I was reproaching myself with not having made some response to the request in relation to Josephine James in the first. It came in a day after I had sent off $105 to Carrie, (as I do every now & then) & at a moment when I was disappointed at not receiving some money which had appeared due this month & on which I was counting for my visit to Paris. It will come next month, (the 1ˢᵗ) & then I will send you a five-pound note. I am sadly afraid you have got poor Josephine & her children rather on your back.—I came here 18 days ago, & remain another week. A month or 6 weeks of Paris, in the year, does me good & helps to keep me going, & this one has been pleasant & profitable, especially as I have been working every day. (I am at this moment writing two short tales for C. A. Dana,² to see how I shall like it,—& he too; *but on this* ABSOLUTE SILENCE.) I have seen more or less of the little American world here, including F. Loring, who asks with much interest after you, & seems as much as ever F.L. & not much more than ever an *artiste-peintre*.³ I have seen several times the gifted Sargent, whose work I admire exceedingly & who is a remarkably artistic nature & charming fellow. I have also spent an evening with A. Daudet & a morning at Auteuil with Ed. de Goncourt. Seeing these people does me a world of good,

& their intellectual vivacity & *raffinement* make the English mind seem like a sort of glue-pot.   But their ignorance, corruption & complacency are strange, full strange.   I wish I had time to give you more of my impressions of them.   They are at any rate very interesting, & Daudet, who has a remarkable personal charm & is as beautiful as the day, was extremely nice to me.   I saw also Zola at his house, & the whole group are of course intense pessimists.   Daudet justified this to me (as regards himself) by the general sadness of life & his fear, for instance, whenever he comes in, that his wife & children may have died while he was out!   I hope *you* manage to keep free from this apprehension.—I have dined with the Crafts & seen them elsewhere once or twice.   They also speak much of you, & are apparently the only pure-minded people here.—I have a good letter from Aunt Kate this a.m. & also a pleasant one from Howells.   A.K. speaks of Alice's going to N.Y. to an electrician & of K.L.s imminent departure.   I hope both things will do her good, &, paradoxical as it may appear, I believe the latter will have its advantages.   She is on my mind much less than she used to be, convinced as I am that, for better for worse, she can take care of herself.   I return to London on the 27ᵗʰ, to stick fast there till the summer.   I embrace Alice & the little Jew & am ever your affectuous

Henry.

ALS: MH bMS Am 1094 (2010)

[1] Herman James was born 31 January 1884 and died 9 July 1885.   In letters announcing his birth, WJ described him as "Jewish-looking."

[2] Charles Anderson Dana (1819–1897), American editor, editor of the *New York Sun.*

[3] Francis William Loring (1838–1905), American painter, lived in Europe for extended periods of time.   He is not to be confused with Aaron K. Loring who in 1880 pirated HJ's *Bundle of Letters*, as was done in *HJL*, 2:270n and *AJB*, 164n.

From Henry James

3 Bolton St W. | March 3ᵈ [1884]

Dear William.

I send you back the three deeds, duly acknow'ged before the U. S. Consul this a.m., & the Covenant duly signed.   If you will send the remaining document I will attend to it promptly.—I send the deeds in another envelope from this, so, that you may be notified in case of loss, I am afraid there will be considerable lawyer's fees (a new batch) to be paid for all this work, & beg you let me know without fail or delay what my share of them is.   I trust that all your bother which must at times have sat heavy on you, with regard to this whole matter of the division is now at an end.[1]   That of the administration of the estate still abides with you; & I can only do my best not to trouble you as far as *I* am concerned.   Do what seems best for yourself & the others, & you have my assent in advance.—I am back from Paris 5 days ago, after a stay of about 4 weeks, from which I derived, as I always do in Paris, many impressions.   There is so much I like there that I sometimes feel it a pity that I don't like it enough to live there altogether.   This however I could not, as the case stands, abide to do. So I must content myself with liking London as much as I do like it, & raging against British density in my hours of irritation & disgust. A glimpse of the intellectual life of some of the men I saw there (Daudet & his lot &c,) renews my sense of the Philistinism of this *milieu* & the degree to which an "artist" is alone in it.   The delicacy of mind of those Frenchmen carries one away, & it is hard to decline, afterwards, upon London talk.   But I might be worse off.   I hope your Alice is by this time quite on foot again & that the babe develops an individuality.   Tender love to both.   I send you the 2 books of father's—2 vols. of one, and return a letter of Carrie's I culpably forgot, a fortnight since.

Ever your   Henry.

ALS: MH bMS Am 1094 (2011)

[1] Division of the estate of Henry James, particularly as it concerns the interests of GWJ who was left out of the will.

From Henry James

REFORM CLUB, | PALL MALL. S.W. March 22ᵈ· [1884]

Dear William.

I have had two or three missives & enclosures from you of late (letters fr. A.K., Alice, Aunt Mary Tweedy &c.   As regards the last— telling of Temple Emmet's death—it has inspired me to write immediately to poor little tragically-situated Elly—of which I am very glad.)[1]   Alice wrote to me, at considerable length—while she was in New York, & whether or no her Russian quack has done her any good,[2] I quite agree with you that she "has spirit enough to survive anything."   Yesterday comes from you the letter about J. La Farge's portrait of me, with your P.S.[3]   As regards the portrait I regret that "the family" should n't possess it—but it can't be helped.   If I had been at home I might have been able to buy it myself; but after this delay I fear it is too late.   I shall perhaps, however, yet write to Stickney on the chance of its still being in his hands.   For your lecture on the subject of my misplaced charities I am very much obliged; those homilies are always useful & suggestive.   What you tell me about Carrie's means is much to the point—it is precisely what I wanted to know.   I have said *nothing* to her about any intention of making up the $2500, & given her no reason to count upon me for the future. Wilkie & she, between them have had from me during the last year— or since January 1883—I shld think, about $1500; & I shall not send her anything more for the present.   The next money I am *irresistibly* impelled to send to Milwaukee shall go to Bob; the trouble is however that Bob will scarcely accept—it is a great job to make him.   I am far more thoughtful of the future than you appear to give me credit for: for the present, however, *n'en parlons plus*.   I am afraid I have no news at all.   I am very busy—very decently well—& this moment much hurried.

Ever yours   H James

ALS: MH bMS Am 1094 (2012)

[1] Ellen Temple Emmet.
[2] For AJ's treatment by William B. Neftel see *AJB*, 227.
[3] No information about this portrait was found.

From Henry James

3 Bolton St W. | March 26th [1884]

My dear William.

I wrote to you a few days ago, but since then I have another missive from you; enclosing a couple of notes from A.K., & another one from Stickney about the La Farge portrait.   I must let this pass, as I haven't £60 now to expend upon it—especially as I don't think it very valuable—as I recollect it;—though if I *could* I would buy it simply for the sake of auld lang syne.   I enclose the £5 note I promised you the other day, to help you to meet the next demand from Josephine. You can easily get it changed the next time you go into State St.—I confess, also to gladness that your helpless babe is not for the (possibly) 80 years of his life to be made a Tweedy!—a cruel little label to tie to him for all the long future.   I don't like *Hagen* (it will eventually be pronounced Haygan & mistaken for the Irish Hagan) much better.[1] I hold in the matter of names to my dislike to the idea of giving children the *whole* names of others.   If one wishes to name a babe after a friend it seems to me enough to give it the friends Christian name— e.g. Edmund or Hermann.   If I wished to gratify certain friends, I shld. name my child after each of them, as they do abroad—Edmund Hermann Francis.   The first would be name he would go by (I put the above in *any* order) & the two others would be dormant save when he signed his name in full—in legal documents &c.   They would however always be a part of him.   Hermann James strikes me as a very pretty name: Hermann H. James (that it will virtually be) as no name at all.   The second[2] is so pretty that it is a pity to spoil it by the second.   I repeat, too, that to give a child the *surname* of a strange family whom he has had had no contact with save the temporary re- lation of his progenitors to *one* member of it, is to saddle him with an awkward element of which he may easily feel the inanity in future years, especially if confronted with the family who rightfully bear it and who may view him with all kinds of obliquity.   Such are my sen- timents on the subject of infant nomenclature—crudely & hastily stated.   I attach great importance to it—& think the appellation of a child cannot be too much considered: it affects his life forever!   I confess that I breathe a sigh of relief that we are not to have a "Tweedy" among us (*Edmund* James I think a very nice name)—affili- ated to all the rest of the Tweedy brood for upwards of a century after poor E.T. of Newport has descended to his rest.   I rejoice too that *our* kind parents didn't make us (for the most part) William P., Henry W., & Robertson F. & urge you to follow their example!—The com- munications in regard to Alice in New York of course interest me much: & I have a letter from her by the same post as yours.   She appears to have such a long road to travel that I sometimes lose cour- age for her—but she doesn't seem to lose it for herself, & so long as she isn't nervous I can think of her with some equanimity.   I fear your wife returns slowly to active life.   I embrace her tenderly.

Ever yours—Henry (P.) James

ALS: MH bMS Am 1094 (2013)

[1]Hermann August Hagen (1817–1893), German entomologist, in 1867 came to Harvard at the invitation of Louis Agassiz and was made a professor in 1870.   Why WJ would consider naming his son after Hagen is not clear since there is no evidence of any friendship.   Several months later some conflict arose between the Jameses and the Hagens; see WJ's letter to AGJ, 13 September 1884 (bMS Am 1092.9 [1384]).   Yet the coincidence of names leaves little doubt that they are thinking of Hermann Hagen.

[2]HJ meant 'first'.

From Henry James

3 Bolton St. W. | April 21st [1884]

Dear William

I receive a note from you of 9th, to which, though it doesn't demand any particular answer I will dash off a few lines of response before taking up the pen of imagination. You enclose an extract from a newspaper purporting to be an article of Matt. Arnold's about Chicago society, & seem to have believe[d] it is his! It doesn't, I must confess, appear to me even a good hoax—full of phrases ("intelligent gentleman," "cultured people," "owner of a large grocery-business," &c), which he is incapable of using. Nor would he talk about "Chicago-society." It seems to me poor as a parody—& it marks the (geographical) gulf that separates Appian Way from—Bolton St!—that this writer should have appeared to you to catch the tone in which a London man of M.A.'s stamp would express himself. The thing, of course, never appeared in the P.M.G.[1] Excuse the invidious style of my acceptance of your offering.—I too am "excited" about the prospect of your getting into John Gray's house. It is a charming idea, but I shld. fear you would find it an expensive place to live in; as you would have to have a man for the grounds.—But I shall hear with great interest of the sequel. As you don't dwell on the character of Aunt Kate's convalescence, besides saying it is slow, I suppose there is nothing particular to hope or fear in regard to it, & nothing to be done for the poor dear woman but to write to her when one can, which I do.—I got your enclosure of Bob's note, a few days since, with news of his curatorship. I hope he may keep it & make it grow. Have you any idea that he has himself this winter advanced in the practice of art?[2] As regards your child's name I am glad the appendage has not yet been fastened. I am afraid *all* "selected" names appear to you "tawdry." If I had a child I would call him (very probably) *Roland*! "Roland James" is very good. If this doesn't suit you—nor Godfrey, nor Gautier, nor any name of chivalry, take something out of Shakspeare: a capital source to name a child from: Sebastian, Prosper, Valentine (I like Valentine though not sure I'd give it;) Adrian, *Lancelot*, Bernard, *Justin*, Benedick, or Benedict, *Bertram*, Conrad, Felix, Leonard, &c. Putting Hagen apart, I like *Herman*. But I don't exactly understand the obligation you seem to feel under to provide Dr. Hagen with a namesake—"because he was never in America"—& has failed to make the provision himself.[3] Did I tell you in my last that I spent at Easter nearly 3 days at the Durdans (Roseberys') with Gladstone, & only two or three others?[4]   Haec olim meminisse juvabit,[5] I suppose; but in the present Gladstone's mind doesn't interest me much: it appears to have no preferences, to care equally for all subjects—which is tiresome!   Look in the *Academy* of April 19th for a notice of your last article in *Mind*.[6]   I would send you the paper, were it not so difficult, & out-of-the-way (time-taking,) to buy.   I have attacked your two Mind articles, with admiration, but been defeated.[7]   I can't give them just now the *necessary* time.   I lunched the other day with Arthur Balfour,[8] & lunch tomorrow (elsewhere) to meet Pasteur, returning from the Edinburgh tricentenary.[9] I am anxious to hear your impression of Alice on her return from N.Y.   Love to your own.

Ever,   H. James

ALS: MH bMS Am 1094 (2014)

[1] *Pall Mall Gazette.*

[2] RJ was appointed curator of the Milwaukee Art Museum in March 1884. The museum was located in the rear of "Poposkey's" store; see *BBF*, 170.

[3] See letter of 26 March 1884.   If he is the Hagen teaching at Harvard, the remark about America cannot be taken literally.

[4] The Durdans is Lord Rosebery's residence at Epsom, used primarily for raising horses and for entertaining friends.

[5] From Virgil's *Aeneid*, 1:203.

[6] *The Academy: A Weekly Review of Literature, Science, and Art*, 19 April 1884, p. 278, commented on WJ's "What Is an Emotion?"   A "brilliant, dashing article," suggesting, however, that the author is more interested in literary effect than in sober search for truth.

[7] WJ, "On Some Omissions of Introspective Psychology"; "What Is an Emotion?" *Mind* 9 (April 1884): 188–205.

[8] Arthur James Balfour (1848–1930), British statesman and philosopher.

[9] The University of Edinburgh was founded in 1583.

From Henry James

3 Bolton St. Piccadilly | May 26th [1884]

Dear William.

I have just closed a letter to Alice, which, by the way, was written in 2 different sittings, at several days apart; but I must add a few lines to you individually, to acknowledge your communication about Carrie Cranch &c.   I know of the hapless condition of the latter—having had three or four crazy—but quite innocent—little notes from her. She was certainly predestined to become insane, & her insanity connecting itself with me must be a pure accident. I say on this on account of the brevity of my contact with her. I saw her but four or five times, in Venice, & never since but once last winter, in Cambridge, when I never dreamed that she was in this state. In Venice I took her two or three times to see some pictures—because the Cranches came to see me, & they—or her father—appeared to be taking her nowhere. It is enough to cure one in future of all meddling—or at least idle—good-nature! It makes me *frémir* to think that she might have disembarked here. I am very sorry that her madness takes such an unhappy form; but it is not a thing about which I can do anything. I do not consider myself obliged to write to Cranch, in the least, or to be anything but ignorant & irresponsible—the whole thing having been so extraneous, as it were, to me—& unprovoked by any relations of mine (save those extremely slight ones, of a single moment, at Venice,) with the unfortunate girl. I can only ignore it, regret it, & being practically useless in the matter, not think of it. I hope she may die—it will be the best thing for her.[1] But she probably won't. Meanwhile I am very sorry you should be oppressed with her. It seems to me you have sorry troubles enough. As regards Bob, I hardly know what to say or how to judge. If he *wishes* to stay in Milwaukee it appears a pity to draw him away. On the other hand it does seem probable that he is competent to do some respectable artistic work. I hope you may have been able to ascertain what he has done this winter, what improvement he has made & how soberly he has lived. If anything *does* offer—or is procurable—for him with La Farge or Crowninshield, I suppose he had better take it.[2] His relations, actual or future, with his wife I give up! I only pray the Lord he may *not* give away his money again. Your quotation from Mary about the $400 a year is very bad. If I can help you with Bob in any definite way—i.e. pecuniarlily—please let me know. I have not heard from Carrie in some time—& have not in some time written to her. Of course I should not object to Mrs. Gibbens taking Carrie's place in the Syracuse property—if Carrie demands to realise. I have the hope—& I think I may say the prospect—of being able, before very long, to buy off one (to begin with) of the Syracuse mortgages—i.e. to take $5000 more worth of the property. I have related to Alice your criticism from Edmund Gurney. I don't see him very often, & I am afraid he is besotting himself with his ghost-hunting. I go on the 15th to spend a Sunday with F. Myers, at Cambridge. I lately received a touching kind of note from J. Warner, acknowledging the receipt of *Portraits of places*. He wrestles with me for my immorality—it is the most New England thing possible.³   I sent a copy of the book to Auguste Laugel, & when I was in Paris, thanking me for it, he said, "Vous êtes un moraliste; des hommes tels que vous font du bien à leur pays!"   So many points of view are there.   Warner's note is a "document."—I am happy to say I am drawing to the close of the various short things I have lately had to write—& am attacking two novels—one series of six months in the Century, & one to run a year (but not to begin till July 1885) in the *Atlantic*.⁴   The subjects of both, thank God, are big & important; & the treatment will be equally so. Therefore I must close this—the scourge of notes & letters here, continuing more or less, always.

Ever your   Henry

ALS: MH bMS AM 1094 (2015)

¹ Caroline Cranch, daughter of Christopher Pearse Cranch, developed insanity in 1884.   Frederick DeWolfe Miller, *Christopher Pearse Cranch: New England Transcendentalist*, unpublished doctoral dissertation (University of Virginia, 1942), 323, reports a Cranch "family tradition" that in London in 1880 HJ paid Caroline enough attention to "awaken her hopes."   When HJ called on them in Venice in 1881, the Cranches were at home but the servants insisted that they were not and "shut the door upon him."

² Frederic Crowninshield (1845–1918), American painter and writer.

³ HJ, *Portraits of Places* (London: Macmillan, 1883).

⁴ HJ, *The Bostonians* was serialized in the *Century Magazine* from February 1885 to February 1886 (vols. 29–31); *The Princess Casamassima* in the *Atlantic Monthly*, from September 1885 to October 1886 (vols. 56–58).

From Henry James

3 Bolton St. W. Oct. 5ᵗʰ [1884]

Dear William.

I have your letter of September 20ᵗʰ, written the day after your return from the country, & speaking alas, of your mysterious fever. How strange & inconvenient are such visitations!—I grieve greatly to hear that they have played such tricks with your holiday.   I had not heard how you were, & hoped everything was propitious; I greatly hope it has all blown over now.   I have been in very little communication with you of late & was just on the point (yesterday) of writing to your Alice when your letter came.   I have wanted to write to her for a long time, & it has only been constant accumulations of other writing that have made it impossible.   Give much love to her from me, & tell her to take this for herself as well as for you.   I have been back in London for ten days, after seven or eight weeks at the seaside (the cocknefied seaside of Dover,) which I greatly enjoyed. I had my time all to myself, there wasn't a creature there I knew, the weather was perfect (though much of the time roasting hot) & the sea charming & crowded with all the entertaining sails that strain through that narrow channel. I had very comfortable lodgings, & achieved what I desired—got on with the novel I am writing for the *Century* & which will begin to appear in February. It is a better subject than I have ever had before, & I think will be much the best thing I have done yet. It is called "The Bostonians." I shall be much abused for the title but it exactly & literally fits the story, & is much the best, simplest & most dignified I could have chosen.—I have been solicitous about the issue of your undertaking to do something for the F. Pollacks in the mountains, & hope that they & your fever were not on you together. But I shall see them when they come back & they will tell me. Wendell Holmes's washing his hands of them is un peu trop fort![1] Alice's advent here is by this time (in prospect) a familiar idea, though I feel naturally a good deal of solicitude about it.[2] It is certainly a good thing for her to do; & if she can adjust herself to a long rythm, as it were, of improvement instead of a short one, I have no doubt, solid results will come to her. But she ought to be prepared to spend *three* years. I don't know what she will do, & don't exactly see how *I* can (when she is alone) be either with her or without her—that is, away from her. But this will doubtless settle itself; & if she learns to become more sociable with the world at large (as I think she will have to, in self-preservation,) the problem will be solved. I have not yet heard from her since K. Loring's return, & don't know when she will sail. The note you enclosed from Bob (from "North Lake, Wis") was the first news of any sort that I have had about him in a long time. It seems to point to a complete rupture of relations with his wife, which I am glad to hear of, as it must much simplify the situation. I am very glad he still paints, but what strange places for the pursuit of art! Perhaps he will become the great Western original artist. I shall write to him before long. Nothing exists in England at present but politics; & as there is to be (for the 1st time in many years) an autumn session of parliament, we shall have still more of it. It is rather an exciting drama, (not—to me—for what is on the surface, but for the tides of change & the manifestations of the Zeitgeist beneath.) I have seen much this summer of a very interesting Frenchman, Paul Bourget, & though he has returned to Paris shall see him more. I hope, devoutly, that by this time your eyes are better.   Much love to Alice & all wishes for your coming exertions.   What have you done toward Father's volume?   Tell me in your next.

Ever your   H. James

ALS: MH bMS Am 1094 (2016)

¹ The Pollocks were in the United States in September 1884 and were invited by WJ to spend a week in Keene Valley in the Adirondacks.   Perhaps Holmes, so as not to interrupt his work, refused to entertain them.   There is no hint of this in the *Holmes-Pollock Letters*, ed. Mark DeWolfe Howe, 2 vols. (Cambridge: Harvard Univ. Press, 1941).

² AJ sailed for England on 1 November 1884, never to return to the United States.

To Henry James

Dictated

15 Appian Way | Cambridge | Oct 18th '84

Dear Harry,

Your letter of 5th was very welcome this A.M.   I am glad you have had six weeks of the country which I think you must have sorely needed, and specially glad that you speak so hopefully, of your forthcoming novel.   Osgood sent me yesterday your Tour in France and Three Cities in their usual spring back binding.   I read part of the Tour in France in the Atlantic & shall reserve the book for next vacation.   Of the "Tales" you already know my opinion¹   The last two are exquisite though of course they will be taken by people of both nationalities as *attacks*.

Things have moved rapidly since my last.   You see Bob is my emanuensis.   All we can say of him in his presence is that he seems in better condition than for a long time back & I should be tempted to say nothing else in his absence.   You speak of Alice's prosperity abroad being contingent upon her willingness to be more sociable than heretofore.   She has already turned over an entirely new leaf this summer in that way, as the record of her life will have shown you.   There is nothing like neccessity to bring us out.   If Alice only stays the first year I can hardly conceive of her not permanently preferring Europe to America.   She can get many more comforts there for her money, and see just as many friends.   However we must leave that all to her.   The progressive simplification of my life by the loss of relatives outside the house is made up in part by the growth of the sweet children of whom the youngest is so far, decidedly the most of a success, a creature of imperturbable good nature & fatness.

Mr Munroe suddenly died a while ago in Syracuse with two months rent in his possession which he had kept back to pay taxes—but I imagine there will only be a slight delay in our extracting. If we can renew the two long leases, now falling in at $800 advance which I have asked the tenants & have no doubt of their accepting I shall be in no hurry to get a new agent, as the business is very simple and a biennial visit to Syracuse will cost at the outside $50 whereas an agent costs 400$ per annum. If we find inconvenience from correspondance &c we can get a resident Agent at any time.

You ask about fathers book.—My introduction will be about 120 pages, more than ½ of it being extracts I worked hard at it for two or three weeks during the summer and felt as if I had never been as intimate with father before. The Book ought to [be] out by middle of November. I let Scudder have the little autobiography for the Atlantic.[2] I thought it would advertise somewhat the book and in this age of publication would on the whole be no sacrifice of dignity.— I trust you feel so likewise.

College work has begun never for me with so little strain. Only six hours a week so far, and subjects I have been over before I hope this will permit me to do something toward my psychology My working day is sadly short however,—do what I will with my eyes I cant get them to do any thing by lamplight without having to pay the piper for it afterwards & the hunger that arises in me for reading in the evening is sometimes most poignantly severe Our housekeeping is running very smoothly—the little house looking charming. Herbert Pratt spent two delightful evenings with us lately. Arthur King is expected at supper to night.

I am glad you have seen Paul Bourget. What was he doing at Dover. His essays de P.C. are a direfully disappointing book.[3] The man has so much ability as a writer and such perceptions that it seems a ten fold shame that he should be poisoned by the contemptible & pedantic Parisian ideal of materialism and of being scientific. How can men so deep in one way be so shallow in another, as if to turn living flesh & blood into abstract formula's were to be scientific St. Beuve's method of giving you the whole of an individual is far more scientific than this dissecting-out of his abstract essence, which turns out after all only a couple of his bones. What strikes me in all this side of Bourgets School is its essential debility—But this is enough for all 3 of us. I look eagerly forward to your a/c of Alice on the other side. Judging by my experience a winter in London will be bad for her.

Affect^ly yours   Wm. James

MLS (RJ): MH bMS Am 1092.9 (2614)

¹ HJ, *A Little Tour in France* (Boston: James R. Osgood and Co., 1885); *Tales of Three Cities* (Boston: James R. Osgood and Co., 1884). The former appeared as *En Provence* in *Atlantic Monthly*, July 1883–May 1884 (vols. 52–53).

² Henry James, "Stephen Dewhurst's Autobiography," *Atlantic Monthly* 54 (November 1884): 649–62, reprinted in *The Literary Remains of the Late Henry James*. Horace Elisha Scudder (1838–1902), American editor and writer, served as editor for the publishers of the *Atlantic*.

³ Paul Bourget, *Essais de psychologie contemporaine* (1883).

From Henry James

3 Bolton St. W. | Dec. 4th [1884]

Dear W^m

Only time for these words. Yours of the 24th ult. came in last night, with news of purchase of land, &c.¹ On this I congratulate you, though I don't quite understand where the territory is situated. It is all right about the rents staying back for F.s book. But *I* shall never take a penny of *repayment*. I INSIST on sharing the expense with you. TAKE ALSO OUT OF MY RENTS THE $*10 you* sent for me to B. Temple. I wrote you in my last that I too had heard from him & sent him money. The main purport of this is to say that I told Edmund Gosse, who is staying with Howells, that I would write & ask you to go in & see him.² I hate to claim your time for such a purpose; but take it easily & go only if you have a spare hour. He is a good fellow, & rather a good friend of mine: but I am under no particular obligations of hospitality to him. Call, only; don't feel obliged to invite him. Alice is still in bed, but lively & cheerful, & I am afraid I wrote you through ignorance, the last time, rather an exaggerated acct. of her gout. It appears she has *not* had it all over her; her head has been very well since she arrived in England, & what she has now been laid up with is catarrh of the bowels of which she can't rid herself. Her stomach is *very* well. In spite of all this she will get on! I am delighted to hear good news of Bob. Tell him I am only waiting a moderate time longer to send him a trunk of draperies. Love to Alice.

Ever your   Henry.

ALS: MH bMS Am 1094 (2017)

[1] In a letter to Katharine James Prince, 2 December 1884, WJ says that he is planning to build a house "out Mount Auburn way." It is not clear whether he means the street of that name or the cemetery, the latter being on the outskirts of Cambridge. The plans were dropped because they did not have the money to build the house they wanted.

[2] Sir Edmund William Gosse (1849–1928), British biographer and critic.

Biographical Register
Textual Apparatus
Index

Biographical Register

Adams, Henry (1838–1918), American historian, married Marian (Clover) Hooper in 1872. Correspondence between WJ and Henry Adams is known from 1882 to 1910.

Adams, Marian (Clover) Hooper (1843–1885). HJ commented that "Mrs. Adams, in comparison with the usual British female, is a perfect Voltaire in petticoats" (*HJL*, 2:307).

Agassiz, Alexander (1835–1910), American naturalist, son of Louis Agassiz by his first wife, married Anna Russell in 1860.

Agassiz, Elizabeth Cary (1822–1907), American author and educator, second wife of Louis Agassiz. Correspondence with WJ is known from 1868 to 1902.

Agassiz, Louis (1807–1873), Swiss naturalist, was appointed to teach zoology and geology at Harvard in 1847, and in 1864–65 headed the Thayer expedition to Brazil, with WJ serving as one of several assistants. In her book, *A Journey in Brazil* (Boston: Ticknor and Fields, 1868), Elizabeth Cary Agassiz's reports of her husband's lectures on board ship leave little doubt that he was in search of evidence to decide the question of the origin of species. One letter to WJ is known (1865).

A.K. *See* Walsh, Catharine

Alice. *See* James, Alice

Allston, Washington (1779–1843), American artist. From 1854 to 1876, the Boston Athenaeum had many of Allston's unfinished paintings, including *Belshazzar's Feast*, described by HJ as "his great strange canvas, so interrupted but so impressive" (HJ, *William Wetmore Story and His Friends*, 2 vols. [Boston: Houghton, Mifflin, 1903], 1:308).

Ames, Sarah Russell, wife of American lawyer and writer James Barr Ames (1846–1910), who was apparently the Sally Russell mentioned in the letters.

Anderson, Frank Eustace (1844–1880), American classical scholar, taught at Harvard.

Andrews. An unidentified American family traveling in Italy in 1873–74. There are references to Mrs. Andrews and to two daughters, Edith and Bessie. The acquaintance might go back to Newport, since at least two Andrews families owned villas there. A Mrs. Loring Andrews, from New York, perhaps a widow, lived on Bellevue Ave., but the names of her children were not discovered. The Newport theory is supported by the fact that WJ knew Edith when she was a child.

Argyll, George John Douglas Campbell, 8th duke of (1823–1900), British politician and author.

Arnold, Matthew (1822–1888), British poet and critic. One letter to WJ is known (1883).

Arthur. *See* Sedgwick, Arthur George

Ashburner, Anne (1807–1894), sister of Grace Ashburner, not to be confused with Annie Ashburner Richards.

Ashburner, Annie. *See* Richards, Annie Ashburner

Ashburner, Grace (1814–1893), sister of Anne Ashburner, with whom she lived in Stockbridge, Mass., and after 1860 in Cambridge. A third sister, Sarah Ashburner Sedgwick, was the mother of Arthur George Sedgwick, Sara Ashburner Sedgwick Darwin, Susan Ridley Sedgwick Norton, and Theodora Sedgwick. After the death of their parents, the Sedgwick children lived with Grace and Anne Ashburner. When WJ mentions visits to the Ashburners, he probably has in mind Grace and Anne. Correspondence is known from 1891 to 1893.

Atkinson, Charles Follen (d. 1915), attended the Lawrence Scientific School in 1861–65, later became a businessman in Boston. He is mentioned in *AJB* as one of WJ's young friends who sometimes called on Alice.

Augier, Émile (1820–1889), French playwright.

Babe. *See* James, Alice

Balzac, Honoré de (1799–1850), French novelist.

Bancroft, John Chandler (1835–1901), American businessman, attended Harvard Law School, traveled extensively in Europe studying art. HJ describes their first acquaintance in *NSB*, 335–39, when they boarded at Miss Upham's. Bancroft was the son of George Bancroft (1800–1891), American historian.

Bartlett, Alice, identified by Edel, *HJL*, 1:329, as a friend of Alice Mason and Elizabeth Boott, who later married someone named

Warren from Texas. In his letter of 25 June 1874 WJ wrote of having been invited to Concord to meet a Miss Bartlett. There were several Bartletts who were friends with the Emerson children.

Bateman, Hezekiah Linthicum (1821–1875), American actor, theatrical producer. His four daughters were actresses, including Kate Josephine Bateman (1842–1917) and Ellen Douglas Bateman (1844–1936).

Beach, Henry Harris Aubrey (1843–1910), Boston physician who treated AJ and other members of the family.

Beesly, Edward Spencer (1831–1915), British writer.

Bellini, Gentile (1429–1507), Venetian painter.

Bellini, Giovanni (c. 1430–1516), Venetian painter.

Bellini, Jacopo (c. 1400–c. 1470), Venetian painter, father of Gentile Bellini and Giovanni Bellini.

Benson, Eugene (1839–1908), American painter and critic, lived in Italy.

Blocqueville, Adélaïde-Louise Davout, marquise de (1815–1892), French writer, daughter of Louis-Nicolas Davout, marshal of France.

Bob (Bobby). *See* James, Robertson

Booth, Edwin (1833–1893), American actor, who portrayed Hamlet in New York City in the fall of 1864 and on many other occasions.

Boott, Francis (1813–1904), American composer, lived mostly in Italy after the death of his wife in 1847. Correspondence with WJ survives from 1892 to 1900.

Boott, Lizzie. *See* Duveneck, Elizabeth Boott

Bornemann, an unidentified young woman whom WJ met in Berlin in 1867–68. She was orphaned and living with her brother, a lawyer.

Boughton, George Henry (1833–1905), English-born painter, moved to the United States at an early age.

Bourget, Paul-Charles-Joseph (1852–1935), French writer, journalist. Correspondence with WJ survives from 1893.

Bowditch, Henry Pickering (1840–1911), American physiologist, professor at the Harvard Medical School. Correspondence with WJ is known from 1867 to 1910.

Broglie, Jacques-Victor-Albert, duc de (1821–1901), French politician and historian.

Bronson, Arthur, husband of Katherine De Kay Bronson.

Bronson, Katherine De Kay (d. 1901), socialite and hostess, owned a villa in Newport in the late 1850s, and later, a home in Venice called Casa Alvisi.

Brosses, Charles de (1709–1777), French scholar and politician.

Broughton, Rhoda (1840–1920), English novelist.

Browning, Robert (1812–1889), English poet.

Bryce, James, Viscount (1838–1922), British historian and politician, married to Lady Marion Bryce. His brother, John Annon Bryce, was a politician and businessman in India. He had two sisters, Katharine and Mary Bryce. Correspondence between WJ and James Bryce is known from 1882 to 1902.

Bushnell, Horace (1802–1876), American clergyman.

Cabot, Lilla. *See* Perry, Lilla Cabot

Carlisle, George James Howard, 9th earl of (1843–1911), from 1881 a trustee of the National Gallery.

Carrie (Carry). *See* James, Caroline Eames Cary

Carter, Alexander, an unidentified friend of HJ. If he can be identified as the husband of the Mrs. Carter who entertained HJ at Kenilworth in August 1880, he died in 1879.

Cary, Caroline Eames. *See* James, Caroline Eames Cary

C.E.N. *See* Norton, Charles Eliot

Cherbuliez, Victor (1829–1899), French novelist.

Child, Elizabeth Ellery Sedgwick, wife of Francis James Child. Correspondence with WJ is known from 1885 to 1903.

Child, Francis James (1825–1896), professor of English at Harvard, fellow boarder with WJ at Miss Upham's in 1861. He married Elizabeth Ellery Sedgwick in 1860. The Childs had three daughters, Helen, Susan, and Henrietta, and a son, Francis. Correspondence with WJ is known from 1878 to 1896.

Childe, Edward Lee (1836–1911) and his wife, Blanche de Triquiti Childe, entertained HJ frequently at their château near Montargis, France.

Clarke, Mary Temple Rose (d. 1913), daughter of Charlotte Temple Rose, a distant relative of WJ.

Cleveland, Mrs., the widow of American educator and scholar Henry Russell Cleveland (1808–1843). The Miss Cleveland whom HJ met in 1873 was her daughter.

Clover. *See* Adams, Marian Hooper

C.N. *See* Norton, Charles Eliot

Coleridge, Samuel Taylor (1772–1834), English poet and critic.

Collins, Wilkie (1824–1889), British writer.

Couture, Thomas (1815–1879), French painter.

Crafts, James Mason (1839–1917), American chemist, a member of the Union Club with WJ.

Cranch, Caroline (Carrie), daughter of Christopher Pearse Cranch. At one time she was in love with HJ.

Cranch, Christopher Pearse (1813–1892), American artist and poet.

Darlington, Miss, an unidentified person traveling in Europe with the Johnstons in 1876.

Darwin, Charles Robert (1809–1882), English naturalist.

Darwin, Sara Ashburner Sedgwick (b. 1839), sister of Theodora Sedgwick, Arthur George Sedgwick, and Susan Ridley Sedgwick Norton. In 1877 she married William Erasmus Darwin.

Darwin, William Erasmus (1839–1914), English banker, eldest son of Charles Darwin, married Sara Ashburner Sedgwick in 1877.

Daudet, Alphonse (1840–1897), French novelist.

Davidson, Thomas (1840–1900), Scottish-born writer. Correspondence with WJ survives from 1880 to 1900.

Delacroix, Ferdinand-Victor-Eugène (1798–1863), French painter.

Dennett, John Richard (1838–1874), American journalist, on the editorial staff of the *Nation*.

Dicey, Albert Venn (1835–1922), British jurist and essayist. In several letters HJ emphasized Dicey's ugliness. Correspondence with WJ is known from 1898 to 1905.

Dicey, Edward James Stephen (1832–1911), British editor and journalist.

Diderot, Denis (1713–1784), French philosopher and encyclopedist.

Dilke, Charles Wentworth (1843–1911), British politician and author. In 1885 he married Emilia Pattison.

Dixey, Ellen Sturgis Tappan (b. 1849), daughter of Caroline Sturgis Tappan and sister of Mary Aspinwall Tappan, married Richard Cowell Dixey in 1875. Two letters to her are known, one undated, one from 1883.

Dixwell, Epes Sargent (1807–1899), headmaster of the Dixwell School attended by many friends of WJ and HJ. He and his wife, Mary Ingersoll Bowditch Dixwell (d. 1893), had six children, one of whom, Fanny Bowditch Dixwell, married Oliver Wendell Holmes, Jr.

Dixwell, Fanny Bowditch. *See* Holmes, Fanny Bowditch Dixwell

Doré, Gustave (1832–1883), French painter.

Doudan, Ximénès (1800–1872), French writer.

Duffy, unidentified American physician, practiced in Italy.

Dumas, Alexandre, *fils* (1824–1895), French dramatist and novelist, whose *Les idées de Madame Aubray* (1867) interested both brothers.

Du Maurier, George Louis Palmella Busson (1834–1896), British novelist and illustrator, drew cartoons for *Punch*, illustrated some of HJ's works. In 1863 he married Emma Wightwick.

Duveneck, Elizabeth Boott (1846–1888), studied painting, married Frank Duveneck, one of her teachers in 1886. One letter to WJ is known (1877).

Duveneck, Frank (1848–1919), American painter, husband of Elizabeth Boott. One letter from WJ is known (1893).

Dwight, Thomas (1843–1911), completed Harvard Medical School in 1867, taught anatomy at Harvard from 1873.

Eckermann, Johann Peter (1792–1854), German reporter of conversations with Goethe.

Eliot, Charles William (1834–1926), in charge of the chemistry laboratory at the Lawrence Scientific School in 1861–63, president of Harvard from 1869. Correspondence with WJ is known from 1875 to 1910. For Eliot's early impression of WJ see *The Letters of William James*, ed. Henry James, 2 vols. (Boston: Atlantic Monthly Press, 1920), 1:31–32.

Eliot, George, pseudonym of Marian Evans (1819–1880), British novelist.

Ellen, a servant of the Jameses in Cambridge in the late 1860s.

Elly. *See* Emmet, Ellen James Temple

Emerson, Edward Waldo (1844–1930), son of Ralph Waldo Emerson, married Annie Shepard Keys. Four letters to WJ are known from 1878 to 1904.

Emerson, Ellen Tucker (1839–1909), daughter of Ralph Waldo Emerson. For an account of the life of the young people in Concord, including visiting Jameses, see *The Letters of Ellen Tucker Emerson*, ed. Edith E. W. Gregg, 2 vols. (Kent State: Kent State Univ. Press, 1982).

Emerson, Ralph Waldo (1803–1882), American author. One letter to WJ is known (1867).

Emmet, Christopher Temple (1822–1884), husband of Ellen Temple Emmet.

Emmet, Ellen (Elly) James Temple (1850–1920), WJ's cousin, wife of Christopher Temple Emmet. She later married George Hunter. For additional information *see* Temple, Mary.

Emmet, Katharine (Kitty) Temple (1843–1895), WJ's cousin, wife of

Richard Stockton Emmet. Correspondence with WJ survives from 1861 to 1868. For additional information *see* Temple, Mary.

Erckmann-Chatrian, pen name of two French authors, Alexandre Chatrian (1826–1890) and Émile Erckmann (1822–1899).

Everett, William (1839–1910), American teacher and writer, Harvard instructor in 1870–77.

Fergusson, Sir William (1808–1877), British physician.

Ferrari, Giuseppe (1811–1876), Italian philosopher and politician.

Feydeau, Ernest-Aimé (1821–1873), French novelist, whose *La Comtesse de Chalis* (1868) WJ reviewed in the *Nation*.

Fiske, John (1842–1901), American historian and philosopher of evolution. Two letters from WJ are known (1880, 1898).

Flaubert, Gustave (1821–1880), French novelist.

Flint, Austin, Jr. (1836–1915), American physician and physiologist.

Garratt, Alfred Charles (c. 1813–1891), American physician, author of two books on the use of electricity in the treatment of nervous disorders.

Gaskell, Lady Catharine Henrietta Wallop (1856–1935), an author.

Gaskell, Charles George Milnes (b. 1842), husband of Lady Catharine Henrietta Wallop Gaskell.

Gautier, Théophile (1811–1872), French critic, poet, and novelist.

Gibbens, Alice. *See* James, Alice Howe Gibbens

Gibbens, Eliza Putnam Webb (1827–1917), WJ's mother-in-law. Correspondence with WJ survives from 1883 to 1910.

Gladstone, William Ewart (1809–1898), British statesman.

Godkin, Edwin Lawrence (1831–1902), American journalist, co-founded the *Nation* in 1865. In 1859 he married Frances Elizabeth Foote. Correspondence with WJ is known from 1885 to 1901.

Goncourt, Edmond-Louis-Antoine Huot de (1822–1896), French author, usually associated with his brother Jules-Alfred Huot de Goncourt (1830–1870), French author.

Gordon, Lady Caroline Emilia Mary (b. 1830), daughter of John Frederick William Herschel.

Gould, James Brewster (1810–1879), American physician, practiced in Rome after leaving the navy.

Gourlay, Jeanette Barber, probably the sister of WJ's paternal grandmother. One letter from WJ is known (1864). WJ maintained ties with one of her children, Catharine, who died in 1896 at the age of eighty-five.

Gray, John Chipman (1839–1915), American lawyer and educator, friend of Mary Temple. Three letters from WJ are known from 1872 to 1899.

Greeley, Horace (1811–1872), American journalist and politician.

Greene, Miss Elizabeth, an unidentified friend whom WJ met while vacationing on the Maine coast in 1872 and 1873.

Greenough. Henry Greenough (1807–1883), American architect, was married to Frances Boott, sister of Francis Boott. Thus their four children, including two daughters, Frances Greenough Blake and Florence Greenough Thorndike, were cousins of Elizabeth Boott. In a letter to GWJ, 16 November 1873, WJ described them as old neighbors from Quincy St. and mentioned a daughter Fanny. HJ also said one of the girls was Fanny (*HJL*, 1:348). Richard Saltonstall Greenough (1819–1904), Henry Greenough's brother, an American sculptor residing in Rome, had at least one daughter. The two Miss Greenoughs mentioned by HJ in the letter of 8 January 1873 are probably Frances and either her sister or her cousin.

Grimm, Herman Friedrich (1828–1901), German critic and author, married to Gisela von Arnim (1827–1889). In 1867 WJ had a letter of introduction to Grimm from Ralph Waldo Emerson and was a frequent visitor at the Grimm household. One WJ letter to Grimm is known (1867).

Grymes, Mary Helen James (1840–1881), daughter of WJ's uncle John Barber James, married to Charles Alfred Grymes (1829–1905), a New York physician whose mother was Suzette Bosch Grymes from New Orleans. Suzette Grymes is the "old" Mrs. Grymes mentioned in the letters. Charles Alfred Grymes, brother of Medora Grymes Ward and Athenais Grymes von Hoffman, had a daughter, Mabel, by a previous marriage.

Gryzanovski, Ernst Georg Friedrich (1824–1888), Polish-born diplomat and writer.

Gurney, Edmund (1847–1888), British aesthetician and psychical researcher. Correspondence with WJ is known from 1882 to 1888.

Gurney, Ellen Sturgis Hooper (1838–1887), wife of Ephraim Whitman Gurney and sister of Marian (Clover) Hooper Adams, suffered periods of mental breakdown.

Gurney, Ephraim Whitman (1829–1886), professor of history at Harvard, dean of the faculty in 1870–75, married Ellen Sturgis Hooper on 3 October 1868. One letter to WJ is known (1877).

Harcourt, Augustus George Vernon (1834–1919), British chemist.

Hare, Augustus John Cuthbert (1834–1903), British writer.

Harrison, Frederic (1831–1923), British jurist, philosophical writer, and editor, married his cousin, Ethel Harrison (d. 1916).

Hawthorne, Julian (1846–1934), son of Nathaniel Hawthorne. He and his sister Una Hawthorne (1844–1877) took part in various social activities with the Jameses in Concord in the early 1860s.

Hawthorne, Nathaniel (1804–1864), American author.

Hayes, Rutherford B. (1822–1893), president of the United States in 1877–81.

Higginson, Henry Lee (1834–1919), American banker, partner in the firm Lee, Higginson and Co., WJ's financial adviser. Correspondence with WJ is known from 1882 to 1910. On 5 December 1863 he married Ida Agassiz.

Higginson, Ida Agassiz, wife of Henry Lee Higginson. Two letters to WJ are known, one undated and one from 1896.

Hill, Frank Harrison (1830–1910), British journalist, editor of the *Daily News*.

Hill, Jane Dalzell Finley, wife of Frank Harrison Hill.

Hillard, Mary Robbins (d. 1932), American educator. One letter to WJ is known (1908).

Hillebrand, Karl (1829–1884), German journalist and essayist.

Hodgson, Shadworth Hollway (1832–1912), British philosopher. Correspondence with WJ is known from 1879 to 1910.

Hoffmann (sometimes Hoffman). The Jameses knew two or three baronesses by that name. Lydia Gray Ward von Hoffman (b. 1843), sister of Thomas Wren Ward, was the wife of Baron Richard von Hoffman. Athenais Grymes von Hoffman (d. 1897), who was married to Louis A. von Hoffman and lived on the Riviera, was the sister of Medora Grymes Ward and Charles Alfred Grymes. Writing from Paris on 14 March 1876, HJ mentioned a Mrs. von Hoffmann, and on 25 April wrote that he was "at the Baronne de Hoffmann's, (late Mrs. L.H. of New York)." No information about her was found.

Holmes, Fanny Dixwell, wife of Oliver Wendell Holmes, Jr. There is evidence that before her marriage WJ had a romantic interest in her.

Holmes, Oliver Wendell, Sr. (1809–1894), American author and physician, one of WJ's examiners in the Harvard Medical School. Two letters to WJ are known from 1884 and 1888.

Holmes, Oliver Wendell, Jr. (1841–1935), American jurist. According to his diary preserved in the Harvard Law School Library, Holmes visited either the James home or WJ and HJ nearly every week in late 1866 and 1867. On 17 June 1872 he married Fanny Dixwell. In later years, relations between WJ and Holmes remained cordial but distant. Correspondence with WJ is known from 1866 to 1910. There are also a number of undated letters.

Holstein, Baron Friedrich von, a German diplomat, suspected of a liaison with Alice Mason.

Holton, Edward Dwight (1815–1892), a wealthy businessman and railroad promoter in Milwaukee, RJ's father-in-law.

Holton, Mary. *See* James, Mary Holton

Hooper, Ellen Sturgis. *See* Gurney, Ellen Sturgis Hooper

Hosmer. There were several Hosmers at Harvard. The best candidate is Edward Downer Hosmer (1843–1912), graduated from Harvard in 1865, later a lawyer in Chicago. Hosmer was in Europe in 1867 and could have been the Hosmer who introduced WJ to the Fischer family in Berlin (see letter of 12 December 1867). He was married in New York in 1871 and may have been the Hosmer, who, according to WJ, had spent the summer of 1869 in Brooklyn (see letter of 1 June 1869).

Houghton, Richard Monckton Milnes, 1st Baron (1809–1885), British politician and book collector.

Howard. *See* Carlisle, earl of

Howe, Julia Ward (1819–1910), American poet and editor. Laura Howe Richards, one of her daughters, was her traveling companion in 1877.

Howells, William Dean (1837–1920), American novelist. Correspondence with WJ is known from 1877 to 1910.

Humboldt, Wilhelm, Freiherr von (1767–1835), German statesman and philologist.

Huxley, Thomas Henry (1825–1895), English biologist and essayist.

Irving, Henry (1838–1905), British actor.

James, Alice (1848–1892), WJ's sister. She moved to England permanently in November 1884. For details about her life see *AJB*. Correspondence with WJ survives from 1861 to 1892.

James, Alice Howe Gibbens (1849–1922), WJ's wife. Correspondence with WJ survives from 1876 to 1910.

James, Caroline Eames Cary (b. 1851), wife of GWJ.

James, Garth Wilkinson (1845–1883), WJ's brother, enlisted in the Union army, became an officer in a black regiment, and was severely wounded in July 1863 in the assault on Battery Wagner, Charleston, S.C. He married Caroline Eames Cary in Milwaukee on 12 November 1873. Their first child, Joseph Cary James, was born on 4 October 1874; their second, Alice James, on 24 December 1875. For details see *BBF*. Correspondence with WJ survives from 1866 to 1883.

James, Henry (1811–18 December 1882), WJ's father. Correspondence with WJ survives from 1860 to 1882.

James, Henry (18 May 1879–1947), WJ's son, a lawyer and biographer. Correspondence with WJ survives from 1882 to 1910.

James, Josephine Worth (1831–1920), wife of Howard James, WJ's father's brother. She had six children, including Florence, Edith, and Howard, Jr. One letter from Josephine James to WJ is preserved (1884).

James, Mary Holton (b. c. 1849), wife of RJ. Correspondence with WJ survives from 1878 to 1907.

James, Mary Robertson Walsh (1810–30 January 1882), WJ's mother. Correspondence with WJ survives from 1861 to 1874.

James, Robertson (1846–1910), WJ's youngest brother, enlisted in the Union army, became an officer in a black regiment. He married Mary Holton on 18 November 1872 in Milwaukee. Their first child, Edward Holton James, was born on 18 November 1873; their second, Mary Walsh James, on 18 August 1875. For details see *BBF*. Correspondence with WJ survives from 1868 to 1909.

James, William (17 June 1882–1961), WJ's son, an artist. Correspondence with WJ survives from 1888 to 1910.

J.L.F. *See* La Farge, John

Johnston. Unidentified family traveling in Europe in 1876. They may have been relatives of John Humphreys Johnston (b. 1857), American painter who studied with John La Farge.

Joukofski, Paul, Russian artist, son of Russian poet Vasili Andreyevich Zhukovsky (1783–1852), friend of Ivan Turgenev. Zhukovsky is the currently preferred transliteration of the family name.

Kate, Aunt. *See* Walsh, Catharine

Kemble, Frances Anne (Fanny, Mrs. Pierce Butler) (1809–1893), British actress, became a close friend of HJ.

King, Arthur, son of Charlotte Elizabeth Sleigh Matthews King and C. W. King, a merchant in Canton, China. Arthur King's grandmother was Charlotte Walsh Matthews, a sister of WJ's maternal grandfather. Arthur King lived in Paris. It was not established whether he was married. The Dr. Kings whom HJ met in 1873 were not identified and may not have been related to the Jameses.

Kitty. *See* Emmet, Katharine Temple

Knowles, James Thomas (1831–1877), British editor, edited the *Contemporary Review* from 1870 to January 1877, then the *Nineteenth Century.*

La Farge, John (1835–1910), American artist, fellow student at William Morris Hunt's studio in Newport in 1860–61. In 1860 he married Margaret Perry, sister of Thomas Sergeant Perry. In the *New York Times*, 2 September 1910, La Farge expressed his view that WJ "had the promise of being a remarkable, perhaps a great painter." Two letters from WJ to La Farge are known, one undated, one from 1909.

Lang, Andrew (1844–1912), British writer. Nine undated letters to WJ are known.

Laugel, Auguste (1830–1914), French engineer and writer, married to Elizabeth Bates Chapman of Boston.

Lecky, William Edward Hartpole (1838–1903), Irish historian and essayist.

Lee, Elizabeth Perkins. *See* Shattuck, Elizabeth Perkins Lee

Lee, Henry (1817–1898), Boston stockbroker, partner in the firm Lee, Higginson and Co.

Leopardi, Giacomo (1798–1837), Italian poet and writer, known for his pessimism.

Lombard. An unidentified American family, consisting of Mrs. Lombard and Miss Fanny, traveling in Italy in 1874–75.

Longfellow, Ernest Wadsworth (1845–1921), American painter, son of Henry Wadsworth Longfellow. In 1868 he married Harriet Spelman, daughter of Israel Spelman, a railroad executive.

Loring, Katharine Peabody (1849–1943), AJ's companion. Correspondence with WJ is known from 1887 to 1893.

Lowell, James Russell (1819–1891), American poet, editor, diplomat. His second wife was Frances Dunlap, whom he married in 1857. Two letters from WJ are known, one undated, one from 1883.

Mary, Aunt. *See* Tweedy, Mary Temple

Mason, Alice, widow of William Sturgis Hooper, married Charles Sumner in 1866. They were divorced several years later, after he suspected a liaison between her and Baron Friedrich von Holstein, a German diplomat. She later resumed her maiden name.

Mathews, Florence Wilkinson, daughter of James John Garth Wilkinson, wife of St. John Mathews.

Mathews, Mary Wilkinson, daughter of James John Garth Wilkinson. Only the last name of her husband is known. Correspondence with WJ is preserved from 1883 to 1908.

Mathews, St. John, husband of Florence Wilkinson Mathews.

Mérimée, Prosper (1803–1870), French author.

Michelangelo Buonarroti (1475–1564), Italian sculptor, painter, and poet.

Michelet, Jules (1798–1874), French historian.

Mill, John Stuart (1806–1873), English philosopher.

Minny. *See* Temple, Mary

Montégut, Émile (1826–1895), French critic and translator.

Morley, John, Viscount (1838–1923), British statesman and author, editor of the *Fortnightly Review* and other magazines.

Morris, Ellen James Van Buren (1844–1929), daughter of Ellen King James Van Buren (1823–1849), WJ's father's sister, and Smith Thomson Van Buren. She was the wife of Dr. Stuyvesant Fish Morris (1843–1925).

Morse, Frances Rollins (1850–1928), a close friend of AJ and WJ. Correspondence between her and WJ is known from 1875 to 1910.

Morse, Samuel Torrey and his wife, Harriet Jackson Lee Morse, were parents of Frances Rollins Morse (b. 1850) and Mary Morse. Three WJ letters to Mrs. Morse are known from 1897 and 1900.

Motley, John Lothrop (1814–1877), American historian and diplomat.

M.T. *See* Temple, Mary

Munroe, Dr., a Boston physician who treated Catharine Walsh. There were two Dr. Munroes in Boston, William H. (d. 1887) and William F. (d. 1912).

Munroe, Allen (1819–1884), business agent of the James family in Syracuse. He served as mayor of Syracuse and as a New York State senator.

Musset, Alfred de (1810–1857), French poet whose plays were often adapted for opera.

Myers, Ernest James (1844–1921), British poet and translator, brother of Frederic William Henry Myers.

Myers, Frederic William Henry (1843–1901), British essayist and psychical researcher. Correspondence with WJ is known from 1885 to 1901.

Norton, Charles Eliot (1827–1908), American art historian, editor of the *North American Review* (1864–68) and cofounder of the *Na-*

tion. Norton with his wife and sisters Jane and Grace sailed for Europe in July 1868, and returned in May 1873. Correspondence with WJ survives from 1864 to 1908.

Norton, Grace (1834–1926), sister of Charles Eliot Norton. An extensive correspondence with WJ is known from 1884 to 1908.

Norton, Jane (1824–1877), sister of Charles Eliot Norton and Grace Norton.

Norton, Susan Ridley Sedgwick (1838–1872), wife of Charles Eliot Norton.

Osgood, James Ripley (1836–1892), American publisher.

O.W.H. *See* Holmes, Oliver Wendell, Jr.

Paget, Sir James (1814–1899), British physician, knighted after 1869.

Pakenham, Elizabeth Staples Clarke, wife of British military officer Thomas Henry Pakenham (1826–1913).

Palgrave, Francis Turner (1824–1897), British poet and critic.

Parkman, Alice, an unidentified friend. The letters indicate that she had a sister Bertha, deceased, a father who had bouts of insanity, and another relative named Theodore.

Parkman, Mary, an unidentified unmarried friend.

Parkman, Mary Elliot Dwight (1821–1880), widow of Samuel Parkman (d. 1854), operated a private school and contributed literary reviews to the *Nation* in competition with HJ.

Pasteur, Louis (1822–1895), French chemist.

Pater, Walter Horatio (1839–1894), British essayist and critic.

Pattison, Emilia Frances Strong (1840–1904), British art historian, widow of Mark Pattison. In 1885 she married Charles Wentworth Dilke.

Pattison, Mark (1813–1884), British scholar, rector of Lincoln College, Oxford, husband of Emilia Frances Strong Pattison.

Peabody. Two different Miss Peabodys are mentioned in the text, but they cannot be identified with certainty because the Jameses knew several Peabody families. The Miss Peabody whom WJ visited in 1876 may have been a sister of Robert Swain Peabody (1845–1917), an 1866 graduate of Harvard who was an architect in Brookline, Mass. Writing from Cambridge on 1 January 1876, WJ mentioned that he "had spent yesterday afternoon with Miss Peabody in Longwood." Since there is a Longwood Ave. in Brookline, that general area may have been referred to as Longwood. The Miss Peabody HJ met on the Isle of Wight in 1877 was a different person. In an unpublished note Alfred Habegger established that she was not Elizabeth Palmer Peabody (1804–

1894), American educator and reformer, whom WJ and HJ may have met on other occasions. In his letter to HJ of 5 January [1891], WJ reported the death of Maria Peabody (bMS Am 1092.9 [2663]). This Miss Peabody, who died on 30 December 1890 at the age of forty-nine, was the daughter of Andrew Preston Peabody and may have been the Miss Peabody on the Isle of Wight.

Peirce, Charles Sanders (1839–1914), American philosopher, married Harriet Melusina Fay in 1862. They separated in 1876 and subsequently divorced. On 30 April 1883 he married Juliette Froissy. From 1861 Peirce was an aide in the United States Coast and Geodesic Survey, and was an assistant at the Harvard College Observatory from October 1869 to December 1872. Correspondence with WJ is known from 1875 to 1910.

Pell-Clarke, Henrietta Temple (b. 1853), WJ's cousin, wife of Leslie Pell-Clarke. For additional information *see* Temple, Mary.

Perkins, Helen Rodgers Wyckoff (1807–1887), sister of Henry Albert Wyckoff and wife of Leonard Perkins. Helen Perkins's grandmother and WJ's maternal grandmother were sisters. Several of HJ's fictional characters were based on Helen Perkins and her husband. Helen was said to be domineering and her husband "negligible." Although the family was wealthy, she is supposed to have placed her brother, Henry Albert Wyckoff, on an allowance of a dime a day.

Perry, Lilla Cabot, wife of Thomas Sergeant Perry.

Perry, Thomas Sergeant (1845–1928), American literary scholar. Perry met the Jameses in Newport in the summer of 1858, and was especially friendly with HJ. From 1871 to 1881 he was associated with the *Atlantic Monthly*. He was editor of the *North American Review* from January 1873 to January 1874. He married Lilla Cabot in April 1874. His mother was Frances Sergeant Perry, his father, Christopher Grant Perry. A sister, Margaret Perry, married John La Farge. Correspondence with WJ is known from 1860 to 1910.

Pollock, Sir Frederick (1845–1937), British jurist and philosophical writer, married Georgina Harriet Deffell in 1873. Correspondence with WJ is known from 1902 to 1907.

Pratt, Herbert James (b. 1841), graduated from Harvard in 1863, military surgeon in the Civil War, completed Harvard Medical School in 1868, a physician and traveler. He was in Europe in 1867 and later. One letter to WJ is known (1885).

Pumpelly, Raphael (1837–1923), American geologist, traveler, and writer.

Pushkin, Aleksandr Sergeevich (1799–1837), Russian poet.

Putnam, James Jackson (1846–1918), American neurologist. Correspondence with WJ is known from 1877 to 1910.

Quaire, Mme de, unidentified French hostess, friend of HJ.

Raphael Santi (1483–1520), Italian painter.

Regnault, Henri-Alexandre-Georges (1843–1871), French painter.

Rembrandt (1606–1669), Dutch painter and etcher.

Renan, Joseph-Ernest (1823–1892), French historian and critic, married to Cornélie Scheffer, niece of the painter Arry Scheffer.

Renouvier, Charles (1815–1903), French philosopher. Extensive correspondence with WJ is known from 1872 to 1896.

Richards, Annie Ashburner, a friend of AJ, married to Francis Gardner Richards. Three WJ letters to her from 1873 to 1878 are known. From his letters it is clear that WJ knew her in Cambridge and that she was a cousin of Sara Sedgwick Darwin, daughter of Anne Ashburner's sister. But since HJ refers to her father as "S.A." in the letter of 4 March 1879, she cannot be the daughter of George Ashburner, the only known brother of Grace and Anne. Either there was another brother or the cousin relation is more remote. Some sources state that her father was named Sam but do not indicate his relationship to Grace and Anne.

Ripley, George (1802–1880), American literary critic and author, married to Sophia Willard Dana.

Ripley, Helen, daughter of Catharine Walsh Andrews Ripley (1806–1865) and Joseph Ripley of Norwich, Conn. Catharine Ripley's mother was a sister of James Walsh, WJ's maternal grandfather.

Ritchie, Harrison (1825–1894), of Boston, married to Mary Sheldon.

Ritter, Charles (1838–1908), Swiss scholar whose friendship with WJ dated from the 1850s. Correspondence is known from 1859 to 1902.

Robeson, William Rotch (1843–1922), attended Harvard in 1860–64, partner in Florida with GWJ, later a railroad executive.

Robinson, Henry Crabb (1775–1867), British lawyer, diarist, friend of many German and English writers.

Rogerson, Christina Stewart, wife of James Rogerson. It was alleged that in 1885 she was scandalously involved with Charles Wentworth Dilke.

Ronalds, Mary Frances Cater (c. 1840–1910), a native of Boston who lived in London, famous for her musical salons, estranged wife of Pierre Lorillard Ronalds.

Ropes, John Codman (1836–1899), American lawyer and military historian, completed Harvard Law School in 1861.

Rose, Charles Day (1847–1913), son of Charlotte Temple Rose, and thus a distant relative of WJ.

Rose, Lady Charlotte Temple (d. 1883), wife of Sir John Rose, sister of Mary Temple Tweedy and thus a distant relative of WJ.

Rose, Mary Temple. *See* Clarke, Mary Temple Rose

Rosebery, Archibald Philip Primrose, 5th earl of (1847–1929), British statesman and author, married to Hannah de Rothschild (d. 1890). In 1878–81 he was Lord Rector of Aberdeen and in 1880–83, Lord Rector of Edinburgh.

Rossetti, Dante Gabriel (1828–1882), London-born poet and painter.

Rousseau, Jean-Jacques (1712–1778), French philosopher.

Rubens, Peter Paul (1577–1640), Flemish painter.

Ruskin, John (1819–1900), British essayist and critic.

Russell. Probably the family of George Robert Russell (1800–1866), a Boston merchant. In 1867 his widow was living in Louisburg Square, off Mount Vernon St. Among their children were Anna Russell, wife of Alexander Agassiz, and Sarah Russell, probably the Sally Russell mentioned in the letters.

Russell, Sally. *See* Ames, Sarah Russell

Sainte-Beuve, Charles-Augustin (1804–1869), French writer and critic.

Sand, George (1804–1876), pseudonym of Amandine-Aurore-Lucie Dudevant, French novelist.

Sardou, Victorien (1831–1908), French playwright.

Sargent, John Singer (1856–1925), American painter, studied in Paris between 1874 and 1884.

Sargy. *See* Perry, Thomas Sergeant

Schiller, Johann Christoph Friedrich von (1759–1805), German poet and dramatist.

Schmidt, Julian (1818–1886), German literary historian.

Schönberg, Elizabeth (Bessie) Ward de, sister of Thomas Wren Ward.

Sedgwick, Arthur George (1844–1915), American lawyer and journalist, from time to time associated with the *Nation*, in which he acquired a part interest in 1872. He was the son of Sarah Ashburner Sedgwick (sister of Grace and Anne Ashburner) and the brother of Theodora Sedgwick, Susan Ridley Sedgwick Norton, and Sara Ashburner Sedgwick Darwin. Correspondence with WJ is known from 1868 to 1893.

Sedgwick, Sara. *See* Darwin, Sara Ashburner Sedgwick

Sedgwick, Susan Ridley. *See* Norton, Susan Ridley Sedgwick

Sedgwick, Theodora (also Marian Theodora) (1851–1916), sister of Arthur George Sedgwick, Susan Ridley Sedgwick Norton, and Sara Ashburner Sedgwick Darwin. Many letters from WJ to Theodora Sedgwick are known from 1874 to 1910. Maud Howe Elliott, *John Elliott: The Story of an Artist* (Boston: Houghton, Mifflin, 1930), 237, quotes Theodora Sedgwick, who claimed that she studied art together with WJ at William Morris Hunt's studio in Newport.

Shaler, Nathaniel Southgate (1841–1906), professor of geology at Harvard. Correspondence with WJ survives from 1868 to 1901.

Shattuck, Elizabeth Perkins Lee, daughter of Henry Lee, married Frederick Cheever Shattuck (1847–1929), a physician, in the summer of 1877.

Shepard, Luther Dimmick (d. 1911), instructor of dentistry at Harvard.

Shinn, Earl (1837–1886), American art critic.

Smalley, George Washburn (1833–1916), correspondent for the *New York Tribune*, whose wife was Phoebe Gamant Smalley.

Spangenberg, Johanna, at whose boarding house, 2 Dohner Platz, Dresden, WJ stayed in 1868. She had spent twelve years in Mexico from which she brought back a collection of interesting objects. Like her other boarders, WJ sometimes addressed her as grandmother. A number of letters to WJ from 1868 to 1874 are known.

Spencer, Herbert (1820–1903), English philosopher. Correspondence with WJ is known from 1879.

Spottiswoode, William (1825–1883), British mathematician and physicist.

Staigg, Richard Morrell (1817–1881), American artist, married Miss Atkinson, a relative of Charles Follen Atkinson.

Steffens, Heinrich (1773–1845), Norwegian-born philosopher.

Stephen, Leslie (1832–1904), British essayist, editor, and critic. His first wife was Harriet Marian Thackeray (d. 1875), daughter of William Makepeace Thackeray. In 1878 he married Julia Prinseps Duckworth. Correspondence between Stephen and WJ is known from 1884 to 1902.

Stickney, Albert (1839–1908), American lawyer, completed Harvard Law School in 1862.

Story, William Wetmore (1819–1895), American lawyer, poet, and sculptor, married Emelyn Eldredge in 1843, lived lavishly in Rome from 1856. His children were Thomas Waldo Story, a sculptor, Julian Russell Story, a painter, and Edith Story, later the wife of the marquis Simone Peruzzi di Medici. HJ wrote *William Wetmore Story and His Friends* (1903).

Strong, Eleanor Fearing (d. 1903), estranged wife of Charles Edward Strong (1824–1897), an American banker, lived in Europe after 1866.

Sumner, Alice Mason. *See* Mason, Alice

Sumner, Charles (1811–1874), United States senator from Massachusetts (1851–74). In 1866 he married Alice Mason, but divorced her several years later, suspecting a liaison between her and Baron Friedrich von Holstein, a German diplomat.

Swinburne, Algernon Charles (1837–1909), British poet and critic.

Taine, Hippolyte-Adolphe (1828–1893), French philosopher, psychologist, and critic.

Tappan, Caroline Sturgis, wife of William Aspinwall Tappan, a friend of Ralph Waldo Emerson. The Tappans lived in Boston, spending their summers on the Tanglewood estate in Lenox, Mass. Her daughter Mary Tappan eventually gave Tanglewood to the Boston Symphony.

Tappan, Ellen Sturgis. *See* Dixey, Ellen Sturgis Tappan

Tappan, Mary Aspinwall (1852?–1941), daughter of Caroline Sturgis Tappan and sister of Ellen Sturgis Tappan. Four letters from WJ from 1870 to 1910 are known.

Temple, Elly. *See* Emmet, Ellen James Temple

Temple, Henrietta. *See* Pell-Clarke, Henrietta Temple

Temple, Kitty. *See* Emmet, Katharine Temple

Temple, Mary (Minny) (1845–1870), daughter of Catharine Margaret James (1820–1854), WJ's father's sister, and Robert Emmet Temple (1808–1854). After the death of their parents, the six Temple children, Mary, Katharine, Henrietta, Ellen, Robert, and William James, were brought up by Edmund Tweedy and his wife, Mary Temple Tweedy, in Newport and Pelham, N.Y. Mary Temple was the favorite cousin of both WJ and HJ, and her early death affected both deeply. For an account of her last meeting with HJ, in February 1869, see Leon Edel, *Henry James: The Untried Years (1870–1881)* (Philadelphia: Lippincott, 1953), 1:279–

80. For a view that WJ was romantically interested in her see Alfred Habegger, "New Light on William James and Minny Temple," *New England Quarterly* 60 (March 1987): 28–53. Two letters from WJ are known (1870).

Temple, Robert (b. 1840), WJ's cousin. In a letter to Julius Hawley Seelye, 22 June 1876, Robert Temple described his erratic life in the army and his problems with alcohol, claiming that he had inherited the habit from "both sides." He stated that when he called on his sister Ellen, then living in San Francisco, he was repulsed at the door (Seelye Papers, Amherst College). To escape his reputation, he reenlisted in the army under the name of Robert Travis. His troubles continued, however, as is clear from two letters: on 8 January [1885] HJ wrote to WJ that he had had an appeal for money from Robert Temple, who was in prison (bMS Am 1094 [2019]), and in an undated letter to AGJ, RJ reported that Robert Temple was in jail in Great Falls, Montana, for forgery (bMS Am 1095.2 [16–17]). One letter to WJ is known (1887). For additional information *see* Temple, Mary.

Temple, William James (1842–1863), WJ's cousin, killed in action. For additional information *see* Temple, Mary.

Tennyson, Alfred, Lord (1809–1892), British poet.

Terry, Louisa Crawford (1823–1897), sister of Julia Ward Howe, widow of American sculptor Thomas Crawford (1814–1857), wife of Luther Terry, mother of American novelist Francis Marion Crawford (1854–1909), Annie Crawford, Mimoli Crawford, and Margaret Terry. The family lived in Italy much of the time.

Terry, Luther (1813–1890), American painter, husband of Louisa Crawford Terry.

Thies, Clara, daughter of Louis Thies, married August von Ekensteen and settled in Germany. Her parents were married in 1843, and Clara probably was in her early twenties when WJ met her in Germany.

Thies, Louis (d. 1871), German pharmacist, curator of the Gray Collection of Engravings at Harvard University. His wife was Clara Crowninshield Thies. When the Thies family traveled to Europe in 1866, they rented their house at 20 Quincy St., Cambridge, to the Jameses. According to Marjorie B. Cohn, *Francis Calley Gray and Art Collecting in America* (Cambridge: Harvard Univ. Press, 1986), 181, the Thies house contained paintings attributed to Van Dyck, Correggio, Raphael, Van der Werft, and Guido Reni.

Tintoretto (1518–1594), Italian painter, whose real name was Jacopo Robusti.

Titian (c. 1490–1576), Venetian painter.

Toy, Crawford Howell (1836–1919), American Orientalist, began teaching at Harvard in 1880. In 1882–83 he rented WJ's house at 15 Appian Way. Correspondence with WJ is known from 1885 to 1910.

Trevelyan, Sir George Otto (1838–1928), British historian and politician.

Trollope, Anthony (1815–1882), English novelist.

T.S.P. *See* Perry, Thomas Sergeant

Tuck, Henry (1842–1904), graduated from the Harvard Medical School in 1867, and in July of that year went to Europe for fourteen months. In later years he was a medical examiner for life insurance companies.

Turgenev, Ivan Sergeevich (1818–1883), Russian writer. HJ met Turgenev in 1875 and corresponded with him extensively.

Turgenev, Nikolai Ivanovich (1789–1871), Russian historian living in exile, in 1825 was condemned to death for his part in the Decembrist Conspiracy.

Turner, Joseph Mallord William (1775–1851), British artist, championed by John Ruskin who had a collection of Turner's work.

Tweedy, Edmund (d. 1901), with his wife, Mary Temple Tweedy, a guardian of WJ's Temple cousins. *See* Temple, Mary. According to his obituary, Edmund Tweedy, an intimate friend of Nathaniel Hawthorne, was eighty-nine years old when he died. The Tweedies lived in Pelham, N.Y., and owned a villa at Bellevue Court, Newport. Edmund Tweedy contributed to the *Harbinger* and in the 1840s served as treasurer of a Fourierist association. Two letters are known from 1867 and 1898.

Tweedy, John, a brother of Edmund Tweedy.

Tweedy, Mary Temple (Aunt Mary) (d. 1891), wife of Edmund Tweedy. She was the sister of Robert Emmet Temple and an aunt of WJ's Temple cousins. Correspondence is known from 1878 to 1889.

Upham, Catharine, WJ's landlady in Cambridge in 1861.

Valery, Antoine Claude Pasquin, known as (1789–1847), French writer.

Van Buren, Ellen James. *See* Morris, Ellen James Van Buren

Van Buren, Smith Thompson, son of President Martin Van Buren.

Ellen King James Van Buren was his first wife. The Mrs. Van Buren HJ met in London in 1882 was his second wife. There were children from the second marriage.

Veronese, Paolo (1528–1588), Venetian painter.

Viardot-Garcia, Pauline (1821–1910), opera singer and music teacher.

Wadsworth, Evelyn Willing Peters (1845–1885), wife of Craig Wharton Wadsworth.

Walsh, Alexander Robertson (1807–1884), WJ's mother's brother.

Walsh, Catharine (Aunt Kate) (1812–1889), WJ's mother's sister, who lived with the Jameses. In 1853 she married Captain Charles H. Marshall but left him in 1855 and returned to the James home. She died 6 March 1889 at 121 W. 44th St., New York City. Correspondence with WJ is known from 1868 to 1888.

Ward, Bessie. *See* Schönberg, Elizabeth (Bessie) Ward de

Ward, Thomas Wren (1844–1940), a banker, graduated from Harvard in 1866, a member of the Thayer Expedition to Brazil. He was the son of Samuel Gray Ward, American banker, and Anna Hazard Barker Ward. His mother was the sister of William H. Barker, who was the husband of Jeanette James, WJ's aunt. Thomas Wren Ward had two sisters: Elizabeth (Bessie) Ward de Schönberg and Lydia Ward von Hoffman. Correspondence between WJ and Thomas Wren Ward is known from 1866 to 1902.

Warner, Joseph Bangs (1848–1923), WJ's attorney. Correspondence survives from 1896 to 1903.

Washburn, Francis Tucker (1843–1873), graduated from Harvard in 1864, attended Harvard Divinity School, a Unitarian clergyman. He is probably the Washburn intended wherever no first name is given, but some references might be to his older brother, William Tucker Washburn. Correspondence between WJ and Francis Tucker Washburn is known from 1867 and 1868.

Washburn, William Tucker (1841–1916), graduated from Harvard in 1862, a lawyer, author of *Fair Harvard* (1869), brother of Francis Tucker Washburn.

Wedmore, Frederick (1844–1921), British art critic.

Wendell (Wendle). *See* Holmes, Oliver Wendell, Jr.

Whitman, J. L., an Englishman related by marriage to Sarah Wyman Whitman.

Whitman, Sarah Wyman (Mrs. Henry Whitman) (d. 1904), Boston hostess and artist. Correspondence with WJ is known from 1888 to 1904.

Whitwell, May. During December 1872 and January 1873, she traveled in Egypt with her parents, her sister Bessie, and Ralph Waldo Emerson. Her parents' first names are not known; neither Emerson nor Ellen Tucker Emerson used first names when referring to May's parents.

Wilkie (Wilky). *See* James, Garth Wilkinson

Wilkinson, Florence. *See* Mathews, Florence Wilkinson

Wilkinson, James John Garth (1812–1899), British homeopathic physician, writer, a Swedenborgian friend of Henry James, Sr. Correspondence with WJ is known from 1871 to 1893. WJ was also acquainted with Wilkinson's son, as well as with his three daughters: Mary Wilkinson Mathews, Emma Wilkinson Pertz, and Florence Wilkinson Mathews.

Wilkinson, Mary. *See* Mathews, Mary Wilkinson

Winslow, Mrs. George Scott, lived at 70 Boylston St., Boston.

Wister, Sarah Butler (1835–1908), daughter of Fanny Kemble, mother of American lawyer and writer Owen Wister (1860–1938).

Wolseley, Garnet Joseph, 1st Viscount (1833–1913), British military officer and writer, married Louisa Erskine in 1867.

Wordsworth, William (1770–1850), English poet.

Wright, Chauncey (1830–1875), American philosopher, advocate of Darwinism, associated with WJ in several philosophy clubs in Cambridge.

Wyckoff, Albert (1840–c. 1899), nephew of Henry Albert Wyckoff. He is described by HJ as "adventurous."

Wyckoff, Henry Albert (1815–1890), brother of Helen Rodgers Wyckoff Perkins. Henry Albert Wyckoff's grandmother and WJ's maternal grandmother were sisters.

Wyman, Charles, brother of Sarah Wyman Whitman.

Zola, Émile (1840–1902), French novelist.

Textual Apparatus

All alterations are recorded here except for strengthened letters to clarify a reading, a very few mendings over illegible letters, and false starts for the same word. Each entry is keyed by page and line number to the individual letter. The line numbers begin anew with each letter and include all elements in the letter, but do not include the editorial heading that precedes each letter or the notes that follow. Alterations in letters dictated by James are in the hand of the amanuensis unless the alteration is noted as '(WJ)'.

In the typewritten letters, all alterations are handwritten unless otherwise noted; handwritten portions of a typed letter are noted. Because of his difficulties with the typewriter, James frequently completed words and added accompanying punctuation at the right margin by hand; these endings are not recorded. Also not recorded as alterations are corrections of typographical errors.

In recording alterations, the reading to the left of the bracket, the lemma, represents the reading of the present edition and is the final version in the manuscript. (A prefixed superior ^{1} or ^{2} indicates which of any two identical words in the same line, or letters in the same word, is intended.) The processes of revision are described in formulaic terms to the right of the bracket. The use of three dots to the right of the bracket almost invariably indicates ellipsis rather than the existence of dots in the manuscript. This is the only violation of the bibliographical rule that material within single quotes is cited exactly as it appears in the original document. The abbreviation *intrl.* is used when an addition is a simple interlineation (with or without a caret); when a deletion positions the interlineation, the *intrl.* is dropped and the formula reads *above deleted* (i.e., *ab. del.* 'xyz'). The word *inserted* ordinarily refers to marginal additions or squeezed-in letters, words, or punctuation on the line of writing that cannot properly be called interlines but are of the same nature; *over* means inscribed over the letters of the original without interlining. The words *altered from* are used to indicate that the letters in a word have been changed and letters added or deleted to form a new word (i.e., 'she' *alt. fr.* 'they'). When a description within square brackets applies to the preceding words, an asterisk is placed before the first word to which the description in brackets applies; thus it is to be taken that all words between the asterisk and the bracketed description are a part of the described material. The full details of this system may be found in Fredson Bowers, "Transcription of Manuscripts: The Record of Variants," *Studies in Bibliography* 29 (1976): 212–64.

The following abbreviations as here defined are used in recording alterations:

ab.	above
aft.	after
alt.	altered
bef.	before
bel.	below
bkt.	bracket
cap.	capital
db. qt.	double quotation mark
del.	deleted
exclm. mk.	exclamation mark
foll.	following
fr.	from
illeg.	illegible
init.	initial
insrtd.	inserted
intrl.	interlined
l.c.	lower case
mrgn.	margin or marginal
orig.	originally
ov.	over
paren	parenthesis
poss.	possible or possibly
qst. mk.	question mark
sg. qt.	single quotation mark
tr.	transposed
underl.	underline
vert.	vertical or vertically
w.	with

To Henry James [7 September 1861]

1.5 not] *aft. del.* '&'
1.13 shall] 'sh' *ov.* 'wi'
1.16 ¹she] 's' *insrtd.*
1.17 absent] 's' *ov.* 'e'
1.18 joke] 'o' *ov.* 'a'
1.20 thought] *aft. del.* 'N'
1.25 over] *aft. del.* 'of'
1.30 linen] *intrl.*
1.32 sofa] *ab. del.* 'window'
1.34 cast] 'c' *ov.* 'a'
2.14 which] *ab. del.* 'with'
2.15 Higginson] *bef. del.* 'too'
2.24 as] *aft. del.* '&'
2.30 at] *aft. del.* '&'
2.41 expenses] *final* 's' *insrtd.*

3.2 poor] 'p' *ov.* 'n'
3.14–17 Address . . . Mass] *insrtd.*
    vert. in upper left mrgn. of first page

To Henry James [27 October 1861]

4.13 it.] *period ov. comma*
4.13 When] 'W' *ov.* 'E'
4.17 left] *ov.* 'gav'
4.19–20 comprehend] *aft. del.* 'take'
4.21 rather] 'r' *ov.* 's'
4.22–23 order] *aft. del. poss.* 'tel'
4.31 Vacation] ²'a' *ov. poss.* 'ti'

To Henry James 3 May 1865

5.3 the Colorado] *aft. del.* 'viz'
6.4 days] *bef. del.* 'may be summed up'
6.16 we] *ab. del.* 'three of us'
6.16 3] *intrl.*
6.18 They] *aft. del.* 'It is'
6.37 trying] *aft. del.* 'th'
6.41 His] *aft. del.* 'There is more charlatanerie & humbug about him & more solid worth too than you meet with'
7.3–4 expedition] 'ti' *ov.* 'sh'
7.5 a] *aft. del.* 'the'
7.6 11] ²'1' *ov.* 'o'
7.16 finish] *aft. del.* 'write'
7.19 we] *aft. del.* 'm'
7.24 the] *ov.* 'a'
7.25 wh.] *written on a new line bel. del.* 'ever saw' *repeated in error fr. the line ab.*
7.33 not] *bef. del.* 'yet'
7.40 over] *aft. del.* 'of'
7.41 Johns] *apostrophe bef.* 's' *del.*
8.5 Agassiz] 'A' *ov.* 'a'
8.9 at] *aft. del.* 'f'
8.9 probably] *intrl.*
8.13 on] *aft. del.* 'our'
8.14 so] *aft. del.* 'I'
8.14 learn] *ab. del.* 'study'
8.30 and] 'an' *ov. poss.* 'th'
8.31 When] 'h' *ov. poss.* 'e'
8.32 I] *ov.* 'O'
8.35 than] 'n' *ov.* 't'
8.38 Harris] *aft. del.* 'Davis'
8.39 Onward] 'On' *ov.* 'on'

To Henry James 15 July [1865]

9.7 Houp] 'H' *ov.* 'D'
10.8 Agassiz] 'A' *ov.* 'a'
10.11 into] *ab. del.* 'over'
10.11 wh. reaches] *intrl.*
10.16 lagoon] 'la' *ov. poss.* 'se'; *bef. del.* 'cov'
10.21 sweet juicy] *intrl.*
10.23 wh.] *bef. del.* 'the'
10.25 wd.] *aft. del.* 'have I'

To Henry James 23 July 1865

10.4 Perkinses] *bef. del.* 'wh'
10.5 had] 'd' *ov.* 've'
11.6 miles] *aft. del.* 'mill'
11.7 there.] *period ov. comma*
11.18 can] *final* 't' *del.*
11.21 Great] *aft. del.* 'Old'

To Henry James 3 May 1867

12.2 après] *intrl.*
12.16 plus] *intrl.*
12.17 ne] *intrl.*
12.17 guère] *aft. del.* 'à peine le'
12.18 et] *ab. del.* 'parce que'
12.22 sente] *aft. del.* 'sentent'
12.22 ou . . . l'ineptitude] *intrl. for del.* 'l'in [*ab. del.* 'la corruption']'
12.24–25 ¹& . . . bête.] *intrl.*
12.33 180] *ov.* '200'
12.38 écrivais] *ab. del.* 'disais'
12.39 de] *ov.* 'à'
12.40 Taylor] *ab. del.* 'il'

From Henry James 10 May [1867]

13.7 be] 'b' *ov.* 'w'
13.8 ³of] *alt. fr.* 'at'
13.10 not.] *period alt. fr. qst. mk.*
14.2 you] *ab. del.* 'they'
14.6 with] 'h' *ov.* 'e'
14.8 were] *ov.* 'are'
14.10 means] 'm' *ov.* 'w'
14.15 ²for] 'or' *ov.* 'ro'
14.24 if] *intrl.*

From Henry James 21 May [1867]

15.1 21] '2' *ov.* '1'
15.16 must] 'm' *ov.* 'f'
15.16 ²not] *intrl.*
15.24 since] *ab. del.* 'when'
15.29 a] *ov. poss.* 'go'
16.2 write.] *ab. del.* 'right.'
16.10 extraordinary] 'ord' *ov.* 's[illeg.]'

To Henry James 27 June 1867

16.9 she] *aft. del.* 'the'
16.11 we] *aft. del.* 'y'
16.11 yore] 're' *ov. poss.* 'u'
17.4 perfection] *aft. del.* 'much'
17.4 course)] *paren ov. dash*
17.7 He] 'H' *alt. fr.* 'I'
17.7 part] *aft. del.* 'place'
17.8 ¹see] *bef. del.* 'f'
17.9 ¹as] *intrl.*
17.16 like] *bef. del.* 'those in Paris'
17.17 I] *ov.* 'A'
17.19 get] *aft. del.* 'have'
17.24 old] 'o' *ov.* 'a'
17.25 melted] *aft. del.* 'is something'
17.26 you] *ab. del.* 'to'
17.27 not] *aft. del.* 'so'
17.29 were] *aft. del.* 'me'
17.30 on] *final* 'e' *erased*
17.37 fat,] *comma ov. period*

To Henry James 26 September 1867

18.1 26] '6' *ov.* '5'
18.6 sitting] *aft. del.* 'swe'
18.7–8 possibly] *aft. del.* 'do'
18.13 thoughts] 'th' *ov.* 'ma'
18.14 judge] *aft. del.* 'sh'
18.14–15 be capable of] *ab. del.* 'have ['any' *del.*]'
18.17 hardly] *ab. del.* 'not'
18.17 this] *alt. fr.* 'the'
18.22 yet] *intrl.*
18.22 In] *aft. del.* 'I'
18.25 with] *bef. del.* 'out the'
18.25 rather a deficiency] *tr. fr.* 'a deficiency rather'
19.5 seem] *final* 's' *del.*
19.7 was] *ov.* 'is'
19.12 By] 'y' *ov.* 'ut'
19.14 get] *init.* 'for' *del.*
19.14 over] *intrl.*
19.23 think] *aft. del.* 'fe'
19.25 over] *aft. del.* 'of'
19.25 remember] *ab. del.* 'think of'
19.25 days] *aft. del.* 'Gr'
19.26 Grandma's] *alt. fr.* 'Grandm'as'

19.26 old] 'o' *alt. fr. poss.* 'a'
19.27 city] 'c' *ov.* 's'
19.28 Europe.] *in MS* 'Europe, [*comma not alt. to period in error*]' *bef. erased* 'at'
19.28 In] *insrtd. bef.* 'The [*cap. in MS retained in error*]'
19.30 flat] *aft. del.* 'cov'
19.31 height] 'i' *ov.* 'a'
19.32 ¹I] *ov.* 'a'
19.32 will] *aft. del.* 'can'
19.34 fundamental] 'al' *ov.* 'le'
19.37 very] *intrl.*
20.3 feel] 'f' *ov.* 'v'
20.7 by staying] *ab. del.* 'at'
20.7 might] *ab. del.* 'wd.'
20.21 These] 'T' *ov.* 't'; *aft. del.* 'But'
20.21 indifferent] 'in' *ov.* 're'
20.21 in] *aft. del.* 'for a'
20.22 insolent] *aft. del.* 'and'
20.33 ²it] *ab. del.* 'the winter'
20.38 would] *aft. del.* 'wh'
20.39 street] *ab. del.* 'way'
21.1 what] *aft. del.* 'the'
21.16 comic] *aft. del.* 'strange'
21.17 delicious] *intrl.*
21.23 will] *aft. del.* 'f'
21.31 Basque] 'q' *ov. poss.* 'k'
21.35–36 distinguished] *aft. del.* 'throug'
21.36 their] *alt. fr.* 'they'
21.40–22.2 I . . . idea] *insrtd. vert. at foot of last page*
22.3–7 ¹I . . . them.] *insrtd. vert. in top mrgn. of first page*

To Henry James 17 October 1867

22.6–7 lightens] *aft. del.* 'burdens'
23.7 He] 'H' *ov.* 'h'; *aft. del.* 'However,'
23.23 its] *ab. del.* 'this'
23.26 or] *aft. del.* 'of'
23.28 There] 're' *insrtd.*
23.29 evidence] 'ce' *ov. poss.* 'ti'
23.32 bust.] *period ov. comma*
23.37 If] *aft. del. poss.* 'A'

23.37 piece] *alt. fr.* 'pice'
23.38 ²it] *aft. del.* 'the'
23.40 very] *ab. del.* 'more'
23.41 jaws] 'j' *ov.* 's'
24.1 like] *aft. del.* 'th'

From Henry James 22 November [1867]

24.9 article] *ab. del.* 'work'
24.15 ¹to] *bef. erased comma*
25.2 ¹as] *intrl.*
25.20 it] *ov.* 'I'
25.30 on] 'o' *ov.* 'i'
25.34 place.] *period ov. poss.* 's'
25.37 A] *ov.* 'a'

To Henry James [December 1867]

26.5 germany] *bef. del. closing paren*
26.6 to know] *intrl.*
27.6 mere] *ab. del.* 'perfect'
27.7 perfect] 'p' *ov.* 'h'; *final* 'l' *del.*
27.7 author.] *period aft. del. comma*

To Henry James 26 December 1867

27.9 writing] *bef. del.* 'I'
27.11 year] *ov.* 'I'
28.6 TS] *alt. fr.* 'The'
28.8,12 that] *intrl.*
28.16 aus] *ab. del.* 'of'
28.18 monthlies] 'ies' *ov.* 'y'
28.28 politeness] 'p' *ov.* 'b'
28.29 *Fischers*] 'i' *ov.* 'a'
28.34 or] *bef. del.* 'be'
28.37 ²a] *intrl.*
28.40 cerate] 'c' *ov.* 's'

To Henry James [January 1868]

30.3 ²of] *ov.* 'in'

To Henry James 12 February 1868

30.10 read] *aft. del.* 'w'
30.12 one] *aft. del.* 'th'

30.23 nice] *aft. del.* 'painstaking.'
31.13 every] *bef. del.* 'german'
31.17 appeal] *bef. del.* 'to'
31.20 a lone] *alt. w. vert. line fr.* 'alone'
31.20 outcast] *intrl.*
31.23 live] *aft. del.* 'am'
31.26 that] *init.* 't' *ov.* 'I'
31.27 on the whole] *intrl.*
31.27 could . . . so] *ab. del.* 'shd.'
31.30 lose] *ab. del.* 'find'
31.30 sense] *aft. del.* 'common'
31.37 run] *aft. del.* 'have'
31.39 beginning] *aft. del.* 'end'
32.2 in] 'n' *ov.* 's'
32.6 am] 'a' *ov. poss.* '&'
32.9 he] *ov.* 'a'
32.19 jealous] *ab. del.* 'cold'
32.20 permit] 'p' *ov.* 'le'
32.23 *les feux*] *aft. del.* 'the passion'
32.23 ²her] *bef. del.* 'h'
32.24 actress,] *bef. del.* 'who'
32.28 late] *aft. del.* 'ex-[start of* 'k'*]*'
32.31 came] *aft. del.* 'all passed first through'
32.35 read] 're' *ov.* 'an'
32.38 ²know] 'k' *ov.* 'n'

To Henry James 4 March 1868

33.1 Bohemia] *intrl.*
33.9 and] 'a' *ov.* 'I'
33.11 countenanced] 'u' *intrl.*
33.12 you] *ov. poss.* 'we'
33.13 youth's] 't' *ov.* 'n'
33.14 whatever] *aft. del.* 'in'
34.3 orbits] 'r' *ov. start of* 'b'
34.28 hair] 'ai' *ov.* 'ea'
34.33 I . . . of] *intrl.*
34.41 in] *insrtd.*
35.1 ¹the] *final* 're' *del.*
35.6–7 old fashioned] *intrl.*
35.13 enters] 'en' *ov.* 'ris'
35.13 so] *ov. poss.* 'th'
35.15 lies] 'e' *ov.* 'l'
35.15 truth] *aft. del.* 'thr'
35.16 before] 'b' *ov.* 'w'
35.18 only] *aft. del.* 'ol'

35.22–23 hypothetical] *intrl.*
35.28 wd.] 'd' *ov. poss.* 'h'
35.28 any] *bef. del.* 'other'
35.37 get] 'e' *ov.* 'o'
35.38 them!] *exclm. mk. ov. comma*
36.3 rather] *intrl.*
36.5 literary] *intrl.*
36.5 an] *intrl.*
36.5 illustration] *final* 's' *del.*
36.6 of the] *intrl.*
36.10 story] 'to' *ov.* 'or'
36.10 certain] 'c' *ov.* 'e'
36.10 &] *intrl.*
36.11 is] *ov.* 'I'
36.13 on] 'o' *ov. poss.* 'n'
36.14 altho'] 'tho' *ov.* 'so'
36.14 first] 'i' *ov.* 'r'
36.15 being] *bef. del.* 'devo'
36.18 to] *aft. del. intrl.* 'or else c'
36.22 if] *ov. closing paren*
36.25 being] *aft. del.* 'f'
36.25 over] *aft. del.* 'abo'
36.29 governs] 'g' *ov.* 'a'
36.32 clinging] *aft. del.* 'gallantly remaing'
36.34 That] *aft. del. opening paren*
36.36 the] *underl. erased*
36.38 the article] *ab. del.* 'it'
36.38 suspect] 'spect' *ov.* 'ppose'
36.40 this] 'is' *ov.* 'e'
36.40 coax] 'o' *ov.* 'a'
37.3 if] *aft. del.* 'in'
37.5 so] *intrl.*
37.7 Lamb] 'L' *ov.* 'h'
37.7 had] 'd' *ov.* 's'
37.13 read] 're' *ov.* 'en'
37.16 trifling] 'ri' *ov. poss.* 'os'
37.21 conscientiously] 't' *ov.* 's'
37.22 little] *ab. del.* 'no'
37.30 problem] *aft. del.* 'literary'
37.31 special] *aft. del.* 'p'
38.2–3 winter] 't' *ov.* 'd'

To Henry James 9 March [1868]

38.7 cleverness.] *bef. del.* 'I should'
39.2 l'apporterai] *final* 's' *del.*

39.3 let] *aft. del.* 'lette'
39.4 ²Renan] 'R' *ov.* 'r'
39.5 représentant] *ab. del.* 'ayant'
39.6 chose] 'c' *ov.* 's'
39.8 do] 'd' *ov.* 't'
39.10 Aggassiz] 'A' *ov.* 'a'
39.10 either] *intrl.*
39.15–17 I . . . house] *insrtd. vert. at foot of last page*

To Henry James 5 April 1868

39.8 still] *intrl.*
40.1 it] *bef. del.* 'once or'
40.4–5 conception] *aft. del.* 'qu'
40.6 together] *intrl.*
40.10 you wd.] *ab. del.* 'wd.'
40.11 Still] *bef. del.* 'it is a'
40.12 sense] *bef. del.* 'of'
40.15 instead.] *ab. del. period*
40.19 side] *ab. del.* 'out'
40.31 old] *intrl.*
40.35 generally] *aft. del.* 'often'
40.39–40 in nature] *intrl.*
41.3 to ones eyes] *intrl.*
41.6 both] *bef. del.* 'sought after *being*'
41.7 Being] 'B' *ov.* 'b'
41.12 ideal] *ab. del.* 'religious s'
41.13 the Germans] *ab. del.* 'they'
41.18 in both cases] *intrl.*
41.18 there] 're' *ov.* 'ir'
41.21 scenes] *alt. fr.* 'scences'
41.25 Venetian] 'V' *ov.* 'v'
41.28 Allston] 'A' *ov.* 'a'
41.30 effortless] *aft. del.* 'infal'
41.35 Homus] *tr. fr. aft.* 'enjoying ['old' *del.*]'
42.1 in spirit] *intrl.*
42.1 Iliad] *aft. del.* 'orig'
42.11 their] 'ir' *ov.* 're'
42.13 joys] 's' *insrtd.*
42.13 or] *ov.* '&'
42.14 coextensive] 'tensive' *ab. del.* 'istent'
42.14 life] *aft. del.* 'existence'
42.17 Homeric] *intrl.*
42.18 ¹its] *ab. del.* 'the'
42.18 very] *intrl.*

42.20 exist.] *period aft. del. comma*

42.20 and] *aft. del.* 'th'

42.23 perfectly] 'p' *ov.* 'a'

42.30 such] *ab. del.* 'wh'

42.34 ¹is] 's' *ov.* 't'

42.39 Book] 'B' *ov.* 'b'

42.40 terrible] *bef. del.* 'and i'

42.41 in our sight] *intrl.*

43.2 modern] *intrl.*

43.5 striking] 'trik' *ov.* 'eal'

43.8 needing] *intrl.*

43.11 behind] *aft. del.* '['beyond' *del.*] he'

43.11 fm] *ov.* 'in'

43.14–15 wd be] *ab. del.* 'is'

43.16 Achilleus] 'A' *ov.* 'a'

43.17 seems] *bef. del.* 'b'

43.17 by] *bef. del.* 'm'

43.18 but] *intrl.*

43.28 you'll] ¹'l' *ov. start of* 'g'

43.31 are] *ab. del.* '&'

43.36 All] *bef. del.* 'are von'

43.36 widowed] *aft. del.* 'married,'

43.38 100] '1' *ov.* 'a'

44.4 altho'] 'a' *ov.* 'I'

44.7 whose] 'w' *ov.* 's'

44.11 cd.] *ov.* 'wd'

44.11 sit] *ov.* 'pay'

44.16 genteel] *intrl.*

44.16 6] *intrl.*

44.31 in] *ab. del.* 'towards the end of'

44.34 Teplitz] 'T' *ov. start of* 't'

44.39 2] *ov.* '1'

44.40 ¹have] *intrl.*

44.40 known] *bef. del.* 'know'

44.40 by] *final* 'e' *del.*

45.2 think] 'k' *ov.* 'g'

45.19 W.J.] *bef. del.* 'Address'

45.20–24 Address . . . correspondence.] *insrtd. vert. in mrgns. of first page*

To Henry James 13 April 1868

46.1 April] *ab. del.* 'March'

46.5 partly] 'l' *ov.* 'y'

46.10 an] *final* 'd' *del.*

46.12 ²of] *insrtd.*

46.17 Some] *bef. del.* 'few'

46.23 gone off] *intrl.*

46.23 sticking] *alt. fr.* 'stuck'

46.23 thumb] *aft. del.* 'fingers'

46.24 fiendishly] ¹'i' *ov.* 'e'

46.25 You] 'Y' *ov.* 'y'; *aft. del.* 'If'

46.25 seem to] *intrl.*

46.25 exhaust] 'a' *ov.* 'e'

46.26 character's] *ab. del.* 'one's'

46.26 articulate displaying] *ab. del.* 'explication'

46.28 which] 'w' *ov.* 'a'

46.31 these] ¹'e' *ov.* 'o'

46.31 body] *aft. del.* 'great'

46.32 fullness] *bef. del. comma*

47.3 succeed.] *period ov. comma bef. del.* 'because if *you must [*ab. del.* 'it'] fail,'

47.3 The] 'T' *ov.* 't'

47.3 fail] *final* 's' *del.*

47.3 that] *ab. del.* 'it'

47.5 much of] *intrl.*

47.8 Richard] *bef. del. closing paren*

47.11 head.] *period ov. comma bef. del.* 'and the young women in both under the second head'

47.11 young] *intrl.*

47.12 been] *aft. del.* 'pe'

47.12 very] *aft. del.* 'f'

47.12 like] *aft. del.* 'he'

47.15 less] *final* 's' *ov.* 't'

47.15 fleshly] *ab. del.* 'solid'

47.15 although] *alt. fr.* 'all though'

47.17 she] 'h' *ov.* 'e'

47.22 no] 'n' *ov.* 's'

47.23 implied] 'ied' *ov.* 'y'

47.23–24 a . . . ¹is] *intrl.*

47.25 know] 'kn' *ov.* 'no'

47.27 the . . . is] *alt. fr.* 'a conception of a story as thorough and passionate is' *alt. fr.* 'a thorough conception of a story as'

47.32 now] 'w' *ab. del. poss.* 'w'

47.32 one] 'o' *ov.* 'w'

47.36 endless] *intrl.*

47.39 yesterday.] *bef. del.* '—but'

47.41 and] *aft. del.* 'but'

48.1 might] *bel. del.* 'wd.'

48.3 another] 'nother' *intrl.*
48.3 ²a] *insrtd.*
48.4 conception] *aft. del.* 'elements'
48.5 race &] *ab. del.* 'the'
48.6 *temperament*] *bef. del.* 'of the
 individual'
48.7 -on-] 'o' *ov.* 'i'
48.7 -dung] 'n' *ov.* 'g'
48.7 e.g.] *aft. del.* 'as'
48.8 poetry of the] *intrl.*
48.9 wh.] *aft. del.* 'to'
48.10 either] *intrl.*
48.10–11 or . . . altogether] *intrl.*
48.16 slip] *bef. del.* 'around'
48.16 "whirl" around] *ab. del.*
 'around'
48.18 nothing] *aft. del. start of letter*
48.19 it] 't' *ov.* 'n'
48.19 vain] *aft. del.* 'fa'
48.24 from] *aft. del.* 'to'
48.26 keeping] *bef. del.* 'the'
48.30 ¹has] 'h' *ov. poss.* 's'
48.34 2] *intrl.*

To Henry James 4 June 1868

49.6 ²avoided] *intrl.*
49.8 has] 'h' *ov.* 'a'
49.20 society generally] *ab. del.* 'this'
50.2 had] *intrl.*
50.2 previously] *ab. del.* 'before'
50.2 his] *bef. del.* 'h'
50.9 -matter] *intrl.*
50.9 perhaps] *init.* 'p' *ov.* 'b'
50.15 weight] 'i' *ov.* 'a'
50.16 to] *aft. del.* 'them'; *bef. del.*
 'embody'
50.21 latter part] *ab. del.* 'second'
50.23 apparent] *intrl.*
50.28 that] *alt. fr.* 'his'
50.33 wh.] *ov.* 'as'
50.33 Emerson] 'E' *ov.* 'e'
50.35 &] *ov.* 'a'
50.36 relates] *alt. fr.* 'realtes'
50.38 the abysses] *aft. del.* 'in Faust'
50.39 fearing] *aft. del.* 'knowing that
 value is in ['the w' *del.*]'
50.41 put] 'p' *ov.* 'b'

51.2 now] *intrl.*
51.3 altho] *in MS alt. to* 'alhto' *fr.*
 'at a'
51.4 raw] *aft. del.* 'yout[*start of* 'h']'
51.4 At] 'A' *ov.* 'I'
51.13 kept] 'k' *ov.* 'g'
51.17 makes] *bef. del.* 'his mind'
51.24 Elegiac] *final* 's' *del.*
51.28 with] *intrl.*
51.33 worked] *ab. del.* 'made'
51.36 Excuse] *alt. fr.* 'Excusse'
51.38 on] *final* 'e' *erased*
51.40 I am] *alt. fr.* 'I'm'

To Henry James 10 July [1868]

52.6 ¹the] *intrl.*
52.6 ²the] *final* 're' *del.*; *bef. del.* 'is'
52.10 curiosity] *aft. del.* 'interest is'
52.15 all] *aft. del.* 'how'
53.4 various] 'v' *ov.* 'r'; *aft. del.* 'some'
53.7 second] *ab. del.* 'premier'
53.9 The] *aft. del. opening db. qt.*
53.16 with] *aft. del.* 'of'
53.30 librorum] *aft. del.* 'articulis,'
53.30 articulis] *bef. del. period*
53.36 ²which] *aft. del.* 'that'
53.39–40 I . . . writing] *insrtd. vert.
 in left mrgn. of first page*

To Henry James 26 August [1868]

54.6 think] 'k' *ov.* 'g'
54.7 got] *ab. del.* 'done'
54.11 expect] *final* 'ed' *del.*
54.13 enclose] *final* 'd' *del.*
54.14 irrelevant] *bef. del. period*
54.17 visible] *aft. del.* 'f'
54.17 rue] *aft. del.* 'grande'
54.17–18 du Rone] *intrl.*
54.19 Kohler] 'h' *ov.* 'l'
54.20 The] 'T' *ov.* 'I'
54.22 kind] 'k' *ov.* 'c'
55.5 unpleasant.] *bef. del.* 'The
 language seemed'
55.12 homesickness] *aft. del.*
 'nostalgia'
55.18 ²me] *aft. del.* 'l'

55.19 they] *bef. del.* 'used to'
55.23 which] *bef. del.* 'we'
55.25 people] *aft. del.* 'lan'
55.29 certain] *aft. del.* 'grea'
55.31 mere] *intrl.*
55.32 their] *bef. del.* 'blindness to the existence of'
55.35 national] *intrl.*
55.37 rather] *intrl.*
56.2 french] *bef. del.* 'in'
56.2 by] *alt. fr.* 'but'
56.4 which] *bef. del.* 'is most'
56.4 his] 'i' *ov.* 'o'
56.4 ²at] *ov.* 'or'
56.9 ¹on] 'n' *ov.* 'r'
56.10 you] 'y' *ov.* 'w'
56.11 write] *ab. del.* 'opine'
56.25 wh.] *intrl.*
56.34 & personal] *intrl.*
56.38 believe] *aft. del.* 'don't'
56.39 if] *ov.* 'I'
57.1 of . . . "motives"] *intrl.*
57.4 ²I] *aft. del.* 'But ['B' *ov.* 'b']'
57.4 very] *aft. del.* 'f'
57.9 will] *aft. del.* 'wl'

To Henry James [22 September 1868]

57.4 Fm] 'm' *ov.* 'or'
58.3 Empty] *bef. del.* 'pu'
58.4 omit] *ab. del.* 'rest'
58.12 mind] *final* 's' *del.*

From Henry James 19 March [1869]

58.11 turning] *ov. poss.* 'acquiring'
59.30 with] 'w' *ov.* 't'
59.35 homme] *bef. erased comma*
59.36 very urgent] *ab. del.* 'picture'
59.36 his] *aft. del.* 'four'
59.39 long-established] *intrl.*
60.1 week.] *bef. del. closing paren*
60.3 paved] *aft. del. illeg.*
60.17 have] *intrl.*
60.18 disappointed] 'ed' *ov.* 'ment'
60.22 you] *aft. del.* 'home'

To Henry James 22 March 1869

61.8 your] *ov.* 'their'
61.9 ²like] *ov. poss.* 'little'
61.10 de suite] *aft. del.* 'of'
61.19 My] *ov.* 'I'
61.21 ¹that] *ov. poss.* 'a an'
61.29 bef.] *aft. del.* 'f'
61.30 She] 'S' *ov.* 'Y'
61.32 her] *aft. del.* 'the'
61.38 without] 'out' *insrtd.*
62.3 It] *aft. del.* 'You'
62.11–13 23rd. . . . gift."] *insrtd. vert. in mrgns. of first page*

From Henry James 8 April [1869]

62.11 once] *intrl.*
63.1 soaring] *intrl.*
63.7 ago,] *ab. del.* 'hence'
63.8 feel] *bef. del.* 'to'
63.8 ease] *ab. del.* 'home'
63.12 have] *ov.* 'of'
63.17 degree)] *bef. del.* 'more or less'
63.36–37 Divonne] *aft. del.* 'Malvern'
64.16 between] *intrl.*
64.16 & 3 weeks] *intrl.*
64.21 too] *ab. del.* 'more'
65.2 one] 'o' *ov. poss.* 'I'
65.41 Remember . . . inquiry.] *insrtd. in top mrgn. of last page*

To Henry James 23 April 1869

66.13 what] 'h' *ov.* 'a'
66.14 Father] 'F' *ov.* 'P'
66.18 such] 'u' *ov.* 'o'
66.21 dols.] 's' *ov.* 'l'
66.26 make] *aft. del.* 'f'
67.2 if] 'f' *ov.* 't'
67.5 a] *intrl.*
67.7 ¹with] *aft. del. poss.* 'i'
67.9 to Paris] *ab. del.* 'West'
67.13 seem] *aft. del.* 'have'
67.15 have] 'av' *ov.* 'op'

From Henry James 26 April [1869]

67.5 say] 'y' *ov.* 'id'
67.12 been] *intrl.*
68.8 These] 'se' *insrtd.*
68.28–29 —in . . . sizes.] *intrl.*
68.34 ²you] 'y' *ov.* 'I'
68.34 poor] *ab. del.* 'rich'
68.35 rich] *ab. del.* 'poor'
68.38 have] *intrl.*
69.4 his] *ab. del.* 'my'
69.8 stood] 'st' *ov.* 'w'
69.11 would] *intrl.*
69.13 You] 'Y' *ov.* 'I'
69.16 lads] *ab. del.* 'youth'
69.19 When] *aft. del.* 'And all this'
70.2 with] *ov.* 'at'
70.4 a] *intrl.*
70.6 ³very] *insrtd.*
70.8 an] *ab. del.* 'our'
70.17 walls, . . . windows.] *comma insrtd.*; 'between . . . windows.' *intrl. w. caret ov. period*
70.27 Blenheim] *bef. del.* 'out to Blenheim'
70.32 with . . . day,] *intrl.*
70.35 &] *intrl.*
70.41 a] *intrl.*
71.1 avenues] *bef. del. period*
71.6 & music] *intrl.*
71.36 abolish] 'b' *ov.* 'l'
72.2 an] *ov.* 'a'
72.4 or . . . it] *ab. del. poss.* 'about'

From Henry James 13 May [1869]

72.4 in] *ov.* 'to'
73.17 ²short] *intrl.*
73.29 fatiguing] *aft. del.* 'very'
73.32 &] *ov.* 't'
73.35 pretty] *intrl.*
74.5 on] *ab. del.* 'with'

From Henry James 30 May 1869

74.4 forgot] *ov.* 'have'
74.11 speech] 'spe' *ov. poss.* 'tal'

74.14 that] *ov.* 'you'
74.19 a] *ov.* 'once'
74.21 still] *intrl.*
75.10–11 imply] *ab. del.* 'involve'
75.16 condition] 'c' *ov.* 'd'
75.17 an] 'n' *added*
75.17 absolute] 'a' *ov.* 'ce'
75.30 part] 'pa' *ov.* 'an'
75.38 ²to] *intrl.*
76.6 beforehand] *intrl.*
76.13 to] 't' *ov. poss.* 'r'
76.14 a new man;] *intrl. w. caret ov. comma*
76.20 ²I have] *alt. fr.* 'The'
76.21 pictures] *bef. del. comma*
76.35 ²to] *intrl.*
76.38 or . . . rather,] *intrl.*
77.2 that] 'th' *ov.* 'm'
77.12 wasn't to] *ab. del.* 'didn't'
77.19 opening] 'op' *ov.* 'm'
77.26–27 I . . . family.] *insrtd. in top mrgn. of first page*

To Henry James 1 June 1869

77.1 69] '9' *ov.* '8'
77.3 week] *aft. del.* 'wit[*start of* 'h']'
77.6 get] 'g' *ov.* 'l'
78.16 I suppose] *intrl.*
78.21 feel] ²'e' *ov.* 'l'
78.24 with] 'w' *ov.* 'I'
78.30 *plomb*] 'om' *alt. fr. poss.* 'ur'
78.38 trying] *aft. del.* 'thr'
79.11 it] *intrl.*
79.12–13 of the treaty,] *intrl.*
79.13 a] *ab. del.* 'the'
79.15 any] 'y' *ov.* 'd'
79.16 dinner] *intrl.*
79.18 undeveloped] 'v' *ov.* 'le'
79.24 ³the] *intrl.*
79.28 thankfully] *intrl.*
79.29 books] *intrl.*
79.31 once] 'o' *ov.* 'n'
79.33 but] *aft. del.* 'f'
79.34 if] *ov.* 'I'
79.34 book] *aft. del.* 'f'
79.35 diffuse] *intrl.*
79.37–38 or . . . birth] *intrl.*

79.40 puts] *aft. del.* 'me'
79.41 men] 'n' *ov.* 'an'
80.7 as] *bef. del.* 'al'
80.10 shall] 'sha' *ov.* 'wi'
80.16 Trying] 'T' *ov.* 't'; *aft. del.* 'By'
80.18 summer] *ab. del.* 'wi'
80.24 congratulate] *aft. del.* 'find'

To Henry James 12 June 1869

81.10 say] *bef. del.* 'you'
81.10 got] *aft. del.* 'h'
81.18 like] *bef. del.* 'a circus in'
82.6 heard] 'h' *ov. start of* 'o'
82.7 is] 's' *ov.* 't'
82.11 be] *bef. del.* 'able'
82.14 very] *aft. del.* 'fr'
82.29 truth] *aft. del. poss.* 't'
82.30 I'll] *bef. del.* 'be dis'
82.35 have] *intrl.*
82.37 but] *ov.* 'and'
83.3 recall] *final* 'y' *del.*
83.12 Russ] *aft. del.* 'gr'
83.17 shape] 's' *ov.* 'c'
83.18 *Streng*] *aft. del.* 'Mus'
83.19 but] 'b' *ov.* 'a'
83.21 get] 'g' *ov.* 'l'
83.21 outside of the] *intrl.*
83.21 building] 'b' *ov.* 'm'
83.26 no] *start of final* 't' *erased*
83.26 writes] 'wr' *ov. poss.* 'as'
83.40 *Whatever*] 'W' *ov.* 'w'; *aft. del.* 'as'
83.40 Italy] *aft. del.* 'Ial'; *bef. del.* 'wh'
84.2 peculiarly] 'c' *ov.* 'r'
84.7 marked] 'r' *ov. start of* 'k'

From Henry James 12 July 1869

84.3 has] 's' *ov.* 've'
85.6 I] *intrl.*
85.23 hour] *intrl.*
85.30 is] *ov.* 'in'
85.31 had] *intrl.*
85.33 comparatively] 'c' *ov.* 'f'
85.37 started] *aft. del.* '&'
86.9 region] 'e' *ov.* 'g'
86.15 at] *ab. del.* 'of'

86.16 starting] *aft. del.* '&'
86.31 Here,] *intrl. bef.* 'At [*cap. in MS retained in error*]'
86.31 I] *aft. del.* 'at Gesteig'
86.41 coupé of the] *intrl.*
87.15 in] *intrl.*
87.19 Having breakfasted] *ab. del.* 'On rising'
87.23 mountains about] *ab. del.* 'scenery of'
87.34 2] *ab. del.* 'four'
88.6 for] *intrl.*
88.6 yet] *bef. del.* 'but'
88.9 My] 'M' *ov. poss.* 'e'
88.12 of] *intrl.*
88.19 have] *aft. del.* 'am to'
88.23 introduced] 'troduced' *ov. poss.* 'creased'
88.24 an] *intrl.*
88.30 so] 's' *ov.* 't'
88.38 for] *ab. del.* 'before'
89.4 am] *ov. illeg.*
89.27 ²her] *intrl.*
89.36 make] *alt. fr.* 'making'

From Henry James 12 August [1869]

90.1 August] 'A' *ov.* 'J'
90.15 try] 't' *ov.* 'b'
90.18 hither] *ov.* 'here'
90.23 ¹the] *ov.* 'of'
90.26 announced] *ab. del.* 'was'
90.28 push] *ab. del.* 'scramble'
91.11 -&-ice-] *ov. erased* 'world'
91.14 opposite] *ab. del.* 'before me'
91.19 the] *ov.* 'my'
91.22 I] *intrl.*
91.28 in] *ab. del.* 'under'
91.35 Send] 'S' *ov. poss.* 'I'
91.36 M.M.] *intrl.*

From Henry James 25 September [1869]

92.4 Venice] 'Ve' *ov. poss.* 'the'
92.6 notes] *underl. erased*
92.11 for] 'f' *ov.* 't'
93.7 that] *intrl.*

93.8 me] 'm' *ov.* 'be'
93.11 Palace] *ov. poss.* 'Place'
93.13 But] 'B' *ov.* 'I'
93.19 something] 'thing' *ov.* 'ing'
93.28 over] *intrl.*
93.30 ¹for] *ab. del.* 'of'
94.8 ²&] *bef. del.* 'by'
94.9 by] *ov.* 's'
94.11 For the present] *intrl.*
94.17 perfect] *ab. del.* 'splendid'
94.20 enough] *intrl.*
94.22 ²&] *intrl.*
94.27 P.] *aft. del. poss.* 'T.G.'
94.35 painter] *aft. del.* 'great'
94.36 own] *intrl.*
94.41 define] *aft. del.* 'the'
95.10 undimmed] 'un' *ov. poss.* 'di'
95.11 a] *ov.* 'the'
95.12 it] *intrl.*
95.12 till] *ov.* 'it'
95.13 one] *intrl.*
95.21 But] 'B' *ov.* 'I'
95.25 touching] *ab. del.* 'about'
95.29 offers] *ab. del.* 'has'
95.36 immense] *ab. del.* 'large'
96.8 mix] 'x' *ov. poss.* 'd'
96.14 facing you,] *intrl.*
96.21 this] *ov.* 'Tin'
96.30 as usual] *intrl.*
97.1 of] *ov.* 'to'
97.9 Read] *ab. del.* 'Get'
97.14 they] *alt. fr. poss.* 'the ri'
97.16–17 you'd . . . fun.] *intrl. ab.
period undel. in error*
97.18 balconies] 'b' *ov.* 'p'
97.26 on the] *ab. del.* 'is under'
97.27 narrow] *intrl.*
97.27 people] *intrl.*
97.30 ²&] *ov. poss.* 's'
97.31 very] 've' *ov.* 'ef'
97.36 sad] *ab. del.* 'melancholy'
97.38 wealth] *ab. del.* 'splendor'
98.4 is conscious] *ab. del.* 'feels'
98.6 of] *intrl.*
98.21 do] *aft. del.* '&'
98.34 Parthenon] 'P' *ov.* 'p'
98.34 think] 'k' *ov.* 'g'

98.35 —the] *ab. del.* '& should'
99.8 no] 'o' *ov.* 'ew'

To Henry James 2 October 1869

100.7 6] *ov.* '7'
100.13 known] *intrl.*
100.39 show] *ab. del.* 'so'
100.39 but] *aft. del.* 'non'
100.40 have] 've' *ov.* 'd'
101.4 splendor,] *ab. del.* 'nature'
101.7 which] *aft. del.* 'even'
101.7 brings] *bef. del.* 'him'
101.13 flowered] 'red' *ab. del.* 'd'
101.13 dress] *final* 'ed' *del.*
101.13 so] 's' *ov.* 'I'
101.16 supine] *aft. del.* 'pe'
101.17 her] *aft. del.* 'the'
101.17 John] 'J' *ov.* 'T'
101.27 start] *aft. del.* 'g'
101.35 ideas] *bef. del.* 'very'
101.39 compunction] *aft. del.* 'p'
101.41 ¹is] *aft. del.* 'I'
102.11 He] *ab. del.* 'This'
102.11 made] 'de' *ov.* 'kes'
102.11 me feel] *ab. del.* 'it'
102.15 is] *ab. del.* 'was'
102.17 Prince] *ab. del.* 'James'
102.17 was] 's' *ov.* 'y'
102.27 doubtfully] *ab. del.
'apparently'*
102.30 rather] *aft. del. start of* 'th'
102.32 cool] *aft. del.* 'wan'
102.32 fabulous] *aft. del.
'tremendous'*
102.34 very] *aft. del.* 'f'
102.41 as] *intrl.*
103.3 him] *bef. del.* 'by'
103.3 sparingly] *alt. fr.* 'sparely'
103.15 religion] *aft. del.* 'reg'

From Henry James 7 October [1869]

104.16 fleeting] *intrl.*
104.16 since] *ov.* 'during'
104.24 in] 'i' *ov.* 'o'

104.27 ¹it] *intrl.*
104.34 &] *intrl.*
104.38 At] 'A' *ov.* 'I'
105.4 stale] *ab. del.* 'plain'
105.13 utterly] *intrl.*
105.14 ³I] *aft. del.* 'Upon my own'
105.30 that] *bef. del.* 'again'
105.35 ³& . . . cauliflower] *intrl.*
106.17 wait.—] *bef. del. poss.* '(Is
 B[*illeg. letters*] suppressed the
 *very [*intrl.*] always i[*illeg.
 letters*]tt[*illeg. letters*] [*two or three
 illeg. words*]'
106.27 from] *insrtd. for del.* 'thro''
106.32 —I] *dash ov. erased* 'If'
107.1 days] *ab. del.* 'time'

From Henry James 16 October [1869]

107.9 sent] 'se' *ov.* 'lo'
107.10 made] *intrl.*
108.7 on] *intrl.*
108.21 me] *intrl.*
108.27 in] *intrl.*
108.27 a] *ov. poss.* 'so'
108.28 if] *ov. erased* 'will'
109.2 ¹of] *ov.* 'in'
109.9 &] *insrtd.*
109.11 of things] *intrl.*
109.11 au] *aft. del.* 'gen'
109.13 than] *bef. del. comma*
109.16 into] *ab. del.* 'with'
109.18 ²the] *ab. del.* 'a contrived'
109.18 same] 'sa' *ov.* 'th'
109.20 which] *intrl.*
109.21 suggests] *ov. poss.* 'is'
109.34 distinct] *intrl.*
109.37 I] *aft. del.* 'While the former
 lasts'
109.41 if,] *bef. del.* 'by'
110.7 when] *intrl.*
110.12 question] 'q' *ov.* 'l'; *aft. del.*
 'reformation'
110.13 condition] *ov. poss.* 'life'
110.17 a] *intrl.*
110.27 Such] 'S' *ov.* 'T'

110.28 under] *aft. del.* 'in such a way,'
111.11 Thence] *alt. fr.* 'There'
111.16 & figs] *intrl.*
111.22 my] *ov.* 'I'
111.25–26 & . . . rate.] *intrl.*
112.15 yourselves] 'ves' *ov.* 'f'

To Henry James 25 October [1869]

112.8 old] *intrl.*
113.6 it] 'i' *ov.* 'a'
113.9 ¹as] *aft. del.* 'with'
113.9 (not . . . scalding)] *intrl.*
113.23 too] *intrl.*
113.31 get] *aft. del.* 'ke'
113.34 is] *bef. del.* 'not'
113.34 only] *ab. del.* 'but'
113.35 can] *final* 't' *del.*
113.38 they] *aft. del.* 'the'
114.5 why] *ab. del.* 'you'
114.14 gone] *alt. fr. poss.* 'goes'
114.20–24 Elly . . . tour."] *insrtd.
 vert. in mrgns. of first page*
114.23–24 Atlantic] 'A' *ov.* 'a'
114.25–27 Bob . . . re-enlisting.]
 insrtd. vert. in mrgns. of second page
114.28–29 Hosmer . . . glasses.]
 insrtd. vert. in mrgns. of sixth page

From Henry James 30 October [1869]

116.3 8] *ov.* '11'
116.16 solus] *ov. erased* 'by myself'
116.23 I wouldn't] *intrl.*
116.25 would] *intrl.*
116.27 Eternal] 'E' *ov.* 'I'
116.32 this] *ov.* 'a'
116.35 loose] *ov. erased* 'self'
117.2 (stupendissimo] '(st' *ov. dash*
117.3 the Capitol] *intrl.*
117.18–19 From the] *ov. poss.* 'I see
 great'
117.20 choir] *ov. poss.* 'pew'
117.25 give] *ov.* 'on'; *aft. del.* 'speak'

To Henry James 1 November 1869

118.3 put] *aft. del.* 'take'
118.4 before] *aft. del.* 'f'
118.10 I] *aft. erased opening paren*
118.16 that] *ab. del.* 'it'
118.18 acquire] *ab. del.* 'become'
118.19 It] *ov.* 'Th'
118.19 on . . . hand] *intrl.*
119.1 you] *aft. del.* 'I'
119.17 Aloes] 'A' *ov.* 'I'
119.18 doses] 'do' *ov.* 're'
119.20 are] *aft. del.* 'find'
119.20 tenesmus] *bef. del. comma*
119.25 but] *bef. del.* 'three'
119.27 such] *aft. del.* 'the[start of 's']'
119.32 you] *aft. del.* 'this'
119.34 trouble] *aft. del.* 'thr'
120.5 our] *alt. fr.* 'on'
120.7 living] 'l' *ov.* 'h'
120.16 a] *intrl.*
120.23 power] *aft. del.* '&'
120.36 want] *bef. del.* 'of'
120.41 your] 'y' *ov.* 'to'

From Henry James 8 November [1869]

121.12 or] *bef. del.* 'not'
121.15 this] 'is' *ov.* 'em'
121.15 change] *intrl.*
121.18 its] *ab. del.* 'their'

From Henry James 30 November [1869]

122.17 & he] *ab. del.* 'who'
123.4 Italian] *intrl.*
123.7 a similar] *ab. del.* 'the same'
123.21 Florence] *aft. del.* 'Rome or'
123.23 now than ever—] *intrl.*
124.1 (as] *paren ov. dash*
124.8 it] *intrl.*
124.11 prolonged] *alt. fr.* 'person'
124.14–15 ²& . . . true] *ab. del.* 'as well as'
124.19 now] *aft. del.* 'then'
124.25 tho'] *ov. dash*

124.36 very] *intrl.*
124.38 be] *intrl.*
125.13 & responsibility] *intrl.*
125.14 &] *ab. del.* 'I'
125.18 (probably)] *intrl.*
125.32 ¹as . . . of] *intrl.*
125.37 remain] *intrl.*
126.3 And] 'A' *ov.* 'In'
126.6 tread] *ov.* 'stride'
126.20 —a bad dream,] *intrl.*
126.22 deal] *intrl.*
126.40 count for] *ab. del.* 'weigh'

To Henry James 5 December 1869

127.3 of Nov 8] *intrl.*
127.5 could] *aft. del.* 'feel'
127.20 about] 'b' *ov.* 'f'
127.21 a third of a] *ab. del.* 'a'
127.22 not,] *comma ov. dash*
128.12 undiscriminating] *intrl.*
128.16–17 rambling] *aft. del.* 'personal'
128.18 visitors] *bef. del. period and* 'I'
128.19 Concord] *bef. del.* 'yester'
128.28 things] *alt. fr.* 'this'
128.28 to storm] *ab. del.* 'at'
128.32 that] *intrl.*
128.32 there] *aft. del.* 'they'
129.6 ¹one] *aft. del.* 'yo'
129.6 have] *bef. del.* 'a'
129.21 injustice] 'in' *insrtd.*
129.34 without] 'out' *insrtd.*
129.35 accented] *aft. del.* 'made'
130.3 ¹world] *aft. del.* 'for'
130.7 giving] *ab. del.* 'being'
130.30 go] *final* 'e' *del.*
131.14 style] *aft. del.* 'sthg'

To Henry James 27 December 1869

132.2 Nov] *ov.* 'Sat'
132.5 one] *ab. del.* 'thing'
132.5 sulf.] *aft. del.* '5 oz'
132.7 perhaps] *bef. del.* 'at the very root'

132.20 Strong] *intrl. bef.* 'Galvanism
 [*cap. in MS retained in error*]'
132.22 and] *aft. del.* 'thr'
132.27 it] *ov.* 'I'
132.28 visit] *aft. del.* 'f'
133.6 took] 'ok' *ov.* 'ld'
133.10 England] *aft. del.* 'a second'

From Henry James 27 [December 1869]

133.16 the] *ov.* 'my'
133.17 is] *intrl.*
133.20 them] *intrl.*
134.1 explicitly] 'exp' *ab. del. poss.* 'suff'
134.3 It] *ab. del.* 'The *Moses*'
134.4 ¹I] *ov.* 'It'
134.6 things;] *semicolon ov.* '&'
134.6 ³seen] *intrl.*
134.10 ever] *init.* 'e' *ov.* 'p'
134.15 limited] *ab. del.* 'definite'
134.21 as] *intrl.*
134.29 up] *aft. del.* 'it'
134.29 the latter.] *intrl. w. caret ov. period*
134.36 was incapable of] *ab. del.* 'lacked'
135.10 interest] 'i' *ov.* 'n'
135.12 it] *intrl.*
135.12 the] *ov. poss.* 'these [*ov.* 'det']'
135.16 for] *ov.* 'from'
135.24 I] *ov.* 'In'
135.29 go] *bef. del.* 'in'
135.31 a] *intrl.*
135.31 ¹of] *ab. del.* 'for'
135.37 28] '2' *intrl.*
136.9 ¹such] *bef. del.* '& such'
136.15 that] *ov.* 'a'
136.25 another,] *ab. del.* 'as'
136.30 church] *aft. del.* 'strict'
136.41 in] *aft. del.* 'tomorrow.'
137.13 into] 'to' *insrtd.*
137.18 Urbino] *ab. del.* 'Umbria'
137.26 But] *bef. del.* 'with'
137.28 rounded] *ab. del.* 'little'
137.40 too] *intrl.*
138.3 so] *ov.* 'too'

138.7 me] *intrl.*
138.16 so happily] *intrl.*
138.21 influence] *ab. del.* 'action'
138.23 to] *aft. del.* 'you'
138.33 leave,] *bef. del.* 'I shall still'
139.2 an insane] *ab. del.* 'Henry'
139.9 I fancy,] *intrl.*
139.26 was] *ab. del.* 'when'

To Henry James 19 January 1870

140.10 chloral] 'lo' *ov.* 'ol'
140.14 for] *aft. del.* 'so'
140.19 the] *final* 're' *del.*
140.19 days] *intrl.*
141.4 with] *aft. del.* 'which'
141.7 sacrés] *aft. del.* 'bayaux'
141.12 I] *aft. del.* 'I t[*start of* 'h']'
141.13 you] 'y' *ov.* 'to'
141.22 of] *ov.* 'to'
141.24 English] 'E' *ov.* 'e'

From Henry James 13 February 1870

142.3 27] *ov.* '19'
142.5 other] *intrl.*
142.5 19] *ov.* 'n'
142.9 A] *ov.* 'I'
142.23 previous] *aft. del.* 'former'
142.32 of] *intrl.*
142.38 on] *ov. erased* 'to'
143.7 my] *intrl.*
143.12 keen] *ab. del.* 'deep'
143.18 of] *intrl.*
143.22 more] *ov. erased* 'in the'
143.27 a] *ov.* 'I'
143.33 echoes] *aft. del. poss.* 'music'
143.37 viz:] *intrl.*
143.39 is] *ab. del.* 'was'
144.9 whole] *intrl.*
144.19 a] *intrl.*
144.20 had] *ab. del.* 'could'
144.33 material] *aft. del.* 'the'
144.34 glorious] *intrl.*
144.39 ²it] *intrl.*
144.41 & exemplify it] *intrl.*
145.6 beside] *bef. del.* 'it'

145.7 -seen,] *comma insrtd.*
145.7 half-felt.] *intrl. w. caret ov.*
    period
145.8 ago.] *period added bef. erased* 'to'
145.10 would] *ab. del.* 'will'
145.16 her] *intrl.*
145.16 (if] *paren ov.* 'to'
145.18 keenly] *ab. del.* 'much'
145.23 expect] *aft. del.* 'gain little &'
145.24 invests with] *ab. del.* 'lends'
145.28 strips] *ab. del.* 'robs'
145.35 ah!] *intrl.*
145.40 if] *aft. del. poss.* 'or'
146.2 yet.] *intrl.*
146.3 ¹the] *intrl.*
146.10 could] *ab. del.* 'gave'
146.13 varies] 'es' *ov.* 'ous'
146.21 the] *intrl.*
146.29 ¹of] *intrl.*
146.39 O.] *ov.* 'W'
147.14 I'll] ''ll' *insrtd.*
147.14 tale] *intrl.*

From Henry James 8 March 1870

148.29 further] *intrl.*
148.31 —up to a certain point.]
    intrl. w. caret ov. period
148.37 individuality,] *bef. del.* '&'
148.40 you] *ab. del.* 'of'
149.3 shall] *alt. fr.* 'should'
149.9 have] *intrl.*
149.13 than . . . Italy.] *intrl. w. caret*
    ov. period
150.5 freedom] *aft. del.* 'taste'
150.22 ²&] *intrl.*
150.26 summer] *ab. del.* 'year'
150.41 see] 'se' *ov. poss.* 'ho'
151.18 what] *ab. del.* 'your'
151.18 in yr. last] *intrl.*
151.18 getting] *intrl.*
151.29 discreetly] 'dis' *ov.* 'my'
151.38 I fancy] *ab. del.* 'probably'
152.20 arrival] *ab. del.* 'engagement'
152.21–22 Florence.] *ab. del.* 'Paris.'
152.27 Tell him] *intrl.*

From Henry James 29 March [1870]

153.1 29] '9' *ov. poss.* '6'
153.8 least] *ab. del. poss.* 'most'
153.18 ¹her] *intrl.*
153.26 feel] 'eel' *ov.* 'ind'
154.7 ever] *intrl.*
154.9 ²life] *aft. del. illeg. word*
154.9 at large] *intrl.*
154.13 had] *ab. del.* 'took'
154.13 permanent] *intrl.*
154.18–19 —as . . . concerned,—]
    intrl.
154.19 that of] *intrl. ab. caret placed*
    bef. dash in error
154.21 the] *ab. del.* 'her'
154.27 had] 'd' *ov.* 've'
154.33 has lost] *ov.* 'or we'
155.2 pure] *aft. del.* 'the'
155.2 with] *ab. del.* 'of'
155.3 happy] *ov.* 'talk'
155.5 illness,] *intrl.*
155.5 &] *ov. dash*
155.8 the] *intrl.*
155.13 the] 'e' *ov.* 'is'
155.14 avail] *ab. del.* 'endure'
155.16 from] *ov.* 'by'
155.16 distance] *ab. del.* 'difference'
155.17 ²not] *intrl.*
155.19 all] *intrl.*
155.30 comply] *aft. del. poss.* 'answer,'
155.34 so intent] *intrl.*
155.36 rummage] *ab. del.* 'rumage'
155.37 —] *ov.* 'a'
155.38 cognizant] *ab. del.* 'conscious'
155.38 action in] *alt. fr.* 'active or'
156.4 lamp] *ov. erased* 'spark'
156.16 ²have] *intrl.*
156.28 a] *ov.* 'she'
156.30 my] *ov.* 'it'
156.39 dearest Minny] *intrl.*
157.6 thought] *ab. del.* 'memory'
157.10 that] *bef. del.* 'as'
157.10 very] *intrl.*
157.13 Now] *ov.* 'It is'
157.19 impatiently] 'im' *insrtd.*

To Henry James 7 May 1870

157.1 May] 'M' *ov.* 'S'
157.5 Eastern] *aft. del.* 'clou'
158.5 its] *ab. del.* 'the'
158.9 old] 'l' *ov.* 'f'
158.10 low] *aft. del.* 'str'
158.15 a week ago] *tr. fr. aft.* 'written to him'
158.34 Of] 'O' *ov.* 'I'
158.39 certain] *bef. del.* 'regularity in'
159.4 idle—] *dash poss. ov. period bef. del.* 'But its'
159.7 live] 've' *ov.* 'fe'
159.10 cooperate] *aft. del.* 'conspi'
159.32 for] *aft. del.* 'of'
160.4 D:] *bef. del.* 'who'
160.6 some] 'om' *ov. poss.* 'ur'
160.7 perhaps] *ab. del.* 'one of'
160.7 of all] *intrl.*
160.10 consult] *aft. del.* '['spe' *del.*] sta'
160.12 waters] *ab. del.* 'bath'
160.17 time] 't' *ov.* 'c'
160.34–35 Mother . . . &c.] *insrtd. upside down at foot of last page*

From Henry James 24 July [1872]

161.15 myself] 'm' *ov.* 'a'
161.23 such] *intrl.*
161.27 as] *intrl.*
161.33 amiability] *ab. del.* 'character'
162.22 I] *ab. del.* 'we'
162.27 Your] 'Y' *ov. poss.* 'T'
162.38 interest.] *period ab. erased comma*
163.2 this] 't' *ov.* 'I'
163.4 now] *intrl.*
163.14 can] *intrl.*
163.14 have] 'h' *ov.* 'c'
163.17 this] *aft. del.* 'in'
163.20 at] *intrl.*
163.27 an] *final* 'd' *del.*
163.33 we] *ab. del.* 'I'
163.39–40 We . . . somewhere.] *written vert. across first page*

To Henry James 24 August 1872

164.15 her] *aft. del.* 'the'
164.17 &c.] *period ov. comma*
164.24 to] *final* 'o' *del.*
165.4 great . . . stooping] *ab. del.* 'line of'
165.21 only] *underl. del.*
165.23 live] *aft. del.* 'lif'
166.4 tendency] 't' *ov.* 'd'
166.23 girl] 'ir' *ov.* 'a'
166.30 condescended] 'c' *ov.* 's'
166.35 She] 'S' *ov.* 'T'
166.40 wrong,] *bef. del.* 'owing'
167.1 D] *intrl.*
167.1 day] 'd' *ov.* 'D'
167.6 symptoms] 'mp' *ab. del.* 's'
167.21 names] *bef. del. poss.* 'are'
167.26–168.4 Home . . . P.O.] *insrtd. vert. in mrgns. of pp. 5–11*
167.34 Aug] *ov.* 'July'; *aft. del.* 'au'

From Henry James 22 September [1872]

168.10 of] *ov.* 'me'
168.14 we] *ab. del.* 'I'
168.14 measure, &] *comma insrtd.*; '&' *ab. del. comma*
168.15 incessant] *intrl.*
169.6 our] *ab. del.* 'my'
169.17 me] *ab. del.* 'the'
169.27 are] 'a' *ov.* 'he'
169.32 at home] *ab. del.* 'impressed'
169.34–35 where . . . criticisms,] *intrl.*
169.37 be] *ov.* 'to'
170.11–12 Luxembourg,] *ab. del.* 'Louvre—'
170.17 by my] *ab. del.* 'of my'
170.18 want] 'w' *ov.* 'A'
170.34 form] *ab. del.* 'learn'
170.40 think,] *ab. del. poss.* 'sense'
171.10 sometimes] 'some' *alt. fr. poss.* 'since'
171.11 of] *ov.* 'in'

To Henry James [10] October 1872

172.12 cultivate] *final* 'ed' *del.*
172.13 care] *aft. del.* 't'
172.17 usual] *aft. del.* 'y'
172.22 he] *aft. del.* 'th'
172.23 or] *aft. del.* 'of'
172.34 entirely] *init.* 'e' *ov.* 'a'
172.34 regards a] *alt. fr.* 'regarded'
172.38–39 this minute] *intrl.*
173.16 his] 'is' *ov.* 'e'
173.24 part . . . universal] *intrl.*
173.28 realize] *aft. del.* 'reall'
173.28 is] *ab. del.* 'was'
173.31 disagreeable] *aft. del.* 'a'
173.32 he] 'e' *ov.* 'is'
173.36 Tappans,] *bef. del.* 'returning night before'
173.39 muffled] 'muf' *insrtd. aft. del.* 'muf-'|
173.41 wh.] *ab. del.* 'and'
174.9 He] 'e' *ov.* 'is'
174.21 winds.] *bef. del.* 'I met a'
174.23–24 Gertrude . . . Jones.] *insrtd. vert. in left mrgn. of first page*
174.25–26 Date . . . time.] *written on back of envelope*

To Henry James 24 November 1872

175.3 Sabbath] ²'b' *ov.* 'a'
175.4 home] *bef. del.* 'and'
175.8 sickly] *aft. del.* 'sl'
175.10 Thermometer] *aft. del.* 'From the'
175.12 hearts] *alt. fr.* 'heart's'
175.13 pluckiness] *aft. del.* 'prettiness'
176.4 is] *aft. del.* 'has'
176.18 Guest's Confession] *ab. del.* 'Griffith Gaunt'
176.19 I] *ov.* 'r'
176.24 identify] *init.* 'i' *ov.* 'I'
176.27 thin] *insrtd.*
176.29 defect] *aft. del.* 'dan'
176.33 Object] 'O' *ov.* 'o'
177.2 will] *ov.* 'wd.'

177.7 wh.] *aft. del.* 'will'
177.11 calling T. a coxcomb] *tr. fm. aft.* 'Huxley &'
177.12 & the magazine] *intrl.*
177.12 their] *ov.* 'his'
177.23 Massive] 'M' *ov.* 'm'; *aft. vert. line insrtd. for new* ¶
177.27 appeals to] *ab. del.* 'pleases'
177.33 stiff] *intrl.*
178.13 giving] *aft. del.* 'ch'
178.18 for constip?.] *intrl.*
178.19 ²is] *intrl.*
178.28 ²the] *final* 'm' *del.*
178.28 editors] *intrl.*
178.34 that] *aft. del.* 'to'
178.35 you] *aft. del.* 'him'

From Henry James [1 December] 1872

180.19 been] *intrl.*
180.37 (it] *paren ov.* '&'
180.41 prodigiously] *ab. del.* 'enormously'
181.12–13 unassimilable] *aft. del.* 'unassimilable'
181.14 society] *ab. del.* 'person'
181.18 a] *ov.* 'n'
181.27 ²a] *ov.* 'an'
181.27 denser] *ab. del.* 'older'
181.32 two] *ov. poss.* 'one'
182.11 of] *intrl.*
182.23 in . . . stud,"] *intrl.*

To Henry James [8] December [1872]

183.7 (before—?)] *intrl.*
183.12 have] *ab. del.* 'can'
183.22 his] 'h' *ov.* 'th'
184.1 for us] *intrl.*
184.2 buying] 'y' *ov.* 'u'
184.4 like] 'l' *ov.* 'h'
184.5 with] *aft. del.* 'of'
184.7 cold] *intrl.*
184.12 views] *bef. del.* 'than'
184.14 in] *intrl.*
184.16 being] *aft. del.* 'in'

From Henry James 8 January [1873]

185.3 ²I] *ov.* 'A'
185.6 now] *intrl.*
185.7 Mr.] *ab. del.* 'what'
185.8 steadily] 's' *ov.* 'e'
185.25 an excellent] *ab. del.* 'a very g'
186.1 one] *ov.* 'in'
186.11 drive] *intrl.*
186.16 dream] 'd' *ov.* 'D'
186.18 *Evening.*] *intrl.*
186.18 visit] *ab. del.* 'affair'
186.19 those] *bef. del.* 'dreary'
186.21 listening] 'l' *ov.* 'I y'
186.31 one's] *ab. del.* 'my'
186.32 more] *intrl.*
186.40 a] *ov.* 'an'
186.40 typical] *ab. del.* 'educated'
186.40 irritating] *alt. fr.* 'irritated'
187.35 will be] *intrl.*
188.6 American] *intrl.*
188.24 attribute] *ab. del.* 'presence'
188.29 haven't] 'n't' *insrtd.*
188.29 any] 'a' *ov. erased* 'n'
188.30 say] 's' *ov.* 'st'
188.31 those] *intrl.*
188.35 ¹to] *ov.* 'in'
188.37 get it] *intrl.*

To Henry James 13 February 1873

189.3 to me] *intrl.*
189.3 Jany] *aft. del.* 'Feby'
189.3 3] *ov.* '2'
189.7 under] *aft. del.* 'in a'
189.9 That] *aft. del.* 'Is there'
189.18 here] *aft. del.* 'the'
190.4 cheer] *final* 'f' *del.*
190.8 the] 'th' *ov.* 're'
190.11 last] *aft. del.* 'latter'
190.14 breadth] 'th' *ov.* 'in'
190.18 a notice] *aft. del.* 'M'
190.21 ¹may] 'm' *ov.* 's'
190.24 make] *aft. del.* 'give you'
190.28 rest] *final* 'e' *del.*
190.28 in it] *intrl.*

190.30 again] *tr. fr. aft.* 'construction'
190.33 which was] *intrl.*
190.33 born] *aft. del.* 'created'
191.4 bkfst.] *aft. del. start of* 'p' *or* 'f'
191.17 Richardson's] 'R' *ov.* 'an'; *aft. del.* 'PO.'
191.18 containing . . . Hawthorne] *intrl.*
191.19 26] '2' *ov.* '3'
191.27 very] *aft. del.* 'f'
191.28 It] 'I' *ov.* 'i'
191.39 A] *ov.* 'I'
192.3 (Agnes)] *opening paren ov.* 'a'
192.3 cleverness] *aft. del.* 'f'
192.17 when] *aft. del.* 'whi'

To Henry James 6 April 1873

193.6 shall have] *intrl.*
193.6 been] *intrl.*
193.7 wallowing] 'ing' *ov. period*
193.10 Usually] 'U' *ov.* 'A'
193.10 wander] 'd' *insrtd.*
193.13 generally] 'g' *ov.* 'd'
193.13 tirade] 'a' *ov.* 'e'
193.17 responsability] 'a' *ov.* 'i'
193.19 he] 'e' *ov.* 'as'
194.6 of] *ov.* 'to'
194.9 & easier] *intrl.*
194.14 such] *intrl.*
194.16 easily] 'e' *ov.* 'h'
194.25 first 3 or 4] *tr. fr.* '3 or 4 first'
194.28 shows] 'ws' *ab. del.* 'uld'
194.28 one] 'o' *ov.* 'w'
194.29 experience] *init.* 'e' *ov.* 'a'
194.33–34 escape] 's' *ov.* 'ex'
194.36 if] *ov.* 'as'
194.37 it,] *comma ov. period bef. del.* 'That is'
194.38 study] 'y' *ov.* 'e'
194.40 vigorous] *alt. fr.* 'vigourous'
195.7 formulated] 'f' *ov.* 'c'
195.8 timidity] *alt. fr.* 'timitdy'
195.11 frenchmen] *aft. del.* 'fe'
195.19 sedgwicks] 'g' *ov.* 'a'
195.20 letter] *aft. del.* 'f'
195.26 mail] 'ma' *ov.* 'se'

195.30 Theodora] 'Th' *ov.* 'an'
195.31 us] *intrl.*
195.34 To] *aft. del.* 'Th'
195.34 females] *aft. del.* 'feel'
195.35 but] *aft. del.* 'by'
195.40 a genuine] 'g' *ov.* 'n' *orig. connected to* 'a'
196.5 dye] 'd' *ov.* 'y'
196.5 call] *final* 'um,' *del.*
196.6 and] 'a' *ov.* 'it'
196.8 from] *aft. del.* 'of'
196.16 in] *intrl.*
196.16 house] *aft. del.* 'th'
196.16 sun] 'u' *ov.* 'o'
196.26 go] 'g' *ov.* 'd'
196.31 & life] ('l' *ov.* 'f'); *intrl.*
196.31 suit] *final* 's' *del.*
196.32 ²to] *intrl.*
197.1 itinerary] ²'i' *ov.* 'e'

From Henry James 9 April 1873

197.1 73] '3' *ov.* '2'
197.6 March] 'M' *ov.* 'Fe'
198.2 I] *aft. del.* 'as they come,'
198.4 should] 'shou' *ov. poss.* 'wil'
198.14 remunerative.] *ab. del.* 'numerous.'
198.14 have] 'h' *ov.* 's'
198.21–22 several times] *intrl.*
198.27 for] *ov.* 'is'
198.30 getting] *ab. del. poss.* 'being'
198.31 spectacle] 'c' *ov.* 'i'
198.37 I] *ov. poss.* 'S'
199.3 my] *intrl.*
199.6 had] 'd' *ov.* 've'
199.14 gave] *ab. del.* 'was'
199.21 heroic,] *ab. del.* 'something'
199.23 away] *intrl.*
199.27 as if,] *intrl.*
199.30 air] *ov. illeg.*
199.37 of] *ov.* 'in'
200.5 These] 'T' *ov.* 'I'
200.5 of] *ov. poss.* 'in'
200.6 it] *ov. poss.* 'th'
200.17–18 acquire . . . firmness.] *ab. del.* 'learn.'

200.30 padrone] 'e' *aft. del.* 'a'
200.40 &] *bef. del. poss.* 'the statement'
201.1 your] 'y' *ov. poss.* 's'
201.32 ²the] *intrl.*
201.39 been] *intrl.*
201.40 is] *ov. poss.* 'wa'
202.7 have] 'h' *ov.* 'n'
202.17 profusion] 's' *ov.* 'ss'

To Henry James 11 May 1873

203.4 seemed] 's' *ov.* 'b'
203.14 a] *final* 'n' *del.*
203.14 big little] *intrl.*
203.23 two] 'wo' *ov.* 'oo'
203.24–25 psychology] 'p' *ov.* 's'
203.29 I'm] 'm' *intrl.*
203.30 penetrating] *aft. del.* 'tho'

From Henry James 19 May [1873]

204.2 for] *ov.* 'in'
204.5 my] *ab. del.* 'the'
204.8 a] *ov.* 'th'
204.9 an] *intrl.*
204.16 two] 't' *ov. poss.* 'a'
204.17 April] 'A' *ov.* 'M'
204.21 Advertiser] 'A' *ov.* 'a'
204.28 with] *intrl.*
204.30 my] *ab. del.* 'the'
204.31 Rome] *ab. del.* 'it'
204.32 write] *aft. del. illeg. letters*
204.33 and] *ov. poss.* 'or'
205.11 a] *ov.* 'on'
205.20 an] 'n' *added*
205.21 inordinate] *ab. del.* 'great'
205.27 intarissable] 'ar' *ov.* 'ers'
205.29 personalities] 'ies' *ov.* 'y'
205.38 contrasted] 'con' *ab. del.* 'sing'
205.40 scientifique."] *db. qt. ov. erased closing paren*
205.40 speak] *ab. del.* 'know'
206.3 shall] 'sh' *ov.* 'w'
206.4 who . . . &] *intrl.*
206.10 have] 've' *ov.* 'd'
206.13 want] *ab. del.* 'propose'
206.17 is] 's' *ov.* 'n'

206.18 whether] *ab. del.* 'that'
206.18 or two] *intrl.*
206.19 in] *ab. del. illeg. word*
206.25 & Anatomy] *intrl.*
206.34 that] *init.* 't' *ov.* 'I'
206.35 does this] *ov.* 'is he'
206.36 are] *ab. del.* 'were'
206.38–39 a moment] *intrl.*
207.4 French?] *ab. del.* 'German?'
207.7 interrupted] 'inter' *ab. del.* 'was'
207.9 a] *intrl.*
207.18 print. I hope] *period insrtd.*; 'I hope' *ab. del.* 'about which'

To Henry James 25 May 1873

208.7 myself] *aft. del.* 'by'
208.7 ²that] *bef. del.* 'this year'
208.13 preparations] ²'a' *ov.* 't'
208.13 recurrence] 're' *ab. del.* 'oc'; *aft. del.* 'of'
208.22 course] *aft. del.* 'g'
208.24 somewhat] *final* 'e' *del.*
208.26 too] *ov. poss.* 'a'
208.26 this] *ab. del.* 'next'
208.27 about] *aft. del.* 'more'
208.28 two] 'wo' *ov.* 'oo'
208.28 is] *aft. del.* 'a'
208.29 are] *ov.* 'is'
208.33 in] *ov.* 'I'
208.39 elsewhere] *intrl.*
208.41 which] *aft. del.* 'of'
209.6 then] *aft. del.* 'so an'
209.7 postponement] 'p' *ov.* 'ne'
209.11 reading] *aft. del.* 'using ['b' *del.*] my'
209.14 suffer] *aft. del.* 'be'
209.17 or] *ov.* 't'
209.23 more than] *intrl.*
209.25 should] 's' *ov.* 'I'
209.32 by] *aft. del.* 'fro'
209.32 I] *aft. del.* 'yo'
209.36 on] *final* 'e' *erased*

From Henry James 31 May [1873]

210.5 One] 'On' *ov. poss.* 'I ha'
210.12 it] *aft. del.* 'to'

210.19 and] *ab. del.* 'but'
210.23 There] 'T' *ov.* 'I'
210.23 to] *ab. del.* 'for'
210.25 as yet] *intrl.*
210.29 after] 'a' *ov.* 'I'
211.1–2 ¹I . . . orange.] *intrl.*
211.3 very] *intrl.*
211.7 that] *bef. del.* 'in proportion'
211.12 ago.]] *bkt. ov. paren*
211.12 Lago Maggiore] *ab. del.* 'the Italian'
211.19 Glion (Montreux)] 'Glion' *intrl.; parens insrtd.*
211.21 Montreux,] *ab. del.* 'Lausanne'
211.24 her] 'h' *ov.* 'I'
211.26 a] *ov. poss.* 'on'
211.38 I] *bef. del.* 'have'

From Henry James 18 June 1873

212.4 (for] *paren ov. comma*
212.15 peculiarly] 'ly' *added*
212.16 many] *ab. del. poss.* 'most'
212.20–21 sitting round] *ab. del.* 'lounging'
212.21 & churches] *intrl.*
212.25 be] *aft. del. intrl.* 'not'
212.32 & . . . nature,] *intrl.*
213.1 (for me)] *intrl.*
213.6 spring.] *ab. del.* 'summer.'
213.16 imagine] 'im' *ov.* 'th'
213.18 ¹you] *bef. del.* 'were to'
213.21 I] *ov. poss.* 'sh'
213.28 papers] *apostrophe bef.* 's' *del.*
213.33 fortnight ago] *ab. del.* 'month ago'
213.39 this] *intrl.*
214.1 shall] *bef. del.* 'also'
214.7 for this] *ab. del.* 'when'
214.8 My] 'M' *ov.* 'I'
214.19 Excuse . . . letter] *insrtd. in top mrgn. of first page*

To Henry James 14 July [1873]

214.3 6] *ov.* 'on'
214.6 4] *ov.* '2'

214.13–215.1 professional development,] *tr. fr.* 'development, professional' *w.* '2' *ab.* 'development' *to indicate position*
215.1 and] *aft. del.* 'or'
215.5 as] 's' *ov.* 't'
215.7 that] *final* 't' *ov.* 'n'
215.7 me] 'e' *ov.* 'y'
215.13 equally] 'q' *ov.* 'x'
215.18 days.—] *bef. del.* 'I begin again after half an hour'
215.27–28 although] *bef. del. comma*
215.28 a] *final* 's' *del.*
215.33 deep] *intrl.*
215.33 revulsion] 'v' *ov.* 'b'
215.35 sounds] *aft. del.* 'breeze'
216.6 new] *intrl.*
216.7 Miss] *aft. del.* 'the'
216.19 had] 'd' *ov.* 've'
216.25 *multa*] *aft. del.* 'ma'

From Henry James 5 August [1873]

217.5 no] *ab. del.* 'to'
217.6 too] *intrl.*
217.8 I] *intrl.*
217.20 touched . . . think] *ab. del.* 'was out of sorts'
217.24 have] *ab. del.* 'am'
218.14 ²in] *ab. del.* '&'
218.15 subsequent] *intrl.*

To Henry James 25 August [1873]

218.2 but one] *intrl.*
219.5 join] *init.* 're' *del.*
219.6 me] 'e' *ov.* 'y'
219.7 be] *aft. del.* 'have'
219.8 If] 'f' *ov.* 't'
219.11 certainly] 'c' *ov.* 's'
219.12 about] 'a' *ov.* 'b'
219.18 lozenges] *aft. del.* 'and'
219.18 &c] *intrl.*
219.19 speak.] *bef. del.* 'or rather I'l'
219.19 writing] 'w' *ov.* 'r'

To Henry James 2 September 1873

219.5 but] *aft. del.* 'f'
220.4 tell] *aft. del.* 'enclose'
220.10 I . . . this] *written vert. on verso of second page*

From Henry James 15 September [1873]

221.5 in] *intrl.*
221.11 Bessie] 'B' *ov.* 'I'
221.31 be] *ov.* 'a'

From Henry James 26 September [1873]

222.16 only] 'o' *ov. poss.* 'n'
222.22 southward] 'so' *ov.* 'in'
222.28 May] 'M' *ov.* 'I s'
223.6 (or] *paren ov. dash*

To Henry James [27 February 1874]

223.14 60] '6' *ov.* '5'
223.16 Southampton] 'a' *ov.* 'h'

From Henry James [28 February 1874]

224.8 for . . . sake] *intrl.*
224.9 incline] *bef. del.* 'for your own sake'
224.22 & cheap] *intrl.*
224.24 dawdling] ¹'d' *ov. poss.* 'D'
225.14 contrary] *ab. del. poss.* 'conntrary'
225.17 if] *ab. del.* 'when'

To Henry James 22 March 1874

225.2 and] *alt. fr.* 'as'
225.2–3 all . . . were] *ab. del.* 'was'
226.8 Perry] *ov.* 'I ca'
226.17 Wendell] *aft. del.* 'Howells I have also seen'

226.35 Instead . . . you,] *intrl. bef.*
'They [*cap. in MS retained in error*]'

From Henry James 22 March [1874]

227.6 ²I] *ab. del.* 'you'
227.20 Dr.] *ov. start of* 'M'
228.1 even] *intrl.*
228.4 as] *ov. illeg.*
228.8 act] 'a' *ov. poss.* 't'
228.16 one] *aft. del. poss.* 'at'
228.20 Davis's] *ab. del.* 'my'

To Henry James 18 April 1874

229.4 its] *aft. del.* 'your'
229.11 the] *intrl.*
229.17 so] *aft. del.* 'but'
229.17 Italian] 'an' *ov.* 'on'
229.28 She] *aft. del.* 'Emerson'
230.4 fall] *aft. del.* 'Sprin'
230.20 fork] *aft. del.* 'cross'
230.25 congeniality] *aft. del.* 'arb'
230.29 possibly] 'y' *ov.* 'e'; *tr. fr. bef.*
'mechanical'
230.30 done,] *bef. del.* 'and does into
which you'
230.33 Merimée] *bef. erased closing
paren*
231.2 can] *intrl.*

From Henry James 3 May [1874]

231.4 has] *ab. del.* 'I see'
231.11 thing] *intrl.*
232.6 Via] *ab. del.* 'Ron'
232.8 go] *final* 'es' *del.*
232.15–16 gratefully] 'a' *ov.* 'ea'
232.28 your] 'y' *ov.* 'h'
232.37 whom] 'who' *ov. illeg.*
232.40 slightly] *bef. del. closing paren*
233.11 the] *ov.* 'one'
233.12 ²the] *intrl.*
233.12 7] *ov.* '6'
233.31 be able] *ab. del.* 'now'

From Henry James 13 June [1874]

234.12 a] *ov. dash*
234.13 At] 'A' *ov.* 'I'
234.13–14 Lombards] 'L' *ov.* 'F'
234.22 am inclined] *ab. del.* 'confess'
235.1 apparently] *intrl.*
235.5 from] *ab. del.* 'in'
235.19 struggling painfully] *ab. del.*
'suffering from'
235.22 into] *ab. del. illeg.*
235.26 lacerated at] *ab. del.* 'ch[*illeg.
letters*] to'

To Henry James 25 June 1874

236.9 passed] ²'s' *ov.* 't'
236.10 but] *bef. del.* 'it is'
236.11 seems] *init.* 's' *ov.* 'a'
236.24 100] '1' *ov.* 'a'
236.26 its] 's' *added*
236.27 beauties] 'ies' *ov.* 'y'
236.38 ²you] 'y' *ov.* 'I'
237.4 vacation] *aft. del.* 'f'
237.10 supped] *ab. del.* 'dined'
237.22 Florence] *aft. del.* 'my'
237.24 infused in] *ab. del.* 'gave'
237.25 thread] *aft. del.* 'that str'
237.25 places] *ov.* 'names'
237.32 Our] *ov.* 'th'
237.39 averse] *aft. del.* 'despair'
237.41 on] *ov.* 'for'

From Henry James 6 July [1874]

239.2 a] *ov.* 's'
239.8 with] *ab. del.* 'in'
239.12 Green] *ab. del.* 'white'
239.17 loveliness] ¹'l' *ov.* 'c'
239.19 Sept.] *ab. del.* 'Aug.'
239.27 these] *ov. poss.* 'thing'
239.29–30 in verden shade] *intrl.*
239.33 departed. I] *period insrtd.*; 'I'
ov. comma
239.39–40 regret] ¹'r' *ov.* 'd'
240.1 attitude] *intrl.*

240.1 toward] *ab. del.* 'to'
240.8 until] *ab. del. illeg. word*
240.10 on] 'o' *ov.* 't'
240.15 expect to] *intrl.*
240.21 uncle.] *ab. del. illeg. word*

To Henry James 26 July 1874

241.7 October] *ab. del.* 'Sept'
241.10 good while] *ab. del.* 'fortnight'
241.15 highest] *ab. del.* 'best'
241.17 York] 'Y' *ov.* '&'; *aft. del.*
    'Portsmouth'
241.20 and] *aft. del.* 'but f'
242.12 genuine] *bef. del.* '*that youth
    should [*written upside down on the
    page at some earlier time*]'
242.15 live] *ab. del.* 'live ['v' *ov.* 'f']'
242.23 Beecher] 'B' *ov.* 'T'

To Henry James 14 November 1875

243.15 an] *bef. erased* 'a'
243.21 making] *ab. del.* 'preparing'
243.23 ²have] 'h' *ov.* 'I'
244.10 fate;] *bef. del.* 'about whom'
244.14 made] 'd' *ov.* 'k'
244.15 scenes] 'es' *ov. poss.* 'se'

From Henry James 3 December [1875]

244.4 three] *ov. poss.* 'two'
244.5 read] *bef. erased closing paren*
244.11 upon] *ab. del.* 'for'
245.31 &c,] *insrtd.*
245.35 family] *bef. del.* ', first
    advance,'

To Henry James 12 December 1875

246.16 Chauncey] 'h' *ov.* 'a'
246.21 one] 'o' *ov.* 'n'
246.21 sat] 'a' *ov.* 'p'
246.23 feel] 'ee' *ov. poss.* 'al'; *final* 's'
    del.
247.5 seems] ¹'s' *ov. poss.* 'b'

247.8 have] *ov.* 'saw'
247.11 by] *ov.* 'at'
247.24 between] 'bet' *ov.* 'we'
247.28 original] *aft. del.* 'a gen'
247.28 ²&] *intrl.*
248.6 the] *ov. poss.* 'as'
248.7 was] 's' *ov.* 'y'

To Henry James 1 January 1876

249.14 30] *ov.* '24'
249.14 and] 'a' *ov. start of* 'h'
249.21 happier] 'ier' *ov.* 'y'
249.28 duly] *aft. del.* 'af'
249.31 the] *ov.* 'an'
249.31 eke] *ov.* 'even'
249.35 Bertha] *bef. del. closing paren*
249.38 by] *bef. del.* 'G.S.'s comfort a'
250.1 other] 't' *ov.* 'f'
250.4 get] *aft. del.* 'wea'
250.14 Dido] 'D' *ov.* 'd'

To Henry James 22 January 1876

251.9 manner] 'ner' *insrtd.*
252.1 out] *intrl.*
252.2 are] *aft. del.* 'have'

From Henry James 8 February [1876]

252.5 am] *ab. del. poss.* 'was'
252.13 Duc] 'D' *ov.* 'd'
252.15 at] *ov.* 'is'
252.21 saw] 'w' *ov.* 'y'
253.13 or too complete,] *intrl.*
253.16 sort] 't' *ov.* 'f'
253.27 agreeable] *final* 'e' *ov.*
    erased 'y'
253.37 is now] *intrl.*
254.1 charming,] *ab. del.* 'pretty,'
254.8 ("Sonny")] *intrl.*
254.11 believe] *final* 'd' *erased*
254.11 just] *intrl.*
254.15 Senatorial] *aft. del.* 'list'

254.15 be] *intrl.*
254.19 hold] *ab. del. poss.* 'hold'
254.22–23 That is "prestige."] *intrl.*
254.23–24 conservative] *ab. del.*
'moderate'

From Henry James 14 March [1876]

255.9 you] *ov. poss.* 'him'
255.26 ²little] *ab. del.* 'weak'
256.1–2 voyais] *ab. del.* 'vois'
256.10 the other day] *intrl.*
256.12 ²the] *ov. illeg.*
256.14 clever] *intrl.*
256.16 invented] *ab. del.*
'manufactured'
256.21 ever] *intrl.*
257.1 ²a] *ov.* '&'
257.8 scribble] *ab. del.* 'scribble'

From Henry James 25 April [1876]

258.16 even] *final* 't' *erased*
258.25 extreme] *intrl.*
258.31 On] 'O' *ov.* 'I'
258.36 little] *intrl.*
258.39 to] *ov.* 'of'
259.8 lieues.] *ab. del.* 'm.'
259.13 ²and . . . man] *intrl.*
259.35 ²a] *intrl.*
259.41 here] *intrl. in error bef.* 'here'
already in text
260.16 it.] *ab. del. period*

To Henry James 3 June 1876

261.1 tell] 'e' *ov.* 'i'
261.12 I] *ov.* 'h'
261.19 Our] *aft. del.* 'As'
261.21 at] *bef. del.* 'at'
261.24 didn't] ²'d' *ov.* 'n'
261.25 3] *ov. poss.* '1' *or* '2'
261.34 thing] 'g' *ov.* 'k'
262.14 sapience] *aft. del.* 'spa'
262.21 restlessness] 'ness' *insrtd.*
262.26 whom] 'm' *insrtd.*

262.30 remarkably] *aft. del.* '['a re'
del.] the'
262.32 she] 'h' *ov.* 'e'

From Henry James 22 June [1876]

263.9 the] *intrl.*
263.14 Bob] 'B' *ov.* 'le'; *aft. del.* 'a'
263.23 a] *ab. del.* 'dinner'
263.25 one of] *intrl.*
264.1 all] *intrl.*
264.4 Strong &] *intrl.*
264.5 annual] *ab. del.* 'great'
264.6 bottomed] *ab. del.* 'backed'
264.15 it is] *intrl.*
264.16 have] *intrl.*
264.26 & Sept,] *intrl.*

From Henry James 4 July [1876]

265.7 send] *ab. del.* 'do it'
265.16 ¹a] *intrl.*
265.20 personally,] *ab. del. comma*
265.20 more] *intrl.*
265.29 mot] 'm' *ov.* 'p'
266.18 the] *intrl.*
266.20–21 passed thro' without] *ab.
del.* 'not turned'
266.23 *e.g.*] *intrl.*

To Henry James 5 July [1876]

267.29 thing] 'thi' *ov.* 'wo'
267.31 "cultured] *aft. del.* 'refined,'
267.35 too] *intrl.*
268.12 painter's] ''s' *ov. period*
268.12 sensibility.] *intrl.*
268.19 showing] 'ing' *intrl.*
268.31 has] 'h' *ov.* 'b'
268.35 article] *aft. del.* 'review'
269.1 three] *ab. del.* 'two & a half'
269.5 stooped] *alt. fr.* 'stopped'
269.8 as it] *intrl.*
269.21 lie in] ('lie' *ov.* 'be'); *aft. del.*
'on both sides'; *bef. del.* 'virtues.'
269.25 Farewell] *aft. del.* 'M'

269.28 Bowditchs] 'c' *insrtd. aft.* 'i'
    undel. in error

From Henry James 29 July [1876]

270.11 were] 'ere' *ov.* 'as'
270.11 purely] *intrl.*
270.13 write] *ab. del.* 'right'
270.20 steal] *ab. del.* 'stole'
270.22 for] *ab. del.* 'forth'
270.29 *acharnement*] 'ac' *ov. poss.* 'a st'
271.2 some] 's' *ov.* 'f'
271.8 layer of] *intrl.*
271.9 the] *intrl.*
271.13 is] *intrl.*
271.17–18 my . . . ingredients] *ab. del.* 'they'
271.24 mercenarily] 'ce' *ov.* 'cer'
271.28 misprint] 'mis' *insrtd.*
271.37 went] *ab. del.* 'got'
271.40 wife] *ab. del. poss.* 'lens'

From Henry James 13 October [1876]

272.14 He] *aft. del.* 'That'
272.19 I . . . reason.] ('farther . . . reason.' *intrl.*); *added*
273.1 have] *intrl.*
273.4 impossible] *aft. erased* 'almost'

From Henry James 23 October [1876]

273.11 notes] *ab. del.* 'letters'
274.6 again] *intrl.*
274.9 a dozen] *intrl.*
274.11 dreariness] *aft. del.* 'stage'
274.15 Adams] *final* "s' *erased*
274.20 continent] 'c' *ov.* 'C'
274.28 see!] *ab. del.* 'cry.'
274.29 is vomiting] *ab. del. poss.* 'fitt'

From Henry James 12 January [1877]

275.3 ¹with . . . ¹cheque;] *intrl.*
275.3 with 2ᵈ cheque;] *intrl.*

275.11 ornamental] *ab. del. illeg. word*
275.13 They . . . envelopes.] *intrl.*
276.2 has] *ov.* 'is'
276.8 practical] *intrl.*
276.10–11 (that . . . to)] *intrl.*
276.16 make] 'e' *ov.* 'es'
276.19 me] *intrl.*
276.28 in] *ab. del.* 'at'
276.37 letter] *intrl.*
276.38 with an] *intrl.*
277.12 (105.)] *opening paren ov.* 'is'
277.17 give] *ab. del.* 'g[illeg.]'
277.19 assembled] *aft. del.* 'the'

From Henry James 2 February [1877]

278.3–4 former] *ab. del.* 'first'
278.21 in] *intrl.*
278.33 The . . . here.] *insrtd. vert. in left mrgn. of first page*

From Henry James 9 February [1877]

279.4 Bob] *final* 's.' *erased*
279.25 B.J.'s] *ab. del.* 'I have'

From Henry James 28 February [1877]

280.7 this process of] *intrl.*
280.8 country] *ab. del.* 'city'
280.11 shall] *ab. del.* 'am'
280.19 meets] *bef. del.* 'there'
280.23 someone who] *ab. del.* 'one who had'
280.32 whom] *ab. del.* 'who'
280.38 out] *intrl.*
281.8 almost] *intrl.*
281.25 The] *alt. fr.* 'It'
281.25 Athenaeum] *intrl.*
281.33 Whatever . . . it.] *intrl.*

From Henry James 29 March [1877]

282.6 no of the] *intrl.*
283.17 a] *intrl.*

283.19 opened] *ab. del.* 'opened'
283.22 excavator] *ab. del.* 'discoverer'
283.23–24 & heard] *ab. del.* 'who'
283.32 my] *intrl.*
283.37 of,] *intrl.*
284.9–10 particularly] *intrl.*
284.19 supremely beautiful] *ab. del.*
 '['horri' *del.*] bleak'
284.22 at] *ab. del.* 'with'
284.25 City] 'C' *ov. poss.* 'c'
284.33 (but] *paren ov. colon*
285.1–2 Ask . . . later.] *insrtd. vert. in*
 left mrgn. of first page

From Henry James 19 April [1877]

285.7 battu] 'b' *ov. erased* 'p'
285.9 right] *init.* 'w' *del.*
285.16 run,] *ab. del.* 'down'
286.6–8 N. . . . connection.] *insrtd.*
 vert. in mrgns. of first page

From Henry James 28 June [1877]

286.4 got] *aft. del.* 'have'
286.7 translator's] *ab. del.* 'German'
286.10 arriving at your] *ab. del.* 'your
 holiday'
286.12 ¹you] *intrl.*
286.12 will] 'w' *ov.* 'I'
286.20 for 24 hrs.] *intrl.*
286.26 little] ¹'l' *ov. poss.* 'C'
287.1 is] *ab. del. poss.* 'has'
287.11 somewhat] *intrl.*
287.15 than] *bef. del.* 'for'
287.19 to] *ab. del.* 'with'
287.21 in] *ab. del.* 'with'
287.35 very clever,] *intrl.*
287.36 appears] 'ap' *ov. poss.* 'is'
287.41 outing] 'o' *ov.* 'v'
288.8–9 one . . . most] *intrl.*
288.19–20 miles away] *intrl.*
288.22 & back,] *intrl.*
288.28 instantly] *intrl.*
288.32 Lawrence] 'L' *ov. poss.* 'S'
288.39 A.] *intrl.*
289.16 day] *bef. del. closing paren*

289.34 (as] *paren ov.* 'to'
289.37 July] *ab. del.* 'the month'
289.38 impossible] *intrl.*

From Henry James 10 July [1877]

291.15 light articles] *intrl.*
291.16 writing] *ab. del.* 'making'
292.4 do] *intrl.*
292.18 a] *ab. del. poss.* 'as'
292.37 straight] *ab. del.* 'directly'
293.8 Edward] 'E' *ov. poss.* 'A'
293.25 of America,] *intrl.*
293.28 nice] *ab. del.* 'wise'
293.35 herself] *intrl.*
293.40–294.1 criticisms] *ab. del. poss.*
 'critizms'
294.4 Tell . . . comes.] *insrtd. vert. in*
 mrgns. of first page

From Henry James 28 January [1878]

294.3–4 another] 'nother' *insrtd.*
294.11 visit,] *comma ov. erased* 's'
295.15 his wife] *ab. del.* 'Sara,'
295.19 from] *intrl.*
295.25 very pretty] *intrl.*
295.41 but] *intrl.*
296.6 sorry] *ab. del.* 'poor'
296.19 less] *ab. del.* 'more'
296.21 at] *ab. del.* 'with'
296.33 again,] *intrl.*
297.3 I] *ov. poss.* 'As'
297.5 with] *intrl.*
297.7 she] *ov.* 't'
297.9 ²a] *intrl.*
297.25 Great] *ab. del.* 'England'
297.26 a] *aft. del. poss.* 'an'
297.27 let] *ov. poss.* 'has'
297.31 for] *insrtd.*
297.36 matter] 'ma' *ov.* 'de'
297.36 mere] *intrl.*
298.2 in] *ab. del.* 'from a'
298.2 material] *bef. del.* 'point'
298.2 to abdicate] *intrl.*
298.7 growing] 'gr' *ov. poss.* 'in'
298.12 as a] *ab. del.* '& she will'

From Henry James 1 May [1878]

299.4 as] *ab. del.* '&'
299.16 women.] *period alt. fr. semicolon*
299.25 Is] 's' *ov.* 't'
300.4 who . . . America,] *intrl.*
300.17 *finesse*] *accent ab.* ¹'e' *erased*
300.35–36 without] *ab. del.* 'to the'
301.5 here.] *period alt. fr. semicolon*
301.12 now] *intrl.*
301.15 greatly] *intrl.*
301.21 believe] *ab. del. poss.* 'belief'
302.21 it] 't' *ov.* 's'
302.31 ²by] *aft. del.* 'from'

From Henry James 29 May [1878]

303.10 nothing] *ab. del.* 'mention'

From Henry James 15 July [1878]

304.12 steady] *ab. del.* 'strong'
304.15 I] *ov. poss.* 'T'
304.17 ²my] *ab. del.* 'her'
305.1 nature] 'n' *ov. poss.* 'h'

From Henry James 23 July [1878]

306.2 has] 'h' *ov.* 'is'
306.7 sell] *ab. del.* 'send'
306.7 in] *ab. del.* 'to'
306.10 but] *intrl.*

From Henry James 14 November [1878]

307.5 servants] *ab. del.* 'members'
307.11 notes,] *comma ov. erased paren*
308.8 comes] *bef. del. closing paren*
308.20 as] *intrl.*
308.23 were] *bef. del.* 'so[*start of* 'm']'
308.27 my] *ab. del.* 'your'
308.29 will] *ab. del.* 'would'
308.33 whomsoever] 'om' *ov.* 'at'

308.41 not] *intrl.*
309.1 is] *intrl.*
309.6 home;] *ab. del.* 'you;'

From Henry James 4 March [1879]

310.6 am] *intrl.*
310.7 put] *ab. del.* 'push'
310.7 rapidly. They] *period insrtd. for comma undel. in error bef. del.* '&'; 'T' *ov.* 't'
310.17 England] 'and' *ov.* 'ish'
310.22 like] 'ik' *ov.* 'ov'
310.22 &] *ov.* 'a'
310.23 regular] *intrl.*
310.27 be] *ab. del.* 'put'
310.30 people.] *ab. del.* 'it.'
311.4 encroachments] 'encroa' *ab. del. illeg. word*
311.23 Radicals] *ab. del.* 'Liberals'
311.37 meant] *ab. del.* 'wrote'

From Henry James 15 June [1879]

312.6 your] *intrl.*
313.38 impression of the] *intrl.*
314.15 in] *intrl.*
314.16–17 (he . . . atrocious)] *parens ov. dashes*
314.28 look] *final* 'ing' *del.*
314.32 life] *intrl.*
314.33 just] *ab. del.* 'only'
315.9 the] *ov.* 'a'
315.11 sort.] *bef. del.* 'From the Episode'
315.17 but] *ab. del.* 'but'
315.21 and] *ab. del.* 'but'
315.34 of] *intrl.*
315.38 him] *ab. del. poss.* 'me'
316.10 night] *intrl.*
316.14 (to] *paren ov. dash*
316.19 staying] *ab. del.* 'staking'
316.26 pleasant,] *ab. del.* 'brilliant,'
316.37 ¹I] *aft. del.* '&'
317.5–6 I . . . me.——] *insrtd. in mrgns. of first page*

From Henry James 19 August [1879]

317.8 *any*] *ab. del.* 'much'
318.21 ¹my] *ab. del. poss.* 'his'
318.21 him] *bef. erased comma*
318.33 relieved me of] *ab. del.* 'took'
318.35 & Cambridge,] *intrl.*
318.40 needn't] *intrl.*

From Henry James 30 August [1879]

319.8 much] *intrl.*
319.14 terrible] ²'e' *ov.* 'y'
319.17 out,] *bef. del.* 'the whole time,'
319.21 de] *final* 's' *del.*

From Henry James 10 November [1879]

320.7 lucubrations] *ab. del.* 'efforts'
320.18 not] *intrl.*
320.25 since] *ab. del.* 'from'
320.27 still] *intrl.*
320.34–35 Munich] 'M' *ov.* 'm'
320.35 with] *ab. del.* 'this'
321.4 two] *ab. del.* 'at'
321.11 of] *intrl.*

From Henry James 16 December [1879]

321.6 also] *intrl.*
322.7–8 I . . . cold.] *intrl.*

From Henry James 9 May 1880

322.13 condition] *bef. erased comma*
322.21 a] *ov.* 'as'
323.7 them] *alt. fr.* 'it'
323.14 interval)] *paren ov. dash*
323.19 write—] *ab. del.* 'work'
323.28 to this place,] *intrl.*
324.11 is] *ab. del. poss.* 'has'

To Henry James 2 August [1880]

324.3 over] *alt. fr.* 'Ober'
324.7 get] 'g' *ov.* 'd'

325.2 where] 'r' *ov.* 'e'
325.7 expedient] *aft. del.* 'most'
325.7 16.] *bef. del.* 'On the other hand I think Aug 21 a little too *early ['y' *ov.* 'ier']. Will it be much trouble for you to find out whether ['either' *del. ab. del.* 'either'] the Britannic goes back between then and the 1st of Sept. If she does and a berth decently'

From Henry James 31 August [1880]

325.8 pleasantest] *ab. del.* 'loveliest'
325.15 writing] *ab. del.* 'right'
326.7 as . . . me.] *intrl. w. caret ov. period*

From Henry James 13 November [1880]

326.8 obviously] *intrl.*
326.8 you] *intrl.*
326.10 see] *ab. del.* 'compare'
326.19–20 —though . . . —of] *intrl.*
326.22 american] ¹'a' *ov.* 'I'
327.7 which] 'w' *ov.* 't'
327.20–21 P. . . . pleasure.] *insrtd. in top mrgn. of first page*

From Henry James 27 November [1880]

327.5 from] 'fr' *ov.* 'to'
328.1 As] 'A' *ov.* 'I'
328.11 book] *ab. del.* 'thing'
328.13 spacious,] *ab. del.* 'leisurely'
328.22 wholly] *intrl.*

From Henry James 21 March 1881

329.11 many charms, but] *ab. del.* 'much to see and'
329.14 there] *intrl.*
329.15 Florence] *bef. del.* 'even'
329.18 would] *ab. del. poss.* 'th'
329.33 too] *ab. del.* 'a'
330.9 interesting] *ab. del.* 'pleasant'

330.14 *recommend*] *ab. del.* 'go'
330.24 having] *ab. del.* 'being'
330.28 be spent] *ab. del. poss.* 'arrange'
330.28 somewhere] 'some' *insrtd.*
330.29 beautifully] *intrl.*
331.1 February] *ab. del.* 'Cambridge'
331.1 decidedly] *intrl.*
331.4 an] *ab. del.* 'your'
331.10 either] *intrl.*

From Henry James 22 March [1881]

332.5 -Florence-] 'F' *ov.* 'P'
332.12 as] *ab. del.* 'if'
332.23–24 or . . . Havre,] *intrl.*
332.25 summer] *bef. del. closing paren*
332.29 in] *intrl.*
332.29 nothing] *bef. del.* 'nothing'
332.40 had] *ab. del.* 'was'

To Henry James 2 October 1882

333.4 in] 'i' *ov. start of* 'a'
333.8 air] 'i' *ov.* 'r'
333.11 altogether] 'a' *ov. start of* 't'
333.27 l'esercito] 's' *ov.* 'x'

From Henry James 15 October [1882]

334.15 want] *ab. del.* 'saw'
334.22 Tomorrow] 'T' *ov.* 'I'
334.23 travel] *ab. del.* 'journey'

To Henry James 16 October 1882

335.8 and . . . clean.] *intrl.*
335.9 7.25] *aft. del. intrl.* 'f'
335.11 style] 't' *ov.* 'y'
335.30 few] 'f' *ov.* 'v'
335.31 I] *ov.* 'a'
336.3 Mrs] *intrl.*
336.4 Also] *aft. del.* 'I exper'
336.9 back] 'b' *ov.* 'to'

To Henry James 22 November [1882]

336.2 the] *ov.* 'in'
336.9 saw] *alt. fr.* 'see'
336.12 The] *aft. del.* 'The h'
336.13 the] *intrl.*
336.18 with] *ab. del.* 'under'
337.1 met] *alt. fr.* 'meet'
337.1 ¹of] *final* 'f' *del.*
337.1–2 cosmopolitan] *aft. del.* 'cosp'
337.6 м.,] *comma added*
337.6 sent] *ab. del.* 'I shall re'
337.14 I] *aft. del.* 'Address'

From Henry James 26 December [1882]

338.6 was to be] *ab. del.* 'had been'
338.15 —not the least—] *intrl.*
338.21 afternoon] *ab. del.* 'for'
338.30 my . . . explain] *intrl.*
339.2 then] *intrl.*
339.11 a . . . refusal] *ab. del.* '['ha *del.*] refusin'
339.11 ²of] *ov. poss.* 'to'
339.14 never] *ab. del.* 'felt'
339.21–22 He . . . died.] *intrl.*
339.24 you] *ab. del.* 'I w'
339.33 into] *ab. del.* 'in'
339.34 ago—] *ab. del.* 'with'
339.36 your] 'y' *ov.* 'A'
339.39 Aunt Kate] *ab. del.* 'your'
340.1 ¹his] *ab. del.* 'this'
340.4 finish this] *ab. del.* 'write mor'
340.5 as . . . many] *ab. del.* 'or send it as it is.'
340.9–10 doesn't . . . to] *ab. del.* 'has lost her appetite, a'

From Henry James 28 December [1882]

340.6 again] *intrl.*
340.8 record] *ab. del.* 'value'
340.12 not] *intrl.*
340.15 During] *ab. del.* 'At'
340.20 also] *intrl.*
341.2 The] 'T' *ov. poss.* 'E'

341.3 assured] *ab. del.* 'told'
341.7 B.C. & Q.] *intrl.*
341.11 This . . . wish.] *intrl.*

From Henry James 1 January 1883

341.3 a] *ov.* 'm'
341.3 after] *ab. del.* 'the day'
342.4–5 wrote . . . to] *ab. del.* 'meant to write you'
342.8 looked at] *ab. del.* 'as I stood'
342.9 difficult] *ab. del.* 'not'
342.13 had] 'ha' *ov. poss.* 'am'
342.32 more] *intrl.*
342.32 ²as] *intrl.*
342.35 I . . . enclosures.] *insrtd. vert. in left mrgn. of first page*

From Henry James 8 January [1883]

343.3 two] *ab. del.* 'a line'
343.5 re-division] 'r' *ov.* 'd'
343.7 me] *ab. del.* 'her'
343.14 This . . . meet.] *intrl.*
343.15 your] *intrl.*
343.18 I] *ov.* 'f'

To Henry James 9 January 1883

343.2 Harry,] *comma added*
343.3 truly] 'ly' *ov.* 'e'
344.2 non-receptivity] *aft. del.* 'recep'
344.3 life,] *comma added*
344.4 closes,] *comma added*
344.15 &] *intrl.*
344.17 money] *intrl.*
344.17 ever,] *comma added*
344.38 course,] *comma added*
345.7 calling or] *intrl.*
345.13 know,] *comma added*
345.17 meanwhile,] *comma added*
345.19 need] *aft. del.* '['is' del.] nor'
345.27 style, beauty,] *commas added*
345.34 its load. It] *tr. fr. aft.* 'moving down the [*illeg. words del.*]'

345.36 filthy, smeary, smoky,] *commas added*
346.1 narrow sort,] *intrl.*
346.3 bystanders!] *exclm. mark alt. fr. period*
346.4 audiences!] *exclm. mark added aft. undel. period*
346.9 you . . . it] *tr. fr. aft.* 'layman & a [*illeg. words del.*]'
346.9 were,] *comma added*
346.13 thus] *ab. del.* 'so'
346.15 has] *underl. added*
346.17 always] *underl. added*
346.26–28 You . . . capitally.] ('Your . . . capitally' *insrtd. vert. in mrgn. of last page*); *handwritten*

To Henry James [9] January 1883

347.12 a piece.] ('a' *ov. period*); *added*
347.14–15 shy, . . . ways,] *commas added*
347.16 it!] *exclm. mk. alt. fr. period*
347.18 club—] *dash ov. period*
347.20–348.14 P.S. . . . W.J.] *handwritten*
347.27 plus] *ab. del.* 'all at'
347.30 7.82] *aft. del.* '12.50.'
348.5 being] 'b' *ov.* 'B'
348.5 if] *aft. del.* 'that'
348.12 of] *aft. del.* 'of h'

From Henry James 11 January [1883]

348.6 ²her] *ab. del.* 'you'
349.1 improvement &] *intrl.*
349.2 it)] *paren ov. dash*
349.13 any necessities] *ab. del.* 'fact'
349.18 There is every] *ab. del.* 'We have the'
349.21 to] *ab. del.* 'off'
349.21 have no] *intrl.*
349.26 as] *aft. del. poss.* '&'
349.28 to] *ab. del.* 'do'
349.29 on] *intrl.*
349.33 your] *intrl.*
349.38 this morning] *intrl.*

349.40 furthest] *ab. del.* 'best'

350.2 even] *bef. del.* 'th'

350.3 surely] 's' *ov.* 'a'

350.12 room] 'r' *ov.* 's'

350.17 you] *aft. del.* 'it'

350.24 your] *ab. del.* 'money'

350.34 There] *aft. del.* 'If you should feel disposed to'

350.36 ¹as . . . definitely,] *intrl.*

351.4 after you] *ab. del.* 'on rec'

351.5 his] *intrl.*

351.8 at] 'a' *ov.* 'i'

351.12 may] *intrl.*

351.13 ¹or] *ov.* '&'

351.14 you] *aft. del.* 'it'

351.17 think] *ab. del.* 'say'

351.18 been] *intrl.*

351.22 curse] *ab. del.* 'see'

351.27–28 & she] *intrl.*

351.29 Mrs] *intrl.*

351.29 about] *ab. del.* 'the'

351.30 Ives] 'Ives' *is written normally on the line, but beneath the* 'I' *HJ placed a caret and above the word, within square brackets, he printed* 'Ives', *in case the original word was illeg.*

351.32–33 on the] *ab. del.* 'about'

351.39 Alice] *aft. erased* 'all'

352.6 painful] *ab. del.* 'purely'

352.10 and . . . ¹the] *ab. del.* 'to live in a'

To Henry James 22 January [1883]

352.3 consent,] *comma added*

352.7 *principle*] *underl. added*

352.10–11 have, . . . me,] *commas added*

352.11 ²and] *intrl.*

352.16 him] *intrl.*

353.7 with] *aft. del.* 'all'

353.10 answer,] *comma added*

353.12 Mrs] *del., then underdotted for stet*

353.22 solve,] *comma added*

To Henry James 23 January [1883]

353.3–4 an hour ago,] *ab. del. illeg. words*

353.5 telegram,] *comma added*

354.6 place,] *comma added*

354.9 long] *intrl.*

354.14 (which . . . dread,)] *parens added*

354.20 simply] *intrl.*

354.26 house, . . . day,] *commas added*

354.28 , is heaven,] *commas added*

354.33 loudly] *intrl.*

355.2 *begun*] *underl. added*

355.8 (To] *paren added*

355.20–21 view, . . . bachelor,] *commas added*

355.23 dont;] *semicolon ov. period*

355.27 all,] *comma added*

355.33 distressing] *intrl. as* 'Distressing'

355.33 so] *typed aft. del.* 'your'

355.35 *status*] *underl. added*

355.36 me,] *comma added*

355.38 having let my] *ab. del.* 'sleepilg out of the'

355.38 to Toy,] *intrl.*

355.38–356.22 (24th . . . Paris.] *handwritten*

355.41 first] 'irst' *ov.* 'lush'

356.15 loving] *ov.* 'bro,'

356.17 Alice] 'A' *ov.* 'a'

356.20 sold] *aft. del.* 'divi'

From Henry James 23 January [1883]

357.2 in Cambridge] *intrl.*

357.2 home] *ab. del.* 'hap'

357.3–4 to . . . now,] *ab. del.* 'that now'

357.8 —i.e. habitation—] *intrl.*

357.17 from] *ab. del.* 'to a'

358.14 (of hers)] *ab. del.* 'do'

358.23 paid,] *bef. del.* 'about'

358.24 us] *bef. del.* 'about'

From Henry James 5 February [1883]

359.3 Jan.] *ab. del.* 'Feb.'
360.3 re-division] 're-' *intrl.*
360.3 were] *intrl.*
360.6 *strong*] *intrl.*
360.6 in . . . degree] *intrl.*
360.11 the money gained] *ab. del.* 'it'
360.14 ¹so . . . pitiably)] *ab. del.* 'so as'
360.19 (as I say,)] *intrl.*
360.20 I] *ov. poss.* 'Th'
360.23 the execution of] *intrl.*
360.25 ¹will] *ab. del.* 'has'
360.26 the] *ab. del.* 'Father's'
360.28 (I . . . Milwaukee)] *intrl.*
360.28 are] *ov. poss.* 'it'
360.30–31 forfeiture by him of] *intrl.*
360.32 be] *aft. del.* 'will'
360.36 do] *ab. del.* 'p'
361.3 in] *intrl.*
361.4 I shall settle] *ab. del.* 'it will go w'
361.9–10 in . . . now,] *intrl.*
361.12 all] *intrl.*
361.14 —I beseech you—] *intrl.*
361.16 now] *intrl.*
361.19 & famy questions] *intrl.*
361.20 can] *ab. del.* 'will'

To Henry James 6 February 1883

361.9 rent,] *comma added*
362.2–3 "the . . . side"] *db. qts. added*
362.6 , *it* is, . . . is,] *commas and underl. added*
362.7 *Kunstwerke*] *underl. added*
362.13–14 "confession] *db. qt. added*
362.14 "appearance] *db. qt. added*
362.15 "failure"] *db. qts. added*
362.27 being] 'ing' *intrl.*
362.28–29 sky, . . . sun,] *commas added*

From Henry James 7 February [1883]

363.6 coming] 'c' *ov.* 'l'
363.15 latter] *intrl.*
363.18 have] *bef. del. poss.* '&'
363.22 has] *ov.* 'is'
363.22 note] *ab. del.* 'let'
363.26 to-day's] *intrl.*
363.27 remain] *ab. del.* 'have'
363.31 than] *ab. del.* 'that'
364.1–2 "skinniness"] *ab. del.* 'aridity'
364.6 with] *ab. del.* 'of'

From Henry James 11 February [1883]

364.11 out] *intrl.*
364.13 treat] *ab. del. poss.* 'treat'
364.19 redivision] 're' *intrl.*
365.2–3 they are] *ab. del.* 'there'
365.4 amount] *ab. del.* 'm'
365.10 both] *intrl.*
365.16,17 as] *intrl.*
365.16 between] 'be' *ov. poss.* 'is'
365.19 that] *ab. del.* 'of'
365.20 ¹the] *intrl.*
365.26 best] *bef. del.* 'to'
365.27 my] *bef. del.* 'new'
365.32 Our] *intrl.*

To Henry James 22 February 1883

366.1 not] *intrl.*
366.11 ¹I] *aft. del.* 'It'
366.23 hardly] *intrl.*
366.23–24 the principle of] *intrl.*
366.24 But] *ov.* 'And'
366.24–25 controlling] 'i' *ov.* 'y'
366.25 not] *intrl.*

To Henry James 26 February [1883]

367.1 26] '2' *ov.* '1'
367.9 felt] *alt. fr.* 'feel'
367.10 earlier] *intrl.*

367.28 Mrs Perry &] *intrl.*
367.31–34 I . . . more.] *insrtd. vert. in mrgns. of first page*

To Henry James 1 August 1883

368.6 ²the] *aft. del.* 'his'

To Henry James 12 August [1883]

369.3 feel] 'f' *ov.* 's'
369.5 too] ¹'o' *ov.* 'w'
369.12 rents] *aft. del.* 'Augus'
369.13 send . . . event.] *intrl.*
369.18 she'll] 'she' *ov.* 'you'
369.20 charming] 'c' *ov.* 'l'
369.27 you] *ov.* 'to'
369.27 hear] *alt. fr.* 'here'
369.31 used] *aft. del.* 'y'
369.31 because] *aft. del. opening db. qt.*
369.31–32 he must] *ab. del.* 'to'

From Henry James 17 August [1883]

370.6 your] *ab. del.* 'm'
370.16 ²the] *ov. poss.* 'his'
370.18 letter] 'l' *ov.* 'c'
370.18 enclosed to] *ab. del.* 'forwarded'
370.18 notified] *bef. erased comma*
370.22 save &] *intrl.*
370.29 remittance,] *ab. del.* 'rent,'
370.38 carry] *ab. del.* 'Carry'
370.39 therefore] 't' *ov.* 's'
371.12 send] *final* 's' *erased*

From Henry James 24 November [1883]

371.3 ¹I] *ov.* 'W'
372.7 comes] *ab. del.* 'coming'
372.10 will] *bef. del.* 'have'
372.27 burial-] 'bu' *ov.* 'la'
372.28 ¹lie] *final* 's' *erased*
372.28 beside] 'be' *ov.* 'lie'

From Henry James 25 January [1884]

373.7 children,] *ab. del.* 'heirs,'
373.18 strikes me] *ab. del. poss.* 'should be'
373.24 Should you] *ab. del. underl. illeg. word*
373.29 verdigreased] *intrl.*
373.31 to . . . mine,] *intrl.*
373.33 as I discover] *ab. del.* 'on [*undel. in error*] account of'

From Henry James 20 February [1884]

374.1 20ᵗʰ] '20' *ov. poss.* '16'
374.4 your] *ab. del.* 'the'
374.9 within] *ab. del.* 'with'
374.10 collez-lui dessus,] *ab. del.* 'puis lui'
374.15 a] *ab. del.* 'the'
374.19 (the 1ˢᵗ)] *intrl.*
374.21 6 weeks] *ab. del.* 'two'
374.22 helps to] *intrl.*
374.22 keep] *final* 's' *del.*
374.24 at this moment] *intrl.*
374.26 American] *intrl.*
375.7 of course] *ab. del.* 'great pessimists'
375.16 appear] *aft. del.* 'be'

From Henry James 3 March [1884]

376.4 still] *ab. del.* 'now'
376.19 ¹2] *intrl.*

From Henry James 22 March [1884]

377.4 my] *ab. del.* 'your'
377.7 of] *ab. del.* 'about'

From Henry James 26 March [1884]

377.11 helpless] *intrl.*
377.13 eventually] *intrl.*

377.15 the idea of] *intrl.*
378.1 one] *ab. del.* 'you'
378.1 wishes] 'es' *insrtd.*
378.2–3 Christian name—e.g.] *intrl.*
378.4 Edmund] *bef. erased comma*
378.11 second.] *ab. del.* 'first.'
378.12 temporary] *intrl.*
378.16 view] 'v' *ov.* 'c'
378.17 infant nomenclature] *ab. del.* 'names'
378.18 I] *aft. del.* 'If I ex'
378.22 upwards] *ab. del.* 'after a'
378.24 didn't] *ab. del.* 'has'
378.24 P.] *final* ''s' *erased*
378.30 ²I] *aft. del.* 'But'

From Henry James 21 April [1884]

379.13 a] *ab. del.* '*the*'
379.14 would] *ab. del.* 'should'
379.33 though . . . it;] *intrl.*
379.36 But] 'B' *ov. poss.* 'b'
380.4 have . . . to] *intrl.*
380.7 (time-taking,)] *intrl. w. caret ov. comma*

From Henry James 26 May [1884]

380.1 26] '6' *ov.* '5'
380.4 several] *ab. del.* 'two'
381.1 must] *ab. del.* 'is a'
381.2 but] *ab. del.* 'three or'
381.15 with] *aft. del.* 'by'
381.22 competent] *ab. del.* 'willing'

381.23 may] *intrl.*
381.24 how] *ab. del.* 'what'
381.25 —or is procurable—] *intrl.*
381.36–37 criticism from] *ab. del.* 'speech about'

From Henry James 5 October [1884]

382.3 day] *ab. del.* 'night'
382.4 of] *ab. del. poss.* 'b'
382.7 everything] 'every' *ab. del.* 'you'
383.7 ¹the] *ab. del.* 'my'
383.19 adjust] *ab. del.* 'resign'
383.32 strange] *ab. del.* 'a'
383.33 great] *final* 'es' *del.*

To Henry James 18 October 1884

384.2 18] '1' *ov.* '2'
384.12 *attacks*] *aft. del.* 'a [*undel. in error*] *tax*'
384.25 is] *bef. del.* 'more than'
385.3 with] *aft. del.* 'whi'
385.34 Parisian] 'P' *ov.* 'p'
385.34 and] *bef. del.* 'the caricature'
385.36 formula's] *aft. del.* 'formel'
385.38 of] *aft. del.* 'a couple'
386.1 eagerly] *aft. del.* 'eg'

From Henry James 4 December [1884]

386.13 only] *intrl.*
386.15–16 Call . . . him.] *intrl.*

Word Division

Each word is keyed by page and line number to the individual letter. The line numbers begin anew with each letter and include all elements in the letter except the editorial heading that precedes each letter and the notes that follow. If there is more than one letter on a page, a superior [1] or [2] before the page-line number indicates to which of the two letters the page-line number refers.

The following is a list of compound words divided at the ends of lines in the manuscripts, which could be read either as one word or as a hyphenated compound. In a sense, then, the hyphenation or the nonhyphenation of possible compounds in the present list is in the nature of editorial emendation.

28.23 maid-servant	213.5 over-relaxation
43.15 super-human	239.7 preoccupies
47.20 over-refine	246.7 bedfellow
55.9 quasi-french	266.12 time-wasting
55.10 firecracker	[2]282.5 brain-lecture
69.3 Christ-Church	284.21 March-wind
70.8 English-woman	293.38 Class-day
70.41 horse-back	308.33 storyteller
86.16 post-chaise	315.4 butter-tub
86.23 snow-crowned	316.10 moon-like
86.34 foot-journey	320.7 a-begging
92.24 homesick	[1]322.14 squab-like
108.5 anti-bilious	323.1 roof-tree
113.15 electro-therapeutist	329.15 house-keeping
145.30 hereabouts	334.3 reenclose
199.31 thick-headed	349.24 today
199.38 booksellers	[2]368.3 tomorrow
202.19 needlework	

The following is a list of words divided at the ends of lines in the present edition which are authentic hyphenated compounds as found within the lines of the manuscripts. Except for this list, all other hyphenations at the ends of lines in the present edition are the modern printer's and are not hyphenated forms in the manuscripts.

23.12 laurel-|crowned-	70.14 Ch.-|Ch.
45.7 -of-|national	85.11 farm-|house

89.37 Good-|bye
91.11 -ice-|world
93.31 full-|streaming
111.6 sight-|seeing
[1]147.10 soft-|looking
[1]147.11 better-|class
149.11 re-|sauntering
253.39 grand-|daughter
269.6 self-|beneficial
271.8 long-|encroaching

274.37 much-|whiskered
276.17 wooden-|faced
288.15 intimacy-|American-
298.5 non-|fighting
299.5 eye-|betterment
299.31 fly-|fishing
[1]327.1 vaguely-|glancing
345.22 Anglo-|Saxon
[1]353.17 *kunst-|producte*
354.28 Punchinello-|existence

The following are actual or possible hyphenated compounds broken at the ends of lines in both the manuscripts and the present edition.

[1]10.7 mule-|path (i.e., mule-path)   232.24 poor-|house (i.e., poorhouse)

Index

James, Robertson (*cont.*)

note to HJ, 179n; financial condition of, 208, 215; HJ on, 210,
276–77, 313–14, 358; WJ's visit,
214, 237; in Prairie du Chien,
238n; retires from railroad, 243;
his farm, 248; suffers back pains,
250; HJ on his letters, 278; his
poems, 278n; estranged from
wife, 331n, 383; his mother on,
332–33; and Syracuse property,
350; GWJ's debt to, 365; his painting, 371, 379; trusteeship, 371;
HJ to send money to, 377; appointed curator, 380n; his art
studies, 381; WJ's amanuensis,
384; mentioned, 1, 3, 8, 37, 45,
65, 71, 103, 151, 180, 192, 202,
203, 221, 240, 245, 261, 264, 266,
296, 329, 344, 347, 353, 368, 369,
370, 372, 373, 386

James, William: in American cultural
history, xvii; early years, xx–xxi;
scientific interests, xxii; and art,
xxiii, 165, 173; his health, xxiii–
xxiv, 67, 72, 78, 83, 100, 130,
132–33, 142–43, 158–59, 167,
179–80, 208, 215, 218, 229, 230–
31, 243, 249, 354–55; and Civil
War, xxv; at Lawrence Scientific
School, xxv; in Brazil, xxvi; medical studies, xxvi, 82–83; studies in
Germany, xxvi; early crisis, xxvi–
xxvii; and HJ, xxvii–xxviii, xliii–
xliv; and the aesthetic, xxix–xxxi;
and philosophy, xxx, 173, 174;
and religion, xxxi–xxxii, xxxiii–
xxxiv; and subjectivity, xxxii; and
the problem of evil, xxxii; and father's religious views, xxxii–xxxiii;
and abnormal psychology, xxxiv;
and Johns Hopkins, xxxiv, 294,
298, 305; career at Harvard,
xxxiv; his marriage, xxxiv–xxxv,
303–5; not an invalid, xxxvi; visits
Milwaukee, xxxvii; and RJ,
xxxviii; appearance of, xxxviii;
and father's death, xxxix, 337,
338–42; and father's will, xxxix–
xli, 344, 347, 352–53, 366; his
farewell letter to father, xli, 342;
urged by HJ not to return, xli–

xlii, 340, 348–52; relations with
AGJ, xlii–xliii; criticizes England,
xliii; fears appearance of vacillation, xliii; on HJ's writings, xliv–
xlvi, 165–66, 170, 190, 194, 247,
261, 267, 268; on women, xlviii,
173; and psychical research, xlix;
Harvard teaching, xlix, 197n, 281,
282n; and Herman's death, xlix–l;
and family deaths, l; his letters, li–
liv; rooms at Mrs. Pasco's, 1–2;
boards at Mrs. Upham's, 2; at the
Lawrence Scientific School, 3n;
HJ's visit, 4; on Germany, 17, 19–
20, 26; sightseeing in Berlin, 20;
reading in Germany, 21; on poetry, 26; on France, 28; tries blisters, 28–29, 57–58, 61; German
reading, 29, 79; on HJ's stories,
30–31, 36–37, 46–47, 52, 103;
cure at Teplitz, 31–32, 33–34; on
German women, 31; meets Jewish
actress, 32; meets Polish liar, 32,
34; reads Balzac, 32–33; on German food, 34; on Teplitz architecture, 35; on Greeks, 38; on tincture of iodine, 38; on art, 39–41,
268; on Homer, 41–43; social life
in Dresden, 43–44; criticism of
HJ, 44–45; on Goethe, 49–51; on
national character, 55–56; on
Gautier, 56; reads Turgenev and
Browning, 61; recommends German language, 66–67; recommends stay in Divonne, 66; medical examination, 78, 82; advises
HJ on European study, 80; reading, 83; interested in HJ's health,
84; on father's philosophy, 102;
on HJ's constipation, 112–14,
118–19, 127–28; compares England and Germany, 120; reads
father's books, 120; HJ on, 126;
on HJ's letters on art, 128–29; experiments with chloral, 140; on
HJ's travels, 141; has tooth extracted, 158; on effects of water
cure, 159–60; appointed at Harvard, 167; on HJ's travel sketches,
172; Harvard opportunities, 174;
first course at Harvard, 175n; on
use of French by HJ, 176; works

THE JAMES FAMILY

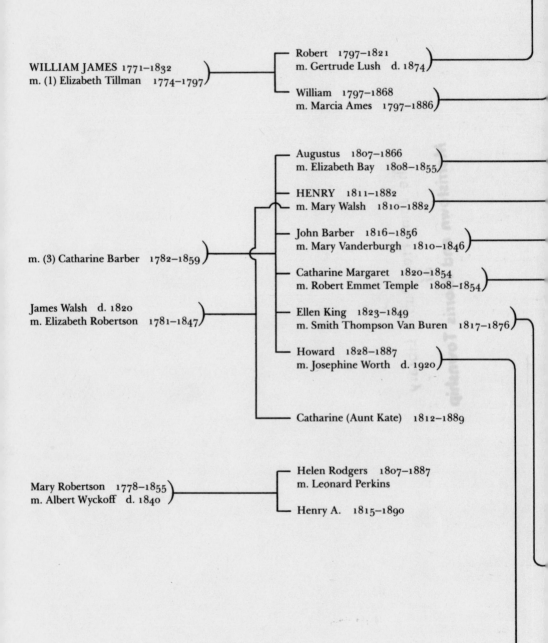

WILLIAM JAMES 1771–1832
m. (1) Elizabeth Tillman 1774–1797

Robert 1797–1821
m. Gertrude Lush d. 1874

William 1797–1868
m. Marcia Ames 1797–1886

Augustus 1807–1866
m. Elizabeth Bay 1808–1855

HENRY 1811–1882
m. Mary Walsh 1810–1882

John Barber 1816–1856
m. Mary Vanderburgh 1810–1846

m. (3) Catharine Barber 1782–1859

Catharine Margaret 1820–1854
m. Robert Emmet Temple 1808–1854

James Walsh d. 1820
m. Elizabeth Robertson 1781–1847

Ellen King 1823–1849
m. Smith Thompson Van Buren 1817–1876

Howard 1828–1887
m. Josephine Worth d. 1920

Catharine (Aunt Kate) 1812–1889

Mary Robertson 1778–1855
m. Albert Wyckoff d. 1840

Helen Rodgers 1807–1887
m. Leonard Perkins

Henry A. 1815–1890

Note: Stemma are simplified to names often mentioned in the letters